An Empire in Eclipse

Japan in the Postwar American Alliance System

A Study in the Interaction of
Domestic Politics and Foreign Policy

JOHN WELFIELD

THE ATHLONE PRESS
London and Atlantic Highlands, NJ

First published 1988 by
THE ATHLONE PRESS
44 Bedford Row, London WC1R 4LY
and 171 First Avenue, Atlantic Highlands, NJ 07716

British Library Cataloguing-in-Publication Data

Welfield, John
    An empire in eclipse : Japan in the Postwar
    American alliance system : a study in the
    interaction of Domestic Politics and Foreign
    policy.
    1. Japan——Foreign relations——
    1945-——Government policy
    I Title
    327.52   DS889.5

    ISBN 0–485–11334–1

Library of Congress Cataloging-in-Publication Data

Welfield, John.
    An empire in eclipse.

    Bibliography: p.
    Includes index.
    1. Japan——Foreign relations——1945—
    2. Japan——Foreign relations——United States.
    3. United States——Foreign relations——Japan.
    4. World politics——1945—   . I. Title.
    DS889.5.W45   1988   327.52073   88-3362
    ISBN 0–485–11334–1

Typeset by TJB Photosetting Ltd
South Witham, Lincolnshire
Printed and bound in Great Britain by
Biddles Ltd, Guildford and King's Lynn

TO MY FATHER AND MOTHER

CONTENTS

PREFACE

This book examines Japanese politics and diplomacy during the years extending from the disintegration of the Greater East Asia Co-prosperity Sphere in 1944–45, through the occupation and the Cold War until the collapse of the American-Soviet *détente* in 1978. While some attempt has been made to sketch developments since 1978 detailed analysis of this more recent period is the subject for a future work.

Japan's postwar policies have developed in the context of an extremely close relationship with the United States. The Japanese-American security treaty system thus provides the principal focus for this study. In recent years, a great deal of nonsense has been written about the Japanese-American relationship, on both sides of the Pacific. A healthy, balanced relationship between Japan and the United States is one of the fundamental conditions of peace and security in the Asian-Pacific region. This is to state the obvious. Yet it is important to view the world as it actually is rather than as one might wish it to be. The fragility of international friendships and the transience of enmities need no elaboration. Nations have neither permanent friends nor permanent enemies. International society has always been complex, fluid and unstable. It will undoubtedly remain so. At any particular moment the alignment of forces within the international community presents its component entities with a choice between several possible courses of action. The choices they make, often depend, ultimately, less on the 'objective realities' of the external world than on the outcome of their domestic political struggles. The nation states of the modern world, like the transnational societies out of which most of them have grown, are not monolithic organizations but intricate and perpetually evolving coalitions of interest groups. Decisions made by their governments tend to reflect the interests of the politically dominant elements or, in democratic or consensus orientated societies, the overall balance of internal forces at any particular point in time. They also reflect the gravitational pull of what might be termed loosely the 'accumulated legacy of history', the continuing, sometimes hidden impact of modes of thought and habits of action derived from the historical experience both of the society as a whole and the particular classes, factions, institutions and individuals within it.

Historical tradition, most certainly, does not operate as a *deus ex machina*, determining the actions of men quite independently of the better judgement of their minds. By and large, historical traditions emerge through a process of natural selection. Those which have produced satisfactory results are remembered. Those which have proved disastrous, or which seem irrelevant to contemporary problems, are gradually, but not entirely, forgotten. However this may be, the 'objective realities' of international society are observed, both by the government of the day and its domestic opponents, by various pressure groups and by the broad masses of the people, through a series of irregularly shaped and rather smoky prisms, layered over and over with virtually unquestioned assumptions about the nation and its place in the world, historical memories, traditional cultural, religious and class loyalties, moral values, hopes, fears and prejudices derived, as often as not, from the very distant, half-forgotten past, and subject themselves to perpetual change under the impact of new experience.

Much recent writing on Japanese society has placed a refreshing emphasis on historical continuity. Discussion of the nation's foreign and defence policies, in contrast, remains firmly enmeshed in the assumptions of the Cold War. The postwar American-Soviet rivalry, however, like the medieval struggles between Rome and Constantinople, the Great Schism or the seventeenth-century wars of religion, is essentially a conflict among societies of Western origin. Some of its implications, no doubt, are universal. The immense power of the two principal protagonists has made it inevitable that the effects of their confrontation have been felt in every quarter of the globe. Yet non-European peoples, like the Japanese, have responded to the Cold War on the basis of their own views about the nature of the world and the place of their society in it. The present volume, by exploring the roots of the Japanese diplomatic tradition, examining the background and objectives of Japan's postwar leaders, tracing the movement of public opinion and carefully analysing the interaction between domestic politics and foreign policy, attempts to demonstrate the essential continuity of the nation's external involvements. This perspective has important policy implications. The United States' pressure on Japan to rearm on an ever larger scale, participate more actively in global strategy against the Soviet Union and adopt a more assertive regional role has rested on the assumption that American and Japanese interests have been, since 1945, totally coincident, that the Japanese government and people share Washington's view of the world, have no independent aspirations of their own and can therefore be relied upon to act as the compliant agents of Western policy in Asia. This view, it is argued, is by no means a self-evident truth. This is certainly not to suggest that the two nations are on a collision course. Yet it is not at all clear that an extremely intimate bilateral strategic relationship, founded on the basis of a *de facto* economic union, is either possible or desirable.

ACKNOWLEDGEMENTS

This work has taken shape slowly as the result of many years' rather solitary research and reflection in Tōkyō, in Canberra, in Brisbane and in the Echigosanzan mountains of northwestern Japan, where I now live. I take full responsibility for the interpretations I have placed on events and for any errors of detail that have crept into the text.

Nevertheless, since I first began the study of Japanese affairs in the late 1960s, I have benefited from the help of many organizations and individuals. The Department of International Relations and the Australia-Japan Research Centre at the Australian National University, the Saionji Hamersley Scholarship Committee, Griffith University, the Japan Foundation, the Kokusai Kyōiku Zaidan and the Australia-Japan Foundation have all provided, at various times, invaluable financial assistance. To my former colleagues and friends at the Australian National University, especially to Professor Anthony Alfonso of the Department of Japanese, to Professor J. D. B. Miller and Mr D. C. S. Sissons of the Department of International Relations, I owe a particularly deep debt of gratitude. I would also like to thank the late Professor Hedley Bull of Balliol College, Oxford, Professor J. A. A. Stockwin, Nissan Professor of Japanese Studies at Oxford, Professor E. O. Reischauer of Harvard University, Professor Ronald Dore of the Imperial College of Science and Technology, University of London and Professor Herbert Passin of Colombia University, for useful comments on earlier drafts of the present manuscript.

In Japan, where I have lived for many years, my debts are innumerable and difficult to repay. I should like to express my sincere thanks to the staff of that venerable institution the Kokusai Gakuyū Kai Nihongo Gakkō, especially to Mrs Shiiba Junko, whose rigorous language training in the spring, summer and autumn of 1967 first provided me with the means to conduct research in Japanese. I would also like to pay my respects to the journalists of the major Japanese language newspapers, whose detailed reporting of domestic and international events has provided one of the fundamental sources for the present study. My understanding of Japanese diplomacy has been deepened by long conversations with several political leaders, Foreign Ministry officials and military officers. In this context I would particularly like to thank the late former Prime Ministers Katayama Tetsu, Kishi Nobusuke and Satō Eisaku; Mrs Aso Kazuko, former Prime Minister Yoshida Shigeru's daughter;

the late Ushiba Tomohiko, who once served as Prince Konoye Fumimaro's private secretary; former Foreign Ministers Fujiyama Aiichirō, Ōkita Saburo and Sonoda Sunao; Kitazawa Naokichi (Yoshida Shigeru's former private secretary) and Utsunomiya Tokuma of the Liberal Democratic Party; Okada Haruo of the Japan Socialist Party; Tagawa Seiichi of the New Liberal Club; Nishimura Kumao, Hatakenaka Atsushi and Nagai Shigenobu of the Ministry of Foreign Affairs; Asakai Kōichirō, former Japanese ambassador to the United States; Kaihara Osamu, former chief of the secretariat of the National Defence Council; Lieutenant-General Tatsumi Eiichi, Imperial Japanese Army (Retired); General Kinugasa Hayao, sometime chairman of the Joint Staff Council and Matsui Akira, formerly of the Atomic Energy Commission. I am deeply indebted to the University of Tōkyō, to Hitotsubashi University, to Hiroshima University, where I have stayed at various times over the past two decades as a Visiting Research Fellow, and to my present employer, the International University of Japan, which has encouraged my work in many ways. Professors Sakamoto Yoshikazu, Rōyama Michio, Itagaki Yōichi, Hosoya Chihiro, Miyasato Seigen, Kuroda Toshio, Yu Chung-hsun, O Sang-won, Iwashima Hisao, Kōsaka Masataka, Kurino Ōtori, Seki Hiroharu, Okudaira Yasuhiro, Etō Shinkichi, Ishida Takeshi, Suzuki Hideo, Mori Yuji and the late Mura Tsuneo have all, over the years, through extensive discussions or through their publications, contributed much to my knowledge of Japanese history, political life and international behaviour. So, too, have many non-academic friends of long standing, particularly Watanabe Hideki, Takayama Haruo, Yazawa Kenji, Yazawa Saburō, Truong Chanh Binh, Nguyen Tri Dung and Tran Viet Hung. Our discussions around the *kotatsu* on snowy winter nights, our talks on the history of East Asia during our trips to the hot springs of Izu and our rambles through the mountains of Okutama will always remain among my most pleasant memories. I also owe much to my former students, both in Australia and Japan, especially to Greg Story, Michael Dutton, Norma Chalmers, Hayden Lesbirel, Jane Deed, Manohar Prasad Bhattarai, Kweku Ampiah, Scott Johnson and Alain Le Ner, who taught me many things I did not know.

Takeda Isami, Namiki Kaoru and Gwen Grey gave me, from time to time, considerable help in gathering materials. Asada Mototsugu was a source of invaluable advice at several critical periods. I would also like to express my deepest gratitude to my wife, Carolyn, who typed much of the original draft, to Mrs Lynne Payne, who typed the final version of the manuscript and to Mark Pearce, who assisted with proof reading.

Finally, I would like to thank the Japan Foundation, the Yoshida Shigeru Memorial Foundation and the Nakayama Sōhei Asian Research Fund for the generous contributions they have made towards the cost of publication.

NOTE ON THE TEXT

(i) All Japanese names have been rendered in the Japanese fashion with the family name first and the personal name second, except in the case of a few writers who have deliberately adopted Western conventions. Chinese, Korean and Vietnamese names have also been rendered in this manner. The romanisation of Chinese and Korean is complicated by the existence of competing systems. The forms adopted in this book are those which the author believes will be most easily recognised by the non-specialist English reader.

(ii) Parts of an earlier version of Chapter I were published as 'Some historical influences on modern Japanese foreign policy', *World Review*, Volume 21, no. 2, June 1982; an earlier version of Chapter II was published as Pacific Economic Paper, no. 94, by the Australia-Japan Research Centre, Research School of Pacific Studies, Australian National University in December 1982; parts of earlier drafts of Chapters VII and IX appeared under the title of 'Japan, the United States and China in the last decade of the Cold war: an interpretative essay', in Peter Jones (ed.), *The International Yearbook of Foreign Policy Analysis*, Volume 2, Croom Helm, 1975.

CHAPTER I

Japanese approaches to foreign policy: the legacy of history, 239 –1945

The past, it seemed, did not die ... but lived on beside the present, and sometimes, perhaps, became the future.

John Galsworthy, *A Modern Comedy*

I Japan and East Asia in ancient and medieval times

Despite the impact of more than a century of frenetic Westernization, Japan remains an Asian country, both by virtue of its geographical location and also because of its history. The Japanese have preserved deep-rooted indigenous traditions that set them somewhat apart from the continental peoples. Yet their political and cultural development has been profoundly influenced by the civilizations of China, Korea, eastern Siberia, the Ryūkyūs and South-East Asia. So, too, has their thinking about international politics, diplomacy, war, peace and revolution.

The most striking feature of Japan's relations with its neighbours during the centuries prior to the Meiji Restoration was their extraordinarily pacific character. The fact that one hundred miles of rough water, swept, at times, by violent typhoons, separate Japan from the mainland gave the ancient Japanese a certain immunity from the vicissitudes of continental politics. Japan, unlike Korea, Vietnam, Tibet and the kingdoms of Central Asia, lay beyond the military reach of the Chinese Empire. The Tsushima Straits also protected Korea and China from Japan. Korea, despite repeated Japanese attacks on its territory between the fourth and the seventh centuries, and again in the sixteenth century, never attempted to invade its eastern neighbour, although it certainly possessed the means to do so. On two occasions, it is true, the Japanese archipelago was threatened by Mongol armies. On another occasion Jurchen forces from eastern Siberia made landings on the north-west coast of Kyūshū. At times Japanese military leaders like Hideyoshi, whose views of world order were largely derived from Chinese classics such as Ssu-ma Ch'ien's *Shih-chi* and the *San Kuo Shih*, attempted, albeit with total lack of success, to forge an extensive continental empire, in much the same way as late medieval European monarchs such as Philip II of Spain aspired to unite the Christian world. These were, however, isolated incidents in a long history of peaceful relations with the continental powers. Centuries of harmonious and mutually beneficial intercourse had fairly predictable consequences. From a relatively early date, both the Japanese ruling classes and the Japanese people came to view their country as an integral and important part of a vast international community embracing the Chinese continent, the Korean peninsula, parts of North-East, Central and South-East Asia, a community bound together, however tenuously, by a common allegiance to Buddhism, Confucianism and the Chinese classics, a sizeable trade in raw materials, manufactured goods, medicinal herbs and *objets d'art*, and a broadly similar lifestyle. Certainly, Japan also experi enced extended periods of isolation from continental affairs. The imperial family, the political and military elite, the Shintō priesthood, all manifested, at times, an attitude of detachment towards the continental peoples that bordered on xenophobia. Yet even at the height of the Tokugawa isolation, few Japanese ques tioned the assumption that East Asia was coeval with the civilized world.[1]

Over the centuries, Japan's feudal ruling classes, conscious of the instability of continental politics, developed particular, characteristic approaches to the prob lems of diplomacy and defence. These Japanese patterns of behaviour differed from those of the neighbouring Chinese. They also differed, significantly, from those which were gradually evolving in Great Britain, that other island empire located on the edge of a disunited and war-torn continent. The Japanese state, as it matured, seldom sought, like China, to employ one barbarian to defeat another. It seldom sought, like Great Britain, to contain the influence of the strongest continen tal society through manipulation of the balance of power. The attempts of other states to involve Japan in balance of power politics also proved singularly unsuccess ful. From the beginning, Japanese governments displayed a marked tendency either to avoid all potentially dangerous international entanglements through adopting isolationist policies or to follow the principle of *nagai mono ni makareyō*, 'move with the powerful', forging amicable ties with whatever foreign society exhibited, in their judgement, the most impressive combination of military prowess, political stability, economic strength and cultural prestige. In order to gain the fullest access to the advantages of association with the paramount regional state, Japanese governments were not averse, where circumstances seemed to demand, to acknowledging publicly its superior international status and formally incorporating themselves within its world order. Thus, in AD 239, Himiko, Queen of Yamatai, the first recognizable Japanese state, concluded an alliance with the powerful Chinese kingdom of Wei, presenting tribute and receiving, in return, a golden seal of office and a purple ribbon of state. During the Yamato period the Japanese allied themselves, first, with the Sinicized Korean kingdom of Paekche, then, when Paekche's influence declined, with the mighty northern state of Koguryŏ, which had established a virtual hegemony of continental North-East Asia and had thrice brought the Chinese Empire to its knees. When, in the mid-seventh century, Koguryŏ was defeated by the combined armies of the T'ang Dynasty and its Silla allies, Japan shifted to a policy of close co-operation with China, completely remodelling its institutions and society along Chinese lines.[2] In 1170 Taira No Kiyomori established intimate ties with the Southern Sung, formally bringing Japan within the Chinese tributary system.[3] The Ashikaga shogunate (1392–1573) developed a similar relationship with the Ming. In

1402 the Shōgun Yoshimitsu even went so far as to have the Chinese ambassador, representing the Emperor Yung-lo, ceremonially invest him with the title 'King of Japan', accepting a crown, royal robes and a Chinese seal of state as a symbol of office.[4] The personal relationship between Yoshimitsu and Yung-lo (they communicated with each other both by letter and in dreams) was at least as amicable as that established more recently by Prime Minister Nakasone Yasuhiro and the United States President Ronald Reagan.

It should be noted that Japan's incorporation into the Chinese world order meant, in political and military terms, very little. The Japanese, while eager to participate in trade and obtain access to the most advanced technology of the age, were generally careful to avoid too intimate a strategic association with their mentors and allies. The Wei emperor's hopes that Yamatai, populous, wealthy and disposing of considerable naval power, might prove a useful ally in his protracted struggles with Wu, Shu Han and the governors of Yen for continental hegemony, proved, in the end, illusory. Japan's military assistance to Paekche was insufficient to alter the military balance on the Korean peninsula. The crushing defeat of the great naval force sent to assist Koguryŏ against the T'ang and Silla at Paekchongang in 663 served only to reinforce the deeply ingrained isolationist sentiments of the Japanese ruling classes. The destruction of the Japanese fleet had a far more enduring impact on Japan than the defeat of the Great Armada had on imperial Spain. There were no further Japanese expeditions to Korea and no more military clashes between Japan and China until the last decade of the sixteenth century, a period of almost a thousand years. Japan's association with the T'ang, the Southern Sung and the Ming in no sense constituted a military alliance. The high point of medieval Sino-Japanese military co-operation was reached when the Emperor Junnin, hearing of An Lu-shan's rebellion against the T'ang, and alarmed at this threat to his fellow Buddhist-Confucian monarch, decided to dispatch military aid to the Chinese court in the form of vast quantities of bullocks' horns (used in the manufacturing of bows).[5] In 1658, when the half-Japanese Ming resistance leader Zheng Cheng-gong (Coxinja), whose navy controlled the China seas, appealed to the Tokugawa shogunate for assistance against the invading Manchus, the Japanese leadership, after careful consideration, decided not to intervene. The outcome of the conflict was uncertain. Discretion, therefore, seemed the better part of valour.

Japanese interest in developing friendly ties with powerful foreign countries, while holding themselves, at the same time, relatively aloof from international affairs, had two causes. First, the Japanese, perhaps as a result of their insularity and geographical isolation, have displayed, from the earliest times, a fascination with brilliant foreign cultures and an intense desire to import and adapt as many of their desirable features as possible. Second, and more importantly, the Japanese archipelago, although well protected by nature from foreign invasion, is divided by the Inland Sea and by rugged mountains into several distinct regions. It resembles, in this respect, Greece or Italy rather than Great Britain. Complete political unification has always proved difficult to achieve. Japanese society, despite its very real continuities, has always been fissiparous and turbulent, rent by regional, class and factional conflicts. These prolonged and bitter struggles made both the central authorities and their rivals eager to acquire the wealth, military technology, administrative skills, ideological trappings and prestige necessary to consolidate their domestic position. More often than not they sought these things in foreign lands. Himiko's alliance with Wei emerged in the context of her rivalry with the patriarchal state of Kuna, which lay to the south of her domains. The alliances with Paekche and Koguryŏ strengthened the position of the Yamato state against its local adversaries, laying the foundations for the Imperial system and military-feudal ruling class that was to dominate Japanese society until the modern era. The tombs of the Yamato rulers and the families most closely allied to them – the Mesuriyama tumulus of the Tomiyama group near Nara, the Ōtsukayama tumulus of the Mozu group near Ōsaka, the Nanakan tumulus and the Ariyama tumulus of the Konda group near Furuichi – all bristle with hundreds of great round-headed Korean swords, iron arrowheads capable of killing men and horses at a hundred paces, North-East Asian iron visored helmets, mobile cavalry armour made from metal medallions laced with thongs, and other equipment obtained, one way or another, from the neighbouring states on the peninsula. These weapons, and the military techniques that went with them – the shower of iron-tipped arrowheads from behind walls of tall, tightly locked shields, the terrible charge of armoured horsemen wielding Korean swords – enabled the Yamato emperors, the direct ancestors of the present imperial house, to extend their sway, however tenuously, over most of south-western, central and south-eastern Japan.[6] Moreover, in Buddhism, imported from Paekche in AD 538, the Yamato rulers found a potent spiritual weapon against their domestic rivals, whose immense prestige, so essential to the maintenance of the status quo within their own domains, rested partly on claims to divine ancestry supported by Shintō. Taira No Kiyomori's association with the Southern Sung was chiefly designed to strengthen his position against the rival Minamoto clan. The Taira, like the Yamato oligarchy, were anxious to gain access to the most sophisticated continental political doctrines, administrative systems and military technology. They were also interested in the revenues derived from the China trade. At least half the income of Kiyomori's court had its origins in this veritable cornucopia. In similar fashion, the Ashikaga's relationship with the Ming developed in the context of their struggles with the great feudal families of the north, south and east.

The initial Japanese discovery of Europe did little to change established patterns of action. Oda Nobunaga's patronage of the Portuguese Jesuits was the direct outcome of his efforts to defeat his feudal rivals, suppress the powerful Buddhist sects and obtain saltpetre for the muskets of his modernized army. Once his successor Hideyoshi had established effective hegemony of the archipelago and seen his schemes to unify the whole of East Asia turn to ashes Japan's 'Christian century' came to an abrupt end. Continued intercourse with the Iberian Catholic powers, not to mention Japanese participation in the kind of East Asian trading community that had existed during the T'ang, Sung and Ming dynasties, by enabling potentially disruptive feudal potentates in western Japan to strengthen their position *vis-à-vis* the shogunate through commerce and access to advanced technology, would undoubtedly have destabilized the nation's delicate internal balance. The Tokugawas, therefore, retreated into watchful isolationism.

II   The impact of the imperial West

The intrusion of Great Britain, imperial Russia, the United States, France and Germany into East Asia during the nineteenth century swept the Japanese Empire into the vortex of Western superpower rivalries, destroyed the Tokugawa shogunate, accelerated the pace of domestic political and economic change and forced the Japanese people to re-examine their traditional concepts of world order. The new imperial powers of Europe and North America were highly civilized, prosperous, technologically advanced and, above all else, disposed of formidable military resources. Their ability to influence events in distant parts of the globe, to impose their own state system, their own diplomatic traditions, their own forms of economic organization and their own ideologies on the non-European world was far greater than that of sixteenth-century Portugal and Spain. This second encounter with the West thus had a profound impact on Japan's political institutions, military organization, economic development, cultural and intellectual life. It was European statecraft, European military technology and the development of a European-style heavy industrial base that enabled the Meiji government, dominated by samurai from the western clans of Satsuma and Chōshū, the old antagonists of the Tokugawas, to defeat the conservative feudal opposition, crush several large-scale peasant uprisings, contain urban working-class dissent and embark on an ambitious programme of domestic reconstruction. The encounter with the West and the imposition of the Western state system onto the old East Asian order also precipitated the emergence of several conflicting streams of thought about the nature of the international community and Japan's place in it. These streams of thought, interacting with a variety of strategic, political and economic considerations, have exerted an important influence on Japanese foreign and defence policies throughout the twentieth century. They remain highly significant today.

(i)   Prewar Japanese 'Westernizers' and foreign policy

One school of thinkers, whose views paralleled, to some extent, those of the dominant groups in the Restoration government, considered that Japan had no alternative but to sever its ties with Asia, remodel itself in the image of the strongest European countries and become an active participant in the Western state system. In general, these people accepted the contemporary European view that Western civilization, based on individualism, private enterprise, industrialism, nationalism and imperial expansion, represented the finest flower of human achievement. Asia, in particular China, was synonymous with squalor, economic backwardness, national decay. Japan could only emerge as a progressive, powerful and respected state by uprooting the nefarious influence of Chinese civilization, with its passive approach to the relationship between man and nature, its pessimistic view of war, its emphasis on stability, hierarchy and order in international society, and substituting more robust and assertive Western models in its place. This required abandoning Japan's deeply rooted sense of community with China and Korea.

According to Fukuzawa Yukichi, the chief academic exponent of the 'escape from Asia' movement in the nineteenth century,

> While it is true that the national territory of Japan lies off the eastern fringes of Asia, the spirit of the Japanese people has already moved away from the rigid framework of Asian civilization towards the civilizations of the Western world. What is unfortunate about this is that Japan has two immediate neighbours. One is China. The other is Korea. From ancient times the people of these two countries have been brought up in the political, educational and cultural traditions of East Asia. In this, of course, they are no different to us Japanese. Yet if we compare the three countries, China, Korea and Japan, [it will be seen] that China and Korea are much closer to each other than either of them is to Japan. It is difficult to say whether this is a result of racial characteristics that have existed from the beginning or whether it is the legacy of East Asian political, educational and cultural traditions. Yet however this may be, China and Korea as nations and Chinese and Koreans as individuals, do not manifest any particular interest in progress. In this world of increasingly easy communications, what they see with their eyes and hear with their ears does not make sufficient impression upon their hearts. Their love for their ancient customs and antique ways has not changed for thousands of years...
>
> It is not only that contemporary China and contemporary Korea are in no position to help Japan. It is also meaningless to do what some civilized Western people do from time to time – that is, to assume that because of the geographical propinquity of the three nations, China and Korea can be measured by the same standards as Japan ...
> In setting our future course, there is no reason at all why we should wait for the development of our neighbours and co-operate with them for the advance of Asia as a whole. Rather, we should escape from Asia and cast our lot in with the civilized countries of the West. We should not allow the fact that we are neighbours to have any influence on our policies towards China and Korea. We should treat these countries exactly the same way as Westerners treat them. People who keep bad company cannot avoid getting a bad name for themselves. We should sever all relations with our bad Asian friends.[7]

Japan's long and bloody internecine conflicts provided an abundant source of inspiration for students of power politics. The basic principles of nineteenth-century international relations had close parallels in the Japanese feudal past. Nevertheless, Japan's Westernizers eagerly studied European traditions of war and diplomacy, assimilating orthodox patterns of thinking and thoroughly familiarizing themselves with the rules of the game. The essence of the Western approach to things, as interpreted by these nineteenth-century thinkers, was summed up in the four-character slogan *fukoku kyōhei*, 'a wealthy country and a powerful army', the creation of which became the principal objective of the prewar Japanese state.

Not surprisingly, most orthodox Westernizers emerged as exponents of imperialism. On the one hand there was the purely strategic argument that foreign bases, overseas possessions and spheres of influence, especially in Korea, the

Ryūkyūs, the northern islands and parts of China, were necessary to defend the territorial integrity of Japan from the depredations of this or that expansionist Western power. As Japan's industrial economy developed, these arguments were reinforced by the demands of the great corporations for raw materials and new markets. Yet as more Japanese came to understand the character of the nineteenth-century European state system and the structure of the international order built up around it, it became increasingly clear that a Japan without an empire would find it as difficult to achieve international recognition as a Japan without locomotives, compulsory education or gas lighting. In this respect, Japan's modern imperial thought, like many of its modern institutions, was heavily influenced by the example of the great Western empires.

Honda Toshiaki, for example, writing in the late Tokugawa period, urged his fellow countrymen to abandon Chinese models and look instead to the examples of Britain and Russia. In Honda's view, the wealth, power, prestige and cultural achievements of these two mighty states were founded on imperialism. Although Honda's most fulsome praise was reserved for Russia, especially for its enlightened Empress Catherine II, he considered the British model most appropriate for Japan's particular circumstances, recommending that immediate steps be taken to create an extensive East Asian empire, centred around the Japanese home archipelago and incorporating Hokkaidō, Sakhalin, the Kuriles, the Aleutians and Kamchatka.* He also proposed expansion into North America. In this way, he argued, Japan would establish itself as a global power, recognized throughout the world as mistress of the eastern seas, just as Britain was recognized as mistress of the West.[8]

The political thought of Yoshida Shōin, who, as the mentor of many of the most important Meiji leaders, exerted an extraordinary influence on Japan's modern history, also involved a rejection of Japan's Asian past, the wholesale adoption of Western institutions and technology, then the creation of a sizeable East Asian empire extending from Kamchatka and the Kuriles in the north through Korea and Manchuria to Taiwan and the Philippines in the south.

In 1854 Yoshida, imprisoned by the shogunate after an unsuccessful attempt to visit America to learn the secrets of Western power, explained his concepts in the following terms:

> If we dispose of sufficient naval vessels and cannon it should be possible for us to bring the [Western] barbarians under control, subdue the feudal lords, seize Kamchatka and [the Sea of] Okhotsk, to absorb the Ryūkyūs, to teach the Koreans a lesson, extract tribute from them and restore our relationship with that country to what it was in the glorious ages of the past, to divide up the territory of Manchuria in the north, to absorb Taiwan, and the Philippines in the south. In fact it will be possible for Japan to establish itself as a power with a gradually expanding sphere of influence. In this way, by carefully guarding our perimeters, we will be

---

* Honda thought that the Kamchatka peninsula, located on approximately the same latitude as England, should prove to be, through a process of sympathetic geography, a more auspicious siting for the imperial capital than Kyōtō. He believed that Kamchatka would eventually emerge as the centre of gravity of Japan's East Asian empire.

able to preserve the greatness of Japan and bring up samurai devoted to the people.[9]

As Yoshida's statement clearly reveals, Japanese Westernizers were not necessarily well disposed towards the Western powers as such. There was no particular reason why they should have been. Westernization was a means to defend Japan from its enemies and to enhance its international prestige. Even Fukuzawa Yukichi did not think that Japan's reconstruction along European lines would make the imperial powers any less dangerous. A 'Westernized' Japan would still be, in some sense, 'Asian' and would thus be regarded as fair game by predatory European powers. 'Japan too', he was eventually forced to concede, 'is one of the nations of Asia. Even if we have not yet suffered misfortune in our dealings with foreign countries we cannot but be apprehensive about the dangers the future might hold.'[10] Itō Hirobumi, too, who as Prime Minister energetically promoted the adoption of European political and economic institutions, military organization, science and technology, shared Fukuzawa's ambivalence towards the West. The European countries and the United States, he was convinced, 'will, in the long run, deceive us. They have little sincere intention of working for our profit and interest ... Whenever East and West confront each other the European nations will act in concert against an isolated Japan to gain the upper hand. This is no more than an expression of fundamental differences in race and religion.'[11]

(ii)   Prewar pan-Asianist traditions

One group of thinkers thus urged abandonment of Japan's Asian heritage and the reconstruction of its society along Western lines. Contact with Europe and America, with civilizations very different from their own, caused other Japanese to place renewed emphasis on their country's links with Asia, not only in matters affecting institutions and culture, but also in the fields of foreign policy and defence.

Prewar Japanese pan-Asianists can be divided into two broad categories. What might be called the imperial pan-Asianist group, contemplating the political fragmentation and economic backwardness of the Asian world, saw no alternative to a regional unity imposed by Japan. They were perfectly happy to countenance the use of force in pursuit of this objective. In this respect the imperial Western powers had already set them several excellent examples. The nineteenth century was not an age of pacifism. After the Restoration of 1868, Saigō Takamori and his supporters urged the government to embark at once on the conquest of Korea as a prelude to creating an Asian federation under the leadership of Japan.[12] Saigō's defeat in the civil war of 1877 did little to reduce the appeal of this idea. If 'Westernist' opinion tended to dominate the Foreign Ministry, imperial pan-Asianism struck deep roots in the armed forces and conservative nationalist circles. The Genyōsha (Dark Ocean Society), founded in 1881 by Tōyama Mitsuru and Hiraoka Kōtarō, two of Saigō's most zealous supporters, and functioning, until its dissolution in 1946, as an immensely powerful subterranean pressure group, with allies in the government, the bureaucracy, the armed forces, the intelligence community, the business world, the

media and the universities, consistently worked towards the establishment of a confederation of East Asian states organized around the Japanese Empire.[13] The
Genyōsha's basic concepts of world order were shared by the Kokuryūkai (Amur
River Society), another influential patriotic organization founded in 1901, and by the
Nichiren Buddhist political philosopher Kita Ikki, whose ideas were to exert a considerable impact on the Young Officers' Movement in the 1930's and, subsequently,
on the ideology of the Co-prosperity Sphere. Kita's domestic programme, with its
rejection of both capitalism and socialism as undesirable Western imports, its vision
of a militant, egalitarian society under the leadership of a divine emperor,
represented, in many respects, a return to the ideals of Prince Shōtoku, the sixth-
century Buddhist aristocrat who presided over the Sinification of the original
Japanese state. In foreign policy Kita saw Japan's sacred mission as the liberation of
Asia from the West. Japan was to play, in particular, a leading role in the destruction
of Russia and the British Empire, the two powers then seen as the principal threats
to East Asia's independence. At the same time, Japan was to co-operate closely with
the fraternal civilization of China to establish a strong East Asian federation, the prelude to the unification of the world in 'feudal peace.'.[14]

Pan-Asianism was one of the many banners held aloft by the conservative
opponents of the Japanese establishment in the Meiji, Taishō and early Shōwa eras.
Yet the ideal of an Asian federation also provided a rallying point for important
sections of the Japanese radical left, for the scores of energetic thinkers and agitators
who had their roots in the peasant and working-class disturbances which had grown
out of the great Tokugawa rebellions and which were gradually merging, along with
other streams of thought, into the Socialist and Communist movements of the twentieth century.

The right wing of the nineteenth-century People's Rights Movement (Jiyū Min-
ken Undō), centring around dissident samurai such as Itagaki Taisuke and Etō
Shimpei, was, from the outset, unashamedly imperialist in its approach to foreign
policy. Nevertheless, several figures associated with the left wing of the People's
Rights Movement advocated, at one time or another, an alliance of Asian powers
against European imperialism. As might have been expected, those whose democratic instincts were the strongest, those who had been most impressed by the radical
reformist thought of eighteenth-century Europe, were also the most ardent in their
denunciation of Western imperialism.

Thus Nakae Chōmin, the translator of Jean-Jacques Rousseau's *Le Contrat Social*,
an exponent, along with Uegi Emori, of a democratic constitution based on the concepts of popular sovereignty, freedom of thought, assembly and association, of the
right of resistance to tyrannical governments, also believed in the necessity of a
defensive grand alliance of Asian peoples, centring on Japan, China and Korea, to
resist the inroads of the West. 'Japan and China should not fight each other', Nakae
urged in April 1881, as Sino-Japanese tension over the Okinawan issue was increasing, 'but combine to resist pressure from the Western powers.'[15] *Kinji Hyōron*, the
newspaper of the left-wing faction of the People's Rights Movement, consistently
promoted the concept of a Japanese alliance with China and Korea.[16] In 1882, when

the murder of Japanese military instructors in Korea exacerbated the already difficult relations with Peking, the *Jiyū Shimbun*, the official organ of the Liberal Party (Jiyūto), urged the Japanese government to avoid confrontation with China and concentrate instead on the more important question of protecting East Asia from the advance of the West.[17] Ōno Azusa, of the Progressive Party (Kaishintō), the author of *An Essay on Foreign Policy* (Gaikōron), also urged the government to devote its attention to protecting the interests of Japan, and those of East Asia as a whole, from the invading Western powers.[18] Tarui Tōkichi, organizer of the Shimabara-based East Asian Socialist Party, which advocated, in internal politics, 'the maximum happiness and maximum interest of the social masses', 'the principle of equality' and 'land to the peasants', urged union of Japan and Korea to form a new Greater East Asia and the conclusion of an alliance between this commonwealth and the Chinese Empire.[19] The objective, once again, was to resist the advance of Western imperialism. Miyazaki Tōten, Sun Yat-sen's leading Japanese revolutionary comrade-in-arms, whose family had been, for many years, involved in the People's Rights Movement, and whose own spiritual odyssey had taken him from radical liberalism and Christianity to socialism and pan-Asianism, considered that

> the world is like a chaotic battlefield, where might is right, where the tyranny of the powerful is becoming increasingly open and brutal, where the rights of the weak are trampled underfoot and their freedom curtailed ... If no defensive measures are taken the Yellow race will continue to be oppressed by the White. All depends on the fate of China. Even if [the present government] of China collapses, its territory is vast and its population is numerous. If the country can be united, maladministration remedied, its [human and physical resources] put to good use, it will be possible not only to restore the rights of the Yellow race, but to command the destinies of the entire world and proclaim the Way to all peoples. The problem is simply to find courageous visionaries equal to the task, men who will be prepared to stand up [and fight for the cause].[20]

(iii) *Japan as a bridge between East and West*

Contact with the West also gave rise to another stream of thought, most eloquently expounded, in the nineteenth century, by the Japanese Christian convert Uchimura Kanzō.

> The Japanese revolution of 1868, I believe, has left its mark on world history. With that revolution as a turning point, two races, representing two very distinct civilizations, encountered each other in an atmosphere of mutual respect and entered into intercourse ... From this time onwards the estrangement between East and West, between pagan and Christian, began to fade away, the whole world moved towards unity in humanity and justice ... Japan has been given the mission of placing relations between Europe and Asia on a correct footing. Japan is presently involved in solving that problem.[21]

Uchimura saw Japan as a nation with a unique potential for forging understanding between the civilizations of Asia and the civilizations of Europe. The Restoration of 1868, in his view, was an event of immense significance for the cause of world peace, for communication across cultures, for the whole general evolution of mankind. Uchimura, his disciples and successors, sought neither to escape from Asia and join the imperial powers in a career of conquest nor to combine with other Asian countries against the West.

Uchimura Kanzō was a Christian and a pacifist. Most of those who saw Japan as the link between East and West were also associated with a pacific approach to the questions of foreign policy and defence. Yet the union of civilizations can be forged in many ways. There were not a few adherents of the Uchimura thesis who saw themselves as modern Alexanders rather than as contemporary Christs or Sakyamunis. The vision of Japan as the Great Unifier was, for example, to appeal strongly to Colonel Ishiwara Kanji, the chief architect of the 1931 Manchurian Incident. In his work *Japan's National Defence – the Present and the Future* (1927), Ishiwara argued that Japan, as the principal vehicle of East Asian civilization, and the United States, as the centre of Western civilization, were destined to contend with each other for the hegemony of the globe. The result of this immense and terrible conflict, the war to end wars, would be the unification of East Asia and the West, the emergence of a new world order and a new civilization.[22]

III Alliances in modern Japanese foreign and defence policies

Prewar Japanese governments, dominated, on the whole, by Westernizing imperialists or conservative pan-Asianists, made skilful use of alliances with European powers both in order to ensure the stability of the Restoration system and to promote their regional objectives. In the selection of allies, Japanese leaders relied on the old principle of *nagai mono ni makareyō*, carefully assessing the relative strengths of the European empires, exploiting their mutual rivalries and seeking to advance the national interest by aligning with the stronger against the weaker.

(i) The Anglo-Japanese alliance: its rationale and consequences.
The impact of empire on relations with the Anglo-American powers,
China and Russia

Japan's long association with Great Britain laid the foundations for its empire on the Asian continent. British capital and technology played a critical role in the Japanese modernization process, enabling the Restoration government to maintain its position against the conservative samurai of the west and north and suppress its opponents on the left. Whitehall's decision to abandon its longstanding policy of equidistance between Peking and Tōkyō and build up Japan as a counterweight to Russian influence in the Far East led directly to the Sino-Japanese war of 1894–5, as a result of which Japan acquired a colonial possession in Taiwan, a strong position on the Korean peninsula and a substantial indemnity enabling it to further accelerate the pace of its industrialization.[23]

British interest in a full-scale alliance with Japan, which increased around the turn of the century, was based on traditional European balance of power concepts. British political leaders and diplomats recognized, correctly, that their empire had entered a period of relative decline. Its industrial supremacy was challenged by Germany and the United States. It was overextended and isolated as a result of the Boer War. Its influence in the Far East had diminished. Russia's position, in contrast, had apparently improved. Confronted with this situation, Great Britain could either attempt to preserve a favourable equilibrium in East Asia through alliance with Japan, involving, perhaps, concessions in areas where British interests were minimal, or endeavour to reach agreement with St Petersburg on mutually acceptable spheres of influence (e.g. British supremacy in the Yangtse Valley in exchange for Russian dominance of Manchuria). The former option appeared to promise greater political, economic and strategic gains, although the idea of an Anglo-Russian *entente* was not without influential exponents. Nevertheless, the British judged the Japanese strong enough to control the Russians locally in North-East Asia but not powerful enough to threaten their own interests in the Far East.

Whitehall's assessment of Japan's objectives and potential proved, in the long term, to be fundamentally mistaken. Tōkyō was not playing balance of power politics. The idea of aligning with the weaker of the great powers against the stronger to preserve the status quo was totally alien to the Japanese tradition. In the inner circles of the Japanese government discussion simply focused on the question of which of the great European empires, the British or the Russian, was superior in overall strength and resolution. Association with the strongest European state, it was argued, would facilitate Japan's continental expansion. A policy of opposition to the paramount European power would not enable Japan to realize its ambitions. Yamagata Aritomo and his protégé, the then Prime Minister Katsura Tarō, maintained that Britain, even in its decline, possessed the world's most extensive empire, the most prosperous economy and the mightiest naval force. It was also the most influential foreign power in China. In North-East Asia, moreover, Britain was essentially a satisfied power, anxious, for reasons of global policy, to limit expansion of Russian influence, but not necessarily hostile to Japanese ambitions. Allied to Great Britain, Japan could dominate Korea, strengthen its position in China and improve its credit in commercial circles throughout the world. The possibilities for economic co-operation with Great Britain were also more attractive than with any other power. 'British colonies', it was noted in a crucial memorandum by Foreign Minister Komura Jūtarō on 7 December 1901, 'extend to the five continents. The benefits which Japan could gain from emigration and trade in these colonies if relations between Britain and Japan became more friendly, would far exceed those to be derived from Manchuria and Siberia.'[24] Alliance with a power hostile to Great Britain, it was contended, would force Japan to maintain parity with the Royal Navy. This would be difficult to achieve. Association with Britain, on the other hand, would merely oblige Japan to maintain naval parity with Russia, an infinitely easier task. Underlying this argument was the assumption that the British navy posed a far greater threat to Japan's continental ambitions than the Russian Far Eastern Fleet and Russian ground forces in Siberia. It was noted, however, that 'since there are grounds for believing Britain has already passed her zenith and will to some extent tend to decline, it would be best to fix a time limit for any British treaty'.[25]

Itō Hirobumi and Inoue Kaoru, on the other hand, argued the case for an *entente cordiale* with Russia. Russia, they believed, would probably accept Japanese supremacy in Korea in return for Japanese recognition of its own position in Manchuria. Japanese alignment with the British Empire, weakened and isolated in the wake of the South African war, coupled with a policy of hostility to Russia, they asserted, could eventually lead Japan, as in 1895, to confront an antagonistic coalition of continental powers. It was far from obvious that the British Empire was stronger than the combination of Russia, France and Germany. The wisest policy, therefore, would be to work with Russia for a peaceful division of North-East Asia into spheres of influence.[26]

Yamagata and Katsura won the day. Their analysis of the European balance of power, too, proved to be correct. Japan's stunning victories over Russia in the war of 1904–5, facilitated by Great Britain's benevolent neutrality and massive loans raised in London, New York and Berlin, temporarily eliminated the Romanov Empire as a factor in North-East Asian politics. As a result of the war, Japan acquired a dominant influence in Korea, the Russian lease of Port Arthur, Dairen and assorted rights on the Liaotung peninsula, Russian railway interests in southern Manchuria and possession of the island of Sakhalin south of the 50th parallel. By 1910, with British consent, Korea had been fully incorporated into the Japanese Empire. During World War I, Japan, as Great Britain's principal regional ally, further extended its influence, seizing the German Pacific islands north of the equator and the German concessions in Shantung, then embarking on a grandiose project to reduce China to satellite status. After the Russian Revolution the Japanese government, again energetically encouraged by Great Britain, dispatched a large expeditionary force to Siberia, where the army attempted to set up a White regime sympathetic to Tōkyō. By the time of the Versailles Peace Conference Japan had clearly established itself as the dominant power in the Far East.

Japan's emergence as a major imperial power had far-reaching consequences, none of which appear to have been foreseen by its British ally.

In the field of domestic politics, two decades of continuous military expansion entrenched the postion of the Satsuma-Chōshū oligarchy, strengthened the influence of the armed forces in the structure of the state and retarded the development of democracy. It was no accident that the first serious democratic challenges to the Satsuma-Chōshū clique coincided with the decline of the Anglo-Japanese alliance and that the period of 'Taishō Democracy' came into being only after it had been abandoned.

Externally, the rivalry between Japan and the United States, for some time evident in the commercial sphere, began to assume serious political and strategic dimensions. Until the advent of Woodrow Wilson's administration, American Far Eastern policy, like that of Great Britain, was conceived in terms of traditional balance of power concepts. Washington's threat perceptions, however, were very different to those of Whitehall. American presidents were not tormented by visions of cossacks pouring down the Khyber Pass. They were principally concerned with protecting their colonial possessions in the Philippines and promoting American commercial activity in China, including Manchuria. Unless the United States established itself as the dominant East Asian power, the latter objective could be realized only through maintenance of the 'Open Door', preserving China's 'independence' and discouraging partition of that country into spheres of influence.

Washington had thus responded to the Japanese victories of 1904–5 on two levels. Under the terms of the secret Taft-Katsura Agreement of 29 July 1905 the United States acknowledged Japan's preponderance in Korea in return for Japanese recognition of the American position in the Philippines. These principles were tacitly reconfirmed in the Root-Takahira Agreement of 30 November 1908.[27] At the same time, from 1906 onwards, Japan became the chief hypothetical enemy for American planners working on Pacific strategy. The world tour of Theodore Roosevelt's Great White Fleet in 1906–7 was primarily designed to impress the Japanese with the awesome potentialities of American power.[28]

In subsequent years, Japanese–American conflict over railway construction in Manchuria, trade with China and immigration into California intensified. By 1908 Theodore Roosevelt was making secret proposals to London, through Prime Minister Mackenzie King of Canada, for an 'Anglo-American coalition against Japan'.[29] He was also interested in Kaiser Wilhelm II's idea of a German-American-Chinese coalition to oppose Japan in East Asia.[30] The Twenty-One Demands crisis and the issue of the German Pacific islands further aggravated Japanese–American tension. The Lansing-Ishii Agreements of 2 November 1917, whereby Japan and the United States jointly recognized the territorial integrity of China, the 'Open Door' and the principle of equal opportunity, was at best an ambiguous compromise, which sowed the seeds for further discord. 'Japan', both parties also conceded, 'has special interests in China, especially the part to which her possessions are contiguous.'[31]

By the end of World War I the die had been cast. The Washington Conference did little to eliminate the underlying causes of Japanese–American friction, despite the agreements on China and naval arms limitations. The Japanese governments of the 1920s outwardly attached great importance to the general principle of co-operation with the United States. Nevertheless, Japan's first postwar long-range defence plan, drawn up, in accordance with constitutional practice, by the Chiefs of Staff, at the request of the emperor, and approved by Cabinet on 28 February 1923, a document which established the basic framework of the country's external policies for the next two decades, observed that

> In recent years the United States, having developed its national power, and disposing of limitless natural resources, has embarked on a policy of economic aggression. In China, especially, American-owned facilities have engaged in scurrilous anti-Japanese propaganda and the United States threatens the position that the empire has acquired as a result of many risks and sacrifices. It is not possible to bear this situation any longer ... The ostracism of Japanese residents in California will gradually spread to other states and develop a more solid base. There are no grounds for optimism concerning the position of our people in Hawaii. These conflicts, growing out of years of economic problems and racial prejudice, will be difficult to solve. In the future, the Japanese residents' feelings of

alienation are bound to grow and the clash of interests become more intense ... In this situation the United States, which possesses immense armaments and has many bases throughout East Asia and the Pacific, will, sooner or later, as part of its Asian policy, provoke a conflict with the empire. From the viewpoint of our national defence we must pay the greatest and most careful attention to the United States.[32]

The rapid growth of Japanese influence in the Far East had also begun to disturb sections of opinion in Great Britain itself. Certainly, political leaders such as Sir Edward Grey continued to believe that British recognition of Japan's preponderance in East Asia was the necessary price for securing Tōkyō's co-operation in other, more important areas. Many, however, considered that Great Britain had given too much and got too little in return.[33]

With the abrogation of the Anglo-Japanese alliance and the signing of the Four Power Pacific Treaty on 13 December 1921, relations between London and Tōkyō entered a long period of ambiguity, punctuated by alternate bouts of co-operation and discord. Yet it could in no way be claimed that dissolution of the Anglo-Japanese alliance precipitated Japan's subsequent drive for regional hegemony. On the contrary, the territorial gains made, with British encouragement, at the height of the alliance, had made further expansion all but inevitable.

The reason for this was fairly simple. Acquisition of a land frontier in Korea and significant interests in Manchuria had transformed the Japanese strategic environment. The new geopolitical realities confronting military planners in Tōkyō at once placed the empire on a collision course with the forces of Chinese nationalism. To protect Korea it seemed essential to control Manchuria. To control Manchuria it was necessary to dominate China. Soon after Korea's formal incorporation into the Japanese Empire, the Governor-General's office in Seoul, therefore, encouraged by powerful elements in Tōkyō, had become involved in schemes to detach Manchuria and sections of Inner Mongolia from China, setting up nominally independent monarchies under Japanese auspices.[34] These efforts had intensified after the fall of the Manchus (greeted with much rejoicing by radical pan-Asianists) confronted the Japanese government, first, with the unwelcome prospect of a Chinese revival under a republican form of government, then, as Sun Yat-sen's administration crumbled, with new opportunities for intervention on the continent through support for the conservative northern warlords. The Twenty-One Demands crisis had further muddied the waters between the Japanese government and the newly emerging forces in China. The Terauchi Cabinet's efforts to restore Japan's fortunes on the continent through negotiation of a conservative Sino-Japanese alliance were a generation too late and fell on stony, inhospitable soil.[35]

The Russian Revolution, Sun Yat-sen's alliance with Moscow, then the founding of the Chinese, Korean and Japanese Communist parties, added new dimensions to the problem. For the generation of revolutionary Chinese nationalists that grew to maturity in the 1920s, the Soviet Union shone like a guiding star on the northern horizon. The Soviet impact on the Korean nationalist movement, too, was very significant. For the old Japanese establishment, in contrast, Russian Bolshevism rapidly became what Iberian Catholicism had been for the Tokugawas – a particularly dangerous foreign creed, antithetic to the principles of Confucian monarchy, propagated, in the interests of a rival Western superpower, by a dedicated and infinitely resourceful international priesthood. Soviet Marxism, to a far greater degree than Anglo-American liberalism, struck at the philosophical roots of the Restoration order. It should not be assumed that this inevitably led the Japanese government to regard the Soviet Union as its most dangerous international antagonist. As we have seen, the postwar Japanese leadership, both civilian and military, was increasingly preoccupied with the threat posed to the empire by the United States. Until well on into the 1930s, the Soviet Union, as a state, was regarded as politically chaotic, industrially backward and militarily weak. Views about its role in Japan's global strategy varied. Nevertheless, in the years after the Russian Revolution, a consensus gradually emerged, both among Westernizing imperialists and in conservative pan-Asianist circles, that while the principal political, strategic and economic threat to Japan's interests in East Asia might come from the United States, the chief ideological challenge came from the Soviet Union.

This position had important implications for Japan's China policy. The nature of the historic Sino-Japanese relationship was such, it was argued, that political developments in China would inevitably affect Japan. In August 1919, a year after the rice riots had severely shaken the self-confidence of the Japanese establishment, Viscount Ishii Kikujiro wrote in his diary:

> ...if China develops into a hotbed of Bolshevism, the existence of European and American states is not directly imperilled. This is not so in Japan's case, however, as she cannot continue her existence without China and as the Japanese people cannot stand alone without the Chinese. Whether it be civil war, or epidemics, or political heresies which afflict China, the contagion will spread to Japan and the Japanese will suffer as well. These considerations are what lie at the bottom of Japan's extraordinary interest in China and make China such a vital concern to her. Whether Japan likes this situation or not, it is one which Heaven and Nature have ordained for her and from which she cannot escape. Nor can European or American nations prevent or alter Japan's particular relationship with China, even though they may wish it, as this relationship is an immutable fact.[36]

Growing Japanese–American rivalry heightened the importance of the Chinese continent. In the months after the Washington Conference, the Japanese government gradually came to the conclusion that the relationship with China was so crucial to the future of the empire that it should be developed, if necessary, by military force. The defence statement of 1923 noted that

> China's abundant natural resources are an indispensable element in both our economic development and our defence. Because of this, our policy towards China must be based on goodwill, mutual assistance, coexistence and mutual prosperity ... Yet the unstable political situation in China, the Chinese policy of using one barbarian to overcome another and China's traditional policy of attempting to win back her rights make it unrealistic to imagine that our expectations will be rapidly realized. There is also no guarantee that the Chinese, taking advantage of a Japanese–American conflict, might not seek to ally with the United States against us. For this reason, the empire needs to be in a position to bring great

pressure to bear [upon China].[37]

Shidehara Kijurō's efforts to reach a *modus vivendi* with the Chinese Nationalists, his willingness to contemplate eventual co-operation with the Chinese Communists, Tanaka Giichi's hardline interventionist policies on the continent, the Kwantung Army's 1931 *coup d'état* in Manchuria, Japan's subsequent expansion south of the Great Wall, the establishment of the puppet state of Manchu-kuo, the full-scale invasion of China that began with the Marco Polo Bridge Incident on 7 July 1937, then the creation of Wang Ching-wei's Chinese Republic as a rallying point for anti-Communist Chinese conservatives opposed to Chiang Kai-shek, were all based on the assumptions contained in this defence statement of 1923. The bitter conflicts between different factions of the oligarchy, the armed forces, the Foreign Ministry, the intelligence services, the business community and the political parties were real enough. Yet they were conflicts over strategy and timing, not basic objectives. The Communists, radical Socialists and left-wing liberals like Ishibashi Tanzan, who opposed military intervention on the continent, also based their thinking on the assumption that the destinies of Japan, China and Korea were inextricably linked, that the wisest policy for the empire lay in accommodation to the inexorable forces of political, economic and social change in Asia and in reform at home.

(ii) The Tripartite Pact

In August 1914 Foreign Minister Katō Takaaki's faith in the inevitable victory of the British Empire had only with some difficulty prevailed over the views of those who argued that Germany, too, was powerful, that the outcome of the conflict was uncertain and that since the alliance with Britain did not specifically require Japanese intervention in European conflicts it might be prudent to adopt an attitude of *de facto* neutrality.

For some years after the Great War the Japanese establishment, while aware of Britain's declining global influence and pessimistic about the long-term future of relations with the United States, remained convinced that the Anglo-American powers would continue to exert considerable influence in world affairs. Japan's objectives in Asia, it was agreed, could not be realized in the face of opposition from London or Washington.

During the 1930s, however, the resurgence of Germany and Italy, the spread of Fascist doctrines in Europe and the pervasive atmosphere of disillusion, nihilism and ennui in the English-speaking world made a strong impression on many Japanese leaders. The Nazi experiment, with its emphasis on the construction of a powerful, authoritarian, hierarchical state, its intense cultural nationalism, its glorification of rigorous discipline, struggle and will, its efforts to combine central economic planning and private enterprise, its vigorous opposition both to Anglo-American liberalism and Russian Bolshevism, seemed by no means incompatible with the ideals of the Meiji Restoration, as they had come to be interpreted. German racism did not alarm Japanese leaders. They themselves entertained extraordinary notions of racial superiority. They also knew, from long observation and experience, that institutionalized racism, accompanied by occasional bouts of genocide, had a hoary tradition in both the British Commonwealth and the United States. By the middle of the decade, a large section of influential Japanese opinion had become convinced that Hitler's Thousand Year Reich was destined to emerge as the world's foremost power, that its political institutions, economic organization, social structure, ideology and cultural forms might therefore provide useful models for Japan's future development, that Japan's objectives in East Asia could best be realized through co-operation with Berlin and Rome. American opposition to the Japanese drive for hegemony of the Western Pacific, the long, bloody and frustrating military operations on the continent, the belief that Stalin's Russia was extending its regional influence through support for the Chinese Communists and Korean nationalist groups, constant anxiety about the activities of the Japanese underground left, the impact of the Great Depression, then the collapse of the global trading and financial system, all combined to increase interest in alliance with the Fascist powers. By and large, however, the Japanese governments of the 1930s drifted towards association with Nazi Germany for the same reasons as their Meiji predecessors had moved towards alliance with the British Empire. As it turned out, the Japanese had this time made a disastrous miscalculation. Yet it was a miscalculation for which they could have been forgiven. The British and the French, along with a large body of opinion in the United States, were also convinced that Germany was emerging as the dominant continental power.

On 25 November 1936, at the height of the Spanish Civil War, the Japanese Empire and the German Reich signed the anti-Comintern Pact in Berlin, providing for wide-ranging co-operation against the 'international Communist conspiracy'. As Yoshida Shigeru, Japanese ambassador to the Court of St James, correctly realized, the real targets of the anti-Comintern Pact were Great Britain, France and the United States. By discouraging a Russian thrust into Manchuria, the anti-Comintern Pact facilitated intensified Japanese military operations in China. Its domestic repercussions were also considerable. A few months before the signing ceremony in Berlin Nosaka Sanzō (code-named Okano), Yamamoto Kenzō (Tanaka) and other Japanese Communists had appealed from Moscow for an anti-Fascist alliance of the left. The Japanese establishment was swept by a new wave of anti-Communist hysteria, accelerating the movement towards construction of a one-party totalitarian state, a trend resisted by liberals and left-wingers alike. It was not long, moreover, before the government and the military forces were torn apart by struggles between exponents of immediate attack on the Soviet Union, a policy favoured by the ferociously Anti-Communist Imperial Way faction (Kōdō-ha) in the army, and advocates of a major drive to incorporate China into the Japanese sphere of influence, the strategy supported by the navy and the Control faction (Tōsei-ha) in the army. This conflict was not finally resolved until the summer of 1939, when the stunning and totally unexpected victory of Soviet forces over the advancing Japanese at the battle of Nomonhan made it clear that an East Siberian empire would be, for the time being, difficult to establish. The Chinese continent, therefore, still seemed to offer the best prospects for expansion, despite the fact that con-clusion of the anti-Comintern Pact had at once impelled Chang Hsueh-liang, the ousted warlord of Manchuria, to kidnap Chiang Kai-shek and force the Nationalist leader to accept Chou En-lai's proposals for joint action against the Japanese.

The Nazi-Soviet pact of August 1939 had made several Japanese leaders uneasy about further co-operation with Berlin. Nevertheless, the outbreak of war in Europe, the rapid German occupation of Norway, Denmark, the Low Countries, then the fall of France and the British retreat from Dunkirk again tilted the balance in favour of close co-operation with the Fascist powers. Imperial Army Head-quarters considered that German forces were now in position to launch a successful invasion of Great Britain.[38] Naval leaders, while doubting Hitler's ability to occupy Britain so long as the Royal Navy remained intact, conceded that Berlin had estab-lished an effective and durable hegemony of the continent.[39] The Japanese embassy in Berlin was convinced that Germany's hour had come. Shigemitsu Mamoru, ambassador to the Court of St James, while maintaining that Great Britain could not be defeated, was also persuaded that it would never regain its former position.[40]

Germany and Italy, it was widely believed, would combine to establish a vast Euro-African empire, exerting a powerful influence in every quarter of the globe, including the Far East. Chiang Kai-shek's armies, it was noted, were counselled by German advisers. The Kuomintang, originally modelled on the Communist Party of the Soviet Union, was increasingly assuming a Fascist colouring. German trade with China was considerable. French Indochina was under a pro-German Vichy administration. Holland, the colonial power of Indonesia, had been occupied by German troops. With the impending fall of Britain it seemed probable that the focus of international conflict would shift to the Indian Ocean and the Western Pacific, with territories dominated by Germany aligning themselves against the remaining British colonies and the United States. 'It must be recognized that the formation of a German-Italian bloc centred on Europe and Africa is now inevitable', wrote Colonel Usui Shideki, Chief of the Eighth Section (Intelligence, Propaganda and Strategy) of the General Staffs on 4 July 1940. 'England will oppose this by reorganizing her strategy around India and Australia and will probably make efforts to keep open communications with the United States by securing the South Pacific sea-lanes. After some years the United States can be expected to realize expansion of its naval power and a strong Anglo-American bloc in the southern regions will emerge.'[41]

It seemed imperative that Japan move decisively. 'The possibility of Japan's *lebensraum* in the Far East and the southern regions again falling into the sphere of influence of [another] great power brings with it the danger of war between that great power [and Japan], thus endangering the peace of East Asia', Shigemitsu Mamoru advised Foreign Minister Arita on 19 June 1941. 'It is necessary for us to move courageously to prevent this now. We should see that Germany and Italy fully under-stand this point ... Since it is clear that European power in the Far East will be very much diminished after the war, I believe that this is the time, taking into account the overall situation, to consolidate our position in the region.'[42]

The new situation thus seemed to necessitate a still closer association with the

Fascist powers, partly to demarcate respective spheres of influence and ensure Hitler's support for Japan's position in the Far East at some future peace conference (just as Lloyd George, Clemenceau and Orlando had supported Japan against Wilson and Wellington Koo at Versailles), partly to discourage the United States from attempting to oppose Japan's accelerated drive for regional hegemony. 'Recently the United States has been taking a rather strong attitude towards our country', the Prime Minister Prince Konoye Fumimaro told the Emperor Hirohito on 19 September 1940. 'This hardening American attitude has influenced the posture of the Chungking government and others ill-disposed towards Japan, making our international position increasingly difficult ... In order to escape from this awkward situation it is necessary to strengthen our international standing ... At the moment, I do not believe there is any way to do this except by consolidating our links with countries with which we share common interests. Germany hopes to forestall American entry into the war. I believe we share their interest in wishing to avoid a difficult situation with the United States.'[43]

On 27 September 1940 Foreign Minister Matsuoka Yōsuke signed the Tripartite Pact in Berlin, five days after Japanese troops, with the consent of the Vichy government, had advanced into northern Indochina. On 13 April 1941 the Japanese government, taking advantage of Stalin's fears of an impending conflict with Germany, further strengthened its position through negotiation of the Japanese-Soviet Neutrality Agreement. By the end of June Japanese troops had completed the occupation of southern Indochina. The subsequent American-British-Dutch economic embargo against Japan forced the Konoye Cabinet to accelerate its war preparations. It was not in itself, except in the most superficial sense, the cause of Japanese entry into World War II. On 8 December 1941 Japanese forces attacked the American naval base at Pearl Harbor. At the same time the Imperial Japanese Army began its advance into Malaya. Within less than a month Japan had occupied Guam, landed troops in the Philippines, captured Hong Kong and concluded an alliance with Thailand. By the northern summer of 1942 it seemed by no means impossible that Japan might absorb China, permanently break the grip of the European powers on South-East Asia, and fight the United States to a standstill, that the whole of East and South-East Asia, from Sakhalin to the Coral Sea, might be incorporated, one way or another, into a Japanese sphere of influence. The Communist Party, left-wing Socialists, the fledgeling Nichiren Buddhist lay organization Sōka Gakkai and a few eccentric Anglophile liberals remained opposed to the government's foreign and domestic policies. By and large, however, men found their own rationalizations for the conflict. Westernizing imperialists rejoiced in the fact that Japan, allied to the mightiest European empire, had reconfirmed its position as a full member of the Western state system and was once again an active participant in a struggle which would determine the shape of world politics for generations to come. Imperial pan-Asianists saw the Greater East Asia Co-prosperity Sphere as the realization of their wildest dreams. Many radical pan-Asianists, too, came to view the conflict as the first and necessary step in the liberation of Asia from the West, the prelude to an Asian cultural renaissance that would eventually transform the sociopolitical order in Japan itself.

CHAPTER II

The postwar international order and the origins of the San Francisco system, 1945–1952

> Can you draw out Leviathan with a fishhook or press down his tongue with a cord ...
> Will he make a covenant with you to take him for your servant for ever?
>
> Job 41:1–4

I The outcome of World War II

In the last weeks of August 1945, the weapons of the great powers fell silent on a world changed almost beyond recognition. The conflict, as His Imperial Majesty Hirohito remarked, had not necessarily developed to Japan's advantage. The German Reich, its armies defeated in the east and in the west, had been reduced to rubble, its territories divided up among the conquerors. Italy was in chaos. The Greater East Asia Co-prosperity Sphere had collapsed under the multiple impact of the American naval victories in the Pacific, the massive air assault on the home archipelago, the Soviet thrust into Manchuria, northern Korea, Sakhalin and the Kuriles, the growing strength of the Chinese Communists and the emergence of anti-Japanese resistance movements in occupied South-East Asia. The vicissitudes of war had also accelerated deep-seated shifts in the balance of power within the anti-Fascist coalition. Great Britain and France, exhausted and deeply in debt, their colonial empires on the verge of dissolution, had entered a period of rapid decline. By the time of the Japanese surrender, despite the polite fictions maintained at Cairo, Teheran, Yalta and Potsdam, it had become abundantly clear that only two of the victorious allies, the United States and the Soviet Union, remained fully independent international actors.

Of the two new global superpowers, Japan's conqueror, the United States, was, overwhelmingly, the stronger. Indeed, in the years immediately after the war the United States, like Rome after the fall of Carthage, seemed on the point of establishing a virtual global hegemony. The American GNP had doubled during the war. By 1945 American factories were producing half the world's goods. In all fields of heavy industry, in steel production, chemicals, shipbuilding, aircraft manufacture, automobiles and electronics, America had achieved unrivalled supremacy over its competitors. American agricultural products and consumer goods flooded the world's markets. The United States possessed, albeit for a brief period, a monopoly of nuclear weapons. It had also demonstrated its readiness to use them. American air power was global in its reach. American naval power seemed unchallengeable. The Pacific, the Atlantic and the Mediterranean had become American lakes. Washington's sphere of influence in Latin America had been unaffected either by the war itself or by agreements reached during its course. American influence in Great Britain, France, Italy, the Netherlands and Belgium was considerable. So, too, was American influence in occupied Western Germany. The United States had replaced Great Britain as the dominant external power in Canada. In the Southwest Pacific Australia and New Zealand, shaken by the Japanese wartime thrust into their region and alarmed at the decline of British imperial power, saw their future in terms of special relationships with Washington. In the Philippines the Americans had been welcomed back as liberators. In Korea they had shared this honour with their Soviet allies. In China, Chiang Kai-shek's moribund regime was increasingly dependent on United States support. In India, Burma, Vietnam and Indonesia, where the long struggle against European colonial domination was entering its final phase, nationalist leaders of all political hues held the United States in high regard. Even Ho Chi Minh, whose fledgeling Democratic Republic of Vietnam was eventually to shake the *Pax Americana* to its foundations, modelled his declaration of independence on its American counterpart. In the Middle East, too, in Saudi Arabia, in Iran and around the periphery of the decaying European empires, both the United States government and American oil companies were vigorously extending Washington's influence. To Foreign Minister Shigemitsu Mamoru, watching the flypast of 400 B-29 bombers and 1,500 fleet aircraft from his vantage point on the *Missouri*, after signing the documents of surrender, it must have seemed that, by some odd twist of fate, the promise of the German Reich would be fulfilled in the American Republic.

The American leadership had a clear idea of the kind of world it wished to create. The United States was seen as the central, dominant and most dynamic component of a vast free enterprise commonwealth embracing the greater part of the globe. Already, the Bretton Woods Conference of 1944, which had established the United States Federal Reserve as the *de facto* World Central Bank, and had tied fully convertible national currencies to the dollar, which in turn was tied to gold, had laid the basis for American hegemony of the postwar international economy. The United States position was further consolidated by the establishment of the World Bank and the International Monetary Fund. The appointment of Secretary of the Treasury, Fred Vinson, as chairman of the board of governors of both organizations in March 1946 underlined Washington's view of its central role in the postwar order and revealed the extent of the influence it was able to wield. So, too, did the success of United States efforts to force Great Britain and France, both desperately in need of postwar reconstruction loans, to dismantle their regional trading blocs, facilitate the free movement of goods and capital throughout their territories, adopt a more cautious approach to the nationalization of industry and abandon the government manipulation and subsidies that had improved the international competitiveness of their export industries in the prewar period.[1] In 1947 the United States sponsored the General Agreement on Tariffs and Trade (GATT), with its headquarters in Geneva, to enforce free trade on a global scale.

American preponderance could endure only so long as the United States remained in a position to contain, and, if necessary, to destroy, rival global systems, to prevent the re-emergence of competing centres of economic, political and military power among its own associates, and to guide the evolution of events in the post-colonial non-European world in directions favourable to its own interests. Realization of these objectives required that American military power remain overwhelmingly strong and effective; that the United States economy remain larger, more dynamic and more efficient than that of any potential rivals; that the world-wide appeal of American civilization, of the American political system and the American way of life remain untarnished.

In the early postwar years there seemed little doubt that the United States would be able to maintain its near hegemonic position indefinitely. The Soviet Union, America's most important wartime ally and only serious potential rival, had emerged from the conflict with a strengthened strategic position in eastern Europe, in continental North-East Asia, the Sea of Okhotsk and the Sea of Japan. Yet the Soviet Union was in no position to challenge the United States. The Russians, in their titanic struggle with Nazi Germany, had suffered immense and terrible losses – 20 million war dead as compared with 545,000 American casualties on all fronts. Their industrial heartland had been devastated, their communications network shattered. Their agriculture, already adversely affected by the enforced collectivization of the 1930s, as well as by climatic factors beyond human control, lay in ruins. Soviet ground forces, it is true, were large, well equipped and battle-hardened. Yet Soviet air and naval power were very much inferior to those of the United States. Soviet cities were highly vulnerable to air attack. Whatever American politicians, diplomats and military planners may have believed, Moscow was in no position to extend its direct influence far beyond its newly established *cordon sanitaire* in Eastern Europe.[2] The Communist victory in the Chinese Civil War, however momentous its historical significance, did not give the Soviet Union any decisive strategic advantage. The Sino-Soviet alliance of January 1950 denied the territory, resources and markets of the Chinese continent to the United States. Yet the Chinese Communists remained intensely nationalistic. Much to Stalin's disappointment, Mao Tse-tung consistently and firmly rejected requests to establish Soviet military bases on Chinese soil.[3]

A breakdown in relations between the United States and the Soviet Union was by no means inevitable. Discussion of the origins of the Cold War lies beyond the scope of the present work. Suffice it to remark that until the death of President Roosevelt in April 1945 it seemed probable that the Grand Alliance would continue to provide the framework for a stable and relatively peaceful postwar international order. Roosevelt and his advisers were pragmatic exponents of enlightened *realpolitik*. They were convinced that, however powerful the United States might appear to be, a lasting peace could be built only on the basis of co-operation with the Russians. They believed that the Soviet Union would demand and, in view of its vital security interests and contribution to the common struggle, was indeed entitled to expect, a dominant role in postwar eastern Europe. At Yalta Roosevelt had conceded Soviet supremacy in this region. Stalin, too, acutely conscious of his country's weakness, showed every indication of willingness to support a concert of the powers based on division of the world into appropriate spheres of influence. The Truman administration's refusal to recognize Soviet preponderance in eastern Europe dealt a fatal blow to this scheme of things. American–Soviet relations deteriorated rapidly during the spring and summer of 1945. By January 1946, less than a year after Roosevelt's death, the United States Joint Chiefs of Staff were unanimously urging the President to prepare for the possibility of a military confrontation with the Soviet Union.[4] The subsequent intensification of the American–Soviet ideological struggle, the enunciation of the Truman Doctrine and the gradual division of Europe into two armed camps impelled Washington to reorganize its planning for the postwar world around the twin pillars of a reconstructed Germany and a revitalized Japan, viewed as the regional centres of two vast, interlocking industrial and trading communities, politically dependent on North America and encompassing, within their respective spheres of influence, the greater part of Africa, the Middle East and South-East Asia.[5]

II   Japan's incorporation into the American global alliance system

Had imperial Japan, like Franco's Spain, maintained a policy of pro-German neutrality in World War II, its postwar leadership, in accordance with well-established historical patterns, would probably have found itself divided between advocates of alliance with the United States, now clearly the dominant world power, and exponents of independent policies based on the concept of a Japan-centred pan-Asianist federation. Advocates of alliance with the United States, Westernizers and Asianists alike, would have argued, privately, that only such an arrangement could protect Japan from its mighty trans-Pacific rival, facilitate the conquest of China and extend the empire's interests still further afield. Publicly, these 'pro-American' factions, taking full advantage of the break-down of United States-Soviet relations in Europe, would have drawn Washington's attention to the similarity of their respective interests in the Far East, stressing the threat posed by the Soviet Union in North-East Asia, protraying the protracted guerrilla war in China as a crusade against Bolshevism, pointing to the dangers posed by the Korean Communists, the Vietminh, radical elements in the Indonesian nationalist movement, and so on. The Truman administration, dominated by hardline anti-Communist ideologues, many of whom had adopted an indulgent attitude to Berlin, Rome and Tōkyō in the prewar period,[6] and increasingly disenchanted with Chiang Kai-shek's performance as an ally, might eventually have decided that a partnership with imperial Japan, despite the considerable risks it entailed, was an essential link in the strategy of containment. Had such an alliance been concluded the Japanese, again in accordance with well-established historical patterns, would have endeavoured to keep their commitments to a minimum, manoeuvring, carefully and diplomatically, to discard the arrangement once they had achieved regional hegemony or when American power had gone into eclipse.

Defeat in the Pacific War made it impossible for the Japanese government to negotiate with the United States from a position of equality. An association along the lines of the Anglo-Japanese alliance or the Tripartite Pact was simply out of the question. Certainly, the San Francisco Peace Treaty, signed on 8 September 1951, after six years of American occupation, was one of the most generous settlements ever offered by a conqueror to a defeated enemy, formally restoring full sovereignty and placing few overt restrictions on Japan's domestic or international activities.* Yet the security treaty, signed by Prime Minister Yoshida at San Francisco under the watchful eyes of United States Secretary of State Dean Acheson, President Truman's Special Ambassador John Foster Dulles, Senator Styles Bridges and Senator Alexander Wiley, made Japan's position as a dependent American client state plain for all the world to see. The security treaty granted the United States the right to maintain, indefinitely, military bases in the Japanese homeland and adjacent areas. Japan, unlike the NATO countries, was given no explicit guarantee of American protection. The treaty simply permitted the United States, on the basis of its own judgement, to use its facilities either to defend Japan from external attack or to pursue its own, independent policy objectives in the Far East. The Japanese government was given no means to influence American decisions in either case. The United States was also granted the right to intervene to suppress domestic disturbances in Japan, a provision remarkably reminiscent of the Brezhnev Doctrine of limited sovereignty for socialist bloc nations promulgated by the Soviet Union some sixteen years later. Japan was 'expected' to build up its own armed forces. It was neither formally committed by the treaty to large-scale rearmament nor to active military support for American policies in Asia and the Pacific. There were no provisions specifically requiring direct Japanese participation in American-sponsored regional security arrangements.[9] Nevertheless, the Yoshida-Acheson Exchange of Notes, concluded after the signing of the treaty, pledged Japan's continued support for American military operations against the Communist forces in Korea.[10] Despite claims to the contrary, Japanese aid to the American war effort was not merely logistical. Japanese minesweepers, manned by Japanese ex-naval personnel, were playing a covert but direct and essential military role in Korean waters. Japanese ex-intelligence officers, familiar with conditions in the neighbouring peninsula, had already, with the full knowledge of the Japanese government, been recruited by the United States forces as special advisers.[11] At every level, the new Japan's links with the United States were at once far more intimate and far less equal than those of the new China with the Soviet Union. The massive American military presence remaining in Japan after the end of the occupation – 260,000 troops manning a total of 2,824 military bases and

* Under the terms of the peace treaty Japan renounced all claims to its former colonial possessions in Korea, Taiwan, Sakhalin, the Kuriles and the Pacific islands.[7] It also recognized temporary but absolute United States sovereignty over the island of Okinawa which, under continued military administration, was rapidly becoming one of America's largest offensive bases in the Far East.[8]

other establishments – ensured that this situation would continue unchanged for many years.

The Japanese-American Security Treaty, as it was concluded in 1951, was an inevitable outcome of the United States victory in the Pacific War, the breakdown of the anti-Fascist Grand Alliance, the Chinese Revolution and Washington's decision to intervene in the Korean civil war. This is to state the obvious. Yet the negotiations that led up to the security treaty, the shape of the final agreement, the interpretations placed upon it, the private views of important individuals about the long-term future of the relationship and their ideas about other options open to their respective nations deserve careful scrutiny. Examined both in the context of Japan's historical traditions and in the light of subsequent developments these reveal, often in a startling fashion, not only the contrasting diplomatic styles of the two new allies but also, more importantly, their differing perceptions of postwar geopolitical realities, their views of probable future trends, the extent to which their perceived interests coincided, the degree to which they were seen to diverge. In 1952, when the United States bestrode the Pacific like a colossus, Japanese views about these matters perhaps seemed of little consequence. Yet they have become increasingly important as America's relative decline, the emergence of a more complex international order and Japan's reassertion of a more significant role in world affairs have precipitated deep and subtle changes in the power relationship between the two countries.

III   American planning for Japan's future, February 1942–June 1950

American planning for Japan's future began shortly after Pearl Harbor, with the establishment of an Advisory Committee on Postwar Foreign Policy in the State Department in February 1942. Shortly afterwards the Joint Chiefs of Staff also began drawing up blueprints for the postwar era. In December 1944 a State-War-Navy Co-ordinating Committee was formed to establish policy guide-lines for the occupation of Germany, Italy and Japan.

With respect to the future of Japan there was, at this stage, a remarkable degree of consensus among American planners, both civilian and military. The Roosevelt administration assumed that the American-Soviet relationship would prove enduring. It also assumed that Japan would fall within a future American sphere of influence. There was no interest in incorporating the Japanese archipelago into the North American strategic defence system. The United States chief objective in the Far East was simply to prevent Japan's re-emergence as a rival military-industrial power. By the end of the 1943 the view had become well established that a reformed, demilitarized and politically stable Japan, stripped of its colonies, guaranteed a reasonable degree of prosperity through participation in world trade and contributing positively to the economic development of China and other neighbouring countries, would be less likely to threaten American interests than a Japan treated harshly by its conqueror. The United States, it was agreed, should dominate the occupation and institute the necessary changes in the Japanese political, economic and social structure. Generally speaking, American planners, heavily influenced by the social democratic philosophies of Roosevelt's New Deal, envisaged establishment of a constitutional monarchy, significant deconcentration of economic power, the dismantling of Japan's military-industrial complex and a substantial programme of land reform.[12] With the exception of the economic deconcentration programme most of these reforms were implemented during the first stage of the occupation.

Truman's decision to confront the Soviet Union in Eastern Europe began to influence American policies in Asia even before the end of the war. In the northern spring of 1945 former President Herbert Hoover urged Truman to regard both Germany and Japan as future allies against Russia. Japan, he suggested, should be granted generous peace terms and be permitted to retain its colonial empire in Korea and Taiwan.[13] Joseph Grew, former United States ambassador to Tōkyō, and Harry Kern, Foreign Editor of *Newsweek* and subsequently founder of the American Council on Japan, an influential grouping of anti-Communist ex-diplomats, businessmen, military officers, academics and journalists, generally shared these sentiments.[14] Truman's decision to co-operate with the Imperial Japanese Army against the Communists in China during the last days of the war perhaps reflected advice he received from these quarters.[15] Nevertheless, Hoover's belief that Japan should be immediately reconstructed as the linchpin of American East Asian strategy did not find much favour at this stage.

The reason for this was perfectly straightforward. Until the summer of 1947, Chiang Kai-shek's Republic of China, not Japan, remained the centrepiece of America's grand design for postwar Asia. China, modernizing along acceptable lines with American capital, technology and educational assistance, spiritually uplifted by American missionary endeavours, armed with American weapons, was to help Washington both prevent a possible re-emergence of Japan as a rival great power and contain the spread of Communist influence in the Far East. In both these fields of activity, particularly the latter, Chiang Kai-shek's record was impeccable. On 7 June 1947 the Joint Chiefs of Staff expressed their conviction that 'the only Asiatic government at present capable of even a show of resistance to Soviet expansionism is the Chinese Nationalist Government'.[16] General Wedemeyer's report to President Truman (19 September 1947) endorsed these views, recommending increased military assistance to the Kuomintang and expansion of the American advisory mission to 10,000 men.[17]

The failure of the Marshall mission (January 1947), the deteriorating military position of the Chinese Nationalists, Soviet withdrawal from Manchuria, reports of Kuomintang corruption and misuse of American aid, together with the consolidation of the United States military position in the Pacific, caused a fundamental, albeit slow and sporadic shift in emphasis. During the latter part of 1947, first, the State Department, then, increasingly, the Joint Chiefs of Staff, the War and Navy departments, General MacArthur's headquarters in Tōkyō and other interested bodies came to believe that the United States relationship with Japan, rather than with the Nationalist Chinese, would eventually constitute the keystone of American policy in Asia. The reorganization of the State Department, the amalgamation of the War and Navy departments, the process leading to creation of the National Security

Council and the Central Intelligence Agency (CIA), delayed, for some time, the translation of these altered perceptions into concrete policy. Nevertheless, the general trend was clear. By February 1948 George Kennan, director of the State Department Policy Planning Staff and principal architect of containment, was advising Secretary of State George Marshall that the United States should 'liquidate unsound commitments to China'. Japan, Kennan argued, was the key to the east, just as Germany was the key to the west. The two former Axis powers should therefore be reconstructed

> to a point where they could play their part in the Eurasian balance of power and yet to a point not so far advanced as to permit them again to threaten the interests of the maritime world of the West.[18]

Japan and the Philippines, Kennan believed,

> would eventually constitute the cornerstones of a Pacific security system adequate for the protection of our interests. If we could retain effective control over these two archipelagoes, in the sense of assuring that they would remain in friendly hands, there could be no serious threat to our security from the east within our time.[19]

There were, however, several possible ways of incorporating Japan into the emerging American global anti-Soviet strategic system. Factional-bureaucratic conflict on this complex issue continued, uninterrupted and without any sign of resolution, from the time of Marshall's return from China in January 1947 until the outbreak of the Korean War in June 1950. Kennan's view, widely accepted in State Department circles, was that Japan would never again be able to emerge as an 'independent entity'. The inescapable realities of postwar international politics required that it would become either an American or a Russian satellite.[20] Given the critical position of the Japanese archipelago in the Eurasian power balance, Washington's objective should be to ensure that its government, however constituted, consistently acted in ways that would advance United States interests. To achieve this goal it would be necessary to design a peace settlement that enabled Washington to retain 'veto power over what she [Japan] does'.[21] If this could be arranged the United States should have no objections to renewed Japanese ascendancy in Korea and other (unspecified) surrounding territories. This would serve to 'counter and moderate Soviet influence there'.[22] An appropriate level of Japanese–Soviet conflict, it was suggested, could be created over the issue of the northern islands.[23] At the same time the Japanese economy should be closely linked with those of the newly independent non-Communist states of South-East Asia, the great arc of resource-rich territories extending through the Philippines, Indonesia and Indochina to the Indian subcontinent and Afghanistan. In this way the United States could construct a solid wall of politically stable, economically viable, anti-Communist states extending all around the periphery of continental Asia.[24] It was essential, of course, to ensure that Japan itself did not re-emerge as an independent and competitive centre of power. Kennan believed that this objective could best be realized by maintaining indirect controls 'foolproof enough and cleverly enough exercised really to have power over what Japan imports in the way of oil and other things'.[25]

Kennan was interested in containing the Soviet Union, not overthrowing it. He was also aware of the complexity of Far Eastern international politics. For this reason he was uncertain about the necessity for a formal Japanese-American security treaty, the stationing of United States forces in Japan after the peace settlement, or the wisdom of encouraging Japanese rearmament. Sometimes he viewed an American-dominated Japan as the politico-military centre of a regional anti-Communist alliance system. At other times he rejected this approach. The draft peace treaty drawn up by John R. Davis in August 1947, under Kennan's supervision, a document which differed little, in essentials, from the 1951 settlement, envisaged the creation of a politically conservative, industrially reconstructed Japan, economically linked to non-Communist South-East Asia, 'amenable to American leadership', garrisoned by United States troops and maintaining a central police force 'susceptible to expansion and use in accordance with American directives'.[26] Two years later, as the dust of the Chinese Revolution settled, Kennan had come to believe that the United States should withdraw its forces from the Japanese mainland to an entirely offshore position, throwing its weight behind a government which would 'maintain normal economic and political relations with the Communist bloc and, in the absence of open hostilities, resist complete identification with either the interests of the United States or the Soviet Union.[27] Such a policy, he felt, might reduce Peking's dependence on Moscow, encourage latent differences between the two Communist powers to come to the surface and pave the way for future political change on the Chinese continent.

General MacArthur, whose position as Supreme Commander of the Allied Powers gave him considerable opportunity to influence United States East Asian policies, was even more convinced that United States interests in the Pacific, and the general cause of regional peace and stability, would best be served by Japanese neutrality. MacArthur unequivocally endorsed Kennan's plan to integrate the Japanese economy with that of non-Communist South-East Asia. Yet he was also inclined to believe that a Japan rearmed against the Soviet Union would not necessarily always act in ways compatible with United States objectives. In May 1950, on the eve of the Korean War, MacArthur told *The New York Times* correspondent C.L. Sulzberger:

> Neither side would profit by the arming of Japan. We don't care to use her as an armed ally but we don't want to see Russia or China use her against us. Japanese neutrality would be a benefit to everyone, including not only Japan but also the United States, Russia and China.[28]

The American position in the Far East, MacArthur thought, could be adequately secured by building a network of bases extending from the Aleutians, through Okinawa, Midway and the former Japanese mandated islands to Clark Field in the Philippines. There was no need for installations in Japan or on the Asian mainland.[29]

The Joint Chiefs of Staff, the War Department and the Navy Department, in contrast, attached paramount importance to the maintenance of a strong United States military presence in the Japanese archipelago. They were also enthusiastic advocates of large-scale Japanese rearmament. Their approach to these matters was a straightforward one, conceived within the simplistic framework of bilateral Russo-American rivalry, untroubled by reflections on the lessons of history or the complexities of regional politics. During the period 1945–54 the Joint Chiefs of Staff consistently (albeit unsuccessfully) recommended that the United States provoke a conflict with the Soviet Union and destroy its superpower rival before the Russians had fully recovered from World War II.[30] American war plans envisaged nuclear and conventional air attacks against the Soviet Union from bases in Great Britain, Egypt, India, Japan and Okinawa.[31] By April 1947 the Joint Chiefs of Staff had come to view Japan as 'the one nation which would contain large armed forces of our ideological opponents in the Far East while the United States and her allies in the West launched a major offensive in that area'.[32] It was also hoped that a rearmed Japan would eventually form the centrepiece of a regional alliance, exerting its political, economic and military influence to ensure that the newly independent countries of South-East Asia remained unreceptive to Communist overtures.[33] These perceptions of Japan's role were generally shared by Harry Kern and his friends, particularly by Lieutenant-General Robert L. Eichelberger, commander of the United States Eighth Army in Japan. A rearmed Japan, Eichelberger told an audience of American businessmen in the northern summer of 1948, 'would force the Russians to consider the possibility of a two-front war'.[34]

The American Council on Japan, like the State Department, believed that Washington's objectives could best be realized through early conclusion of a peace treaty. This assessment was rejected by the Joint Chiefs of Staff. From the military point of view, it was argued, absolute American control of the Japanese archipelago through continued occupation was essential. The Chinese Revolution (not generally regarded in military circles as an irreversible historical development) caused the Chiefs of Staff to dig in their heels. Proposals for Japanese neutrality, too, were regarded as highly dangerous, all the more so since the Russians might accept them, depriving the United States of a valuable forward base and establishing a disturbing precedent for settlement of the German problem.[35]

It was in the context of this debate that both the State Department and the American Council on Japan, concurring with the military view of the strategic importance of the archipelago, yet conscious of the political need for an early peace settlement, gradually drifted towards the idea of negotiating a separate, bilateral Japanese-American security treaty. This treaty would permit United States forces to remain in Japan after the end of the occupation. It would also contain provisions for rearming Japan with a view to using the nation's fighting manpower in any future conflict with the Russians.[36]

IV   Japanese planning for defeat, June 1942–February 1945

From 1941 to 1945 those Japanese officially charged with planning the postwar world order, like their American counterparts, thought only in terms of victory.

Nevertheless, shortly after the battle of Midway (5 June 1942) a small group of court nobles, elder statesmen, senior diplomats, high-ranking military officers and business leaders, centring around Prince Konoye Fumimaro (b. 1891, Prime Minister at various times between 1937 and 1941), the Marquis Kido Kōichi (b. 1889, grandson of the Restoration oligarch Kido Takayoshi, Minister for Education and later for Social Welfare in the 1937 Konoye Cabinet, Home Minister in the 1939 Hiranuma Cabinet) and Yoshida Shigeru (b. 1878, see below) began unofficial and highly secret discussions about the possibility of an unfavourable outcome to the war. The group gradually expanded to include such figures as Baron Harada Kumao (b. 1888, sometime private secretary to Prince Saionji Kimmochi, Member of the House of Peers), Hatoyama Ichirō (b. 1883, Seiyūkai politician, Minister for Education, 1931–4), Ikeda Seihin (b. 1867, former director of the Mitsui Bank and governor of the Bank of Japan, Finance Minister and Minister for Commerce and Industry at various times during the 1930s), Iwabuchi Tatsuo (b. 1892, critic and journalist, associated at various times with the *Mainichi*, *Yomiuri* and *Kokumin* newspapers), Admiral Kobayashi Seizō (b. 1877, retired), Count Makino Nobuaki (b.1861, son of the Restoration leader Ōkubo Toshimichi, father-in-law of Yoshida Shigeru, close imperial adviser), General Mazaki Jinsaburō (b. 1876, reserve), Rear Admiral Mazaki Katsuji (b. 1884, reserve), Major-General Obata Toshishirō (b. 1885, reserve), Admiral Suzuki Kantarō (b. 1867, retired), Ueda Shunkichi (b. 1890, former Finance Ministry official), General Ugaki Kazunari (b. 1868, War Minister at various times between 1924 and 1931, Governor-General of Korea, Foreign Minister in the 1938 Konoye Cabinet) and Wakatsuki Reijirō (b. 1866, Minseitō politician, Prime Minister, 1926–27, 1931).

These men were not, on the whole, anti-imperialists, 'little Japanists', pacifists or Wilsonian idealists. They came from the core of the old establishment. They believed profoundly in imperial Japan and its values. The majority of them had supported, enthusiastically, Japan's expansion on the Asian continent. Some, like Yoshida, had regarded the alliance with Germany and the war with the Anglo-American powers as a tactical mistake. Their 'anti-war movement', nebulous and ineffectual as it was (particularly in comparison to their later resistance to the occupation reforms) had two objectives. Mistrustful of the Soviet Union, lacking confidence in their ability to deal simultaneously with China and the United States in the Pacific, they were anxious to conclude peace rapidly, on favourable terms, before the military situation turned against them. Uneasy, as always, about Japan's own internal stability, apprehensive about the manoeuvrings of rival factions, they hoped to wind up the war before the political, social and economic contradictions of which they were only too well aware erupted into full-scale revolution.[37]

Less than a week after the battle of Midway, on 11 June 1942, Yoshida Shigeru discussed with the Marquis Kido the possibility of sending Prince Konoye to Switzerland to sound out the prospects for a settlement. Yoshida, whose devotion to Anglo-American values was always subordiante to his practice of a *realpolitik* based on the principle of *nagai mono ni makareyō*, thought that Konoye's past record of sympathetic interest in the United States, together with his current devotion to the German alliance, could prove useful to Japan whichever way the military situation in Europe developed.[38] General Ugaki Kazunari also supported the idea of a mission to Europe led by Prince Konoye. He suggested, in addition, that Tōyama Mitsuru, the conservative pan-Asianist and co-founder of the Genyōsha, lead a similar delegation to China.[39]

Nothing appears to have come of these discussions, although a great deal of agonizing continued throughout the course of 1942 and 1943. By the end of 1943 it was clear that the days of the Axis were numbered. Those who had maintained, in prewar days, that the Anglo-American powers and the Soviet Union were stronger than Germany and Italy had clearly been correct. Still, all was not lost. The neutrality agreement with the Soviet Union was still operative. The Japanese position in Korea and Manchuria appeared stable. The war in China could be regarded as a stalemate. It was by no means certain that the United States and its allies could mount an invasion of Japan. On 6 January 1944, therefore, the Marquis Kido drew up a plan which he considered could form the basis for a just and realistic peace settlement.

–   Questions relating to the Pacific to be settled by countries bordering on the Pacific.
–   A Joint Japanese-Soviet-Chinese–American–British Commission to be formed.
–   Territories occupied by Japan, as well as islands in the Pacific, to be made into a demilitarized zone.
–   With the exception of great powers, all independent countries in the region save Manchukuo to declare perpetual neutrality on the Swiss model. All other occupied territories to be disposed of by the joint commission.[40]

Obviously, Kido was not thinking in terms of Japanese integration into a postwar world order dominated by the United States. Japan was to survive as an independent great power, preserving intact its large North-East Asian empire in Korea and Manchuria. Security in the Pacific was to be guaranteed by a combination of great power accords and demilitarized zones. Again, nothing appears to have come of these proposals.

During the course of 1944–5, as the military situation worsened, Japanese exponents of a negotiated settlement tended to divide into three broad streams. To some extent these schools of thought reflected different views about the likely configuration of power in the postwar world. They also reflected differing hopes and fears about the domestic outcome of the conflict.

One group, centring around such figures as General Umezu Yoshijirō, the Army Chief of Staff, Tōgo Shigenori, sometime Foreign Minister in the Tōjō Cabinet, and Shigemitsu Mamoru, also Foreign Minister in the Tōjō Cabinet, thought in terms of negotiating a special relationship with the Soviet Union. This view, apparently, had a particularly strong appeal in sections of the armed forces. It will be recalled that the leading elements in the uncompromisingly anti-Soviet Kōdō-ha, or Imperial Way faction, had been decimated in the wake of the 26 February affair in

1936. After that time, leadership of the army had been assumed by the Tōsei-ha, or Control faction, which had adopted a generally more indulgent attitude towards the Soviet Union and saw Japan's imperial destiny lying in China and the South Seas. The war had clearly revealed Russia's staggering military potential. There were also rumours that the United States and Germany might soon negotiate a separate peace and join together in a crusade against Bolshevism.

It was against this background that Foreign Minister Shigemitsu Mamoru declared, in December 1944, that Japanese interests in Asia were much more compatible with those of the Soviet Union than with those of the Anglo-American powers. Similarly, Russian interests were much more compatible with those of Japan than with those of Great Britain or the United States.[41] In February 1945 General Umezu reportedly told the emperor that Japan

> must under no circumstances make peace with the United States. The Americans have a contempt not only for Japan as a state but for the Japanese as a race... The only people we can ask favours of now are the Russians ... we have no alternative but to prepare for a decisive battle on the continent with the Soviet Union at our rear.[42]

Even that doughty old conservative Admiral Nomura Kichisaburō apparently believed that a pro-Soviet position was 'one possible policy'.[43]

It was, however, a totally unrealistic policy. Perhaps things might have been different had Soviet, rather than American, forces taken the lead in the Allied drive against Japan. Yet as it was, Stalin, like Roosevelt, saw Soviet-American co-operation as constituting the fundamental axis of the postwar order. His own interests were limited largely to Eastern Europe. He apparently considered both Japan and China as falling within a future American sphere of influence.[44] There was no possibility of his abandoning the American alliance for association with a crumbling, exhausted and defeated Japan.

Others within the Japanese elite envisaged a special agreement with the Chinese Nationalists. This, too, was an untenable position. A defeated Japan and a China teetering on the brink of renewed civil war were in no position to form a conservative pan-Asianist alliance.

Prince Konoye and his colleagues, on the other hand, thought in terms of a peace settlement with the Anglo-American powers. Their position was outlined in a Memorandum to the Throne presented by Prince Konoye on 14 February 1945, seven months before the surrender.

An awareness of the strategic, political and ideological basis of their recommendations is of considerable importance to any understanding of postwar Japan's foreign policies, defence posture and domestic politics. The Konoye Memorandum also throws much light on the links between Japan's domestic politics and its external relations at this most critical moment.

> I believe that defeat is, unfortunately, rapidly becoming inevitable. It is on the basis of this assumption that I make the following petition [to Your Imperial Majesty].
> Defeat will undoubtedly cause cracks to appear in the edifice of Japan's Sacred National

Polity [*kokutai*]. Nevertheless, opinion in Great Britain and the United States has not, at least until the present time, gone so far as to demand changes in this order. Certainly, extremist elements do exist [in the Anglo-American powers] and it is difficult to know what changes the future may bring. Still, I believe that defeat itself gives us little grounds for concern about preservation of the Sacred National Polity. What we need to fear, far more than defeat, is the Communist revolution that will follow it.

Internationally, Konoye argued, the Soviet Union had made extraordinary advances, installing pro-Communist regimes in countries all around its periphery. The anti-Fascist resistance in Europe, too, was increasingly dominated by radical elements. What was happening in Europe was bound to happen in the Far East. The Japanese Empire was undoubtedly the next target for the international Communist conspiracy. At this very moment, Konoye warned the emperor,

> a group of Japanese centring around Okano,* who has arrived from Moscow, are setting up a Japanese Liberation League in Yenan. This group is establishing ties with the Korean Independence Alliance and the Taiwanese Vanguard Army. It is beginning to beam propaganda to Japan.

These developments might have been of little significance, Konoye suggested, had not defeat in the Pacific War dramatically altered the character of Japan's domestic political life.

> If we turn to consider the Japanese domestic situation, it is clear that the conditions necessary for a successful Communist revolution are being created day by day. I refer to the deterioration in the standard of living, the increasing outspokenness of the working class, the pro-Soviet feelings that have grown up in the wake of sentiments of enmity towards Great Britain and the United States, the radical movement in sections of the military, the so-called New Public Servants Movement, which is taking advantage of this, and the secret activities of left-wing elements who are manipulating the whole thing from behind the scenes.
>
> Of these various factors, the radical movement in the armed forces is particularly worrying. The majority of young soldiers seem to believe that Communism and Japan's Sacred National Polity are by no means incompatible...I have heard that there are even members of the Imperial Family who are showing some interest in this view. The great majority of professional soldiers are from middle class or lower class families. Their circumstances are such that Communist doctrines will have a ready appeal...
>
> Even if these military radicals do not aim to precipitate a Communist revolution, the bureaucrats and civilian sympathizers who surround them, whether they be called 'right-wingers' or 'left-wingers' (the so-called 'right-wingers' are only advocates of Communism

---

* Pseudonym for Nosaka Sanzō, b. Yamaguchi prefecture, 1892; graduate of Keio University; member of the Yūaikai; joined the British Communist Party while a student in England (1919); founding member of the Japanese Communist Party (1922); active in the Japanese Communist underground throughout the 1920s and 1930s; fled to the Soviet Union in 1933; member of Comintern Secretariat; engaged in anti-Japanese propaganda work in Sian, 1940–5; formed an anti-war alliance among Japanese prisoners of war in China; returned to Japan in 1946; active in Communist movement throughout the postwar period, serving, for many years, as chairman of the Japanese Communist Party.

dressed up as the Sacred National Polity) consciously cherish the intention of bringing about a Communist revolution and it would not be mistaken to believe that the simple, ignorant soldiers will be made to dance to their tune.

Recently, elements urging total national resistance have become increasingly vociferous. Despite the fact that these views are being put forward by so-called right-wing elements, I suspect that they are increasingly being manipulated from behind the scenes by the Communists, who hope to throw the country into confusion as a prelude to realizing their revolutionary objectives. While they are enthusiastically calling for the total destruction of Great Britain and the United States, pro-Soviet feelings are gradually spreading. There are even people in the armed forces who urge that Japan should join hands with the Soviet Union. Others are thinking in terms of co-operation with Yenan ... If the military situation continues to deteriorate I believe these trends will develop still further.

As far as the future of the military situation itself is concerned (leaving aside the possibility of some breakthrough, some possible ray of hope), and working on the assumption that defeat is inevitable, it is my conviction that to continue the conflict beyond this point, with no prospect of victory, is to play into the hands of the Communists. Thus, it is my firm conviction that if our objective is to preserve the Sacred National Polity we must begin discussing ways to end the war as quickly as possible.[45]

What Prince Konoye is saying, in effect, is that imperial Japan has come to resemble the Russian Empire in the last months of World War I. The conflict with the Anglo-American powers and with China, a struggle for Asian-Pacific hegemony which he himself had actively encouraged, cannot continue, either in the direction of victory, or towards defeat, without disturbing the political, economic and social status quo. Preservation of the established order, with all its attendant moral sanctions, symbolized, above all else, by the imperial institution, is now the most important objective, to which all other goals must be subordinated. To forestall the impending Communist revolution the emperor should consider an immediate and far-reaching purge of the armed forces, which have, because of the deteriorating military situation, the growing economic crisis and the class origins of their officers and men, ceased to be bastions of the established order and have become, instead, the greatest threat to it. Once this purge had been carried out it might be possible to negotiate a favourable peace settlement with the Anglo-American powers and China. These essentially conservative states, Konoye felt, had little interest in tampering with Japan's domestic order.

> Once this group has been disposed of, the army will look very different. Perhaps I am excessively optimistic but might it then be too much to expect that the attitude of Great Britain, the United States and Chungking government towards us might change? From the beginning Great Britain, the United States and the Chungking government have declared that their only objective is the destruction of the Japanese military cliques. If the Japanese armed forces were to change in character and alter their policies it is not unthinkable that these powers might consider terminating the war. In any case, to sweep aside this group and implement a reconstruction of the army is an essential prerequisite for saving Japan from Communist revolution. I urge Your Majesty to take a courageous decision.

Prince Konoye's audience with the emperor continued in the following vein:

Emperor: The Chief of the General Staff has also made a petition. He claims that if Japan concludes peace at the present time the Americans will inevitably demand abolition of the Imperial system and thus endanger the Sacred National Polity ... General Umezu and the Navy believe that we can strike at the enemy if we succeed in drawing him towards Taiwan.

Konoye: I do not consider that Grew and the American leadership are thinking in terms of destroying the Japanese Imperial House. But if the war continues, and if the domestic and external situation worsens, I believe it will have implications for the Imperial system.[46]

Prince Konoye's petition made a greater impression on the emperor than that of General Umezu. Within a few months Japanese diplomats in Switzerland were telling Allied representatives that they would be prepared to negotiate a settlement on condition that the imperial institution be preserved as a bastion against Communism.[47] On 9 September 1945, in a letter to the Crown Prince, Hirohito explained that his agonizing decision to surrender had been made 'in order to preserve the seeds of the [Japanese] nation ... If Japan had continued the war the Three Sacred Treasures of the Imperial House could not have been preserved and the people would have to have been killed.' As sovereign and supreme commander, he complained, he had not been blessed with thoughtful military leaders.[48]

Yoshida, who helped Konoye compose his memorandum, did not over-estimate the international influence of the Soviet Union. The Anglo-American powers, he believed, would inevitably dominate the postwar world. Yet Yoshida, too, was deeply troubled by the spectre of revolution. Neither Konoye nor Yoshida, both reared in the old school of imperial power politics, understood that the American leadership, no less than the Soviet, was determined to reconstruct the international order and recreate both its allies and its former enemies in its own image. Yet their implicit assumptions about the future development of American-Soviet relations proved remarkably accurate. In so many ways, moreover, their perceptions of the Soviet Union paralleled those of the American policy-makers who came into prominence after the death of Roosevelt. On the Japanese side, at the highest level, the psychological basis for a limited, tactical co-operation between a defeated imperial Japan and a triumphant imperial America, a new variant of the Anti-Comintern Pact, was laid even before the occupation had begun.

Konoye's obsession with the possibility of Communist revolution had been evident since at least 1942. He believed that the Communists had not only penetrated the armed forces but were also active in the Finance Ministry, the Ministry of Railways, the Planning Agency and other key organs of government. His fears had been intensified by discussions with the Communist renegade Sano Manabu (introduced through Iwabuchi Tatsuo).[49] In April 1944 Konoye had told Prince Higashikuni, only half jokingly, that

> Someone had recently said that the Soviet Military Attaché had declared that the Japanese were lately becoming increasingly communistic, that there was no stopping them and that if this tendency continued the Soviet Union itself would have to adopt a containment of Communism strategy.[50]

Were Konoye's perceptions of the domestic situation correct? Was a Communist revolution, or at least a radical nationalist military *coup d'état*, imminent? Konoye's private secretary, Ushiba Tomohiko, considered such fears to have been 'totally unrealistic'. Konoye was a credulous man, easily influenced by the wild tales of men like Sano Manabu. Yet it is difficult to come to any definite conclusion about this matter. There has been no study of the Japanese army in the last years of the war. Nor has there been any detailed examination of the climate of Japanese opinion during this period. Powerful currents of anti-establishment sentiment always moved beneath the surface calm of Japanese life during the Meiji, Taishō and early Shōwa periods. Radical reformist doctrines had exercised considerable influence on the Japanese armed forces in the 1930s. In Indonesia and other parts of South-East Asia, in 1944 and 1945, high-ranking Japanese army and navy officers, well versed in Marxist doctrines, had actively facilitated the work of local Communists. They had told their Indonesian colleagues of the inevitability of Communist revolution in Japan and of an impending Russo-Japanese alliance against the United States and the imperialist powers.[51] The letters of young Japanese soldiers, of both middle-class and peasant origin, in the last years of the war, suggest a profound disillusionment, war weariness and bitterness towards the established order.[52] After the collapse of the empire the reconstructed and increasingly radical Socialist Party, together with the Japanese Communist Party, attracted an extraordinarily high degree of popular support. Nosaka Sanzō, whose activities in Moscow and Yenan had so alarmed Konoye, was given a tumultuous welcome on his return to Tōkyō. He remains, to this day, a popular and highly respected figure, among Communists and non-Communists alike. Had Japan been occupied by Soviet, rather than American forces, history might have followed a very different course.

The reforms initiated during the occupation were far too radical for men like Konoye and Yoshida to stomach. Konoye, accused of war crimes, bitterly disillusioned and weary of life, committed suicide. Yoshida soldiered on as Prime Minister and president of the newly founded Liberal Party. Still, the Americans tampered less with the established order than the Russians would have done. They also performed at least one sterling service. If the emperor's renunciation of his divinity, the new Constitution, the legalization of the Communist Party, land reform, the threat to dissolve the great corporations, changes in the education system, the encouragement given to the trade union movement and the new position of women mortified the old establishment, the armed forces, which Prince Konoye had regarded as the greatest threat to the status quo, had finally been dissolved, not by the Japanese emperor himself but, as good fortune would have it, by the foreign conqueror. Yoshida Shigeru and his circle were not anxious to see them reconstructed in a hurry.

V   Yoshida Shigeru's vision

The Japanese governments which held office during the occupation, while theoretically preserving some domestic autonomy, were not permitted to conduct independent foreign relations. They were almost totally insulated from the debates about the future of the Far East taking place in Washington. Nevertheless, three Japanese leaders – Yoshida Shigeru, Ashida Hitoshi and Katayama Tetsu – played a significant role in negotiating the security treaty and setting the course of Japan's subsequent foreign policy. Of these three, Prince Konoye's associate Yoshida Shigeru was by far the most important. His background, assumptions and objectives thus need to be examined in some detail.[53]

President of the Liberal Party from the purge of its postwar founder Hatoyama Ichirō until his own retirement from active politics in 1955, Prime Minister during the greater part of this critical decade, patron of a group of young conservatives that included such figures as Ikeda Hayato, Satō Eisaku, Ōhira Masayoshi and Miyazawa Kiichi, Yoshida was an extraordinarily complex figure. His roots in Japan's modern history were deep. His connections with the old court aristocracy, the political elite and the business establishment were at once extensive and intimate. He had been born in Yokosuka, near Tōkyō, in 1878, the fifth son of Takeuchi Ko, an aristocratic but poverty-stricken Liberal Party activist from Kochi, on the island of Shikoku, in the old Tosa domain. His natural father had been a friend of Itagaki Taisuke and Saigo Takamori. His mother had been a geisha. Almost immediately after birth he had been adopted by the wealthy shipping magnate Yoshida Kenzō, Japanese agent for the Jardine Matheson Steamship Company. Yoshida Shigeru's education, first at the Kangakujuku (School of Chinese Learning) near Kamakura, then at the Gakushūin (Peers School) had been typical of the upper echelons of the Meiji elite. His marriage to Setsuko, the eldest daughter of Baron Makino Nobuaki (himself the second son of the Satsuma Restoration leader Ōkubo Toshimichi) had enabled him to move into the inner counsels of the small oligarchy that still effectively ruled Japan.

In some respects Yoshida Shigeru's views were characteristic of his class. In other ways he remained, throughout his life, an outsider. He was intensely patriotic, an unrepentant conservative, a staunch believer in private enterprise and a dedicated monarchist. (His granddaughter was eventually to marry into the imperial family.) He was not necessarily an enthusiast for popular democracy. He was also a totally unabashed and incorrigible racist, believing that the Japanese were inherently superior to all other peoples except, perhaps, the British and the Chinese. He had scant regard for Germans, Russians, Indians and Koreans, among others. His distaste for Communism was so great that he refused even to read about it. His hostility towards the Soviet Union was legendary. While certainly not a pacifist he had maintained, throughout his life, an ambivalent attitude towards the Japanese armed forces, regarding them with suspicion as hotbeds of peasant and working-class radical nationalism. After the defeat of the empire (for which he naturally blamed the military) he was determined to ensure that economic recovery took precedence over rearmament.

In the prewar period Yoshida had been well known as an exponent of good relations with the British Empire and the United States. It was this background that made him acceptable to the occupation. His attitudes had excluded him from the 1936 Hirota Cabinet and led to his recall as ambassador to Great Britain after the signing of the anti-Comintern Pact. On the eve of the Pacific War he had been involved in efforts to avoid conflict with the Anglo-American powers. It was his suspected participation in secret peace negotiations that led to his arrest by Japanese military police in April 1945, shortly after the presentation of Konoye's Memorandum to the Throne. During his brief confinement he energetically attempted to persuade his Kenpeitai interrogators that 'Japan is completely incapable of prospering without a close relationship with the United States and Great Britain ... the war against the Anglo-American powers cannot be terminated a day too soon'.[54]

Yoshida had espoused the cause of good relations with the Anglo-American powers for two reasons, neither of them sentimental ones.

First, like so many Japanese of his era, he had believed that Japan's fundamental national interests, indeed its very survival as an independent great power, necessitated the creation of an extensive, Western-style empire on the Asian continent, in Korea, Manchuria and Mongolia. He had also believed that Japan's destiny lay in close association with a politically and economically dependent China. These two objectives had not seemed to him, at the time, incompatible. The Chinese Nationalists, he had judged (correctly) would be prepared to relinquish Manchuria and Inner Mongolia to Japan. China's political fragmentation, military weakness, technological backwardness, the natural interdependence of the Chinese and Japanese economies, mutual hostility towards the Soviet Union and Communism, together with the close cultural ties between the two countries, would provide a more than adequate basis for Sino-Japanese co-operation. Nevertheless, unlike many of his pan-Asianist contemporaries, Yoshida had believed that Japan's continental ambitions could *not* be realized in the teeth of British and American opposition. Great Britain and the United States enjoyed considerable influence in China. Politically, economically and, perhaps, even militarily, they were in a position to frustrate Japan's plans for 'management of the continent'. The Soviet Union, Germany and Italy did not pose a serious threat in this regard. As far as North-East Asia was concerned, Japan's principal rival was the Soviet Union, not Great Britain or the United States. For strategic and ideological reasons significant elements in the Anglo-American powers were also potentially hostile to the Soviet Union. This fact could be exploited in Japan's interests. Certainly, nothing could be gained by alienating London, Washington and Moscow all at once. Yoshida had therefore considered that Japan should go about building its Asiatic empire in a way that would not offend the Anglo-Saxons. In the context of the 1930s this had meant placing a moratorium on expansion south of the Great Wall.[55]

The second reason for not alienating the Anglo-American powers was that they were highly organized and immensely wealthy, controlled vast resources and, more importantly perhaps, dominated the sea-lanes of the world. Japan's position as an industrial and commercial island nation, without substantial resources and dependent on the sea-lanes for its survival, made it fatal to ignore British and American naval supremacy.[56] It is evident from Yoshida's advice to Prince Konoye in June 1942 that his interest in maintaining good relations with Great Britain and the United States would have faded rapidly had World War II resulted in the establishment of a global *Pax Germanica*. Yoshida admired the Anglo-Saxons for their power, not for their virtues.

Yoshida's attitude to China was qualitatively different. It is often forgotten that he was, by training, not a Europeanist but a China specialist. He had spent two years of his professional life as ambassador to Italy and three years as ambassador to Great Britain. He had spent some twenty-two years in China and Korea. For Yoshida, China was not simply an indispensable piece of strategic real estate, a source of raw materials and a market for the empire's manufactured goods. His respect for Chinese civilization surpassed, if anything, his admiration for that of the Anglo-American world. He himself had been brought up in an intensely traditional Confucian atmosphere. His old headmaster from the Gakushūin had been the noted imperial pan-Asianist and founder of the Tōa Dōbunkai (East Asian Civilization Society) Prince Konoye Atsumaro, Fumimaro's father. Yoshida's knowledge of the Chinese classics was extensive. He was well versed in Chinese poetry. His calligraphy was highly regarded. He wrote formal classical Chinese with ease, grace and elegance. His command of English, in contrast, was poor.[57]

The defeat had seemed to vindicate Yoshida's view of international politics. Because of this his thinking about the basic principles of foreign policy and defence did not change radically in the postwar period.

The collapse of the Greater East Asia Co-prosperity Sphere, the loss of Korea and Manchuria and the bitter legacy of the Sino-Japanese war had destroyed, temporarily at least, Japan's great power status. On this issue, as on others, Yoshida took a long-term view, remaining confident that, given sound leadership and astute diplomacy, Japan would be able to re-emerge as an independent power in its own right. Japan might have become a temporary American colony, he told Cloyce Huston, counsellor at the American Embassy in Tōkyō in April 1950, but it would eventually come out on top, just as the United States itself had at last established its own supremacy over the British Empire.[58] Yoshida and his circle were generally agreed that recovery required preservation of the imperial institution, a carefully planned programme of economic reconstruction, containment of the Socialist and Communist parties and relegation of the armed forces to a relatively minor position in the constellation of state power. It was also essential to end the occupation rapidly and to ensure that Japan, while adequately protected from the Communist menace (here Yoshida was thinking of the Japan Communist Party rather than the Soviet Union, whose power he did not rate highly), was not drawn too deeply into the American strategic orbit. 'I want Japanese sovereignty restored as quickly as possible', he told a high-ranking official on 29 May 1946. 'I want the occupation forces to leave. GHQ, as some people have noticed, is the abbreviation for "Go Home Quickly". In order to encourage them to go home we have to give the Allied powers a sense of security by abandoning rearmament and instituting a thoroughgoing democratization of Japanese society.'[59]

A close relationship with the Anglo-American powers, Yoshida believed, would remain an essential component of any conceivable Japanese foreign policy. Short-term considerations might even necessitate a special security arrangement with the

United States. Even at the height of the occupation, however, Yoshida did not abandon his conviction that Japan's long-term future lay not with North America but with the Asian continent, above all with China. In 1947 Yoshida, like Truman and Stalin, fully expected Chiang Kai-shek's Nationalists to remain in control of the Chinese continent. Yet while he viewed the Russians with an almost pathological suspicion, and while the activities of Japanese and Korean Communists sent him into paroxysms of anxiety, the growing strength of the Chinese Communist Party seldom disturbed his equanimity. The Chinese, Yoshida firmly believed, on the basis of his long experience on the continent, were a pragmatic, materialistic and highly individualistic people. Unlike the Russians, the Koreans and the Japanese, they could not become *real* Communists. The Nationalist collapse and the foundation of the People's Republic in 1949 thus did not cause Yoshida to lose much sleep. He did not care, he told an American journalist, 'whether China was red or green. China is a natural market, and it has become necessary for Japan to think about markets.'[60] Nor was he unduly alarmed by the Sino-Soviet alliance. Chinese civilization and Marxism, he thought, were essentially incompatible. China would ultimately reject or transform Communism, just as it had rejected or transformed foreign creeds in past ages. The Chinese and the Russians had different cultural traditions and potentially conflicting national interests. Their strategic association would therefore prove to be a transient one.

The Liberal Party leader had no objection to developing economic relations with the countries of non-Communist South-East Asia. Yet for Yoshida, as for Ishii, Shidehara, Tanaka and the other figures who had shaped continental policy in pre-war days, China remained an essential element in Japan's strategy towards both the United States and the Soviet Union. Throughout the postwar period he never abandoned his private conviction that at some future time, after the Sino-Soviet alliance had collapsed and when a Japan strong enough to negotiate with Peking on an equal footing had freed itself from American tutelage, the two great East Asian powers could resume their natural historic relationship. The age of imperialism had clearly come to an end. Japan's empire in Korea, Manchuria and Mongolia could never be recreated, even if it were desirable to do so. Yet, as a long-term future prospect, the old pan-Asianist dream of a conservative Sino-Japanese alliance was by no means impossible to contemplate.[61]

VI   Ashida Hitoshi and Katayama Tetsu

Ashida Hitoshi, president of the Democratic (Progressive) Party during the occupation period, shared Yoshida's intense nationalism, anti-Communism and hostility to the Soviet Union. A graduate of Tōkyō University he had spent several years as a diplomat in Europe and America. In 1932 he had returned to Japan to stand as a Seiyūkai candidate for the Diet. In the years before the war Ashida had been a persistent advocate of expansion into China. Like Prince Konoye, he had been convinced that the prospects for continental empire would be enhanced by alliance with Hitler's Germany, the probable victor in the oncoming struggle in Europe. The ease with which Ashida had subsequently adjusted to the idea of American world hegemony undoubtedly helped him escape the 1946 occupation purge. His conversion to democracy was viewed by many conservative leaders as blatant and unprincipled opportunism.[62] As the American-Soviet Cold War deepened, Ashida, whose Russophobia had been intensified by Stalin's claims to an exclusive sphere of influence in central Europe, the advance of the Chinese Communists, the emergence of a socialist state in northern Korea and the rise of the Vietminh, concluded that Japan's interests would best be served by alliance with the United States, a substantial programme of rearmament and an active foreign policy as a member of the emerging 'Free World'. To judge from his public statements, Ashida totally accepted American Cold War orthodoxy.[63] No doubt he saw some form of incorporation into the American-centred world order as desirable. Yet Ashida, like Yoshida, was a complex and subtle man. It also seems possible that his chief immediate objectives were to restore Japan's full independence by facilitating withdrawal of American forces, to encourage the United States to support a large-scale Japanese rearmament programme, and, perhaps, to lay the basis for a future reassertion of Japanese interest in Korea, a country he regarded as being of fundamental strategic importance.

Katayama Tetsu, Japan's first and only Socialist Prime Minister (April 1947–October 1948) shared Yoshida's profound suspicion of the military, albeit for different reasons. A native of Wakayama prefecture, one of Japan's most depressed areas, a graduate of Tōkyō University and a lawyer, he had spent his entire prewar political life struggling in the faction-ridden Socialist movement. Katayama, like many Japanese Socialists of the old school, was a Christian and a pacifist. In 1940 he had been expelled from the increasingly pro-expansionist Socialist Masses Party because of his opposition to the Sino-Japanese War and his support for the anti-militarist stand of Saitō Takao.[64] The war, the defeat and the occupation had strengthened his convictions. Unlike Yoshida he identified strongly with the occupation reforms. He shared General MacArthur's vision of a neutral, unarmed Japan. He was hostile neither to the United States nor to the Soviet Union. Like Yoshida, he believed Japan's long-term future interests required good relations with the Chinese continent. He was not, however, an enthusiast for any kind of exclusive Sino-Japanese relationship. A deeply religious man, he was to devote much of his later life to the cause of world federation. [65]

VII Developments during the first Yoshida and Katayama Cabinets

It was during Yoshida Shigeru's first Cabinet (16 May 1946–23 April 1947), after the enunciation of the Truman Doctrine and MacArthur's call for an early peace settlement, that Japanese officials began to give serious attention to the nation's future foreign and defence policies. Japanese leaders were, at this stage, only vaguely aware of the storms raging through the White House, the State Department, the Department of Defence and SCAP about the regional impact of the Cold War and the direction of policy towards Japan. This ignorance made them particularly susceptible to manipulation by rival American factional-bureaucratic interests. Three things, however, were clear. First, the United States seemed likely to remain the dominant external influence in North-East Asia for some time to come. Second, full Japanese recovery would take many years to accomplish. Third, Japan's domestic situation would remain extremely unstable. Australian and British officials (as ignorant of American intentions as the Japanese themselves) hinted at a punitive peace settlement and suggested that some form of Allied control would be maintained indefinitely.[66] The terms of the Potsdam Declaration and of the Initial Post-Surrender Policy Directive for Japan, as well as various documents published by the Far Eastern Commission, also suggested a punitive peace treaty with severe restrictions on Japan's future international activities. Yoshida and his group agreed that should such a punitive treaty materialize, Japan would be best advised to declare its perpetual neutrality and request security guarantees from the United States, the Soviet Union, China and the nations of the Far Eastern Commission.[67] Various plans were drawn up on the basis of these assumptions. At the same time, the breakdown of the American-Soviet relationship suggested opportunities for negotiating a more favourable peace agreement. Japanese officials made discreet enquiries about the possibility of 'an alliance with a third power'.[68] These overtures, whatever their purpose, aroused no official interest among the occupation authorities who were approached.[69]

In the April 1947 elections, held in the wake of an abortive general strike, amid mounting economic chaos and popular unrest, Yoshida's Liberal-Progressive Party coalition lost control of the Diet. While the Japan Socialist Party won the largest number of seats, increasing its Diet representation from 92 to 143, and its share of the national vote from 17.78 per cent to 26.23 per cent, it did not gain an absolute majority. Yoshida's Liberals had won altogether 131 seats, the Democratic Party (which had changed its name from the Progressive Party on the eve of the elections) had gained 126, the National Co-operative Party 31. Eventually, the Socialist and Democratic parties agreed to form a coalition government with Katayama as Prime Minister and Ashida Hitoshi as Foreign Minister.

During the Katayama Cabinet further consideration was given to the question of postwar foreign policy. It was during this period that the first tentative expressions of Japanese interest in a bilateral security agreement with the United States came to the surface.

Ashida had agreed to the coalition with the Socialists on the understanding that he would be given considerable freedom of initiative in foreign policy matters.[70] Shortly after assuming office, in close consultation with Yoshida (now leader of the Opposition) and a number of Foreign Ministry officials, he prepared a memorandum on future peace and security arrangements. It is uncertain whether the Prime Minister was consulted about its contents.[71] Even so, the document would not have been inconsistent with Katayama's ideals. There was no mention of rearmament (despite Ashida's strong views on this subject) although strengthening of the police forces in the interests of internal security was suggested. Japan was specifically described as an 'unarmed' state, 'totally committed to the way of peace'. Nor did the Ashida memorandum propose a Japanese-American security treaty. Japan's security, it was implied, could best be guaranteed by the United Nations. Ashida's memorandum (which probably reflected Yoshida's views as much as his own) concerned itself chiefly with Japan's expectations for the peace settlement, mentioning, among other things, its hope that the treaty might be executed 'voluntarily'. This was an indirect indication of the desire of both Ashida and Yoshida to *avoid* the continued presence of Allied armed forces or control organizations in Japan after the settlement.[72]

Copies of the memorandum were given to the American ambassador George Atcheson and to General Courtney Whitney, Chief of the Government Section of SCAP. Both copies were returned to the Japanese Foreign Ministry almost immediately. Atcheson and Whitney stressed that it was not an appropriate time either for Japan to draw up, or for General Headquarters to receive, such documents.[73] Similar proposals were made to various American and Allied officials from time to time. All, without exception, proved abortive.[74]

In July 1947 the United States formally proposed the convocation of a preliminary conference on the Japanese peace settlement. In the context of the factional-bureaucratic struggles raging in Washington it now became advantageous for American exponents of an anti-Communist military alliance with Japan to elicit some demonstration of Japanese support for their ideas. MacArthur's strong commitment to Japanese neutrality, Katayama's pacifism and the lack of any direct channel to Ashida all made it necessary to proceed cautiously. Shortly after news of the preliminary conference was announced, Lieutenant-General Eichelberger met informally with Suzuki Tadakatsu, director of the Central Liaison Bureau (the former Japanese Foreign Ministry), a distinguished career diplomat with whom he was on intimate terms.[75] United States forces, Eichelberger said, had been ordered to prepare to leave Japan by the spring of 1948. Meanwhile, the Soviet Union was consolidating its military position in Siberia. The outlook for the anti-Communist forces in China was, to say the least, bleak. Once American forces had left Japan, Soviet airborne units would be in a position to occupy Hokkaidō within three or four hours. What measures, Eichelberger wondered, did the Japanese government contemplate to deal with this threat?

Suzuki, avoiding a direct response, reported Eichelberger's remarks (through Mr Yoshizawa, deputy director of the Central Liaison Bureau) to Foreign Minister Ashida. Ashida then requested Vice-Foreign Minister Okazaki Katsuo to prepare a paper on the subject. The Chief Cabinet Secretary Nishio Suehiro and one or two key Foreign Ministry personnel were also consulted. Neither Prime Minister Katayama nor the Liberal Party leader Yoshida Shigeru were approached in any way. Katayama, in fact, was not even aware that the document was being drawn up.[76] Ashida's decision to bring the Socialist Chief Cabinet Secretary Nishio Suehiro into the discussions can possibly be explained by the fact that Nishio, unlike Katayama, had supported Japanese military expansion on the Asian continent in the years before the war. Like Ashida he had also supported the Tripartite Pact and the General National Mobilization Law. The Foreign Minister therefore probably regarded him as 'sound' on matters related to defence policy.[77]

Ashida's memorandum was presented to Eichelberger (as Suzuki's personal opinion) on 13 September 1947. The document is remarkable for its clear, concise, dispassionate and non-ideological analysis of the international situation and the problems confronting Japan. It posited two scenarios. If American-Soviet relations were to improve and the two superpowers work constructively for world peace, it argued, Japan's independence could be guaranteed by the United Nations. If relations between the superpowers continued to deteriorate, Japan's security could be protected either by prolonged stationing of American forces in connection with supervision of the execution of the peace treaty or by conclusion of a 'special specific arrangement between Japan and the United States by virtue of which the former's defence is entrusted in the hands of the latter'.

In the case of such a 'special specific arrangement', it was argued, continued stationing of American forces in Japan would *not* be necessary. The United States could maintain forces in Okinawa and the Bonins. The Japanese government could construct air and naval bases in Japan for use by these forces in times of emergency.[78]

According to Nishimura Kumao, who was closely involved in the negotiations, this idea of a security treaty with the United States was not only designed to provide protection for a defenceless Japan in an increasingly polarized and unstable world. *It was also designed to remove American troops from Japanese soil, thus avoiding Japan's total incorporation into the emerging American global security network.* At the time, both the Japanese government and the Japanese people believed that Okinawa and the Bonins, like the former German Pacific islands and the Kuriles, had been lost to Japan forever.[79]

This memorandum, which Eichelberger presumably discussed with his friends in the Defence Department and the Japan Lobby on his return to the United States, had no discernible influence on the evolution of American policy at the highest level. If it was noted it was politely ignored. On the other hand, in the context of the deteriorating international and domestic situation, Ashida's proposals exerted a decisive impact on Yoshida's thinking. By the time he resumed office as Prime Minister in October 1948 Yoshida had become convinced that circumstances beyond Japan's control might necessitate some form of temporary alliance with the United States. Still, like Ashida, he remained hopeful that American forces could be removed from Japan.[80]

In the months that followed, encouraged by Ashida's response to Eichelberger's *démarche*, advocates of Japanese-American military co-operation in Washington continued to cultivate the impression that the United States was preparing to wash its hands of North-East Asia. On 11 February 1949 the Secretary for the Army, Kenneth C. Royall, on an official visit to Tōkyō, told reporters that 'Japan would have to be written off in the event of a war with Russia'. Many strategists argued, he said, that America's real interests lay in Europe, not in the Far East, and that bases in Japan were therefore a liability.[81] A number of similar statements were made during the course of 1949–50, creating an atmosphere of unease and uncertainty among anti-Communist circles in Tōkyō. Even Secretary of State Dean Acheson's announcement on 12 January 1950 that the United States Pacific defence perimeter extended from the Aleutians through Japan and Okinawa to the Philippines did little to assuage these anxieties.

VIII   Prime Minister Yoshida Shigeru's secret offer of a Japanese-American security treaty, May 1950

Yoshida had decided in October 1948 that Japan's interests might best be served by a temporary alliance with the United States, involving the stationing of American forces in Okinawa and the Bonins. In the months that followed, increasing American–Soviet tension, the formation of the North Atlantic Treaty Organisation (NATO), the Sino-Soviet alliance, the impact of peasant and urban revolt on the moribund Rhee Syngh Manh regime in South Korea, the beginnings of the first Indochina war, popular unrest within Japan itself and the growing strength of the Japanese Communist Party combined to convince the Liberal Party leader that some form of military association with the United States would be unavoidable.

In May 1950, in the wake of the remarkable Communist advances in the 1949 general elections (Communist strength had jumped from four to thirty-five seats in the House of Representatives) and the equally remarkable self-decimation of the party in a campaign of ill-conceived revolutionary violence, and at a time when the South Korean regime was obviously crumbling, Yoshida dispatched a secret mission to Washington to propose formally the conclusion of a bilateral security treaty.

The decision to send this mission had been made by Yoshida alone. The Foreign Ministry, much to its dismay, had been in no way consulted.[82] The three members of the delegation – Ikeda Hayato, Minister for Finance, Yoshida's most senior disciple and trusted Cabinet associate, Miyazawa Kiichi and Shirasu Jirō – all believed, right up to the time they boarded the aircraft bound for Washington, that they were visiting the United States to discuss economic problems. This extreme secrecy was probably intended to keep the purpose of the visit hidden from MacArthur and other exponents of neutrality.

In Washington, Ikeda gave the following message from Yoshida to Joseph M. Dodge, formerly Special Financial Adviser to SCAP and at that time working as an adviser to both the State and Defence departments. Dodge also enjoyed good relations with several members of the Japan Lobby.

> The Japanese government herein formally expresses its desire to conclude a peace treaty with the United States as early as possible. In the case of such a peace treaty being concluded, the Japanese government thinks it will be necessary to station American forces in Japan in order to preserve the security of Japan and the Asian area. If it is difficult for the United States to make such a request, the Japanese government itself is prepared to make the offer. As far as this point is concerned, we have been asking the opinion of Japanese constitutional scholars. They tell us that the problems will be minimal if reference to this course of events is included in the peace treaty. Yet even if this is not done and the Japanese-American covenant is concluded in a separate arrangement, it will not be contrary to the Japanese Constitution.

Dodge promised to pass the message on to the appropriate authorities. He assured Ikeda that there was a strong opinion in Washington against leaving Japan unprotected after the peace treaty and that the reduction of American military capability in the Far East would be to the advantage of neither the United States nor Japan.

Copies of the notes taken at this meeting, together with the text of Yoshida's message, were subsequently sent to the Assistant Secretary of the State Department, to Dulles and to General MacArthur in Tōkyō. MacArthur, realizing that he was being outmanoeuvred by the Chiefs of Staff and the Japan Lobby, was incensed by the news of Ikeda's visit.[83]

There was no direct causal connection between Yoshida's secret mission and the peace and security treaties concluded in 1951. Advocates of Japanese-American military co-operation were naturally gratified to learn the new trend of Japanese thinking on the subject. That was all. Yoshida's letter (contrary to Miyazawa's impression) did not pour oil on the troubled waters of American interdepartmental factional-policy conflict. President Truman's appointment of John Foster Dulles as special ambassador to conclude a peace settlement with Japan in May 1950 was made against a background of continuing struggle both within the State Department and between the State Department and the Pentagon. In Tōkyō MacArthur remained a law unto himself. The visit of Dulles, Secretary of Defence Louis Johnson and Chief of Staff Omar Bradley to Tōkyō on 22 June 1950 for talks with MacArthur represented yet another attempt to find a way out of the confusing labyrinth of complex and mutually incompatible options promoted by conflicting bureaucratic interests. Yoshida had doubtless expected a formal reply to his 3 May offer. If he did he was disappointed.

IX   The impact of the Korean War on American and Japanese thinking

Full-scale civil war broke out in Korea on 25 June 1950, three days after Dulles, Bradley and Johnson arrived in Tōkyō. Two days later President Truman ordered American military intervention. At the same time the United States reversed its previous policy of non-interference in the Chinese civil war by sending the Seventh Fleet into the Taiwan Straits. Truman also promised additional aid to the French in Indochina and to the American-sponsored Philippine government in its campaign against Communist insurgency. In one sweeping set of interconnected decisions the United States thus became, overnight, a direct participant in four Asian civil wars.

The immediate origins of the Korean conflict and the reasons for American involvement remain something of a mystery. However this may be, United States intervention in Korea, the Taiwan Straits, Indochina and the Philippines transformed Japan's strategic position. The Japanese archipelago now became America's most crucial forward base of operations in the Far East. Truman's decision to intervene in Korea brought to an end the confrontation between the State Department, the Pentagon and MacArthur's headquarters. Maintenance of bases in a Japan militarily allied to the United States was now America's minimum demand. Within the State Department, support for a settlement permitting Japan to maintain normal relations with the Communist powers on the Asian mainland evaporated. MacArthur abandoned his hopes for Japanese neutrality. Dulles and MacArthur were able to convince the Joint Chiefs of Staff and the military bureaucracy that a swift, generous peace settlement would secure maximum Japanese co-operation.

At the same time the President, the State Department and the National Security Council all swung around to the view, long promoted by the Joint Chiefs of Staff and Harry Kern's friends, that a rearmed Japan, closely linked to the United States, should be set up as the pivotal element in an Asian-Pacific regional security organization modelled on NATO. The terms of reference for Dulles' second mission to the Far East, in the winter of 1950–1, this time as Special Representative of the President with the rank of ambassador, gave him authority not merely to negotiate a Japanese peace treaty but also to organize a collective defence agreement embracing all the offshore island chains of Asia, including Japan. He was also to persuade the Japanese to rearm. Already, shortly after the outbreak of the Korean War, MacArthur had ordered the creation of a 75,000-man Japanese National Police Reserve Force.

The Japanese government, while dutifully repeating the United States version of the origins of the war, did not necessarily see the conflict as the first step in a Soviet master plan to take over the Far East.[84] Yet it was overjoyed at the prospective economic boons offered by the conflagration. The conflict in the neighbouring peninsula, Prime Minister Yoshida proclaimed, had been 'a gift of the gods'.[85]

The Korean War and the decisions that followed in its wake made it clear to the Japanese government that the Americans would remain in North-East Asia. If this solved a number of short-term problems it also created serious long-term ones. Yoshida could now confidently plan on the assumption that Washington would continue to assist him in maintaining the domestic status quo and protecting Japan from whatever threat might be posed by the Russians. There was now little possibility of Japan becoming a Democratic People's Republic allied to Moscow. The principal remaining danger was that Japan might become *too* involved in United States Far Eastern strategy, jeopardizing its chances of re-emergence as a genuinely independent great power, friendly towards Washington but able to make its own arrangements with its continental neighbours. It was for this reason that Yoshida was anxious to avoid large-scale rearmament and involvement in an American-centred regional anti-Communist alliance system. He began an intensive campaign against both these options and laid out an elaborate strategy in preparation for his talks with Dulles.

In his public campaign against rearmament, sustained throughout the autumn and winter of 1950–1, Yoshida concentrated on three themes: the fears of Japanese militarism still prevalent in Asia and the Pacific, the incompatibility of massive rearmament with economic recovery and the state of public opinion. No opportunity was lost to ensure that Washington understood his position.

In late 1950, after consultations in August and September with a small number of intellectuals, business leaders and former military officers,[86] Yoshida had the Foreign Ministry compose two draft treaties. The first, drawn up in October, envisaged an arrangement of fifteen years' duration whereby the United States would maintain bases in Japan to protect the country from external attack. Japan was to enjoy the right of self-defence and would co-operate militarily with the United States to safeguard the Japanese archipelago. There were no provisions for large-scale rearmament, overseas military service or participation in regional security arrangements. Only in respect to the fifteen- year time limit and mention of Japan's right of self-defence did this treaty draft differ from Yoshida's secret offer of 3 May. The second draft treaty, completed in November, was based on radically different principles. It envisaged demilitarization and neutralization of Japan and Korea with security guarantees from the United States, the Soviet Union, China and Great Britain. The forces that all these powers could maintain in and around the demilitarized area were to be strictly limited. Nishimura Kumao, who composed the two drafts, recalls Yoshida's remark that 'he would produce either the first or the second draft' during his talks with Dulles, 'depending on the time and circumstances'.[87] The objective circumstances produced by the Korean War had made neutrality, for the time being, an unrealistic option. What Yoshida probably meant, therefore, was not that he would decide on alliance or neutrality 'depending on the time and circumstances', but that if Dulles' pressure for Japanese rearmament and participation in some sort of Asian-Pacific regional military arrangement became too strong, he would produce his neutrality plan and refuse to budge until Washington relented.[88] The Americans would then have to face either the prospect of a continued occupation, with the probability that political unrest and leftist agitation would grow, further undermining their precarious position in North-East Asia, or accepting the Yoshida proposal of a bilateral security treaty without substantial Japanese rearmament or Japanese participation in a regional defence pact.

X   The 1951 Dulles-Yoshida negotiations: Japan's refusal to rearm for regional security and the shape of the final treaty

On 8 September 1950 President Truman authorized Dulles to begin negotiations on a Japanese peace treaty and some form of comprehensive defence arrangement in the Asian-Pacific area. It was now almost universally assumed in Washington that the Soviet Union and its allies would be excluded from the peace treaty, just as the United States had been from the Balkan settlement and the Russians had earlier been from Italy. It was also assumed that while consultations would take place with America's allies and with Japan the final agreement would reflect Washington's thinking.

The first assumption proved correct. The Russians did not sign the San Francisco Peace Treaty. The second assumption proved ill-founded. Both America's allies and the Japanese government refused to accept some of the most crucial elements in Dulles' conception of the postwar Asian-Pacific order. The United States had, in the end, no alternative but to negotiate a workable compromise, albeit one generally favourable to its perceived interests.

Early in January 1951 Dulles left Washington on an extensive negotiating tour of East Asia, Oceania and Europe. The 'principal purpose' of his mission, as defined by his letter of instructions from President Truman, was 'to secure the adherence of the Japanese nation to the free nations of the world, and to assure that it will play its full part in resisting the further expansion of Communist imperialism'. For this reason, the peace settlement was to be a generous one, with no restrictions on Japanese economic activities or on rearmament. Dulles was also to make clear that the United States was prepared to conclude mutual defence agreements with the Philippines, Australia, New Zealand, and, perhaps, Indonesia, as well as Japan.[89]

In the Philippines, Australia, New Zealand, Great Britain and France, Dulles stressed that there could be no question of large-scale Japanese reparations. This most of the allies accepted, either because they were persuaded by his eloquence or because they had no choice. Dulles rejected British proposals that the People's Republic should be invited to San Francisco and that Taiwan should be returned to China. The British had been anxious to facilitate Japanese recognition of Peking, partly because they believed this would make long-term peace in the Far East more likely, partly because they hoped to channel the economic activities of a revived Japan away from their own colonies in South-East Asia and the Pacific. In the end, Dulles agreed that Japan's China policy should depend on 'the exercise of the sovereign and independent status contemplated by the treaty'.[90]

America's allies were generally uneasy about the concept of a regional anti-Communist alliance. Australia and New Zealand declined to enter any arrangement that included Japan. Japan, rather than the Soviet Union, remained, for many years, the principal source of their anxieties. Great Britain insisted that inclusion of the Philippines would make it logical to include its own colonial possessions in South-East Asia and the Pacific. It also seemed possible, much to Dulles' chagrin, that the French and Dutch might advance this argument with respect to their dependencies.[91]

Dulles arrived in Tōkyō on 25 January 1951 and spent the first few days of his visit conferring with General MacArthur and other occupation officials. His first of five meetings with Prime Minister Yoshida took place on 30 January. Mutual contempt did not prevent agreement on basic matters. Yoshida was, if nothing, a realist. It was quickly decided to conclude a security treaty separately from the peace treaty. There was no conflict over permitting the proposed American bases to be used to further American policies in Asia as well as to protect Japan. Yoshida's secret offer 3 May 1950 had envisaged American bases in Japan acting 'to preserve the security of Japan and the Asian area'. Nor was it likely that the Japanese Prime Minister demanded such luxuries as the right of prior consultation and the power of veto over American actions from Japanese bases. The earlier Ashida proposal and the secret Yoshida note had requested no such control and Japan was given none in the final treaty. These early Japanese proposals had, however, all envisaged autonomous responsiblity for domestic security. Nishimura Kumao told the American historian Weinstein that the clause in the 1951 treaty giving Washington the right to intervene to put down insurrections in Japan was inserted at Dulles' request, despite Yoshida's strong protest.[92] Perhaps this is so. Yet it can also be suspected that Yoshida felt his long-term plans would best be served by the inclusion of a few blatantly unequal clauses in the treaty. Once Japan had recovered from the defeat, a scandalously humiliating treaty would be easier to jettison or renegotiate than a just and equitable one. Even if the internal riots and disturbances clause *was* Dulles' brainchild, Yoshida's protests may have been largely ritual.

The main points of controversy in the 1951 Dulles-Yoshida negotiations were Japanese rearmament, participation in regional security arrangements and the question of an explicit American guarantee to defend Japan. These three questions soon became inextricably intertwined.[93]

At the talks on 30 January, Dulles, as Yoshida had anticipated, strongly requested large-scale Japanese rearmament (mention was apparently made of a 350,000-man army) and participation in some kind of regional alliance.[94] The Japanese Prime Minister flatly refused to consider either matter. After ninety minutes of futile discussion the two referred the problem to General MacArthur.[95] Yoshida had already persuaded a none too unwilling MacArthur to support him against the President's special ambassador on this issue. MacArthur told Dulles that in his view Japan could best contribute to the security of the Free World by non-military means.[96]

After this confrontation, Yoshida refused to discuss questions of rearmament and regional military co-operation. On the night of 30 January he outlined Japan's economic demands at the coming peace conference to a few officials from the Foreign Ministry.[97] He then retired to his seaside villa at Ōiso, declining to take part in further talks with Dulles.[98] This inflexible stance and two or three more days of fruitless negotiations with Foreign Ministry officials at last convinced the Americans that Japanese participation in a regional security organization would be, for some time, difficult to realize.[99] Dulles made one last plea at a dinner given by the Japan-America Society on 2 February.[100] The matter was then dropped. When the Foreign Ministry produced the plan for a simple Japanese-American treaty drawn up in October 1950 the Americans, conscious also of the lack of enthusiasm among all their Asian-Pacific allies except Taiwan and South Korea, temporarily shelved the idea of a regional organization.[101]

Dulles was still determined to commit the Japanese to some measure of rearmament. Yoshida eventually showed him 'a project, long under consideration, for increasing both our land and sea forces and placing them under the control of an embryo Ministry of Defence'.[102] This did not satisfy Dulles. The American special ambassador therefore insisted that reference to America's 'expectation' of Japanese rearmament be included in the treaty preamble. Subsequent events made it impossible for Yoshida to avoid rearmament. Nevertheless, he did have considerable success in his initial bargaining with Dulles over the scale of the Japanese military effort. The result of Yoshida's tough stand on the rearmament issue, however, was that the United States declined to undertake any *formal* obligations to defend Japan.[103] Dulles referred the Japanese Prime Minister to the Vandenberg Resolution, adopted by the United States Senate in June 1948, proclaiming American willingness to join only such 'regional and other collective arrangements as are based on continuous and effective self-help and mutual aid'.[104] Dulles refused to accept Yoshida's argument that Japanese contributions of bases, labour and industrial power could play a critical role in United Stated efforts to contain the expansion of Communist influence in Asia.[105]

Yoshida was not at all worried by America's refusal to extend an unequivocal guarantee to defend Japan. He did not share Washington's view either of the global strategic situation or of Japan's military requirements. It was clear that the United States intended to remain in the Far East for some time. Bases in Japan would continue to be vital to American strategy. Yoshida was satisfied that 'if Japan were invaded while United States forces were actually stationed in that country they could hardly adopt a neutral attitude'.[106] A written guarantee was therefore unnecessary.

By 9 February substantial agreement on the shape of the future security treaty had been reached. Minor adjustments were made at the time of Dulles' third visit to Japan in April and in June a few amendments suggested by the Allied powers were introduced. Nevertheless, the security treaty signed on 8 September was essentially the outcome of a long period of gestation in the State Department and the Dulles-Yoshida talks in January. Its generally unbalanced character reflected the realities of the new power relationship between the two countries. The American refusal to give Japan a clear-cut guarantee of protection, it must be stressed, was *not* the result of Japanese capitulation before overwhelming American pressure. On the contrary, it was a result of the United States having *failed* to impose its views on Japan in one critical area.

The differences between the two new allies, so clearly revealed during the course of the negotiations, were also very much in evidence at the signing ceremony. Secretary of State Dean Acheson, John Foster Dulles, Senator Styles Bridges (for the Republican Party) and Senator Alexander Wiley (for the Democrats), in the traditional display of national solidarity and bipartisanship, signed the treaty on behalf of the United States. Prime Minister Yoshida, alone, signed on behalf of Japan. There were two reasons for this. First, the conservative opposition Democratic Party and the Socialists were opposed to any military alliance with the United States. Second, Yoshida himself hoped that the security treaty would be a transient affair. The fact that he alone signed the agreement was meant to indicate to his successors, and to the Japanese people at large, that he alone took responsibility for it. 'It was the only thing that could be done at the time, really', his daughter told the present writer. 'Yet he always knew that it was a very unnatural position for us to be in.'[107] These subtleties were perhaps lost on the American signatories. So, too, was the significance of the Prime Minister's remarks after the signing ceremony. Dean Acheson, representing the United States, declared that the treaty with Japan represented the first step towards security in the Pacific. Yoshida, in his reply, observed simply that 'the treaty safeguards a Japan deprived of her own defences'.[108]

XI   Ratification of the peace and security treaties: Japanese recognition of China and the Yoshida Letter

On one crucial question Yoshida found himself totally outmanouevred by Dulles. The results of his defeat were to have far-reaching consequences.

Yoshida's long-term strategy for Japanese recovery required a close relationship with the Chinese continent. While surprised by the Nationalist collapse of 1949 he hoped to normalize ties with Peking as rapidly as possible, both to lay the politico-economic foundations for a more independent Japanese policy towards the United States and to encourage the Chinese Communists to rely less on Moscow.

Dulles, in his talks with the British Foreign Secretary Herbert Morrison in June 1950, had agreed that Japan itself should decide whether to recognize Peking or Taipei. Immediately after the San Francisco Conference, however, Dulles told Morrison that it would be difficult to 'suppress indefinitely the natural desire' of the Japanese government, which was 'strongly anti-Communist', to recognize Chiang Kai-shek's Republic of China. Lest the Japanese government have any doubts about where its 'natural desires' lay, a letter from fifty-six United States Senators to President Truman stated bluntly that any Japanese ambiguity on the China question could jeopardize Senate ratification of the San Francisco Peace Treaty.[109] Even so, Japan carefully avoided any move to establish diplomatic relations with Taipei. In Yoshida's view, Chiang Kai-shek's group was in no way representative of China.[110]

In December 1951 Dulles, accompanied by Senator John Sparkman and Senator H. Alexander Smith, respectively the ranking Democratic and Republican members of the Senate Foreign Relations Committee's Far Eastern Subcommittee, flew to Tōkyō. The United States Senate, Yoshida was informed, 'would doubtless want to have clarification of Japan's attitude, in view of the large number of practical post-treaty problems between the United States and Japan that would involve Congressional action'. The United States, it was pointed out, was assuming

> a certain responsibility for Japan's security and ... inasmuch as the threat to that security came primarily from Communist China, already convicted by the United Nations of military aggression in Korea, the Senate would doubtless want to know whether or not Japan contemplated giving moral, political or economic support to the aggressor regime against which the United States would be expected to defend Japan.[111]

Dulles then presented the Japanese Prime Minister with a letter to sign. This document, subsequently known as 'the Yoshida Letter', had almost certainly been written by Dulles himself.[112] It was to exert an extraordinary influence on Japan's policies towards both the United States and China for over two decades. The letter stated, in part, that the Japanese government 'is prepared as soon as legally possible to conclude with the National Government of China, if that government so desires, a treaty which will re-establish normal relations between the two governments'. This treaty would be 'applicable to all territories which are now, or which may hereafter be, under the control of the National Government of the Republic of China'.[113] The letter also noted that Peking had been condemned by the United Nations as an aggressor and that Japan 'is now concurring and expects to continue to concur' in United Nations' sponsored sanctions against the regime.

Yoshida decided he had no alternative but to accept American dictation on this issue, central as it was to his plans for Japanese reconstruction. The most important immediate problem was the peace treaty with the United States and its allies.

Nothing, he believed, could be permitted to jeopardize its ratification. As for China, the Japanese Prime Minister probably considered it best to be guided by the wisdom inherent in the old Taoist proverb *taiki bansei*, 'great vessels cannot be constructed in a single day'. In any case, whatever Dulles may have felt, the Yoshida Letter, even more than the security treaty, bound Yoshida, and him alone.

XII   Japanese reactions to the security treaty system

The settlement with the United States and its allies split Japanese society from top to bottom. These new fissures, cutting across and interlocking with other, pre-existing cleavages, have remained until the present day.

The Socialist and Communist parties, as was to be expected, vehemently opposed Japan's alignment with the West, advocating, instead, policies based on unarmed or lightly armed neutrality. Among the Conservative parties, the general principle of association with the United States was widely accepted. Yoshida, elitist and secretive, did not tell many of his Liberal Party colleagues about his private vision of Japan's future outside the American strategic system. In the short term the alliance was vital. It was necessary to encourage public acceptance of this fact. Within the Liberal Party itself, Yoshida's personal dominance, a long tradition of Westernist thought, America's extraordinarily powerful position in postwar international society, anti-Soviet sentiment and fear of Communist subversion all combined to ensure almost total support. For the back-benchers and the party rank and file adherence to the Japanese-American Security Treaty became, and remained, for over two decades, a virtual article of religious faith.

In the Democratic Party, the other main Conservative grouping to emerge in the postwar period, the situation was more complicated. The party, originally formed around the remnants of the prewar Minseitō and the Nakajima faction of the Seiyūkai, was made up of widely disparate elements. Ashida Hitoshi's early ascendancy proved transitory. The fall of his Cabinet in 1948, amid economic troubles and corruption scandals, led to his rapid political demise. The Democratic Party thereafter divided into three main groups of factions, popularly known as the 'radicals', the 'neutrals' and the 'conservatives'. The 'radicals' centred around two large factions led respectively by Kitamura Tokutarō and Miki Takeo. Associated with these factions were distinguished elder statesmen such as Matsumura Kenzō and aspiring young leaders like Nakasone Yasuhiro. The two 'neutral' factions, which included personalities such as Furui Yoshimi, were also influential and active. The 'conservatives' consisted of a small and declining group around Ōasa Tadao and Ashida's remaining followers.

In domestic policy, the 'conservatives' urged union with Yoshida's Liberals against the Socialists. In foreign affairs, following the Ashida tradition, they advocated energetic Japanese participation in America's global struggle against Communism. Most of the 'radicals' and several prominent members of the 'neutral' factions, in contrast, openly espoused pan-Asianist policies. The prospect of a military alliance with the United States filled them with deepest unease.[114] In their view,

China, not the United States, was Japan's natural trading partner and ally. In retrospect, it would appear that the differences between these groups and Prime Minister Yoshida revolved largely around questions of priorities, emphasis and timing. Even at the height of the occupation, Matsumura Kenzō, Kitamura Tokutarō and their colleagues were not convinced that a peace settlement with the United States should take precedence over Japanese rapprochement with China. The immediate result of this controversy was that while both the Liberal Party and the Democratic Party eventually endorsed the San Francisco Peace Treaty, the Democratic Party refused to support the military relationship with Washington.

These Conservative differences on foreign and defence policy to some extent reflected divisions within the Japanese business community. Organized business had responded favourably to both the peace and security treaties. Support for the American alliance soon became the official policy of Keidanren, Nikkeiren, Keizai Dōyūkai and Nisshō, Japan's four largest employers' organizations. From the standpoint of the business community, Washington's decision to reconstruct Japan as the centrepiece of its Asian-Pacific alliance system, to encourage its former enemy 'to reopen some sort of empire to the south',[115] the generous terms of the peace settlement, the important role played by American Korean War special procurements in the Japanese economic recovery and the continuing threat posed by the radical opposition to the domestic status quo combined to make any other policy unthinkable.[116] The Japanese economic establishment, however, was a complex amalgamation of interlocking competitive interest groups. Generally speaking, the strongest support for the American alliance came from finance and heavy industry, both hard hit by the loss of empire and the destruction of the armed forces. Shipping, textiles, agriculture and fisheries, while not denying the importance of good relations with Washington, were also anxious to normalize ties with the Socialist bloc. Regional differences, too, were apparent. The dominant elements in the Kantō business community emphasized the overriding importance of ties with the American alliance system. Kansai business interests remained fascinated by the possibilities of the Chinese continent. Business leaders in the smaller regional centres around the Japan Sea, such as Niigata, hoped for improvement of ties with the Soviet Union and Korea. For the inhabitants of these remote and snowy regions, Washington, London and even Tōkyō were far away; Vladivostok, Khabarovsk, Seoul and Pyongyang were near neighbours.

Attitudes to the American alliance in both the Conservative and the radical opposition were also influenced by the academic debate on foreign policy that began in the northern spring of 1949. The Confucian tradition has ensured that the stand taken by leading academics on important public issues has always carried considerable weight in Japan. In the early postwar period an overwhelming majority of Japanese intellectuals, acutely aware, from personal experience, of the immense destructive potential of modern warfare, conscious of Japan's extreme vulnerability, and also of their country's complex, interpenetrating ties with East Asia and the West, became convinced that non-alignment offered the most realistic foreign policy option. In March 1949 the magazine *Sekai* published a statement on the causes of war by some sixty prominent Japanese scholars.[117] A year later a second statement, drawn up by the newly formed Peace Problems Discussion Council and signed by thirty-five academics, urged conclusion of a peace treaty with all the former Allied powers, including the Soviet Union and China.[118] A treaty with the American bloc alone was opposed. A third statement appeared in December 1950, on the eve of the Dulles-Yoshida talks.[119] The Dulles visit, then the conclusion of the peace and security treaties, unleashed a flood of books, articles, statements and manifestos denouncing Japan's military involvement with the United States. There were also some who defended the alliance. Yet the Peace Problems Discussion Council and other opponents of the San Francisco system undoubtedly dominated the high ground. For the next thirty years they constituted the Japanese intellectual mainstream.[120]

The Japanese political elite, the business establishment and the principal luminaries in the academic world, whatever their philosophical differences, had their roots in the same soil. They came from the same social classes, attended the same schools and graduated from the same universities. Their network of personal connections was intricate and extensive. The political institutions set up under the 1946 Constitution made it necessary for Japanese leaders, on both the right and the left, for the first time in history, to take some account of popular opinion. In the early postwar period, and for many years afterwards, the attitude of the general public towards foreign affairs tended to strengthen the hand of those who argued the case for a cautious, passive association with the United States or for a policy of lightly armed neutrality. The general public, its confidence in imperial institutions and values shattered as a result of the defeat, had adjusted rapidly to the realities of the new world order. The United States soon established itself, in the minds of many Japanese, from all sections of society, as the political, economic and cultural centre of the universe. For the Japanese middle classes, in particular, Washington became, on an even grander scale, what Chang'an had been for the aristocrats of the Heian period. The utter destruction of the Imperial Japanese Navy, the devastation of Japan's major cities, the nuclear bombings of Hiroshima and Nagasaki, the terrible casualties sustained in the battle for Okinawa had clearly revealed the incomparable material superiority of American civilization. The occupation reforms had aroused widespread and genuine enthusiasm. The behaviour of the occupation forces had been, on the whole, exemplary. By August 1950, five years after Hiroshima, 65.7 per cent of Japanese interviewed by the *Yomiuri Shimbun* were declaring that the United States was their 'favourite country'.[121] For the next three decades, whatever their attitude to the policies of the American government, the Japanese people were to remain among the most fervent admirers of American civilization to be found anywhere in the world.

America's superpower rival, in contrast, had a poor image. The *Yomiuri Shimbun* poll of August 1950 found 67.9 per cent of respondents identifying the Soviet Union as the nation they most disliked. This was not necessarily an indication either of abiding popular Russophobia or hostility to Communism. In the prewar period, antagonism towards the Soviet Union had been no more intense than antipathy towards the United States. Deep-seated, ideological anti-Communism, too, as Prince Konoye realized, was not widespread among the Japanese people. In the early postwar years, popular attitudes towards the two superpowers were largely expressions of judgements about their relative strengths. The Japanese may have abandoned the concept of *fukoku kyōhei*, 'a wealthy country and a powerful army', as a standard for measuring themselves. They had not necessarily discarded it as a yardstick for measuring others. More than 40 per cent of those polled by the *Yomiuri Shimbun* confidently asserted that the United States was the world's greatest power. Only 27.2 per cent thought that the Soviet Union was in any way comparable. A mere 10 per cent considered that the Soviet Union would eventually eclipse the United States. Had the Soviet Union been more obviously powerful, its people more conspicuously wealthy, their lifestyle more glamorous, popular perceptions might have been rather different.

Wartime experiences, of course, were not without some influence on public opinion. Large numbers of Japanese had been taken prisoner by the Russians in Manchuria during August and September 1945. Many had been treated well. Much to the alarm of the Japanese government some groups of prisoners returning from Siberia had marched down the gangways of their repatriation vessels singing the Internationale. Others had experienced the full horrors of the Stalinist labour camps. Like British Commonwealth prisoners of the Japanese in South-East Asia, they remained, for the rest of their lives, implacably hostile to their former captors. The conflict with the Americans in the western Pacific, in contrast, had not lent itself to the large-scale taking of prisoners. Few returned to tell their stories of suffering and deprivation. The experiences of Japanese Americans during the war went, for many years, unnoticed. Memories of Hiroshima, Nagasaki and the terrible fire bombings of Tōkyō rapidly faded in the general enthusiasm for all things American.

The fascination with American institutions, value systems and fashions, together with the generally negative attitude towards the Soviet Union, did not imply that the Japanese people unconditionally welcomed the prospect of incorporation into the United States global strategic system. There was a widespread feeling that a peace treaty with all the former Allied powers, including the Soviet Union and China, would be preferable to one with the American camp alone. A *Yomiuri Shimbun* poll conducted in April 1951, for example, found 57.1 per cent of respondents in favour of a comprehensive settlement, 21.2 per cent supporting a peace treaty exclusively with the United States and its allies. (Only 5.5 per cent of respondents thought that a comprehensive peace treaty was really possible.)[122] At the same time there was no overwhelming enthusiasm for the security treaty and American bases. One substantial minority favoured a base-lending agreement with the United States. Another minority regarded the presence of American bases unavoidable. Another large minority inclined towards neutrality in the Cold War and opposed the presence of foreign bases on Japanese soil. A *Mainichi Shimbun* poll of November 1949, for example, found 48.4 per cent of respondents in favour of neutrality, 20.5 per cent advocating alignment with the United States and 14 per cent favouring some kind of collective security arrangement.[123] In September 1950 another *Mainichi Shimbun* poll found 10.9 per cent of respondents supporting total reliance on the United States in matters of security, 32.7 per cent in favour of reliance on America and an independent defence build-up, 9.6 per cent in favour of reliance on the United Nations and 26 per cent supporting reliance on the United Nations and additional independent Japanese defence efforts. Another 7.4 per cent believed Japan should build up its own forces and rely on no one.[124] This can probably be taken as 43.6 per cent in favour of a security treaty with the United States and 43 per cent in favour of some kind of neutrality. The same poll, significantly, showed 40.4 per cent of respondents opposing the presence of American bases.

Popular ambivalence towards the American alliance had several causes.

First, the general public, like the political elite, could not ignore the fact that the outcome of the Greater East Asia War had transformed Japan's strategic situation. It was abundantly clear, to the most ill-informed peasant in the remotest mountain village, that Japan was no longer the centre of a large and potentially autarchic empire, but had become, instead, a small, vulnerable island chain in the strategic canyon between two mutually antagonistic Western superpowers. For obvious reasons, the implications of military nuclear technology were better understood in Japan than in any other country. World War II had also touched off a massive popular reaction against the militarist values that had dominated Japanese society since the Meiji Restoration. The nature of American plans for postwar Japan was well understood. In this context, alignment with the United States in the Cold War was seen as facilitating restoration of the *ancien régime* at home and increasing the danger of involvement in futile military adventures abroad.

Second, a Shinto-Buddhist cultural tradition, together with the observable facts of recent history, have made the Japanese people acutely aware of the evolutionary possibilities inherent in any situation, of the fluidity of international politics, the transience of worldly power. The United States, despite its unparalleled military strength and the material abundance of its civilization, was merely the most recent arrival in a long line of aspiring candidates for global hegemony. There was no reason to suppose that its supremacy would prove any more enduring than that of the British Empire or the German Reich. The Chinese Revolution and the Korean War, indeed, were already revealing the limitations of its power. In international politics, as in everyday life, wisdom lies in making appropriate obeisance to the powerful, avoiding excessively close commitments and keeping all options open. In the wake of the Korean War some kind of military relationship with the United States was clearly unavoidable. A longer-term partnership might also prove to be in the national interest. Yet neutrality, too, offered another equally realistic alternative, in every way compatible with Japan's historical traditions, permitting the nation to withdraw from the American-Soviet conflict, enhance its security, husband its strength and adjust rapidly to the ebb and flow of world politics.

Third, the issue of alliance with the United States inevitably became entangled in the wider debate about Japan's place in the world and its role in international society. The collapse of the Greater East Asia Co-prosperity Sphere had dealt a crushing blow to the pan-Asianism embraced by the ultranationalist right, the Imperial

Japanese Army and Navy and the secret societies. The victory of the United States in the Pacific War had doubtless seemed, to many, the ultimate vindication of Fukuzawa Yukichi's 'escape from Asia' philosophy, of the belief that Japan's future lay with the modern, industrial powers of the West, in acceptance of the philosophical concepts and forms of social organization that were believed to underpin their strength. The conflict between the extreme pro-American Conservatives and the pro-Soviet wing of the Communist Party was, in one sense, simply a struggle about which Western power and which Western state doctrine provided the most appropriate model for Japan. Yet Westernism did not gain an overwhelming victory. The very facts of the nation's history, geography and strategic situation dictated otherwise. Pan-Asianist sentiment, both conservative and radical, did not disappear, either among the broad masses of the Japanese people or among the political elite. After all, as we have seen, even the Prime Minister who negotiated the American alliance was a *kakure Ajiashugisha*, a closet Asianist. The Chinese Revolution, the conflicts in Korea and Vietnam, were struggles of truly epic proportions, for which large numbers of Japanese felt a deep, intuitive and fraternal sympathy. Despite the new enthusiasm for North American civilization it was impossible for many Japanese to feel comfortable about supporting Washington's efforts to crush what were widely viewed as popular, progressive and very necessary revolutions.

CHAPTER III

Japanese rearmament, 1945–1955

Come, little ones, and get your arms!

Wu Ch'eng-en, *The Journey to the West*

In the northern autumn of 1945 there seemed every possibility that the mighty imperial Japanese Army and Navy, so intimately linked, in so many ways, to Japan's emergence as a major world power, would disappear as completely as the empire they had helped to create. In the United States advocates of an anti-Soviet military alliance with Japan, such as former President Herbert Hoover, found their advice largely ignored, at least in the highest echelons of government. The Initial Post-Surrender Policy Directive for Japan, issued by President Truman to General MacArthur on 29 August 1945, explicitly stipulated that

> Japan will be completely disarmed and demilitarized. The authority of the militarists and the influence of militarism will be totally eliminated from her political, economic and social life ... Disarmament and demilitarization are the primary tasks of the military occupation and shall be carried out promptly and with determination ... Japan is not to have an army, navy, air force, secret police organization, or any civil aviation. Japan's ground, air and naval forces shall be disarmed and disbanded and the Japanese Imperial General Headquarters, the General Staff and all secret police organizations shall be dissolved.[1]

Within Japan itself there was widespread support for disarmament. Certainly, as Lord Mountbatten's political adviser Elsar Denning complained, the Japanese higher officer corps 'do not consider they have been defeated ... say so quite openly' and are determined 'to preserve the military spirit'. In this respect, Denning lamented, 'the war has been fought in vain'.[2] Yet among the broad masses of the Japanese people the imperial armed forces had been totally discredited. The old court aristocracy, together with important sections of the conservative political leadership and the business community, had come to view the military as a breeding ground for revolution. A handful of military leaders had begun to share their anxieties. Rear-Admiral Yamamoto Yoshio, chief of the Military Affairs Bureau of the Naval Ministry during the short-lived Koiso Cabinet (July 1944–April 1945), urged total abolition of Japan's army and navy.[3] Many members of Colonel Ishiwara Kanji's East Asia League (Tōa Renmei), disillusioned not only by the outcome of the war but even more by the way it had been conducted, began to adopt positions in favour of pacifism and disarmament.[4] Even steely-eyed old hawks like Vice-Admiral Hoshina Zenshirō, chief of the Military Affairs Bureau in the Naval Ministry during the last stages of the conflict, argued for significant reductions in the size of Japan's armed forces.[5]

On 2 September 1945, in accordance with the provisions of the Potsdam Declaration and the Initial Post-Surrender Policy Directive for Japan, SCAP issued orders for Japanese demobilization and disarmament. On 13 September the Imperial General Headquarters (Dai Honei), one of the principal nerve-centres of the empire, was formally abolished. The General Staffs (Sanbō Honbu) were disbanded a little over a month later. The Imperial Japanese Army and Navy were dissolved in November. Japan's remaining naval vessels and aircraft were subsequently destroyed, reduced to scrap, transferred to Allied navies or to the Japanese merchant marine. With the exception of a small group of officers kept on by SCAP in the Demobilization Bureau, all professional soldiers, sailors and airmen, of all ranks, then became subject to the restrictions of the purge. Within a year of the surrender Japan had adopted a constitution formally renouncing the maintenance of military forces and resort to war as an instrument of national policy.

There was no logical reason why the onset of the Cold War and the conclusion of the security treaty should have led to Japanese rearmament. After all, Iceland, a nation no less strategically placed than Japan, was able to join NATO in 1949 without abandoning its traditional opposition to the maintenance of armed forces. Nevertheless, American interest in promoting Japan's demilitarization evaporated as tensions in the Far East mounted. By 1954, two years after the end of the occupation, Japan had been provided with a new, fully fledged army, navy and air force. By the middle of the 1960s, while the pacifist constitution remained intact, Japan had re-established itself as a substantial military power, with a defence budget consistently ranking among the world's top ten, a growing military industrial complex and a number of interlocking intelligence agencies operating throughout the Asian-Pacific region.

The new defence forces differed, in several respects, from the Imperial Japanese Army and Navy. Their place in the domestic constellation of power, in particular, was in no way comparable to that of their prewar counterparts. The Defence Agency Establishment Law, the Self Defence Forces Law (June 1954) and the Law Concerning the Structure of the National Defence Council (July 1956), which formulated the legal framework for the forces and defined defence policy decision-making procedures, all laid heavy influence on the principle of civilian control. The 1889 Constitution, by placing the Chiefs of Staff on an equal footing with the Prime Minister and Cabinet, had created a position of special privilege for the armed forces. The right of direct access to the imperial presence had enabled the Chiefs of Staff to operate independently of the Cabinet in all matters affecting military planning and operations. The imperial ordinance of 1900, stipulating that the Minister for War and the Minister for the Navy should be serving generals and admirals, subject to military discipline while in office, had further strengthened the position of the Chiefs of Staff *vis-à-vis* the Cabinet, enabling them to destroy governments at will by the simple device of forcing the service ministers to resign. Under the 1954–6 laws, the Prime Minister enjoyed the 'right of supreme command and control' of the forces. Defence planning and the day-to-day administration of the forces were theoretically the responsibility of a civilian-dominated National Defence Council and a Defence Agency, headed by a junior Minister of State responsible to the Prime Minister. Mobilization was to be decided by the Prime Minister after consultation with the National Defence Council. Subsequent Diet approval of the Prime Minister's action was necessary. Despite the existence of a Joint Staff Council military officers were, in principle, given no active role in defence policy decision-making at any level.[6] At the same time, a unanimous resolution of the House of Councillors on 2 June 1954 opposed the dispatch of forces overseas on constitutional and other grounds.[7]

The process leading to Japan's re-emergence as a major military power was a complex one, providing a fascinating field of research for students of pressure groups, secret organizations, conspiracy and intrigue. It also sheds much light on the question of continuity and change in modern Japanese history. Three points, in particular, should be noted.

First, at a time when the United States government, General MacArthur, all the Allied powers and the legally constituted Japanese authorities were energetically promoting disarmament under the terms of the Potsdam Declaration and the Initial Post-Surrender Policy Directive for Japan, certain elements in SCAP, apparently on their own initiative, but working in close co-operation with former Imperial Japanese Army and Navy officers, were actively laying the foundations for future rearmament. In this way they sought to present both Washington and Tōkyō with a series of irreversible *faits accomplis*. A legal basis for the present forces was surreptitiously laid by the Government Section of SCAP and the then Democratic (Progressive) Party leader Ashida Hitoshi in the phrasing of Article 9 of the 1947 Constitution. The Intelligence Section of SCAP began assembling the personnel for a future Japanese army and navy, and for a new intelligence service, almost immediately after the dissolution of Imperial General Headquarters and the General Staffs. As far as can be judged from documents currently available, most of these activities remained hidden from the United States government, the Supreme Commander of the Allied Powers and the Japanese authorities of the day.

Second, while Prime Minister Yoshida, among others, envisaged the eventual re-establishment of independent military forces, and began making his own discreet preparations for rearmament as early as 1947, all the steps leading to the creation of the Self Defence Forces in their present form were the result of very heavy American pressure on rather unwilling Japanese governments. Neither General MacArthur nor Prime Minister Yoshida was anxious to consider rearmament until Japan's economic recovery had been completed. Both had strong ideas about the character and scale of Japanese rearmament. The forces that emerged in the wake of the ferocious institutional, factional and policy conflicts of the early 1950s conformed, on the whole, rather more closely to the pattern envisaged by MacArthur and Yoshida than to that advocated by the Intelligence Section of SCAP, the old General Staff group, and John Foster Dulles.

Third, while the United States, for historical and ideological reasons, insisted on the principle of 'civilian control', the overall character of the 1954–6 defence laws was not the result of American hectoring but of talks between Yoshida's Liberals and the Democratic Party. Before these talks began, internal changes in the Democratic Party had to some extent undermined the position of Ashida Hitoshi and the extreme anti-Communist right. This had caused the party to abandon some of the more hawkish aspects of its defence policy. As a result, the defence laws that eventually emerged reflected the Yoshida view rather than the Democratic Party's original programme.

I   The Government Section of SCAP and Ashida Hitoshi modify General MacArthur's pacifist Constitution, January–October 1946[8]

In October 1946 an American-inspired Constitution, the enduring popularity of which has caused successive governments to approach the question of revision with caution, was approved almost unanimously by the Japanese Diet.

Article 9 of this Constitution states:

> Aspiring sincerely to an international peace based on justice and order, the Japanese people forever renounce war as a sovereign right of the nation and the threat or use of force as a means of settling international disputes.
>
>   In order to accomplish the aim of the preceding paragraph, land, sea, and air forces, as well as other war potential, will never be maintained. The right of belligerency of the state will not be recognized.

The Potsdam Declaration and the Initial Post-Surrender Policy Directive for Japan envisaged complete Japanese disarmament and demilitarization. All official State Department planning for Japan's future, from 1942 until the outbreak of war in Korea, was based on the assumptions embodied in these documents. Neither the State Department, nor the State-War-Navy Department Co-ordinating Committee, however, seem to have contemplated a Japanese *constitutional* renunciation of war.[9]

The idea of a pacifist constitution appears to have originated either with Baron Shidehara Kijurō, Prime Minister during the immediate post-surrender period, or with General MacArthur himself. MacArthur claims the idea was suggested to him by Shidehara.[10] This view has been disputed by a number of Japanese conservatives, largely on the grounds that Shidehara, as a Japanese nationalist and an experienced statesman, would never have contemplated such follies. Certainly, Baron Shidehara was a patriot and a realist. Neither of these qualities has ever been incompatible with pacifism. Shidehara's policies as Foreign Minister in the prewar Katō, Wakatsuki and Hamaguchi cabinets, his advocacy of good relations with both the Anglo-American powers and the Soviet Union, his reluctance to countenance military intervention in China and his support for disarmament had alienated him from the military and the extreme nationalists. It would not be surprising if he had come to believe that a constitutional renunciation of war could have its advantages.

On 3 February 1946, MacArthur directed his Government Section to prepare a draft constitution for the 'guidance' of the Shidehara Cabinet. After an informal talk with Baron Shidehara MacArthur drew up a three-point draft to 'guide' the Government Section.

The second point of MacArthur's draft stated that

> War as a sovereign right of the nation is abolished. Japan renounces it as an instrumentality for settling disputes *and even for preserving its own security,* [emphasis my own]
>
> No Japanese Army, Navy, or Air Force will ever be authorised and no rights of belligerency will ever be conferred upon any Japanese force.[11]

Despite MacArthur's suggestions to the contrary in his memoirs,[12] published many years later, it is clear that at this time he did envisage Japan's total and permanent disarmament. Nevertheless, the pacifist clause drafted by the Government Section and handed to Shidehara on 13 February was significantly different to that drawn up by the Supreme Commander. The Government Section draft read:

> War as a sovereign right of the nation is abolished. The threat or use of force is forever renounced *as a means of settling disputes with any other nation.*[13] [emphasis my own]

The 'threat or use of force' was now not explicitly forbidden in cases where the objective was not 'settling disputes with any other nation'. It might, therefore, perhaps, be regarded as permissible in cases of crushing domestic revolution or, albeit rather more tenuously, in defending the nation from external aggression.

The proposed pacifist clause was strongly attacked by Admiral Nomura Kichisaburō at a meeting of the Privy Council held in the presence of the emperor to discuss the new Constitution. Nomura argued that submission to the Potsdam Declaration necessitated disarmament. It did not require 'renunciation of armaments forever'. Neutral countries like Switzerland maintained military forces. Japan, he noted, was now even weaker than Korea. It would certainly need some future military protection against that country.[14] Since the emperor had already consented to the basic principles of the new Constitution Nomura's appeal was in vain.

Nevertheless, the Government Section's modified draft underwent a further significant change during discussions between SCAP and representatives of the Japanese Cabinet on the night of 4–5 March 1946. After this meeting it read:

> War, as a sovereign right of the nation, and the threat or use of force, is forever renounced as a means of settling disputes with other nations.[15]

Now, 'war', as well as the 'threat or use of force', was not *explicitly* forbidden as a means of advancing objectives other than 'settling disputes with other nations'.

Orders to implement these changes cannot possibly have come from the responsible authorities in Washington. The White House remained committed to the principles set out in the Initial Post-Surrender Policy Directive for Japan. State Department planning for the peace settlement also envisaged a demilitarized Japan. General MacArthur, too, would hardly have requested his Government Section to introduce fatal flaws into the pacifist constitution at the moment of its birth. He remained, until the outbreak of the Korean War, the most enthusiastic American exponent of Japanese unarmed neutrality. Perhaps the SCAP representatives at the critical Cabinet meeting on the night of 4–5 March, lulled into somnolence by the lateness of the hour and the dronings of their Japanese colleagues, were unaware of the significance of the changes being proposed. Perhaps they did understand the changes and supported their inclusion, fearing that if Japan were constitutionally disarmed as a result of American pressure, the United States might be morally obliged to enter into a mutual defence treaty with its former antagonist, a step not contemplated, at this stage, by any senior officials in the State Department. Perhaps, unknown to the Supreme Commander, they were acting as surrogates for other interests. The United States Joint Chiefs of Staff, important groups in the War and Navy departments, along with Harry Kern and his circle, were already, by this stage, coming to see Japan as an active future ally in the global struggle against Bolshevism.

The radically altered 'pacifist clause' underwent further transformation at the hands of a Japanese Select Committee at the time of its passage through the Diet. At the suggestion of Ashida Hitoshi, who had close links with Admiral Nomura Kichisaburō, the two phrases

Aspiring sincerely to an international peace based on justice and order ...

and

In order to accomplish the aim of the preceding paragraph ...

were added to the revised draft.

Ashida later claimed that he had devised these two phrases to make it clear that war potential could be maintained for defensive purposes – 'the aim of the preceding paragraph' referring to 'war as a means of settling international disputes'.[16] In the revised version, in fact, Japan's entire commitment to pacific and defensive policies could be interpreted as being dependent on the emergence of 'an international peace based on justice and order'. To date, such an interpretation has not been advanced, although, in the view of the present writer, it is theoretically possible and was probably consistent with Ashida's intentions. Ashida's role in altering Article 9 was particularly significant, not only because of his prewar background, his association with Admiral Nomura and, through him, with Harry Kern's American Council on Japan, but also because of his attempts in 1947 to ally Japan with the United States and his strong stand on rearmament in the 1950s.

II Lieutenant-General Willoughby's interest in Japanese rearmament

Despite the provisions of the Potsdam Declaration and the Initial Post-Surrender Policy Directive for Japan, the Japanese military forces did not completely disappear after the dissolution of Imperial Headquarters, the General Staffs, the Army and Navy Ministries and the demobilization of the officers and men they administered. A small group of high-ranking officers was, of necessity, kept on by SCAP in the

Demobilization Bureau. Other groups were quickly absorbed by Lieutenant-General Willoughby's Intelligence Section, G–II. Within SCAP G–II was very much a law unto itself. Willoughby's views on several matters differed significantly from those of the Supreme Commander. He guarded his operations both from MacArthur and from other sections of SCAP with jealous secrecy. Born in Germany, profoundly influenced by Prussian military thought, elitist, intensely conservative (he served as adviser to General Franco after his retirement from the United States Army in the early 1950s) Willoughby observed the occupation's attempts to restructure and democratize the Japanese state with ill-concealed horror. Like former President Herbert Hoover, Joseph Grew and Harry Kern, he believed that the global struggle against Communism should have first priority. On 5 September 1945, three days after the beginning of the occupation, Willoughby, seemingly on his own initiative, enlisted the services of Lieutenant-General Arisue Seizō, the director of Japanese Military Intelligence, in his own organization. He also had Arisue arrange a meeting with Major-General Nishimura Toshio, Chief of Special Intelligence.[17]* Within a few months, under Willoughby's direction, several overlapping groups of Japanese officers were engaged in various kinds of covert intelligence work on behalf of G–II. Lieutenant-General Arisue and his associates were busy gathering information about the Soviet Union, Manchuria and Korea. Another group, under Rear-Admiral Nakamura Shōhei and Rear-Admiral Ogawa Saburō, was involved in cartographic work. Yet another group, centring around Lieutenant-General Yoshiwara Kane, former Chief of Staff of the Eighteenth Army in New Guinea, and including the future Chief of Staff of the Ground Self Defence Forces, Sugiyama Shigeru, was involved in mapping military strong points and transport routes in the Japanese archipelago. These groups, although formally dissolved at the end of the occupation, actually continued in existence until the 1970s, providing vital channels of communication between the Japanese and American intelligence services. Another organization, headed by the former Deputy Chief of the General Staff, Lieutenant-General Kawabe Torashirō, and including such prominent figures as General Shimomura Sadamu (former Minister for the Army), Lieutenant-General Tatsumi Eiichi (former Military Attaché in London, Commander of the Eastern Army in Japan, Commander of the Third Division in China), Lieutenant-General Yoshinaka Kazutarō (former Military Attaché in Turkey and Hungary, Staff Officer of the Western Army, Divisional Commander in southern Kyūshū), Major-General Yamamoto Shigeichirō (former Military Administrative Inspector in Java), Colonel Saigo Shōgo (former Military Attaché in Austria, later attached to the German Section of Imperial Headquarters), and Lieutenant-General Arisue Seizō himself, together with about a hundred other senior officers, engaged in domestic intelligence work from the vantage point of an office set up in the old Yūsen Building. The principal target of this group's operations was the Japan Communist Party. Kawabe's organization continued to function until 1956.[18] Willoughby, again, apparently, without MacArthur's knowledge, was also instru-

* Nishimura was the adopted heir of the prewar Prime Minister General Tanaka Giichi, an exponent of hardline expansionist policies on the Chinese continent.

mental in arranging immunity from war crimes prosecution for Japanese chemical and biological warfare experts on condition that they turn over to him the results of their grisly research on living human victims (including American prisoners or war).[19]

Willoughby developed an early interest in large-scale Japanese rearmament. In the aristocratic Lieutenant-General Arisue, an intimate of the imperial family, implacably anti-Communist and, in prewar days, one of the principal channels of communication between Japan and Mussolini's Italy, he found a kindred spirit. Towards the middle of November 1945, a few weeks after Arisue had begun his new work in Willoughby's office, the two men went on a day's trip to Chiba prefecture to pay a courtesy call on Prince and Princess Kaya, who had been evacuated to Kashiwa. During the return journey, after a day spent enjoying the beauties of the late autumn countryside, the conversation turned to domestic politics. The threat of Communism continued to preoccupy the old establishment. The imperial family had already expressed their concern to Arisue about the security of the palace in the troubled times they believed lay ahead. Arisue earnestly requested Willoughby to persuade the occupation authorities to permit the maintenance of at least one division of Imperial Guards 'for the preservation of internal security and out of respect for the emperor'. Arisue, of course, was not simply thinking about the safety of the imperial family:

> Naturally, I was thinking secretly of the precedent of defeated Germany after World War I, where the 100,000-man militia permitted by the Allies had formed the basis for German rearmament.[20]

Willoughby replied that he completely understood Arisue's sentiments. As a man devoted to the profession of arms he deeply regretted the destruction of the Imperial Japanese Armed Forces. Nevertheless, occupation policy was directed towards the weakening of Japan. Dissolution of the armed forces was central to that policy. After a moment's silence, however, Willoughby asked Arisue how many men he thought would be necessary 'to form a gendarmerie [*keisatsugun*], openly called a gendarmerie, for the maintenance of internal order throughout Japan'. Arisue suggested 250,000 men would be sufficient.[21]

Early next year the occupation authorities authorized Japan to maintain a police force of 125,000 men. There is no need to suspect (as Arisue does) that there was any connection between these two events. The occupation remained, at this stage, totally dedicated to destroying the institutions of the *ancien régime*. The reorganized Japanese police force, in its structure, functions and personnel, did not, in any way, resemble an army.[22]

In the middle of 1946 another secret organization took shape in Willoughby's headquarters. This organization, centring around Lieutenant-General Kawabe Torashirō, Lieutenant-General Arisue Seizō, Rear-Admiral Nakamura Shōhei and Professor Araki Kōtarō, former Professor of Economics at Tōkyō University, was initially set to work on the production of a large-scale history of the Pacific War. An American historian, Dr Gordon Prange, later to achieve fame as the author of the best-selling novel and Hollywood extravaganza *Tora, Tora, Tora*, also co-operated in this task. A book based on their research was eventually published by the United States Government Printers' Office in 1966. Willoughby, however, came to conceive of this organization not as an historical research society but as the nucleus of a future Japanese army.[23]

In May 1946 the group was joined by Lieutenant-Colonel Hattori Takushirō. Hattori, a graduate of the Officers Staff College (Rikugun Shikan Gakkō), a protégé of Colonel Ishiwara Kanji (also a native of Yamagata prefecture and Hattori's senior at the Officers Staff College), had served as Japanese military observer during Mussolini's Ethiopian campaign, as Principal Staff Officer with the Kwantung Army at the battle of Nomonhan and as General Tōjō Hideki's private secretary. Throughout the greater part of the Pacific War he had been chief of the Operations Section at the General Staffs. In the last months of the conflict he had been transferred to China, where he had won considerable prestige conducting the withdrawal of Japanese forces from the interior. Hattori saw himself, and was quickly seen by Willoughby, as the future Japanese von Seeckt. Hattori, an unbending nationalist, intensely loyal to the emperor, yet not necessarily an enthusiastic supporter of the free enterprise system, was the very embodiment of that military-political tradition that had caused Prince Konoye and Yoshida to lose so much sleep in the dark days of 1944–5. Like Yoshida, Hattori had accepted the inevitability of defeat, looked realistically at the future options open to Japan, kept his innermost thoughts to himself and was determined to make use of the American occupation to advance the national interests as he saw them.

Hattori believed that the breakdown of the American-Soviet alliance presented Japan with important opportunities. The United States and Great Britain, he argued in a memorandum dated 10 July 1946, would almost certainly launch a pre-emptive strike against the Soviet Union before that country had completed its defence preparations under the then current five-year plan. The Anglo-American powers would first 'occupy the vital political and strategic areas of the Far East, then attack [the Russians] from all sides.'[24] Hattori's thinking, it should be noted, closely paralleled that of the United States Joint Chiefs of Staff. The probability of a large-scale American-Soviet conflict in the Far East, Hattori contended, again echoing the Joint Chiefs of Staff, gave Washington a strong reason for promoting Japanese rearmament. This was obviously a welcome development. Over the next few years, with Willoughby's encouragement, but unknown to either General MacArthur or the Japanese government, Hattori gradually built up a nationwide organization of like-minded officers. Altogether Hattori's agency consisted of about fifty or sixty officers scattered throughout Japan. By the beginning of 1949, it had produced detailed plans for the reconstruction of a vast Japanese army. Hattori's old comrade-in-arms, Lieutenant-Colonel Tsuji Masanobu, the radical pan-Asianist, a man whose place in modern Japanese history somewhat resembles that of T. E. Lawrence in Great Britain, did not participate in this work. In the post-occupation period Tsuji, as a writer and conservative politician closely linked to imperial officers' groups, became well known as an advocate of armed neutrality and a foreign policy based on Asianist principles. Between 1945 and 1951, however, he was slowly making his way back to Japan through Burma, Thailand, Laos and Vietnam disguised as a Buddhist monk, a journey described in his epic work *Senkō Sanzen Ri*.[25]

It was, perhaps, on the basis of conversations with Willoughby, Hattori and their circle that Harry Kern informed the readers of *Newsweek* on 4 August 1947 that the American-Soviet Cold War had stimulated a growing interest in Japanese rearmament. The Japanese, he suggested, would welcome the prospect of war with the Soviet Union. Given American naval and air support Japanese forces, he explained, could occupy Siberia. This scenario doubtless reflected Willoughby's hopes rather than Hattori's. Whatever Hattori may have thought about the likely outcome of an American-Soviet confrontation, he would hardly have been, in the aftermath of Hiroshima and Nagasaki, anxious to involve his country so directly in a clash with one of the two new super-powers. This despite the manifest weakness of the Soviet Union and the opportunities this situation might appear to offer. Japan itself, in the northern summer of 1947, was hardly in much better shape than Russia. No responsible Japanese military officer, least of all Hattori Takushirō, could forget that the Soviet Union had also been judged to be weak and overextended on the eve of the battle of Nomonhan.

Various projects for naval rearmament were drawn up by a group of former imperial officers seconded to the Demobilization Bureau.[26] This group, organized under the protective wing of Admiral Nomura Kichisaburō (who had good connections with Harry Kern's group, especially with Admiral William V. Pratt and Rear-Admiral D.W. Beary) functioned independently of Willoughby's organization. Its members, Captain Yoshida Eizō, Captain Nagaishi Masataka and Commodore Terai Yoshimori, drew up secret rearmament plans in their spare time. These plans, passed on to Admiral Nomura, were discussed from time to time both with sympathetic Americans, such as Rear-Admiral Beary and the retired Chief of Naval Operations William H. Standley, and with Japanese politicians such as Yoshida Shigeru and Ashida Hitoshi.

As noted above, the greater part of the Imperial Japanese Navy had either been destroyed in the Pacific War, sunk after the surrender, scrapped, transferred to Allied navies or to the Japanese merchant marine. The Allies, however, had no alternative but to enlist the services of Japanese naval personnel for minesweeping operations in and around the former territories of the empire. The Japanese minesweeping force, which rapidly became the largest and the most efficient in the western Pacific, consisted of 350 small vessels, 773 officers and 9,227 enlisted men, directed by Admiral Yamamoto and commanded by Captain Tamura Kyūzō. After 1 May 1946 this force conducted all minesweeping operations in Japanese waters. Yet however it may have been viewed by Admiral Nomura and the ex-naval officers' group, it was not intended by SCAP, at any time, to form the nucleus of a future navy. Captain Tamura, 91 of his officers and 1,324 of his enlisted men did, nevertheless, join the Maritime Safety Force in 1952.[27]

Nor did the occupation authorities regard the Maritime Safety Board (Kaijō Hōan Cho), set up in 1947 to prevent smuggling, illegal entry and harassment of

Japanese fishing boats, as an embryonic navy. The need for some kind of coastguard (which Japan had never before possessed) was obvious and pressing.

As with minesweeping operations there was no reasonable alternative but to employ former Japanese navy personnel.[28] Once again, this encouraged Japanese interested in rearmament to view the Maritime Safety Force as the forerunner of a new navy. Ashida Hitoshi officially proposed, in October 1947, that the coastguard be established as an armed, uniformed force, without limitations as to size.[29] Ōkubo Takeo, head of the Sailors Bureau in the Transport and Communications Ministry, who worked with Captain Meals of the United States Navy in drawing up plans for the force, also saw the coastguard as the basis for a future navy. Captain Meals, very emphatically, did not.[30] Nor did the Government Section of SCAP, the Allied Council for Japan or the Far Eastern Commission. The Maritime Law sponsored by the occupation in March 1948 permitted only a 10,000-man uniformed Maritime Safety Force (Kaijō Hōan Tai) equipped with sidearms.[31] There is no particular significance in the fact that this force was set up separately from the Water Police. There was scope for two organizations with somewhat different functions. According to the provisions of the Maritime Law, the vessels under the control of the Maritime Safety Board were limited in number to 125 and to a gross total of 50,000 tons. No individual vessel was to exceed 1,500 tons. Stringent restrictions were placed on speed and equipment. It was explicitly stated that

> Nothing in this law shall be construed so as to permit the Maritime Safety Board or its personnel to be trained or organized as a military establishment or to function as such.[32]

III   Yoshida Shigeru's tentative preparations for rearmament

Yoshida Shigeru had rejoiced at the dissolution of the Imperial Japanese Army and Navy. He was determined that rearmament should not take precedence over economic recovery. Yet he did not believe Japan should remain permanently without military forces. When the time was ripe the country should rearm.[33] Still, the question needed to be approached with the utmost caution. Yoshida was particularly anxious to avoid rearmament of a kind that would revive the influence of the old officer corps. He was also determined to avoid, as far as possible, the kind of rearmament that would bind Japan inextricably into the framework of American Far Eastern strategy.

Until 1950, Prime Minister Yoshida, like General MacArthur, appears to have been totally unaware of the secret organizations that had grown up around Willoughby's offices in the Yūsen Building. Nevertheless, in 1947, shortly after the inauguration of his first cabinet, this wily old Japanese politician began to make his own discreet preparations for the future by establishing an intelligence organization, euphemistically known as the Cabinet Research Office (Naikaku Chōsa Shitsu), within the Prime Minister's Office. The Cabinet Research Office, which has continued to operate until the present day, was placed under the direction of Yoshida's former private secretary Murai Jun, then chief of the Police Affairs Section in the Police

Agency. It was advised by two separate groups of military officers, all hand-picked by Yoshida, specializing in Soviet affairs. The first group centred around Vice-Admiral Maeda Minoru (former Military Attaché in Moscow and Nanking, chief of the Second Mobilization Bureau), Colonel Yabe Chūta (former Military Attaché in Moscow), Captain Suezawa Yoshimasa (former chief of the Military Affairs Bureau, Second Section (Intelligence), and Colonel Asai Yū (a Soviet specialist in the General Staff, former special assistant to the Military Attaché in Moscow). The second group consisted of about ten people from the former intelligence section of the General Staff.[34] The fact that the Cabinet Research Office was, from its inception, strongly influenced by these men, with their generally hostile attitude towards the Soviet Union, together with the fact that it contained, for many years, no specialists on American affairs, on Europe, China, South-East Asia or the Middle East, was to have much the same impact on official Japanese attitudes as the domination of the United States State Department's East European division by Robert F. Kelley's 'Riga Group' had on American policies.

In creating the Cabinet Research Office, and in selecting its personnel, Yoshida had two objectives in mind. One was to set up an intelligence organization which could, to some extent at least, provide the Japanese government with independent assessments of Soviet policies. The other objective was probably to groom the higher officer corps of a future Japanese army and navy. If Yoshida did not have some such scheme in mind it is difficult to understand why he did not staff the Cabinet Research Office entirely with ex-Foreign Ministry officials. He did not, after all, particularly like military men, and mistrusted their judgement almost as a matter of principle.

IV The Police Reserve Force and the expanded Maritime Safety Force, July 1950–January 1952

In Washington, the collapse of the Chinese Nationalists did not produce a decisive swing of official opinion in favour of Japanese rearmament. The Joint Chiefs of Staff, the Defence Department and Harry Kern's American Council on Japan intensified their campaign to undermine the pacifist constitution. MacArthur continued to argue the case for Japanese unarmed neutrality. Opinion in the State Department vacillated. In October 1948 George Kennan recommended to the National Security Council that the United States establish a 150,000-man Japanese National Police Force.[35] His thinking on the subject, at this stage, had apparently been influenced by Harry Kern's widely circulated paper 'American Policy towards Japan'.[36] Within less than a year Kennan's enthusiasm for Japanese rearmament had waned. The Communist victory in China, the emerging relationship between Moscow and Peking, together with the unstable situation in South-East Asia, made it essential, he felt, for the United States to avoid a provocative stance. Nothing would be gained by turning Japan into an armed camp. The State Department's revised draft peace treaty of 13 October 1949 thus supported continued disarmament and demilitarization, although it suggested that these policies might be reviewed in five years' time.[37]

Truman's decision to intervene in the Korean civil war created an entirely new situation. On 8 July 1950 MacArthur ordered the Yoshida government to create a Police Reserve Force (Keisatsu Yōbitai) of 75,000 men. He also ordered that the Maritime Safety Force be strengthened by 8,500 men.

After an urgent Cabinet meeting held to discuss MacArthur's order the Yoshida government announced that the Reserve would be established *outside* the framework of the existing police forces. The Police Reserve was to be a highly centralized force administered by a specially established headquarters (Keisatsu Yōbitai Honbu) directed by an official responsible to the Prime Minister. Detailed plans were drawn up over the next few weeks in close collaboration with SCAP. On 10 August 1950, a month after receiving MacArthur's instructions, the Japanese Cabinet proclaimed the Police Reserve Force Order (Keisatsu Yōbitai Rei). A supplementary Police Reserve Force Organization Order (Keisatsu Yōbitai Soshiki Rei) was issued on 26 August 1950. Appointments of high-ranking officials to Police Reserve Headquarters were announced in October. Recruitment and training of officers and men began almost immediately. By May 1951 units of the new force had been disposed in a state of readiness throughout the country.[38]

The Police Reserve and the expanded Maritime Safety Force formed the basis for all Japan's subsequent rearmament. Both organizations were rather more ambiguous in character than is often supposed. There is considerable evidence to suggest that MacArthur and Yoshida, at least, had been reluctant to establish the new organizations, viewed them as no more than paramilitary police forces, were anxious to check their development into a full-scale army and navy and, in case this should prove impossible, carefully to guide their evolution in directions compatible with Japan's long-term interests as they saw them. Other people had different ideas. The establishment of the Police Reserve and the expansion of the Maritime Safety Force created new opportunities for those Americans and Japanese interested in genuine and immediate large-scale rearmament. Between July 1950 and January 1952 intense, behind-the-scenes struggles for control of the new forces took place. The outcome of these struggles had an important influence not only on the character and direction of Japanese rearmament but on the evolution of postwar Japanese society itself.

MacArthur's support for Japan's unarmed neutrality had been based partly on his belief that the Soviet Union had neither the intention nor the capability to invade the archipelago. A Chinese attack on Japan, too, he felt, was totally out of the question.[39] He continued to hold his position after the outbreak of war in Korea, despite wild rumours of Soviet-trained Japanese divisions of 'indoctrinated' prisoners of war massing in Sakhalin.[40] MacArthur had every reason to believe, however, that anti-war elements in Japan, particularly the Japanese Communist Party and its sympathizers, would attempt to make the American position as difficult as possible. Political and economic conditions in Japan in 1950 remained highly volatile. Japanese conservative leaders, including Yoshida Shigeru, had long been critical of the 1947 police law, which had established a decentralized force under the control of elected Municipal Safety Commissions and a separate National

Rural Police Force for duty in sparsely settled areas. Fearful of Communist activity rather than conventional crime, Yoshida and his colleagues advocated the restoration of something akin to the prewar system, where a highly centralized and efficient police force under the control of the Home Ministry had operated throughout the empire to eradicate political unorthodoxy and crush dissent. In January 1950 the Japanese Communist Party, in the face of increasing American pressure on the embryonic labour movement and intense criticism from Moscow, had embarked on a course of action which seemed to justify the conservatives' arguments, abandoning its previous policy of working for change within the occupation system and launching a campaign of demonstrations, strikes and industrial sabotage. This in turn, precipitated the occupation purge of Communist leaders in June 1950, on the eve of the Korean War, a month before the creation of the Police Reserve. The Communist campaign subsequently intensified, reaching a peak in 1951–2. Police stations and other facilities were attacked. Desultory attempts were made to create rural liberated areas on the Chinese model. These efforts ultimately ended in failure. By 1953 Communist electoral support had temporarily evaporated. Within the party, changes were taking place which would eventually lead to more realistic policies. Yet in the summer of 1950, with full-scale war raging in Korea, it was no more clear to MacArthur and Yoshida than it was to Moscow and the Communist Party leadership that the new tactics would fail. The United States and the Japanese governments had seen what had happened in China. They had seen the growth of peasant and worker movements in southern Korea.[41] There was also the example of French Indochina. In the tense situation created by the outbreak of war in Korea and the hasty departure of American occupation troops for the battlefronts, MacArthur and Yoshida had every reason to fear the outbreak of domestic Communist revolution.[42] They also had every reason to believe that the war in Korea would drastically increase the flow of refugees and illegal immigrants across the Tsushima Straits, aggravate the problem of smuggling and encourage the neighbouring Communist powers to land intelligence agents on Japan's long, exposed coastline. Only a paramilitary police force and an expanded coastguard could adequately deal with these problems. The Far Eastern Commission, under the terms of the Potsdam Declaration, had authorized a total Japanese police strength of 200,000 men. At the time of the outbreak of hostilities in Korea the Japanese police force comprised 125,000 men. The creation of a special gendarmerie to deal with insurrection, MacArthur probably reasoned, would not fall outside the scope of the occupations's original objectives. If the activities of the Japanese Communist Party intensified, or if the United States wished to put pressure on the Soviet Union in the northern islands or Siberia, the Police Reserve could be transformed into an army. If the Korean War resulted in an American victory and Japan's domestic situation could be stabilized, the force could remain as it was or even be merged with the regular police.

On 8 July 1950, on receiving MacArthur's orders, the Yoshida Cabinet, uncertain about the Supreme Commander's intentions, despatched Chief Cabinet Secretary Okazaki Katsuo to General Headquarters to speak with Lieutenant-General Courtney Whitney, head of the Government Section. It was from Whitney, *not* from

MacArthur, that Okazaki gained the impression that the United States was thinking *not* in terms of a simple increase in police strength but of an embryonic army, eventually to be equipped with tanks and heavy artillery.[43] The Yoshida government was thereafter anxious to make it clear that the decision to create the new force was not its own. Thus on 26 July 1950 the Minister for Justice Mr Ōhashi told the House of Representatives Foreign Affairs Research Committee that

> General Headquarters did not act in response to any request from the Japanese government. I consider that [the establishment of the Police Reserve Force] should be viewed in the same light as other orders previously issued to the Japanese government by the Supreme Command of the Allied Powers.[44]

His own convictions and the uncertainties of the situation prompted Yoshida to proceed as cautiously as possible. On 18 July 1950 a joint American-Japanese meeting was held to discuss plans for the development of the force. The United States, represented by Major-General Shepherd, who had been appointed Chief Military Adviser to the Police Reserve, pressed for urgent action. The Japanese Cabinet, represented by Okazaki and Ōhashi, resisted. Okazaki expressed a desire to see some reference to the Potsdam Declaration (which specifically forbade Japanese rearmament) incorporated into the legal framework for the new force. In any case, he argued, it would be prudent to wait until the opening of the Diet (scheduled for 3 August 1950) in order to avoid Opposition attacks and public confusion. It was for this reason that the proclamation of the Police Reserve Force Order was eventually postponed until 10 August. Even then, many of Yoshida's Cabinet colleagues, not knowing whether the Police Reserve Force was a gendarmerie or an army, wanted to advance slowly, allowing time for consolidation of public opinion and the construction of a proper legal framework.[45]

Yoshida, probably with the objective of exercising as much personal control as possible over the development of the forces, appointed Masuhara Keikichi as the first director-general of Police Reserve Headquarters. Masuhara, governor of the small, rural and relatively remote prefecture of Kagawa, was an unknown figure nationally and had no experience of military affairs. The Prime Minister had pounced on him with the job offer while he was in Tōkyō on prefectural business.

Yet whatever the intentions of MacArthur and Yoshida the Police Reserve Force *looked* like a future army. In General Headquarters and in the Japanese political world there were many people who were anxious to effect the final transformation as rapidly as possible.

Major-General Shepherd assured his second-in-command Colonel Frank Kowalski, that the force was the precursor to a new Japanese army.[46]

Masuhara Keikichi also recalls that Shepherd

> from the first considered the Police Reserve Force to be an army. He used the words 'police, police', but as far as adopting a military type organization was concerned he spoke without the slightest reserve.[47]

The pressures were not just from the American side. Masuhara also remembers that

My friends and various others believed that now, after the tragedy of defeat, an army should be established. In particular they believed that an army should be built up with the Soviet Union in mind ... it was a matter of life or death. There were many serious people who kindly came and gave me advice to this effect.[48]

The problem of staff appointments provoked an early clash between the two opposing tendencies. General MacArthur, supported by Yoshida, insisted on the principle of civilian supremacy. A staff of one hundred civilians at Police Reserve Headquarters was, under the Prime Minister, given complete administrative and operational control of the force. All appointments to this staff were made from among former police officers and civil servants, especially men with experience in colonial administration.[49]

However, since the conduct of operations to suppress large-scale civil disorders would require considerable military experience, this policy could not be followed in all appointments of uniformed officers. Thus, when applications for the 800 uniformed officer posts were called in September 1950, unpurged former officers of the Manchurian National Army were specifically invited to apply. These officers, it should be noted in passing, were much more likely to have developed an anti-Soviet outlook than men who fought in China proper, South-East Asia and the Pacific. Others eligible for officer postings were police superintendents, police inspectors and certain classes of civil servants.[50]

The creation of the Police Reserve Force made it imperative for Willoughby to act quickly if his schemes were to be implemented. Late in July 1950 Major-General Shepherd, at Willoughby's suggestion, introduced Hattori to Kowalski as 'the future commander of the Police Reserve'. Kowalski, understanding something of Willoughby's methods and somewhat surprised at the speed with which Hattori drew up a list of officers for four divisions, quietly consulted with MacArthur's aide-de-camp, Colonel Bunker. It quickly became evident that neither MacArthur nor the Government Section of SCAP knew anything about Hattori and his group. Not a man to be easily discouraged, Willoughby then wrote a memorandum commending Hattori's anti-Communist spirit and warning of the dangers posed by Communist infiltration of a Police Reserve Force under incompetent leadership.[51]

Around about the same time, at Willoughby's suggestion and through the agency of Major-General Shepherd, Hattori approached the newly appointed director-general of the Police Reserve and offered his services. Several conversations were subsequently held between Hattori, Masuhara and Ōhashi. Willoughby and Shepherd, for obvious reasons, insisted that there was no reason for the Prime Minister to know the substance of these talks. Masuhara, nevertheless, reported the matter to Yoshida, who flatly refused to deal with Hattori.[52] Yoshida, in turn, approached MacArthur and obtained the Supreme Commander's support. Willoughby's plans thus came to nothing. So too did Hattori's, despite the fact that, in the years that followed, his organization developed close links with Shigemitsu Mamoru (sometime Foreign Minister in the Tōjō Cabinet and later president of the Democratic Party) and with Yoshida's Liberal Party rival Hatoyama Ichirō.[53] In this way, indirectly, he exerted a certain amount of influence on the development of Japan's postwar foreign and defence policies.

The Hattori incident had shocked Yoshida profoundly. Sensing that American pressure for genuine, large-scale rearmament might soon become irresistable, despite MacArthur's support for his own position, he decided to offer the command of the Police Reserve Force to his old friend Lieutenant-General Tatsumi Eiichi, who had spent ten years as Military Attaché in London and was by no means typical of the prewar military establishment. Yet Tatsumi, although approached a number of times, declined to accept the offer, arguing that his generation should take responsibility for the war. The reconstruction of the armed forces, if it was to take place, was something for younger men.[54]

In the end, after several weeks of tortuous negotiations, MacArthur and Yoshida agreed to sponsor the candidature of Hayashi Keizō as uniformed head of the Police Reserve. Hayashi was the son of Lieutenant-General Hayashi Mizokichi. He himself had no military experience. At the time of his appointment to the Police Reserve he was serving as an official of the Imperial Household Agency. Hayashi stayed on as commander of the National Security Force, became the first chief of the Ground Self Defence Forces in 1954 and finally retired, after long service as chairman of the Joint Staff Council, in 1964.[55] His appointment as commander of the Police Reserve, vigorously opposed by Willoughby, demonstrates the attitude of MacArthur and Yoshida to the force at this time. That this was not simply a matter of Yoshida's personal hostility to Hattori (he was suspicious of all people associated with Tōjō) was shown by the lively resistance put up by both the Japanese Prime Minister and MacArthur to Dulles's demands for large-scale Japanese rearmament in January 1951, six months *after* establishment of the Police Reserve.

By the end of October 1950, after an intensive national recruitment campaign, some 75,000 men had been assembled. Advised by American officers, whose language they did not understand, commanded by Japanese who knew little of military procedures or discipline, dressed in American uniforms and armed with American weapons, they appeared, to the general public, little more than a disorderly rabble. Hayashi Keizō, subjected himself to perpetual ridicule from Willoughby and Hattori, became increasingly concerned about the public acceptability of what was obviously no more than an American puppet force. Tatsumi, also disturbed by the situation, eventually persuaded Yoshida to employ a certain number of hand-picked former military officers newly released from the restrictions of the purge.[56] In June 1950 some 300 former imperial second-lieutenants were taken into the Police Reserve. They were followed in October by 400 lieutenant-colonels. Later, Tatsumi, on the advice of Lieutenant-General Inada Masazumi, urged Yoshida to appoint a further thirty experienced officers of colonel rank as regimental commanders or section chiefs at Police Reserve Headquarters. This move was fiercely opposed by the police officials and former colonial administrators who dominated the headquarters. Eventually, in June 1952, Yoshida used his personal authority to have ten of Inada's men appointed.[57]

The character of the Police Reserve Force was thus the outcome of a series of compromises. Yet to the end it remained a gendarmerie rather than an army. Until the autumn of 1951 the only weapons issued to the reserve were rifles and light machine-guns. Early in October 1951, units were supplied with 60mm mortars and 75mm bazookas. These light weapons would have been useless if the force were intended to have a counter army role, to oppose large-scale amphibious landings on Japanese territory, or launch a Japanese attack on the Kuriles, Sakhalin, Kamchatka, the Siberian Maritime Province or Korea with American air and naval support.

The Police Reserve Force Pledge, recited by the entire organization at 6.00 a.m. every morning, referred merely to the duty of 'maintaining peace and order in our country and preserving the public welfare'. The most significant indicator of Yoshida's intentions, however, was the fact that the new force was concentrated in areas where support for the Japanese Communist Party was strongest, around the sprawling, grey and bombed-out industrial cities of the Kantō plains, the Kinki region and northern Kyūshū. Somewhat less than a quarter of the force was stationed in Hokkaidō and northern Honshū, where support for the Communists was weak, but which were relatively close to Soviet territory. Thus, of the thirty units making up the four District Forces (Kankutai) of the Police Reserve, seven were sent to Hokkaidō and one to northern Honshū. Only four were placed along the entire western coast of Honshū. In contrast, five units were located in the immediate vicinity of Tōkyō, two more within easy reach of the capital. Another seven units (as many as in the whole of Hokkaidō) were stationed around the Kinki area, near the industrial cities of Ōsaka, Kobe and Nagoya and the ancient capital of Kyōtō, well known as a centre of radical left-wing activity. Three units were stationed around the city of Hiroshima, two others within easy reach of either Hiroshima or the Kinki region. Another seven units were stationed near the mining and industrial belt of north Kyūshū. Only one unit was stationed on the remote and staunchly conservative southern coast of this island, the part of the Japanese archipelago closest to Korea.[58]

The expanded Maritime Safety Force was a similarly ambiguous organization. Much the same sort of struggles took place between American and Japanese exponents of large-scale rearmament and advocates of more cautious policies.

In 1950–1, Yoshida and Lieutenant-General Tatsumi believed that the 1948 Maritime Safety Force was adequate for Japan's current requirements. They had also been given to understand that this view was shared by the highest authorities in the United States Navy and also by SCAP. Admiral Nomura and his organization, however, had developed increasingly intimate connections with senior American naval officers, including Vice-Admiral Turner Joy and Rear-Admiral Arleigh Burke. Both Burke and Joy, impressed by the assistance rendered the United States Navy by Japanese minesweepers during the Korean War, became enthusiasts for Japanese rearmament. Some time towards the end of 1950 Joy told Nomura that the United States could make available to Japan a force of eighteen frigates returned by the Soviet Union after World War II and currently awaiting repairs in Yokosuka harbour. Thus encouraged, Nomura and his friends busied themselves drawing up a variety of comprehensive plans for large-scale naval rearmament. Private discussions between Nomura and Burke, in no way authorized by either the Japanese government or the United States, continued during the winter of 1950–1. By February 1951 the Japanese ex-naval officers and their American friends had reached agreement on a detailed rearmament plan. Admiral Sherman, United States Chief of Naval Operations, agreed to sponsor this plan if Nomura could persuade Yoshida to adopt it officially. Nomura met Yoshida on 7 February and gave him a copy of the project. The Prime Minister reacted in a generally negative fashion, stating, enigmatically, that he had already told Joy that Japan could not remain indifferent if American forces were fighting in defence of Hokkaidō or Kyūshū. Nomura, undeterred, presented his plans to a highly impressed John Foster Dulles later in the month. Admiral Burke also continued to make representations in the United States.[59] In this way, an increasingly powerful American-Japanese military lobby sought to undermine the policies of SCAP and the Japanese government.

V   The Yoshida-Dulles talks and the creation of the National Security Force

Despite the setbacks experienced by those Americans and Japanese favouring rapid, large scale rearmament, it is conceivable that internal pressures could eventually have propelled both the Police Reserve and the Maritime Safety Agency towards regular military status.

The next concrete step towards rearmament, however, came in 1952, again as a result of American pressure.

At the Yoshida-Dulles talks in January-February 1951 the Japanese Prime Minister, supported by General MacArthur, had successfully resisted Dulles' more extravagant demands for rearmament and participation in an Asian-Pacific collective security organisation. He had, in particular, put up spirited opposition to American proposals for placing the Police Reserve Force 'and all other Japanese armed forces' under 'a Supreme Commander designated by the United States Government' in the event of hostilities. He recognised that the new military forces could easily emerge as a Trojan horse within the structure of the Japanese state, opening the way for the permanent transformation of the archipelago into an American military colony. Nevertheless, Dulles' attitude had disturbed Yoshida. A totally negative stance on rearmament, he felt, could place the peace treaty negotiations in jeopardy and cast a long shadow over the future of Japanese-American relations. At last, therefore, in order to pacify the President's Special Envoy, Yoshida had produced 'a project ... for increasing both our land and sea forces and placing them under the control of an embryo Ministry of Defence'. It is the present writer's informed impression that Yoshida, at this stage, gave Dulles a private undertaking to establish a National Security Force and some kind of Joint Staff Council, under the control of a National Security Agency. Even so, he was unable to avoid a reference in the security treaty to America's 'expectation' that Japan would 'increasingly assume responsibility for its own defence'.

Rearmament was not written into the Treaty as an explicit Japanese duty. Nevertheless, MacArthur's dismissal in April 1951, a mere two months after the Dulles-Yoshida talks, probably destroyed any illusions the Prime Minister may have entertained about postponing implementation of the 'project'. He had now lost his most powerful American ally. General Ridgway, MacArthur's successor, did not share Yoshida's opposition to rapid, large scale rearmament and Japanese participation in regional security arrangements. Dulles probably did not fail to impress the significance of these changes on Yoshida when he visited Japan in April 1951, immediately after MacArthur's fall.[60]

During the course of 1951, in the wake of the Yoshida-Dulles talks, a vigorous debate on foreign and defence policies took place in Japan. Supporters of rearmament put forward various schemes for development of the Police Reserve Force. At the same time, Nomura's organisation intensified its lobbying efforts in Japan and the United States.

Shortly after the signing of the peace and security treaties in September 1951, Yoshida found himself confronted with the necessity of doing something about the promise made to Dulles in January. On 19 October General Ridgway formally offered Japan the 18 patrol frigates returned by the Soviet Union and, as an additional bonus, 50 landing craft still in the United States. Yoshida accepted.

While the Prime Minister was certainly aware that his Government was embarking on the development of a small navy it is difficult to know whether he had any firm views on the relationship between the new force and the existing Maritime Safety Force. Nomura's group and its American supporters, however, were determined, at the very least, to set up an autonomous organisation within the Maritime Safety Force, controlled and manned by ex-naval personnel and able to split off, at the appropriate time, to form a regular navy. Yamamoto Yoshio, Assistant Naval Attaché in London during Yoshida's years as Ambassador to Great Britain, only agreed to organise a committee to examine the use of the new frigates and landing craft on the understanding that a *navy*, not a coast guard, was being established. At the first, informal meeting of the American-Japanese committee to study the matter (26 October 1951) Captain Noble W. Abrahams, the chief American advisory officer, told Yamamoto that '*a new navy was being born* as an autonomous organisation, which, for political and financial reasons, had to be temporarily included under the MSA in the Transportation Ministry'.

In line with Nomura's thinking, Abrahams and Yamamoto devised an elaborate strategy to realise their objectives. This provoked an immediate clash with the existing Maritime Safety Force bureaucracy, which hoped to assume control of the new vessels itself. Not unexpectedly, victory went to the Imperial Naval officers group.[61]

Further development of the Police Reserve proved to be a simpler matter. Some time after the Dulles-Yoshida talks it was decided to expand the force from 75,000 men to 110,000. On 31 January 1952 Yoshida announced that 'with the internal situation and the state of affairs abroad in mind' the Police Reserve would be transformed into 'something along the lines of a Self Defence Force'.[62]

Early in March, after struggles between exponents of unified ground and naval forces and advocates of the traditional policy of separation, Yoshida announced plans to establish a National Security Agency (Hōan Cho). Details were drawn up by Cabinet during April in close collaboration with American officials. Like Police Reserve Headquarters the new agency was to be dominated by civilian bureaucrats. An Outer Bureau of the Prime Minister's Office, headed by a minister responsible to the Prime Minister, it was charged with 'preservation of Japan's peace and order, and, where special need arises, protection of life and property'. The military character of the National Security Agency was emphasized by the fact that its director-general and five internal bureaux (Equipment, Administration, Personnel, Security and the Secretariat) administered the affairs not of a gendarmerie but of forces commanded by the so-called First and Second Chiefs of Staff (Dai-ichi to Dai-ni Bakuryō Cho), the First Chief of Staff commanding an enlarged and transformed Police Reserve, the Second Chief of Staff leading a reorganized, re-equipped and expanded Maritime Safety Force.[63]

The forces controlled by the First and Second Chiefs of Staff were themselves, in form at least, very different to the Police Reserve and the Maritime Safety Force. From the spring of 1952, a time when the prospect of Communist revolution in Japan itself was receding, the National Security Force was equipped with both field (105mm) and heavy (155mm) artillery, medium tanks (20-ton class) and a variety of other military vehicles obtained from the United States.[64] Most of this equipment was unsuitable for suppressing purely domestic disturbances in a country such as Japan. Many units, it is true, were still concentrated around the Kantō plain, in the Kinki region and near the industrial cities of northern Kyūshū in readiness to put down internal disorder. Yet the most heavily armed and highly mechanized units were organized into a special Northern Regional Force (Hokubu Hōmen Tai) with headquarters at Sapporo in Hokkaidō. The impressive array of tanks and artillery maintained by the Northern Regional Force was not intended merely to overawe the disaffected Hokkaidō proletariat.[65] One of the functions of the National Security Force, in the eyes of its planners, was to protect Japan from a hypothetical Soviet invasion from Sakhalin and the northern islands. However, in view of the fact that Soviet forces in these areas were fairly small and could only be supplied either by means of the highly vulnerable one-track trans-Siberian railway, or across vast oceans where American naval and air supremacy was overwhelming, it must be assumed that at least some United States and Japanese officials saw other uses for the National Security Force. Geographical factors made it inevitable that a capacity to defend Hokkaidō from external attack, and to move forces from one Japanese island to another, also implied a capacity, given American naval and air support, to launch an invasion of the Kuriles, Sakhalin, Kamchatka and, perhaps, the Korean peninsula or the Siberian Maritime Province. It was, perhaps, recognition of this fact that made the Yoshida government even more determined to resist Washington's demands that all Japanese forces be placed under an American-designated supreme commander in times of crisis.

Whatever its purpose, the National Security Force was clearly an army. Equally remarkable was the transformation of the Maritime Safety Force into a navy under the name of the Maritime Patrol Force (Kaijō Keibitai). In March 1952 the 1948 Maritime Safety Law was amended to abolish limits on the total number of personnel and the tonnage of vessels. On 26 April the new Maritime Patrol Force, commanded and manned, on the whole, by former Imperial Navy personnel, was formally established within the Maritime Safety Agency of the Ministry of Transport. With the creation of the National Security Agency in August, the Maritime Safety Agency was transferred to its administration under the Second Chief of Staff.[66] A Charter Party Agreement, signed on 12

November 1952 and approved by the Diet towards the end of December, formalized the transfer of the eighteen frigates and fifty landing craft from the United States.[67]

The National Security Agency established, Yoshida considered the rearmament question closed. He had carried out his commitment to Dulles. At the same time he had avoided concessions on the issue of an American supreme commander. Japan could now concentrate on economic recovery. At some time in the future, a substantial, independent arms build-up might be necessary. That day was still a long way off. While some groups in the business community welcomed the prospect of an immediate and heavy arms build-up, there was evidence that the small-scale rearmament so far undertaken was alienating wide sections of the public from the Conservative camp. Certainly, two of the three great Tōkyō daily newspapers, the *Mainichi* and the *Yomiuri*, had from the beginning adopted a hawkish stand in favour of rearmament. Only the *Asahi* remained consistently opposed to a major arms build-up and Japanese participation in United States regional strategies. The dominant groups in the academic community, however, opposed rearmament in the same way as they had opposed the security treaty. Rearmament was seen as a threat to peace in Asia and the Pacific, the first step towards revival of Japanese militarism and restoration of the *ancien régime*. These views were shared by many outside the universities. A *Yomiuri Shimbun* public opinion poll taken in August 1950 showed 37.4 per cent of respondents supporting rearmament, 34.8 per cent opposed.[68] While later polls showed a clear majority supporting the establishment of military forces (but strongly opposed to overseas service), a substantial minority remained opposed to rearmament and hostile to unconditional expansion of the existing forces.

The October 1952 general elections, conducted two months after establishment of the National Security Agency, were fought partly on the rearmament issue.[69] The Liberal Party suffered substantial losses, reducing its representation in the House of Representatives from 285 to 240 seats. The Democratic Party, increasingly dominated by old-style nationalists such as Shigemitsu Mamoru and advocating an independent foreign policy backed by substantial rearmament, made impressive gains, increasing its representation from 64 to 85 seats. The two Socialist parties, campaigning with variations from left to right on a disarmament platform, increased their representation almost threefold, from 46 to 111 seats.[70]

Thus, when the director of the National Security Agency, Kimura Tokutarō, at a Cabinet meeting on 14 November 1952, urged a 'more positive' attitude to defence, Yoshida rebuffed him, claiming that the international situation was tending towards relaxation of tensions.[71] A week later, after a reconciliatory meeting between Yoshida and Kimura, the Chief Cabinet Secretary Ogata Taketora told the press that the time was not ripe for rearmament. 'Emphasis should be placed on improving the lives of the masses, giving them a nation worthy to defend.' Ogata referred approvingly to Yoshida's opposition to rearmament on political, diplomatic and economic grounds. He stressed there were no differences on this question between Kimura and the Prime Minister.[72] Three days later it was reported that Japan had turned down American requests for further increases in the National Security Force.[73]

VI   The establishment of the Defence Agency and the Self Defence Forces, March 1954

Throughout the spring and summer of 1953 Yoshida continued to oppose further expansion of Japan's military forces. Yet in March 1954 his government submitted the Defence Agency Establishment Bill to the Diet, thus initiating the most sweeping changes in Japan's defence policy since the creation of the Police Reserve Force in 1950. When the two Bills became law in May 1954 Japan was provided with a *de facto* Ministry of Defence, National Defence Council, army, navy, air force and Joint Staff Council.

Once again, direct pressure from the United States played a decisive role in forcing the Japanese government to implement these changes. The 1954 defence laws were closely linked with the 1953 decision to accept Mutual Security Assistance (MSA) military aid from the United States. This decision had been made reluctantly. Indeed, it had not been made until it was clear that Washington was insisting that Japan avail itself of the benefits of the scheme.

The following is Yoshida's own explanation of the background to the 1954 laws:

> In order to benefit from the provisions of MSA Japan had to undertake to fulfil the obligations set forth in the [MSA] law. And this had been primarily designed to apply to countries possessing an army and a navy, to which Japan alone happened to be an exception. Something needed to be done in order to bring Japan into line with the law's requirements ... and ... it was decided to include among the duties of the new Security Forces [i.e. the National Security Force and the Maritime Patrol Force] that of repelling foreign invasion, and to frame a new law for that purpose.[74]

What Yoshida does not reveal is that the Japanese government, when applying for an MSA grant in 1953, was apparently unaware that 'something needed to be done to bring Japan into line with the law's requirements'. As far as one can judge from the published record, the Americans only explained this during the first round of MSA negotiations in July 1953, when it was too late for the Japanese to retreat. Japan was, of course, aware of the provisions of the MSA Act. However, until the first round of negotiations the Japanese appear to have believed that the Americans would be willing to modify the Act to suit Japan's special needs. Thus on 24 April 1953, after Ikeda Hayato's first visit to Washington to discuss MSA aid, Kamimura Shinichi declared on his return from a diplomatic posting in the United States that

> As regards the MSA plan, which is linked to the question of Japanese rearmament, the United States is going ahead with plans to amend the law so that the scheme can also be applied to Japan.[75]

This impression subsequently took firm root. Later government statements gave no indications of plans to alter the status of the National Security Agency. On 28 May 1953 a high-ranking Foreign Ministry official told the House of Representatives Foreign Affairs Committee that he believed Japan, like Iran and Yugoslavia, would be able to accept aid without incurring additional military responsibilities. The Foreign Ministry spokesman emphasized the economic and technical rather than military aspects of the MSA scheme.[76] Nor did the American Embassy's reply to Yoshida's later enquiries about MSA aid suggest that acceptance would necessitate legal changes. On the contrary the embassy assured the Japanese that they could fulfil their duties under Article 51 Clause 1 Part A3 of the MSA Act merely by 'carrying out [their] obligations under the security treaty'.[77]

Although the communiqué issued after the Japanese-American MSA talks on 15 July gave no indication that a new legal framework for the National Security Force had been discussed,[78] it was only *after* this meeting that the government began to speak of impending legal changes.

The policy shift after 15 July was striking. The day before Foreign Minister Okazaki had told the House of Councillors Foreign Affairs Committee that it would be 'correct' to assume Japan's duties under the MSA agreement would *not* be of military character.[79] Two days after the first round of MSA talks Okazaki told the House of Councillors that in accepting aid Japan would, in fact, incur duties different to those already undertaken in the security treaty. These new duties would necessitate establishment of defence forces able to resist both 'direct' and 'indirect' aggression.[80] The following day the director-general of the National Security Agency announced that acceptance of MSA aid would inevitably change the character of the existing forces. Because of this alterations in the National Security Force Law would become necessary.[81]

VII The Liberal-Democratic Party defence talks, Conservative party merger and the character of the 1954 defence laws, September 1953–March 1954

From the establishment of the Police Reserve onwards, the United States, asserting that the Pacific War had been caused exclusively by 'irresponsible Japanese militarism', insisted on the principle of civilian control of all new armed forces. Nevertheless, the character of the 1954 defence laws, in particular the provisions concerning the role of the forces, the functions of the National Defence Council and the Joint Staff Council, the details of the civilian control system, the principle of voluntary service and the ban on duties overseas, took shape during talks in 1953–4 between the Liberal Party and the Democratic Party. As far as can be established at the present time, these talks were *not* the outcome of American pressure but of unconnected events in the Japanese political world. In particular, they were a response to three trends that dominated political life during the first part of the 1950s – the continued growth of popular support for the Socialist parties, the corresponding decline in Conservative electoral strength and the increasing factional fragmentation of the Conservative camp. As a result, pressure for Conservative unity mounted, not only within the two parties themselves but also among their sponsors in the business and financial world.* The MSA negotiations and the imminent necessity of framing new defence laws made agreement on defence policy a convenient starting-point on the long and difficult road to Conservative merger, which

---

* It is only reasonable to assume that the United States also took considerable interest in the question of Conservative party unity.

was finally achieved in November 1955 with the formation of the Liberal Democratic Party.

The Liberal Party's heavy losses and the astonishing Socialist gains in the October 1952 general elections have already been noted. The April 1953 House of Representatives elections saw further increases in Socialist strength (from 116 to 138 seats, the left-wing Socialists increasing their representation from 56 to 72 seats, the right-wing Socialists from 60 to 66, the small Worker Farmer Party gaining 5 seats and the Communists 1), and a continued decline in support for the Conservatives (Yoshida's Liberals lost 23 seats, the Democrats lost 12, although Hatoyama Ichirō's breakaway Liberal group (see below) increased its strength from 22 to 35 seats).[82]

Equally significant was the emergence of disruptive factionalism in the Conservative camp. The Democratic Party had been, from the beginning, highly factionalized. The situation was further complicated by the return *en masse* of prewar politicians after their release from the purge in 1952. The reappearance of the Old Guard, with their robust nationalist convictions, strong personalities and extensive connections, had its most divisive effect in the Liberal Party, where Yoshida's dominant position was rapidly eroded.

During the April 1953 elections a major crisis was precipitated when the depurged founder of the Liberal Party, Hatoyama Ichirō, unable to co-operate further with Yoshida, left the party with a group of thirty-five followers. As a result Yoshida found himself at the head of an isolated, minority government.

Throughout the summer of 1953, moves to stem the Socialist advance and promote political stability through Conservative merger gathered momentum. The fact that the two Socialist parties were also engaged in merger negotiations added a note of urgency. Secret talks between representatives of the Liberal and Democratic parties took place in August, apparently through the offices of business leaders such as Katō Takeo, former president of the Mitsubishi Bank.[83] On 27 September Yoshida met the Democratic Party leader Shigemitsu Mamoru and discussed the defence problem as a step towards Conservative collaboration.[84] Formal defence talks between the Liberals, the Democrats and Hatoyama's group began on 3 December, continuing over nineteen sessions until 8 March 1954, just before the Defence Agency Establishment Bill and the Self Defence Forces Bill were submitted to the Diet.[85] The basic principles and individual provisions of both bills were hammered out in the course of these discussions.

Under Ashida Hitoshi's influence the Democratic Party had, for a time, emerged as the most enthusiastic exponent of large-scale rearmament within the context of the American global anti-Communist alliance system. The appointment of Shigemitsu Mamoru as party president after his release from the purge in 1952 put the party on a rather different course. Like most of his generation, and like Yoshida, Shigemitsu believed that Japan's future lay in the development of a special relationship with China. Unlike Yoshida (but like Itō Hirobumi) Shigemitsu appears to have considered that Japan's interests on the Asian continent required, above all else, amicable relations with Russia. He had never believed that Japan's destiny lay in exclusive association with the Anglo-American powers. In the prewar period, and even during the war, he had shown considerable interest in the development of relations with the Soviet Union. He was to retain this interest throughout the postwar years. Yet like de Gaulle, he believed that independent diplomacy and *rapprochement* with the Socialist powers could not take place without a substantial arms build-up. (It was for this reason that he was sceptical of Hatoyama's attempts to reach agreement with the Soviet Union in the mid-1950s.) Shigemitsu's convictions had probably been reinforced by his association with Hattori Takushirō. If the views of a few near-pacifists like Matsumura Kenzō[86] are excluded, defence was thus a very important issue for the Democrats. Yet it was an issue on which the party remained, for some time, divided. One group, centring around Shigemitsu, saw rearmament as a means of asserting a degree of independence from Washington and normalizing relations with the Socialist powers. Another group, centring around Ashida, saw a heavily armed Japan as the pivot of the American anti-Communist alliance system in Asia. These two views, one inclining towards Gaullism, the other stressing solidarity with the United States, embodied very different concepts of the character and role of Japan's armed forces.

The party leadership could be well pleased with its electoral performance since 1952. With the passage of time, the decline of Ashida's influence, the increasing strength of the old-style nationalist factions, an awareness of the essentially pacifist nature of Japanese public opinion and the prospect of merger with Yoshida's Liberals, all combined to modify the Democrats' defence platform. By the time of the Yoshida-Shigemitsu talks in September 1953 the Democrats had abandoned their earlier demands for an immediate, large-scale military build-up, with *de facto* conscription, establishment of a Home Guard and provisions for overseas service. They had emerged, instead, as the champions of balanced, autonomous forces (i.e. not completely integrated into the American Far Eastern military alliance system), the voluntary service principle and a total ban on operations overseas. They had also come to believe, like Yoshida, that rearmament should not take priority over economic reconstruction.[87]

Although events had thus brought the two parties closer, differences still remained. The most important of these concerned the role of the forces to be created by the new laws, the status of the controlling agency and the character of defence policy decision-making machinery. The latter centred around the fundamental issues of civilian control and Cabinet responsibility. During the Liberal-Democratic Party defence talks, Yoshida made substantial concessions on the first point but eventually managed to impose his own views on the second and third.[88]

While the National Security Force and the Maritime Patrol Force constituted, in effect, an army and navy physically capable of engaging in hostilities with foreign powers, Yoshida opposed all but minimal legal recognition of this fact. Despite his gradually expanding interpretation of Article 9, the Prime Minister still maintained that possession of 'war potential' was unconstitutional. In his view, to placate the Americans and make Japan eligible for MSA aid it was merely necessary to amend the existing National Security Force Law, adding provisions for an Air Self Defence Force and changing the names of the Security Force and Maritime Patrol Force into the Ground and Maritime Self Defence Forces. The amended law could indicate that these forces were to oppose both foreign attack and domestic disorder. There was no need to elevate the National Security Agency to the status of a full Ministry. Nor was there need for such institutions as a National Defence Council or a Joint Staff Council.

The Democratic Party, in contrast, held that Article 9, as amended by the Government Section of SCAP and Ashida Hitoshi, was compatible with the maintenance of regular military forces. Two entirely new laws, one creating a National Defence Force and the other a Ministry of Defence, both clarifying that the principal objective of these new institutions was resistance to foreign attack, were thus preferable to piecemeal amendments of existing legislation.

The Democrats also proposed radical changes in the existing defence decision-making machinery. A powerful Joint Staff Council was to be established and a National Defence Council was to be set up separately from the Cabinet and Ministry of Defence. The Joint Staff Council, made up of the three Chiefs of Staff, was to be charged with coordinating the strategies of the three services and was also to be invested with certain rights of command. The National Defence Council, comprising the Chiefs of Staff, leading members of the Defence Ministry, the Cabinet and certain private individuals 'of learning and experience' (here Shigemitsu was doubtless thinking of his friend Hattori Takushirō) appointed by the Prime Minister, all sitting with equal status, was to be given extensive, direct influence on defence planning, defence industries and the vital question of mobilisation in time of crisis.

These proposals were resisted by the Liberals on the grounds that a strong Joint Staff Council would undermine the principle of civilian control and constitute a dangerous step towards restoration of the prewar system. It was also feared that inclusion of private individuals of 'learning and experience' in the National Defence Council would enable a variety of undesirable pressure groups (here Yoshida, too, was doubtless thinking of Shigemitsu's friend Hattori Takushirō) to exert direct influence on defence and foreign policy outside the normal democratic process.

Towards the end of December 1953 the shape of the final compromise began to emerge. The Liberals accepted the Democrats' scheme for two new laws instead of partial amendments to the existing legislation. In return the Democrats abandoned their insistence on creation of a full Defence Ministry. Both parties agreed that the new Self Defence Forces should be equipped and trained to counter 'direct' and 'indirect' aggression. There was to be no indication of where their principal duties lay. The Liberals were prepared to set up a Joint Staff Council provided its functions were confined to 'assisting' the Defence Agency director-general in the drawing up of defence plans and related matters. These concepts were all incorporated into the final laws.

The Liberals also showed willingness to establish a National Defence Council, provided the Chiefs of Staff sat in a subordinate, advisory capacity and that there was no participation by private individuals 'of learning and experience'. On this point immediate agreement with the Democrats proved impossible. While the 1954 laws provided for a National Defence Council there was no mention of its role or structure. Negotiations continued until 1956, long after Yoshida's fall and the merger of the Liberal and Democratic Parties. The Law Concerning the Structure of the National Defence Council promulgated by the Hatoyama government in July 1956 represented, ironically, a triumph for the Yoshida view. The National Defence Council established by this law was chaired by the Prime Minister and comprised the Foreign Minister, the

Minister of Finance, the Defence Agency director-general, the director of the Economic Planning Agency and several other members of Cabinet. The Prime Minister was obliged to consult it on all matters relating to national defence. However, since the council differed little, structurally, from the Cabinet itself, its existence could hardly be claimed to undermine the principle of cabinet responsibility or facilitate the penetration of outside undemocratic influences. 'At times when the necessity was recognized' the council could 'hear' the opinions of the chairman of the Joint Staff Council. Yet he was to sit in a subordinate capacity and have no part in decision-making. The idea of having civilians 'of learning and experience' as permanent, full members of the council had been abandoned. The principle of civilian control was thus firmly established. How it was applied in practice will be discussed in a later chapter.

CHAPTER IV

Japan and the United States Pacific alliance system, 1952–1958

It's a great game of chess that's being played all over the world.

Lewis Carroll, *Through the Looking Glass*

I Japan's place in American post-occupation global strategy

On 17 May 1951, four months before the signing of the San Francisco Peace Treaty, the United States National Security Council approved a memorandum on post-occupation policy towards Japan. This document, embodying the consensus that had gradually emerged since 1947, recommended continued efforts to realize Japan's total integration, political, economic, military and psychological, into the American global anti-Communist alliance system. Particular emphasis was placed on the development of Japan's relations with non-Communist Asia and on its future regional military role. Specifically, the National Security Council recommended that the United States should continue to promote Japanese economic recovery and

1) assist Japan in the development of appropriate military forces

2) assist Japan in the development of low-cost military material in volume for use in Japan and in other non-Communist countries of Asia

3) take all practical steps to assure Japanese membership in the United Nations and participation in a regional security arrangement

4) establish appropriate psychological programmes designated to further orient the Japanese towards the free world and away from Communism.[1]

American policies could not succeed unless Washington was in a position decisively to influence the political evolution of all the newly independent countries of non-Communist Asia, persuading them, too, actively to participate in its global strategy. Three areas, in particular, were regarded as being of critical importance. The Korean War had made it inevitable that Washington would regard preservation of an anti-Communist government in Seoul as essential to its regional position. In South-East Asia, American interest focused on Indonesia, Malaya and the three states of Indochina. These countries were viewed by geostrategic planners as formidable barriers against further Communist expansion in the region, as convenient springboards for a possible future offensive against China[2] and as sources of raw materials indispensable for Japanese economic growth. In accordance with these perceptions Washington had, from a relatively early date, adopted a sympathetic attitude towards the Indonesian Republic. It had also moved rapidly to establish close relations with Bao Dai's Vietnam, extending substantial economic aid to this French client state and laying the basis for a growing military involvement throughout Indochina. The indivisibility of America's North-East Asian and South-East Asian strategies was explained by the National Security Council early in 1952 in the following terms:

> The loss of any of the countries of South-East Asia to communist aggression would have critical psychological, political and economic consequences. In the absence of effective and timely counteraction, the loss of any single country would probably lead to relatively swift submission to or an alignment with communism by the remaining countries of this group ... South-East Asia, especially Malaya and Indonesia, is the principal world source of natural rubber and tin, and a producer of petroleum and other strategically important commodities ... The loss of South-East Asia, especially Malaya and Indonesia, could result in such economic and political pressures in Japan as to make it extremely difficult to prevent Japan's eventual accommodation to communism.[3]

Or as President Eisenhower was to tell a press conference a month before the French collapse at Dien Bien Phu:

> In its economic aspects, the loss of Indochina would take away that region that Japan must have as a trading area, or it would force Japan to turn towards China and Manchuria, or towards the Communist areas in order to live. The possible consequences of the loss of Japan to the free world are just incalculable.[4]

At the same time, George Kennan's belief that the United States could control Japan through its influence over the nation's oil supply had considerable impact on Washington's thinking about the Middle East.

II Japanese foreign policy in the 1950s – the partial accommodation with American strategic objectives

In the years immediately after the occupation the Yoshida, Hatoyama and Ishibashi Cabinets continued to steer a careful course between the policy of total integration with American global strategy advocated by Washington and the more autonomous line recommended by traditional Japanese nationalists, pan-Asianists and the radical left.

The intensity of the Cold War, the apparent solidity of the Sino-Soviet alliance, the vigilance of the United States and the fragility of Japan's own domestic political base combined to make unilateral *rapprochement* with the Communist bloc impossible. Nevertheless, in October 1956, despite Yoshida's reservations, the Hatoyama Cabinet normalized diplomatic relations with the Soviet Union, paving the way for Japan's entry into the United Nations and facilitating a limited expansion of bilateral trade. A compromise settlement of the northern territories issue was prevented both by pressure from extreme nationalist elements and by Dulles' declaration that the United States would be entitled, under the terms of the San Francisco treaty, to remain in permanent occupation of Okinawa if Japan recognized Soviet sovereignty over any of the southern Kuriles.[5] The United States thus ensured that it would continue to exercise a decisive influence on the development of Japan-Soviet relations. Hatoyama and his successor Ishibashi Tanzan also made desultory attempts to improve ties with the People's Republic of China.

The immediate political and economic returns from these ventures were limited. Close alignment with Washington and participation in the expanding network of organizations that had begun to link the countries of the non-Communist world, in contrast, produced immediate and tangible benefits. It was largely as a result of American assistance that Japan became, after India, the second largest borrower from the World Bank. It was the American procurement programme in Japan during the Korean War that first put the Japanese economy back on its feet, increasing the nation's foreign exchange holdings by more than 450 per cent in the space of three years and bringing the GNP back to prewar levels. The Japanese were also able to take advantage of United States Import and Export Bank short- and medium-term credits and the concessionary terms of America's surplus disposals programme to pay for their increasingly large imports of food and raw materials. Washington sponsored Japanese membership of the GATT and the OECD. American investment, too, flowed into Japan, although it never became a major factor in the nation's economic recovery. The strategic heights of the Japanese economy remained firmly under Japanese control. Japan also obtained access to the latest American advances in science and technology. Japanese students flocked to American universities, learning new skills and initiating a process that was significantly to alter the nation's cultural orientation. Most important of all, the United States government, despite resistance from established industrial interests and wide sections of public opinion, continued to open its domestic markets to Japanese goods. It also encouraged its allies in Europe, South-East Asia, Australasia and Oceania to do likewise. By the end of the decade the United States had consolidated its position as Japan's most important trading partner, purchasing over 27 per cent of the nation's exports and supplying some 35 per cent of its imports. A further 32 per cent of Japan's exports were being shipped to the non-Communist countries of Asia and the Pacific. Non-Communist Asia was the source of more than 20 per cent of Japan's imports. Trade with the entire Socialist bloc, in contrast, accounted for less than 2 per cent of Japan's exports and 3 per cent of its imports.[6]

While Japan's Conservative leaders were prepared to accept a high degree of economic integration into the new American-centred world order they remained determined to eschew any course of action that might lead to direct military participation in Washington's regional strategies. In particular, they were anxious to avoid too intimate an association with America's protégé the Republic of Korea, to ensure that Japan's involvement in South-East Asia remained essentially economic in character and to give Washington no grounds for supposing that resistance to participation in a NATO-style regional collective defence system had abated.

(i)   *Japanese relations with the Republic of Korea*

From its inception the Republic of Korea developed, in virtually every respect, as an American client state, dependent on Washington for its military security, political stability and economic survival. With the outbreak of the Korean War its armed forces, acting under *de facto* American command, trained by American officers and equipped with American weapons, were almost totally integrated into the United States Far Eastern strategic system.

For the United States, the cost of containment in Korea had been staggering. Even before the war high-ranking American officials had made little secret of their desire to encourage renewed Japanese political, economic and military involvement in the area. In October 1949 George Kennan had told Dean Rusk that the United States should have 'no objection' to Japanese preponderance in Korea. Japanese control, Kennan suggested, 'was to be preferred to Korean mis-management, Chinese interference, or Russian bureaucracy'.[7] It was assumed, of course, that the United States would continue to exercise a decisive influence over Japan's behaviour. According to Mun Hak Bong, the late President Rhee Syngh Manh's private secretary and political adviser, the United States drew up plans early in 1950 to have a reconstructed Japanese army dispatched to the peninsula in the event of possible hostilities, encourage Japanese nationals to join the South Korean forces, have the South Korean officer corps trained in Japan and a South Korean armaments industry developed on Japanese territory, under Japanese management.[8]

These projects, conceived in total disregard of historical circumstances and geopolitical realities, came to nothing. Nevertheless, during the Korean War, the Japanese Maritime Safety Force, under the orders of SCAP, had seen active service in Korean waters. The United States Army had also recruited former Japanese colonial officials and ex-servicemen familiar with conditions on the peninsula as special advisers. The Japanese intelligence agencies secretly established by Lieutenant-General Willoughby had devoted considerable attention to gathering information about Korea. Japanese industry, too, had played a vital role in supplying munitions and equipment to the United Nations forces. President Truman's opening address at the San Francisco Peace Conference specifically referred to his hope that Japan's future armed forces would work in close association with the forces of other non-Communist nations in the region.[9] The Yoshida-Acheson Exchange of Notes after the signing of the 1951 security treaty committed Japan to 'permit and facilitate' continued United Nations military action in the Korean peninsula.

Prime Minister Yoshida, it will be recalled, had strenuously resisted American attempts to involve Japan in regional military organizations. While eager to exploit the economic opportunities provided by the Korean War, he was especially hostile to any suggestion of a Japanese military role in the peninsula. His attitude was founded neither on narrow, parochial self-interest nor on strategic myopia. Certainly, Yoshida displayed a lively prejudice against all Koreans, considering them 'ungrateful' for the 'benefits' bestowed upon them during thirty-five years of Japanese colonial rule. Yet his attitude towards the Korean issue was almost certainly connected with his long-term view of the development of Sino-Japanese relations. It can be assumed that he did not want Japan's future relationship with China, so central to his plans for the nation's recovery as an independent great power, to be disturbed, as it had invariably been in the past, by conflicts over spheres of influence in Korea. In any case, reflection on the history of the prewar era had led him to regard the peninsula not as 'a dagger pointed at the heart of Japan' but as a one-way street to disastrous continental entanglements. Colonel Frank Kowalski, deputy chief of the American military advisory mission to the Police Reserve Force, told John Dower of a conversation with an unidentified Japanese official during the Korean War:

> 'I can't understand', I began, 'why the Prime Minister refuses to increase the defence forces of your country when we are willing to assume the costly burden of supplying weapons and equipment. Surely this is all to the advantage of Japan. All you're asked to furnish is manpower and you have a lot of that.'
> 'Ah, so', responded my friend, 'we will strengthen our forces, but not until 1955.'
> 'Why 1955?' I asked.
> 'By then the Korean War will be over.'
> 'But why must you wait until the war is ended?' I persisted.
> 'Because Mr Yoshida does not want Japan to become involved in the Korean War. If we organize 300,000 troops as your Mr Dulles wants us, your government will insist that we send some of these troops to Korea. That is why the Prime Minister agreed to expand our forces only to 110,000.
> 'Mr Yoshida shudders every time he recalls how the Japanese army was bogged down in China. In that the people share his fears. Should Japan have 300,000 ground troops, a strong argument would be made that we don't need that many to defend Japan from attack and the United Nations, under your influence, would ask us to co-operate by sending at least 100,000 to Korea. Once those troops are dispatched, there is no telling when they will be withdrawn.'[10]

Throughout the 1950s, South Korean President Rhee Syngh Manh's intense anti-Japanese sentiment* also frustrated Washington's attempts to promote a wider measure of politico-strategic co-operation between its two North-East Asian allies. The atmosphere of Japanese-South Korean relations during this period was well illustrated at the secret meeting between Prime Minister Yoshida Shigeru and Rhee Syngh Manh organized by General Mark W. Clark, commander of United Nations Forces in Korea, on 5 January 1953. When Clark, who had arranged the meeting without Yoshida's knowledge or permission, left the two leaders to talk in his Tōkyō headquarters, hoping, no doubt, that they would quickly perceive their common strategic interests, both sat bolt upright in their chairs, silent and sullen. Neither wished to be the first to initiate a conversation. Finally, Yoshida, remembering that Rhee Syngh Manh was, in some sense, a guest in Japan, asked, 'Are there

* Rhee Syngh Manh, like his northern rival Kim Il Sung, had played a leading role in the long and bloody anti-Japanese independence struggle.

any tigers in Korea?' 'No', Rhee retorted, 'the Japanese took them all.' With that the conversation stopped. Press speculation that Yoshida and Rhee had discussed bilateral military co-operation was entirely baseless.[11]

Yoshida's disinclination to develop ties with South Korea was shared by most of his successors. The United States insisted that the two countries move towards a strategic *rapprochement* and made every effort to promote negotiations. Yet when the fourth round of Japanese-South Korean talks drew to a close on 15 April 1960 the two sides remained as far apart as they had been at the end of the occupation. The Japanese refused to accept Seoul's claim to be the only lawful government in the peninsula. They also declined to regard all Korean residents in Japan as South Korean citizens, arguing (correctly) that the Koreans in Japan were divided in their allegiance. In 1959, Japan went so far as to conclude an agreement with Pyongyang permitting Koreans of both northern and southern origin to be repatriated to the Democratic People's Republic under the supervision of the International Red Cross. The deeply ingrained anti-Korean sentiments of the Japanese Conservative leadership reinforced its view of the national strategic interest, further alienating opinion in Seoul. The Japanese, while eventually abandoning their own claims to compensation for property damage sustained at the end of World War II, refused to admit that any Korean government had a right to compensation for losses incurred during the period of colonial rule. As Kubota Kitarō, the Japanese plenipotentiary at the third round of negotiations (6–21 October 1953), disarmingly explained to his South Korean counterpart, Japan's imperial rule 'had been of great benefit to the Korean people',[12] and the question of reparations therefore did not arise. The Japanese refused to recognize the 50 nautical-mile exclusive fishing zone claimed by Seoul. The two sides also remained at loggerheads over the possession of Takeshima (Dokto), a tiny, barren and totally useless group of islets in the Sea of Japan. Opponents of Japanese participation in American global strategy could at least console themselves with the thought that prejudice, ignorance and folly occasionally conspire to promote the common good.

(ii)   Japanese relations with South-East Asia

American hopes that Japan, in return for the restoration of an economic sphere of influence in South-East Asia, might eventually come to share the politico-military burdens of containment in that part of the world, also proved to be without foundation. Japanese political and business leaders had no objection to developing economic links with non-Communist Asia. They were fully conscious of the rich natural and human resources of the region. They were aware that the countries of the south could become a valuable market for Japanese manufactured goods. They were as concerned as their American counterparts about the growth of Communist influence in the region. While having no intention of participating in military containment themselves, Japan's leaders were generally sympathetic to American efforts to strengthen local non-Communist governments. If Washington's policies led to increased American procurement of goods and services in Japan, so much the better.

The American conviction that the newly independent states of non-Communist South-East Asia would inevitably view the world in terms of the Truman Doctrine, accept United States leadership and adjust their foreign policies to the requirements of containment also proved erroneous. Japanese leaders, whose own background gave them some insight into the forces at work in South-East Asia, could not fail to observe that, despite Washington's attempts to set up a broadly based regional anti-Communist alliance, several of the most important local powers, notably India, Indonesia and Burma, had, from the beginning, enthusiastically embraced neutralist policies. They could not overlook the epochal significance of the battle of Dien Bien Phu. They could not help noticing that when the South-East Asia Treaty Organization (SEATO) was eventually formed, in September 1954, the only non-Anglo-Saxon regional powers to participate, apart from the three 'protocol states' of Indochina, were Pakistan, the Philippines and Thailand. Nor could they overlook the fact that, with the consolidation of President Sukarno's leadership in the mid-1950's, Indonesia, a country of crucial importance to America's regional strategies, began to incline rather more decisively towards non-alignment. In the wake of the Bandung Conference (April 1955), held just eleven months after Dien Bien Phu, interest in neutralism among the countries of South and South-East Asia mounted. In April 1956, with the demise of the conservative Siri Kotha (United National Party) government, Sri Lanka declared its neutrality in the Cold War. Great Britain was obliged to withdraw its naval base at Trincomalee and its air base at Katunayake. In September 1956 Prince Souvanna Phouma proclaimed his desire to make Laos (one of SEATO's 'protocol states' and the recipient of an annual $US50 million in American aid) into 'the Switzerland of the Far East'. At the same time, following Prince Norodom Sihanouk's victory in the Cambodian general election, that country, too, moved rapidly towards non-alignment. In September 1956 Pakistan, one of the three Asian members of SEATO, also began to emerge as a *de facto* neutral. Then in October 1956 Nepal signed a commercial treaty with China and agreed to an exchange of ambassadors.

These developments in no way affected Japanese perceptions of the overall American-Soviet strategic balance. The United States clearly remained the world's mightiest power. Nevertheless, it was apparent that Washington was in no position to arrange affairs in South-East Asia according to its own liking. This fact reinforced the arguments of those who contended that Japan's long-term interests did not lie in too close an identification with America's regional policies, that a politico-strategic role in Asia, in particular, would be highly dangerous and destabilizing. Obviously, however, there was much to be gained by encouraging a greater degree of economic involvement with the countries of South and South-East Asia. A large-scale Japanese aid programme, promoting economic growth and regional trade, would undoubtedly win approval in Washington. It might, conceivably, raise local living standards, help stabilize non-Communist governments, check the growth of political radicalism and prevent any undesirable drift towards Moscow or Peking. Carefully negotiated it might even be made to hasten Japan's own economic recovery. It might also lay the groundwork for the development of autonomous relations with a more independent South-East Asia at some time in the future. In this way it could help facilitate Japan's re-emergence as an independent great power, provide the basis for a more equal relationship with the United States, inside or outside the San Francisco system, and pave the way for an eventual *rapprochement* with China.

The issue of war reparations, left pending after the San Francisco Peace Conference, provided a convenient springboard for launching Japan's regional strategy. In November 1954, two months after the formation of SEATO, the Yoshida cabinet concluded an agreement with Burma (which, together with India, had boycotted the gathering at San Francisco) on peace terms, economic co-operation and war reparations. Over the next twenty years, in accordance with a series of bilateral agreements, the Japanese government paid out more than $US1,012 million from the public purse in 'reparations' and $US490 million in unrestricted economic aid to Burma, Indonesia, the Philippines, South Vietnam, Laos, Cambodia, Malaysia, Singapore, South Korea and Micronesia. The question of reparations agreements with the Democratic Republic of Vietnam and the Democratic People's Republic of Korea touched off a vigorous internal debate. In the end, partly out of deference to the United States, no negotiations were conducted with these countries.*

The Japanese reparations programme, negotiated by the government in close association with the business community, made a small but significant contribution to the postwar economic development of non-Communist Asia. It also provided considerable stimulus to the Japanese steel, shipbuilding, automobile, electrical goods and construction industries. In Burma, Japanese firms engaged in the construction of the Balu Chaung power station, in railway restoration work, in setting up assembly plants for automobiles and in the supply of electrical equipment, pumps, trucks, rails, railway rolling stock and ships. In the Philippines, Japanese firms built rolled steel, cement and paper production plants and an ammunition factory, and supplied general machinery, automobiles, ships and the fuselages of military training aircraft. In Indonesia, by far the largest beneficiary of the reparations programme, Japanese industry played a dominant role in comprehensive development plans for the Berantas river area in East Java and the Riam Kanam region in South Borneo. Paper, textile and plywood plants were constructed. Japanese firms also supplied agricultural equipment, motor vehicles and ships and engaged in an extensive programme of hotel construction. In South Vietnam, some 70 per cent of Japan's reparations payments were channelled into the construction of the Da Nhim power station south of Da Lat. Indirect military aid to the American-backed government was also provided. In Laos and Cambodia Japanese aid was directed principally towards the construction of water supply systems for the capital cities, towards road and bridge building and towards a variety of pastoral, agricultural and medical projects. In Thailand, Malaya and Singapore, Japan provided materials for railway construction, textile factories, shipyards and cargo vessels. In South Korea (with which an agreement was

---

*   The United States itself, along with the Soviet Union, India, the Kuomintang on Taiwan, Australia, New Zealand and, later, the government of the People's Republic of China, unilaterally waived the right to claim reparations.

not concluded until the mid-1960s), most of Japan's reparations payments were channelled into the construction of the Pohang steel complex, into the establishment of textile factories and into various projects for the revitalization of agriculture and fisheries.[13]

During the 1950s, Japanese economic involvement in South-East Asia outside the reparations framework also grew steadily. Japanese interest in iron ore deposits in India, Portugese Goa, Laos and the Philippines was considerable. By 1960, Japan was importing 27.8 per cent of its iron ore needs from India and Goa and another 43.2 per cent from various Asian countries.[14] In 1952 the first yen loans were advanced to India. In April 1954 Japan joined the Economic Commission for Asia and the Far East (ECAFE). In October 1954 it joined the Colombo Plan. The Japanese Import-Export Bank also set up a special South-East Asian Development Fund. Japanese investment throughout the region grew, although its total volume remained relatively small.[15] In 1957 a commercial treaty was signed with Australia, paving the way for the development of a flourishing economic relationship with that most loyal of American allies.

(iii) *Japan's shift to an oil economy and relations with the Middle East*

In the prewar period Japan's industrial economy had been sustained largely by domestic supplies of coal and hydro-electricity. Its immediate postwar recovery, too, had been based on these energy sources. By the end of 1950, however, domestic coal production had reached its limits. The possibilities for new hydro-electric power developments were few. With the encouragement of the United States the Japanese government thus began to convert to an oil-based economy. Acute shortage of foreign exchange forced Japan to import crude oil rather than the more expensive oil products. This strategy, in turn, necessitated modernization of the country's existing oil refineries, all of them small, backward and inefficient. Japan, lacking both the capital and the technology required for this task, had no alternative but to consent to the establishment of joint ventures between American multinationals and local oil companies. Under these arrangements the multinationals secured the right to supply, in perpetuity, all the oil that would ever be required by the Japanese refinieries.[16]

These agreements were negotiated against the background of America's increasingly powerful position in the Middle East. Washington's influence in Saudi Arabia had been, for sometime, considerable. Its influence around the Persian Gulf was growing. On 19 August 1953 an American-sponsored *coup d'état* in Iran overthrew the Mossadegh government, restoring the Shah and the multinational oil companies after a brief period of nationalist ferment. United States refusal to support Great Britain and France in the 1956 Suez War increased Washington's prestige throughout the Arab world. On 5 January 1957 Congress gave President Eisenhower authority to use armed force in the Middle East 'to secure and protect the territorial integrity and political independence of such nations requesting aid against overt armed aggression from any nation controlled by International Communism'. American troops landed in Lebanon on 15 July 1958. By the end of the decade it doubtless seemed to many Japanese that the United States, whatever setbacks it had experienced in South-East Asia, was destined to emerge as the heir to all the European empires in the Middle East.

The impact of America's new position on the supply and price of oil throughout the non-Communist world, together with the United States dominance of the sea-lanes, locked Japan, politically and economically, into the Western alliance system far more effectively than the five clauses of the security treaty. It ensured that Japan's freedom of manoeuvre would remain limited so long as its economy was dependent on oil, the United States retained its near hegemony of the Middle East and the American navy dominated the seas.

Throughout the 1950s Japan's reliance on oil steadily increased. In 1950, 60 per cent of Japan's energy requirements had been supplied by coal, 33 per cent by hydro-electricity and 7 per cent by oil. During the 1950s oil consumption increased by an average of 15 per cent per annum. By 1958 Japan was the seventh largest oil consumer in the world.[17] By 1960 oil was of equal importance to coal in the Japanese economy, each accounting for 37.7 per cent of the nation's energy supplies.[18] Eighty per cent of this oil was imported from the Middle East, 15 per cent from South-East Asia (chiefly Indonesia) and 5 per cent from the Soviet Union.[19]

III   Japanese-American military relations, 1952–60

Japanese attempts to avoid integration into the American Far Eastern alliance system obviously required a cautious approach to the question of military co-operation with Washington. The defeat, the occupation and the circumstances surrounding the establishment of the Self Defence Forces made it inevitable that Japan's efforts to retain a high degree of military autonomy would not be as successful as those of France to escape absorption into NATO. Nor could they be as successful as China's attempts to maintain its military independence *vis-à-vis* the Soviet Union. Yet they were not entirely fruitless. While very close links were developed between the Japanese Self Defence Forces and their American counterparts, several years of careful negotiations and a strong stand on the question of overseas service placed Japan, militarily speaking, in a rather more independent position than that of some other American allies in the region. Nevertheless, it remained uncertain whether this independence could survive a major crisis.

(i)   *Japan's decision to apply for MSA aid, September 1952–June 1953*

The issue of a more intimate military relationship with the United States came to the fore towards the end of the occupation when Washington began to urge the Japanese government to take advantage of the MSA aid scheme. The Mutual Security Assistance (MSA) Act, passed by Congress in October 1951, had been designed to consolidate the American alliance system through the supply of weapons and equipment, participation of allied officers in training programmes in the United States and the overall co-ordination of military strategies.

On 12 January 1952, shortly before the establishment of the National Security Force, General Hickey, Chief of Staff at SCAP, requested Prime Minister Yoshida to attend a special briefing at Supreme Headquarters. Yoshida, suspecting the nature of the exercise, refused, sending instead his military adviser, Lieutenant-General Tatsumi Eiichi. As the Prime Minister had anticipated, American officials explained to Tatsumi that the defence of Japan required a much larger army, preferably one of at least 325,000 men [20] Yoshida dismissed this proposition as totally absurd. The National Security Force created on 31 January 1952 consisted of 110,000 men. After the establishment of the National Security Force Yoshida considered that he had fulfilled his commitments to Dulles and did not wish to pursue the matter of rearmament any further.

Washington had other ideas. The prospect of a Japanese-American Mutual Defence Assistance Agreement was first raised in September 1952, some months after the creation of the National Security Force, when Yoshida's close associate Ikeda Hayato conferred with United States Secretary for the Treasury John W Snyder and the State Department Special Adviser Joseph Dodge in Mexico City. The Americans urged expansion of the National Security Force from 110,000 to 180,000 men by the end of 1952, with the ultimate objective of creating a 325,000-man army by 1954–5. Dodge and Sneider expressed their willingness to request $US300 million from Congress in the next budget to arm and equip the enlarged Japanese force.[21]

As was to be expected, the Yoshida government reacted unenthusiastically to these overtures. On 21 November the director-general of the National Security Agency told American military officials that it would be difficult to increase the strength of Japanese forces beyond the existing level of 110,000 men.[22] The Prime Minister's policy speech at the new session of the Diet in November had little to say about rearmament.[23] Nevertheless in January 1953 the director of the Foreign Ministry's International Co-operation Bureau was sent to Washington to explore American intentions. He was reportedly told that the United States would like to see at least 150,000 Japanese under arms (presumably by the end of the year).[24] Early in March Yoshida sent Ikeda to Washington for further exploratory talks.[25] Ikeda apparently returned convinced that acceptance of MSA aid would necessitate formulation of a detailed defence plan.[26] This news was probably responsible for Yoshida's continued negative attitude towards the question.

From the summer of 1953 onwards strong pressure was exerted on Yoshida from two directions. On 5 May Dulles told a joint Senate-Representatives Foreign Relations Committee hearing in Washington of a plan to extend MSA aid to Japan.[27] The American Secretary of State later gave the Japanese to understand that the aid would enable Japan to establish ten army divisions and place 350,000 men under arms.[28] The Japanese government, taken by surprise, immediately instructed its ambassador in Washington to sound out American intentions.[29] Yet Washington's attitude was abundantly clear. The Japanese were not simply being *invited* to avail themselves of the benefits of MSA aid. Even though Yoshida's attitude to further expansion of the military forces was known to be hostile and while no formal negotiations had taken place, Japan's participation in the scheme was regarded as a foregone conclusion. Budgetary provisions were already being made and the United States had formulated plans for Japanese use of the aid to be extended.

At home, deteriorating economic conditions associated with the end of United States Korean War special procurements prompted business leaders to urge acceptance of MSA aid. On the one hand it was felt that a properly negotiated agreement could direct much aid into economic reconstruction rather than strictly military channels, raising the level of Japanese technology and improving industrial competitiveness. On the other hand it was felt that refusal of MSA aid would damage Japanese-American political and, ultimately, economic relations. It might also adversely affect Japanese trade with America's allies in South-East Asia and the Pacific.[30]

Despite these pressures, Yoshida held his ground for some time. A week after Dulles' announcement, Foreign Minister Okazaki told a meeting of foreign correspondents in Tōkyō that it would be 'premature to say anything definite about MSA aid'.[31] On 26 May Yoshida told the House of Councillors that 'we are not at present considering increasing the strength of the National Security Force, nor do we wish to do so'.[32] On 29 May, in an obvious reference to the Dulles speech, the Prime Minister told the House of Councillors Budget Committee that since there had been 'no formal communication' from the United States government on the question he could not speculate about the possibility of Japanese participation in the MSA scheme.[33]

The following day, Senator Everett Dirksen, a prominent member of the Senate Budget Committee, arrived in Japan for talks with Yoshida.[34] The Dirksen visit seems to have convinced Yoshida that the long-term cost in American goodwill of refusal to accept MSA aid might be greater than the price of a carefully negotiated acceptance. By the middle of June, Japanese government spokesmen were hinting that participation in the scheme would be 'desirable'.[35]

Enquiries at the American Embassy suggested there might be considerable flexibility in negotiating the quantity and type of aid. The Americans gave Yoshida to understand that the MSA scheme would have favourable effects on Japanese-American economic relations. They stressed they were not insisting on a degree of rearmament beyond Japan's economic and political capacity to absorb. Japan could comply with the requirements of the MSA act by maintaining internal security, fulfilling its duties under the security treaty and effectively exercising its right of individual and collective self-defence. Thus the Japanese gradually formed the impression that MSA aid would have as much economic as military significance and would not necessarily involve them in new military responsibilities.[36] After further promptings from the United States they announced their 'inclination' to accept MSA assistance,[37] although Okazaki took care to tell the Diet (16 June) that he was thinking of the 'economic' rather than the 'military' aspects of the scheme.[38] The Cabinet finally decided to apply for aid on 30 June and the first round of negotiations began a fortnight later (15 July) in the Foreign Ministry.[39]

(ii)   The first round of MSA negotiations, July–September 1953

When the negotiations opened it became apparent that American demands were more far-reaching than had been expected. The Japanese soon found themselves committed to instituting legal changes affecting the status of the National Security Force and its administrative agency. Yet the Yoshida government was extremely reluctant to make concessions on other grounds. The negotiations that began in July 1953 dragged on acrimoniously for more than eight months, until the spring of the following year. Although the final agreement committed Japan to a defence expansion programme that the Prime Minister would have preferred to avoid, it by no means represented an unconditional capitulation before American demands.

As in January–February 1951 the Americans appeared anxious to involve Japan in heavy rearmament and wider responsibilities.[40] Conflict soon arose on the question of how to express the relationship between MSA aid and Japanese economic stability. There was also disagreement on how Japan's military duties should be described. The United States hoped to see explicit reference to Section 511, Part (a) of the MSA Act incorporated into the text of the final agreement. Point four of Part (a) obliged the aid-receiving country to

> make, consistent with its political and economic stability, the full contribution permitted by its manpower, resources, facilities and general economic condition to the development and maintenance of its own defensive strength and the defensive strength of the free world.[41]

The Japanese side opposed this, on the grounds that it would be tantamount to committing their forces to overseas service. On this critically important issue the talks remained deadlocked, despite the fact that agreement was soon reached on a number of peripheral technical matters.

As time passed and the negotiations made little headway Japan's attitude began to cause much annoyance in Washington. A week after the inconclusive end of the fifth session of talks, Dulles, during a stopover in Tōkyō (8 August 1953) on his way home from South Korea, strongly urged Japan to view its membership of the Western alliance more positively. The Secretary of State compared Japan's contributions to Free World security unfavourably with those of Italy and recalled that even South Korea, economically weak and beset with internal problems, already supported seventeen army divisions and was preparing to raise another three.[42] Yoshida's response was predictably unsatisfactory and when Dulles returned to the United States he again publicly gave vent to his extreme dissatisfaction.[43]

Pressure of this kind failed to weaken Japanese resistance. Three days after the Dulles-Yoshida confrontation, with the opening of the sixth session of MSA talks (14 August 1953), the Japanese presented the Americans with a draft appendix they hoped to attach to the final agreement.[44] The appendix quoted the text of sections of the MSA law, as the Americans desired, adding the caveat that Japan 'will fulfil her obligations within the limits permitted by her Constitution'. In the context of current interpretations of the Constitution this was meant to indicate that the Japanese government would not permit its forces to serve outside Japan. At the same time a vast battery of economic demands was advanced, apparently in an attempt to broaden the MSA talks into general economic discussions. The United States was requested to procure as much MSA-aid material as possible in Japan and to assist in establishing domestic Japanese defence industries. Japan's interest in the output of raw materials in various parts of Asia was stressed and mention was made of a general technical assistance programme. So wide-ranging were the Japanese demands that at the next session of the talks (19 August 1953) the United States negotiators felt obliged to point out that the MSA programme was basically concerned with defence, not economic development. The Americans suggested that Japan's economic demands should, therefore, be omitted. The Japanese declined to retreat from their original position and no conclusion was reached.

The negotiations dragged on throughout September with no significant progress on basic issues. Yoshida's attitude continued to irritate the Americans. On 3 September Dulles delivered another blast from Washington.[45] When Foreign Minister Okazaki and the director-general of the National Security Agency Kimura Tokurarō met General Clark on 24 September their reluctance to discuss long-term defence plans was so obvious that the general repeatedly banged the table in anger.[46] Thus by the time the twelfth session of talks ended on 30 September no more than a tentative agreement on a number of technical issues had been reached, although the joint communiqué spoke of 'complete accord'.

(iii)   The Ikeda–Robertson talks, October 1953

Discussion of Japanese military responsibilities, the amount and character of aid to be received and the details of defence planning was reopened at the talks between Ikeda Hayato and the United States Under-Secretary of State Walter S. Robertson in October 1953.

Yoshida's attitude to the negotiations was revealed in the composition of the delegation he sent to Washington. The delegation did not include a single member of the National Security Agency. It contained no strategic studies experts or specialists on military affairs. Ikeda, his most senior political disciple, was a former Finance Minister. At the time of the talks, he held no Cabinet post and was theoretically in no position to speak on behalf of the government. Aichi and Miyazawa, too, although important members of the Liberal Party, were not Cabinet Ministers. The other two delegates, Suzuki and Kamimura, were both Finance Ministry officials.

The Ikeda mission left Japan on 29 September after receiving strict instructions from the Prime Minister to make as few concessions on rearmament as possible.[47] Serious talks began on 5 October with Ikeda assuring the Americans that 'there were certain special circumstances that made increased defence outlays difficult for Japan'.[48] These pleas made little impression on the Americans, who devoted the next session of talks (8 October 1953)[49] to an analysis of the world situation, then proceeded to outline their views on the future development of Japan's defence forces (12 and 15 October).[50] They spoke in terms of a Japanese army 'some three times the size of the present National Security Force'. The Chairman of the Joint Chiefs of Staff, Admiral Radford, suggested expansion of Japanese ground forces to 300,000 men over a five-year period. The Japanese adamantly refused to consider rearmament on this scale. Ikeda's modest counter-proposal of 180,000 men (only 70,000 more than the National Security Force) built up over five years caused the Americans to express 'extreme dissatisfaction' and the talks came to an uneasy deadlock.

For a time the Japanese sought to avoid discussion of military matters. They also expressed 'interest' in the fact that whereas the MSA aid earmarked for Japan appeared to be strictly military in character, assistance extended to various European countries under the Economic Co-operation Administration (ECA) scheme (the forerunner of MSA) had been partly economic. The Americans offered no more than a 'useful explanation' of this point.[51]

At his press conference of 16 October 1953, Ikeda made no attempt to conceal his differences with the United States. America and Japan were agreed, he said, that present Japanese military strength was insufficient. There had been, however, no agreement on the scale of the planned expansion. Moreover, while maintenance of strictly defensive military power could be reconciled with the Constitution, establishment of armed forces for overseas service simply could not be considered. Expansion of the existing forces could not be taken to the point where they became potentially aggressive.[52]

Ikeda's stubbornness brought the talks with Robertson to a premature end. The Americans felt nothing could be gained by further discussion. Just before the opening of the sixth session (schedule for 19 October) the United States informed the Japanese that it was preoccupied with the Korean problem and would like to conclude the talks as quickly as possible. The Japanese accordingly drew up a summary of their views and handed it to the State Department.[53] This memorandum emphasized Japan's interest in the economic aspects of MSA aid and contained no concrete reference to future military responsibilities and planning. In response the United States, on the pretext that Robertson was obliged to leave Washington 'on a trip', cancelled another meeting scheduled for 22 October.[54] The final session of talks on 30 October failed to break the deadlock and Japanese government spokesmen, in assessing the significance of the negotiations, were reduced to declaring that they had 'deepened mutual understanding'.[55]

(iv)   Japanese defence planning – the origins of the First Defence Plan, September 1952–October 1953

The principal reason for the breakdown in the Ikeda–Robertson talks was Japan's failure to produce a long-term defence plan that the United States could regard as satisfactory.

Despite the continuing efforts of Admirals Turner Joy, Burke and Nomura to establish a small Japanese navy the United States appeared, at this stage, chiefly interested in large-scale expansion of the Japanese ground forces.[56] There was little discussion of sea power at the MSA talks. No pressure was put on Japan to establish an air force. Washington's attitude had been evident since Ikeda's talks with Snyder and Dodge in the autumn of 1952, when the Americans had apparently confined discussion entirely to expansion of the National Security Force.

American interest in the creation of a powerful Japanese army was closely linked to the military, economic and political lessons of the Korean War. By the time the conflict had come to an end it was evident that American military power was not omnipotent. It was also clear that the cost of containment was having a deleterious effect on the health of the American economy. Certainly there was no immediate prospect of the United States losing its newly acquired global primacy or abandoning containment. In terms of economic strength and political influence the United States still towered above both its rivals and its allies. Nevertheless, per capita growth in the American GNP had dropped. The American public, while intensely anti-Communist, was increasingly war-weary. In the 1953 presidential elections, therefore, Eisenhower had campaigned on a platform designed to appeal, simultaneously, to the American public's desire to roll back the forces of Communism, to avoid direct involvement in future military conflicts, to reduce government expenditure and restore the health of the American economy.[57] All these things, the Republicans argued, could be accomplished by reliance on John Foster Dulles' massive retaliation strategy. Overwhelming American nuclear superiority, along with appropriate application of air and naval power, would contain Communism, consolidate the Western alliance and permit reduction of American ground forces stationed abroad to a level acceptable to the Treasury and to the public.

Yet if economic necessities and the post-Korea domestic political climate required reduction of American ground forces overseas, the Korean War itself had made American military planners acutely aware of the importance of these forces.[58] In the Far East reliance on nuclear weapons, air and sea power alone was inadequate. If American policies were to be successful it was also imperative that Soviet and Chinese ground forces, and those of their allies, be confronted by substantial 'Free World' armies. As with the later Nixon Doctrine, Dulles' new strategy meant, in practice, that the United States would provide the nuclear shield, the air and naval power. The hand-to-hand fighting was to be done, as far as possible, by its Asian allies. It was, of course, explained to Japanese reporters in Washington that the United States was *not* thinking of a potential combat role for the forces of its allies. Rather, their 'political value' in negotiations with the Communists was stressed.[59] This explanation cut little ice with Yoshida, who was well aware of American interest in involving Japanese forces in the Korean peninsula and other parts of Asia. From the Japanese point of view, Eisenhower's election promise that wars for Asian freedom would, in future, be fought by Asians, could mean only one thing.

Constitutional issues apart, Japan's conservative leaders, anti-Communist as they were, had little inclination to see the nation's emerging military forces act as America's Asian watchdogs. The intellectual climate of postwar Japan was generally hostile to the concept of rearmament. Nevertheless, creation of the Police Reserve and the National Security force had been followed by the appearance of a few writers and private organizations actively interested in defence planning.[60] In the business community activity centred around the special Defence Production Committee (Bōei Seisan Iinkai) set up by the Federation of Economic Organizations (Keidanren) in 1952. Private plans were also drawn up by various conservative politicians, academics and former imperial army and naval officers. All these unofficial defence planners concurred that domestic and foreign Communism constituted the chief threats to Japanese security They were all particularly concerned about what they saw as growing Soviet influence in the world. The majority supported the security treaty, although there were a few proponents of Swedish-style armed neutrality. It can probably be assumed that many of these people, like Prime Minister Yoshida himself, envisaged Japan's eventual re-emergence as an independent great power, outside the framework of the American alliance system. However this may be, all were agreed that Japan's military forces should *not* become mere vehicles for the implementation of American Far Eastern policy. There were stern warnings against creation of 'a deformed, ambiguous and fragmented defence organization' dependent on the United States.[61] Japanese-American military relations should be based, as far as possible, on co-operation, not dependence.

To achieve the desired degree of autonomy within the security treaty system, Japan, it was believed, needed powerful air and naval as well as ground forces. The Federation of Economic Organizations group envisaged a navy of 290,000 tons (manned by 70,000 men), an air force of some 3,750 aircraft (including 900 medium-range bombers) as well as an army of 300,000 men organized into fifteen divisions.[62] Colonel Hattori Takushirō proposed a 225,000-man army, a 387,000-ton navy and an air force of 1,800 aircraft.[63] The prominent former Communist Nabeyama Sadachika, who had wide connections in the business world and ties both with Hattori and the ultranationalist ideologue Kodama Yoshio,[64] advocated a 200,000-man army, a 180,000-ton navy and an air force of 2,500 aircraft.[65] The conservative economist Watanabe Tetsuzō (whose Watanabe Economic Research Institute was connected with Hattori and Admiral Nomura Kichisaburō) envisaged a 200,000-man army, a 300,000-ton navy and an air force of 2,000 aircraft.[66] Admiral Nomura himself proposed a navy of 387,000 tons, an air force of 1,800 aircraft and a 225,000-man army.[67] Lieutenant-General Inada Masazumi, also associated with Hattori, Nomura and Watanabe, advocated a 250,000-ton navy, an air force of 1,500 aircraft and a relatively small army of 100,000 men.[68] Colonel Tsuji Masanobu, an opponent of the security treaty, hoped for a 200,000-man regular army, a substantial navy and an air force of 1,000 fighter-bombers.[69] There were differences of opinion on whether possession of long-range air and naval strike capacity would complicate relations with Australia and South-East Asia, but the common emphasis in all these plans was on balanced, potentially autonomous land, sea and air forces.[70]

Official defence planning began in September 1952, with the establishment of a special secret committee within the National Security Agency.[71] While pressure for research into defence planning had probably existed in the National Security Agency for some time, this committee (euphemistically called the Systems Research Committee) was presumably set up after Ikeda's talks with Dodge and Sneider had convinced Yoshida that further wide-ranging American demands were imminent and could only be resisted by a well-prepared case.

The Systems Research Committee was chaired by the director-general of the National Security Agency, Masuhara Keikichi. Its members included the agency's secretary-general, the various sectional chiefs and other important civilian officials. However, on Masuhara's own admission the civilian members of the committee were 'mere novices' as far as military matters were concerned. They had no alternative but to entrust the actual planning to the former Imperial Army and Navy officers who had entered the new forces in 1951–2.[72]

The character of Japan's postwar military leaders will be examined in a later chapter. Suffice it to remark that the degree of continuity, both personal and ideological, between the prewar and postwar military elite appears to have been far greater than many observers have imagined. That the uniformed officers of the National Security Agency shared the preoccupation of the unofficial planners (including some of their former colleagues who had remained aloof from the new militia) with balanced, potentially autonomous forces, is evident from the character of the Systems Research Committee's successive draft plans. The first draft, completed late in March 1953, placed particular emphasis on the development of air and sea power. Without the security treaty, it was argued, Japan's defence would require an army of 1 million men, a 1.5 million-ton navy and an air force of 10,000 aircraft. In the context of the treaty the committee envisaged an army of 300,000 men, a navy of 455,000 tons (367 vessels, 112,000 men) and a powerful air force of 6,744 aircraft (202,000 men) built up over thirteen years. While the size of the proposed army was the same as that recommended by the Americans and the Federation of Economic Organizations group, the huge air force and navy exceeded the wildest expectations of even the most ambitious private defence planners. As far as defence expenditure was concerned, it was planned to devote 3.8 per cent of the GNP to defence during the first year of the plan and increase this to 8.3 per cent by 1965, on the assumption that the GNP would increase at an annual rate of 3.5 per cent. The committee anticipated that about 25 per cent of Japan's defence requirements would be met by American MSA aid.[73]

Yoshida did not object to the *basic principles* of this plan. The construction of balanced, potentially autonomous forces was a necessary component of his own policy of temporary alliance with the United States, strict avoidance of military commitments outside Japan and the gradual development of an independent role in world affairs. He himself did not want to press forward too quickly with rearmament. Nevertheless, he was aware that the creation of the National Security Force had not satisfied America's 'expectations'. It was evident that the healthy condition of the security treaty, so essential in the short- to medium-term future, could only be preserved by greater Japanese military efforts. Yet to succumb to American pressure and concentrate exclusively on building up large ground forces would not only result in the semi-permanent satellization of Japan; it would bring closer the day when

Washington would request the deployment of those forces to other parts of Asia. On the other hand, investment in naval and air forces geared, as far as possible, to home defence, might temporarily placate opinion in Washington, reduce the possibility of American-sponsored Japanese involvement in wars in other parts of Asia and make easier the eventual transition from junior alliance partner to independent great power.

The Japanese Prime Minister, supported by the Ministry of Finance, *did object*, however, to the *scale* of the Systems Research Committee's rearmament proposals. Within two months, therefore, the committee had compiled another more modest draft. The new plan envisaged a 205,000-man army (100,000 men less than the force Dodge had suggested to Ikeda in 1952), a 142,960-ton navy (32,000 men) and an air force of 1,536 aircraft (46,000 men).[74]

During the course of 1953 this draft was revised numerous times. At the insistence of the Ministry of Finance, presumably with Yoshida's backing, the estimates for the size of the three forces and the scale of defence spending were progressively reduced.[75] While the project Ikeda showed Robertson at the October 1953 talks, and which formed the basis for the later First Defence Plan, envisaged balanced development of ground, air and sea power, the combined efforts of Yoshida and the Finance Ministry had drawn the teeth from the Systems Research Committee's original blueprint. The army had been cut in half, the navy reduced by two-thirds, the air force slashed to a fraction of that originally planned.

(v) The character of the final MSA agreement, March 1954

After Ikeda's return from the deadlocked Washington talks early in November, no further negotiations took place until the arrival of Robertson and the chairman of the Joint Chiefs of Staff, Admiral Radford, in Tōkyō in December.[76] Further negotiations took place in February 1954[77] and led directly to the signing of a Mutual Defence Assistance Agreement in March.

The two months between the breakdown of the Ikeda-Robertson talks and the opening of the new series of negotiations saw a shift in official American opinion towards acceptance of the Japanese position on military responsibilities and the amount and character of aid. This was a result of the Yoshida government's intractability, not of changes in the international situation. The Korean armistice had been signed on the eve of the Ikeda-Robertson talks but it was clear that a state of extreme tension would continue indefinitely along the 38th parallel. While the final Japanese-American negotiations were in session, the stage was being set for the battle of Dien Bien Phu. A month after the signing of the MSA agreement in Tōkyō the French position in Indo-China collapsed, the Eisenhower administration began to fear that its entire Asian-Pacific strategy was threatened,[78] Dulles and Radford began examining a plan to intervene in Vietnam in association with forces from America's Asian and Pacific allies.[79]

Nevertheless the preamble of the 1954 agreement, while 'reaffirming' that 'Japan as a sovereign nation possesses the inherent right of individual or collective self-defence' and 'recalling' America's expectation that 'Japan will itself increasingly assume responsibility for its own defence', recognized that

> in the planning of a defence assistance program for Japan, economic stability will be an essential element for consideration in the development of its defence capacities, and that Japan can only contribute to the extent permitted by its general economic condition and capacities.

The importance of economic stability was again stressed in Article 1. More significantly, Article 8, while committing Japan to fulfil the requirements of Section 511, Part (a) (4) of the MSA Act, was immediately followed by a provision stipulating that 'the present Agreement will be implemented by each Government in accordance with the constitutional provisions of the respective countries'.[80]

Although no clause *specifically* prohibited dispatch of Japanese forces overseas, Foreign Minister Okazaki explained at the signing ceremony on 8 March that

> In carrying out the duties and contributions promised in this agreement, adequate consideration must be paid to the conditions that exist in, and the separate interests of, the two countries. As was made clear in the course of the negotiations, the duties undertaken by Japan on the basis of this agreement will be completely fulfilled by her carrying out the commitments already undertaken in the Japanese–American Treaty of Mutual Security. There are no new and separate military duties. Overseas service and so on for Japan's internal security force [*jian butai*] will not arise.[81]

His words were echoed by the American ambassador, John Allison, who signed the agreement on behalf of the United States.[82]

Moreover, although no formal agreement was published, United States MSA aid was subsequently extended to Japan on the basis of the defence plan shown by Ikeda to Robertson in October 1953. After minor modifications this plan was officially adopted as the First Defence Power Consolidation Plan by the National Defence Council on 14 June 1957. As such it formed the basic framework for the Japanese defence power expansion programme and American military assistance to Japan during the next decade.

Japan was thus able to limit its military obligations under the scheme. Its efforts to channel MSA aid into economic development also met with some success. In Annexe A the United States promised to 'give every consideration ... to the extent that other factors will permit' to procuring supplies and equipment in Japan. The United States also undertook to provide information and facilitate the 'training of technicians from Japan's defence production industries'.[83] It could be expected that the techniques and skills thus acquired would also stimulate the development of non-military industries. A separate Agreement between the United States of America and Japan regarding the Purchase of Agricultural Commodities[84] gave Japan access to large quantities of cheap surplus grains. Another agreement encouraged the flow of further American capital into Japan.[85] The conclusion of these agreements activated Japan's military-related industries and had a far-reaching impact on the Japanese economy as a whole, helping overcome the stagnation brought on by the end of the Korean War.[86]

(vi)　The Shigemitsu–Dulles talks, August 1955: Japanese participation in regional defence arrangements as a condition for revision of the 1951 security treaty

Despite Allison's assurances, the MSA negotiations apparently did not persuade Washington that active Japanese participation in a regional military alliance was impossible. Japanese–American differences over the vexed question of overseas service for the Self Defence Forces surfaced again in August 1955, when Shigemitsu Mamoru, Foreign Minister in the new Hatoyama Cabinet, went to Washington to discuss the Far Eastern situation and press the case for revision of the 1951 security treaty. At this meeting, Dulles countered Shigemitsu's complaints about the inequities of the 1951 arrangement with the argument that from Washington's standpoint, too, the treaty was an unequal one. Japan, he observed, was under no obligation to come to America's aid in time of crisis. The treaty could only be revised, the Secretary of State insisted, if Japan changed its Constitution to permit overseas service for its military forces.[87]

Shigemitsu, eager to embark on a major, independent military build-up and conclude an agreement with the Soviet Union as a prelude to a closer relationship with China, was not enthusiastic about the idea of a closer strategic relationship with Washington. Like Prime Minister Hatoyama, however, he hoped to move forward on the question of constitutional revision. What Shigemitsu said to Dulles on this occasion is not altogether clear. Nevertheless, the joint communiqué issued after the talks suggested that Japan had promised not only to assume primary responsibility for its own defence but also to undertake certain unspecified military commitments for 'the preservation of international peace and security in the Western Pacific'. The communiqué clearly linked Japan's assumption of such responsibilities to revision of the 1951 treaty, stating, in part, that 'when such conditions were brought about it would be appropriate to replace the present security treaty with one of greater mutuality'.[88] Immediately after the talks senior American State Department officials told the press that Japanese forces would now be available for service overseas.[89] The story was featured prominently in *The New York Times* and other newspapers.[90]

The Shigemitsu-Dulles Joint Communiqué caused unprecedented uproar in Japan.[91] Washington's interpretation of its significance was firmly rejected by Shigemitsu himself. Prime Minister Hatoyama, too, insisted that he would not be prepared to countenance overseas service for Japanese forces. In rapid succession the entire Cabinet, the Foreign Ministry and the Defence Agency issued statements opposing Japanese participation in the kind of mutual defence treaty envisaged by the United States.[92] When the House of Councillors Foreign Affairs Committee resumed its hearings on 14 September 1955 the government explained that the communiqué was to be interpreted as meaning that Japan would contribute to the security of the Western Pacific by accepting increased responsibility for its own defence. The committee then resolved unanimously that

In view of the fact that the joint communiqué published after the recent Japanese–American talks has invited misunderstanding, both at home and abroad, this Committee recognizes, once again, the 2 June 1954 House of Councillors' resolution against the Self Defence Forces being sent overseas.[93]

On this fundamental issue Japan and the United States thus remained as far apart as ever. No further developments took place until Prime Minister Kishi Nobusuke's visit to Washington in June 1957. (See Chapter VI.)

(vii) The 'New Look' strategy, changing patterns of MSA aid and the development of the Self Defence Forces, 1954–60

The ink had hardly dried on the MSA agreements when developments at home and abroad produced important changes in American strategic thinking. The cost of containment had clearly begun to affect America's economic vitality. President Eisenhower, as Townsend Hoopes observes, was 'overridingly concerned that he might inadvertently spend the country into bankruptcy'. Shortly after his accession to office in 1953 the new President commissioned a group of senior officials, centring around the Under-Secretary of State, General Walter Bedell Smith, the director of the CIA, Allan Dulles, the vice-president of *Time*, C.D. Jackson, and the chairman of the National Security Council, Robert Cutler, to re-examine America's basic foreign policy objectives. At the same time he set the new chairman of the Joint Chiefs of Staff, Admiral Radford, to work on a reconsideration of the 1954–5 military budget. Eisenhower insisted that Radford and his team, in their deliberations, strike a proper balance between perceived military necessities and the economic realities confronting the United States.

By October 1953 both groups had prepared their initial recommendations. Walter Bedell Smith's team had concluded that containment, as practised by the Truman administration, should be continued. An overt 'spheres of influence' approach to dealings with the Soviet Union was rejected. So too was the concept of 'liberation' or 'rollback', although it continued to figure prominently in the rhetoric of the Eisenhower administration. Radford's group, meanwhile, had decided that the military budget could be reduced if nuclear weapons could be used in all situations where it was advantageous to employ them.[94]

The 'New Look' strategy, which began to take shape during this period (although it was not completely implemented until 1957) was, essentially, Dulles' 'massive retaliation' doctrine further modified to suit a domestic situation demanding additional cuts in military spending and an international situation where unco-operative allies refused to raise armies to stem the Communist tide under the protection of America's 'nuclear umbrella'. Since neither Eisenhower nor the American public would tolerate direct involvement in foreign wars Radford (whose motto in the war against Japan had been 'kill the bastards scientifically') was forced to do without armies.[95] As with Dulles' original scheme, Communism was to be held in check by the threat of instant nuclear retaliation launched from air and naval bases around the periphery of the Eurasian continent. Yet now even localized brushfire wars were apparently to be countered by massive nuclear strikes.[96] More than ever before, the emphasis was on the foreign-based strategic bomber, the missile and the naval air arm. America's overseas ground forces would be reduced to a minimum.

Implementation of this 'New Look' strategy necessitated sweeping changes in the deployment of American forces all over the globe. In Japan, as elsewhere, the level of American ground forces was rapidly reduced.[97] When the Radford strategy was first formulated there were 210,000 American military personnel in Japan. The first large-scale withdrawals were announced in December 1955 and by the end of 1957 only 77,000 men remained. Over half of these were air force personnel. By 1960 only 48,000 Americans, of whom 30,000 were attached to the air force, remained in Japan. At the same time the entire Far Eastern command structure was reorganized. By July 1957 responsibility for the vast area stretching from the west coast of the United States to the rimland of continental Asia was vested in a single Pacific milit-ary command located in Hawaii. Within this framework, responsibility for aerial operations from Japan, Korea and Okinawa was vested in the American Fifth Air Force, with headquarters at Fuchū, near Tōkyō.

The Japanese government formally refused to permit the entry of American nuc-lear weapons.[98] It would appear, however, that American nuclear weapons *were* brought into Japan, either with or without the knowledge of the Japanese authorities.[99] At the same time, in November 1956, to 'fill the vacuum' left by the departure of United States ground forces, supersonic F100 Super Sabres capable of carrying nuclear weapons were stationed at Japanese bases.[100] Moreover Okinawa, the importance of which had suffered a minor eclipse since the end of the Korean War, was rapidly transformed into a huge strategic nuclear air and missile base.[101]

These developments profoundly altered Washington's perceptions of the character and role of Japan's armed forces. After 1955–6 the United States abandoned its previ-ous preoccupation with the Japanese army and, in a complete reversal of policy, directed its efforts towards the creation of Japanese air and naval forces. This change naturally affected the volume and character of aid channelled into Japanese rearmament. In 1954 more than 80 per cent of MSA aid to Japan went to the ground forces. The fledgeling Japanese air force had received only 4 per cent, the navy 15 per cent. With the applica-tion of the Radford Doctrine in 1956–7 the change was dramatic. Aid to the Japanese army underwent a sharp decline, falling to 15 per cent of the total in 1956, 6 per cent in 1957, rising briefly to 25 per cent in 1958, dropping to 6 per cent in 1959 and standing at about 20 per cent of the total at the time of the 1960 security treaty crisis. In contrast, aid to the air force rose from a mere 4 per cent of the total in 1954 to well over 60 per cent in 1956. Aid to the navy increased from 14 per cent of the total in 1954 to 50 per cent in 1957, 28 per cent in 1958, 50 per cent in 1959. These trends continued until the aid programme itself gradually trailed out in the mid-1960s.[102]

In view of the early interest in 'balanced' forces, the changing emphasis of Ameri-can policy was welcomed by Japanese political leaders and defence planners. The spring of 1960 saw Japan in possession of an air force of 1,050 aircraft (including trainers and miscellaneous craft) and a navy of 99,400 tons.

Yet while the new Japanese army appears to have retained a certain degree of independence, neither the navy nor the air force were the autonomous bodies that the mainstream defence planners in 1954–5 had envisaged. They were, in fact, integral parts of the new American strategic system in the Far East. By 1962, 98 per cent of the weapons held by the Self Defence Forces, 99 per cent of their ammunition, 82 per cent of their communications equipment and 70 per cent of their vehicles had been obtained from the United States under the MSA aid scheme. So, too, had 70 per cent of Japan's military aircraft and 60 per cent of its naval vessels. Between 1954 and 1961 almost 3,000 Japanese army, navy and air force officers were trained at American military schools and academies.[103]

American naval vessels transferred to Japan under the terms of the MSA agreement remained the property of the United States. Even in 1967–8, the United States legally owned 40 per cent of the tonnage of the Japanese navy and 40 per cent of the naval air arm. Moreover, a United States Military Assistance and Advisory Group (MAAG–J), comprising some twenty officers (several of them Japanese linguists) and twenty-seven enlisted men, kept a close watch on all the activities of the new Japanese force, 'from its annual fleet exercises down to the cost of its band instruments'.[104] Needless to say, strategic and tactical planning developed in close co-operation with the United States. It was apparently not until the 1970s that the Military Assistance and Advisory Group adopted a somewhat lower profile.

The Japanese Air Force, too, became inextricably linked into the American Far Eastern strategic network. No one was more acutely aware of this than Air Marshal Genda Minoru, planner of the Pearl Harbor operation and first chief of the postwar Air Self Defence Force Staff. According to Genda

> At the present time ... the Air Self Defence Forces make their preparations within the framework of an extremely intimate co-operation with the United States forces ... The greater part of the American forces stationed in Japan – at Mitaka, Yokota, Atsugi and Iwakuni and the Seventh Fleet around Japan – are offensive in character and very different from Japan's Self Defence Forces. Their exercises are carried out with the greatest emphasis on attack ... The main objective of Japan's air defence network is to protect America's retaliatory power, to guard the bases from which America's retaliatory power will take off. Our radar network and so on have the same function.[105]

The character of the new Japanese air force became evident as early as 1957, when its headquarters was moved from Hamamatsu to Fuchū, where the headquarters of the American Fifth Air Force were located. Indeed, the Air Self Defence Headquarters were installed in the same building as those of the Fifth Air Force. English, not Japanese, became the operational language of the Japanese force. The interdependence of the two allies was deepened by reliance on the same radar network.[106] Finally, on 2 September 1959 Lieutenant-General Robert W. Burns, commander of the United States Fifth Air Force, and Air Marshall Matsumae Masuo, commander of the Japanese Air Defence Command, signed a secret agreement establishing procedures for joint action in case of emergency and arranging exchange of information with aerial warning and other facilities in South Korea and Okinawa.[107] This agreement had grave implications both for Japan's ability to make independent decisions in time of crisis and for the operation of the Self Defence Force laws. While the specific details of the Matsumae-Burns agreement remain unknown, it is difficult to escape the conclusion that an American decision to intervene militarily in Korea (for example) would automatically place at least the Japanese Air and Naval Self Defence Forces on the alert. The Japanese Prime Minister might have no time to consult with the National Defence Council before hostilities involving Japan actually commenced. The Diet, regardless of the provisions of the Self Defence Forces Law, might subsequently be in no position to influence the situation one way or another.

From the mid-1950s onwards the Japanese Ground Self Defence Forces increasingly assumed a counter army role against the Soviet Union. Northern defences were further consolidated. After 1955, with the establishment of the Western Region General Inspectorate in Kyūshū, efforts were also made to strengthen military preparedness along the southern coast of the Sea of Japan, in the areas closest to Korea. The greatest concentration of strength, however, remained in Hokkaidō. Less emphasis was placed on dispositions to suppress internal disorder, although this function remained important. Of the six regional forces (*kankutai*) (each of 12,700 men) and four mixed brigades (*konseidan*) (6,000 men each) established by the end of 1959 only one regional force was stationed around Tōkyō, the Kantō plains and the Kōshinetsu area. Only one regional force and one mixed brigade were stationed in the Chūbu, Kinki, Chūgoku and Shikoku area.[108] The extent to which these dispositions were made after consultation with the United States is unknown.

The end of the decade thus found Japan involved in an extremely close, albeit complex and ambivalent relationship with the United States.

The United States, preoccupied with the global containment of Communism, saw a Japan linked politically, economically and, hopefully, militarily, to the nations of non-Communist Asia as the sheet anchor of its Far Eastern strategy. To keep Japan within the American orbit Washington was prepared to facilitate its entry into the international trading community, to open the United States market to Japanese goods, to persuade other Asian-Pacific nations to do likewise and to involve itself deeply in the internal politics of South-East Asia.

Japanese leaders viewed the world in somewhat different terms. Certainly, there was a widespread consensus in the conservative political elite that the American alliance offered Japan the best prospects for economic recovery. There was general agreement on the importance of developing relations with non-Communist East and South-East Asia. The changeover to an oil-based economy, against the background of Washington's strong position in the Middle East, further integrated Japan into the American global strategic system.

Nevertheless, the Yoshida, Hatoyama and Ishibashi Cabinets, supported by the opposition parties, the press and public opinion, resolutely refused to join any American-sponsored regional security arrangement. Yoshida and his successors declined to rearm on the scale and in the manner considered appropriate by Washington. They would not transform the country into an arsenal producing 'low-cost military material in volume for use in Japan and in other non-Communist countries of Asia'. Japan's military planners were also insistent that the country build up the kind of balanced, potentially autonomous forces that distinguished allies from satellites. The task that confronted them was not an easy one. While Eisenhower's 'New Look' strategy succeeded, superficially, in resolving Japanese-American differences over the character and role of the Self Defence Forces, critical ambiguities remained. Japanese and American interpretations of the bilateral military relationship were fundamentally divergent. Contradictions between the Japanese Constitution, the Japanese-American security treaty, the Yoshida–Acheson Exchange of Notes, the Defence Agency Establishment Law, the Self Defence Forces Law, the Law Concerning the Structure of the National Defence Council, the Matsumae–Burns agreement and similar arrangements raised, for both parties, frightening possibilities.

Officially, the Japanese government believed that the scale and character of the rearmament it had undertaken was sufficient to fulfil its duties under the security treaty within the limits of the Constitution. Japan, with its developing, albeit purely defensive, army, navy and air force, had at least the appearance of military autonomy. And, as the old proverb goes, *banri no kō wa ippō de hajimaru*, 'even a journey of ten thousand *ri* must begin with a single step'.

Nevertheless, for the Japanese, the 1958 Matsumae-Burns agreement and the involvement of United States naval personnel in virtually every aspect of the Maritime Self Defence Forces strategic planning at least raised the possibility that Japan could suddenly find itself drawn into a conflict without the necessary constitutional and legal procedures having been observed. These arrangements also made some form of overseas service (e.g. Japanese fighters escorting American bombers to Korea, Kamchatka or eastern Siberia and back) by no means unthinkable. America's legal ownership of a large proportion of Japan's military aircraft and naval vessels also posed difficult questions. Postwar Japanese Prime Ministers, like their prewar predecessors, have had to consider the possibility that the armed forces might not be, in the last analysis, subject to Cabinet control. It has not been possible for them to dismiss altogether the unsettling thought that they sit with a time bomb in their desk, that this time the controlling device is not in the Imperial Japanese General Headquarters in Ichigaya, or in Kwantung Army Headquarters in Manchuria, but in Washington DC.

The Americans, too, had their worries. They believed that the security treaty and the Japanese rearmament programme had given them a Japanese air force to help protect their offensive power in North-East Asia, a Japanese navy to assist in operations against the Soviet Far Eastern fleet and the maritime forces of its local allies, and a Japanese army able to crush domestic Communism and co-operate generally in the region. They probably considered that, under the Matsumae-Burns agreement and similar arrangements, Japanese and American military efforts in North-East Asia would be closely co-ordinated. Nevertheless, governmental and popular support for the pacifist Constitution, together with the provisions of the 1954–6 Defence Laws, stipulating that Japan's new armed forces could go into action only on orders issued by the Prime Minister, after obligatory consultation with the National Defence Council, and that subsequent Diet approval of the Prime Minister's action was essential for continued operations, raised the real possibility that political developments in Japan could paralyse the alliance in time of crisis.

CHAPTER V

Liberal Democratic Party factionalism and foreign policy, 1957–1960

Observe the instincts that guide these men; the ends they struggle for; the grounds on which they like and value things. In short, picture their souls laid bare.

Marcus Aurelius, *Meditations*, IX, 34

The Americans had some cause for concern. Yoshida Shigeru, that devious old autocrat, had been difficult enough to deal with. Yet with Yoshida's eclipse, while the external constraints binding Japan to the Western alliance remained compelling, the reassertion of traditional modes of political thought and behaviour became increasingly apparent. The merger of the Liberal and Democratic parties in November 1955 had done little to promote an acceptable consensus on foreign and defence policy, either within the political elite or among the people at large. By the time Kishi Nobusuke formed his first cabinet in February 1957, a little over a year after the merger, it had become clear that the new Liberal Democratic Party, far from being a unified political organization committed to free enterprise at home and unequivocal support for American Cold War strategies abroad, was no more than a coalition of eight large factions, backed by different interest groups, each associated with a somewhat different approach to domestic and foreign policy.[1]

These eight factions, led respectively by Prime Minister Kishi Nobusuke himself, Ishii Mitsujirō, Ikeda Hayato, Satō Eisaku, Ōno Bamboku, Kōno Ichirō, Miki Takeo and Matsumura Kenzō (jointly) and Ishibashi Tanzan, had all grown directly out of the former Liberal and Democratic parties, themselves reincarnations of the prewar Seiyūkai and Minseitō. Equipped with their own headquarters, their own research committees and academic advisers, publishing their own journals and enjoying a membership that fluctuated according to the fortunes of the leader, the factions functioned virtually as separate political parties, bound together by a common opposition to socialism, yet competing openly against each other in elections and engaging in prolonged and bitter struggles for the fruits of office. Despite a general tendency towards philosophical homogeneity, each faction contained within it several subsidiary constellations of power. Like the courts of Japan's feudal *daimyō*, the postwar Conservative Party factions were also subjected to an unremitting process of diplomatic white anting by allies and rivals alike. This process, together with the desire of foreign powers, great corporations and assorted interest groups to influence policy decisions, contributed significantly to the massive corruption that gradually came to characterize Japan's postwar political society. The behavioural patterns established in the late 1950s were to continue, virtually unchanged, for the next thirty years.

Each faction had its own connections and sources of funds in the business community, built up over the years through a long process of natural selection and mutual accommodation of interests. Each faction leader had his friends in the Ministry of Finance, the Foreign Ministry, the Ministry of Agriculture and other organs of the bureaucracy. To some extent the views of individual faction leaders on important issues paralleled those of their financial backers and bureaucratic associates. At least some of the major factional-policy struggles in the Liberal Democratic Party, therefore, reflected the antagonisms between the great corporations and small-scale enterprises, conflicts between heavy and light industry, the differing interests of industrial, financial and commercial capital, agriculture and fishing, struggles within the bureaucracy and so on. Yet it would be incorrect to view the postwar Conservative leadership simply as obedient servants of their masters in the business community and the bureaucracy. Quite clearly, they could not attempt to implement policies fundamentally at variance with the interests of their financial supporters. They were unlikely to ignore consistently all the advice they received from their friends in the bureaucracy. Yet most faction leaders were men with forceful personalities, strong views and substantial personal reputations. They were power centres in their own right. Their policy positions were hammered out through a complex process of consultation with the senior members of their faction, supporters in the business community, contacts in the bureaucracy and various academic advisers, in the light of their private assessment of domestic and international conditions. Sometimes the views of their financial backers or bureaucratic associates prevailed. Sometimes they did not. Generally speaking, the position taken by factional leaders on any major issue represented the consensus of the entire factional machine and the conglomeration of interest groups clustered around it. For this reason their public pronouncements tended to be clouded in ambiguity, their dealings with other factions intricate and byzantine to an extreme degree, their movements across the political stage crab-like and unpredictable.

The ultimate goal of each faction leader was election as Liberal Democratic Party president. In a situation where the Conservative Party dominated the Diet this ensured subsequent election as Prime Minister. However, the complexity of the party's factional structure and the size of individual groupings made it impossible for one faction to dominate the stage. The result was a continually shifting pattern of transitory alliances and the division of the Conservative Party into warring camps, with the temporary ascendancy of one factional coalition challenged by a hostile confederation of other groups. At times, the leader of the dominant coalition might be in a position to distribute government and party posts exclusively to members of those factions that had supported his election. Generally speaking, however, party presidents did not find themselves in this happy position and could only maintain their supremacy by accommodating the demands of at least some neutral or opposing groups. On highly controversial issues the party leadership usually found it difficult to ignore altogether the attitudes of dissident and neutral groups. It is of considerable importance, therefore, to examine the background, personal connections, financial links, political philosophies and international outlook of the Conservative leaders who rose to prominence during the latter part of the 1950s. For many years afterwards the Japanese government's decisions on most major domestic and foreign policy issues were to be heavily, often decisively, influenced by the compromises reached during the course of their interminable factional-policy struggles.

I   The Kishi faction

Kishi Nobusuke had joined the Liberal Party after his release from the restrictions of the purge in 1953. His faction, however, was based largely on the extreme right wing of the old Democratic Party, where it had absorbed the groups formerly led by Ashida Hitoshi and Ōasa Tadao. By the late 1950s it had established itself as the largest and most influential grouping in the Liberal Democratic Party, claiming the loyalty of some seventy to eighty members of the House of Representatives and thirty or forty members of the House of Councillors. Financial support came chiefly from heavy industry – from Uemura Kōgorō, vice-president of the Keidanren, Kishi's senior by two years at Tōkyō University, from Nagano Shigeo, president of Fuji Steel, from Doi Masaji, president of Sumitomo Chemicals and from the Prime Minister's old friend Fujiyama Aiichirō (see below). Kishi was also connected with a wide range of ultra-nationalist and underworld organisations, some of which may well have contributed to his faction's financial upkeep.[2]

Kishi Nobusuke represented a very different stream of Japanese conservatism to that of the Yoshida school. Yoshida's outlook reflected that of the old court aristocracy and the financial establishment. Kishi, born in Yamaguchi prefecture in 1896, the second son of Kishi Hidesuke, a former clan official and sake brewer, was the heir and successor of the Chōshū military-bureaucratic clique that had exercised such a tenacious grip on the sinews of power since the Restoration of 1868. He had been brought up by the Satōs, a prominent Chōshū family into which his father, Hidesuke, had been adopted to marry a daughter, Moyo. The leading families of Yamaguchi prefecture, like the Prussian *junkers*, whose culture they so much admired, were intensely conscious of the fact that their sons dominated the army and held powerful positions in the bureaucracy, the academic world, the secret societies and the political parties. The Satōs were unusually well connected. Kishi Nobusuke's maternal great-grandfather, Satō Nobuhiro, the founder of the dynasty, had known Yoshida Shōin and enjoyed close connections with Itō Hirobumi and Inoue Kaoru. Two of his three sons had risen to high rank in the Imperial Japanese Army. The third son had been active in the Yamaguchi Prefectural Assembly. Kishi's mother, the redoubtable Moyo, a cultivated, autocratic and ambitious matriarch, produced two Prime Ministers (Nobuske and his younger brother Eisaku*) and one Rear-Admiral, something of a record, even by Chōshū standards.[3]

Post-Restoration Chōshū had remained, for many decades, a region of tremendous social and intellectual ferment. Its ideological confrontations were unusually intense. The region produced an extraordinary number of conservative elder statesmen, high-ranking military officers and imperial civil servants. It also gave birth to a disproportionate number of eminent Communists. Kishi's most formidable postwar political opponents, Nosaka Sanzō, chairman of the Japan Communist Party and Miyamoto Kenji, secretary-general of the party, were also Chōshū men. As such, they were perhaps the only members of the Opposition the Prime Minister took seriously.

Young Kishi's philosophical orientations had been apparent at an early date. He imbibed, with his mother's milk, the vision of Japan as a unique national polity, ruled by a divine emperor, entrusted by the gods with a sacred imperial mission. His childhood heroes had been energetic Chōshū Restoration leaders, military men and imperialist philosophers such as Takasugi Shunsaku, Kusaka Gentan, Nogi Maresuke and Yoshida Shōin. The fall of Port Arthur during the Russo-Japanese War had sent him into transports of joy. He had immediately resolved to become a great military leader, and spent much time afterwards reading biographies of Field Marshal Ōyama, Generals Nogi, Kurogi and others.[4] In 1912, during his third year at middle school, angered by the judgement of *The London Times* on the suicide of General Nogi and his wife after the Meiji emperor's funeral, little Kishi had written an essay expressing his admiration for his eminent fellow clansman's heroic self-sacrifice. His teacher had rewarded his efforts with a 'very good'.[5] At high school, Kishi had been an outstanding student in a brilliant year. Among his classmates at the Tōkyō Dai-Ichi High School, then one of the most famous secondary institutions in Japan, were the future Socialist Party leader, Miwa Jusō, and the future eminent legal scholar (and defender of the pacifist Constitution), Wagatsuma Sakae. It was during these years, as World War I raged in Europe, that Kishi first became acquainted with German philosophy and literature. It was not long before he was reading Goethe, Schiller, Hauptmann, Schopenhauer, Hegel, Nietzsche and Kant in the original. He also read Bergson, Tolstoy and Dostoyevsky in German. Yoshida Shigeru's conservative Confucianism had been tempered by his admiration for Britain. Kishi Nobusuke, throughout his life, retained an immense respect for Germany.

In 1917 Kishi entered Tōkyō University, that most prestigious seat of learning in the empire, studying for a time under Professor Hatoyama Kazuo, father of the future Prime Minister, Hatoyama Ichirō. At university, as at high school, Kishi revealed himself to be a first-class intellect, vying with his old friend Wagatsuma for the highest academic honours and attracting the attention of the conservative

---

* In his youth Nobusuke had been adopted by his paternal uncle, Kishi Nobumasa, to marry his daughter Yoshiko. After this he again assumed the old family name of Kishi. This explains why his family name is different to that of his younger brother Eisaku.

pan-Asianist Professor of Law, Uesugi Shinkichi, soon to achieve prominence as the chief opponent of Minobe Tatsukichi's 'organic theory' of the emperor.

The intellectual ferment at Tōkyō University in the years after World War I, the Russian Revolution and the rice riots brought the boys from Tōkyō Dai-Ichi High School to a parting of the ways. Their interest was focused on developments in Europe, particularly Germany, the former Austro Hungarian Empire and Russia. Miwa joined Professor Yoshino Sakuzō's social democratic Shinjinkai and threw himself into the socialist movement. Kishi, thoroughly alarmed at the trend of international and domestic events, joined Professor Uesugi's Mokuyōkai (Thursday Club) and the Gokoku Dōshi Kai (Association of Comrades to Defend the Fatherland), organizations dedicated to the defence of the Imperial system, the Sacred National Polity and conservative pan-Asianism against the rising tides of liberal, socialist and communist ideas. As the contradictions in Japanese society deepened, and the ideological conflicts on campus became more intense, Kishi moved further towards the radical right. He was particularly influenced by Kita Ikki.

> Kita Ikki was the greatest influence on me in my student days. He was later executed by firing squad as one of the chief conspirators in the 26 February 1936 Incident. But he died as he had lived, a dedicated revolutionary since the time of Sun Yat Sen's revolution against the Manchus. The right-wingers who came after him simply could not compare in knowledge and judgement. Kita's *Proposal for the Reconstruction of Japan*, the work of a socialist converted to nationalism [kokkashugi], outlined, in a structured, concrete fashion, a project for implementing immense social and poltical changes within the context of the Sacred National Polity. This was very close to my way of thinking at that time. I think that the young officers who took part in the 26 February Incident were more than a little moved both by Kita's personal charisma and by the perceptions of his *Proposal for the Reconstruction of Japan*.[6]

Under Kita's influence, Kishi came to believe that Japan's historic mission was to defend East Asia from those two most nefarious manifestations of twentieth-century Western civilization, Russian Bolshevism and Anglo-American capitalism. He also came to believe that while the Imperial system was central to the Sacred National Polity, the concept of private property was not. It was the adherents of this philosophical position, it will be recalled, who later caused so much distress to Prince Konoye Fumimaro and his circle, including Yoshida Shigeru.

According to Kishi, he arrived at the conclusion, during this period of his life, that

> the question of private property and the question of the Sacred National Polity are two entirely different matters. Changes in the former would not lead to changes in the latter. In one sense, the concept of the absolute right of private property, which dervies from Roman Law, would need to be abolished if the Sacred National Polity is to be brought to its finest flowering. The system of private property must change with the passage of time. The protection of private property must not be confused with defence of the Sacred National Polity.[7]

Kishi thus ended his university career as a convinced National Socialist. Rejecting offers from Professor Uesugi to succeed him in his Chair at

Tōkyō University, Kishi entered the Ministry of Agriculture and Commerce under the patronage of then dominant Chōshū faction.* During his years in the public service he built up a wide circle of useful acquaintances, some of whom, like Fujiyama Aiichirō, Shiina Etsusaburō and Akagi Munenori, were to join his faction in the postwar period. In 1936, following urgent requests by the Japanese army, Kishi was transferred to Manchuria. Manchuria gave him an opportunity to experiment with the ideas he had developed at university. Thanks to his innate ability and to the assistance of his close relatives Matsuoka Yōsuke, president of the Manchurian Railway Company, and Ayukawa Yoshitsuke, president of Manchurian Heavy Industries, his rise in the power structure of the satellite state was swift. Within a few months of his arrival, Kishi, as deputy director of the Manchurian Industrial Ministry, had become, along with General Tōjō Hideki, Commander-in-Chief of the Kwantung Army, Hoshina Naoki, Matsuoka and Ayukawa, one of the five most powerful men in the colony. Philosophically, he felt at home with the military officers and civil servants who presided over all aspects of life in Manchuria. Like them, he was convinced that Manchuria, constructed according to the principles of the Imperial Way, with its planned economy, militant anti-Sovietism and rejection of Anglo-American liberalism, would eventually provide a model for the development of Japan itself, for China and, ultimately, for the rest of Asia.

In 1939 he returned to Tōkyō to take up an appointment as Vice-Minister of Commerce and Industry in the Abe Nobuyuki Cabinet. His advocacy of long-range economic planning and tighter government control of the economy eventually forced the resignation of his minister, Kobayashi Ichizō. In October 1941 he entered the Tōjō Cabinet as Minister for Commerce and Industry and Vice-Minister for Munitions. Two months later, along with his other Cabinet colleagues, he signed the Declaration of War against the United States. There is no evidence to suggest that he did anything to halt the drift to war. He was firmly convinced of the justice of the Japanese cause. Japan's destiny was to establish itself as the dominant power in Asia. The Anglo-American powers, he believed, by opposing Japan's special position in China, had left no alternative but war.[8] Intellectually his whole life had been a preparation for just such a conflict. Throughout the war, he struggled, with a certain degree of success, to bring the economy under stricter central control. Nevertheless, with the fall of Saipan, he realized, like Prince Konoye, the Marquis Kido, Yoshida Shigeru and many others, that a Japanese victory was impossible. A negotiated peace would be necessary if the empire and its institutions were to be saved from total destruction.[9] Kishi, unaware of developments in Konoye's circle, linked up with Fujiyama Aiichirō, his closest friend in the business community, and a group of naval officers centring around Admirals Yonai Mitsumasa, Okada Keisuke and Suetsugu Nobumasa, who were plotting to overthrow the Tōjō Cabinet. His resignation from the Cabinet in 1944 prepared the way for Tōjō's political demise. This rather ambiguous 'anti-war' movement did not altogether save Kishi from the wrath of the

* Here his immediate superior was Itō Hirobumi's adopted son, Itō Fumikichi, also a native of Yamaguchi prefecture.

occupation authorities, although his treatment was more generous than that of comparable German political leaders such as Albert Speer. In 1946 he was interned in Sugamo Prison as a Class A war criminal. Never one to pass up a useful opportunity, he immediately struck up an acquaintance with his fellow prisoner Kodama Yoshio, the ultranationalist underworld personality. The relationship established in Sugamo was to serve both men well throughout the postwar period.

After three and a half years Kishi was released from prison, took up a position in Fujiyama Aiichirō's chemical company, then re-entered politics after the end of the purge in 1952, founding the League for Japanese Reconstruction (Nihon Saiken Dōmei), joining the Liberal Party at the invitation of his brother Satō Eisaku, then linking up with Hatoyama's breakaway group. By the time of the Conservative merger his extraordinary organizational capacity, strong financial base and extensive network of personal connections had established him as one of the most significant figures in national politics.

It soon became apparent that Kishi's basic approach to domestic and foreign policy had not changed dramatically since 1945.* During the early 1950s he emerged as one of the most forceful exponents of dismantling the occupation reforms, espousing the causes of constitutional revision, large-scale rearmament, stronger internal security laws, patriotic education, more effective government control over the contents of school textbooks and, in general, a greater measure of social discipline and order. Democracy, he believed, could only function in a politico-social context characterized by strong leadership, hierarchy and respect for authority. 'Democracy is not just flattering the masses', he once told the present writer, 'but if there is no leader willing to show the way to the public and to the Diet this is all we will really have.'[10] His approach to national economic policy, too, remained essentially *dirigiste*. He did not believe in either the absolute right of private property or in the untrammelled operation of market forces. The idea of close and continuous co-operation between government and business had widespread support among the financial backers of his faction. Like their counterparts in imperial Germany, Japan's great steel, chemical, shipbuilding and munitions manufacturers had always seen themselves as virtual organs of the state.

With the political demise of his colleague Ashida Hitoshi, Kishi also established himself as the foremost Japanese exponent of active co-operation with United States Far Eastern policies. This necessitated the transformation of Yoshida's 1951 security treaty into a full and equal military alliance. His position represented the synthesis of his own strategic judgement and the requirements of Japan's heavy industrial sector, which was then chiefly interested in developing the North American market and securing access to raw materials.[11] Kishi was implacably hostile to any accommodation with the Soviet Union. He consistently opposed the development of ties with the People's Republic of China. Unlike Yoshida he had little confidence in the possibility of concluding a special relationship with China. The Communist Revolu-

* Here again he formed an interesting contrast with his German counterpart Albert Speer.

tion, he thought, had destroyed Japan's position on the continent forever.[12] Japan had no alternative, therefore, to active participation in an economically integrated politico-strategic alliance with the United States and the countries of non-Communist Asia. Having accepted this position Kishi energetically set about forging close personal ties with regional leaders. He served, for many years, as president of the Japan America Society, president of the Japan-Great Britain Parliamentarians' Association, president of the Japanese-Australian Parliamentarians' Association, chairman of the Japanese Division of the Asian Parliamentary Union, president of the Japan-Republic of Korea Co-operation Committee, president of the Japan-Philippines Association and vice-president of the Japan-Republic of China Co-operation Committee. He was also active in the Asian Peoples' Anti-Communist League. His first overseas visit, as Prime Minister, was, significantly, to South-East Asia and Oceania.

Kishi made no secret of the fact that he hoped to see the development of military ties between Japan and the countries of non-Communist Asia. This position was implicit in his earliest postwar policy statements.[13] It did not change substantially during the remainder of his political life. In 1975 he told the present writer:

> I'm not one of those who believe in attacking others, in employing military power to invade other countries. Those things are bad. They ought not to be done. But I don't believe it is correct to close our eyes in the case of the region being unjustly invaded by outside military force ... At the moment, the Constitution is interpreted as meaning that Japan cannot participate in United Nations forces. But I believe it is very peculiar that one member of the international community should seek to set itself apart from the rest and refuse to bear sacrifices on behalf of others. I don't mean to suggest that we settle international problems through arbitrary use of military power as the Communists are doing at present. Yet I think it very strange that we cannot participate in United Nations forces to defend the peace and security of a particular region.[14]

Revision of the Constitution, or even its reinterpretation to permit Japanese participation in United Nations peace-keeping activities, would, of course, enable Japan to contribute militarily to maintenance of the status quo on the Korean peninsula. This cause, which, in the 1950s recommended itself to Kishi largely on strategic grounds, became particularly close to his heart after the military *coup d'état* that brought Major-General Pak Chung Hi to power in Seoul in May 1961, just twelve months after Kishi's own resignation as Prime Minister of Japan. Pak Chung Hi, a graduate of the Japanese Military Academy in Manchuria and a former officer of the Imperial Japanese Army (where he had served under the name of Okamoto Minoru), at once began a programme of political and economic reconstruction under strong military-bureaucratic control reminiscent of Kishi's own experiments in Manchuria.[15]

Kishi's views on Japan's regional role mirrored, almost perfectly, those of former President Herbert Hoover, Joseph Grew, John Foster Dulles, Harry Kern and the American Council on Japan. For this reason the 'Japan Lobby' assiduously cultivated Kishi's friendship. He became, in a very real sense, their principal asset in Tōkyō. Harry Kern always personally arranged the details of Kishi's visits to the

United States. He provided a business colleague, Kawabe Michio, who had previously worked with both SCAP and the United States Embassy in Tōkyō, as Kishi's press secretary for overseas affairs. Kern's close associate Compton Pakenham helped guide the Germanophile Kishi through the intricacies of written and spoken English. [16]

There was no contradiction between Kishi's prewar opposition to the United States and his strong support for Washington after the collapse of the Co-prosperity Sphere. His anti-Communism was intense and genuine.* The United States, as the dominant Western power, was Japan's logical choice for an alliance partner, the security treaty the natural successor to the Anglo-Japanese relationship and the Tripartite Pact. Provided the American-Soviet Cold War continued unabated, a reconstructed Japan might eventually be able to establish itself as the residuary legatee of the *Pax Americana*, in much the same way as the Anglo-German conflicts during the first part of the twentieth century had facilitated its emergence as the heir to the British Empire in the Far East.[17] Kishi's strong and continuing interest in conservative pan-Asianism is probably to be interpreted in this context. 'I do not believe that [pan-Asianism] in its purest form was mistaken', he told the present writer, 'not by any means.'[18]

Kishi's views were not necessarily shared by all his factional colleagues. Fukuda Takeo, a graduate of Tōkyō University and former Finance Ministry official, who was eventually to take over leadership of the faction, endorsed his mentor's emphasis on order, hierarchy and social discipline. He also agreed that the right of private property was not absolute. In the early 1970s his assertion that 'land is the people's property' and that private ownership 'should only be recognized within the limits consistent with its public nature'[19] was to highlight, once again, the fundamental differences between Anglo-American conservatism and important streams of traditional Japanese thought. Fukuda found no quarrel with his leader's anti-Communism, his hostility towards the Soviet Union and China, his emphasis on the importance of special ties with South Korea, Taiwan and the nations of non-Communist South-East Asia. Yet Fukuda, the son of a wealthy farmer from Gunma prefecture, in Central Honshū, had no connections with the old Chōshū military-bureaucratic clique. His dealings with the Imperial Japanese Army in the years after the Manchurian Incident had left him with a considerable antipathy towards the military.[20] Unlike his leader he was not enthusiastic about the prospect of large-scale rearmament. Akagi Munenori, too, Minister for Agriculture during the first Kishi Cabinet and subsequently director-general of the Defence Agency, opposed large-scale rearmament, was not eager to see the Self Defence Forces serve abroad and was anxious to limit their influence on Japan's domestic politics. The most significant differences within the Kishi faction, however, were between the Prime Minister and his Minister for Foreign Affairs, Fujiyama Aiichirō.

Like Kishi, Fujiyama (b.1897), the eldest son of Fujiyama Raita, a self-made

---

* Even so, Kishi's political philosophy, especially his attitude to economic planning and private property, contained elements that would not have made accommodation with the Soviet Union difficult, had circumstances been different.

sugar industry magnate and local politician from Saga prefecture, in Kyūshū, had been deeply involved in the politics of the Japanese Empire. His family background, education and business interests placed him firmly in the mainstream of prewar conservative pan-Asianism. His father had considered that Japan's diplomacy should revolve around the twin axes of a special relationship with China and the avoidance of conflict with the United States. As a dedicated modernizer, he had dispatched all his sons, with the exception of Aiichirō, to be educated in America. The family's American connections were extensive. The basis of its fortunes, however, lay in Japan proper, in Taiwan and on the Chinese continent. Fujiyama Raita had been a firm believer in the old pan-Asianist principle of 'same people, same literature'. Together with Iizawa Shūji, he had even established a company, the Daitō Dōbun Kyoku, to produce common textbooks for Chinese and Japanese schools.[21] He had been careful to ensure that Aiichirō became acquainted with China at an early age, sending him on a long tour of the continent in 1918, during his first year as a student of politics at Keiō University. The heroic struggle of the Chinese people to free themselves from feudalism and foreign domination made considerable impact on the young Fujiyama.[22] While he subsequently travelled extensively in North America, Europe and South-East Asia, China remained the focus of his interests. In 1937, after succeeding his father as president of the Greater Japan Sugar Manufacturing Company (Dai Nippon Seitō), he participated in a Japanese economic delegation to China led by Kodama Kenji, of the Yokohoma Seijin Bank, meeting Chiang Kai-shek and other luminaries of the Kuomintang. In Shanghai, representatives of the *Asahi Shimbun* and *Dōmei Tsūshin* arranged for him to exchange views with younger, more radical members of the party. He also made contacts with the new generation of Chinese businessmen.[23] Fujiyama, like many wealthy armchair revolutionaries, was a victim of his circumstances. He sympathized with the aspirations of Chinese nationalism. He understood that Japanese expansion on the continent would continue to meet with fierce resistance. Yet he seems to have believed that Japan, because of its complex relations with the other powers, had no alternative course of action.

Imperialism also had its consolations. Throughout the Sino-Japanese War, Fujiyama's continental interests continued to expand and prosper. He constructed new sugar refineries at Soochow and in Hong Kong.[24] He also took over the Nittō Chemical Company. His interests diversified. By the time of Pearl Harbor, Fujiyama, at the relatively youthful age of forty-five, had become one of the most prominent figures in the Japanese industrial and financial community. His links with the government and the military forces were close. In addition to managing the family business, he served as president of the Tōkyō Chamber of Commerce and Industry, the Japan Patriotic Trade Association and the Japan Chamber of Commerce and Industry, and as chairman of the Japan Sugar Industry Association. He sat on the board of directors of the Tōkyō Stock Exchange, the Sino-Japanese Insurance Company, the Yūrin Insurance Company, the Kyōdo Trust Company, the Ōsaka Kaikan, Nihon Shoken, the Alcohol Transportation Company, East Manchurian Industries, Korean Chemical Industries, East China Metal Processing, Manchurian Sugar, Japan Special Steel Tubing and Kurao Steel. He was auditor of the Taiwan Development Corporation and the Greater Japan Machine Industry Company. He also served as a director of the Conscription for National Glory Association.

During the war, Fujiyama worked as a director of the Imperial Rule Assistance Political Association, a member of the Discussion Group for the Construction of Greater East Asia and an adviser to the Naval Ministry, in which capacity he made an extensive tour of South-East Asia.[25] It would thus have been difficult for him to claim that he had not supported the war effort wholeheartedly. Yet once defeat became inevitable, the flexible and pragmatic Fujiyama was quick to see the importance of a negotiated settlement.[26]

Fujiyama had entered politics in July 1957, as Foreign Minister in the first Kishi Cabinet, with the greatest reluctance.[27] In the immediate postwar period, after his release from the restrictions of the purge, he had devoted himself to rebuilding the family fortunes, re-establishing his position in the business community, promoting Conservative unity and endeavouring to ensure, as far as possible, that key sections of the Japanese economy did not fall under American control. He had played a central role in the battle to establish Japan Airlines as a purely Japanese concern, rather than as a joint venture with United States capital.[28] He developed a close friendship with Yamashita Tarō, founder of the Arabian Oil Company, formed with the aim of breaking the grip of the American multinationals on Japan's energy supply.[29] He had accepted Kishi's insistent offers of a portfolio largely because he respected his old friend's nationalism and believed that his support might allay business suspicions of the new Cabinet.

Fujiyama's views on foreign policy had developed naturally from the interaction of his prewar experience with the realities of the postwar world. Like most Japanese Conservatives, he had accepted the defeat philosophically, regarded the security treaty as its inevitable legacy and believed that maintenance of good relations with the United States was an important national interest. Like the Prime Minister, he considered the 1951 security treaty to be humiliating in the extreme and was anxious to put Japanese-American relations on a more equal footing. Unlike Kishi, he did not wish to see Japan co-operate more actively with United States Far Eastern strategy. There appear to have been three reasons for this. First, like Yoshida, he continued to believe, as he had in the prewar period, that Japan's long-term future lay with the Chinese continent. Second, like Kishi, he believed that Japan had important interests in South-East Asia, the Middle East and, more generally, throughout the Third World. Unlike the Prime Minister he felt that Japan could gain nothing by joining the United States in a futile crusade against the tides of political, social and economic change sweeping these vast regions. While the relationship with the United States would, of necessity, remain the corner-stone of Japanese foreign policy for some time, Japan also had no choice but to come to terms with the newly emerging forces of the non-European world.[30] Third, Fujiyama was not especially anti-Communist. Even his attitude to the Soviet Union was more tolerant than that of many other Japanese Conservatives. He was convinced that the Communist

Revolution had been good for China.[31] He believed that the collapse of the Japanese empire on the continent had made it possible for the two nations to begin a new era in their historic relationship. He also considered that Japan had no long-term political, economic or strategic interests in Taiwan.[32] He was particularly gratified to discover that his perceptions of China were shared, in general terms, by the then British Prime Minister, Sir Harold Macmillan, and his Foreign Secretary, Selwyn Lloyd.[33]

Unlike Yoshida, Fujiyama was prepared to confront the United States on China policy and Third World issues. His first speech to the United Nations General Assembly in the autumn of 1957 had emphasized Japan's interest in the emerging Afro-Asian bloc.[34] He refused to support the United States during the offshore islands crisis of 1958. At the time of the Lebanon crisis, Fujiyama spoke strongly in support of Arab nationalist aspirations. Much to the annoyance both of John Foster Dulles and the Japanese Foreign Ministry, he declined to co-sponsor American proposals for a Middle East settlement, urging that any agreement concluded without the adherence of the Arab League would be unworkable.[35]

II Ishii Mitsujirō

In the late 1950s, Ishii Mitsujirō (b.1889), a native of the village of Kurume, in Fukuoka prefecture, north-western Kyūshū,[36] headed a faction consisting of some fifteen to twenty-five members of the House of Representatives and about thirty to forty members of the House of Councillors.

Ishii, like Kishi, was an ardent nationalist. He also advocated a strong anti-Communist line in foreign policy. There the resemblance stopped. Ishii had entered postwar Conservative politics as a 'party man', not as an ex-bureaucrat. His origins, and his electoral base, were in the traditional, populist, conservative political culture of western Japan. His family had been small shopkeepers. He had been brought up as a Nichiren Buddhist. He had not studied at elite high schools and prestigious universities. He had not entered the Imperial Civil Service. His connections with the Imperial Armed Forces had been tenuous. His education had been a traditional one. A physically robust and genial personality, his happiest memories of his years at Kōbe Commercial High School revolved around his activities in the judo club, the sumo club, Japanese poetry groups and his study of Zen Buddhism under Takaji Ryūen, abbot of Tenryūji in Kyōtō. Despite his youthful admiration for Germany, he had always found European languages difficult and never succeeded in mastering any. Unlike the young Kishi, he had in no way been associated with the radical right. As a student he sympathized with Minobe Tatsukichi's 'organic theory' of the emperor (although he had felt it prudent to avoid making this explicit in his final examination). He had been shocked by the assassination of Abe Shintarō, then one of the leading exponents of conciliatory policies towards China.[37] These incidents seem to have represented the full extent of the youthful Ishii's exposure to politics. He was not a man of ideas.

After graduation, Ishii served briefly with the Police Department in the Home Ministry. His duties had been in the area of traffic control, not ideological surveillance. In 1915 he was appointed private secretary to General Andō Sadami, Governor-General of Taiwan, serving altogether five years on the island. This appointment, together with his childhood friendship with Ishibashi Shōjirō, founder of the Bridgestone Tyre Company, and his marriage to Hisako, daughter of Hisahara Fusanosuke, president of the Ōsaka Steel Foundry (the precursor to Hitachi Shipbuilding) and one of the earliest proponents of a Japanese alliance with Hitler's Germany, had a decisive influence on his subsequent career. In 1920, Ishii, convinced of the beneficence of Japanese colonialism, joined the *Asahi Shimbun*, where he made the acquaintance of such figures as Ogata Taketora, Hatoyama Ichirō and Kōno Ichirō. Japan's drift to military fascism, then the onset of the war, disturbed him, although he could scarcely oppose the views of his wealthy and strongminded father-in-law. He decided to sit the conflict out, having neither the inclination nor the connections to engage in anti-war activities. The collapse of the empire came as a merciful relief. 'The military politicians of that time were completely dictatorial, just the same as Communists', he lamented.

Immediately after the war he had drifted into politics, joining the Liberal Party at Hatoyama's request. He was instrumental in arranging the smooth transition to Yoshida's leadership after Hatoyama's purge. In 1947, before he could take up his position in the first Yoshida Cabinet, he himself was purged. Three and a half years later he was back in the mainstream of Conservative political life. In 1951, on the eve of the San Francisco settlement, along with Hatoyama Ichirō and Ishibashi Tanzan, he urged an already fully committed Dulles not to treat Japan as a defeated nation but as a vital element in the world economy. He pleaded with Dulles that no restrictions be placed on the shipbuilding industry, in particular. The success of these representations doubtless pleased his father-in-law. From October 1952 until December 1954, as Minister for Transport in the fourth and fifth Yoshida Cabinets, he played an important role both in the reconstruction of the shipbuilding industry and the establishment of Japan Airlines, quarrelling bitterly with Fujiyama in the process.[38] In 1955–6 Ishii threw himself with gusto into the negotiations leading to Conservative Party merger.

In August 1956 he led the first large delegation of Japanese politicians, businessmen and cultural figures to visit the Kuomintang regime on Taiwan. His meeting with Chiang Kai-shek made a profound impression on him. He subsequently founded the Japan-Republic of China Co-operation Committee, a pressure group that was to exert considerable influence on Japanese foreign policy in the 1960s and the 1970s. For Ishii, the Taiwan connection, rather than the Japanese-American security treaty, came to constitute the principal axis of Japanese diplomacy. He took over responsibility for Taiwan largely out of a sense of personal loyalty towards his old friend Yoshida Shigeru, who had an uncanny ability for placing harmless men in potentially dangerous positions. According to Ishii's own testimony:

A long time before [I led the delegation to Taiwan], I was talking to Yoshida at Ōiso. 'You've got good connections with Taiwan. I'd like you to take the main responsibility for looking after the Taiwan problem for us. As far as the problem of South Korea is concerned, young Kishi comes from Yamaguchi prefecture, which is near to there, and it would be good if he looks after that side of things. I'd like you and young Kishi to help each other.' Thus it came about that I became the chief figure in the Japan-Republic of China Co-operation Committee. Kishi became second in command. Kishi was the leading light in the Japan Republic of Korea Co-operation Committee. I worked as its Vice-President.[39]

In the ebb and flow of Conservative factional politics, one thing led to another. In September 1957 Ishii accepted Kishi's offer of appointment as Deputy Prime Minister. In this capacity he attended the Colombo Plan Conference in Saigon, making the acquaintance of Ngo Dinh Diem and his family. He also visited the Philippines, making contact with pro-Japanese elements in the political and business establishment. He subsequently became involved in the talks to normalize relations with South Korea. In this way, the genial and good-natured Ishii, guided largely by his innate, deep-rooted conservatism, vague concepts of 'Asian morality' and loyalty to his colleagues, gradually extended his involvement with the family dictatorships and right-wing military regimes of East and South-East Asia.

In May 1958 he was dropped from the Cabinet and reluctantly severed his ties with Kishi. 'As Deputy Prime Minister I didn't do much work', he recalled. 'Kishi himself was always very active. Perhaps he judged my attitude to be unreliable.' By the end of 1958 Kishi's attitude to the law and order issues had made Ishii feel more than a little uneasy.[40] It savoured too much of the 1930s.

III Ikeda Hayato and Satō Eisaku

The Yoshida faction had split in December 1956 over the question of Ishibashi Tanzan's election as party president. Yoshida and Ikeda Hayato had supported Ishibashi. Satō Eisaku had supported the candidature of his elder brother Kishi. Of the two groups descended from the old Yoshida school, the Ikeda faction was by far the stronger, claiming the allegiance of some forty to fifty members of the House of Representatives and about thirty members of the House of Councillors. Ikeda Hayato was Yoshida's principal disciple and chosen successor.[41] He was closely advised by Maeo Shigesaburō, Ōhira Masayoshi, Miyazawa Kiichi and other Yoshida aides. The faction's financial base was securely implanted in the inner sanctums of the Japanese economic establishment. If Kishi's strongest support came from heavy industry, Ikeda's most important backers were bankers and financiers. In July 1960, shortly before Ikeda's election as president of the Liberal Democratic Party, it was reported that the faction's sponsors included Yamagiwa Masamichi, president of the Bank of Japan, Kobayashi Ataru, president of the Development Bank of Japan, Hamaguchi Iwane, president of the Japan Long Term Credit Bank, Hotta Shōzō, president of the Sumitomo Bank, Okumura Tsunao, president of Nomura Securities, Ōgami Hajime, president of Yamaichi Securities, Fukuda Chisato, president of Daiwa Securities, Kan Reinosuke, president of Tōkyō Electrics, Kikawada Kazutaka, vice-president of the Tōkyō Electric Power Company, Matsunaga Yasuzaemon, director of the Electricity Research Institute, Nagano Shigeo, president of Fuji Steel, Sakurada Takeshi, president of Nisshin Bōseki, Imazato Hiroki, president of Nihon Seikō and Horikoshi Teizō, chief of the Keidanren Secretariat.[42]

Notably absent from this impressive list were representatives from small and medium enterprises, agriculture and fishing.

The Satō faction, in which men such as Tanaka Kakuei and Hori Shigeru played a leading role, comprised some thirty-five to forty members of the House of Representatives and about twenty members of the House of Councillors. Satō was Yoshida's second disciple, destined, in the old man's view of things, to succeed Ikeda as Prime Minister at some future date. He was also Kishi's younger brother. The links with Yoshida and Kishi gave the faction extraordinary influence. So too did its wide connections in the financial, industrial and business worlds.

Ikeda and Satō, unlike the other faction leaders in the Liberal Democratic Party, had no prewar political experience. They were relatively young men, with bureaucratic and technological backgrounds, hand-picked and carefully trained by Yoshida to guide the destinies of the party and the nation after his retirement.

Ikeda, born in Hiroshima in 1899, the son of a prominent local landlord, had attended the Kumamoto Dai-go High School, where he had been a contemporary of Satō. Neither of the young men possessed exceptional intellectual powers. Both had hoped, like Satō's brilliant elder brother, Kishi, to gain admission to the Tōkyō Dai-Ichi High School. Both had been disappointed. Satō, by dint of sheer hard work, had eventually managed to enter the Faculty of Law at Tōkyō University. Ikeda, an easy-going youth, managed to make it to the somewhat less prestigious Kyōto University. At Tōkyō, Satō, overshadowed by Kishi, and acutely conscious of the family honour, plodded on dutifully to the end of his degree, then joined the Ministry of Transport, spending altogether eleven years as a provincial railway official in various parts of Japan. At Kyōto, Ikeda gained fame for his relaxed lifestyle and his abilities as a drinker rather than for his scholastic achievements. After graduation he entered the Ministry of Finance. Here his rise had been gradual, hampered by long bouts of illness.

As students, and as young civil servants, both Ikeda and Satō had held, as far as can be judged, purely conventional opinions. The epic struggles of the 1920s and the 1930s had left them unmoved. They had not been radical ultranationalist activists like Kishi. Yet they had certainly not been liberals. Their attachment to the values and institutions of imperial Japan was deep, instinctive and unquestioning.

The end of the war had found Ikeda working as director of the Department of Taxation in the Ministry of Finance. The day Japan's surrender was announced, Ikeda, together with his friend Maeo Shigesaburō and several other young officials, had joined the weeping crowds in the square before the Imperial Palace. Here they apologized to the emperor for their failure to fulfil their duty, then walked silently back to their offices.[43] Ikeda, like all Japanese, had been relieved to find that the occupation forces did not embark on a rampage of indiscriminate murder, rapine and plunder. Nevertheless he had quickly been made aware of the realities of the new Japanese-American relationship. Once, at Sukibayashi, in the full view of Japanese police, an American serviceman had stopped Ikeda's car, ordered the young Finance Ministry official out onto the street, got in and driven off at high speed. The Japanese police, with their ingrained respect for all superior authority, had been reluctant to investigate the case. Even the highest-ranking officers at

Police Headquarters had treated the future Prime Minister's protestations with disdain. What had he to complain about? He had only lost a car. He had been lucky he had not lost his life.*[44] There is no record of what conclusions Ikeda drew from this incident, either about the American people or his fellow countrymen.

August 1945 had found Satō working in Ōsaka, as chief of the Railways Section of the Ministry of Transport. Here, in the chaos of a devastated city, he was responsible for directing the flow of military supplies, troops, industrial materials, foodstuffs and refugees along a shattered communications network. In later years, Satō made little attempt to conceal his support for the imperial Japanese cause in the Greater East Asia War. Yet for the Satōs, as for all Japanese, the war had been a terrifying experience. In Ōsaka, Satō himself was constantly exposed to American air attacks. His wife and children, staying with the Kishis in Tōkyō, were bombed out of their home in the Great Tōkyō Air Raid, fleeing to Ōsaka just in time to experience an attack of similar proportions in that city. Satō's nephew was killed in the nuclear bombing of Hiroshima. The horrors of the war, the humiliation of defeat and the intensity of these personal family tragedies were not without their impact on Satō's political thought. In later years, as Prime Minister, he revealed an extraordinary preoccupation with national security and a determination to prevent any breakdown in Japan's relations with the United States. 'Japan's defeat has made it necessary for us to maintain good relations with the United States', he told the present writer in 1975. 'In that respect we are just like defeated Germany.'[45]

The occupation purge of senior politicians and bureaucrats accelerated the advance of younger, relatively uncompromised middle-ranking officials. By February 1947 Ikeda was Vice-Minister of Finance. In 1948 he entered politics, joining the Popular Liberal Party (Minshū Jiyū-tō), a small conservative grouping. In January 1949 he gained a seat in the Diet. Here he caught Yoshida's eye. Appointed Finance Minister in the third Yoshida Cabinet, he was primarily responsible for the nation's economic management for almost four years. Under Yoshida's guidance, his hitherto undiscovered political judgement, administrative skills and diplomatic sense developed rapidly. Yoshida used his talents to the fullest extent in several crucial rounds of political and economic negotiations with the United States.

Ikeda repaid Yoshida with an intense personal loyalty. He continued to consult closely with him long after the old man's retirement. His views on most matters closely paralleled those of his mentor. In both domestic and foreign policy Ikeda gave the highest priority to the demands of economic reconstruction. He was solidly anti-Communist, although, apparently, somewhat less hostile towards the Soviet Union than Yoshida had been. Like Yoshida, he opposed rapid rearmament and was disinclined to see Japan acting as a tool of United States Far Eastern policy. He regarded

---

*   Prime Minister Yoshida Shigeru's car, too, had once been stopped by an American serviceman on the road from Ōiso to Tōkyō. Yoshida, initially apprehensive, had been pleasantly surprised to find that the man was merely a hitch-hiker. The Japanese Prime Minister obligingly gave him a lift, for which he was rewarded with chocolate and chewing gum. Yoshida frequently recounted this incident to illustrate his views on the American character.

the alliance with the United States as essential in the short to medium term. At the same time he believed that Japan needed to develop ties with the People's Republic of China as rapidly as possible. 'After revision of the security treaty, the next thing is trade with the People's Republic', he was heard to remark some time before he became Prime Minister in the summer of 1960.[46] This view, too, was in accordance with the long-range thinking on which Yoshida's policies had been based.

Satō, after failing to obtain a portfolio in Yoshida's first Cabinet because of the purge of his brother, entered the second Yoshida Cabinet as Chief Cabinet Secretary in October 1948. He gained a seat in the Diet in the January 1949 election. He proved an energetic and competent administrator. Along with Ikeda he was extremely successful in raising funds for the Yoshida faction in the business community. Yoshida guided his progress with paternalistic solicitude. Yet he rarely employed Satō in delicate international negotiations. As a result, Satō's international experience remained, until the early 1960s, somewhat undeveloped. It is difficult to escape the conclusion that, apart from a strong anti-Communist sentiment,* a fierce nationalism inherited from his family background and a healthy respect for the sensitivities of the United States, Satō had, in the late 1950s, no particular view of Japan, its place in the world, and the future options open to it. In any case, unlike Yoshida, he was a man who preferred to move with the tide. He was reluctant to commit himself on most issues until he knew in which direction the tide was moving.

IV　Ōno Bamboku

Ōno Bamboku, Kōno Ichirō, Ishibashi Tanzan, Matsumura Kenzō and Miki Takeo, like Kishi Nobusuke, had all been active in prewar political life. Yet unlike Kishi, Ikeda and Satō they were not former bureaucrats but professional party politicians, with backgrounds in agriculture, fishing, local government and journalism. Their roots were to be found in the popular conservatism of prewar Japan, with its robust nationalism, its rather more nebulous pan-Asianism, its tenacious sense of community self-interest, its instinctive hostility to Chōshū and Satsuma domination of the government, its suspicion of Westernized bureaucrats, its preference for earthy, populist leaders, embodying traditional cultural values, who lived and worked in their communities, understood their constituents and were prepared to fight energetically on their behalf.

Ōno Bamboku, born the fourth son of a village headman in Gifu prefecture in 1890, was a veteran of the great political struggles of the 1920s and the 1930s.[47] In

---

* Satō's anti-Communism and Russophobia declined after his first visit to the Soviet Union in 1974. In 1975, just before his death, he told the present writer of the profound impression made on him by his visit to Leningrad. 'A Russian explained to me that Hitler's armies had laid siege to Leningrad for two and a half years, that the defences had not been broken, the city had not surrendered. I think that was a wonderful thing. The Soviet Union is usually said to be a totalitarian country but those problems are fading away ... In Communist countries too, totalitarianism is on the wane.'

his youth, he had abandoned his studies at Meiji University, joined the Seiyūkai, entered local politics through the Tōkyō City Council, then developed a close association with Hatoyama Ichirō. A tough and resilient grass-roots politician, he had emerged as one of the chief warriors of the Hatoyama faction. His clashes with Katō Takaaki had several times brought him into conflict with prewar Japan's stringent internal security laws. Along with Hatoyama and Ōzaki Yūkio he had refused to join the Imperial Rule Assistance Association. In the postwar period he had helped Hatoyama found the Liberal Party, then, after Hatoyama's purge, groomed Yoshida to take over as successor. In the subsequent conflict between Hatoyama and Yoshida, Ōno, a man of strong personal loyalties, had unhesitatingly supported his old benefactor. In 1948, his alleged involvement in the Shōwa Denkō scandal led to a brief term of imprisonment. He returned to politics, cleared of all charges against him, to find his position within the party increasingly eclipsed by Yoshida's young technocrats. He did not believe bureaucrats could make good politicians. 'Politics is more than legal codes and electric calculators. You can't learn about it as a bureaucrat. It needs experience and judgement.'

In foreign affairs, Ōno was an exponent of alliance with South Korea and Taiwan. Yet unlike Kishi he was also committed to the preservation of liberal democratic values in Japan. This despite his extensive ties with ultra-nationalist groups, Yakuza families and other dubious elements. In his view, the rivalry between the Conservative Party and the Opposition was not a life-and-death struggle of incompatible opposites. No political or economic system could outlive its usefulness. Friendly competition between different ideologies was necessary for the healthy development of the body politic.

V   Kōno Ichirō

Like Ōno, Kōno Ichirō (b.1898) had been a close associate of Hatoyama and a veteran of the struggles of the 1930s. In 1960 his faction commanded the allegiance of about thirty or thirty-five members of the House of Representatives and eighteen members of the House of Councillors.[48] His chief lieutenants were young men like Nakasone Yasuhiro and Sonoda Sunao.[49] Kōno's funds did not come from the financial and industrial capital at the centre of the Japanese economic establishment. Generally speaking, Japan's major bankers and industrialists regarded him with suspicion. His strongest support came from fishing, agriculture, small and medium enterprises and newly established industrial concerns, from Nakabe Kenkichi, president of Taiyō Fishing, Suzuki Kyūhei, president of Nihon Fishing, Hagiwara Kichitarō, president of the Hokkaidō Coal and Steamship Company, Nishiyama Yatarō, president of Kawasaki Steel, Nagata Gaichi, president of Daiei, Kawai Ryōsei, president of Komatsu, Fujiyama Katsuhiko, president of Dai Nippon Seitō, Anzai Hiroshi, president of Tōkyō Gas and Komamura Sukemasa, president of Eshō. Most of these men stood somewhat apart from the mainstream of the business community. Kōno also enjoyed a wide network of connections with traditional regional magnates and local city power-brokers. Like Kishi, Ōno and several other Conservative leaders, he had easy access to the murky world of rightists, extreme nationalist groupings and gangster organisations.[50]

Kōno was, in every way, a formidable figure, physically powerful, a persuasive speaker, a superb political tactician, a seasoned manipulator. Like Yoshida and Kishi, he was also a man with a grand vision, blessed with uncanny political realism, immense reserves of energy and considerable ruthlessness.

Politics and agriculture were in the blood of the Kōno family. Kōno's father, Jihei, a wealthy farmer from the Odawara district in Kanagawa prefecture, had been active in local politics for many years, eventually becoming president of the Kanagawa Prefectural Assembly. His mother's family had also been substantial farmers. His early education had been at local schools. After graduating from the Faculty of Politics and Economics at Waseda University (he had failed to enter the Engineering Faculty because of his poor English) he joined the *Asahi Shimbun*, that bastion of prewar Japanese liberalism, as a reporter specializing in agricultural matters. Agriculture, and the future of the Japanese farming community, remained for him issues of passionate concern throughout his life. In 1931 he obtained a position as private secretary to Yamamoto Teijirō, Minister for Agriculture in the Inukai Cabinet. The following year he won a seat in the Diet, joined Hatoyama in the Seiyūkai and remained in politics almost continually until the end of the war. During the war, he followed Hatoyama's example and refused to join the Imperial Rule Assistance Association. He did, however, become a member of the Parliamentarians League for the Revitalization of Asia. Like Hatoyama, he was purged during the occupation. In 1952 he was re-elected to the Diet, subsequently joining Hatoyama's breakaway Liberal group and eventually becoming Minister for Agriculture in the Hatoyama Cabinet. Hatoyama's illness and Kōno's own domineering personality had made him virtual Prime Minister during this period.

Kōno had strong views on foreign policy. These were closely linked to his position on domestic political and economic issues. His philosophy was essentially a Gaullist one. His nationalism was intense, transcending ideologies and political parties. While rejecting Marxism he displayed a lively philosophical interest in reform of the capitalist system. He maintained amicable ties with many members of the Opposition. He believed that an independent economy, with a proper balance between agriculture and industry, was an essential prerequisite both for the livelihood of the Japanese people and for the reassertion of an autonomous role in world affairs. The San Francisco system, which brought with it close links between Japanese and American financial and industrial capital, and which exposed Japan to constant pressure from the United States agricultural lobby, endangered this balance. It also jeopardized relations with countries like the Soviet Union and China, whose goodwill was essential for the future of the Japanese fishing industry. Kōno was especially interested in re-establishing sound relations with the Soviet Union. During the Hatoyama Cabinet he had played a leading role in the negotiations to normalize ties with Moscow. He had many personal friendships among Soviet officials and regarded himself as something of a Soviet specialist.

While Kōno believed that a friendly relationship with the United States was important for Japan, he was lukewarm towards the American alliance. Japan's future, he considered, lay not with the United States but with an independent pan-Asianist community incorporating the developing non-Communist nations to the south. The simple, bipolar order created by World War II could not endure. Four vast blocs, centred on the United States, the Soviet Union, Europe and China, would inevitably emerge.

> For reasons of geography Japan cannot be part of the European community. If she is not to become a Communist society, she can therefore either join hands with the United States, or, in accordance with her destiny, think of forming an Asian community ... Of course, it is perfectly possible to blindly follow everything the United States says. It would be quite simple to hoist the stars and stripes here, like they do in Hawaii, and make Japan into the fiftieth or the fifty-first state. If we tear down the walls between us and the United States, a quick calculation on the abacus will show us that our incomes will increase enormously. The entire nation might rapidly achieve unprecedented bliss. There may well be people who think like this ... But we have a consciousness of ourselves as Japanese. Because of this, the only road open to us is to build an Asian community ... It is certainly not too much to imagine that Japan can best fulfil its role by forming a fifth, new bloc and, through the power of this organization, strive for world peace.[51]

Such a community could never be constructed if Japan, behind the shield of the security treaty, simply acted as the surrogate for American interests in the Far East. Nor could it be formed unless Japan maintained amicable, equidistant relations with the Soviet Union and China.

VI Miki Takeo and Matsumura Kenzō

In 1960 the faction jointly led by Miki Takeo and Matsumura Kenzō was estimated to contain somewhere between thirty and fifty members of the House of Representatives and about a dozen members of the House of Councillors. Its business support, like that of the Kōno faction, came less from the financial and heavy industrial sectors than from medium and small enterprises. Miki, connected, through marriage, with the powerful Mori (Shōwa Denkō, Japan Metallurgy) and Anzai (Tōkyō Gas) families* had many admirers in Keizai Dōyūkai. He also enjoyed friendly personal relations with Kudo Shōshirō, president of the Tōkyō Tōmin Bank, and Shōji Takeo, president of Asahi Denka. Matsumura's group attracted support from agricultural interests, fertilizer companies and some pharmaceutical firms.[52]

Miki, born in 1907 in Tokushima prefecture, in the old Tosa domain, the son of a prosperous fertilizer merchant, had entered politics immediately after graduating from Meiji University in 1937.[53] He had taken a leisurely approach to his education, spending altogether five and a half years in the United States and Canada during his student days. As a young member of parliament in the days before World War II, he had been known as an advocate of a pacific foreign policy, a man in the tradition of Shidehara Kijūrō. After World War II he had joined the Democratic Party. Miki was

---

* By virtue of Anzai Takeyuki's marriage to Shoda Emiko, sister of the Crown Princess, Miki was also connected to the Japanese Imperial Household.

neither a Cold War warrior nor an extreme nationalist. Like most members of the Democratic Party, he had not been happy with the security treaty. Yet it was not altogether clear what kind of arrangement he proposed to substitute in its place. His attitude to improving relations with the surrounding Communist powers was generally positive. By the beginning of the 1960s he had become increasingly attracted to the idea of Pacific Basin co-operation, a concept that appealed to his sense of economic rationalism, his distaste for the Cold War, his friendly sentiments towards the United States and the Soviet Union, his longstanding interest in the Chinese continent and his growing concern for North-South issues.

Miki was a liberal internationalist. Matsumura Kenzō, in contrast, was a Sino-centric pan-Asianist. China had fascinated him ever since his youth. Born in 1883, in Toyama prefecture, the son of a dealer in medicinal herbs, he had been steeped since childhood in the traditions of old East Asia. He had made his first visit to China in 1905, in the last years of the Ch'ing Dynasty, while still a student at Waseda University. After graduation, he had spent time as a journalist, then entered local politics. In 1928 he joined the Minseitō, was elected to the House of Representatives, and held his seat continuously (except for the five years of the occupation purge) until his retirement in 1969.[54]

A conservative of the old school, cultivated, sensitive, and incorruptible, Matsumura was not a crusading anti-Communist. He established excellent personal relations with the Chinese Communist leadership, understood their viewpoint and sympathized with the broad aims of the revolution. His pan-Asianism had both cultural and geopolitical aspects. He believed in the historical unity of East Asian civilization and in the necessity of defending its values and institutions. He also believed that Japan's political, economic and cultural autonomy could not be preserved without close relations with China. In this sense, his long-term vision was very similar to that of Yoshida. He was under no illusions that the security treaty could be easily jettisoned. He was convinced, however, that future changes in the international order would precipitate the gradual disintegration of both the San Francisco system and the Sino-Soviet relationship, permitting East Asia to develop in accordance with its own historical patterns.[55] Matsumura found Yoshida's apparent subservience to the United States, whatever its motives, utterly intolerable. He believed that Japan should resist American pressure vigorously, even at the risk of offending Washington.[56]

Matsumura's attitude to China, unlike that of many Japanese Conservatives, was far from patronizing. In his view, China and Japan were the two great powers of the Orient. Japan could make a significant contribution to the industrial and agricultural development of the People's Republic. The new China, in turn, had much to teach Japan. Significantly, it was the more authoritarian aspects of the Chinese Revolution, as Matsumura saw it, the strict control of the trade unions, the curbing of wayward egotistical impulses among the masses, the inculcation of patriotism and virtue through the education system, that most excited his attention.[57] Matsumura was, after all, an old-fashioned East Asian conservative, not a liberal. In this sense, he differed from Ishibashi Tanzan, that other indefatigable advocate of Sino-Japanese amity within the Liberal Democratic Party.

VII Ishibashi Tanzan

Former Prime Minister Ishibashi Tanzan's supporters, who in 1960 totalled about ten to fifteen members of the House of Representatives, comprised the smallest faction in the Liberal Democratic Party. They had no significant support in the business community, although Ishibashi's personal friendship with Matsunaga Yasuzaemon, of the Electricity Research Institute, may, perhaps, have occasionally done something to prop up the faction's shaky finances.[58] Nevertheless, the Ishibashi faction, more than any other Conservative grouping, existed because its members had sufficient personal prestige to win elections on shoe-string budgets.

Ishibashi, born in 1884, a native of Yamanashi prefecture, the son of the Nichiren Buddhist monk Sugita Tanei, who later became the abbot of Sōhonzan Minobusan Kūonji, had been, since his youth, a thorn in the side of successive Japanese governments.[59] He was the leading maverick of the Liberal Democratic Party, a man of unusual learning and experience, brilliant, unconventional, respected by his constituents and admired by the Opposition.

His involvement in public controversy extended back to the beginning of the Taishō period. The essential elements of his political philosophy had remained substantially unchanged for over half a century. After graduating from the Faculty of Law at Waseda University in 1907 (two years after the end of the Russo-Japanese war) Ishibashi had joined the staff of the *Tōkyō Mainichi Shimbun*. In 1911 he had entered the *Tōyō Keizai Shinpō*, becoming its chief editor in 1925 and president in 1941. In the *Tōyō Keizai* he soon established his reputation as a radical liberal, 'little Japanist' and anti-imperialist. In the 1920s and 1930s he also took the lead in introducing Keynesian economics to Japan.

Believing Sino-Japanese amity to be an essential condition of Japan's political and economic security, he had vigorously opposed Japanese expansion in China during World War I. Throughout the 1920s he continued to support the cause of revolutionary Chinese nationalism, although he eventually came to accept Japanese supremacy in Manchuria as a *fait accompli*. The experience of World War II made him bitterly regret this slight compromise with the establishment. In the immediate postwar period he moved rapidly to the left. In 1945–6, together with Communists, pro-Communists and members of the old left such as Arahata Kanson, Kobori Kanji, Takano Minoru and Yamakawa Hitoshi, he was involved in unsuccessful attempts to organize a Popular Front. In 1946 he was a sponsor of the rally in Hibiya Park to welcome the exiled Communist leader, Nosaka Sanzō, back from Yenan. Appointed Minister of Finance in the first Yoshida cabinet in May 1946, he was elected to the Diet in the April 1947 general elections only to be purged almost immediately afterwards. He re-entered politics in October 1952, holding his seat in Shizuoka continuously until his retirement in 1963.

Ishibashi, while insisting that friendship with the United States formed one essential corner-stone of Japanese diplomacy, was less than enthusiastic about the security treaty. Strategic and economic realities, he believed, also required development of good relations with the Soviet Union and China. In September 1959, he visited Peking and, in a joint communiqué with Chou En-lai, called for the development of political, economic and cultural relations between China and Japan on the basis of the Bandung Conference declaration.[60] The following year he became president of the Japan-Soviet Co-operation Society.

Unlike Yoshida, Kishi and Fujiyama, Ishibashi did not hope for Japan's re-emergence as a great power. He did not see the future in terms of an exclusive political and economic relationship with China or a new Co-prosperity Sphere in South-East Asia. He remained, as he had been for the greater part of his life, a 'little Japanist', convinced that his country could best survive, and make its contribution to world peace, by developing as a liberal, prosperous, modern industrial and trading nation, with a solid agricultural base, a modest defence capacity, friendly ties with the United States, the Soviet Union and the People's Republic of China and mutually beneficial relations with the emerging countries of Asia and the Pacific.

CHAPTER VI

The 1960 security treaty crisis

Wisdom cries aloud in the street;
in the markets she raises her voice;
on the top of the walls she cries out.

Proverbs 1: 20–1

I. The crisis[1]

On 19 January 1960, in the East Room of the White House, Prime Minister Kishi Nobusuke, his Foreign Minister Fujiyama Aiichirō, Ishii Mitsujirō, chairman of the Liberal Democratic Party Executive Board, Adachi Tadashi, president of the Japan Chamber of Commerce and Industry and Asakai Kōichirō, the Japanese ambassador to Washington, signed a new Treaty of Mutual Co-operation and Security between Japan and the United States to replace the agreement negotiated by Prime Minister Yoshida Shigeru and John Foster Dulles in 1951. Kishi was convinced that his new treaty had eliminated the most humiliating features of the old agreement, assuring Japan's position as a full and equal partner of the United States in the Pacific. The beginning of the 'new era' in Japanese-American relations was to be symbolized by President Eisenhower's visit to Japan after formal ratification of the treaty. The Emperor Hirohito's eldest son, Crown Prince Akihito, the first member of his ancient line ever to marry a commoner, was to pay a return visit to the United States later in the year.

San gun mo sui o ubau beshi, hippu mo kokorozashi o ubau bekarazu, 'The Supreme Commander may attempt to impose his will through overwhelming force but he cannot succeed in changing the views of ordinary men'. So goes an old proverb. Contrary to Kishi's expectations the issue of treaty revision plunged Japan into its greatest political crisis since World War II, exposing the latent ambiguities in the Japanese-American strategic relationship, the deep fissures within the Conservative camp, the extraordinary organizational power of the Opposition parties and the degree of public support for their neutralist platforms. Once treaty revision became a major issue the Prime Minister's opponents in the Liberal Democratic Party, the Socialists, the Communists, the mainstream of the trade union movement, the intellectual establishment, student and religious organizations, supported by a

large body of public opinion, launched a full-scale assault on the military relationship with the United States. The storm of protest, almost unparalleled in modern
Japanese history, reached its peak on the evening of 19–20 May 1960, when the new
treaty was approved by the House of Representatives. Several important Conservative Party leaders, including former Prime Minister Yoshida, deliberately absented
themselves from this critical session of parliament.[2] Before the vote could be taken,
the entire Opposition, which had attempted to block the proceedings by staging a
sit-down demonstration, was removed bodily from the Diet by a force of 500 police-
men ordered into the chamber by the Speaker. For the next month the Socialist and
Communist parties boycotted parliamentary proceedings. Outside the Diet the
demonstrations, protest marches and strikes reached unprecedented proportions.
The Prime Minister's residence was attacked, rioting students fought pitched
battles with police in the Diet compound, 6 million men and women went out on
strike two times in as many weeks. On 18 June, the day the treaty was automatically
approved by the House of Councillors, a crowd of some 330,000 protestors gathered
in front of the Diet. Ratification of the treaty by the Japanese Cabinet on 21 June and
its approval by the United States Senate the following day precipitated another
massive strike involving an estimated 6.25 million workers, the largest in the nation's
history. In the summer of 1960 Japan showed every indication of emerging as
America's Hungary.

The mounting scale of public unrest forced the Japanese government to conduct
the formal Exchange of Ratifications with the United States ambassador, Douglas
MacArthur II, secretly in the Foreign Minister's official residence in Shibashira-
gane-machi. Fearing that student activists might attempt to capture the ambassador,
Fujiyama made arrangements with the owners of two adjoining properties to permit
MacArthur to escape by scaling fences and running across gardens into a waiting
limousine. Beer crates had been thoughtfully stacked in strategic places to facilitate
his exodus. The Foreign Minister's apprehensions were not entirely groundless.
Nevertheless, both MacArthur and Fujiyama were able to retire gracefully by the
front entrance, after celebrating the Exchange of Ratifications with champagne. Five
minutes later students from nearby Meiji Gakuen milled around the residence,
shouting their opposition to the alliance.[3]

Immediately after the Exchange of Ratifications, Prime Minister Kishi, under
intense pressure not only from the Opposition, the demonstrators and the press but
also from within his own party, announced his resignation. Already, a week earlier,
lamenting that this was 'not the appropriate time to welcome a state guest', Kishi had
been forced to cancel President Eisenhower's scheduled visit to Japan. The first
projected Japanese tour by a serving American president thus failed to eventuate.

The 1960 security treaty crisis, like the rice riots of 1918, left an indelible impression on Japan. It marked the beginning of new chapters both in the development of
the nation's political life and in the evolution of its foreign policy. In the six months
between the signing ceremony in the White House and Prime Minister Kishi's
resignation, the tactics employed by both the government and the Opposition to
advance their objectives were such that observers began to speak of the impending

collapse of the postwar constitutional order.[4] As the crisis deepened, many Conservatives became convinced that Japan was again teetering on the brink of a violent Communist revolution. Socialists, Communists and other opposition groups increasingly began to fear the possibility of a right-wing *coup d'état*.

Both sides could find ample evidence to justify their anxieties. From the winter of 1959–60 the Ground Self Defence Forces began to intensify their anti-riot training. The Joint Staff Council and the Defence Agency drew up plans for mobilization.[5] By June 1960 Japan had come perilously close to civil war. It was saved from this appalling tragedy* by the political common sense of Akagi Munenori, the then director-general of the Defence Agency, the respect of the Self Defence Force leadership for the principle of civilian control, the restraint of the Socialist, Communist and trade union leaders, and by Kishi's willingness to listen to sound, reasonable advice, despite the very great pressures to which he was subjected. The Japanese talent for compromise, one of the nation's greatest assets, was seldom more urgently needed, and rarely more effectively employed, than it was in the summer of 1960.

Akagi Munenori recalls that

> The question of mobilizing the Self Defence Forces was not formally discussed in the Cabinet. In informal discussions, however, the then Minister for Finance, Mr Satō (Eisaku), the Minister for International Trade and Industry, Mr Ikeda (Hayato) and others, asked me from time to time whether it would not be possible to mobilize the Self Defence Forces ... Because the situation was an urgent one, opinion within the Liberal Democratic Party became more and more impatient. The Liberal Democratic Party Secretary-General, Mr Kawashima Shōjirō, arrived at the Defence Agency, via the underground passage network, urging that the Self Defence Forces be mobilized, somehow or another, to facilitate Eisenhower's visit ... I think that was on 14 or 15 June. I was called to the Prime Minister's home at Nampeidai-machi and was strongly requested by Mr Kishi to mobilize the forces. The demonstrators massed outside the Prime Minister's residence were shouting 'Oppose the Security Treaty!' and 'Down with Kishi!' Despite this situation, however, I stated frankly that I did not think Eisenhower's visit warranted mobilization of the forces. For a moment Mr Kishi pathetically held his breath. He sat quietly, listening, his arms still folded. At last, he understood what I was trying to tell him.[6]

Akagi's resistance to the party hardliners brought sighs of relief from moderate elements. When Foreign Minister Fujiyama heard that Akagi had been able to persuade Kishi not to mobilize he hurried to congratulate him personally. 'I think Akagi did a tremendous thing', he notes in his memoirs.[7]

The Socialist and Communist leaders, too, tirelessly urged moderation. Like the liberals in the Conservative camp they understood the fragility of the postwar parliamentary system, the latent strength of the anti-democratic forces gathering on the wings of the political stage, the comparative ease with which popular anti-treaty organizations and the radical student movement had been infiltrated by the firebrands of the ultra-right. At the height of the crisis Miyamoto Kenji, secretary-

---

* And, perhaps, from a fate similar to that which befell neighbouring South Korea less than a year later.

general of the Communist Party, vigorously and effectively opposed plans by extremists to break into the Prime Minister's residence, seize Kishi, force his resignation and physically prevent ratification of the treaty. Miyamoto, whose attitudes bore comparison with those of his Italian counterpart Togliatti, argued that the party should take a longer perspective, consolidating the gains it had made after the disasters of the late 1940s, building up its electoral strength and reconstructing its popular image with a view to gaining power through the parliamentary process.[8] This strategy was to serve the Japanese Communists well in the following decades.

Nevertheless, the atmosphere in June 1960 was electric. The night before the treaty was to go into effect, the superintendent-general of the Metropolitan Police visited the Prime Minister with a warning that it would be impossible to guarantee the security of his residence. Kishi declared that he would not move elsewhere. If the Prime Minister's home could not be secured, no place in Japan was safe. Just then his younger brother Satō Eisaku came along, declaring grimly that they were both of them, perhaps, fated to die in the residence that night. Kishi replied that if that were to be so, it would be good if they died together.[9]

Yet neither the Prime Minister's life, nor that of any other Japanese political leader, was seriously endangered by the demonstrations organized by the Socialist and Communist parties, or the wild snake-dancing and rock-throwing of the radical students. The left was anxious, above all else, to preserve the postwar constitutional order. The real threat to representative institutions, as at all times in Japan's modern history, came from the extreme right, whose shadowy, labyrinthine organizations, suppressed during the occupation, had cautiously begun to reassert themselves, penetrating the political parties, the business community, the armed forces, the media and other centres of influence. On 14 July, Aramaki Taisuke, a well-known ultra-nationalist with a long prewar record, unsuccessfully attempted to assassinate Kishi (now viewed, because of his 'weakness', as a traitor to the ultra-nationalist cause) at a reception organized to celebrate Ikeda's victory in the party presidential election. Less than three months later, on 12 October, the secretary-general of the Japan Socialist Party, Asanuma Inejirō, was stabbed to death by Yamaguchi Otoya, a former member of the Great Japan Patriotic Party (Dai Nippon Aikoku Tō). In February 1961, another rightist assassin, also connected with the Great Japan Patriotic Party, broke into the home of the president of the Chūō Kōron publishing company, killing a maid and seriously injuring the president's wife. Then in December 1961 police uncovered a plot by former military officers and ultra-nationalist groups to assassinate Prime Minister Ikeda, physically eliminate several other members of his Cabinet and take over the government, reconstructing Japan on firm anti-Communist principles. The token sentences meted out to some of the figures involved in these incidents caused widespread popular outrage.[10]

The men and women who participated in the 1960 struggles were convinced that the Prime Minister was determined not simply to revise an unequal treaty but to further strengthen the Japanese-American military alliance, paving the way for constitutional revision, a greater degree of integration with United States global strategy and eventual dispatch of the Self Defence Forces overseas. Their assessment of the Prime Minister's intentions and the dangers inherent in a more intimate Japanese-American strategic relationship was probably correct. Their understanding of the nature of the new treaty and of the forces that had shaped it was not. Despite Kishi's rhetoric there were few important practical differences between the 1960 treaty and the 1951 arrangement. The new treaty was, in almost every respect, just as unequal as the old. Yet like the old treaty it did *not* require direct Japanese military participation in United States Far Eastern strategy. A careful study of the Japanese-American negotiations on treaty revision during the period 1958–60, the concomitant factional struggles in the Liberal Democratic Party, the views of the Foreign Ministry and the Defence Agency would suggest that the Prime Minister, despite his strong interest in a more militant anti-Communist alliance, had found it impossible to break with Yoshida's policy of a limited, passive, tactical association with the United States. Kishi was unable to negotiate a genuine bilateral military alliance with Washington, not so much because of opposition from the Socialist and Communist parties, but because of resistance from within the Liberal Democratic Party itself. However much they valued the political and economic relationship with the United States, a treaty involving closer Japanese-American military co-operation did not recommend itself to many of Kishi's conservative colleagues. To a far greater extent than they would have cared publicly to admit, their views of Japan's national interests in this matter coincided with those of the Opposition parties. The massive popular anti-treaty movement of 1959–60 thus strengthened the position of those Japanese Conservatives who, whatever they might say in the Diet, were convinced that Japan and the United States were different societies, with different cultural backgrounds, located in different parts of the world, facing different strategic problems and moving, ultimately, towards different destinies.

II The treaty[11]

On the surface of things, the Kishi government's claim that the 1960 treaty differed significantly from the 1951 agreement, establishing the framework for a more balanced and equitable relationship with the United States, had much to support it.

Certainly, the new treaty, like the old, was essentially a base lending agreement. The United States was granted facilities on Japanese territory for its land, sea and air forces which, as before, could be used both to 'contribute' to the defence of Japan and in pursuit of America's wider Far Eastern policies.[12] Yet the 1960 treaty had a definite time limit and could be abrogated by either party after ten years on twelve months' notice.[13] There were no formal provisions enabling Washington to intervene in Japan to suppress domestic disorders. Moreover, Japan was given the unequivocal promise of American protection against external attack that Dulles had refused to extend to Yoshida in 1951.

Article V of the 1960 treaty stated that

Each Party recognizes that an armed attack against either Party in the territories under the administration of Japan would be dangerous to its own peace and safety and declares that it would act to meet the common danger in accordance with its constitutional provisions and processes.

This formulation, while weaker than the NATO treaty, involved the United States in a commitment to Japan that differed little from the guarantees extended to its other Asian and Pacific allies. Conversely, it involved Japan, for the first time, in a formal commitment to contribute to the defence of American installations on its territory. An Agreed Minute initialled by Prime Minister Kishi and the United States Secretary of State Christian Herter implicitly excluded Okinawa and the Bonins from the area of mutual responsibility but established a basis for Japanese support for the 'welfare' of the islanders in the event of war.[14] The Kishi-Herter Exchanges of Notes recognized the continued validity of the 1951 Yoshida-Acheson notes on Japanese support for United Nations forces in Korea.[15] However, nothing in the new treaty required direct Japanese military support for South Korea or Japanese participation in regional security organizations.

Finally, Article IV of the new treaty, the Kishi-Herter Exchanges of Notes and the Kishi-Eisenhower Joint Communiqué established various provisions for Japanese-American consultation, apparently giving the government a degree of control over American dispositions, weapons and use of bases in Japan not enjoyed under the 1951 arrangement.[16]

According to Article IV of the new treaty:

> The Parties will consult together from time to time regarding the implementation of this Treaty, and, at the request of either Party, whenever the security of Japan or international peace and security in the Far East is threatened.

In the Kishi-Herter Exchanges of Notes it was agreed that

> Major changes in the deployment into Japan of United States armed forces, major changes in their equipment, and the use of facilities and areas in Japan as bases for military combat operations to be undertaken from Japan other than those conducted under Article V of the said Treaty, shall be the subjects of prior consultation with the Government of Japan.

Japanese government spokesman explained that the phrase 'major changes in their equipment' referred, among other things, to the hypothetical introduction of American nuclear weapons. As early as June 1955 Washington had assured the Japanese government that United States forces stationed in the archipelago were not equipped with nuclear arms. From February 1957 onwards, Japanese cabinets had publicly adopted the position that while neither the Constitution nor the security treaty gave them any influence over American actions they would do what they could to prevent the introduction of nuclear weapons. After 1960, Japanese governments consistently claimed that they were now in a position to veto any American requests to bring nuclear arms into Japan.*

---

* In December 1967, Prime Minister Satō Eisaku formalized Japan's policy towards all nuclear issues around the 'three non-nuclear principles' and the 'four nuclear policies'. According to the three non-nuclear principles, Japan would not manufacture, possess or permit the

Regarding Article IV and the Kishi-Herter Exchange of Notes, the Kishi-Eisenhower Joint Communiqué stated:

> In this connection the Prime Minister discussed with the President the question of prior consultation under the new treaty. The President assured him that the United States Government has no intention of acting in a manner contrary to the wishes of the Japanese Government with respect to matters involving prior consultation under the treaty

Undoubtedly, the ten-year time limit and the new provisions governing abrogation of the treaty were real and significant changes. Yet it seems highly probable that the three other major changes – the enunciation of Washington's duty to protect Japan and of Japan's obligations to protect American bases on its territory, the removal of clauses enabling the United States to intervene to suppress internal disorders and the various arrangements for Japanese-American consultation – were either meaningless or did not represent genuine innovations.

It will be recalled that in Yoshida's view the size and importance of American military installations in Japan, was, in itself, a sufficient guarantee of American protection for as long as Japan wanted it. In any case, Yoshida was far from convinced that Japan actually faced any serious external threat. He had quite cheerfully sacrificed the security of a written guarantee in order to avoid large-scale rearmament and direct involvement in any American-sponsored regional alliance system. At the same time, the close links forged in the 1950s between the Self Defence Forces and United States forces in Japan, in particular the provisions of Article 24 of the 1952 Administrative Agreement and the ties between the Air Self Defence Force and the American Fifth Air Force under the 1959 Matsumae-Burns agreement, made it virtually inevitable that Japan would give armed support to the United States in the event of an attack on American facilities in its territory. Article V of the new treaty can thus be regarded as merely formalizing arrangements already in existence.

While the growing strength of the Self Defence Forces made American intervention to suppress 'large-scale internal riots and disturbances' highly improbable, the 1960 treaty, despite appearances to the contrary, did, in fact, leave a way open for such intervention. In the event of internal insurrection either party could presumably have requested consultations under Article IV, raising the matter as a question affecting 'the security of Japan or international peace and security in the Far East'. The 'armed attack' of Article V was not necessarily armed attack from without. Government spokesmen usually claimed that the 'armed attack' mentioned in the new treaty was the same as that referred to in the NATO treaty. This was highly signific-

entry of nuclear weapons. The four nuclear policies committed Japan to adhere to the three non-nuclear principles, to promote nuclear disarmament, to advance the peaceful uses of nuclear energy and to rely on the American nuclear deterrent for protection against 'international nuclear threats'. The Japanese government's opposition to the entry of United States nuclear weapons, apparently strengthened by the provisions of the 1960 security treaty, thus came to be closely linked to its policies on a wide range of nuclear issues, including the question of the development of an independent deterrent.

ant. On 7 May 1960 the director of the Foreign Ministry Treaties Bureau told the House of Representatives Security Treaty Committee that while the NATO treaty did not provide for joint military action against 'ordinary [domestic] upheavals' it did go into force in case of 'revolutionary uprisings' and 'attacks by armed groups instigated from outside'. If this represented the government's official interpretation, the new treaty theoretically permitted exactly the same kind of American military intervention under exactly the same circumstances as provided in the 1951 agreement.[17]

The most problematical features of the 1960 treaty and its concomitant understandings were the provisions for Japanese-American consultation. As we have seen, two kinds of consultation were established. Article IV of the treaty itself provided for periodic consultation on the implementation of the agreement and, at times of crisis, on questions affecting the security of Japan or the Far East. The United States was not bound to follow Japanese recommendations in either instance. In contrast, the Kishi-Herter Exchanges of Notes and the Kishi-Eisenhower Joint Communiqué implicitly committed the United States to obtaining Japan's prior consent for major changes in the deployment of its forces into Japan, major changes in their equipment and the use of Japanese bases for combat operations outside Japan. No prior consultations were necessary, it should be noted, if these changes or operations were undertaken to protect Japan itself, or American bases in Japan, from direct, external attack.

The fact that the provisions for prior consultation have never been invoked, either by Japan or the United States, is in itself of very great significance.[18] It is, perhaps, idle to speculate about what would happen if they were invoked. The evidence that is publicly available, however, would suggest that Japan's ability to exert any influence over the deployment of United States forces in its territory, on the character of their equipment, or on their operations beyond Japan, let alone on the general development of American Far Eastern policy, has been, from the beginning, negligible. The 1960 security treaty, whatever the intention of those who negotiated it, did not improve the Japanese position in any way.

President Richard Nixon's decision to initiate a policy of *détente* with the People's Republic of China in 1971, an event that had a far-reaching impact on the entire Japanese-American relationship, was made without any prior consultations with the Japanese government. Prime Minister Satō Eisaku's Cabinet, which, contrary to the better judgement of some of its members, had vigorously supported the containment of China, was told of the change in Washington's policy only after Dr Kissinger had left Peking. Certainly, it is debatable whether the terms of the 1960 treaty, interpreted in a strictly legalistic fashion, actually *obliged* the United States to consult with Japan about such matters. Yet the *spirit* of the treaty certainly did, and the long-term effectiveness of alliances depends, to a large extent, on the feelings of trust and mutual confidence entertained by the parties involved in them. In this context, the shock and disillusionment of Satō and his colleagues was understandable. (See Chapter XI.)

In May 1981, moreover, in an exclusive interview with the *Mainichi Shimbun*, Professor Edwin O. Reischauer, the former United States ambassador to Japan, revealed that a secret verbal agreement, concluded at the time of the 1960 security treaty negotiations, had permitted Washington to bring nuclear weapons freely in and out of its bases on the archipelago. This corroborated earlier assertions by Admiral Gene Laroque (United States Navy, retired), and Daniel Ellsberg, among others, that American nuclear weapons had been stored in, or had passed through, Japan at various times in the postwar period, the formal provisions of the 1960 security treaty notwithstanding.[19] Despite strenuous denials by the then Japanese Prime Minister Suzuki Zenkō and former Foreign Minister Fujiyama Aiichirō,[20] the Japanese government's claims that the 1960 security treaty enabled it to exclude United States nuclear weapons from the territories under its administration, and that it effectively exercised this right, appear to have been without foundation.

Next, what of the government's ability to influence American use of bases for combat operations outside Japan but not directly connected with the defence of the home archipelago from external aggression?

Setting aside the difficult questions of whether meaningful prior consultations could always be arranged in the context of modern warfare, and of whether the established links between the United States Fifth Air Force and the Air Self Defence forces might not, through a process of chain reaction, involve Japan almost instantaneously in conflicts originating in Korea or other areas of the western Pacific, without prior consultations ever being invoked, two points should be noted.[21]

First, as the former Japanese ambassador to the United Kingdom (and previously to Australia), Nishi Haruhiko, pointed out at the time:

> It is simply not possible for Japan to stand on the same power level and negotiate with the United States ... it is easy to imagine situations where Japan would be obliged to follow the United States.

The main reason for this was that

> Japan has no access to independent military intelligence with which it could counter [the contentions] of the United States side, and, putting aside all questions of forms and theories, what will in fact happen [at prior consultations] is that Japan will, in the end, perhaps reluctantly, defer to the views of the Americans.[22]

Second, the Japanese interpretation of the treaty left numerous loopholes enabling United States forces to take action outside Japan without prior consultations being invoked. It is difficult to escape the conclusion that this was done deliberately. During the Diet debates preceding ratification of the treaty, government spokesmen made it clear that

1) the 'United States armed forces' referred to in the treaty and subject to prior consultations were 'those forces stationed in Japan, using Japanese bases and facilities'. They were thus distinct from 'forces stationed in Japan for short periods for other objectives, or forces passing through Japan'.[23] It was thus possible for forces usually stationed in other areas to stop over briefly in Japan *en*

route to military combat operations, in other parts of the world, without the right of prior consultations being invoked.

2)   the departure of American forces stationed in Japan for other areas, regardless of the size of the transfer, could not become subject to prior consultations unless the forces were bound for an actual area of combat. On 4 May 1960 the director of the Legislative Bureau explained that even this latter provision might be over-come simply by altering the posting of the forces prior to their departure.

> If, when the forces set out from Japan, they have been invested with the responsibility of engaging in military combat operations, they will become the objects of prior consultation, even if (for example) they refuel at Okinawa. However, if they change their posting to Okinawa or Taiwan, then leave, there is no need for Japan to say anything. After the milit-ary combat operations are over, these forces will be subject to prior consultations, in another sense, if they change their posting once again to Japan.[24]

It is thus difficult to see what effect Japanese protestations could have had on a United States committed to certain objectives in Korea, the Taiwan Straits, South-East Asia, or even more distant areas, defined without reference to Japanese interests, and determined to pursue them to the logical conclusion. It was perhaps for these reasons that Kusumi Tadao, chairman of the Okinawa Base Problems Research Council (Okinawa Kichi Mondai Kenkyū Kai) and one of Prime Minister Satō Eisaku's closest private defence advisers, told the *Nihon Keizai Shimbun* in 1969 that

> if you read the security treaty carefully you will see that it does not say that all United States actions can be checked, even if prior consultations are held. Some people consider that prior consultations under the security treaty provide a check against involvement in war. However, the check is not provided by prior consultations. Rather, the security treaty itself provides the vital check preventing the Far East from being drawn into a great war.[25]

In short, the differences between the first and second security treaties were inconse-quential. For this reason it is difficult to escape the conclusion that the treaty Prime Minister Kishi eventually signed in January 1960 was *not* the treaty he had set out to negotiate in the summer of 1957.

III   The negotiations

(i)   *Prime Minister Kishi Nobusuke accepts Washington's conditions for treaty revision, February 1957–August 1958*

The United States had made it clear at the Shigemitsu-Dulles talks in August 1955 that Japan's acceptance of military commitments for 'the preservation of inter-national peace and security in the Western Pacific' was an essential precondition for renegotiation of the 1951 security treaty. It had also been apparent that the United States assumed such commitments would involve dispatch of the Self Defence Forces overseas. The strong and unambiguously negative Japanese reaction to the

Shigemitsu-Dulles Joint Communiqué did not alter Washington's attitude (see Chapter IV).

Kishi Nobusuke's long-standing interest in revision of the 1951 agreement, a more equal Japanese-American relationship and Japan's assumption of an active regional military role have already been discussed (see Chapter V). Shortly after taking office in February 1957 Kishi embarked on a highly symbolic tour of South-East Asia and Oceania. He formally raised the question of treaty revision in June, at the time of his first visit to Washington.

> I explained that the development of sound, long-term, friendly ties between Japan and the United States required a relationship based on the principle of equality, even though the power of the two countries was vastly different. Both President Eisenhower and the Secretary of State Mr Dulles appreciated this. We incorporated these sentiments into the Joint Communiqué. I felt that now this splendid new era in Japanese-American relations had been inaugurated, it was necessary to revise what was, without any doubt, an extremely unequal treaty ... Two years earlier, when Shigemitsu had raised the subject, Dulles had opposed revision of the treaty on the grounds that it was premature, that Japan was not yet strong enough. But when I approached him he agreed completely.[26]

During these discussions, Japan and the United States agreed to set up a joint committee, composed of the Japanese Foreign Minister, the director-general of the Defence Agency, the commander-in-chief of American forces in the Pacific and the American ambassador to Japan, to study the question in detail. The committee met for a year, examined a number of possibilities and produced a report generally favourable to the concept of revision.[27]

Kishi persuaded Fujiyama Aiichirō to enter his Cabinet as Foreign Minister in the summer of 1957. Fujiyama, too, was attracted by the idea of negotiating a new treaty. As soon as the May 1958 general elections had secured him a seat in the Diet he decided that revision of the 1951 agreement would be his principal task as Foreign Minister.

> As Foreign Minister I could not help but think that the treaty was a preposterously unequal one, and that it was most peculiar for Japan, seven years after independence, to be in the same situation as it was under the occupation. That is to say, my intention in proceeding with revision of the security treaty was, if I may employ words we often used at the time, to correct occupation policy and occupation administration. I had absolutely no idea that public opinion would later become so divided.[28]

Despite their long personal association it is by no means clear that Kishi and Fujiyama held the same views either about the place of the Japanese American relationship in Japan's diplomacy or the shape of the new treaty. 'I don't quite know what Mr Kishi meant by a new treaty', Fujiyama confessed many years later, when questioned on this matter by the present writer.[29] Nevertheless, shortly after the general elections, the two men agreed to begin serious study of revision.[30] In July 1958, after the formation of Kishi's second Cabinet, Fujiyama raised the subject at a conference of Japanese ambassadors, taking particular care to hear the views of Asakai Kōichirō, ambassador to the United States, and Ōno Katsumi, ambassador to Great

Britain. On Fujiyama's instructions, Asakai then informed Washington of the Japanese government's intention to request renegotiation of the 1951 treaty. Douglas MacArthur II subsequently visited Fujiyama and explained that, in the American view, revision could take one of three forms. Japan and the United States could

1) conclude a completely new treaty,

2) amend the existing treaty,

3) retain the existing treaty, adding to it a new explanatory appendix.[31]

Fujiyama discussed these alternatives with the Prime Minister. Then, on 1 August 1958, Kishi, Fujiyama and MacArthur met in the Foreign Minister's official residence to study the question further. MacArthur again outlined American thinking on the three alternative modes of revision. The Prime Minister replied, unhesitatingly, that he wished to negotiate a completely new treaty. MacArthur promised to return to Washington at once and discuss the matter with Secretary of State Dulles.[32]

On 25 August, Kishi, Fujiyama, Kawashima Shōjirō (secretary-general of the Liberal Democratic Party) and Kōno Ichirō (chief of the party's General Affairs Bureau) met to consider the forthcoming negotiations.[33] The concrete details of the proposed new treaty were not examined at this meeting. On 29 August Fujiyama again talked with MacArthur and reached agreement on a number of procedural matters.[34] The intention of both parties to renegotiate the 1951 treaty was made public on 11 September 1958, after Fujiyama, Ambassador Asakai and Mori Haruki, director of the Foreign Ministry's North American Bureau, met with Dulles in New York.[35]

Both Kishi[36] and Fujiyama have insisted that they had no intention of concluding a treaty that would conflict with Article 9 of the Constitution or involve overseas service for the Self Defence Forces. Even the United States, Fujiyama maintains, did 'not once ... raise the question of overseas service for the Self Defence Forces'[37] during the negotiations. These protestations cannot necessarily be taken at face value. Asakai, who served as ambassador to the United States from 1958 to 1964 and played a central role in the revision negotiations, recalled that all issues in Japanese-American relations during these years remained subordinate to America's desire to fit Japan more firmly into its Asian grand strategy. This strategy, Asakai maintained, continued to envisage establishment of an East Asian alliance system, modelled on NATO and incorporating Japan, South Korea, Taiwan and, perhaps, some other Western Pacific countries.[38] When Secretary of State Dulles met with Fujiyama, Asakai and Mori on 11 September 1958 he complained, as at the time of his talks with Shigemitsu in August 1955, that 'under the present treaty Japan is not obliged to do the slightest thing to defend us in the case that the American continent is attacked. There are many things that we think are unequal and one-sided too.'[39] Fujiyama's own account of the negotiations reveals that the United States, as as the time of the Ikeda-Robertson talks, was anxious to see the text of the Vandenburg

Resolution incorporated into the revised treaty.[40] This can only be interpreted as revealing a continued interest in committing Japanese forces for service overseas. It is thus fairly reasonable to assume that when Kishi proposed to MacArthur that Japan and the United States conclude a completely new treaty, he realized he was embarking on a course of action which would commit Japan to contribute actively to 'the preservation of international peace and security in the Western Pacific', in the sense that this had been understood by Washington since the Yoshida-Dulles talks of 1951. In this way he prepared to challenge both the established policies of his own party and the mainstream of national opinion.

Political developments in Japan during the summer of 1958 might easily have suggested that opposition to more complete integration into the United States global alliance system was declining. The May 1958 general elections, while not completely reversing the drift away from the Conservatives and towards the Socialists, had at least stabilized the situation. The Liberal Democrats won a total of 287 seats in the House of Representatives, only three less than the number they had held before dissolution. The Socialists gained only eight seats, bringing their total to 166. Of the 12 independents elected, ten were associated with the Liberal Democrats and only two with the Socialists.[41] Analysts unfamiliar with the complexities of Japanese politics might have interpreted these trends to mean that popular unease about the United States alliance, opposition to rearmament, hostility to overseas service and interest in neutralist policies had somewhat abated. Newspapers in the United States and Great Britain optimistically predicted the beginning of a new era of 'stable government' in Japan.[42]

At the same time, the election consolidated Kishi's own factional base. The Ishibashi Cabinet, in which Kishi had served as Foreign Minister, had been founded on an alliance of the Ikeda, Ishibashi, Ishii and Miki-Matsumura factions, with Kishi, Kōno, Ōno and Satō forming the dissident group. Kishi's accession as Prime Minister had meant that the roles of the dominant and dissident factions had been to some extent reversed. Nevertheless, Kishi's first Cabinet had been largely inherited from Ishibashi. The new Prime Minister had not always been in a position to impose his views.[43] Kishi's first Cabinet reorganization, announced on 10 July 1957, shortly after his visit to Washington, had strengthened his hand considerably. Fujiyama Aiichirō had been brought in as Foreign Minister. Akagi Munenori became Minister for Agriculture. Five men from the Kōno faction, including the redoubtable Kōno Ichirō himself, had also been given positions. At the same time, Tanaka Kakuei, from the Satō faction, had been appointed Minister for Posts and Telegraphs. Even so, the dissident factions had still maintained a strong position.[44] After the 1958 general election the situation changed dramatically. The second Kishi Cabinet, details of which were announced on 12 June, was overwhelmingly dominated by the Prime Minister and his supporters. Kishi had also moved to tilt the power balance within the Cabinet away from Kōno in favour of his own followers and those of his brother Satō Eisaku. The Prime Minister's faction retained its grip on the Ministry of Foreign Affairs (Fujiyama Aiichirō) and the Ministry of Agriculture (Miura Kunio). In addition, Kishi appointed Akagi Munenori as director-general of the Defence Agency and Endō Saburō as Minister for Construction. Satō Eisaku was brought into the Cabinet as Minister for Finance. Satō's supporters were also installed in the Ministry of Justice (Aichi Kiichi) and in Posts and Telegraphs (Terao Yutaka). Ikeda was present as Minister without Portfolio. Miki was appointed director of the Economic Planning Agency. Nadao Hirokichi, from the Ishii faction, which had now gravitated to a neutral position, became Minister for Education. One member of the Kōno faction and one of Ōno's supporters also received Cabinet posts. Ishibashi and his supporters were totally excluded.[45] Kishi's distribution of posts in the Liberal Democratic Party followed a similar pattern.[46] The Prime Minister's success in installing his supporters in vital Cabinet and party posts doubtless convinced him that opposition to his policies would be easily contained.

(ii)　The Liberal Democratic Party and bureaucracy react to Prime Minister Kishi's Démarche

If Kishi imagined that Japanese electoral trends and his redistribution of party and Cabinet posts had opened another era of 'one man rule', permitting the development of a more active Japanese-American strategic partnership, he was gravely mistaken. The mere suspicion that the Prime Minister intended to negotiate a genuine, mutual defence treaty with the United States, involving, perhaps, provisions for the eventual dispatch of Japanese forces overseas, provoked a bitterly hostile reaction within the Liberal Democratic Party.

From early September 1958 until the end of November, almost all factions in the party, both dominant and dissident, encouraged from behind the scenes by former Prime Minister Yoshida Shigeru, and supported by the Foreign Ministry and the Defence Agency, exerted intense pressure, through a variety of channels, to dissuade the Prime Minister from pursuing courses of action that could result in wider Japanese political and military commitments. This campaign reached its climax just as the first round of formal Japanese-American negotiations on the shape of the new treaty began, in the greatest secrecy, in the Teikoku Hotel.

Towards the end of November 1958, with the apparent success of the Conservative opposition in forcing the government to realize that any agreement linking Japan more closely to the United States would be totally unacceptable, interest turned to the details of the proposed new treaty. In the wake of the party crisis over the Police Duties Performance Bill (October–November 1958) this provided a fertile field for factional manoeuvre and intrigue. The result of this process was that, whatever the Prime Minister's original intentions, Japan and the United States were left with no alternative but to conclude a treaty that differed little, in substance, from the 1951 arrangement.

On 4 September 1958, the day Foreign Minister Fujiyama left for Washington for preliminary discussions with the United States, a group of twenty-two Liberal Democratic Party politicians from the dissident factions gathered at the Grand Hotel in Nagatamachi to establish a Diplomatic Problems Research Council (Gaikō

Mondai Kenkyū Kai). The sponsors of the council at once declared themselves hostile to the Prime Minister's plans for treaty revision.[47] The first general meeting of the council, attended by representatives of the Ikeda, Ishibashi, Ishii and Miki-Matsumura factions, was held two weeks later, after the contents of Fujiyama's talks with Dulles had become known through the press and other channels. Ikeda's presence was widely, and correctly, taken to mean that Yoshida took a dim view of the government's plans. At the meeting, strong opposition was voiced to any treaty involving the possibility of more active Japanese participation in American Far Eastern strategy.[48]

Uneasiness about the government's intentions was not confined to the dissident factions. On 2 September, two days before Fujiyama left for the United States, the Foreign Affairs Research Council (Gaikō Chōsa Kai), a formal organ of the party's Policy Affairs Research Council, and very much under the influence of the dominant factions,[49] announced that while 'ideally' the 1951 treaty should be revised, as 'an actual question' the time was 'not yet ripe for revision'. It would therefore be 'inappropriate' for Fujiyama to raise the matter during his talks with Dulles and other American officials. The main source of anxiety appears to have been the possibility of involvement in wider military commitments at a time when the offshore islands crisis had brought about a serious escalation in Sino-American tension. As far as the offshore islands were concerned, the council recommended that American views should be 'heard' but that a 'cautious approach should be adopted'.[50]

At another meeting, on 18 September, the council closely questioned the director of the Foreign Ministry's North American Bureau, Mr Tanaka. Tanaka also adopted a 'cautious' attitude towards a treaty revision. The council, while declaring its support for the 'rationalization' of certain features of the 1951 agreement, endorsed his stand. Alarm at the possibility of overseas service for Japanese troops was also expressed at this meeting.[51] On 24 September the Foreign Affairs Research Council, after hearing the testimony of Yoshida's old protégé, General Hayashi Keizō, chairman of the Joint Staff Council, again drew attention to its 'reservations' on treaty revision.[52] General Hayashi's comments at this meeting were not revealed to the press. Yet since the Defence Agency was later reluctant to have Okinawa and the Bonins included in the area of joint responsibility under the new agreement, on the grounds that Japanese military strength was 'insufficient' to undertake 'additional burdens', it can be assumed that the Chief of Staff would have opposed any suggestion of a genuine mutual defence treaty.

Fujiyama later came to believe that Yoshida had been behind most of the Conservative opposition to the new treaty. Yoshida, the Foreign Minister was convinced, opposed the idea of a new agreement simply because he was senile, wilful and cantankerous, believing no one could do anything better than he could.[53] Yoshida's hostility to Kishi's plans was undoubtedly sustained and ferocious. Yet his position was the logical outcome of his long-range strategic judgement. Yoshida had, from the very beginning, opposed any arrangement linking Japan too closely to the United States Far Eastern alliance system. In his view, the 1951 treaty had been a temporary arrangement, providing Japan with a breathing space to reconstruct its political system, rebuild its economy and lay the foundations for re-emergence as an independent great power. He may well have believed that an obviously unequal arrangement, externally imposed, would be easier to jettison, at the appropriate time, than one which had some appearance of mutuality. That is to say, a bad treaty was more compatible with Japan's long-term interests than a good one. Although Yoshida's public support for the American alliance was still unwavering, he had, by September 1958, emerged as an advocate of an independent Japanese nuclear deterrent.[54] Other Conservatives from the old Konoye circle, too, were moving towards broadly similar positions.[55] Yoshida was also, at this stage, giving serious thought to his long-term projects for the development of relations with China. Perhaps he had heard, through private channels, that the People's Republic had recently rejected Soviet overtures for closer military co-operation in the Far East.[56] In any case, when Fujiyama visited him at Ōiso in the autumn of 1958 the old man was busily thinking up schemes to lure Peking away from its alliance with the Soviet Union. He even asked the Foreign Minister if it would not be possible for Japan to set up a Consulate-General in Shanghai.[57]

After Fujiyama's return from the United States on 26 September 1958 strenuous attempts were made to win over party opinion. On 30 September, Kishi and Fujiyama discussed their plans with Matsumura Kenzō. On 2 October the two leaders conferred with Ishii Mitsujirō and Ashida Hitoshi. On the afternoon of 2 October, Fujiyama addressed the Foreign Affairs Research Council and the Diplomatic Section of the Policy Affairs Research Council.[58] These efforts apparently met with little success. A few days later, on 7 October, a meeting of Liberal Democratic Party members of both Houses, while expressing 'understanding' of Kishi's efforts to have the treaty revised, resolved that the appropriate organs of the party should have the final word on the shape of the agreement. It was noted at this meeting that the Foreign Minister did not stand up well to close questioning about the character of the proposed treaty. When Kawasaki Hideji asked Fujiyama specifically whether revision could lead to dispatch of the Self Defence Forces overseas, Fujiyama apparently avoided a direct reply, declaring merely that the new treaty would 'tend to strengthen Japanese-American ties even further'.[59]

(iii)   The impact of the Police Duties Performance Bill

On 8 October 1958 Prime Minister Kishi's government, to the surprise of some of its most senior ministers, presented the Diet with a bill to revise the Police Duties Performance Law.[60] The proposed legislation would have significantly extended police powers. Among the Opposition parties and large sections of the general public it was believed that this legislation was closely linked to the question of treaty revision. A powerful, centralized police force, with wider powers of search, interrogation and arrest, was to emasculate the influence of the Socialist and Communist parties, the trade unions, the peace movement and the mass media, facilitating conclusion of a new and more aggressive military alliance with the United States, paving the way for changes in the educational system, constitutional revision and, eventually, overseas service for Japanese troops.[61]

The Opposition parties, the trade unions, the mass media and an impressive array of citizens groups mounted a determined campaign against the Bill. Throughout October and November 1958 the Diet was paralysed, the country torn by strikes and demonstrations.

The Police Duties Performance Bill aggravated the divisions within the Liberal Democratic Party. Many Conservatives were alarmed by the implications of the proposed legislation for the future of parliamentary government. Others saw an opportunity to advance personal and factional interests. The extent of the opposition eventually forced Kishi to shelve his plans. Nevertheless, by the end of 1958, a major factional realignment had taken place. Ikeda Hayato, Miki Takeo and Nadao Hirokichi (Ishii faction) had all resigned from the Cabinet. Ōno Bamboku was wavering in his support. The conflict of interests among the Prime Minister's opponents was too great to prevent his victory in the January 1959 party presidential elections. Nevertheless, his position within the Liberal Democratic Party became more and more precarious during the last months of 1958.

(iv)   The impact of Conservative party factional-policy conflicts on the Japanese-American negotiations, October 1958–January 1959

The groundswell of opposition from within the Liberal Democratic Party to any suggestion of more active military co-operation with the United States, the factional struggles touched off by the Police Duties Performance Bill, then the gathering momentum of the popular anti-treaty movement exerted considerable influence on the Japanese-American negotiations that began in the Teikoku Hotel on 4 October 1958 and continued, over fourteen or fifteen sessions, until basic agreement on the shape of the new treaty was reached in February 1959. Prime Minister Kishi, however much he believed that public opinion should be led, not followed, could not risk totally isolating himself within the party. He therefore gradually retreated from his original position. Similarly, the United States, whatever Secretary of State Dulles may have desired, could not risk alienating its strongest supporters in Japan. Throughout the postwar period, American officials, irritated by Japanese dilatoriness, indecision and vacillation, have frequently been tempted to ride roughshod over their trans-Pacific ally. The best way to deal with Japan, it has been thought, is to present its government with a series of irreversible *faits accomplis*. In Douglas MacArthur II Washington enjoyed the services of a far-sighted and skilful diplomat who understood, in the Japanese context, what was possible and what was not. MacArthur showed himself, throughout the negotiations, unusually sensitive to Japanese opinion. He struggled hard to explain the Japanese situation to the more intransigent elements in Washington. He did not hesitate to approach President Eisenhower personally in the hope of obtaining decisions that would protect United States perceived interests and at the same time accord with Japanese realities.[62]

(a)   The duration of the treaty and the area of joint responsibility

Agreement was quickly reached on the establishment of a ten-year time limit for the new treaty.[63] The question of the area of joint responsibility was not so easily settled. While both Kishi and Fujiyama deny that the United States formally requested Japan to commit itself to wider military responsibilities at this time, other authoritative accounts suggest that Washington at first proposed an agreement applicable to the entire Western Pacific region, as far south as Guam. Fujiyama, stressing the limitations placed upon Japan by its Constitution, declined to consider this proposal.[64] Shortly afterwards Kishi, too, appreciating the strength of the resistance in the party and the nation, declared himself opposed to a mutual security treaty covering the western Pacific.[65] As far as one can judge from the published record, the idea, once firmly rejected by the Japanese side, was not raised again during the course of the negotiations, although the United States did argue for inclusion of some reference to the Vandenberg Resolution in the revised agreement. Since this could have been taken as committing the Self Defence Forces to service overseas, the Japanese side would only consent to its inclusion if appropriate references to the Constitution were also made (Article III).[66]

The Prime Minister appeared, for a time, interested in including Okinawa and the Bonins within the sphere of joint military responsibility. This proposal meant, in fact, that the Self Defence Forces would be responsible for the protection of United States conventional and nuclear strike forces stationed on these islands. On 23 October Kishi told the House of Representatives Cabinet Committee that 'constitutionally' there would be no objection to joint Japanese-American defence of Okinawa. Indeed, the extension of Japanese military responsibilities to the islands under the terms of the new treaty 'should be interpreted as a partial restoration of administrative rights'.[67]

These remarks provoked strong reactions both from the Liberal Democratic Party and from the Defence Agency. Foreign Minister Fujiyama himself did not believe it would be wise to include the islands within the scope of the treaty.[68] Miki, Matsumura and Ishibashi, too, opposed inclusion of the islands on the grounds that this would increase the risk of confrontation with the Soviet Union and China.[69] Then, on 31 October, the director-general of the Defence Agency told the press that the agency was 'not enthusiastic' about the Prime Minister's proposals. Japan's existing defence capability was inadequate even for the defence of the homeland. Responsibilities extending beyond the four main islands would lead to greater military expenditure. The necessary funds were not available. Moreover, since the United States treaties with South Korea and Taiwan also covered the defence of Okinawa, incorporation of the islands into a new Japanese-American security treaty would be tantamount to the establishment of a NATO-type alliance.[70]

Prime Minister Kishi's original position was thus rapidly eroded. By 3 December, within a week of his initial pronouncement, he had reluctantly come to agree that it would be prudent to exclude Okinawa and the Bonins from the area of joint responsibility.[71]

No sooner had this decision been taken than Kōno Ichirō declared that in his view

Okinawa and the Bonins *should* be included in the treaty area.[72] He stressed, however, that Japan should have no actual obligation to defend the islands until full administrative rights had been returned. There was thus little practical difference between Kōno's position and that of groups opposed to inclusion of the islands. As Chief Cabinet Secretary Fukuda told a Nagoya audience on 1 February 'no one' in the party considered Japan should *actually* be responsible for the defence of Okinawa. 'I'he problem was merely one of 'expression'.[73]

Nevertheless, Kōno's stand had important consequences. The Police Duties Performance Bill controversy had weakened Kishi's control over the party. Kōno had been critical of the Prime Minister's handling of the crisis. He had resented Kishi's attempts to circumscribe his influence in the June 1958 Cabinet reshuffle and had subsequently begun to act with considerable independence. Yet, unlike Ikeda, Miki and Ishii, he had not yet broken with the dominant coalition. Because of this Kishi became, from the autumn of 1958, increasingly dependent on Kōno's support. The Prime Minister's victory in the January 1959 party presidential elections would probably have been impossible without Kōno's assistance and advice.[74] After the election, too, Kishi continued to rely on Kōno.

This made it impossible for the Prime Minister to disregard Kōno's views, either on Okinawa and the Bonins, or on other aspects of the new treaty. Washington, alarmed by the mounting popular opposition to the negotiations and aware of Kishi's delicate position, probably judged it better to take a neutral stand on this issue. Talks with the United States and adjustment of opinion within the party continued through the spring of 1959. Foreign Minister Fujiyama's statements on Okinawa became more and more equivocal, moving gradually, albeit ambiguously, towards the Kōno position. The draft treaty drawn up by Fujiyama and approved by Cabinet on 9 April stated vaguely that the new arrangement should be applicable to 'all Japanese territory' (*Nihon zen ryōchi*).[75] Basic agreement with the United States on the text of the new treaty seems to have been reached by the end of May 1959, just before the House of Councillors election. During the final stages of these negotiations it was decided to limit the treaty specifically to 'territories under the administration of Japan' (in accordance with majority opinion in the party) but to exchange notes clarifying that Okinawa and the Bonins *were* Japanese territory and would be incorporated into the treaty after the return of administrative rights.[76] This formula, coinciding with the private view of the Foreign Minister himself, and reflecting the factional balance within the Liberal Democratic Party between the Police Duties Performance Bill crisis and the 1959 House of Councillors election, was eventually incorporated into the treaty signed in January 1960.

(b) The operational range of United States forces in Japan – the scope of the 'Far East'
Conservative Party factional-policy conflict, the attitude of the Opposition and an extraordinarily unprofessional approach to the negotiations with the United States were responsible for the government's continually shifting views about the range within which American forces stationed in Japan would be free to operate. The uncertainties surrounding the meaning of the term 'Far East', as employed in Article

VI of the treaty, had the gravest implications for every aspect of Japan's foreign and defence policies.

On 10 November 1959, towards the end of the first stage of the negotiations with the United States, Fujiyama provoked a nation-wide outcry when he defined the 'Far East', under Article VI, to include coastal China and parts of Siberia. Both the Opposition and important groups within the Liberal Democratic Party were aghast at the possibilities raised by this definition. On 8 February 1960, after two months of turmoil within the government, a 'Unified View' was announced, defining the 'Far East' as the area centring on Japan, north of the Philippines, including South Korea, Quemoy, Matsu, the southern Kuriles, Shibomai and Hakotan (claimed by Japan) but excluding continental China and Siberia.[77] This definition can be seen as representing a compromise between the minimum demands of the United States on the one hand, and the views of Kōno, Miki, Matsumura, Ishibashi and Fujiyama himself on the other. Nevertheless, government explanations of the Unified View remained evasive. On 10 February 1960 for example, the Prime Minister told the Diet that while the whole of North Korea was not included in the scope of the Far East, it was impossible to say whether the boundary between North and South Korea would always remain stationary.[78] After heated debate, both inside and outside the Diet, the government retreated to the position that the Far East was intrinsically a 'vague and abstract concept'. It was 'not appropriate' to discuss which areas were included and which were not.[79]

The government would have spared itself a great deal of trouble if it had thought more carefully about this vital issue, prepared a negotiating position in accordance with its perceptions of Japanese national interests and attempted to unify opinion within the party before the talks with the United States began.

According to Fujiyama's own testimony:

> It was only after the security treaty debate in the Diet had intensified that we actually sat down with the Americans in front of a map and thought about the concept of the Far East. At the time military interest was centred on the Korean peninsula and the Taiwan Straits. The Americans, however, were most interested in whether Vietnam could be included or not. From the beginning, the Japanese side was of the opinion that Vietnam, which we regarded as the tinder-box of Asia, should not be included within the scope of the Far East. For this reason the Far East came to be defined as the area around Japan, north of the Philippines.[80]

(c) A Japanese right of veto over American actions

Party opinion was unable to ensure that the new treaty gave Japan unequivocal right of veto at prior consultations. Kōno, in particular, insisted that Japan ought to be able to approve or reject American actions under Article VI on a case-by-case basis.[81] His views were shared by many in the Conservative camp. Yet Kōno, powerful, tough and shrewd as he was, proved no match for the Pentagon.[82] Fujiyama recalls that the United States Defence Department tenaciously resisted the inclusion of any form of prior consultations clause in the new treaty. Analysis of the realities of the 1960 agreement would suggest that the Pentagon had its way.

(d) American military intervention to suppress Japanese internal disturbances

The United States indicated, from the beginning, that it would have no objections to removing the clause permitting its intervention in cases of 'large-scale internal riots and disturbances'.[83] Kishi, Fujiyama, Kōno Ichirō and others were all determined to abolish this clause, regarding it as incompatible with Japan's status as an independent nation. Others hesitated. For a surprisingly large number of Japanese Conservatives, nationalist sentiment remained subordinate to anti-Communism and the desire for independent great power status was emasculated by the fear of uncontrollable domestic upheaval. Prince Konoye's ghost continued to haunt the inner sanctums of the party. The draft treaty shown by Fujiyama to Kishi, Fukuda and Akagi on 18 February 1959, and drawn up on the basis of the negotiations with the United States, contained no provisions for external intervention in time of crisis.[84] Doubts about removing the 'internal riots' clause were first openly expressed at a combined meeting of the Liberal Democratic Party's Foreign Affairs Research Council and the Diplomatic and Defence Sections of the Policy Affairs Research Council on 19 February 1959, the day after Fujiyama released his draft.[85] Two days later, on 21 February, the director-general of the Defence Agency called on Fujiyama and urged that provisions permitting Japan to request American military assistance in cases of 'large-scale indirect aggression supported by a foreign power' be included in the new treaty. Fujiyama was non-committal about leaving the provisions in writing but eventually agreed that even if the old clause were eliminated some avenue for obtaining American assistance might be left open.[86] On 3 April the Liberal Democratic Party Executive Council also expressed opposition to plans to eliminate the clause. Kozawa Sadoki, Funada Naka, Hamada Yukio, Yamamoto Katsuichi, Tomabechi Hideyuki and even Kimura Tokutarō, many of them stalwarts of the dominant factional alliance, all argued that removal of the clause would be 'premature', since it was difficult to draw a sharp distinction between 'insurrection', 'indirect aggression' and 'direct aggression'.[87] The day before, a meeting of the Foreign Affairs Research Council and the Diplomatic and Defence Sections of the Policy Affairs Research Council had agreed that while the Self Defence Forces might be in a position to deal with simple 'insurrection', Japan would have no alternative but to request help from the United States in cases of 'indirect aggression'.[88] The treaty proposals drawn up by the Foreign Minister and shown to party leaders on 3 April 1959 thus envisaged retention of provisions for requesting American assistance in cases of riot and insurrection.[89] This draft was approved by the party 'Leaders' Meeting' and 'Advisers' Meeting' on 8 April.[90] It has been already noted that the text of the 1960 treaty can be interpreted as permitting the Japanese government to appeal for American assistance in times of internal crisis.

After the May 1959 House of Councillors election, a number of factors conspired to frustrate further attempts to influence the shape of the new treaty. First, Fujiyama and MacArthur had reached substantial agreement on the provisions of the treaty just before the election. For any factional confederation or individual factional leader to have forced major alterations after June 1959 would have necessitated substantial renegotiation. The United States may have been disinclined to take such a step and the Japanese government would certainly have been reluctant to propose it. Second, after the House of Councillors election, factional alignments within the Liberal Democratic Party changed radically. Kishi, in an apparent effort to re-organize the dominant coalition and replace the truculent and unpredictable Kōno with more amenable allies, refused to accede to Kōno's request for appointment as party secretary-general. Kōno consequently withdrew from the dominant alliance. In place of Kōno, Kishi brought Ikeda into the Cabinet as Minister for International Trade and Industry and appointed Ishii as chairman of the Executive Board. Ikeda's public opposition to the government at once subsided. Kōno's ability to exert direct pressure on the Prime Minister was circumscribed.[91] Third, after the election, Kishi began to take an increasingly firm stand on the revision issue. An extremely hostile attitude was adopted to any form of opposition. Outside the Diet, the massive national protest movement against the new treaty was gathering strength day by day. The looming crisis was now perceived not so much as a debate about the nature of Japan's ties with the United States but as a test of strength between the Conservative camp and the Opposition. Once the battle to convince the nation of the wisdom of the government's policies had begun, the Liberal Democratic Party closed ranks. Many faction leaders hitherto sceptical of the treaty, or of particular aspects of it, rallied to the cause. By September the Prime Minister was declaring that all oppos-ition to the new treaty had been inspired by the forces of international Communism and that even the dissident groups within the Conservative Party were being 'used' by China and the Soviet Union.[92] Personalities like Admiral Nomura Kichisaburō, who had earlier been critical of the new treaty, now urged that, if necessary, it be forced through the Diet, regardless of the opposition.[93] Even former Prime Minister Yoshida half-heartedly came around.[94] Factions that had opposed the treaty from the beginning became increasingly subdued. They realized that the government was determined to go ahead with its plans and decided to withdraw and await develop-ments.[95]

After the election, Kōno continued his campaign to ensure that American rights under the 'Far Eastern' clause of the new treaty were accompanied by a Japanese right of veto. He also asserted that the ten-year time limit was 'too long', advocating greater 'flexibility', so that Japan could abandon or renegotiate parts of the treaty at will, 'in accordance with the international situation'. Yet the new circumstances frus-trated his efforts to initiate further changes. Kishi eventually gave Kōno to under-stand that something might be done about the time limit.[96] After his return from the United States on 4 October 1959 Fujiyama also expressed a willingness to look into this matter.[97] These were hollow promises. Kōno, realizing that his opposition was becoming less and less effective, gradually lost interest. Complicated negotiations within the party dragged on throughout October. In the end no conclusion was reached. The final report of the Security Treaty Revision Sub-committee set up by the party to investigate Kōno's proposals was vague about the meaning of 'prior con-sultations'. Noting that the duration of the treaty would be ten years, it simply re-called a 'strong request' in 'some quarters' for greater flexibility.[98] This report was accepted by the Liberal Democratic Party Executive Board on 21 October[99] and approved by a meeting of Conservative members from both Houses on 26 October.[100] Kōno's last efforts to influence the shape of the treaty thus ended in failure.

IV Japanese reactions to the revised treaty

The Japanese business community, regarding the security treaty as the symbol of a stable and mutually beneficial economic relationship with the United States, initially gave considerable public support to the government's plans for revision. As in the early 1950's, however, organized business remained divided on the question of what kind of a relationship with the United States was in Japan's best interests. The views of Kishi's supporters in heavy industry and those of Kōno's backers in small-scale enterprises, agriculture and fisheries remained poles apart. Nevertheless, all groups in the business community had a common interest in the maintenance of stable Conservative government. Once it became apparent that the Prime Minister's policies were beginning to endanger the constitutional order his support in financial and industrial circles rapidly evaporated. It was widely believed that organized business played a decisive role in engineering Kishi's political demise.[101]

Virtually the entire Japanese academic and cultural establishment united to oppose the new treaty. As in the period 1950–2, only a handful of intellectuals were prepared to argue in favour of close alignment with the United States. It was generally assumed that the new treaty would mean even deeper involvement in American Far Eastern strategy, *de facto* constitutional revision, large-scale rearmament, introduction of nuclear weapons, and, ultimately, overseas service for the Self Defence Forces. Japan would be forced into closer co-operation with the Kuomintang regime on Taiwan, South Korea and America's other client states in the Far East. It would be prevented from opening a meaningful dialogue with China and the Soviet Union. As in 1950–2, it was thought that Japan could best preserve its own security and make some meaningful contribution to world peace by breaking out of the American alliance system and declaring its neutrality.[102]

On the far left Hatada Shigeo, dedicating his book *Shin Ampo Taisei Ron* 'to all my old school-friends whose lives were lost in the Pacific War', argued that the new treaty 'rather than facilitating Japan's gradual liberation from a dependent position in a military alliance system actually rivets her more securely into a joint defence system with the United States'. Its domestic implications, he contended, were in every way as alarming as its ramifications in the field of foreign policy and defence. It was by no means unthinkable, Hatada declared, that the United States might encourage Japan to develop a limited military nuclear capacity within the context of the new treaty. This would threaten all that had been achieved since World War II.

First, the necessity of protecting the secrets of nuclear missiles will move the government to proclaim a National Secrets Protection Law and an anti-Espionage Law. This could invite a situation in which [the government might be tempted] to reintroduce the Police Duties Performance Bill. It is probable that the United States, on the pretext that the prior consultations system [demands the maintenance of the strictest secrecy in inter-governmental communications] will also request such legislation ... This will lead to very great restrictions on the democratic rights of academic research, freedom of thought, expression and association. The second point relates to the economic burdens of nuclear missiles. Since nuclear weapons require the expenditure of vast sums of money, taxation can be expected to increase rapidly. At the same time, spending on social welfare, education, scientific research and disaster relief can be expected to decline. Increases in military expenditure will accelerate inflation and, by reducing real wages (through rising costs) render the livelihood of the Japanese people extremely difficult.[103]

These apprehensions, some of them far-fetched, some of them very well grounded, were not confined to left-wing circles. As we have seen, they were shared, to one degree or another, by a wide range of opinion within the Liberal Democratic Party itself. Conservative intellectuals, too, were by no means eager for Japan to join the United States in a global crusade against Communism. As George R. Packard has so aptly pointed out, the character of the arguments put forward by America's foremost academic supporters in 1960 reveals the extent to which the intellectual mainstream remained impervious to Cold War perceptions of the world. Fifteen years of unprecedented exposure to American politics, culture and society, ten years in the vortex of United States Far Eastern strategy, an incessant barrage of anti-Communist propaganda both from Washington and from the Japanese government, had failed to make any serious impact on the way Japan's academics viewed the international system and their country's place in it. There remained a staggering gap between the world as seen by educated Japanese and the world as seen by their American counterparts.

Professor Ōhira Zengo, one of the most illustrious Japanese supporters of the new treaty, appealing for 'moral neutrality' within the context of alignment with the United States, argued that:

The guide to our action must first of all be the 'maintenance of the balance'. But morally, we must be neutral, and with regard to the action of both East and West, we must take a realistic view of diplomacy. I think that we must not let our judgement be affected by ideologies, but rather that we should, freely and fairly, become the conscience of the world, and in the UN General Assembly form a healthy floating vote. It is wrong to say that either Russia or China – being red dictatorships – are morally evil by nature, or conversely, that the US is an imperialist aggressor. We must look at both sides impartially, and rejecting totally pro-US or totally pro-Soviet positions, make judgements objectively, based on the national interest. This is a theory of moral neutralism, and I think this form of neutralism is tenable even though we belong militarily to the joint defence structure of the free world. It is a mistake to brand those who favour treaty revision as pro-American, ideologically. Only when we are ideologically neutral can we make impartial judgements on our foreign affairs.[104]

The anti-treaty demonstrations, unprecedented as they were, represented no more than the activities of a substantial minority of the Japanese population. Supporters of the Prime Minister's policies could justly point out that the general elections of November 1960 returned the Liberal Democratic Party to power with 297 seats in the House of Representatives – 10 more than it had won in 1958. (The Socialist Party won 144 seats, an increase of 22, largely at the expense of the splinter Democratic Socialist Party; the Communists won 3 seats, an increase of 2 over the total in the previous general election.) Government spokesmen could also point out that the demonstrations were confined largely to the Tōkyō metropolitan area, that even at the height of troubles the majority of the Japanese people went peacefully about their ordinary business.

All this is to obscure the issue. The Japanese people were well aware, albeit in general terms, of the philosophical differences between Prime Minister Kishi and the old Yoshida school. Kishi's fall and Ikeda Hayato's victory in the party presidential elections were widely, and correctly, interpreted as heralding a return to Yoshida's policy of essentially passive alignment with the United States. The Liberal Democratic Party victory in the November general election might therefore be viewed as a popular endorsement of Yoshida's brand of conservatism and a rejection of the Kishi position.

Opinion polls taken at the time of the crisis showed that the public remained, as it had been in 1950–2, sharply divided. It could certainly not be claimed that the government had been forced by public opinion to revise the treaty or that it had a popular mandate to do so. The new treaty clearly did not have overwhelming support. As in 1950–2, one large minority supported the alliance with the United States, another substantial minority opposed it and advocated some kind of neutralism. There was evidence, in some quarters, of the strong swing towards neutralism that was to be a feature of many polls taken in the 1960s. Again, as in 1950–2, there was no significant popular interest in association with the Socialist bloc.

However public opinion is to be interpreted, there can be little doubt that the 1960 security treaty crisis confirmed, in a more dramatic fashion, and on a more grandiose stage, the lessons of the 1951 Yoshida-Dulles talks. Whatever Prime Minister Kishi's inclinations, the dominant groups in the Japanese political establishment and the most articulate sections of the Japanese public were fundamentally opposed to participation in a regional military alliance. Supporters of the security treaty were persuaded that wisdom lay in continued association with the United States. Yet there was little desire to provoke America's opponents unnecessarily. In 1951 Yoshida had told Dulles that to accede to American demands on security and rearmament would lead to the collapse of his government and his own assassination.[105] Kishi's fall in June 1960 and the disturbing events that followed demonstrated the soundness of Yoshida's judgement.

Sample public opinion polls on various aspects of the 1960 security treaty*

TABLE VI. 1 Alignment with the United States or neutrality? Ways of guaranteeing Japanese security

Newspaper	Date	Support alignment with the United States	Support neutrality		Support alignment with Socialist camp
Tōkyō Shimbun	19 July 1959	45.3%	36.0%		1.6%
Yomiuri Shimbun	4 October 1959	26.0%	50.0%		1.0%
Asahi Shimbun	18 January 1960	14.0%	Rely on United Nations	Japanese neutrality	Security through good relations with Socialist camp
			24.0%	35.0%	8.0%

TABLE VI. 2 Support for revision of the 1951 security treaty

Newspaper	Date	Favour immediate revision	Favour eventual revision	Favour status quo	Favour immediate abolition	Favour eventual abolition
Tōkyō Shimbun	19 July 1959	31.1% in favour of revision		10.8%	16.9% in favour of abolition	
Mainichi Shimbun	26 August 1959	7.2%	20.6%	12.5%	6.4%	13.0%

* Certain liberties have been taken with the exact forms of questions to facilitate preparation of the tables.

Newspaper	Date	Support revision	Oppose revision
Asahi Shimbun	18 January 1960	29.0%	25.0%

Newspaper	Date	Satisfied with new treaty	Dissatisfied with new treaty
Mainichi Shimbun	5 April 1960	21.6%	36.0%

Newspaper	Date	Hope the Diet ratifies the new treaty	Hope the Diet does not ratify the new treaty
Yomiuri Shimbun	3 April 1960	21.0%	28.0%

TABLE VI. 3 The revised treaty and involvement in war

Newspaper	Date	The new treaty increases likelihood of involvement in war	There is no such risk/or the new treaty guarantees Japan's security
Tōkyō Shimbun	19 July 1959	44.5%	21.5%
Asahi Shimbun	18 January 1960	38.0%	27.0%

CHAPTER VII

Japan, the United States and China, 1960–1967

I sent a message to the fish:
I told them 'This is what I wish'.
The little fishes of the sea,
They sent an answer back to me.
The little fishes' answer was
'We cannot do it, Sir, because ——

Lewis Carroll, Through the Looking Glass

I The erosion of the Cold War alliance systems

When Ikeda Hayato assumed office as Prime Minister of Japan on 19 July 1960, during the last months of the Eisenhower administration, it was evident that forces beyond Washington's control had begun to erode the near hegemonic position achieved by the United States in the period 1942–52. The first cracks had also begun to appear in the Soviet alliance system. By the middle of the decade NATO was in disarray, the foundations were being laid for the re-emergence of an autonomous Western Europe and China, despite its severe domestic problems, had formally repudiated Soviet leadership of the world Communist movement.

The relative decline of American power was the outcome of closely related international and domestic developments. By 1960 the Soviet Union had largely recovered from the ravages of World War II. Its postwar economic growth, while not spectacular, had been solid and sustained. Russia's launching of the first man-made earth satellite in October 1957, then of the first manned spacecraft in April 1961, demonstrated the strength and sophistication of its industrial, scientific and technological base. The expansion of the Soviet nuclear arsenal and the development of an intercontinental ballistic missile system ushered in a long period of *de facto* strategic parity between the two superpowers, undermining the advantages the United States had hitherto derived from its larger nuclear stockpiles, forward-based bomber force and considerably greater naval capacity. While United States superiority in terms of the number and accuracy of nuclear weapons, as well as in air and naval power, remained unassailable, the new vulnerability of the North American continent to Soviet missiles effectively destroyed the credibility of massive retaliation. American-Soviet nuclear confront-ation became increasingly difficult to contemplate, a fact highlighted by the outcome of the Cuban missile crisis, when both sides withdrew from the precipice after mak-ing hitherto unthinkable concessions. The Cuban crisis marked the beginning of a relatively stable period in superpower relations. A 'hot line' was installed between the White House and the Kremlin. A partial nuclear test ban treaty was concluded in 1963. In 1964 the United States, the Soviet Union and Great Britain agreed to limit the amount of military plutonium manufactured in both new and existing reactors. It was not long before the three powers were engaged in negotiations on a nuclear non-proliferation treaty.

The new decade also saw the first challenges to American leadership in the non-Communist world. The postwar devastation of Western Europe had obscured the divergence of national interests within the Atlantic Community. Recovery caused old ambitions to resurface. In 1959 General de Gaulle, determined to restore the French Republic as a fully independent great power, had withdrawn the French Mediterranean fleet and several fighter squadrons from the Allied High Command, banned United States nuclear warheads from French territory and refused Washington permission to use French rocket sites. De Gaulle's ultimate goal, he declared, was the dissolution of the Cold War alliance systems, the creation of 'a new order on our continent', the economic, political and strategic integration of a Europe united 'from the Atlantic to the Urals'.[1] The United States, Great Britain and the Commonwealth were peripheral to de Gaulle's grand vision. His determination to push ahead with the development of an independent nuclear strike force and the long campaign to exclude Britain from the Common Market reflected his desire to ensure that a united Europe, when it eventually emerged, would develop outside the American global system. With the end of the Algerian War in 1962 de Gaulle began to pursue a highly independent line in world affairs, initiating policies of unilateral *détente* with the Soviet Union and China, attempting to interest West Germany in his concepts of European solidarity and energetically cultivating nationalist forces in Latin America, Africa, the Arab world and South-East Asia. By March 1966 the French Republic, regarded, in 1950, as one of the keystones of American strategy in continental Europe, had formally withdrawn from the military wing of NATO, forc-ing the transfer of the Supreme Headquarters of the Allied Powers in Europe from Paris to Brussels.[2] NATO remained, in every respect, a formidable military alliance. Yet the French example was not without its impact on other European powers, not-ably the Federal Republic of Germany and Italy. United States relations with several smaller NATO allies were, during the same period, strained by conflicts over the use of bases for aerial reconnaissance of Soviet territory and port calls by nuclear sub-marines.

De Gaulle's challenge to United States supremacy in the West took place against the background of important changes in the economic relationship between Washington and its European allies. With the exception of Great Britain, the major European powers had recovered rapidly from World War II. By 1960 it was evident that declining domestic productivity, vast military expenditure and lavish foreign aid programmes had begun to undermine America's hitherto overwhelming economic pre-eminence. The United States share of world export trade decreased from 16.5 per cent in 1955 to 15.9 per cent in 1960. By 1965 it had dropped to 14.6 per cent. During the same period the combined share of France and West Germany alone had increased from 11.8 per cent to 15 per cent. Between 1953 and 1958 the annual average growth in industrial productivity in the United States had been 2.9 per cent. In West Germany it had been 5.6 per cent, in Italy 6.4 per cent, in France 7.7 per cent.[3] The United States balance of payments position had deteriorated badly. By the winter of 1960–1 American gold reserves, too, had reached a dangerously low level. The Eisenhower administration, in one of its last acts, had initiated urgent measures for dollar defence, giving priority to American goods, services and shipping in foreign aid programmes, curtailing Pentagon and State Department procurement of foreign products and ordering large-scale reductions in military forces stationed overseas. Kennedy followed with measures to persuade America's allies to further open their markets to United States goods and capital, assume greater defence burdens and participate more actively in Washington's military and civilian aid projects. These measures met with only limited success. In the decade that followed the problems grew in magnitude and complexity.

America's position in the non-European world also suffered serious setbacks. In the Middle East and around the Horn of Africa, United States relations with Israel, Saudi Arabia, Iran and Ethiopia remained close. Elsewhere in these strategic regions American influence retreated. The first part of the decade also saw unprecedented challenges to United States authority in Latin America, in Cuba, the Dominican Republic, Brazil and Argentina. A succession of conservative military *coups d'état*, direct intervention in the Dominican Republic and a massive injection of economic aid under Kennedy's Alliance for Progress eventually restored Washington's fortunes. Even so the region remained highly unstable.

It was the erosion of American influence in the Western Pacific, however, that caused the greatest concern to United States policy-makers during this period. American efforts to isolate and overthrow the Chinese Communists had met with a singular lack of success. By 1960 the leadership of the People's Republic, despite the strains produced by the Korean War and the disastrous setbacks of the Great Leap Forward, seemed well on the way to reasserting China's traditional position as the pre-eminent East Asian state. The Chinese Revolution, like the Russian, was clearly irreversible. Washington's relations with Peking, exacerbated by successive offshore islands crises, the bloody suppression of the 1959 Tibetan rebellion, then the prolonged Sino-Indian border dispute, continued to deteriorate. Communist movements throughout the region, it was argued, were essentially instruments of Chinese expansionism. Characteristically, local events were viewed in apocalyptic terms. Towards the end of May 1961, Vice-President Lyndon B. Johnson, returning from a whirlwind tour of South-East Asia, told Kennedy that

The battle against Communism must be joined in South-East Asia with strength and determination to achieve success there – or the United States, inevitably, must surrender the Pacific and take up our defences on our own shores.

Asian Communism is compromised and contained by the maintenance of free nations on the subcontinent. Without this inhibitory influence, the island outposts – Philippines, Japan, Taiwan – have no security and the vast Pacific becomes a Red Sea.

Continued European reluctance to support United States policies in the region, Johnson argued, made it futile to expect decisive action from SEATO. This moribund organization should be replaced by a new 'alliance of all the Free nations of the Pacific and Asia' who are willing to 'join forces in the defence of their freedom'.[4] Within a month Kennedy was telling a sceptical de Gaulle of American plans to intervene decisively in South-East Asia, to build an impregnable bulwark against China's expanding influence.[5] By the end of the year, the Secretary of State, Dean Rusk, the Secretary of Defence, Robert S. McNamara, and General Maxwell D. Taylor, the President's military adviser and later chairman of the Joint Chiefs of Staff, were all recommending a tougher line against Peking, further consolidation of the United States Pacific alliance system and direct military intervention against the Communists in Indochina.[6] During the northern spring of 1962 the administration, encouraged by Chiang Kai-shek, Chiang Ching-kuo, the Pentagon, the CIA and the domestic 'China lobby' examined proposals to support a Nationalist Chinese reconquest of the mainland. This idea was abandoned, on the grounds that the chances of success were slight. So, too, was the idea of initiating large-scale covert operations against the People's Republic.[7] The compromise between the extreme anti-Communist hardliners and more moderate elements in Washington eventually took the form of promoting a massive build-up of air and naval power in the Pacific and a policy of active military intervention in Vietnam. Further developing the strategic doctrines established by the National Security Council early in 1952 General Maxwell D. Taylor declared that

> The Joint Chiefs of Staff are increasingly mindful that our fortunes in South Vietnam are an accurate barometer of our fortunes in all of South-East Asia. It is our view that if the US program succeeds in South Vietnam it will go far toward stabilizing the total South-East Asia situation. Conversely, a loss of South Vietnam to the Communists will presage an early erosion of the remainder of our position in that subcontinent ... In a broader sense, the failure of our programs in South Vietnam would have heavy influence on the judgements of Burma, India, Indonesia, Malaysia, Japan, Taiwan, the Republic of Korea and the Republic of the Philippines with respect to U.S. durability, resolution and trustworthiness. Finally, this being the first real test of our determination to defeat the communist wars of national liberation formula, it is not unreasonable to conclude that there would be a corresponding unfavourable effect upon our image in Africa and in Latin America.[8]

The installation of Mace-B missiles in Okinawa in March 1961 had already brought the greater part of eastern and central China within the range of American nuclear strike power.[9] In March 1964 American B-52 strategic bombers were stationed on Guam. After the first Chinese nuclear test in October 1964 American Polaris submarines were dispatched to the Pacific, the nuclear-powered aircraft carrier *Enterprise* was attached to the Seventh Fleet, air bases in Taiwan and Thailand were strengthened.[10] At the same time the Kennedy administration transformed Eisenhower's cautious, limited involvement in Indochina into a total commitment of American resources, manpower and prestige. In the spring of 1961 the President ordered 400 United States Special Forces troops and 100 additional military advisers into South Vietnam. He also ordered wide-ranging clandestine operations against the Democratic Republic of Vietnam and south-eastern Laos. By the time of Kennedy's assassination in November 1963 the number of United States military personnel engaged in combat operations against the Vietnamese Communists had reached nearly 17,000. Within a year of President Johnson's accession to office the United States, increasingly frustrated in its attempts to defeat its opponents on the ground, had launched an aerial bombardment of North Vietnam on a scale unprecedented in the history of warfare. By the middle of 1967 the number of United States troops involved in the war had climbed to well over half a million. Despite the optimistic predictions of imminent victory, it was clear that the Vietnam War was accelerating the decline of American global influence, eroding popular support for NATO in Europe, tarnishing the American image throughout the Western Pacific, further undermining the health of the American economy and threatening the stability of America's political life itself.

The slow disintegration of the American-centred order in the West was paralleled by the erosion of Soviet authority in the Communist world. As Yoshida Shigeru had long predicted, the Sino-Soviet alliance proved to be an edifice of clay. Khruschev's insistence on the necessity for superpower *détente*, his reluctance to give Peking unconditional support during the 1958 offshore islands crisis, then his refusal to share military nuclear technology destroyed Mao Tse-tung's conviction that China's interests would best be served by close alignment with the Soviet Union. By the summer of 1960 a massive exodus of Soviet technicians from China had begun. The Cuban missile crisis, viewed in Peking as further evidence of Soviet weakness, then Khruschev's open support for India during the 1962 Sino-Indian border war, drove the last nails into the coffin of the alliance. By the end of 1962 the Sino-Soviet conflict had become open. China, like France, embarked on a drive to establish itself as a fully independent great power. At the same time the international Communist movement was racked by acrimonious ideological disputes. By October 1964 the People's Republic had emerged as the world's fifth military nuclear power. Its leadership had also come to regard the Soviet Union as a serious threat to China's security, a decision that precipitated, in its turn, a substantial redeployment of Soviet ground, naval and air power to the Far East.[11]

China's emergence as a rival centre of Communist orthodoxy, the economic recovery of Eastern Europe and the spread of polycentralist philosophies among the Communist parties of the West combined to threaten the cohesion of the Warsaw Pact. The process was accelerated by de Gaulle's vigorous East European diplomacy. Romania drifted away from the alliance. Poland remained restless. Even Bulgaria displayed highly independent tendencies. By the late 1960s Czechoslovakia was experimenting with a radical programme of domestic reform. While the Soviet Union and its allies were eventually able to reassert their authority through armed intervention (21 August 1968), following the example set by the United States in the Dominican Republic three years earlier, the situation in Eastern Europe remained, for Moscow, a source of perennial concern.

'Windows of opportunity' in the Third World created by American folly and Chinese dogmatism provided some consolation. American intervention in Indochina helped consolidate the Soviet position in Hanoi. Until the 1965 *coup d'état*, Moscow competed with Washington, Peking and Tōkyō for influence in Sukarno's Indonesia. In the wake of the Sino-Indian border crisis Russia's ties with New Delhi also became increasingly cordial. In the Islamic world, Moscow's position was improved considerably by the development of relations with Egypt, Syria, Iraq, Yemen and the new revolutionary government in Algeria. These gains, significant as they were, could in no way compensate for the emergence of a hostile China along the Soviet Union's long inner Asian frontiers.

II Japanese domestic political struggles, high economic growth, American pressures and the failure to establish an independent relationship with China, 1960–7

(i) *The foreign and domestic policies of the first Ikeda Cabinet, July–November 1960*

Ikeda saw his principal immediate task as repairing the damage done by the security treaty crisis. His election as president of the Liberal Democratic Party had been made possible by the support of the Kishi and Satō factions, backed by Yoshida. He therefore had no alternative but to give these groups a central role in his new Cabinet. This, in turn, necessitated continued efforts to exclude Kōno and his supporters from access to the seats of power. Nevertheless, it was clearly necessary to improve the government's image. To achieve this objective, important posts were given to relatively liberal and, in many cases, rather youthful Conservatives. Thus it was that Ikeda's own associate, Kōsaka Zentarō, became Foreign Minister, Ishibashi Tanzan's former Minister for International Trade and Industry, Mizuta Mitsugi, became Minister for Finance, Esaki Masumi director-general of the Defence Agency, Ishida Hirohide[12] Minister for Labour and Mrs Nakayama Mara (Japan's first woman Cabinet Minister) Minister for Welfare.

The new Cabinet's policies were cautious and conciliatory.While the Prime Minister made it clear that the American alliance would remain the corner-stone of Japan's external relations, he stressed the importance of improving ties with the Soviet Union, China and other Communist countries. In domestic affairs he announced his intention to reform the Liberal Democratic Party, initiate dialogues with the Opposition, work for normalization of parliamentary government and make efforts to improve popular living standards. Ikeda's efforts to dissociate himself from Kishi's foreign and domestic policies brought an immediate response. A public opinion poll conducted by the *Asahi Shimbun* on 1–2 August 1960 revealed that 51 per cent of Japanese were favourably disposed towards the new Cabinet. This was the highest rate of support for any new Cabinet since 1945.

The Prime Minister's attempts to restore the fortunes of the Conservative Party were made easier by troubles in the Opposition camp. Unity of the left did not long survive the 1960 crisis. Even before the last demonstrators had dispersed, the anti-treaty coalition had begun to founder in the treacherous waters of ideological controversy. The Opposition could agree neither in their analysis of the Japanese-American relationship, nor on their assessment of the 1960 struggle or the agenda for future action. The Socialist Party, arguing that Japanese capitalism was an independent growth, allied to American imperialism, maintained that the principal objective of Opposition struggles should be domestic political, economic and social reconstruction. The Communist Party, reiterating its traditional view that postwar Japanese capitalism was subordinate to that of the United States, argued that the destruction of the security treaty system should take priority over domestic reform. By the beginning of 1961, moreover, serious internal conflicts had developed in both parties. The Socialist Party, swept up in struggles over structural reform, turned in upon itself. In July 1961, the Communist Party faced a serious crisis when Kasuga Shōjirō and seven followers were expelled for their attacks on party 'bureaucratism'. The party was subsequently rocked by the impact of the Sino-Soviet dispute. These conflicts, in turn, wrought havoc with the Japanese peace movement. By the mid-1960s, three rival anti-nuclear weapons organizations, each linked indirectly to one of the major Opposition parties, were engaged in bitter struggles for supremacy. In these circumstances, large numbers of intellectuals, religious leaders, students and ordinary citizens, disillusioned by the rising crescendo of fruitless theoretical debate, drifted into political agnosticism and began to dissociate themselves from the organized peace movement.[13]

(ii)   High Economic Growth and its long-term consequences

On the eve of the 1960 general elections Ikeda decided to embark on an ambitious project of national economic reconstruction. The Prime Minister's objectives were twofold. First, like de Gaulle, Ikeda was convinced that a solidly based, modern industrial economy was a fundamental precondition of independent great power status. Second, he believed that rising material standards of living would promote domestic stability, undermine support for the Socialist opposition and prevent a recurrence of crises like that experienced in 1958–60.

Early in 1961, the Japanese government, much to the surprise of several prominent Conservatives, who had regarded Ikeda's talk of a new era of high economic growth as little more than an election slogan[14], began preparations for a large-scale reorganization of industry and a rationalization of agriculture. Following the traditions established in the Meiji era the state was to play a decisive role in this process. In the years that followed, Japan's industrial base was modernized and diversified. New, dynamic, capital intensive industries were targeted for special assistance. Technological innovation was actively encouraged. Old, declining industries were deliberately phased out. Particular attention was paid to the development of internationally competitive heavy and chemical industries and cost efficient, technology-intensive consumer durables, especially steel, shipbuilding, oil refining, petro-chemicals, automobiles, machinery, electrical goods, and synthetic fibres. An extra-ordinary high level of capital formation, stimulated by minimal government welfare expenditure, facilitated the constant upgrading of plant and equipment, reduced production costs and increased productivity, all of which heightened the inter-national competitiveness of Japanese industry. Growth was further encouraged by fiscal and monetary policies, a tolerant attitude towards the provisions of the 1947 Anti-Monopoly Act, generous development loans, government purchases, import restrictions, regulation of capital flows and subsidies. The government also assisted private industry to launch an aggressive and sustained export drive, providing easy credit, depreciation allowances and tax incentives. The reconstruction of agriculture was designed both to increase efficiency and provide a continuous flow of labour for the booming industrial and commercial sectors. The Basic Law on Agriculture (June 1961) envisaged a 70 per cent reduction in the agricultural population (from 15,750,000 to 4,560,000) over ten years, relaxation of restrictions on land transfer to encourage larger holdings, and the development of agricultural co-operatives.[15]

At one level, Ikeda's policy of high economic growth, pursued even more forcefully by the Satō and Tanaka Cabinets, was remarkably successful. In less than a decade Japan had become, after the United States and the Soviet Union, the world's third greatest economic power. By the beginning of the 1970s Japan's indust-rial output had increased more than eightfold, its agricultural production had almost doubled. Between 1960 and 1965 Japan's real GNP grew at an average annual rate of 10 per cent, compared with 4.8 per cent for the United States, 5.8 per cent for France, 5.0 per cent for West Germany and 3.4 per cent for the United Kingdom. These trends were accelerated during the latter part of the decade.[16] The nation's share of world export trade jumped from a mere 2.1 per cent in 1955 to over 7.0 per cent in the early 1970s.[17] Between 1960 and 1970, Japan's exports, increasingly dominated by heavy industrial products, grew at an average annual rate of 17.5 per cent, more than double that of the United States and three times that of the United Kingdom.

The Prime Minister's efforts to lay the economic foundations for renewed great power status had important strategic implications, many of which may not have been foreseen in the autumn of 1960. High economic growth required assiduous cultivation of existing trading alliances and an energetic search for new markets and sources of raw materials. While it improved the long-term prospects for Japan's reassertion of a posi-tion of complete equality *vis-à-vis* its trans-Pacific ally, it also entailed the risk of increased short-term dependence on American technology, sources of raw materials and markets. The rapid growth of the Japanese economy, too, produced an ambivalent response in the United States. On the one hand, American political and business lead-ers continued to view Japan as an indispensable ally in the global struggle against Com-munism, a United States-sponsored free enterprise success story, a model for the rest of Asia. On the other hand, Americans became increasingly disturbed both by the relentless Japanese thrust into their own markets and by the growing imbalance in bilateral trade. As the Japanese economy developed, the United States began to urge its ally to lift import restrictions, relinquish currency controls and remove barriers to foreign investment. The Ikeda Cabinet, uncertain of Japan's strength and fearful of foreign domination, responded with a policy of artful procrastination varied by tactical, piecemeal concessions. Japan's increasingly powerful position in the world economy, the favourable balance of payments position that emerged in the mid-1960s and the appearance of a massive imbalance in bilateral trade with the United States made this strategy difficult to continue. During the late 1960s, therefore, as the international competitiveness of Japanese industry increased, Japan progressively reduced tariffs to a level somewhat below that of the United States, phased out controls on currency transactions and eased restrictions on foreign investment.[18] Yet even these measures proved, in the end, unable to satisfy Washington's expectations.

The domestic repercussions of high economic growth were also complex. Rising material living standards did not necessarily lead to greater political conservatism. On the contrary, public dissatisfaction with the status quo, stimulated by spiralling land costs, bad housing, rising consumer prices, growing income disparities, poor welfare facilites and catastrophic environmental destruction grew rapidly throughout the 1960s. Anxiety about the direction of the government's foreign policy also mounted. By the end of the decade, popular unrest had reached levels comparable to those of the security treaty crisis.

(iii)   Conservative Party factional manoeuvrings, November 1960–July 1962

After the Conservative victory in the 1960 general elections and the launching of his programme for economic reconstruction, Ikeda made a concerted effort to promote party unity and political stability by enlarging the factional base of his government.[19] In the reorganized Cabinet announced on 7 December 1960 four posts were occupied by members of the Prime Minister's own faction, two each by followers of Kishi, Satō and Fujiyama. The Miki-Matsumura faction and various other small groups obtained one post each. Members of the House of Councillors, unattached to any faction, also received several portfolios. The Kōno faction remained in the political wilderness.

The Prime Minister saw these arrangements as necessary to harmonize purely factional interests. Yet the structure of the new Cabinet also reduced the slight margin of superiority that groups advocating a foreign policy closely aligned with that of the United States had hitherto enjoyed over those committed to improvement of ties with the Communist powers on the mainland.

In July 1961, Ikeda decided to invite all powerful faction leaders, including Kōno, to accept Cabinet portfolios or high office in the party.[20] Thus it was that Ōno became Deputy Prime Minister, Satō Minister for International Trade and Industry, Kōno Minister for Agriculture, Fujiyama director of the Economic Planning Agency, Miki director of the Science and Technology Agency and Ishii director of the Administrative Management Agency. Kōsaka retained his position as Foreign

Minister. Mizuta stayed on as Minister for Finance. In the Liberal Democratic Party, Ikeda's close associate Maeo was appointed secretary-general, Satō's confidant Hori Shigeru director of the General Affairs Bureau and Kishi's second-in-command Fukuda director of the Political Affairs Bureau.

The new constellation of power, above all the reappearance of Kōno in the Cabinet, again tilted the factional balance marginally in favour of those advocating a more independent foreign policy. By the winter of 1961–2 'nationalist' and 'Asianist' groups had gained further ground. The Kishi faction, the centre of opposition to *rapprochement* with Moscow and Peking, split and went into temporary eclipse.[21] While the mainstream of the faction, led by Fukuda, remained committed to an uncompromisingly anti-Communist foreign policy, two of its derivative groups, the Fujiyama and Kawashima factions, gradually dissociated themselves from the attitude of their former leader. Fujiyama decided to devote the remainder of his political life to improving relations with the Chinese Communists. Kawashima, too, began to display a cautious interest in the People's Republic. After 1960 the Ishii faction also entered a period of attrition, stagnation and decline.[22] These developments somewhat offset the break-up of the Ishibashi faction, which began to occur about the same time.[23]

The debate between exponents of greater independence and advocates of close association with the United States was soon caught up in the struggle between the Kōno and Satō factions. Both groups had grown rapidly in the wake of the 1960 crisis. By 1961 the tension between them had become acute. Kōno, impressed by the example of de Gaulle, emerged as the principal Conservative Party advocate of a foreign policy based on 'national interests'. Immediate dissolution of the security treaty, he declared, would be 'unrealistic'. Nevertheless, he urged Japan to negotiate a unilateral *détente* with the Soviet Union and China, to expand trade with the Communist bloc and to embark on a large-scale project for the economic reconstruction of South-East Asia.[24] In July 1962, after his third visit to the Soviet Union, he recalled: 'Mr Mikoyan, at a party given in my honour, stated that "Young Kōno is a nationalist. He will not become pro-American, nor is he anti-Communist. We can talk together easily." I was satisfied to hear it put that way.'[25] His easy-going attitude towards Communism alarmed the extreme right. In July 1963 his private residence at Hiratsuka was burned to the ground by ultranationalist gangsters.[26] Satō, in contrast, remained convinced that Japan's interests lay in continued identification with Washington.[27]

The Kōno-Satō rivalry was not simply the outcome of different views on foreign policy. It was well known that Yoshida, now established as the Conservative Party's elder statesman, intended to have Satō elected as Ikeda's successor. This prospect did not arouse universal enthusiasm. The appointment of Satō as acting Prime Minister during Ikeda's 1961 Asian tour was particularly galling to other factional leaders.[28] By the end of the year, Kōno, Ōno, Fujiyama and Kawashima were attempting to organize an anti-Satō coalition to frustrate Yoshida's plans.[29] In retaliation a group centring around the Kishi-Fukuda and Satō factions established a League for Uplifting Party Morale (Tōfū Sasshin Renmei), ostensibly for the pur-

pose of modernizing the party by combating factionalism, in reality as a move to isolate Kōno.[30] Early in 1962 the Simple Hearts Society (Soshinkai), an association of
Liberal Democratic Party extreme conservatives, requested Ikeda to crush 'neutralist' views within the government and re-establish his administration on firm anti-
Communist principles. The Prime Minister, anxious to avoid alienating Satō, yet not
wanting to precipitate conflict with Kōno and his supporters, adopted a non-committal attitude.[31] The polarization of the party continued throughout the spring and
summer of 1962, with Ikeda striving desperately to preserve his 'all-faction' structure and maintain a precarious balance between the warring camps.

The crisis came with Ikeda's Cabinet reorganization in July 1962. Satō, accusing
Kōno of advocating policies favourable to the Soviet Union and China, refused to
participate unless his rival were excluded.[32] Fujiyama, who had begun to doubt the
wisdom of Ikeda's economic strategies, tendered his resignation.[33] Fukuda, Ishii
and Miki, either because of hostility to Ikeda's policies or opposition to Kōno, or in
the hope of securing more bountiful rewards for their eventual support, also
declined to be directly associated with the new Cabinet. After much haggling, Satō's
protégé Tanaka Kakuei was installed as Minister for Finance. Nakagaki Kunio, one
of Ishii's supporters, was appointed Minister for Justice. Shiga Kenjirō, of the Miki-
Matsumura faction, became director-general of the Defence Agency, Ayabe Kentarō of the Fujiyama faction Minister for Transport. Otherwise, the major Cabinet
posts were monopolized by the Ikeda, Kōno, Ōno and Kawashima factions. Ikeda's
close associate Ōhira Masayoshi took over the Foreign Ministry. Miyazawa Kiichi
became director of the Economic Planning Agency. Both these men had always felt
uncomfortable with simplistic Cold War views of the world. Fukuda Hajime, of the
Ōno faction, a man with considerable interest in promoting Sino-Japanese trade,
was appointed Minister for International Trade and Industry. Ōno's supporters also
received two other Cabinet posts. Kōno Ichirō became Minister for Construction.
His protégé Shigemasa Masayuki took over the Ministry of Agriculture. Kawashima
retained his previous position as director of the Administrative Management Agency.
That is to say, despite the existence of important restraining influences, the new
Cabinet was dominated by groups opposed to open-ended support for the United
States in the Cold War, sympathetic to the cause of better relations with the Communist powers, especially China, and determined to assert a more independent role
in world affairs.[34]

(iv) The Ikeda Cabinet's efforts to formulate an independent China policy, July 1960–July 1962

The establishment of the Ikeda Cabinet had brought an immediate change in the
climate of Sino-Japanese relations. Despite the strong position of the Kishi and Satō
factions in the dominant coalition, the new Prime Minister made his own intentions
clear the day he assumed office. While he certainly did not contemplate immediate
recognition of Peking, Ikeda indicated that he did not intend Japan's China policy to

be made in Washington. The Sino-Soviet dispute, the failure of the Great Leap Forward and Japan's anticipated requirements for new markets and raw materials in the coming era of high economic growth suggested that the time had come to begin exploring the possibilities for a unilateral *détente* with the People's Republic.

> As far as China policy is concerned, there is no need for Japan to adopt the same attitude as the United States. For the past six or seven years I have been saying that it is necessary for us to have good relations with Communist China. But things just haven't gone well. In diplomacy, we can't just think of China policy. The most important thing for us is to increase our credibility in the Free World. In addition, we must also improve Japan's domestic political situation ... We must become a country that will be taken seriously by the Chinese Communists, that will not be easily manipulated by them ... We are watching China carefully and quietly. At the present stage we are in a position to open cultural and economic relations. I want to encourage such relations on a large scale.[35]

The breach with Moscow, by no means complete in 1961, had intensified the deep-seated factional-policy conflicts within the Chinese leadership. The contours of the Chinese political landscape during these years remain unclear. It seems probable that while Mao Tse-tung, the Communist Party leadership and the armed forces remained profoundly hostile towards Japan, the ideologically flexible 'economic pragmatists' who wielded considerable influence during the early 1960s were anxious to establish a mutually beneficial relationship with Tōkyō. Undoubtedly, historical experience inclined Chinese of all persuasions to caution in their dealings with Japan. The Chinese were also well aware of the international and domestic restraints on the Ikeda Cabinet. Nevertheless, within three weeks of the Japanese Prime Minister's statement Chou En-lai had informed Suzuki Kazuo, director of the Japan International Trade Promotion Council, that while the long-term development of Sino-Japanese trade would be conditional on the climate of political relations, it might be possible, in the short term, to adopt a flexible approach. China insisted merely that Japan should not regard it with hostility, support Washington's schemes to create two Chinas or deliberately place obstacles in the way of normalization of relations. If Tōkyō found immediate diplomatic recognition impossible, the People's Republic would be prepared, for the time being, to co-operate with private firms.[36]

Chou En-lai's attitude impressed Ikeda. In October 1960 the Japanese Prime Minister gave his unofficial sanction to a private visit to Peking by Matsumura Kenzō and Takasaki Tatsunosuke, the wartime president of Manchurian Heavy Industries. In Peking, Takasaki, rejecting Chou En-lai's contention that Japan's alliance with the United States was indicative of a hostile attitude to China, strongly urged the conclusion of air, maritime, postal, radio, cultural and trade agreements between the two countries.[37] While the Chinese avoided a direct reply on this occasion, Liao Cheng-chi, chairman of the Afro-Asian Regional Committee of the Ministry of Foreign Affairs in Peking (and, like Matsumura Kenzō, a graduate of Waseda University), shortly afterwards made an unofficial visit to Tōkyō to explore Japanese intentions further. Then, in December 1960, after the formation of Ikeda's second Cabinet had reduced the influence of factions antagonistic to China, the Japanese Prime Minister set up a special advisory committee to examine relations with Peking.

In December 1961, Japan reasserted its close identification with United States China policy in the United Nations General Assembly (UNGA) by co-sponsoring a new American resolution to make Peking's entry into the world body an 'important question', requiring a two-thirds majority vote.* The Japanese decision to co-sponsor the American resolution, which brought fierce criticism from Peking, shocked groups sympathetic to China within the Conservative Party and scandalized the Opposition, was perfectly consistent with Ikeda's statement of 19 July 1960. In the short to medium-term, Japan had no alternative but give priority to relations with Washington. Relations with the People's Republic, whatever their long-term potential, could only be constructed slowly. The economic facts of the situation alone had a compelling logic. During the course of 1961, Japanese exports to China had risen to $US31 million. This was only half the volume of trade with Taiwan and a mere fraction of Japan's vast trade with the United States.[39]

Yet while the Ikeda Cabinet, like its predecessors, was prepared to support United States efforts to exclude China from the United Nations, it clearly did not share Washington's perceptions of the People's Republic as the principal threat to the security of the Asian Pacific region. Nor did the Foreign Ministry, the Cabinet Research Office or the Defence Agency entertain such views. Japanese diplomatic, intelligence and military assessments of the situation on the continent during these years were more concerned with the future of the People's Republic as a viable political entity than with any threat China might pose to its neighbours. The dominant view at a conference of Japanese ambassadors in Asia and the Pacific held in May 1962 was that the Chinese economic situation was serious and that China's international influence had, for the time being, reached its limits.[40] Two months later, the Foreign Ministry and the Cabinet Research Office, in a detailed report, stressed the serious nature of the external and domestic problems facing the Peking government. Sino-Soviet tension, it was argued, based on historical, geographical and strategic rather than purely ideological factors, would continue to grow. So, too, would China's sense of insecurity. The People's Republic feared, in particular, the creation of an American-sponsored North-East Asian Treaty Organization and could be expected to respond to this threat by making overtures to neutral countries in South-East Asia.[41] The report implicitly rejected the American view that China was about to launch a major military campaign to incorporate East Asia within its sphere of influence. Tension along the Sino-Indian border was apparently seen as local in it origins. A situation analysis prepared by the Japanese Defence Agency in June 1961, while predicting a further increase in Sino-Soviet tension, concluded that the possibility of

---

*   The United States had decided to adopt this strategy because the increasing number of countries recognizing Peking made it seem probable that the previous tactic of excluding the People's Republic by forcing postponement of a General Assembly vote on the China question would soon prove futile.[38]

direct Chinese military aggression against Japan was 'practically unthinkable'.[42] In January 1963, four months after the United States had warned Japan of China's military nuclear development programme at the Security Consultative Committee meeting in August 1962,[43] another Defence Agency report dwelt at length on China's difficult domestic situation, alleging erosion of popular support for the regime and needless dissipation of military strength along the Sino-Indian border. Communist China, in the view of the Defence Agency, was teetering on the brink of another revolution.[44] All this suggested that the country was incapable of posing a direct military threat to Japan.

These attitudes were widely held among those groups within the Conservative Party most hostile to the People's Republic. On 15 May 1961, the China Subcommittee of the Liberal Democratic Party's Foreign Affairs Research Council, a body traditionally dominated by the most 'pro-American' elements in the party, after hearing evidence from the Foreign Ministry, the Ministry of International Trade and Industry (MITI), Takasaki Tatsunosuke, representatives of the Kuomintang and various individuals interested in the Chinese continent, submitted a long report to the Ikeda Cabinet. This report, stressing the paramount importance of continued, close alignment with the United States, recommended against recognition of the People's Republic of China. Peking, it noted, had been condemned by the United Nations as an aggressor. There was no guarantee that the regime did not pose a threat to international peace. Japan maintained diplomatic relations with the Kuomintang and regarded it as the legally con-stituted government of China. The report also took a cautious line on the expansion of Sino-Japanese trade. 'Japan's economic base lies in the Free World; trade with Com-munist China is a problem that must be considered from this perspective ... from the viewpoint of our trade expansion, Sino-Japanese trade is to some extent useful; it will not, however, become a decisive element.' Yet there was no suggestion that the Chinese Communists posed any particular threat to Japan.[45] The American-oriented Conserva-tives on the Foreign Affairs Research Council, it may be suspected, viewed China as an undesirable associate largely because of its Asianness, economic backwardness and military weakness, not because of its strength.[46]

(v) The Matsumura and Takasaki missions and the resumption of Sino-Japanese trade, August–November 1962

In August 1962, a month after Ikeda's Cabinet reorganization had precipitated Satō's withdrawal and weakened the position of groups advocating close identifica-tion with United States East Asian policies, the Prime Minister again expressed his interest in expanding Sino-Japanese trade. This despite the storm clouds on the Sino-Indian border, the unequivocal support for India's position in Washington and the increasingly intimate links between Moscow and New Delhi. It can be assumed that Ikeda had discussed these developments with Yoshida and had weighed his mentor's advice carefully before making his decision public. On 12 September 1962, at the invitation of Prime Minister Chou En-lai, a large Japanese delegation led by

Matsumura Kenzō left for Peking. The Matsumura mission, despite its formally unofficial character, had the full personal backing of Prime Minister Ikeda himself. It was also supported by Kōno, Fujiyama and Miki. It was not viewed favourably by Kishi, Fukuda, Satō, Ishii, or Ōno. Despite these divisions, the Prime Minister, as an indication of his personal interest in the mission's success, included Ogawa Heiji, a member of his own faction, among the thirty-three delegates. Tabayashi Masakichi, from the Japan Long Term Credit Bank, one of Ikeda's principal financial supporters, also took part. The objective of the mission was to discuss the development of Sino-Japanese trade, cultural relations, an exchange of journalists and the possibility of opening a Tōkyō-Peking air route.[47] Late in October 1962, at the height of the Cuban missile crisis and the Sino-Indian border war, a second Japanese delegation, led by Takasaki Tatsunosuke and Okazaki Kaheita, left for the People's Republic for talks with Chou En-lai, Liao Cheng-chi and other Chinese officials. The result was the signing, on 9 November 1962, of the Takasaki-Liao Memorandum on Trade. This was not a formal government-to-government trade agreement but one providing for an expansion of commerical activity through the agency of private Japanese firms prepared to accept Chou En-lai's three principles of trade. This was as far as the Ikeda Cabinet, in the light of current international and domestic circumstances, judged it prudent to proceed. While the Japanese 'friendly firms' lacked long-term credit facilities, the Takasaki-Liao Memorandum established the basis for a considerable growth in bilateral trade over the next few years. The Chinese were especially keen to acquire Japanese chemical fertilizers, agricultural chemicals, farm equipment, high-quality steel, metal alloys and synthetic fibre plants. Japan, in turn, was interested in Chinese coal, iron ore, soya beans and other grains, medicinal herbs and salt. While it proved impossible to negotiate the opening of a direct air link between Japan and China, cultural exchanges were increased significantly and journalists from the major Japanese newspapers were eventually permitted to operate in the People's Republic.

The 1962 Memorandum Trade talks provided both Japan and China with a valuable opportunity to assess each other's long-term intentions. The Japanese Conservatives were gratified to discover that the Chinese position, throughout the negotiations, was pragmatic and flexible. Chou En-lai made it clear that he did not subscribe to Ikeda's view that political issues could be separated from economic ones. Japan's refusal to recognize Peking and its support for Washington in the United Nations, he said, were unacceptable. Moreover, while China had no objection to Japan's development f a legitimate self-defence capability, it was disturbed by the prospect of the country assisting the United States 'to impose its military rule on Asia'. The long-term development of Sino-Japanese relations, Chou insisted, would depend on Japan's breaking with Washington, recognizing Peking, facilitating China's entry into the United Nations and arranging for the withdrawal of American military forces from the archipelago. In the short term, however, China recognized that changes in established Japanese policies were unlikely. 'We recognize that the Ikeda Cabinet is somewhat different to the Kishi Cabinet. But the changes have not yet become qualitative changes.' For this reason, it was obviously best to begin by negotiating limited small-scale agreements and carefully monitoring future developments.[48] On this matter, at least, the Japanese Prime Minister and the Chinese Premier were in complete agreement.

Despite the extremely modest nature of the commercial agreement being negotiated, it was difficult for the Japanese delegates and their Chinese counterparts to avoid discussing the possible future development of the relationship. The sentiments expressed by both sides during these talks in the autumn of 1962 were compatible neither with the Japanese-American security treaty nor the Sino-Soviet alliance. Chou En-lai set the tone with a rousing speech on Asian solidarity at the banquet to welcome Matsumura Kenzō held on the evening of 15 September. Matsumura, in his reply, characterized Japan and China as 'two brother nations of East Asia'. Commending the heroic achievements of the great pan-Asianists, of Sun Yat-sen, Inukai Bokudō, Tōyama Mitsuru, Ōkuma Shigenobu and Miyazaki Tōten, he expressed the hope that Japan and China could rebuild their ancient relationship on foundations that would endure 'from generation to generation ... for the sake of our children and our children's children'.[49] In November, during the Memorandum Trade negotiations, Chou En-lai advised Okazaki Kaheita over dinner that Sino-Japanese relations should be developed slowly and carefully. In the recent past, he declared, terrible mistakes had been made. Yet Sino-Japanese co-operation was essential both for the reconstruction of Asia and for the protection of the region against outside influences.

> For eighty years after the Sino-Japanese war [of 1894–5], Japan invaded our country, causing immense loss of life and property. After the Manchurian Incident, especially, we suffered terrible losses. We are very bitter about this. Yet, compared to two thousand years of Sino-Japanese friendship, eighty years of bitterness is a very short time indeed. We are trying hard to forget our bitterness. Let us forget our bitterness and join together to strengthen Asia as a whole. The power of a revitalized Asia would not be used to threaten [countries] outside [our region] but to defend ourselves in case we are ever again subjected to external pressures.

Okazaki, his heart already warmed by the consumption of a considerable quantity of *mao tai*, was captivated by Chou En-lai's grand vision. It coincided almost exactly with his own.

> I remember replying that since my student days I had hoped that Japan and China could join hands and work together for the independence and cultural advance of Asia and for the abolition of poverty.[50]

(vi)   American reactions to Ikeda's new China policy, October 1962–January 1963

The Cuban missile crisis erupted on 23 October 1962, just three days before Takasaki's party left for Peking. Chinese and Indian troops had already been engaged in heavy fighting on the North-East frontier for some days. While Japan's moral support for the United States stand on Cuba was all that could have been expected from an ally, its enthusiasm for the Indian cause in the border war was not great. After the first full-scale Chinese offensive on 20 October Ikeda sent a note to

Nehru declaring his 'sympathy' for India's difficulties and his support for efforts to settle the problem 'by peaceful means'. However, the Japanese Ministry of Foreign Affairs declined to recognize the McMahon line. Japanese diplomats recalled India's attack on Goa in 1961. China's unilateral suspension of hostilities created a favourable impression in many quarters.[51] Although the United States Assistant Secretary of State Averell Harriman urged the Ikeda Cabinet to extend more aid to India,[52] Japan's assistance remained strictly non-military and limited in scope.[53]

The Kennedy administration, gearing up for a major confrontation with China over Vietnam, found the Japanese attitude alarming. Kennedy had discussed China at some length with Ikeda during the Japanese Prime Minister's visit to Washington in June 1961. At that time, Ikeda had appeared to endorse Washington's view of the Asian situation. At the meeting of the United States-Japan Joint Committee on Trade and Economic Affairs in December 1962, therefore, Kennedy strongly requested Japanese co-operation in efforts to 'contain' Communist China. The Americans criticized Japan's indulgent attitude towards Peking and attacked its apparent lack of enthusiasm for improving ties with South Korea, Taiwan and other non-Communist Asian countries.[54] A week later Averell Harriman told correspondents from the *Mainichi Shimbun* that the United States could not possibly approve of Sino-Japanese trade.[55] On 9 January 1963 the United States, perhaps acting in accordance with agreements believed to have been reached with the Kishi Cabinet in 1960, renewed a request, already made unsuccessfully in 1961, that American nuclear-powered submarines be permitted to call at Japanese ports.[56] Finally, at the Security Consultative Committee of 19 January 1963, the United States urged Japan to consider seriously the implications of the Chinese nuclear programme and co-operate more positively with the Western alliance. In particular, United States officials made it clear that they hoped to see increased Japanese economic aid to South Korea, South Vietnam and other nations directly engaged in the struggle against Communism.[57]

The Kennedy and Harriman statements were the opening shots in a campaign whose ultimate objective was to align Japan more closely with American policies in Asia and halt the drift towards *rapprochement* with Peking. This campaign, conducted against the background of Chinese nuclear development, the deepening crisis in Vietnam and continued tension on the Korean peninsula, succeeded in aggravating the factional strife already existing in the government and Liberal Democratic Party. Yet it did not produce concrete results until Conservative Party factional struggles had brought about a new configuration of power, and illness or death eliminated the principal opponents of fuller co-operation with the United States.

(vii)   Japanese reactions to the new emphasis in American policy, December 1962–October 1963

The Japanese government at first pretended to misunderstand Washington's intentions. The Foreign Ministry's official translation of Kennedy's speech to the Joint

Committee on Trade and Economic Affairs avoided the use of the usual Japanese word for 'contain' (*fujikomu*), replacing it by 'to limit' or 'to check' (*soshi suru*).[58] After the Kennedy statement, Ikeda told the press that while it was 'natural' for Japan to join hands with the other nations of the Free World, the President had actually been speaking of 'checking the expansion of Stalinism'. This should not be linked to the question of trade with China, which was a matter for Japan to settle independently.[59] On his return from the Joint Committee meeting in Washington Foreign Minister Ōhira, explaining how United States hostility to China had increased because of the Cuban crisis and the Sino-Indian border conflict, stated that

> Japan has an alliance with the United States and extensive ties of co-operation with that country. Therefore there will be no problems at all even if Japan, to a degree not inimical to these relations, sorts out her affairs with Communist China, conducts trade, establishes cultural and economic ties. This is the Government's view and there will be no need to change it in the future.[60]

While it was 'natural' to oppose further expansion of Communist power, there were no plans for Japanese–American consultations on future policy towards the People's Republic.

These were the attitudes of Ikeda, Kōno and the dominant coalition. The impact of Kennedy's stand on factions emphasizing the paramount importance of co-operation with the United States was different. Shortly after the Trade and Economic Affairs Committee meeting, Satō returned from a tour of Europe and North America stressing the intensity of the East–West conflict, the need for Western unity and the desirability of 'caution' in relations with China.[61] By the spring of 1963 controversy over Sino-Japanese relations within the Liberal Democratic Party had become acute. The 'pro-American' Westernist groups argued that the 'world trend' was to make approaches to the Soviet Union and isolate China. Japan should, accordingly, co-operate faithfully with the United States and abandon efforts to improve ties with Peking. Naturally, in accordance with established Japanese policies, most Conservatives drew the line at actual military co-operation. The 'pro-China', 'Asianist' factions, in contrast, maintained that for historical, geographical and economic reasons Japan would be obliged to improve relations with Peking, whatever the trend of American policy.[62]

Apart from the fact that independently minded nationalists and groups sympathetic to China were strong in the dominant factional alliance, certain international developments in the spring and summer of 1963 improved the position of those favouring a flexible policy towards Peking. The visit of the American special envoy Christian Herter in April made it clear that the United States was not interested in increasing imports from Japan. Washington declined to recognize any 'special relationship' with Tōkyō, announcing that its foreign trade policy was determined 'from a global standpoint'.[63] Many Japanese business and political leaders, moreover, were disturbed by the rapid growth of Chinese trade with Western Europe and the United Kingdom. The visit of the British Foreign Secretary Lord Home in

April provided an opportunity to exchange views on the China question with another conservative American ally. Lord Home made a favourable impression on the Japanese government by appealing for joint efforts to persuade Washington that a more positive approach to trade with the People's Republic was ultimately in the interests of the non-Communist world.[64]

It was these factors that lay behind Ikeda's decision of August 1963 to permit the export of a vinylon plant to China on a deferred payment basis,[65] despite American threats of dire consequences if the negotiations were carried through.[66] Within months a number of similar contracts were either being negotiated or examined. Despite the explosive reaction of Taipei,[67] the hostile attitude of Washington and the cautious stand of the Japanese Foreign Ministry, Sino-Japanese trade continued to expand during the autumn and winter of 1963. In September the Japan Economic Research Council (Nihon Keizai Chōsa Kyōgikai), an influential research organ operated jointly by Keidanren, Nikkeiren, Nisshō and Keizai Dōyūkai, released a report explicitly recommending increased trade with all Communist bloc nations, including the People's Republic of China.[68]

In October 1963, in symbolic culmination of these developments, the largest Japanese trade fair ever held in China was opened in Peking. The president of the sponsoring organization, which employed a staff of over 300 Japanese in the Chinese capital, was the former Prime Minister Ishibashi Tanzan. More than 500 companies contributed exhibits to the value of 170 billion yen. Over a thousand Japanese visited Peking for the fair itself, including representatives of political parties, religious groups and cultural organizations. The grand opening banquet was attended by 400 Japanese and 600 Chinese guests. Together with Ishibashi Tanzan, Chou En-lai and other distinguished Chinese leaders moved among the guests, shaking hands, chatting with visitors and drinking toasts.[69] Six months later, in April 1974, a large Chinese trade fair opened at Harumi in Tōkyō. Groups sympathetic to China began organizing a petition, which eventually collected 30 million signatures, calling for immediate restoration of diplomatic ties with Peking.[70] Yet what appeared to be the beginning of a new era in Sino-Japanese relations was, in fact, the end of a brief Indian summer.

(viii)   Postponement of visits by American nuclear-powered submarines, December 1963

Parallel to the debate on relations with China a conflict developed within the government on the advisability of permitting port calls by American nuclear-powered submarines. Generally speaking, factions supporting one cause adopted a cautious attitude towards the other. The American request put Ikeda in a difficult situation. The 1960 security treaty provided no grounds for refusing such port calls. The only condition Japan could place on the entry of naval vessels and aircraft was that they be not equipped with nuclear weapons, which would constitute a 'major change in equipment'. The United States believed it had already secured the Japanese government's permission to bring nuclear weapons in and out of the country. Nevertheless, it informed Tōkyō that, in this case, the nuclear submarines in question were not of the Polaris type, equipped with nuclear missiles, but carried only conventional warheads.[71] There were precedents for American allies refusing to permit port calls. In 1958 Denmark had barred the entry of nuclear submarines on safety grounds.[72] In Japan's case, however, continued refusal to permit port calls on these grounds would have been difficult. Japan itself was planning construction of a nuclear-powered merchant vessel.[73] There was also a view that, in the aftermath of the 1960 crisis and Japanese-American friction over a number of issues during the first years of the Ikeda Cabinet, closer co-operation was necessary to restore American confidence in Japan.[74] Quite clearly, however, recognition of port calls would complicate relations with China. The only solution to Ikeda's dilemma was to placate the Americans with a promise that port calls would in principle be permitted, but to postpone the actual decision as long as possible.

Thus, in announcing Washington's request, the Chief Cabinet Secretary stated (24 January 1963) that there was 'no reason to reject the United States representations', adding that a Japanese-American agreement would soon be drawn up.[75] However, despite discussion of the Chinese nuclear programme at the meeting of the Japanese-American Security Consultative Committee in January 1963[76] and the firm attitude reportedly shown by the Deputy Secretary of Defence Roswell L. Gilpatric when he visited Japan in February,[77] the Ikeda government intimated that its final decision would depend on Washington's furnishing adequate proof of the vessels' safety.[78] Various enquiries on safety were subsequently made but the American replies failed to satisfy the Ministry of Science and Technology and the Atomic Energy Commission.[79] On 11 March the Chief Cabinet Secretary announced that the Japanese decision would be delayed for some time.[80]

Refuge in the safety question was a fortunate stratagem. Within less than a month one of the newest of America's *Nautilus*-type submarines, the *Thresher*, was lost in the Atlantic. In the Atomic Energy Commission opinion against the visits hardened.[81] At the same time, opposition gathered momentum not only in the Socialist and Communist parties but also in scientific circles. Several of Japan's most eminent nuclear scientists publicly protested against the proposed port calls, emphasizing the hazards of radio-activity and the dangers of contamination. On 25 March a committee of nuclear scientists, headed by the Nobel Prize-winning physicist Yukawa Hideki, appealed directly to the government.[82] On 27 March another 154 leading scientists issued a joint statement condemning the visits.[83] On 19 April the President of Tōkyō University handed Ikeda a note of protest[84] and on 26 April the Japan Science Council (Gakujutsu Kaigi) announced its opposition to the proposed port calls.[85] At the same time, there was every indication that the mounting wave of popular protest could precipitate a national crisis on the scale of the 1960 upheaval. These ominous developments proved a boon to opponents of the visits in the Liberal Democratic Party and the bureaucracy. Towards the end of April the government moved towards the view that negotiations could not advance until the reasons for the sinking of the *Thresher* had been disclosed.[86] This shift in opinion corresponded with the emergence of a view in Washington that it would be unwise to provoke the Japanese public too far and that, for the time being, the whole question should be put to one side.[87]

The debate continued inconclusively throughout the summer and autumn of 1963. In December a new complication arose with the United States Navy's announcement that its nuclear submarines were to be fitted with Subroc anti-submarine offensive missiles. These projectiles could be equipped with either conventional or nuclear warheads. It was soon revealed, however, that all Subrocs would be nuclear-tipped.[88] Thus the question was now not merely one of safety, but of whether nuclear weapons could be admitted to Japan.

(ix)　Factional realignments and outside pressures – vacillation on China policy and the decision to permit port calls by nuclear-powered submarines, November 1963–October 1964

The period extending from the general election in November 1963 (a month after the opening of the Japanese trade fair in Peking) until Ikeda's retirement in October 1964 (just after the first Chinese nuclear test) was characterized, on the domestic front, by intensified factional conflict and the first signs of an important shift in the Liberal Democratic Party factional balance. On the international front the period was marked by French recognition of China, heightened Sino-American tension and the rapid escalation of the American war effort in Vietnam. These events were accompanied by an increase in pressure on Japan from Washington and Taipei. The result was an erratic China policy and the decision to permit the entry of American nuclear-powered submarines, subject to certain conditions.

The rise of Kōno, the eclipse of the Kishi-Fukuda faction and the temporary isolation of Satō have already been traced. Despite Satō's readmission to the Cabinet in June 1963 and the partial return to the 'all-faction' structure of 1960–1, Kōno's influence continued to grow. The 1963 general election, in which the Liberal Democratic Party effectively lost a total of thirteen seats,[89] saw a further erosion of Satō's strength. Members of the House of Representatives associated with the Satō faction decreased from over fifty to forty-five or forty-six. In contrast the Kōno faction recruited some fifteen new members and now surpassed both the Satō and Ikeda factions in size and potential influence. After the election, Ikeda moved closer to Kōno than ever before and found it prudent to obtain his understanding on every issue.[90]

Kōno's very success proved to be his undoing. The reaction it inspired undermined not only his own position but also the Ikeda Cabinet and its policies. When Satō had been powerful and seemed destined as Ikeda's successor, faction leaders such as Miki and Fujiyama had, in varying degrees, inclined towards *rapprochement* with Kōno. Now that it seemed probable Kōno would be the next Prime Minister, these factions gradually increased their reserve towards the Ikeda-Kōno-Ōno axis and began to repair their relations with Satō, Fukuda and Ishii. The smaller factions saw their future in support for the weaker contender for party leadership.

Thus within a week of the general elections 117 representatives of the Satō, Ishii, Miki and Fujiyama factions established an organization grandly styling itself as the Headquarters for the Renovation of the People's Minds and Dissolution of the Factions (Jinshin Isshin Habatsu Kaishō Suishin Honbu). The ostensible objective was 'renovating' Cabinet personnel and liquidating internal factions. The real purpose was to undermine Kōno's position in the government.[91]

The Ikeda structure was dealt its first major blow with the sudden death of Ōno Bamboku, just before the July 1964 party presidential election. Together with Kōno, Ōno had been one of the chief pillars of Ikeda's Cabinet. After his demise, his faction divided into pro- and anti-Satō elements, although it did not officially break up until some months later.[92] The significance of these developments was clearly spelled out in the July elections, when Ikeda, with 242 votes, was re-elected party president by a slender majority of ten. Satō gained 160 votes, Fujiyama, who made a last-minute decision to run, polled an unexpectedly high total of 72.[93]

Ikeda's precarious victory would have been impossible without the support of the Kōno faction. In view of the balance of forces revealed by the election, Ikeda hoped to return to the 'all-faction structure' established in 1960. Kōno resolutely opposed this. As a result, the party and Cabinet posts of Ikeda's last, ephemeral administration were monopolized by the dominant factions. Ōno's absence meant that Kōno's weight had increased out of all proportion. Appointed Minister without Portfolio, he emerged as virtual Deputy Prime Minister.[94] Paradoxically, this ensured that the Ikeda Cabinet, had it survived, would have been unable to undertake important new policy initiatives, in view of the intense resistance to be expected from the now powerful dissident groups.

Ikeda's resignation because of ill health on 26 October and Satō's accession as Prime Minister, radically altered the factional configuration in the party. The changes were, however, no more than the reaction to Kōno's dominance would have led one to expect. Miki made strenuous efforts to smooth the path for Satō's accession to power. The Ikeda, Kawashima and former Ōno factions also threw in their lot with Satō. Fukuda and Ishii, who had conscientiously supported Satō during his months in the political wilderness, rode with him into power, insistent that they, too, receive a place in the sun as a reward for their fidelity. It was now Kōno's turn to wander in the pathless waste of political dissidence.[95]

In mid-October 1963 Takasaki Tatsunosuke and Liao Cheng-chi had reached agreement in Peking to extend the Memorandum Trade arrangements negotiated the previous year. This had heightened concern about Japan's future policies in both Washington and Taipei. Towards the end of October the Kuomintang began to apply increasingly intense economic pressure on Japan. A pretext was provided by the Ikeda Cabinet's refusal to hand over Chou Hong-ching, an interpreter with a Communist Chinese technical delegation who had sought refuge in the Soviet Embassy in Tōkyō, then successively requested political asylum in the Soviet Union, Taiwan and Japan before eventually deciding to return to the People's Republic. Officially organized anti-Japanese protests swept Taiwan. Japanese goods were boycotted.

The visit of the then Deputy Prime Minister Ōno Bamboku to Taipei on 30 October had done little to pacify Nationalist opinion.

In January 1964, just as the anti-Kōno alliance was forming in the Liberal Democratic Party, it became evident that France intended to further distance itself from the United States and recognize the People's Republic. The Kuomintang, fearful that Tōkyō might follow suit, but hopeful that the factional struggle in the Liberal Democratic Party might be turned to its own advantage, stepped up its campaign of economic warfare against Japan. On 11 January 1964, just before the French decision to recognize Peking was announced, Taipei proclaimed its intention to suspend imports of government purchases from Japan. About half of Japan's exports to Taiwan fell into this category.[96]

These events hardened the divisions in the Liberal Democratic Party. The Ikeda Cabinet, not wishing to abandon its policy of incremental *rapprochement* with Peking, yet unwilling to sacrifice a healthy trading relationship with Taipei, dominated by groups favouring greater independence from the United States and better relations with the People's Republic, yet unable to ignore the influence of the powerful 'pro-American' elements in the party, swung wildly from one position to another. The first news of the French decision threw the government into confusion. The Chief Cabinet Secretary, Kurogane Yasuyoshi, told the press: 'It puts me in a difficult position, a difficult position.' He kept repeating this phrase throughout the interview.[97] Faction leaders sympathetic to Peking applauded de Gaulle's far-sightedness and courage.[98] Conservatives hostile to China made no attempt to conceal their view that the French move had been 'premature'.[99] The Foreign Ministry sought refuge in muddled ambiguity.[100]

Ikeda's administrative policy speech at the opening session of the new Diet became the focus of the controversy between the contending camps. The Prime Minister referred to the 'stern reality' (*genzen taru jijitsu*) that the Chinese continent, 'inhabited by over 600 million people', was separated from Japan by 'only a narrow strip of water'.[101] The speech announced no new policy (the party factional balance made this virtually impossible) but the wording represented a marginal victory for the 'pro-Peking' forces. When the draft of the speech was being studied by Cabinet the anti-Peking elements had insisted that 'it was not especially necessary to say that there were over 600 million people on the Chinese continent'.[102]

Over the next three weeks government spokesmen made a number of statements interpreted as conciliatory to Peking. On 31 January the Prime Minister told the House of Representatives Budget Committee that while Japan's position was 'different' to that of Peking, Japan entertained 'friendly sentiments' towards the Chinese people. Relations between Japan and China were 'different' to Sino-American relations.[103] On 6 February Foreign Minister Ōhira told the House of Representatives Foreign Affairs Committee that Peking was 'not adventurous' but 'cautious' and 'pursuing realistic policies'.[104] On 12 February Ōhira announced that while Japan still intended to support the American resolution regarding China's admission to the United Nations as an 'important question', relations with Peking would be normalized as soon as the People's Republic entered the world body.[105] Finally, on 18

February, Ōhira told the House that he did not think Communist China was 'a threat to Japan either militarily or economically'.[106]

These statements further alarmed Washington, caused outrage in Taipei and provoked a vigorous counter-offensive on the part of the 'pro-American' groups in the Liberal Democratic Party. After his speech on 12 February Ōhira was summoned before the Party Executive Council and the Foreign Affairs Research Council and informed that it was 'ridiculous' to say that China posed no threat. 'Such statements', the Foreign Minister was told, 'undermine the very foundations of the security treaty system.'[107] The source of anxiety, in these quarters, was not so much China itself as Washington's possible reaction to a Sino-Japanese *rapprochement*. The Foreign Ministry was divided. Nevertheless, the dominant view was that nothing should be done to jeopardize relations with the United States and Taiwan,[108] although influential figures such as Asakai Kōichirō, the Japanese ambassador to Washington, consistently advised the government to adopt more independent policies on China.[109]

It was probably about this time that Yoshida Shigeru, the *éminence grise* behind Ikeda's cautious exploration of the prospects for unilateral *détente* with the People's Republic, decided that the situation might be defused by making a personal visit to Chiang Kai-shek. Since Yoshida himself held no official post in the Japanese government, Ikeda's policy of incremental *rapprochement* with Peking, he might have reasoned, would in no way be compromised. A heart-to-heart talk with the Generalissimo, a few ambiguous promises from an ailing old man, might help placate Washington, salvage a useful trading partnership and repair relations between the Prime Minister and 'pro-American' groups in the Liberal Democratic Party, thus reducing his reliance on Kōno. If Yoshida could heal the breach between the Prime Minister, Kishi, Fukuda, Satō and Ishii, then drive a wedge between Ikeda and Kōno, it would be difficult for Hatoyama's followers to seize control of the party. This project, which relied for its success on both American and Nationalist Chinese misunderstanding of the realities of Japanese political culture (and of Yoshida's own long-term objectives) was a classical product of the crafty old man's scheming mind. The only danger was that the Chinese in Peking might also mistakenly believe that he was going to Taipei as a great and powerful genro, able to override Cabinet decisions and turn the Japanese ship of state around at will. Any misunderstanding in Peking might, however, be cleared up during Matsumura Kenzō's visit to the Chinese capital, scheduled to begin in mid-April.[110]

In preparation for Yoshida's trip to Taipei, the Ikeda Cabinet subtly changed the emphasis (but not necessarily the meaning) of its earlier pronouncements on relations with the People's Republic. On 20 February Foreign Minister Ōhira told the Diet that he did not think there was 'no possibility of aggression by the Communists'.[111] In an interview with the *Mainichi Shimbun* he went to considerable lengths to establish his credentials as a man aware of the importance of relations with Taipei.[112] Then, on 4 March, shortly after Yoshida's return, Ikeda told the House of Councillors Budget Committee that Japan would have 'no obligation' to recognize the People's Republic even if it were admitted to the United Nations.[113]

With the release of the Liberal Democratic Party's 'Unified View' on China policy on 5 March the pendulum began to swing back in the other direction. This 'View', like most such documents, was not 'unified' in the sense that it incorporated any logically consistent strain of thought. It appeared, in many ways, little more than an attempt to reduce tensions within the party by stating, side by side, the contentions of the two warring camps. A careful reading of the text, however, will reveal that while many concessions in principle were made to those groups advocating continued solidarity with the United States, the operative parts of the document tended to reflect the thinking of elements sympathetic to Peking. Thus, to satisfy the 'pro-American' camp China was first described as 'a Communist regime which aims eventually at communizing the world'. It was noted that Asian nations, including Japan, were feeling 'uneasy' about Communist China's military, ideological, political and economic expansion. Yet whether China's *actual policies* were aggressive was 'a different question'. China appeared, in fact, to be taking a 'prudent' attitude towards the outside world. There was little possibility of Peking's direct, military intervention on the Sino-Soviet border, in Korea or the Taiwan Straits. Chinese military intervention in Laos, Vietnam and South-East Asia was 'hardly conceivable'. Moreover, 'at the present stage', China was considered not to harbour 'any intention of direct, armed aggression against Japan'. This despite its long-term, avowed objective of destroying the Japanese-American security treaty.

As for Japan's policy towards China, it was argued that Japan had concluded a peace treaty with Chiang Kai-shek and maintained formal diplomatic relations with Taipei. Yet Japan's special circumstances demanded 'various kinds of *de facto* relations' (*jisshitsujō no kankei*) with the Chinese mainland. China's population of 600 million was again specifically mentioned. So too were Japan's historical links with China. Because of these factors Japan's position was 'fundamentally different' from that of the United States, which need not have 'any relations with the Chinese continent at all'. Nevertheless, it could not be denied that recognition of Peking would 'impair the solidarity of the Free Camp' and thus 'endanger the peace and stability of Asia'. This would be 'contrary to Japan's national interests'. Since the solution to the Peking-Taipei conflict was not in Japan's hands, it was recommended that Japan continue its policy of maintaining '*de jure*' relations with Taipei and '*de facto*' relations 'in trade and other fields' with Peking. Japan would continue to regard China's entry into the United Nations as 'an important matter', and would therefore support the American-sponsored resolution based on this premiss. However, if China were admitted to the United Nations, Japan would 'consider' the question of recognition.[114]

Two days after publication of the 'Unified View' the government announced plans to permit the export to China of a vinylon plant by the Dai Nihon Bōseki Company, presumably on the deferred payment basis with Export-Import Bank credit that had been resisted by the 'pro-American' groups within the party ever since the Kurashiki Rayon Company plant decision of 1963.

This proved to be one step too far. Japanese relations with Taiwan sank to a nadir. On 18 March Vice-Foreign Minister Mori returned from an overseas trip with the warning that if the Dai Nihon Bōseki decision were officially announced, relations with the Kuomintang would 'reach a point of complete break-off'.[115] Kishi and Ishii protested to Ikeda in the strongest terms.[116] The 'pro-American' groups in the party closed ranks and marshalled their forces for a concerted attack on the Cabinet.

These moves, coming on the eve of the party presidential elections, inclined Ikeda to caution. No official announcement on the Dai Nihon Bōseki plant was made. The idea was, presumably, to announce the deal after the election had confirmed Ikeda in power and subsequent Cabinet reshuffles had reduced the influence of groups hostile to the development of relations with Peking. In the weeks that followed, Japanese policies continued to oscillate wildly. On 2 April the government's decision to refuse entry to a Hsinhua News Agency journalist (on the grounds that he had criticized Japanese foreign policies during a previous visit)[117] was greeted warmly in Taipei. The applause had scarcely subsided when Matsumura Kenzō and Liao Cheng-chi concluded an agreement in Peking on exchange of journalists and establishment of Memorandum Trade offices in the Chinese and Japanese capitals.[118] Rumbles of disapproval came from Washington. Taipei was outraged.

Once again, Yoshida Shigeru came to Ikeda's rescue. On 30 May 1964 Yoshida dispatched a private letter to Chiang Kai-shek, apparently assuring the Nationalist leader that he would use his personal influence to ensure that the Japanese government exercised caution in any decisions regarding plant exports to Peking on Export-Import Bank credit.[119] On 5 July 1964, five days before the Liberal Democratic Party presidential elections, Taiwan lifted its restrictions on trade with Japan.[120]

In later years, especially after Yoshida's death, the 'pro-American' groups in the Liberal Democratic Party came to regard this second Yoshida Letter with much the same kind of exaggerated reverence as certain Buddhist sects view the Lotus Sutra. Unilateral *rapprochement* with Peking was impossible not just because of the American alliance but because Yoshida had given his personal word to Chiang Kai-shek. Yet like the Lotus Sutra, the second Yoshida Letter must be seen in context. In the higher interests of the state Yoshida had always been willing to sacrifice his own reputation and act as a diplomatic lightning conductor. It seems highly probable that the 1964 Yoshida Letter was intended simply to help Ikeda escape from a rather sticky situation. No doubt the former Prime Minister expected his disciple to ignore it as soon as a convenient opportunity arose.

The feeble Cabinet formed after Ikeda's narrow victory, however, found it extremely difficult to undertake new intitiatives on China. The weeks before and after the election had been marked by a series of portentous international developments. The Japanese government had carefully observed the escalation of American involvement in Indochina. Ikeda had been fully aware of the possible implications of Kennedy's policies. Yet by the middle of 1964 it was evident that a large-scale (and notably unsuccessful) anti-guerilla operation was about to develop into a major war with far-reaching international repercussions. On the eve of the 1964 Liberal Democratic Party presidential elections President Johnson appointed the former Chief of Staff General Maxwell Taylor as ambassador to Saigon. The Tonkin Gulf incident occurred on 2 August. Within less than twelve hours United States bombers were winging their way towards North Vietnam. The Tonkin Gulf resolution, passed by Congress on 7 August, gave the American President virtually unlimited authority 'to take all the necessary steps, including the use of armed force, to assist any member or protocol state of the Southeast Asia Collective Defence Treaty requesting assistance in defence of its freedom'.[121] In both the United States and Japan the possibility of Chinese intervention in the conflict began to be taken very seriously. These events gave force to the contention of 'pro-American' groups in the Liberal Democratic Party that now was not the most appropriate time to improve relations with Peking. Japan would be best advised to batten down the hatches and ride out the storm. In the House of Representatives Foreign Affairs Committee the new Foreign Minister, Shiina Etsusaburō, faithfully repeated Washington's version of the Tonkin Gulf incident, expressing his full 'understanding' of President Johnson's reaction. The Foreign Ministry Treaties Bureau hastened to assure the Diet that the Gulf of Tonkin was not in the Far East. For this reason, events there could not become the subject of prior consultation under the 1960 security treaty.[122] In rapid succession high-ranking American officials visited Japan, emphasizing the need for greater Japanese awareness of the Communist threat, expressing disapproval of Sino-Japanese trade and urging Japan to give greater assistance to the countries of non-Communist Asia.[123]

The heightened tension in the Far East and the new balance of power in the Liberal Democratic Party had several important consequences. First, in the area of China policy, no decision on the Dai Nihon Bōseki plant export was announced, although Sino-Japanese trade continued to expand. Second, Japan took immediate steps to increase aid to non-Communist Asia. On 11 July, in one of its first acts, the new Ikeda Cabinet decided to dispatch $US500,000 worth of medical supplies to South Vietnam.[124] On 18 August Cabinet announced that Japan would export $2 million worth of raw materials, plant and machinery to South Korea on a deferred payment basis.[125] Third, on 28 August 1964, the Japanese government announced that it would welcome port calls by American nuclear-powered submarines.[126] Fourth, as an inevitable outcome of these developments, the dialogue between the government and the Opposition, so assiduously cultivated by the Ikeda Cabinet, began to break down. The Opposition intensified efforts to reconstruct the anti-treaty coalition that had exercised such a powerful influence on national affairs in 1960. On 10 July, the day of the Liberal Democratic Party presidential election, representatives of the Socialist Party, the Communist Party, the General Council of Trade Unions and 137 other organizations met in Tōkyō to plan joint action against American involvement in Vietnam and Japanese support for Washington's policies.[127] Despite continued ideological dissension in the Opposition camp, this meeting laid the basis for what was to become one of the largest, best organized and most influential anti-war movements in the world.

(x)   Reactions to the Chinese nuclear test, October 1964

China conducted its first nuclear test on 16 October 1964, a week before Ikeda's retirement. China's emergence as a nuclear power had little impact on attitudes within the government and the Liberal Democratic Party. The 'pro-American' groups did not consider Chinese nuclear weapons posed a direct military threat to Japan's security. Conservatives sympathetic to Peking did not believe China's image as a cautious and realistic international actor had been damaged. Nor was there any particular alarm in the Defence Agency or Foreign Ministry.

Immediately after the test the Chief Cabinet Secretary issued a statement regretting China's decision to become a nuclear power. He emphasized, however, that Chinese nuclear weapons could pose no threat to a Japan protected by the United States.[128] Similar statements were made by Defence Agency spokesmen.[129] There was no panic in the Foreign Ministry. Some Foreign Ministry officials, in fact, expressed hopes that China, its sense of security now increased, might adopt a more flexible and conciliatory attitude to the outside world.[130]

Two months after the test the Liberal Democratic Party Security Research Committee (Anzen Hoshō Ni Kansuru Chōsakai), an organ virtually dominated by groups opposed to *rapprochement* with Peking, prepared a report on the Chinese nuclear programme. This report concluded that

> The success of China's nuclear test does not mean we are faced at once with a Chinese military nuclear threat. Moreover, even if the Chinese do, after several years, succeed in developing some kind of nuclear weapons system, this will increase only slightly the threat to which Japan has previously been exposed by Soviet military power. There should be no cause for alarm or agitation.[131]

This attitude remained one of the most striking features of reports compiled by the committee from 1964 onwards. The long 'Interim Report on Japan's Security' prepared in June 1966, for example, followed broadly similar lines. China's military power, including its nuclear arsenal, was dismissed as a factor of little significance in world affairs. Noting with satisfaction the overwhelming nuclear superiority of the United States the committee observed that

> Even if China, after ten years or so, were to possess strategic nuclear strike power in the form of intercontinental ballistic missiles, these, like the present Soviet intercontinental missiles, will be effectively prevented from threatening the American continent.

China's conventional power, according to the 1966 report, was even more limited. Its armies were poorly equipped, its naval and air forces antiquated, its industrial base backward and exposed. The nuclear weapons programme would inevitably retard its economic growth. In these circumstances it could pose no direct military threat to areas beyond its immediate borders.

This relatively sanguine assessment of China's power did not lead the committee to recommend establishment of normal ties with Peking. Nor was there any apparent interest in persuading Washington that the People's Republic was not the principal cause of global instability. On the contrary, the committee's reports, almost without exception, manifested acute hostility towards China, opposed the development of political, economic and cultural ties with Peking and recommended that Japan play a more active (but not necessarily military) role in American Far Eastern strategy.[132]

If Chinese nuclear weapons failed to overawe the 'pro-American' groups in the Liberal Democratic Party, they did not, as later events were to show, cause any lessening of interest in improved Sino-Japanese relations among independently minded nationalists and Asianists.

(xi)   The emergence of the Satō Cabinet and the deterioration of Sino-Japanese relations, October 1965–September 1966

The factional realignments that followed Ikeda's retirement on 26 October might have had greater repercussions had not reaction to Kōno's growing power impelled Ikeda, Miki, Kawashima and the remnants of the Ōno faction to co-operate in the transfer of party leadership to Satō. While the new Prime Minister was able to find places for representatives of the Kishi, Fukuda and Ishii factions, his first Cabinet contained many elements inherited directly from the Ikeda years. The nucleus of the new structure was formed by Satō and his followers, and by the Miki, Ikeda, Kawashima and former Ōno factions. Kōno played no part, but took up a position with his huge faction on the flanks, ready to take advantage of the first signs of internal dissension in the dominant alliance.[133]

This had important effects on Satō's initial policies. The Chinese Communists, with their Confucian-Marxist view of the world, were intensely suspicious of Satō.[134] He was, after all, Kishi's younger brother, and Kishi had been hostile to China. His connections with heavy industry were also close. China's misgivings were not entirely without foundation. In 1964 Satō did believe that Japan's recovery as a great power could best be realized through continued co-operation with the United States and its Asian-Pacific allies. Unlike Yoshida, Hatoyama, Ishibashi and Ikeda he does not seem to have had much interest in continental Asia. With the passage of time, he increasingly looked south, towards Indonesia and the Malay world, Australia and Oceania. Nevertheless, Satō was, above all else, a slow-moving, consensus politician. Just as Ikeda had been obliged to act cautiously so as not to antagonize basically 'pro-American' elements, like Ōno, in his own camp, or to provoke powerful dissident faction leaders such as Kishi and Satō, so, too, Satō had to satisfy the demands of his supporters without totally alienating Miki, Kawashima and Ikeda, or giving Kōno an opportunity to revive his political fortunes. For this reason, the first few months of the new administration saw a continuation of the erratic policy towards China that had characterized the last eight months of the Ikeda Cabinet. On 21 November 1964, Satō informed the Diet that he would continue Ikeda's policy of separating politics and trade and would seek to build bridges to Peking, despite China's emergence as a military nuclear power. 'It must be said that the importance of the China question is continually increasing. Taking into consideration the development of the international situation I intend to examine this matter cautiously and seriously.'[135] The very same day, however, the Japanese government refused to permit the entry of a Chinese Communist Party delegation headed by the then Mayor of Peking, Peng Chen.[136] The Chinese Foreign Ministry, already highly critical of Japan's decision to permit port calls by American nuclear-powered submarines, issued a strong statement condemning the decision. The *People's Daily* attacked the Satō Cabinet's 'reactionary policy hostile to China' and 'aggressive policy towards South-East Asia'.[137] The growing *rapprochement* between Tōkyō and Seoul was also the subject of hostile comment. Early in December China refused to permit the entry of Kuno Chūji, the Satō faction's only 'China specialist'.[138] Liao Cheng-chi cancelled plans to visit Japan and it soon became apparent that an all-party Japanese parliamentary delegation scheduled to visit China in December would not be invited.[139] Nevertheless, Satō strenuously denied viewing China with hostility.[140] His Chief Cabinet Secretary spoke tirelessly of the government's hopes for increased Sino-Japanese trade, personal and cultural exchanges.[141]

After the Prime Minister's return from talks with President Johnson in January 1965, there was a perceptible hardening in policy towards Peking. Johnson was well known for his ability to twist the arms of recalcitrant allies. Within a week of the talks the Japanese government announced that Export-Import Bank finance would not be available for the proposed Dai Nihon Bōseki vinylon plant export to China.[142] Shortly afterwards the government disclosed that Export-Import Bank funds would also be denied to the Hitachi Company for the export of a freighter to China.[143]

The Prime Minister's first major Cabinet reorganization, announced on 6 June 1965, strengthened the position of the Satō, Kishi-Fukuda and Ishii factions. Fukuda's appointment as Finance Minister and Ishii's appointment as Minister of Justice were particularly significant. Yet with Fujiyama's installation as director of the Economic Planning Agency and Miki's appointment as Minister of International Trade and Industry it could not be said that groups advocating a conciliatory policy towards Peking had been totally pushed aside.[144]

The decisive blow to the cause of improved Sino-Japanese relations at this stage was dealt shortly after the Cabinet reshuffle, with the sudden deaths of Kōno in July and Ikeda in August. The break-up of the former Ōno faction was also not without significance. The Kōno faction was immediately paralysed by internal dissension. One group of more elderly members, led by Shigemasa Seishi, gravitated towards co-operation with Satō. The others, led by Nakasone Yasuhiro, opposed Satō and advocated continuation of the Kōno tradition.[145] The youthful Nakasone, however, while intensely nationalistic, was much more influenced by the anti-Communist ethos of the Cold War era than his mentor had been. The Ikeda faction was subjected to little internal stress after its leader's demise. Maeo Shigesaburō was at once appointed heir and successor.[146] Yet Maeo had neither the prestige nor the experience to pursue Ikeda's policies forcefully. The effects of the split in the Ōno faction (which became open in August 1965, about the time of Ikeda's death)[147] were more difficult to evaluate. It seems probable, however, that this eliminated one of the principal channels of communication between various groups within the Liberal Democratic Party. These events left the 'pro-American' elements temporarily in command of the field. Advocates of improved Sino-Japanese relations in the dominant alliance, like Miki and Fujiyama, found their freedom of manoeuvre increasingly restricted.

It was just at this time that the United States, perhaps sensing its opportunity in the altered complexion of the Liberal Democratic Party, began a major drive to bring Japan more into line with American policies in the Far East. The Japanese were subjected to an intensive campaign of official and semi-official American criticism. The American barrage began early in October 1965 when Ambassador Reischauer publicly attacked the coverage of the Vietnam War given by two leading Japanese newspapers, the *Asahi Shimbun* and the *Mainichi Shimbun*.[148] This incident was followed up by a speech attacking Japan's 'dangerously mistaken views' on China given by Assistant Secretary of State William Bundy at a meeting of the American Assembly in New York.[149] A few days later Bundy again condemned the Japanese view of China in a speech to the Japan-United States Mayors' Conference.[150] Then on 22 December James Reston in *The New York Times* strongly criticized Japan's refusal to help lighten the American burden in South-East Asia.[151] The January 1966 edition of *Foreign Affairs* (released on 22 December 1965) carried a long article by the editor-in-chief, Philip Quigg, attacking Japanese attitudes towards China, Vietnam, defence and the American alliance.[152] Even more alarming was America's reported disinterest in promoting Japanese candidature for non-permanent membership of the United Nations Security Council.[153] In business circles, it was increasingly felt that some gesture of support for the United States was necessary if Japanese-American economic relations were not to be further damaged.[154]

Shortly after Reischauer and Bundy had delivered their initial volleys, therefore, the Prime Minister told the House of Councillors Special Committee on Relations with the Republic of Korea that China's attitude was 'very worrying'. A nuclear-armed China was a 'threat' to Japan.[155] He developed this theme at greater length the following day.[156] Satō's remarks were followed up on 11 December 1965 by an interview with Foreign Minister Shiina published in the *Nihon Keizai Shimbun*. Shiina spoke of China's 'expansionist policies' presenting 'a serious problem for Japan'. He prognosticated gloomily on the future of Sino-Japanese trade (there were not many items Japan wanted to purchase from China; Chinese coal and iron ore were of 'poor quality'; China's foreign currency reserves were 'weak').[157] Then, on 29 March 1966, the government refused to issue entry permits for members of a Chinese delegation invited by the Socialist Party. This was the first time an entire delegation had been summarily barred.[158] After the Chinese hydrogen bomb test in May 1966 the Defence Agency director-general spoke with the press about 'the Communist threat' and the necessity for 'strengthening the security treaty system'.[159] At the same time, Foreign Minister Shiina was telling the House of Councillors Foreign Affairs Committee that while the security treaty would be upheld, Japan would take no part in American strategic planning.[160] As the Prime Minister had remarked some months earlier: 'Just because I said I feel threatened, this does not have to be reflected in our immediate policies.'[161]

It is thus difficult to know whether the Japanese were relieved when United States Secretary for Defence Robert McNamara assured the strategic studies expert Wakaizumi Kei in September 1966 that there were no limitations on the kind of weapons America would use to fulfil its treaty obligations to Japan.[162] Japan's decision to regard China as a threat had, after all, been made solely with an eye to the effect it would produce in Washington.

During the course of the next few months the Chinese leadership embarked on the Great Proletarian Cultural Revolution. Preoccupied with internal factional conflicts, the People's Republic gradually lost touch with the realities of the outside world. Even if Satō's cabinet had wished to reverse its own policies it is doubtful whether it could have succeeded in improving the climate of Sino-Japanese relations.

III The development of informed and popular opinion

Soviet-American strategic parity, estrangement between France and the United States, the Sino-Soviet split, intensified containment of China and the Vietnam War coincided with the emergence of a new generation of Japanese international relations and strategic studies specialists. From the mid-1960s onwards two new groups, the 'neo-idealists' and 'neo-realists', dominated the foreign policy debate, making the greatest and most original contributions to its development. The 'neo-idealists' centred around such figures as Sakamoto Yoshikazu, Seki Hiroharu, Ishida Takeshi and Fukushima Shingo. The principal luminaries among the 'neo-realists' were scholars such as Kōsaka Masataka, Nagai Yōnosuke, Etō Shinkichi and Wakaizumi Kei. Writers such as Rōyama Michio and Kishida Junnosuke occupied an intermediate position between the two camps.

The 'neo-idealists', like their mentors in the 1950s, opposed rearmament, advocated peaceful coexistence and espoused policies of unarmed or lightly armed neutrality. What distinguished them from their predecessors was not so much the substance of their ideas but their mode of expression, which was strongly influenced by new developments in the social sciences in the United States and Western Europe. The focus of their interests, however, remained East Asia, above all China. The Sino-Soviet split, China's emergence as a nuclear power, then the onset of the Cultural Revolution, caused some initial confusion. Yet a consensus soon emerged that while the international environment had become at once more complex and more dangerous, Japan's interests lay in continued efforts, as a neutral and unarmed state, to reduce tensions among the surrounding great powers. 'Neo-idealist' writing, during this period, was characterized by an admirably balanced approach to American-Soviet strategic rivalry, a cool-headed assessment of the implications of the Chinese nuclear programme and a profound uneasiness about United States policies in South-East Asia. The Vietnam War generated considerable anti-American sentiment. Throughout the 1960s, 'neo-idealists' continued to oppose Japanese participation in containment, rearmament, American military bases, *rapprochement* with South Korea, support for Taiwan, involvement in Indochina and indirect co-operation with SEATO.[163]

The 'neo-realists', like their predecessors in the 1950s, supported Japan's alignment with the United States, regarded military power as a vital factor in international relations and rejected unarmed neutrality. By the mid-1960s, however, the rationale for maintenance of the security treaty had shifted from ideological anti-Communism to balance of power theories. The changes in the global equilibrium and the erosion of the Cold War alliances produced, in turn, a far more conditional support for the San Francisco system. Most of the new 'realists' were guarded against unnecessarily making an enemy of either the Soviet Union or the People's Republic of China.[164]

China's nuclear weapons programme was not generally seen as constituting, in itself, an immediate military threat to Japan's security. A minority of the 'neo-realists', typified by Wakaizumi, saw a nuclear-armed China with great power status as posing a potentially serious long-term political, diplomatic and military challenge. They recommended, as a temporary measure, closer ties with the United States. They also urged massive investment in space research and civilian nuclear energy programmes. It might one day be necessary, they argued, for Japan to develop a fully independent nuclear strike force. There was some interest in economic, political and, perhaps, military co-operation with Asian and Pacific nations seen as hostile to China, such as Australia and India.[165] Nevertheless, a majority of the 'neo-realists', typified by Kōsaka, Etō and Nagai, considered that uncritical association with American policies was driving Japan needlessly into a position of confrontation with the People's Republic. They urged greater Japanese autonomy within the security treaty system. This necessitated a weakening of military ties with the United States and a substantial independent defence build-up.[166] At the same time, there was little feeling, even in these circles, that the American connection should, or could be, abandoned. The global balance of power may have been changing, but it had not yet changed decisively. The United States still remained the world's mightiest nation. This simple fact, the neo-realists believed, compelled Japan to act in particular ways. As Nagai Yōnosuke remarked:

> We must always bear in mind that the first principle of Japan's defence and diplomatic policy is to ensure that the United States does not become an enemy ... If we put it in the language of the left-wing camp, the question becomes, 'Is Japan comparatively safer as the first line of defence against "American imperialism" or as a target for attack by "peace-loving" China?' This problem is, for me at least, the greatest lesson of the Vietnam War.[167]

By the spring of 1968 an overwhelming majority of the Japanese public was in favour of neutrality. The 5 April 1968 *Shūkan Asahi* poll found 66 per cent of respondents supporting some form of neutrality and only 19.6 per cent in favour of the security treaty. The 1 July 1968 *Mainichi Shimbun* poll found 21 per cent in favour of the security treaty, 38 per cent advocating armed neutrality, 28 per cent supporting unarmed neutrality. By the end of 1969 interest in neutrality had somewhat declined. A *Tōkyō Shimbun* poll in December 1969 found 37.4 per cent in favour of security through ties with the United States, 34.5 per cent supporting neutrality. This was roughly the same division of opinion that had existed in 1949–51, on the eve of the first security treaty. Polls on the contribution of the treaty to Japan's security yielded more erratic results, but by 1970 large, approximately equal minorities were apparently convinced either that the treaty had a beneficial effect, or that it was unnecessary or dangerous.

Table VII. 1 Sample public opinion polls on neutralism and the security treaty in the 1960s

Newspaper or Organ	Date	Strengthen security treaty	Maintain present security treaty and military forces	Security treaty and increasing autonomous military power	Armed neutrality	Unarmed neutrality	Security treaty with Communist powers	Other
Prime Minister's Office poll (as reported in *Tōkyō Shimbun*)	31/01/63	38.0% favour general co-operation with Western powers			36.0% favour neutrality		1.0%	
Mainichi Shimbun	13/06/65	question not asked	7.9%	19.2%	11.4%	11.5%	question not asked	13.2%
Mainichi Shimbun	13/06/66	question not asked	9.6%	22.5%	11.5%	10.8%	question not asked	14.6%
Shūkan Asahi	5/04/68	question not asked	19.6%	question not asked	66.0% for neutralism		question not asked	6.6%
Mainichi Shimbun	1/07/68	question not asked	21.0%	question not asked	38.0%	28.0%	2.0%	11.0%
Asahi Shimbun	5/01/69	question not asked	24.0%	question not asked	56.0% for neutrality		question not asked	6.0%
Mainichi Shimbun	12/05/69	question not asked	21.0%	19.0%	43.0% for various types of neutrality		question not asked	17.0%
Yomiuri Shimbun	1/06/69	question not asked	27.0%	28.0%	8.0%	9.0%	question not asked	
Asahi Shimbun	1/10/69	question not asked	17.0%	23.0%	28.0%	20.0%	question not asked	
Mainichi Shimbun	4/11/69	question not asked	22.0%	21.0%	33.0% for various types of neutrality		question not asked	
Tōkyō Shimbun	10/12/69	question not asked	22.1%	15.3%	21.3%	13.2%	question not asked	

Table VII. 2 The security treaty – a contribution to Japanese security or a possible danger

Newspaper or organ	Date	The treaty is (has been) necessary for (contributes to) Japan's security.	The treaty is (has been) unnecessary for (has not contributed to) Japan's security.	The treaty is (has been) dangerous
Mainichi Shimbun	3/10/67	28.2% (Respondents were asked whether US bases were necessary.)	28.4% (Respondents were asked whether US bases were necessary.)	19.7% (Respondents were asked whether US bases were necessary.)
Yomiuri Shimbun	22/04/68	55.0%	17.0%	question not asked
Mainichi Shimbun	1/07/68	18.0%	question not asked	33.0%
Asahi Shimbun	5/01/69	28.0% (Respondents were asked whether US bases were necessary.)	56.0% (Respondents were asked whether US bases were necessary.)	question not asked
Asahi Shimbun	5/01/69	33.0%	29.0%	question not asked
Mainichi Shimbun	12/05/69	33.0% (Respondents were asked whether US bases were necessary.)	59.0% (Respondents were asked whether US bases were necessary.)	question not asked
Mainichi Shimbun	12/05/69	52.0%	23.0%	14.0%
Sankei Shimbun	13/05/69	23.0%	38.0%	question not asked
Chūō Chōsa (government-sponsored poll – results in *Yomiuri Shimbun* 1/06/69)	20–25/5/69	65.0%	10.0%	question not asked
Asahi Shimbun	1/10/69	41.0% (Respondents were asked whether US bases were necessary.)	45.0% (Respondents were asked whether US bases were necessary.)	question not asked
Asahi Shimbun	1/10/69	37.0%	34.0%	

The number of variables involved makes it virtually impossible to isolate the causes of the pronounced swing to neutrality in the mid-1960s and the return to the traditional distribution of opinion by 1970. The rise of neutralist sentiment took place against the background of the realization of Soviet-American strategic parity, the rise of Gaullism in Europe, China's nuclear development, the Cultural Revolution and the escalation of the Vietnam War. The swing away from neutralism coincided not only with increasing evidence of American decline, but with the Warsaw Pact intervention in Czechoslovakia and the beginning of the student struggle in Japan. The latter, in particular, may have alienated large sections of the public from causes espoused by the left. It could not be *conclusively* shown that any of the changes during this critical decade were caused by the Soviet Union's emergence as a power equal to the United States, the example of France, the Chinese nuclear programme or American policies in South-East Asia. The opinion surveys of the period throw virtually no light on popular attitudes to the changing Soviet-American balance or de Gaulle's break with Washington. The interest of the journalists and scholars responsible for compiling public opinion polls centred almost exclusively on the Far East. Here two general trends were evident.

First, while a majority of the public felt 'threatened' by the Chinese nuclear strike force (35 per cent of those interviewed by the *Yomiuri Shimbun* in April 1968 felt the danger 'strongly', 37 per cent felt it 'a little', only 17 per cent felt 'no danger'),[168] there was, apparently, little belief that China posed a military threat comparable with that of the Soviet Union or, potentially, the United States. Fear of Chinese nuclear weapons was, in fact, fear of nuclear weapons in general, not of China. The January 1969 *Asahi Shimbun* poll revealed that only 12 per cent of respondents 'felt at ease' to know Japan was protected by the American 'nuclear umbrella'. An overwhelming majority of 67 per cent feared the 'nuclear umbrella' would lead Japan into nuclear war.[169] At the same time, there was an extraordinarily strong popular interest in promoting friendly relations with the People's Republic. A *Yomiuri Shimbun* poll of 14 April 1968 showed 35 per cent advocating 'more friendly' relations with China, 34 per cent in favour of normalizing diplomatic ties. Only 10 per cent believed the existing situation to be satisfactory and a mere 8 per cent wished to avoid involvement with China.[170] Second, there was intense popular opposition to the Vietnam War, no widespread belief that American policies in South-East Asia contributed to Japanese security and considerable fear that escalation of the conflict could eventually involve Japan. This strongly suggests that the interest in neutralism may have been an Asianist reaction to American policies but the complexity of the situation makes definitive conclusions impossible.[171]

CHAPTER VIII

Japan, the United States and the Great Crescent, 1960–1967

Ah, take the Cash in hand waive the Rest;
Oh the brave Music of a distant Drum!

The Rubaiyat of Omar Khayyam, XII

I Japanese relations with South Korea

The struggles over China policy within the government, the Liberal Democratic Party and the nation at large were paralleled by controversies over normalization of ties with the Republic of Korea. These disputes reached a climax during the Ikeda and Satō Cabinets. With the overthrow of Rhee Syngh Manh in the spring of 1960 the United States had intensified its efforts to normalize relations between Tōkyō and Seoul. The Kennedy administration, on the eve of its massive intervention in South-East Asia, was anxious to consolidate the American alliance system in the north-east. Washington's long-standing interest in promoting Japanese military involvement in the Korean peninsula remained essentially unchanged. On 17 April 1963 the United States Assistant Secretary for Defence, Roswell L. Gilpatric, after his return from a visit to Tōkyō, told a closed meeting of the Overseas Writers Club that he expected Japan to develop naval and air power sufficient to defend a region 'including part of the Korean peninsula'.[1] On 3 October 1964, Assistant Secretary of State William P. Bundy, during a visit to Seoul, told the press that in the event of another Korean war, 'Japan too, within the limits permitted by its Constitution, will assist South Korea to repel the Communist armies'.[2] American strategies for 'bottling up' the Soviet Pacific fleet in the Sea of Japan assumed a high level of military co-operation between Washington, Tōkyō and Seoul. On the basis of previous experience, however, there could be no grounds for optimism about the feasibility of establishing overt Japanese-South Korean military links. In the early 1960s, therefore, Washington, itself confronted with an increasingly difficult economic situation, directed its attention towards persuading Japan to underwrite South Korea's economic development. It was doubtless assumed that Japanese interest in undertaking responsibility for containment in and around the peninsula would be stimulated by increased economic involvement, trade and investment.

Ikeda and his colleagues, while unable to abandon an attitude of arrogant paternalism in their dealings with Seoul, were by no means opposed to economic co-operation with the new South Korean regime. The Chang Myon government, formed after Rhee Syngh Manh's retirement, was dominated by Japanese educated technocrats. It appeared relatively liberal, popular and stable. It was also responsive to mounting popular pressure in favour of talks with the North. In the spring of 1960, the beginning of an era of *détente* and peaceful coexistence on the Korean peninsula seemed closer at hand than ever before. Prime Minister Chang Myon, for his part, was eager to enlist Japanese co-operation in rebuilding his country's shattered economy. In the spring of 1961 a Japanese parliamentary delegation visited Seoul to assess the situation. On 12 May the director of the Foreign Ministry's Asian Bureau, Mr Iseki, returned from South Korea with a glowing account of the prospects for Japanese-South Korean economic co-operation under the new democratic government. 'The Chang Cabinet is extremely stable', he assured the Prime Minister.[3]

Four days later Colonel Pak Chung Hi, a graduate of the Japanese military academy in Manchuria, led a military *coup d'état*, overthrowing the Cabinet and reinstating the hardline anti-Communist policies of the Rhee Syngh Manh regime. Martial law was proclaimed, the national and provincial assemblies were dissolved, political parties, trade unions and student organisations were forcibly disbanded, newspapers and publishing companies shut down. Mass arrests of political leaders, academics, students and journalists followed. At the national and local level, military officers replaced civilians in all significant administrative positions.[4]

Despite the negative attitudes towards Seoul displayed by most Japanese Cabinets during the 1950s, the Liberal Democratic Party, the business community, the Foreign Ministry and the military establishment were as deeply divided on the question of relations with South Korea as they were on China. As with Sino–Japanese relations, Cold War views of the international order were superimposed on a procrustean bed of prejudices, ambitions, hopes and fears derived from recent experience as well as the remote past. Pak Chung Hi's military *coup d'état* (and the possibility that it had been encouraged by Japan's ally the United States) further complicated an already complex situation.

Within the Liberal Democratic Party, perspectives on the Korean question, like attitudes to China, were to some extent differentiated along factional lines. As far as can be judged from documents currently available, Prime Minister Ikeda, like Yoshida, while convinced of the importance of preserving a non-Communist government in southern Korea, was determined to avoid military involvement in the peninsula. This also appears to have been the position of Satō Eisaku and Kawashima Shōjirō.[5] Kishi Nobusuke, Fukuda Takeo, Ōno Bamboku, Funada Naka, Kitazawa Naokichi, Kaya Okinori, Nakagawa Ichirō and several other Conservative leaders, all of whom strongly opposed any compromise with Moscow or Peking, took a more activist view of Japan's role in the peninsula. Former Prime Minister Kishi's views have already been examined. Fukuda, like Kishi, saw South Korea as 'Japan's outer moat'.[6] The genial Ōno Bamboku, who regarded his relationship with Pak Chung Hi as 'that of a father to his son',[7] unreservedly embraced George Kennan's view of Japan's role in the peninsula, declaring expansively that 'the security of the Far East cannot be achieved until we have established a United States of Japan incorporating South Korea and Taiwan'.[8] Funada, too, constantly criticized Japan's leaders for being too hostile to the concept of a 'NEATO alliance' involving South Korea and Taiwan.[9] Nakagawa considered that Japan should dispatch troops to the peninsula in the event of another Korean war. 'It is my conviction that leadership of Asia can only be achieved by continuously involving ourselves in such matters', he was reported as saying.[10] Kōno Ichirō, Miki Takeo, Matsumura Kenzō and Fujiyama Aiichirō, in contrast, displayed little overt interest in developing relations with South Korea.[11] Like Yoshida, they perhaps believed that renewed involvement in the peninsula would obstruct the development of better relations with the People's Republic of China and tie Japan too closely to American Cold War strategies.

In the early 1960s Japanese business leaders, increasingly confident of their own country's economic future, viewed South Korea as one of several potential markets and fields for investment. They also held high hopes for China. While some may have entertained a genuine ideological sympathy for the Pak Chung Hi regime, their interest was basically a commercial one. Like businessmen in any country, they were anxious not to be outdone by their competitors. On 23 September 1962, Uemura Kōgorō, then president of Nikkeiren, lamented that 'at the present time, American, West German and Italian industrial concerns are advancing into South Korea at an astonishing rate. If Japan's advance is delayed we will probably lose the market in that country.'[12]

Opinion in the Foreign Ministry was divided. One group of officials argued that Japan should take advantage of the opportunity offered by the United States to re-establish a presence in the peninsula and build up the Republic of Korea as a bulwark against Communism. Their views were hawkish in the extreme. Sawada Kenzō, for example, leader of the Japanese delegation at the fourth round of talks with Seoul (15 April 1958–15 April 1960), in a statement widely interpreted as encouraging a South Korean attack on the North, expressed his hope that 'the 38th parallel dividing Korea into two will be pushed back northwards as far as the Yalu'.[13] Others advocated a cautious approach, either because they did not wish to antagonize Moscow, Peking and Pyongyang unnecessarily, or because they considered that the situation in Korea was complex and fluid, that Japan's real interests embraced the entire peninsula, and that these interests differed significantly from those of the United States.[14]

The reticence of many postwar serving military officers to comment publicly on foreign policy makes it impossible to obtain an overall view of attitudes to Korea within the armed forces. Two incidents, however, suggest that at least some elements within the Self Defence Forces retained a high degree of interest in reasserting Japanese political and military influence in the peninsula.

First, General Sugita Ichiji, Chief of the Ground Self Defence Force Staff from 11 March 1960 until 12 March 1962, consistently urged the Japanese government to regard maintenance of the status quo in South Korea as an essential national security interest. While convinced that the American alliance offered the best prospects for preserving a favourable balance in the peninsula, he also seemed prepared to countenance Japanese military intervention, if necessary, to support an anti-Communist regime in Seoul. So strongly held were General Sugita's convictions that he did not hesitate to act, in his capacity as Chief of the Ground Staff, contrary to the spirit of official Japanese government policy. In April 1960, for example, at the time of the collapse of the Rhee Syngh Manh Cabinet, the Japanese government – in accordance with established practice–adopted an attitude of complete neutrality. It maintained this attitude throughout the course of 1960 and 1961. General Sugita took a somewhat different approach. The demise of Rhee Syngh Manh authoritarian, anti-Communist regime, the leftward drift of the South Korean student movement, the calls by the University League for National Reunification for North-South talks, Pyongyang's favourable response to these overtures, then the deteriorating economic situation in Seoul all disturbed him greatly. Increasingly, the Chief of Staff began to view Self Defence Force exercises in the context of the evolving situation in the peninsula. Claims in the South Korean media that he had made statements that could be construed as an interference in domestic politics were, he asserted, based on 'misunderstanding'.[15] Nevertheless, according to his own account,

> in the [Japanese Ground] Staff, from about 8 April onwards, preparations were carried forward for the command exercises to be observed by the Ground Staff Inspectorate (Chief Inspector Vice Chief of Staff Hosoda). The exercises began in earnest on 15 April. The exercises [*kunren*] were given added significance [*kami shitsutsu*] by the global situation and the state of affairs in various neighbouring countries, particularly South Korea.[16]

In the spring of 1961, a few months before Prime Minister Ikeda's visit to the United States, the Japanese Joint Staff Council prepared a paper on Korea's importance to Japanese security. This document, submitted to Ikeda by the then director-general of the Defence Agency, Esaki Masumi, was based on the hoary Meckelian proposition that the Korean peninsula was a 'dagger pointed at the heart of Japan'. While its detailed recommendations remain unclear it seems to have envisaged the possibility of Japanese military intervention, in certain circumstances. This prospect did not appeal to the Prime Minister or to any senior official in the government. The prevailing view, Sugita lamented, was that 'defence means defence within [the limits of] Japanese territory and events outside the country are of no interest'.[17]

> The dominant opinion [in the government] was that it would be sufficient for the Ground Self Defence Forces to carry out exercises with a view to fighting within Japan itself. However, if one thinks dispassionately [it is clear] that in the present day and age a nation's defence is greatly dominated [*sayū sare*] by the global situation. In particular the [very] basis of national defence can be totally destroyed by the trend of events in neighbouring countries. These trends cannot be taken lightly, especially when we recall that there are more than 600,000 Koreans living in Japan. Yet, at the time, no matter how much these things were explained, the view seemed to be that it was merely a stratagem to increase the Ground Self Defence Force budgets.[18]

General Sugita was not, however, a man easily diverted from his long-term objectives. On 15 June 1961, a month after Pak Chung Hi's *coup d'état*, Sugita met the new

South Korean Defence Minister, General Song Hyo Chan, in extreme secrecy, in Tōkyō. General Song had made a stop-over in the Japanese capital *en route* to Seoul after a visit to the United States. The two discussed 'the situation in Korea' and parted 'promising to keep in touch in future'. Contacts were kept up, although it is not clear by what means.[19] In view of the fact that General Song had many friends in the United States military establishment and was highly trusted in Washington, it is possible that the contacts were maintained, perhaps even originally arranged, by the Americans. It seems by no means impossible that the Japanese government knew nothing of these contacts until some days later, when Sugita, at the request of former Prime Minister Yoshida, prepared another memorandum on the Korean question for Ikeda.

Sugita's memorandum, after drawing the Prime Minister's attention to America's expectations of Japan's military role in the Asian area and the importance Washington currently attached to South Korea, portrayed the 38th parallel as 'the front line of Japan's defence'. The destinies of Japan and South Korea, the Chief of Staff argued, had been inseparable since the Meiji Restoration. They remained, in every respect, intimately linked. The continued health of the Japanese-American relationship and Japan's own vital security interests, therefore, made it imperative that Ikeda assure Kennedy, in the strongest terms, of his commitment to Seoul. If Japan acted 'contrary to American expectations' on this matter, Washington might relax its position in the peninsula, paving the way for a Communist seizure of power in the south. Sugita, conscious of Ikeda's sensitivities, did not raise the question of a Japanese military role. General Song, he explained, had expressed an interest in Japanese economic assistance during their recent secret talks. He had also spoken of an exchange of intelligence.[20]

The Chief of Staff's submission failed to impress the Prime Minister. Ikeda was well aware that the assumptions underlying Sugita's argument and the course of action he proposed would eventually lead to some form of Japanese military involvement. Three months later General Song invited Japanese military representatives to attend the South Korean armed forces day celebrations in Seoul as a first step towards future co-operation 'to oppose the infiltration of Communist power in the Far East'. Despite Sugita's urgent pleas to the director-general of the Defence Agency and the Joint Staff Council the Japanese government refused to permit any Self Defence Force personnel to travel to Seoul for the festivities.[21]

Two years later, in February 1963, the Joint Staff Council commissioned a group of some thirty-six army, navy and air force officers, under General Tanaka Yoshio, to draw up detailed plans for a Japanese response to heightened tension in North-East Asia brought about by a hypothetical collapse of the government in Seoul. General Tanaka's group, working in the greatest secrecy, examined seven possible contingencies. The first scenario considered Japanese responses to a situation created by 'an insurrection within the South Korean armed forces', requiring 'the dispatch of American troops', leading, in time, to increasing tension along the 38th parallel and a 'deterioration in Japan's internal security'. The seventh scenario envisaged escalation of tension to such an extent that war with the Communist powers became probable. According to Okada Haruo (Japan Socialist Party), who revealed the contents of the so-called 'Three Arrows' exercise (*mitsuya kenkyū*) to the House of Representatives Budget Committee on 10 February 1965, the countermeasures envisaged by the Joint Chiefs included proclamation of a state of emergency by the Prime Minister, combined military action with the United States under the terms of the security treaty, mobilization of the Self Defence Forces to ensure 'domestic security' (*jian*) (widely believed to involve the mass arrest of Japanese Communists, opponents of the American alliance and of Koreans sympathetic to the Democratic People's Republic) and the expedited passage of a large body of emergency legislation through the Diet. The Joint Staff Council certainly assumed that a Korean crisis would permit the armed forces to play a far greater role in national affairs that at any time since 1945 (critics charged that the exercise read like a plan for a military *coup d'état*). Yet while oblique reference was made to joint American-Japanese military operations against North Korea, Sakhalin, the Kuriles, the Maritime Province of Siberia and other Soviet territories in the Far East, the exact division of allied responsibilities was unclear. It was simply noted that unless Japan resolved the question of overseas service for the Self Defence Forces the major role in any occupation of Sakhalin and the Kuriles would be undertaken by American troops. During the subsequent Diet debates over the Three Arrows exercise, government spokesmen pointed out (correctly) that the Joint Staff Council was required, as part of its normal activities, to consider possible Japanese responses to a wide variety of hypothetical situations. It was never made clear, however, whether the Ikeda Cabinet had specifically authorized, or even been aware of, this particular research project.[22] Certainly, Prime Minister Satō, on first hearing Okada's revelations in the Diet, visibly paled, declaring that 'this kind of thing is impermissible. I believe it is regrettable that this kind of planning has been undertaken without the government's knowledge.'[23] Subsequent government explanations lapsed into nebulous ambiguity, reinforcing the widespread belief that the relationship between the Self Defence Forces and United States global strategy was beyond Japan's control.

A month after Pak Chung Hi's military coup Prime Minister Ikeda left for Washington for talks with President Kennedy (20–21 June 1961). The Americans, strongly commending the new South Korean government, urged Japan to normalize ties with Seoul as soon as possible and contribute positively to the reconstruction of the South. Ikeda, reaffirming the importance Japan had traditionally attached to the maintenance of a non-Communist regime in South Korea, and fearing that Washington had come to regard his Korean policy as the litmus test of his commitment to the Western alliance, indicated a willingness to begin serious negotiations with Seoul.[24] Contacts between Tōkyō and Seoul became more frequent during the summer of 1961. On 15 August Pak Chung Hi, facing a rapidly deteriorating economy, rampant inflation, high unemployment, peasant unrest and, in many areas, real starvation, announced a Five Year Economic Development Plan. The success of this plan was premissed on a vast inflow of Japanese capital, aid and technology. On 30 August 1961 Kim Yu Tek, director of the South Korean Economic Planning Agency, visited Tōkyō for exploratory talks. Other informal discussions followed.

As we have already seen, groups determined to assert a more independent Japanese role in world affairs and improve relations with Peking had greatly strengthened their position in Cabinet by the end of 1961. While normalization of ties with Seoul was not necessarily incompatible with their objectives, South Korea's near-total dependence on the United States, China's relationship with North Korea and the complex issues involved in Japanese policy towards Pyongyang suggested the desirability of a cautious approach. Not only that, but many Japanese, of all political colourings, were disturbed by the character of the Pak Chung Hi regime. The Opposition parties were forming a solid front against co-operation with Seoul. Liberal elements in the Conservative Party recoiled at the prospect of collaboration with what was clearly a repressive and possibly unstable right-wing military dictatorship. The academic establishment and the press were not enthusiastic about *rapprochement* with Seoul. Public opinion became increasingly agitated. Against this background, the sixth round of Japanese-South Korean negotiations, which began in October 1961, made little progress on fundamental issues. At the annual meeting of the Japanese-American Joint Committee on Trade and Economic Affairs held at Hakone on 2–4 November 1961 Prime Minister Ikeda felt it necessary to point out to Dean Rusk that

> Japan will work hard to help South Korea recover. However, as far as Japan is concerned there are two problems. First, we do not know whether or not the Pak regime is stable. Second, the question of property claims involves vast expenditures. The Opposition parties, including the Democratic Socialist Party, are strongly against it. South Korea is a military regime and can quickly put the decisions [of its leadership] into effect. In Japan all questions have to be settled by the Parliament. We can't do things as simply as they do them in South Korea. For this reason, the debates on Japanese-South Korean co-operation in the Diet will be extremely difficult. We run the risk of a replay of the [1960] security treaty crisis. I am trying hard to think of ways to avoid that. However, our lively concern for the stabilization of South Korea in no way differs from that of the United States.[25]

Despite his reservations, Ikeda agreed to meet Pak Chung Hi (12 November 1961) and Kim Jong Pil (21 February 1962). A Japanese-South Korean Foreign Ministers' meeting was held in March 1962. On 22 March, however, the Japanese-South Korean talks received a major setback when President Yun Po Son, whose continuation in office after the coup had given some semblance of legitimacy to the Pak Chung Hi regime, resigned in protest at the authoritarian character of the new government. In the Diet, Opposition claims that Japan's negotiating partner was, in fact, an unconstitutional military regime, became more difficult to refute. Within the Liberal Democratic Party advocates of a cautious approach further strengthened their position. The anxieties of these doubting Thomases were not entirely quelled by Pak Chung Hi's resounding victory in the October 1962 general elections, hailed in Washington as a triumph for democracy and a demonstration of public confidence in the military government.

The United States, sensing a return to the impasse of the 1950s, responded with a major campaign to convince Japanese leaders of the importance of reaching rapid understanding with Seoul. On 3 May 1962 President Kennedy personally urged Yoshida Shigeru, that most unrepentant of anti-Korean Japanese Conservatives, to use his good offices to facilitate the negotiations.[26] It is difficult to evaluate the impact of Kennedy's pleas on this wily old fox. After his return from Washington, Yoshida, who was at the same time encouraging Ikeda to move ahead on the China issue, began to display an extraordinary degree of public enthusiasm for the development of ties with Seoul. Perhaps he had experienced a genuine conversion. Yet in a major speech to the Japan-America Society on 12 July 1962, ostensibly on the subject of Japanese-South Korea relations, Yoshida drifted off on a Gaullist tangent which could only have caused the greatest consternation in Washington. Japan, he reminded his audience, had the capacity to produce nuclear weapons within ten years. It should be prepared to do so, if necessary, 'not only to take care of our own defence, but also to defend the Orient from the unfortunate threat of Communism'.[27]

South Korea was one of the main topics discussed at the Japanese-American Security Consultative Committee meeting held in Tōkyō on 1 August 1962.[28] On 6 August *The New York Times*, in an editorial, commended the development of Japanese-South Korean relations as an important factor in the political and military stability of the Far East. President Kennedy's appeal for a more serious Japanese commitment to American containment of China at the meeting of the Japanese-American Joint Committee on Trade and Economic Affairs in December 1962 has already been noted. These calls were renewed at the Security Consultative Committee meeting on 19 January 1963[29]. In February, Gilpatric came to Tōkyō bearing the same message.[30] In March, Ambassador Edwin O. Reischauer criticized those Japanese leaders who were dragging their feet on the Korean question.[31] In April Roger Hilsman called on Japan to do more for non-Communist Asia.[32] The issue was raised again at the Security Consultative Committee meeting in October.[33]

Japanese resistance was gradually worn down. Washington's pressure might perhaps have been less effective had not Ikeda felt it necessary to balance his support for the 'pro-Peking' factions in the Liberal Democratic Party with concessions to extreme anti-Communist groups advocating greater solidarity with the United States. Even so, the Japanese Government approached the talks with the utmost caution. On 20 November 1962 Japan and South Korea reached tentative agreement on property claims. By the summer of 1963 some progress had also been made on the fisheries question. Yet on more fundamental issues the two sides remained deadlocked. Moreover, in the spring of 1964, despite continued American pressure on both Tōkyō and Seoul, the negotiations were further complicated by a massive eruption of popular protest in South Korea and growing unease in Japan. On 24 March 1964 student demonstrations against the prospective settlement with Japan in Seoul spread to Kwangju and Taegu. Within a few days the demonstrators were demanding the resignation of Pak Chung Hi, the restoration of democracy, the release of political prisoners, a reassertion of true political and economic independence and national reunification. The demonstrations, strikes and peasant unrest continued to grow throughout April and May. In Japan, the Socialist Party, the Communist Party and the General Council of Trade Unions also began to organize a mass movement against the treaty. This temporarily strengthened the position of those Conservatives who argued that it was unwise for Japan to be stampeded into a *de facto* alliance with the military regime in Seoul.

By the summer of 1964, however, both the international situation and the Liberal Democratic Party factional balance had changed dramatically. If the escalation of the Vietnam War and the rise of the anti-Kōno coalition had forced Ikeda to adopt a more cautious policy towards the People's Republic of China, they also tended to facilitate the development of relations with South Korea. Ikeda's retirement and Satō's accession to office in October 1964 produced conditions favourable to a rapid settlement with Seoul. Nevertheless, opponents of too intimate an association with South Korea still retained considerable influence. The Basic Treaty between Japan and the Republic of Korea (initialled 22 February, signed 22 June, ratified 18 December 1965) touched off the largest popular demonstrations since the 1960 security treaty crisis. It in no way represented unconditional Japanese acceptance of American and South Korean demands.

Despite strong pressure from both the United States and South Korea, Japan did not, for example, unequivocally recognize Seoul as the only legitimate government on the peninsula. The Japanese insisted that the agreement specifically incorporate the terminology of United Nations Resolution 195 (III), defining the area of Seoul's jurisdiction as 'that part of Korea where the Temporary Commission was able to observe and consult'.[34] Despite Seoul's protests, Prime Minister Satō made it clear in October 1965 that although Japan would not establish relations with the Democratic People's Republic, it would not deny the existence of a separate government in Pyongyang and would continue to trade with the North Koreans.[35] No agreement was reached on the question of sovereignty of Takeshima (Dokto). At the same time, the Japanese government refused to recognize all Koreans resident in Japan as citizens of South Korea. Prime Minister Satō gave a personal commitment to Seoul that he would attempt to persuade Japanese Koreans to change their allegiance from the North to the South. He also made it clear that he would permit Japanese South Koreans sympathetic to the North to change their allegiance to Pyongyang if they felt so inclined.[36]

As far as property claims were concerned, Japan agreed to provide South Korea with $300 million in outright grants, $200 million in government loans and $300 million in private commercial credits. The Japanese declared that these funds were to be regarded as 'economic co-operation'. The South Koreans insisted that they were compensation for losses sustained during the period of colonial rule. The fisheries question was settled by both sides agreeing to observe a 12 nautical mile limit, certain areas for joint operations and a number of zones reserved exclusively for South Korean use. Japan also agreed to provide $90 million in private credits for the development of the South Korean fishing industry.

Japanese assistance rendered under the terms of the basic treaty contributed to the stabilization of the Pak Chung Hi regime, the growth of the South Korean economy and the strengthening of the country's military capability. Indirectly, it created the conditions that enabled Pak to dispatch a total of 312,000 troops to assist the United States in Vietnam. The Japanese government strenuously denied that it had any intention of developing direct military links with Seoul. Before the initialling of the treaty the then Foreign Minister, Shiina Etsusaburō, told the *Tōkyō Shimbun*[37] and the *Nihon Keizai Shimbun*[38] that Japanese participation in any NEATO-type military pact would be unconstitutional. He later told the *Asahi Shimbun*[39] that he had rejected South Korean proposals for a 'Free Asian Foreign Ministers' Solidarity Meeting' specifically on these grounds.

During the course of the Diet proceedings prior to the initialling of the treaty, the Opposition claimed that while the treaty itself might be devoid of references to military co-operation, Japan's obligation to co-operate with the United Nations (implied in Article 98 of the Constitution), the security treaty and the Yoshida-Acheson Exchange of Notes would eventually make some form of military involvement in the peninsula inevitable.

Prime Minister Satō categorically denied this.[40] By the winter of 1965 it was evident that the government's public position was

1) that Japan's co-operation with the United Nations forces under the Yoshida-Acheson notes was limited to the supply of material;[41]

2) that Japan could only co-operate with the United Nations provided it did not violate its own Constitution in doing so. The Constitution prohibited use of force to settle international disputes and Japan could not dispatch military forces abroad.[42]

The Japanese Constitution, Prime Minister Satō assured a television audience on 13 May 1966, made military co-operation with the United States outside the home archipelago impossible. Japan simply could not join with the Republic of Korea, Taiwan and the Philippines to form a multilateral Far Eastern security organization akin to NATO.[43] Satō forcefully emphasized the same points in discussions with the present writer on 16 May 1975, just after the demise of the Lon Nol government in Cambodia and immediately prior to the final collapse of South Vietnam.

At the time, there was a general consensus among conservative Japanese military analysts that the treaty would not alter the strategic equilibrium in North-East Asia. Saeki Kiichi, former commandant of the National Defence College, considered that normalization of diplomatic relations would enable Japan and South Korea to exchange views on the military situation in the region. These exchanges, however, would be 'of little direct benefit'.[44] Shortly after conclusion of the treaty a Japanese military attaché was posted to Seoul. Yoshie Seiichi, then chief secretary of the Joint Staff Council, believed that this would enable Japan to obtain a better view of the situation in North Korea, assess the strength of the South Korean forces and profit from their experience.[45] The concrete benefits derived from contacts of this sort would seem to have been rather peripheral. Needless to say, the conduct of joint exercises with the South Korean forces would have radically altered the situation, but there is little evidence to suggest that these were seriously contemplated by any Japanese government in the late 1960s and 1970s, despite the attitude of the United States and interest in some sections of the Self Defence Force officer corps. By the end of the 1960s, however, exchanges of the type envisaged by Generals Sugita and Song had become commonplace. It remained to be seen what the conclusions reached during these discussions might have on Japanese government policy in time of crisis. The informal talks with French officers conducted by the British director of military operations Sir Henry Wilson in the years before World War I, it will be recalled, had a decisive influence on the British Cabinet in August 1914.

II   The Vietnam War and the polarization of the Liberal Democratic Party

From the beginning Prime Minister Satō, persuaded of the wisdom of continued alliance with the United States, publicly justified virtually every aspect of American policy in Indochina. While Japan did not participate directly in the conflict, the government did everything possible to facilitate United States military operations from bases on its territory. The Japanese procurements industry, stagnant since the end of the Korean War, entered a new period of rapid expansion. Profits were staggering. In the late 1960s Washington's annual military expenditure in Japan was almost invariably larger than its expenditure in Vietnam itself.[46] Japanese-American technological co-operation intensified. At the same time, the diversion of much United States industrial effort into military production enabled Japanese exporters to increase their share of the North American market. Throughout non-Communist South-East Asia, the boom conditions created by the conflict inflated demand for Japanese products.

America's Indochina adventure, like the Korean War, accelerated Japan's revival as a major world power. Nevertheless, Japanese attitudes to the Korean and Vietnamese conflicts were different. Both conflagrations, no doubt, were viewed in the wider context of United States rivalry with China. For the Japanese Conservatives, in particular, both were essentially proxy wars. Yet there had been little overt Japanese opposition to United States intervention in Korea. Conservatives had supported the American military effort either because, like Yoshida, they saw the war providing an opportunity for economic recovery, or because, like Ashida, they accepted the Meckelian doctrine regarding the strategic importance of the peninsula. The sufferings of the Korean people, those 'ungrateful' former subjects of the Japanese Empire, had not caused overmuch concern. The Japanese Socialists and Communists had opposed American intervention in Korea. The occupation made it impossible for them to do much about it. As Ambassador Reischauer was quick to perceive, however, the Vietnam War made close association with the United States seem 'less desirable to many Japanese, and the confrontation between left and right ... took on a new heat'.[47] As with China policy, the conflict was not simply one between 'left' and 'right'. The Vietnamese cause, and the issues it seemed to symbolize, aroused the sympathetic interest of large, very disparate groups in Japanese society, in much the same way as the Greek independence struggle against the Turks had fired the imagination of early nineteenth-century Europe. Japanese attitudes towards the Vietnamese exhibited few of the socio-historical pecularities that characterized attitudes towards Koreans. Western-orientated Japanese, no doubt, viewed the Vietnamese with the same haughty disdain as they regarded all non-European peoples. For Asianists, on the other hand, it seemed as if the apostolic flame had passed to North Vietnam and the Viet Cong. Marxist leadership of the Vietnamese nationalist movement ensured the automatic hostility of a wide spectrum of Japanese conservative opinion. It also guaranteed the dedicated support of the Japanese Communist Party, important elements in the Socialist Party, the General Council of Trade Unions, the major student organizations and other radical groups. Yet the spectacle of a Western superpower unleashing the full terrors of modern technological warfare against a small, developing Asian society in defence of a puppet regime regarded with contempt even by its patron was as disturbing to many Japanese conservatives as it was to men and women on the left. At the same time, the extraordinary sacrifices of the Vietnamese Buddhists in the movement against the Ngo Dinh Diem regime were noted with satisfaction by their Japanese co-religionists.

Within the Liberal Democratic Party, American policies aggravated existing tensions. The majority of Japanese Conservatives accepted the American view that the struggle was essentially one between Communist China and the West. They had little interest in the indigenous origins of the Vietnamese Revolution. The complexity of Vietnam's historical relations with China was unknown to them. There was little confidence that the United States would emerge victorious from the conflict. Even so, the full implications of the eventual American defeat were foreseen only by a few exceptionally far-sighted individuals such as Yoshida and Okazaki.[48] Advocates of continued Japanese association with the United States supported the war effort, albeit often with considerable reluctance. 'Asianists' and exponents of a more independent foreign policy quickly dissociated themselves from the United States. One of the first Japanese Conservatives publicly to express his opposition to American policies in Vietnam was former Prime Minister Yoshida.[49] After the initial bombings of Hanoi, Yoshida's close associate, Miyazawa Kiichi, issued a strongly worded statement advising against further escalation of the war.[50] Some months later, Miyazawa wrote an impassioned personal appeal to the new American ambassador, U. Alexis Johnson.[51] In January 1965, Foreign Minister Shiina Etsusaburō, one of the most conservative figures in the party, publicly compared American policies in Vietnam with those of the Japanese army in China in the 1930s.[52] In April, Matsumoto Shunichi, former ambassador to Great Britain and special adviser to the Foreign Ministry, returned from a government-sponsored fact-finding mission to Vietnam and openly attacked the whole direction of American policy.[53] Less surprising was the opposition of such figures as Fujiyama Aiichirō, Matsumura Kenzō, Takasaki Tatsunosuke, Okazaki Kaheita and Utsunomiya Tokuma.[54] As the war continued there was, in all sections of the Japanese establishment, a perceptible erosion of confidence in Washington's leadership and judgement.

It was against this background that the Liberal Democratic Party gradually began to polarize around two organizations. The larger of these organizations was the Asian Problems Study Association (Ajia Mondai Kenkyū Kai) formed in December 1964, two months after Satō became Prime Minisiter. This body centred around the Satō, Ishii, Fukuda and Kishi factions. Estimates of the size of its membership varied. Some observers put the figure as low as 70, other spoke in terms of 140, 150 or 170 members.[55] The Asian Problems Study Association adopted the view that Japan's interests would best be served by encouraging the United States to maintain a strong and actively interventionist presence in Asia. It advocated continued exclusion of Peking from the United Nations, preservation of the status quo in Taiwan, minimal contact with the Chinese mainland, close association with the Republic of Korea and support for Washington's involvement in Indochina.

In January 1965 a rival organization, the Afro-Asian Problems Study Assocation (Ajia-Afurika Mondai Kenkyū Kai), was set up by groups opposed to uncritical endorsement of American policies.[56] Founded initially by some twenty-four members of the Matsumura, Fujiyama and Utsunomiya factions, this organization eventually attracted a membership of 100 to 120 Diet members. All of Matsumura's small group, most of the former Kōno faction and a significant number of Miki and Fujiyama supporters associated themselves with this body.[57]

Once established, the two associations began a campaign of protracted trench warfare designed to discredit the views of their opponents and win new support both within and outside the party. Debates and seminars were organized, fact-finding missions dispatched to various countries. Visits to North Vietnam, areas under Viet Cong administration and the war zones in Laos were obviously difficult to arrange. Generally speaking, tours of these dangerous regions were left to the Socialists, the Communists, trade union activists and adventurous journalists such as Honda Katsuichi. In September 1966 the Afro-Asian group sponsored a tour of China led by Furui Yoshimi. Included in this group were the former Foreign Minister, Kōsaka Zentarō, the former Defence Agency director-general, Esaki Masumi, and former Finance Minister Fukuda Hajime. The delegates talked with Chou En-lai, Chen Yi and other dignitaries. Kōsaka returned full of enthusiasm for Japan's role in easing Sino-American tension, viewed as the chief cause of the troubles in Indochina. He announced a plan to visit Washington armed with an 8mm cinematographic record of his experiences in the People's Republic.[58] Other matters of mutual interest had been discussed. Chou En-lai told Esaki that while China objected to the revival of 'reactionary military cliques', it was 'only natural' for Japan to defend itself.[59] Esaki, after inspecting military installations near Tientsin, came to the conclusion that the People's Liberation Army was trained 'solely for defensive war'.[60] Fukuda was optimistic about the future of Sino-Japanese trade.[61] After their return to Japan, Kōsaka, Esaki and the others made desultory efforts to establish links with the American Senate 'doves' led by Senator Fulbright.[62] While the Afro-Asian team was in Peking a party of nineteen members from the rival Asian group visited South

Korea to attend a meeting of the Asian Parliamentary Union.[63] Many trips were organized to South Vietnam, culminating in Prime Minister Satō's official visit to this American client state in October 1967. In the summer of 1966 the two associations clashed bitterly over the question of the 'Interim Report on Japan's Security' drawn up by the party's Security Problems Research Committee. With the passage of time, meetings attended by members of both organizations became increasingly heated. The traditional decorum of Conservative political debate was thrown to the winds, voices were raised, fists brandished, bottles of beer and soft drink upset in unseemly scuffles, pieces of *sushi** hurled across rooms.

So acrimonious did these disputes become that there were rumours of possible defections from the party. In March 1966 Esaki Masumi, Furui Yoshimi, Ishida Hirohide, Mori Kiyoshi, Nakasone Yasuhiro and Sakurauchi Yoshio, all associated, in one way or another, with the Afro-Asian group, became involved in secret negotiations with members of the Democratic Socialist Party. There were reports that luminaries from the old Ikeda faction, in particular Kōsaka and Miyazawa, were displaying more than a passing interest in these discussions. By June 1966 Matsumura had begun to speak openly about the formation of a second Conservative Party. His sentiments were echoed by Furui and Nakasone. It was widely believed that Conservative Diet representation could drop below 260 seats after the next general election. In these circumstances, the government could expect to lose control of the Diet if only twenty or thirty members left the party.[64]

Predictions of a split in the Liberal Democratic Party eventually proved to be unfounded. Yet the situation clearly demanded caution. The partial redrafting of the 'Interim Report' and the reorganization of the Foreign Affairs Research Council were the first of a series of steps taken by the party leadership to appease the internal opposition.[65] The situation became delicate in the months preceding the party presidential elections in December 1966. The government was thrown into turmoil by a succession of corruption scandals. The groups most active in the Afro-Asian Problems Study Association formed themselves into a new Party Rectification Group, with the objective of 'purifying' the party by opposing Satō in the election.[66] Satō's victory in December was comfortable: 289 votes were cast in favour of the Prime Minister, 89 for Fujiyama and 47 for Maeo.[67] The Cabinet formed after the election was dominated totally by the groups that had supported Satō's candidature. Members of the Prime Minister's own faction took four posts, Miki received three, the Kishi-Fukuda faction two and Ishii, Kawashima and Funada one post each.[68] The new Cabinet was, as before, confronted by powerful and well-organized dissident forces. This, together with Miki's strong position, led initially to the adoption of an aloof but not markedly hostile attitude to Peking, more restrained public support for America's Vietnam adventure and an attempt to placate exponents of greater autonomy by concentrating on issues that aroused less hostility in Washington. In particular Miki, as Foreign Minister, sensing that international and domestic condi-

---

* Japanese steamed rice balls, wrapped in seaweed paper and filled with choice morsels of raw fish.

tions made unilateral *rapprochement* with China, for the time being, difficult to achieve, saw in the promotion of 'Asian-Pacific diplomacy' a means to rally an increasingly fragmented party, satisfy the 'pro-Americans' without alienating the 'Asianists' and bring Japan's diplomacy more into line with current economic realities.

III   Relations with Indonesia, Oceania and the Middle East

The issues involved in relations with the United States, China, the Korean peninsula and Vietnam aroused deep political emotions in Japan. In contrast, Japan's ties with the countries of non-Communist South-East Asia, Oceania, the Indian subcontinent and the Middle East, central as these had been to Washington's strategic design for Japan, were, for most Japanese, almost entirely non-controversial.

Throughout the 1960s Japanese business, encouraged by the Japanese government, continued the cautious but determined economic advance into South-East Asia that had begun in the early 1950s. By the end of the decade Japan had emerged as the first or second trading partner of every country in the region, a process greatly accelerated by the Indochina war. Non-Communist South-East Asia furnished approximately 12 per cent of Japan's imports, including some 14.5 per cent of its resources imports. The region had further consolidated its position as a vital source of tin (96 per cent of total national requirements), natural rubber (98 per cent), lumber (50 per cent), bauxite (46 per cent), copper (45 per cent) and oil (10 per cent). While Japanese economic assistance to non-Communist Asia was extensive (by 1968 Japan ranked fourth among the major aid-giving nations, after the United States, France and West Germany), Japanese investment was to remain, until the early 1970s, relatively modest.[69]

By the beginning of the 1960s, Indonesia, with its rich and varied natural resources, vast potential markets and strategic location across the oil routes through the Straits of Malacca, at the confluence of the Indian and Pacific Oceans, had come to be seen as the centrepiece of Japanese policy in the region. The Japanese government, like that of the United States, professed a vital interest in the maintenance of a non-Communist Indonesia, informally linked, politically and economically, to the Western alliance system.

In reality, Japanese policies were more complex. President Sukarno's active commitment to the Non-Aligned Movement, his suspicion of the Anglo-American powers, together with the growing strength of indigenous Communist forces had made it difficult, from the beginning, for the United States to use Indonesia as an instrument for the indirect control of Japan. Sukarno's policies created problems for Tōkyō. They also created opportunities. In some areas Japan's interests overlapped with those of the United States. In other respects they did not. From the late 1950s the Japanese government, together with a variety of individuals, factions and special interest groups, emerged as important participants in a great, unfolding drama, the ultimate outcome of which was to determine whether the Indonesian Republic would become a genuinely independent influence in world affairs, whether its policies would be non-provocative or expansionist and whether it would seek a special relationship with the United States, with the Soviet Union, with China or with Japan itself.

Indonesian policy, unlike policy towards China, Korea or Vietnam, was seldom drawn into the maelstrom of Liberal Democratic Party factional conflict. The dominant groups in the Japanese government, the bureaucracy and the business community, from the time diplomatic relations were first established in 1958, all actively encouraged support for Sukarno's regime through the reparations programme, deferred payment import credits and private capital investment. Indonesia rapidly emerged as the largest recipient of Japanese overseas aid. President Sukarno, however erratic his policies, whatever his personal idiosyncrasies, was viewed as the only individual capable of uniting this sprawling, racially and linguistically diverse archipelago and preventing the precarious balance between the armed forces, the Communist Party (PKI), nationalist and Muslim groups from collapsing into bloody civil war. The reparations strategy of the Kishi government served, albeit indirectly, to buttress the Sukarno regime and pave the way for the President's assumption of dictatorial powers. Japanese capital and technology played a central role in the development of the Indonesian national oil company PERMINA, set up in 1957 to exploit the North Sumatran oilfields and break the virtual monopoly over the Indonesian resource hitherto enjoyed by Caltex, Shell and Texaco. Even at the height of Sukarno's anti-Anglo-American period, Japanese companies, supported by the Japanese government, continued to invest heavily in Indonesian resources development projects.[70]

Sukarno's complex ambiguity offered something to everyone. Within the Japanese government and business community, 'pro-American' groups viewed the special relationship with Indonesia as a means of containing Soviet and Chinese influence in Asia and preventing the Republic's drift to the left. Independently minded nationalist elements, on the other hand, believed that a special relationship with a non-aligned Indonesia might help Japan to escape from the constraints of the San Francisco system and increase its freedom of manoeuvre *vis-à-vis* the United States. Either way, Indonesia seemed destined to become a new and greater Manchuria. Pan-Asianist groups felt a natural sympathy for Sukarno's ebullient anti-Western nationalism. The Japanese Socialist and Communist parties, sections of the trade union movement, radical student organizations and 'progressive' intellectuals, too, came to view Indonesia, along with Vietnam, as the spearhead of the continuing struggle against Western imperialism in South-East Asia.

By the early 1960s a sizeable 'Indonesia Lobby', incorporating elements of the government, the Liberal Democratic Party, the Foreign Ministry and the business community had emerged in Tōkyō. The Indonesia Lobby overlapped, to some extent, with both the China and South Korean lobbies, but was, to all intents and purposes, a separate organization, with different historical roots, different personnel and somewhat different strategic perspectives. Many of the central figures in the

Indonesia Lobby had played an important role in Japan's imperial expansion into South-East Asia during the Pacific War. In the prewar period they had been adherents of the 'advance south' school of thought, rather than exponents of a special relationship with China. Others had been deeply involved in Manchuria. The membership of the Indonesia Lobby, in fact, read like an honour roll of the Japanese Empire. Its connections with the Indonesian leadership bore the indelible imprint of an earlier age. Former Prime Minister Kishi Nobusuke, the most senior member of the Liberal Democratic Party associated with the group, had come to know President Sukarno partly through the good offices of C. M. Chow, a former Shanghai businessman who had worked for Japanese military intelligence in North China in the 1930s, migrated to Indonesia after the war, joined Indonesian intelligence, then set himself up in the import-export trade. Chow was also an acquaintance of Kishi's enterprising business colleague, Kinoshita Shigeru, president of Kinoshita Trading, whose fortunes had been made in Manchuria in the 1930s, and whose aggressive business strategies had given him a strong position in postwar Indonesia, at least until the collapse of his trading empire in 1964.[71] Kishi's old friend from Sugamo days, the ultranationalist gangster Kodama Yoshio, also paid considerable attention to Indonesian affairs, providing President Sukarno with private bodyguards during his many visits to Tōkyō.[72] Kawashima Shōjirō, secretary-general of the Liberal Democratic Party during Kishi's tenure of office as Prime Minister and vice-president of the party at various times until his death in 1970, in contrast, had few prewar connections with the continental expansionists or the 'advance south' school. His central position in the Indonesia Lobby had developed from contacts made with Sukarno during his years as Minister of State for the Tōkyō Olympic Games between 1962 and 1964, and from his personal belief that it was in Japan's long-term interests to cultivate ties with non-aligned countries.[73] Kōno Ichirō, Ōno Bamboku, Fujiyama Aiichirō, Matsumura Kenzō and Utsunomiya Tokuma, for various reasons, all adopted positions interpreted as sympathetic to Sukarno's Indonesia.[74] Kawashima's old friend, Saitō Shizuo, director of the Planning Section of the General Affairs Department during the Japanese occupation of Indonesia (when he had first become acquainted with Sukarno) and ambassador to Djakarta in the mid-1960s, was generally regarded as the chief representative of the Indonesia Lobby within the Foreign Ministry. During his years as Japanese ambassador to Indonesia, Saitō was assisted by several wartime colleagues, including Nishijima Shigetada, who had once worked in the Imperial Japanese Navy Djakarta Liaison Office, Shimizu Hitoshi, a former propaganda officer, and Captain Yanagawa Tomoshige, who had served in the Sixteenth Army's Special Intelligence Task Unit.[75] These men enjoyed a wide range of contacts in Indonesian political, military and business circles. Matsunaga Yasuzaemon, president of the Japan Chamber of Commerce and Industry, Ayukawa Yoshitsuke, wartime president of the Manchurian Heavy Industries and later of the Imperial Oil Company, Ishihara Hiroichirō, president of the South Seas Mining Company and the conservative industrialist Kajima Morinosuke, president of the Kajima Construction Company, president of the Japan-Indonesia Association and prominent advocate of a pan-Asianist Federation,[76] also occupied important positions in the Indonesia Lobby.[77] Japanese trading companies interested in Indonesian affairs, such as Kubo Masao's Tōnichi Trading Company, whose board of directors included Ōno Bamboku, Kōno Ichirō and Kodama Yoshio, vied with each other in introducing Sukarno to attractive young ladies. One of these, Miss Nemoto Naoko, became the Indonesian President's third wife, taking the name Ratna Dewi Sari. She subsequently emerged as a significant political influence in her own right, cultivating ties with Kawashima Shōjirō, ambassador Saitō and other key figures.[78] Tōyama Tatsukuni (Tōyama Mitsuru's grandson), head of the Keio University Indonesia Society, also played an important role in organizing Japanese support for Sukarno and his policies.[79]

The Japanese government's interest in fostering the development of a politically stable, friendly and non-Communist Indonesia did not lead it to endorse all aspects of Sukarno's diplomacy. Japan adopted, in principle, a neutral stand towards the West New Guinea dispute, although some individual members of the Liberal Democratic Party, along with the Socialist Party and the Communist Party, sympathized with Indonesian efforts to incorporate this Dutch colony into the national territory. In September 1960 the Ikeda Cabinet refused to permit the Dutch aircraft carrier *Karel Doorman*, based at Hollandia in West New Guinea, to enter Japanese ports for refuelling. The Japanese government also succeeded in persuading the Netherlands to abandon the practice of sending military personnel to West New Guinea on regular KLM flights through Tōkyō.[80] While these actions were consistent with Japan's neutral attitude (Indonesian requests to dispatch military vessels to Japan for repairs would also certainly have been refused), it is possible that the Ikeda Cabinet might have adopted a different position had not its dominant factions, faced with the prospect of Indonesian boycotts of Japanese goods, come to the conclusion that relations with Djakarta were, in the long term, more important than ties with The Hague.

Indonesian opposition to the newly established Malaysian Federation during the period 1963–6 confronted the Japanese government with a more serious dilemma. The Malaysian Federation was supported, politically, economically and militarily, by Great Britain, Australia and New Zealand. The United States, in return for British endorsement of its Vietnam policies, had also expressed its support for Kuala Lumpur. Sukarno's *Konfrontasi*, in turn endorsed, for a variety of reasons, both by the Indonesian armed forces and the Communist Party, was regarded sympathetically in Moscow, Peking, Pyongyang and Hanoi.

Both the Ikeda and Satō Cabinets, while attaching much importance to the Indonesian connection, had no desire to see Djakarta establish a virtual hegemony of insular South-East Asia, although Japanese policies would certainly have made appropriate adjustments had such a situation come about. As the conflict between Indonesia and Malaysia grew in intensity, Japan also became concerned about the possible impact of hostilities both on the passage of its tankers through the Straits of Malacca and on its oil development projects in North Sumatra. From the beginning, therefore, the Japanese government made strenuous efforts to act as a mediator. Between 31 May and 1 June 1963, just four months after Indonesia's announcement of its opposition to the proposed federation, President Sukarno and the Malaysian Prime Minister Tunku Abdul Rahman met in Tōkyō, at the suggestion of the then Japanese Foreign Minister Ōhira Masayoshi, in an attempt to reach a mutually acceptable compromise. These talks, the subsequent discussions at Manila among the Foreign Ministers of Indonesia, Malaysia and the Philippines (which had also decided to oppose the federation), then the three-nation summit attended by President Sukarno, Prime Minister Rahman and President Macapagal, failed to produce substantial agreement, despite vacuous talk of a grand federation of Malay peoples.[81] By the end of 1963 Indonesian and British Commonwealth forces were engaged in hostilities in Sarawak and Sabah. Nevertheless, the Japanese government, convinced that direct superpower involvement in the conflict would be disastrous, that co-operation with Djakarta was vital for Japan's future and that Sukarno, for all his faults, was the best bulwark against the PKI, ignored British efforts to enlist its support for 'containing' Indonesia. For quite some time it continued to see its role as that of a mediator. Ikeda extended his good offices to a sceptical President Macapagal during his visit to Manila (23–6 September 1963) and to the Australian Prime Minister Robert Menzies in Canberra (3 October 1963).[82]

The Japanese Prime Minister's optimistic belief that Indonesia, Malaysia and the Philippines, if given an opportunity to talk, would soon settle their differences, proved to be unfounded. By the time Ikeda returned to Tōkyō the situation had further deteriorated. It was around this time that the United States began to show an interest in Japan's initiatives. It can probably be assumed that Washington requested Japan to throw its weight behind British efforts to preserve the Malaysian Federation and, at the same time, to help prevent Indonesia's drift towards association with Peking. The Japanese government, accordingly, redoubled its efforts. In November 1963 Ikeda sent Oda Takio, a former ambassador to Indonesia and counsellor to the Foreign Ministry, on a fact-finding mission to Malaysia.[83] On 16 January 1964 President Sukarno, on a private visit to Tōkyō, accompanied by Foreign Minister Subandrio, the Army Chief of Staff General Yani and the Indonesian ambassador to Japan Bambang Sugeng, met with Ikeda, Ōhira, Kurogane and other Japanese officials. At this meeting, the Japanese Prime Minister apparently urged the Indonesians to abandon confrontation, advising them to devote their resources to the peaceful reconstruction of their country rather than to military adventures abroad.[84] On 17–18 January Ikeda, Ōhira and Sukarno met with the United States Attorney-General Robert Kennedy, also on a private visit to Japan.[85] These discussions failed to produce tangible results. Nevertheless, by the middle of the year, United States pressure and the growing strength of the Malaysian Federation had persuaded the Philippines, at least, to modify its stand. Djakarta, however, remained obdurate. In June 1964, another meeting between Indonesian, Malaysian and Filipino leaders in Tōkyō ended in failure.[86] By January 1965, two months after Ikeda's retirement, Indonesia had withdrawn from the United Nations and was aligning its policies more closely with Peking.

The Satō Cabinet's scepticism about the prospects for an *entente cordiale* with the

People's Republic of China, coupled with its lingering desire to reassert a more independent role in world affairs, despite the unpromising conditions created by the Vietnam War, encouraged it to place even greater emphasis on relations with Indonesia. This heightened Japanese interest came at a time when the United States had all but washed its hands of Sukarno. The Japanese government, in contrast, made it clear that its Indonesian policy would not be affected by Sukarno's withdrawal from the United Nations. It continued to examine projects for economic co-operation with Indonesia, studying Djakarta's request for long-term credits and planning joint ventures to import Sumatran crude oil directly, rather than through the Western oil majors, long after Sukarno's seizure of British and American oil interests.[87] By the time of the *gestapu* affair, Japan's economic aid to the Indonesian Republic was considerably greater than that to any other nation. The Japanese government also redoubled its efforts to mediate in the dispute with Malaysia, dispatching Kawashima Shōjirō to Djakarta, Kuala Lumpur and Bangkok in April 1965, to the second Afro-Asian conference in Algiers in June and to the Indonesian Independence Day celebrations in August.[88] All these efforts ended in failure.

Colonel Untung's attempted *coup d'état* of 30 September 1965, General Suharto's conservative military counter-coup, then the massacre of Communist supporters and the fall of Sukarno caught the Japanese government by surprise. During the first days of October, when it seemed as if Untung's *coup* had been successful, the Japanese Embassy in Djakarta was apparently resigned to a major shift to the left in Indonesian politics.[89] There was a general belief that Sukarno's position was impregnable, despite his failing health. General Suharto's counter-coup did not shake the Embassy's confidence in Sukarno's power. Ambassador Saitō reportedly believed that Sukarno would be able to reassert his authority over the military within three to six months.[90]

Nevertheless, as the situation developed, the Japanese government, following long-established practice, cautiously shifted its support from Sukarno to Suharto. The firm anti-Communist stance of the new military regime, its break with China, the physical destruction of the PKI and the signs of a willingness to end the dispute with Malaysia were welcomed by the Satō Cabinet. Towards the end of January 1966 Foreign Minister Miki announced that 'Japan should play a leading role in constructing the Indonesian economy and to do that Japan would have to make a bold political judgement'.[91] This presumably meant bringing the full weight of its political and economic influence down on one side or the other in Indonesian internal affairs. Early in March 1966 Ushiba Nobuhiko,* Deputy Vice-Foreign Minister, visited Djakarta to discuss Japan's role in Indonesia's future economic development, China policy and other delicate matters with the new military leadership.[92] Shortly afterwards, on 11 March 1966, these same leaders formally removed Sukarno from office, thus bringing to an end a long and turbulent chapter in Indonesian history.

* Ushiba Nobuhiko was the younger brother of Prince Konoye's former private secretary, Ushiba Tomohiko.

On 12 March, the day General Suharto formally replaced Sukarno as President of the Indonesian Republic, Kawashima Shōjirō, welcoming the eclipse of Chinese Communist influence in Djakarta and perceiving a tendency in the new military leadership to look towards Tōkyō rather than Peking, declared that the basic principles of Japan's Indonesian policy remained unaltered. Despite the change of leadership, Kawashima stated, Japan's objective was still to harness Indonesia's vast natural resources with Japanese economic power and technology to promote the prosperity of both countries.[93]

Japan's new Foreign Minister, Shiina Etsusaburō, too, publicly commended the 'realistic policies' of the Suharto government.[94] By the end of March Japan had proposed the establishment of a new international consortium to reschedule Indonesia's debts and negotiate new credits. The Japanese government worked hard both to encourage Suharto to bring confrontation to an end and to enlist Indonesian co-operation in the South-East Asia Ministerial Conference on Economic Development. The Satō Cabinet's offer of $US30 million credit to Djakarta in May 1966 carried with it the condition that Indonesia end confrontation and return to the United Nations as expeditiously as possible.[95] Shirahata Tomoyoshi, a former Japanese consul in Djakarta, and Kai Fumihiko, the Japanese ambassador to Malaysia, played an important role in arranging the Bangkok talks between the new Indonesian Foreign Minister, Adam Malik, and the Malaysian Deputy Prime Minister, Tun Razak, which paved the way for the peace agreement of 11 August 1966.[96] In the years that followed, Japan's political and economic relations with Indonesia became more intimate than ever before.

With the fall of Sukarno, the old 'Indonesia Lobby' in Tōkyō gradually faded away. Its place was taken by a new group, ideologically more conservative, whose members had also been active in South-East Asian affairs in the prewar and early postwar periods.

Former Prime Minister Kishi retained his strong interest in Indonesian affairs, establishing good relations with the new men in Djakarta. His heir and successor Fukuda Takeo, who had for many years enjoyed close personal and financial ties with the anti-Sukarnoist Sumatran separatist Sumitro Djojohadikusumo,[97] also emerged into prominence in the new constellation of power. So too did Ishii Mitsujirō, the principal luminary in the Taiwan Lobby.* The Japanese business community rapidly threw its weight behind the Suharto regime. The years before the *gestapu* affair had seen the development of close contacts between anti-Communist Indonesian military officers opposed to Sukarno and various Japanese ultranationalist

---

* In 1956 Ishii's father-in-law, Hisahara Fusanosuke, assisted by Iwakura Takeo, a former Imperial Army intelligence officer who had worked with pro-Japanese Indian independence movements in World War II, Nakata Fusahide, adviser to the Society for Economic Co-operation with Asia, Obata Tadayoshi, sometime secretary-general of the Imperial Rule Assistance Association and Tanaka Tatsuo, Tanaka Giichi's son and prominent member of the Kishi faction, had apparently encouraged, and, perhaps, materially assisted, Colonel Lubis's unsuccessful attempt to raise an anti-Sukarnoist rebellion in Sumatra.[98]

organizations. While the evidence is not conclusive it seems by no means impossible that these mysterious connections had some impact on the 1965 upheaval. For this reason, several prominent Japanese rightists came to occupy important positions in the new Indonesia Lobby. These included Fujiwara Iwaichi, an Imperial Army intelligence officer who had served in Sumatra, Burma and India,* Yanagawa Tomoshige (see above), Miura Giichi and Migami Taku, both of whom had been involved with ultranationalist assassination squads in the 1930s.[99] Generally speaking, such men were deeply anti-Western as well as uncompromisingly anti-Communist in outlook.

The 1960s also witnessed a notable expansion of Japanese trade with Australia. The growth of the Japanese economy, and, in particular, of the Japanese steel industry, coincided with the discovery of large iron ore, coking coal and other mineral deposits in Australia. It also coincided with Great Britain's continued decline as a world power, its preparations for entry into the European Economic Community (EEC) and the consequent loss of Australia's traditional markets. The demands of a rapidly expanding economy, the difficulty of establishing a relationship with the People's Republic and the heavy pressure on Japan's traditional suppliers of iron ore such as India and Malaysia, combined to turn Japanese interests increasingly towards Australia. By the beginning of 1970s, Japan was dependent on Australia for some 44 per cent of its imported iron ore, 38 per cent of its imported coal and 38 per cent of its bauxite. Australia, in addition, supplied 82 per cent of Japan's wool and 16 per cent of its wheat. Japan, in turn, had become Australia's single most important market. Within a short time the Australian-Japanese trading relationship had become the seventh-largest in the world.[100]

At the same time, Japan's industrial expansion and the change-over to an oil-based economy led to increased involvement in the Middle East. In 1960 coal and oil had been of approximately equal importance as energy sources, each supplying 37.7 per cent of Japan's needs. By 1965 coal supplied 27.5 per cent of Japan's needs, oil 58.4 per cent. By 1970 coal supplied only 20.7 per cent of Japan's requirements. In contrast, 70.8 per cent of Japan's energy needs were obtained from oil. Saudi Arabia, Iran, Kuwait and the Persian Gulf states had emerged, for the first time in history, as major Japanese trading partners.

The overwhelming importance of the North American market, the pro-Western neutrality of Suharto's Indonesia, Washington's strong position in Australia, the Philippines, Thailand and South Vietnam, its powerful influence in Saudi Arabia, Iran and the Persian Gulf, strengthened the matrix of constraints binding Japan to the San Francisco system. For a few years, this offset the impact of the decline of American influence in other parts of the world. This did not enable Washington to persuade the Japanese government to pursue policies seen as contrary to the long-term national interest. It did, however, make foreign policy options outside the American alliance, for the time being, increasingly difficult to contemplate.

* In the postwar period Fujiwara had joined the Self Defence forces, rising to the rank of Divisional Commander.

CHAPTER IX

Domestic politics, foreign policy and the reversion of Okinawa, 1960–1972

Our promises are made in proportion to our hopes
but kept in proportion to our fears.

La Rochefoucauld, *Maxims*, 38

I The problem

Strategic assets acquired in war are not readily abandoned by any great power. The importance of the Ryūkyū chain had been recognized by both Japanese and American policy-makers since at least the time of Commodore Perry's expedition. The formerly independent Ryūkyūan kingdom had been forcibly incorporated into the Japanese empire in 1879, partly because of fears that it might fall under the influence of a hostile power. Sixty-four years later United States forces had wrested the territory from Japanese control in one of the bloodiest battles of the Pacific theatre. The San Francisco peace treaty, while recognizing Japan's 'residual sovereignty' over Okinawa and the Bonins, had placed the islands under a United Nations trusteeship administered by the United States. Their legal status was thus fundamentally different to that of Taiwan, southern Sakhalin, the Kurile chain, the Marshalls, the Marianas, the Carolines, the Spratleys and the Paracels, to which Japan had renounced, in perpetuity, 'all rights, titles and claims'. The 'residual sovereignty' formula had been devised by Dulles as a compromise between those United States officials who insisted on outright annexation of the islands and those who were prepared to contemplate their eventual reversion to Japan, on certain conditions.

In the early postwar period American strategists were generally agreed that a strong position on Okinawa was essential to prevent Japan's revival as a hostile power. With the breakdown of the American-Soviet relationship, Okinawa emerged as the military linchpin of containment in the Asian-Pacific area. The administration of the island was entrusted to a special bureaucracy directly responsible to the Army Chiefs of Staff. The huge Okinawan bases played an important role in United States contingency planning for possible operations against the Soviet Union in Siberia, the Sea of Japan and the Sea of Okhotsk. They were vital for the implementation of United States policies towards China, the Korean peninsula and the newly independent states of South-East Asia. By the 1960s Okinawa had become the largest offensive nuclear base in the Far East. Vital training, communications and intelligence-gathering facilities had been constructed. After the outbreak of the Vietnam War the island's role as a strategic bomber base became increasingly significant. So too did its position as a storage depot, repair facility, rest and recreation centre and staging point for troops bound for Indochina.

Eisenhower had shown no inclination to return either the Ryūkyūs or the Bonins to Japan. During the Kennedy administration, partly in response to the 1960 security treaty crisis, partly as a result of constant promptings by the newly appointed American ambassador, Professor E.O. Reischauer, Washington's attitude underwent a subtle change.[1] In June 1961, Prime Minister Ikeda, in his talks with President Kennedy, managed to obtain American reaffirmation of Japan's 'residual sovereignty' over the Ryūkyūs.[2] A special commission chaired by presidential assistant Carl Kaysen subsequently recommended some relaxation in United States military control of the islands, a more extensive American aid programme and increased Japanese involvement in settling local problems. The Kaysen Report alarmed the Pentagon. Its implementation was effectively frustrated by the opposition of General Caraway, the United States Military High Commissioner on Okinawa, who argued that any tampering with the established system of military administration, any concessions to Japanese opinion, would undermine the entire basis of American Far Eastern policy, not only towards the Communist powers on the mainland but also towards Japan itself. Japan, Caraway suggested, had been taking advantage of America's regional policies to re-establish its position as a fully independent great power with an expanding sphere of influence. It was by no means clear that this was in Washington's long-term interest.

> Japan, its people, political and economic structure, and its government are tough physically and are equally tough-minded ... Far from adopting an isolationist, inward-looking policy, Japan was wholly expansionist in the 1930s, and indeed to the end of World War II – and beyond.
>
> The Japanese still cannot believe that the United States could have been so foolish as to set them up in business again, and/or that the United States could be so timorous, really, in asking that this country have a fair shake from Japan in the Western Pacific. Japanese unbelief and astonishment have not prevented them from taking full advantage of the openings given.[3]

America's position *vis-à-vis* all the powers in the Far East, Caraway argued, was dependent on its ability to deploy military forces, rapidly and effectively, anywhere in the region. Political influence and economic leverage were of secondary importance. In this sense, Okinawa, rather than Japan, Korea, Taiwan, the Philippines or Indochina, remained the key to control of the Western Pacific. It was essential, therefore, that the United States did not lose the grip on the island.

Caraway's position, especially his suggestion that American and Japanese interests might not necessarily always coincide, represented the beginning of a significant reassessment of the assumptions that had guided United States policy makers since the late 1940s. Advocates of returning Okinawa to Japan stood Caraway's logic on its head and carried the reassessment still further. In a long essay on United States regional objectives written in 1969 Professor Reischauer argued that a self-sustaining balance of power had already been established in Asia. America's position depended less on its military involvements than on its political, economic and cultural ties with the countries of the region. The Soviet Union, locked in confrontation with a politically disorganized, economically weak but nationalistic China, did not constitute a direct, immediate threat to American interests in the Western Pacific. China, in turn, was effectively prevented from establishing a regional hegemony by the intensity of Korean and Vietnamese nationalism, particularly in the Communist-controlled areas of those nations. Japan's position in the regional balance, however, was changing dramatically. Japan had already re-established itself as a major economic power. Its technological base was highly developed. Its military potential was by no means inconsiderable. While Japanese interests appeared to be generally compatible with those of the United States it was also possible that differences over China policy, trade friction and territorial issues could cause the two nations to drift apart. It was therefore essential, in an age of relative American decline, that Washington make prudent concessions to convince the Japanese that their real interests lay in continued association with the United States, rather than in independent great power status, armed neutrality or alliance with some other country. These propositions, Reischauer argued, had important implications for American policy towards Okinawa.

> The greatest of the irritations [in the present Japanese-American relationship] is Okinawa ... One can hardly imagine a more unsound situation than for the United States to be ruling almost one million citizens of its major Asian ally in the only 'semi-colonial' territory created in Asia since the war. This situation is intensely irritating to Japanese of both the left and the right.
> For long the Okinawan situation was justified on the grounds that an uncertain political climate in Japan endangered the future of our bases there and that, therefore, a firmer grip was necessary on our Okinawan bases, just in case we lost our bases in Japan. But this is to state the problem backwards. If we were to lose our bases in Japan, our 'colonialist' grip on Okinawa would be one of the major reasons for this disaster, and if the mutual security treaty were broken, the 960,000 Japanese living in and around our bases in Okinawa would soon make them quite ineffective, if not untenable. We shall either continue to have a friendly defence relationship with Japan and bases in both Japan proper and Okinawa, if these are needed, or we shall have effective bases in neither and a hostile Japan to boot. It is high time we solved the Okinawan problem. The islands must be returned to Japan by 1970, or at least a clear, early date for their return must be fixed by that time.[4]

In Japan and in Okinawa popular movements demanding return of the islands had grown steadily in the 1950s and the 1960s.[5] These movements were essentially expressions of rising nationalist sentiment, opposition to the American alliance, hostility to the presence of foreign bases and a more generalized scepticism about the direction of United States Far Eastern policy. The Socialist and Communist parties had included demands for the return of Okinawa in their policy platforms at a relatively early date. The Liberal Democrats, in contrast, while increasingly agitated over the southern Kuriles, occupied by the Soviet Union during the closing stages of World War II, had been reluctant to press Japan's rather more substantial claims to the Ryūkyūs. It was Satō Eisaku, that shrewd judge of popular opinion, who first decided to place the issue on the Conservative Party agenda.[6] On 4 July 1964, in an announcement that stunned his Liberal Democratic Party colleagues, the Foreign Ministry and the Defence Agency, Satō solemnly proclaimed that only a settlement of 'the territorial question' could bring the postwar era to an end. His assessment of the strength of public feeling was confirmed during his tour of the Ryūkyūs in the summer of 1965, less than a year after he became Prime Minister. Everywhere, angry crowds of demonstrators demanding return of the islands to Japan and the removal of United States facilities disrupted his schedule, forcing him, in one particularly humiliating incident, to take refuge behind the armed guards and barbed wire fences of an American military base. On his return to Tōkyō, Satō began to think more carefully about the possible international and domestic consequences of reversion.[7] Eighteen months later, in the course of a campaign speech at Ōtsu, on the eve of the 1967 general election, the Prime Minister announced his intention to work for the recovery of all administrative rights over Okinawa.

Okinawa's critical position in American Far Eastern strategy made it inevitable that the prospect of reversion would force Japan to examine, once again, the basic character of its relations with the United States, Washington's Asian allies and the Communist powers on the continent. In view of the trend of American policy, interest centred, in particular, on three issues. First, would the return of Okinawa at last herald the establishment of the Japan-centred, anti-Communist, Asian regional alliance that Dulles had attempted to create in 1951? Would Japan inherit not only the American administrative rights, but also, perhaps unwittingly, Okinawa's military role and the policies on which this was based? Was the return of Okinawa compatible with a policy of peaceful coexistence with the Soviet Union and China, or would Japan be drawn, despite its traditional attitudes, into closer diplomatic and, ultimately, military co-operation with South Korea, the Kuomintang, South Vietnam and the SEATO powers? Second, even if a regional alliance were not immediately established, would Japan agree to facilitate the conduct of American Far Eastern policies by formally surrendering, as far as Okinawa was concerned, its rights of prior consultation under the 1960 treaty? The uncertainties surrounding prior consulatations have been examined in an earlier chapter. The existence of the giant Okinawan bases, close to Japan but outside the scope of the 1960 treaty, had enabled both Tōkyō and Washington to avoid testing the reality of the consultations clauses. What would happen when Okinawa once more became, legally and administratively, Japanese territory? Would Japan make a special exemption permitting virtual free use of the Okinawan bases to further American policies in the Far East? Would the Japanese government attempt to assert its theoretical right to approve or reject American military action from Japanese bases on a case-by-case basis? The former solution would inevitably complicate relations with the Soviet Union and deepen the rift between Japan and China. The latter raised the possibility of serious friction with the United States, on the one hand, and the undying enmity of America's opponents on the other. Third, would Japan abandon its traditional hostility to the overt entry of nuclear weapons and formally permit retention of American nuclear bases on Okinawa after reversion? Or would the United States itself, in the light of the evolving global strategic balance, developments in military technology and the changing character of its relationship with Japan, agree to alter its own policies?

After almost three years of tortuous negotiations an American promise to return the Ryūkyūs to Japan was secured at the Satō-Nixon talks in November 1969. The islands formally reverted to Japanese administration in May 1972. Much obscurity surrounded the precise terms of the agreement. In retrospect it seems by no means impossible that the settlement involved several competing interest groups, in both countries, in an intricate exercise in mutually deceptive multiple diplomacy; that significant details of the agreement were either not revealed to, or were deliberately ignored by, some of the principal negotiating parties; that other aspects were consciously interpreted in different ways, in the hope that events which might test the reality of the understandings would never arise. Yet whatever its provisions meant, in practice, the Okinawan agreement can only be understood in the context of the changing balance of power, both global and regional, the evolution of the Japanese-American relationship and the development of domestic political conflicts. It is to discussion of these matters that we will now turn.

II   The prelude to the Okinawa negotiations, June 1966–April 1969

(i)   *The development of American policy, 1966–7*

In June 1966 the Johnson administration, in accordance with recommendations made by Ambassador Reischauer in 1965, set up a special Ryūkyū Islands Study Group to examine the future of the United States position on Okinawa. Chaired by Richard Sneider, the State Department's Japan Country Director, the study group included Morton Halperin, Deputy Assistant Secretary of Defence for International Security Affairs; Norman Orwat, Deputy Director of J-5 (of the Joint Chiefs of Staff) for Regional Affairs; Thaddeus Holt (soon replaced by James Siena), Deputy Under Secretary of the Army for International Affairs and, from time to time, representatives of the White House and the Central Intelligence Agency. Despite Reischauer's important role in its inception it can be assumed that the group viewed both the relationship with Japan and the Okinawan question in a Cold War context. Sneider, in particular, was known as a tough anti-Communist hard-liner on defence and foreign policy issues.

By the end of 1967, Sneider and his colleagues, working in close collaboration with U. Alexis Johnson, the new American ambassador to Japan, had produced a report on the probable impact of Okinawan reversion on the United States military position in the Far East. This report, while deliberately avoiding discussion of the island's nuclear bases, concluded that the return of Okinawa to Japan would have surprisingly little effect on the conventional balance of power in the region. Sneider's findings had considerable influence on the Secretary of Defence Robert S. McNamara, reinforcing his long-held conviction that the development of military nuclear technology had rendered the Okinawan bases obsolescent, and that the issue had become a political one between Japan and the United States. The Ryūkyū Islands Study Group Report also went some way towards persuading the Joint Chiefs of Staff, hitherto the most implacable opponents of reversion, that the islands could be returned to Japan without destroying the United States strategic position in the Western Pacific. It was on the basis of Sneider's report that the White House and the United States Embassy in Japan began to prepare for Prime Minister Satō's visit to Washington in November 1967.[8]

(ii) Domestic politics, foreign policy and the Okinawan issue in Japan, 1966–7

In Japan thinking about the Okinawan question evolved within the framework of the wider foreign policy debate. The polarization of the Liberal Democratic Party over co-operation with Washington's Far Eastern strategies has already been examined. The limited United States–Soviet *détente* had facilitated some improvement in Japan's relations with Moscow. For this reason interest remained focused on the China question. From the winter of 1966–7, the factional stalemate within the Conservative camp, the onset of the Cultural Revolution and public hostility to American intervention in South-East Asia combined, for a time, to frustrate attempts either to improve relations with Peking or to align Japan more unequivocally with the United States. In the Conservative Party, individuals and organizations hostile to the People's Republic continued to denounce China's policies. Groups sympathetic to China continued to call for improved relations with Peking. Yet chaotic conditions in China made visits there difficult. Proponents of *détente* with Peking thus turned their attention to consolidating their political base at home and establishing contacts with American Congressmen sharing similar views. The road to better relations with China was seen to lie through Washington, not directly to Peking.

Despite Satō's victory in the 1966 party presidential elections, the dominant factional coalition was not unchallengeable, although the Prime Minister's position had been made somewhat more secure by the factional proliferation that continued as a result of the breakup of the Ōno and Kōno groups. However, by the time of the January 1967 general election the dominant coalition (now composed of the Satō, Miki, Fukuda, Kawashima and Ishii factions) found itself confronted by virtually equal numbers of neutral and dissident Members of Parliament. The Funada, Mori-Shigemasa and Murakami factions (derivatives of the Ōno and Kōno groups) and the large Maeo (former Ikeda) faction all stood aloof from the Cabinet. The Nakasone, Fujiyama, Akagi-Ishida and Matsumura factions actively opposed Satō.[9]

This factional configuration was not a simple case of dominant 'pro-American' versus dissident 'nationalist' or 'Asianist'. Each camp contained 'pro-American', 'nationalist' and 'Asianist' elements which could, when factional interests permitted, be expected to press for implementation of their ideas. Within the dominant coalition, Satō, Fukuda and Ishii inclined, in varying degrees, towards the concept of close co-operation with the United States. Miki and Kawashima advocated more independent, 'Asianist' policies. Among the neutral and dissident groups, the Funada faction was identified with extreme anti-Communist, 'pro-American' policies, the notoriously opportunistic Nakasone with a 'Gaullist' stance, Maeo with the Yoshida-Ikeda tradition of temporary, limited co-operation with Washington as a prelude to eventual *rapprochement* with Peking. The Mori Shigemasa and Murakami factions were of indeterminate colouring. Fujiyama, Akagi and Matsumura continued to press for immediate reconciliation with China, even at the risk of offending Washington.

In the first quarter of 1967 Prime Minister Satō found himself embarrassed by a series of electoral reverses. These paved the way for a split within the dominant coalition along policy lines. The performance of the Liberal Democratic Party in the January 1967 general elections was uninspiring. The percentage of the national vote secured by Conservative candidates dropped, for the first time, below 50 per cent, reaching a record low of 48.8 per cent. The Conservatives succeeded in maintaining the number of seats (278) held prior to the election. Socialist representation actually declined from 141 to 140 seats. Yet these figures were deceptive. Just before the election the number of seats in the House of Representatives had been increased by 19, of which the Liberal Democrats had expected to win 15. The fact that they succeeded only in maintaining their previous position meant, in reality, a significant loss in Diet strength.[10] The party was dealt an even more devastating blow in April when, for the first time in the twenty years since the institution of gubernatorial elections, the Liberal Democrats lost the governorship of Tōkyō to a candidate sponsored jointly by the Socialists and the Communists. Almost immediately after his inauguration, the new Governor of Tōkyō, Dr Minobe Ryōkichi, the radical son of Professor Minobe Tatsukichi, that old *bête noir* of the Conservative establishment, began a vigorous campaign against the government's support for American policies in East and South-East Asia. The defeat of the Liberal Democrats in Japan's greatest city, like the gradual decline in the Conservative vote at general elections, reflected trends that had been evident for some years. In 1959 the Liberal Democrats had polled an average of 53 per cent of the vote in elections for the forty-four Prefectual Assemblies. This had subsequently dropped to 50.7 per cent, then finally to 48.3 per cent in the April 1967 elections.[11]

These events aggravated the factional-policy conflicts within the Liberal Democratic Party. Satō, Fukuda and the 'pro-American' elements in the dominant coalition saw, behind the declining Conservative electoral fortunes, the sinister machinations of the Japanese Communist Party, and, beyond that, the leviathan tentacles of an international conspiracy directed from Peking. The rot could only be stopped and the balance rectified by an immediate, far-reaching confrontation with the radical camp.[12] The 'nationalist' and 'Asianist' components of the dissident coalition, dismissing such interpretations as sheer fantasy, maintained that the government's policies themselves were at fault.[13] Fujiyama, Furui, Matsumura and Nakasone bitterly attacked the Satō Cabinet's attitude to China and its support for the Vietnam War. These, it was claimed, were alienating an increasingly substantial proportion of the electorate from the Conservative camp.[14]

It was against this background that a split over defence and foreign policy developed in the ruling coalition itself. By the summer of 1967 it was clear not merely that the Liberal Democrats were divided, but that Prime Minister Sato and Foreign Minister Miki were quite openly pursuing different policies. While the Prime Minister gave vociferous support to the American stand on China, Korea and Vietnam, the Foreign Minister thrust himself forward as the apostle of *détente* and peaceful coexistence with the Communist powers. Early in July Satō visited South Korea, the first visit to Korea by a Japanese Prime Minister since the Pacific War. While in Seoul he participated in an unscheduled conference with high-ranking officials from South Korea, Taiwan and the United States.[15] In September he visited Taiwan for talks with Chiang Kai-shek. In October he left for a tour of South Vietnam, amid some of the most violent popular demonstrations since 1960. On 13 October, during the course of a visit to Australia, he openly expressed his support for the bombing of North Vietnam.[16] Finally, in November, at Satō's invitation, Chiang Kai-shek's son and successor, the Nationalist Chinese Defence Minister Chiang Ching-kuo, visited Japan, making a series of fiery speeches on reconquest of the mainland.[17]

While the Prime Minister jetted between the capital cities of Washington's Asian allies, the Foreign Minister, at the ASPAC meeting in Bangkok in July 1967, propounded a policy of reconciliation with China.[18] At other international forums he decried the persistence of the Cold War mentality, stressed the folly of attempting to solve the political and economic problems of South-East Asia by military means, emphasized new trends and other possibilities in world politics.[19] This stand was maintained throughout the summer and autumn of 1967, despite the intensification of the Cultural Revolution, reports of Sino-Soviet border clashes, Sino-British tension in Hong Kong and the breakdown in relations between China and several South-East Asian countries. Quite apart from the fact that Miki had always seen *détente* with the Communist powers and efforts to reduce tension among Washington, Moscow, Peking and Tōkyō as the best guarantee of Japan's long-term security, the Foreign Minister clearly judged that Satō's 'pro-American' stance had reached a degree unacceptable to the party as a whole. He was therefore manoeuvring to capture the party presidency with the support of the 'nationalists' and 'Asianists' in the dissident coalition.

The Okinawan issue, too, gradually split the Japanese establishment along the familiar lines of cleavage. Within the Liberal Democratic Party, those groups giving exclusive priority to relations with the United States, if they supported the concept of reversion at all, inclined towards retention of the island's nuclear bases and untrammelled American use of all facilities. Exponents of *détente* with the Communist powers, advocates of a more independent foreign policy and groups well disposed towards Peking urged removal of all nuclear weapons or recommended postponing the island's return until this should prove possible. Within the dominant coalition, Miki emerged as a proponent of the latter alternative. For some time, however, the great mass of the party, including the powerful Maeo and Nakasone factions, gave no indication of their stand.[20]

The Foreign Ministry, dominated by hardline 'pro-American' anti-Communists contemptuous of domestic Japanese opinion, insisted that reversion itself would prove difficult, removal of nuclear weapons impossible and application of the 1960 security treaty to the military bases remaining on the island totally out of the question. In general, the attitudes of the North American Affairs Bureau director, Tōgo Fumihiko, and the Japanese ambassador to Washington, Shimoda Takezō, closely paralleled those of the most intransigent Cold War warriors in the Pentagon.[21] So rigid had their thinking become that neither the Japanese Foreign Ministry nor the embassy in Washington made any attempt to assess the subtle changes taking place both in United States Far Eastern policy and in perceptions of the Okinawan issue.[22] It was, significantly, from the *Asahi Shimbun*, not the Foreign Ministry, that Prime Minister Satō, in September 1967, first learned of the Ryūkyū Islands Study Group Report.[23]

The Prime Minister, while giving the highest consideration to Japan's relationship with the United States, was determined to negotiate an agreement acceptable to the party, the Diet and the nation. He was not anxious to jeopardize Japan's long-term interests as he saw them. Nor did he wish to endanger his own political future, or that of the faction he led. For these reasons, he moved cautiously. In April 1967, sceptical of the pessimistic reports from the Japanese Embassy in Washington, Satō dispatched Ōhama Shinsen, chairman of the unofficial Okinawan Problems Study Council, on a fact-finding mission to the United States. After interviewing a large number of State and Defence Department officials, members of the Council on Foreign Relations and influential academics, Ōhama returned to Tōkyō convinced that serious negotiations on reversion were possible.[24] Yet the signals from Washington were confusing. When Foreign Minister Miki visited the American capital early in September to attend the United States-Japan Joint Committee on Trade and Economic Affairs he received the impression that the return of Okinawa would be considered only if Japan agreed to undertake wider military responsibilities in the North-East Asian area. His impressions were confirmed in talks with Secretary of State Dean Rusk held in the first part of October.[25] For Japan, additional military responsibilities were simply out of the question. Nevertheless, in late October, after a number of working seminars attended by both Satō and Miki, Ōhama's Okinawan Problems Study Council produced a report recommending that the Prime Minister reach 'fundamental understanding on concrete reversion plans' during his negotiations with President Johnson in November. Japan, it was argued, should attempt to fix a definite reversion date and work for removal of nuclear weapons and full application of the 1960 security treaty to United States bases remaining on the island. The last two points were removed from the report, without Ōhama's knowledge, by Foreign Ministry officials prior to its submission to the Prime Minister on 1 November. In its edited version, the report became the basis for Japan's negotiating position at the November summit.[26]

(iii)   The Satō-Johnson Joint Communiqué, America's terms for return of Okinawa and their domestic political impact, November 1967–March 1968

Despite the findings of Ōhama's committee,* Satō himself remained undecided about the questions of nuclear weapons on Okinawa and application of the security treaty to American bases on the island. In any case, in November 1967, he merely wished to persuade the Americans to begin examining the issue of reversion. The concrete conditions could be negotiated later, in the context of the evolving international situation and the state of public opinion in Japan. Nevertheless, Satō found himself increasingly irritated by the attitude of the Japanese Foreign Ministry. On the eve of the summit, therefore, he sent a private emissary to Washington with a draft joint communiqué somewhat different to that already drawn up by the Foreign Ministry and the United States Embassy in Tōkyō. Satō's draft explicitly committed both parties to begin negotiations on early return of Okinawa. In Washington, this document was accepted by the State Department, the Joint Chiefs of Staff and other interested parties. The chairman of the Senate Armed Services Committee, however, refused to countenance it. This was sufficient to ensure its rejection *in toto*.[27]

The outcome of the November summit thus fell somewhat short of the Japanese Prime Minister's expectations. The Okinawan problem was discussed 'frankly'. President Johnson expressed his 'understanding' of the Japanese position. Nevertheless, it was 'recognized that the United States military bases on these islands continue to play a vital role in assuring the security of Japan and other free nations in the Far East'.[28] The American intention eventually to return administrative rights to Japan was expressed more strongly than ever before, but no time-table was given, no concrete formula enunciated.

Despite this, the United States, delighted by Satō's unequivocal public endorsement of its Far Eastern policies and eager to consolidate the domestic position of such a strong ally, agreed to begin negotiations immediately on return of the Bonin islands, taking into account 'the intention of the Government of Japan ... gradually to assume much of the responsibility for the defence of the area'.[29] These islands had no nuclear bases and were of little military value either to the United States or Japan. America's willingness to return them, separately from Okinawa, had been conveyed to Prime Minister Satō, through former Vice-Admiral Hoshina Zenshirō, on the eve of his departure for Washington.[30]

The Washington talks gave Satō the impression that return of Okinawa would be facilitated by a less hostile public attitude to American nuclear bases, a more positive approach to defence and Far Eastern policies still more closely aligned with those of the United States. The rejection of his draft joint communiqué by a single hawkish senator, despite its acceptance by the bureaucracy and the Joint Chiefs of Staff, suggested that the Foreign Ministry, rather than Ōhama's group, had correctly assessed the realities of power in the American establishment. After his return to Japan, therefore, Satō began to speak with unparalleled enthusiasm on the twin

* Of which the Prime Minister was certainly aware.

themes of 'eradicating the nuclear allergy' and 'increasing popular defence consciousness'. There was also much discussion of 'the China threat'. Satō fired the first volleys of the new campaign as soon as he stepped down from the aircraft that had brought him from Washington. Drawing attention to the 'threat' posed by Soviet and Chinese nuclear weapons the Prime Minister castigated the Socialist Party for its belief that the pacifist Constitution alone provided a sufficient basis for national defence. A more resolute popular attitude to the defence issue, he declared, would facilitate return of Okinawa 'within three years'. Reversion of the island with nuclear bases intact, he hinted, was something that 'should be discussed hereafter'.[31]

Taking their lead from the Prime Minister, government spokesmen expounded and developed these new themes throughout the winter of 1967–8. At the meeting of the Liberal Democratic Party Executive Council on 14 December Fukuda Takeo declared that the time had come to remove the Japanese people's 'nuclear allergy'.[32] This provided Satō with a new slogan. By the end of the month the Prime Minister was telling the House of Councillors Special Committee on the Okinawa Problem that 'the people must have an accurate knowledge of nuclear power and rid themselves of the nuclear allergy'.[33] The Education Minister, Nadao Hirokichi, stressed the need to increase infant defence consciousness, outlining plans to incorporate lessons on national security in a revised primary school syllabus. He later spoke of projected alterations to history textbooks, the object being to reveal 'clearly ... the good points' of the national past. This, he asserted, would increase children's 'self-confidence'.[34] The Liberal Democratic Party's Draft Action Policy, published on 16 January 1968, was characterized by a heavy emphasis on defence and related topics. This document decried the 'confusion of thought', 'the decline in public order and salutary customs' and the 'loss of the innate features of the Japanese nation' brought about by the postwar education system and leftist propaganda. These pernicious influences were directly responsible for the spiritual deficiencies of modern youth. Firm action would be necessary to resurrect the Japanese spirit, which, according to the Draft Action Policy, was based on the five pillars of 'human love', 'public spirit', 'love for the homeland', 'national spirit' and 'defence consciousness'. Many young people, it was noted, were inclining towards support for the radical Opposition parties. A complete overhaul of the education system would be necessary to counteract these tendencies. Particular emphasis should be laid on physical education, inculcation of patriotism, respect for democratic order (*minshūteki chitsujō*) and traditional moral values. Only when national defence consciousness had been revived through a reconstruction of the moral order could Japan begin acting in a way 'worthy of an independent great power'.[35] From January 1968 the government began preparations for a massive publicity campaign to stimulate popular interest in defence.[36]

These developments were accompanied by a renewed emphasis on 'the China threat', discussion of which had somewhat subsided since 1966. The Satō-Johnson Joint Communiqué had spoken of 'the importance of creating conditions wherein Asian nations would not be susceptible to threats from Communist China'. The Japanese Prime Minister had also endorsed President Johnson's conditions for a halt in the bombing of North Vietnam and spoken of 'widespread support' in South-East Asia for American policies. At a general meeting of Conservative Members of Parliament on 24 November the Prime Minister held forth at some length on China's nuclear development.[37] On 7 December Satō told the House of Representatives that his greatest 'responsibility and duty' was to 'ensure the security of Japan'. Reviewing his recent South-East Asian tour the Prime Minister recalled the 'great interest' shown in Chinese nuclear development. It was 'natural' that Japan, too, should share this interest.[38] On 18 December Defence Agency director-general Masuda told the House of Councillors Budget Committee bluntly that

> Mao Tse-tung is, just as Khruschev said, an expansionist and a militarist [uproar in the House]. So I say that [China? Mao Tse-tung? (inaudible)] is a threat.[39]

These statements did not mean, however, that the Satō government had at last come to regard China as an *actual* military threat to Japan. In his statement to the House of Councillors Budget Committee on 18 December, Masuda was careful to explain that

> Chinese nuclear weapons are primitive ... Judging from her national strength and internal situation, China is in miserable shape. That China, whose national strength [Masuda was presumably thinking in terms of gross national product] is only half that of Japan, should use these weapons, is a ridiculous proposition.[40]

As Miki told the House of Councillors Budget Committee on 21 March 1968:

> The Satō-Johnson Joint Communiqué [in referring to the threat of nuclear China] was speaking in an abstract way, about the psychological side of things. It was not referring to any concrete reality.[41]

As in the period 1965–6, references to the 'China threat' were, essentially, expressions of ideological hostility to China as a revolutionary Asian power, reinforced by fear of Chinese-inspired subversion in Japan. Most importantly they were, as before, made with an eye to their impact in Washington.

The new policy emphasis also had far-reaching implications for the factional struggles within the Conservative Party. The Satō-Johnson Joint Communiqué, with its clearly enunciated hostility towards China and endorsement of American policies in Vietnam, was a direct challenge to the dissident nationalists and the Asianists. It was also a challenge to Foreign Minister Miki. There was every indication that the party's right wing was preparing for a head-on clash with its opponents. The closely related issues of Okinawa, nuclear bases, defence and China policy would be used to antagonize, divide and break the dissident forces, to dominate the party and government, restore public confidence in the Conservative camp and, ultimately, purge society of left-wing influence and the more undesirable legacies of the occupation.

On his return from the United States the Prime Minister, in preparation for the anticipated upheaval, embarked on a major Cabinet reorganization. Dissident factions regarded as potentially amenable were given Cabinet and party posts, factions regarded as intractable were isolated. Thus Nakasone was appointed Minister for

Transport and Communications, Ogawa Heiji of the Maeo faction became Minister for Labour and Maeo's close associate Ōhira Masayoshi was appointed chairman of the Party Policy Board. No new posts were given to Miki's supporters. Fujiyama and Matsumura were left out in the cold.[42]

(iv)   The Enterprise visit, the Pueblo incident, the Viet Cong Tet offensive and the dissident factions' counter-attack, January–November, 1968

Satō's decision to eradicate the 'nuclear allergy', prepare the way for the possible return of Okinawa with nuclear bases intact, align Japan more closely with the United States and confront the dissident forces in the Conservative Party proved particularly inopportune. The tumultuous events of 1968 – the aggravation of the base problem within Japan itself, exacerbated tension in Korea and the development of the Vietnam War – revealed the tenacity of the 'nuclear allergy', increased anxiety about close co-operation with the United States, made even Satō's closest supporters begin to doubt the wisdom of 'nuclear-attached' reversion and enabled the dissident forces to launch a counter-offensive that proved a formidable challenge to the Prime Minister's position. By the end of the year it would have been politically impossible for any Japanese leader to open negotiations on Okinawa with the United States on the basis of reversion with nuclear bases attached.

Within the Liberal Democratic Party, erosion of support for 'nuclear-attached' reversion began after the visit of the American nuclear-powered aircraft carrier *Enterprise* in January 1968. The *Enterprise* visit, approved shortly before Satō's trip to Washington, was widely interpreted as an American attempt to cure the Japanese 'nuclear allergy' by shock innoculation.[43] Its impact proved entirely counter-productive. Despite government denials that nuclear weapons were on board, the general belief that the vessel was, in fact, nuclear-armed, together with its role in the bombing of North Vietnam, aroused the Opposition parties, the press, academic circles, students, the labour movement and large sections of the general public to a pitch of hostility comparable with the 1960 crisis. Local authorities also opposed the visit. When the vessel entered Sasebo naval base, a stone's throw from Nagasaki, massive demonstrations brought the city and the surrounding region to a standstill. Demonstrations of sympathy were staged throughout the nation. The *Enterprise* was still in port, its crew unable to proceed ashore, when an American B-52 bomber, laden with nuclear weapons, crashed in Greenland, scattering its bombs across the ice, dispersing their plutonium content and contaminating a wide area.*

Popular Japanese fear of nuclear weapons reached new levels of intensity. These events were not unnoticed by the Prime Minister. In Cabinet Satō observed despondently that 'even housewives participated in the demonstrations or made statements sympathetic to the [demonstrating] students'.[45] The government's public relations campaign, he felt, had been inadequate.[46] As the disorders spread throughout

---

*   In February 1968 a joint US-Danish report announced that the accident had produced no danger from radiation. Eighteen years later, more than 500 workers who participated in the clean-up operation were seriously ill, 98 of them with cancer. An unknown number of workers had apparently died as a result of exposure to plutonium.[44]

Japan, daily growing in magnitude, the Prime Minister's position shifted. Eradication of the 'nuclear allergy' clearly had little promise as a vote-catching issue. On 22 January, after five days of continuous riots and demonstrations, Satō's close confidant, the Chief Cabinet Secretary Kimura Toshio, announced that while Japan, because of its obligations under the security treaty, was prepared to welcome future visits by the *Enterprise*, if requested,

> both the Japanese and American governments must take cognisance of the fact that the *Enterprise* visit precipitated a popular reaction different to that caused by the earlier visits of nuclear submarines. Although there may have been many who went along merely out of curiosity, the government must attach importance to the fact that the citizens of Sasebo showed a certain degree of hostility to the police. Friendly relations between the two peoples is the basis of the Japanese-American security treaty system. It is the belief of both governments that incidents damaging to future friendly relations should be, if possible, avoided.[47]

This announcement split the government along the usual lines.[48] While the Prime Minister remained formally aloof, pressure from Kishi, Fukuda and the 'pro-American' right eventually forced Kimura to retract his statement. At the very moment the Fujiyama, Maeo, Matsumura, Miki and Nakasone factions were planning a counter-attack, the United States naval intelligence vessel *Pueblo* was seized by North Korean patrol boats off Wonsan and taken into custody. The *Enterprise*, which had just left Sasebo, was diverted to the Sea of Japan, nuclear-armed B-52 bombers flew in large numbers into Okinawa, American air bases in Japan went on the alert and President Johnson announced a call-up of reservists.

These events caused unparalleled alarm in Japan. On 25 January 'a high Foreign Ministry source' announced that, 'depending on the development of the situation', Japan might request prior consultations with the United States.[49] After the Cabinet meeting of 30 January the Chief Cabinet Secretary, in a carefully worded statement, told the press that while Japan 'had no alternative' but to support the American version of the incident, 'the Japanese government had no way of verifying the facts'. The reports on which Japan based its judgement had come, it was stressed, entirely from American sources. In response to questioning, Kimura further emphasized that

> Support for the United States version of the facts of the incident is not support for the intelligence-gathering activities of the *Pueblo* or for the threatening actions [*shii kōdō*] of the United States after the *Pueblo*'s capture.[50]

This was perhaps the strongest stand yet taken by Japan towards the United States on any foreign policy issue since the end of the Pacific War. It was also the signal for the beginning of a major reappraisal of the Okinawan base question within the government. Even in conservative 'pro-American' circles, support for removal of nuclear weapons from the island prior to its return increased. So, too, did interest in Japan's asserting some degree of real control over American actions from bases on its territory. On 7 February, disturbed by the new trends in the Liberal Democratic

Party, a 'high Foreign Ministry spokesman' warned that insistence on non-nuclear bases and full application of the security treaty would make reversion of Okinawa 'difficult'.[51] The Chief Cabinet Secretary promptly requested the 'high source' to exercise more discretion.[52]

The *Enterprise* visit and the *Pueblo* incident took place against the background of the 1968 Viet Cong Tet offensive. The destruction of numerous South Vietnamese towns and cities, the occupation of the American Embassy by Viet Cong commandos and Saigon's reverses in the country-side made it clear, even to those who identified closely with the fortunes of the United States, that the war would ultimately end in a North Vietnamese victory. The impact was heightened on 1 April by the announcement of President Johnson's decision to begin de-escalation of the American military effort and not to run as a candidate in the next presidential elections. By millions of Japanese, Johnson's decision was seen as a triumph for American democracy, a victory for the good nature and commonsense of the American people. For countless others it represented a victory for Asian nationalism over the last of the great European empires, further evidence that Iwakura Tenshin, Miyazaki Tōten and Tōyama Mitsuru, not Fukuzawa Yukichi, had correctly divined the future. Others, again, saw the American reverses as a vindication of Marxist Leninism, the prelude to a further extension of the Socialist Commonwealth. Yet however it was interpreted, the fact that America's immense resources, awesome military power and sophisticated modern technology had been unable to subdue the peasant armies of Indochina was obviously a development of historic significance, requiring a substantial revision of established conceptions of international order. Although the final *débâcle* did not come for another seven years, the collapse of the *Pax Americana* in continental South-East Asia, like the Roman withdrawal from Britain, made it apparent to thoughtful observers everywhere that the world was entering a long period of transition, that a new and more complex configuration of power was replacing that to which men had grown accustomed.

The Johnson statement threw Satō and the 'pro-American' wing of the Liberal Democratic Party into disarray. Predictably, the Prime Minister, with an eye to the future, hastened to proclaim that he had always doubted the wisdom of American policies in South-East Asia and had never supported the bombing of North Vietnam.[53] For the most part, however, the 'pro-American' factions in the Conservative Party fell silent. The 'nationalist' and 'Asianist' groups, in contrast, basked in the balmy light of vindicated prescience and reflected glory. The new turn of events was believed to herald the emergence of a more reasonable climate of opinion in Washington, a general relaxation of tensions, the dawn of an age of peace and harmony in the Far East. Former Foreign Minister Ōhira Masayoshi told the press that 'we have come to a turning point in world history'. The Vietnam War had taught Washington 'a valuable lesson'. The Americans might hopefully lose their crusading mentality, adopt a more realistic understanding of Asia, become less willing to intervene in the affairs of other countries.[54] Nakasone foresaw the demise of the *Pax Americana*, a new era of independence for the nations of Asia and the Pacific.[55] Miki predicted that American withdrawal form Vietnam would reduce Chinese fears of encirclement and attack. Peking would respond with a more flexible foreign policy, tensions would be reduced throughout the Far East.[56]

The Tet offensive and the Johnson statement had important effects on the balance of power within the Liberal Democratic Party. Foreign Minister Miki dissociated himself even more decisively from the government. Maeo and Nakasone, whom the Prime Minister had attempted to win over in the November 1967 Cabinet reorganization, gravitated towards the dissident camp. By the middle of the year a powerful anti-Satō coalition had emerged.

It was, ironically, the very day the Viet Cong occupied the United States Embassy in Saigon that the dissident forces established a New Policy Discussion Council (Shin Seisaku Konwa Kai) to spearhead the attack on Satō's foreign and defence policies.[57] The new organization was closely linked with the Afro-Asian Problems Study Association and similar bodies. What made the New Policy Discussion Council a more formidable challenge to the party leadership than the earlier dissident organizations was the fact that it was virtually dominated by the powerful Maeo, Miki and Nakasone factions. Of the seventy-four members of the Diet who joined in the first few weeks, seventeen were from the Maeo faction, thirteen from the Miki faction, eighteen from the Nakasone faction. Fujiyama dispatched eight representatives, the Matsumura, Murakami, Kawashima and various neutral factions four each.[58] Some weeks later a related organization, the Domestic and Foreign Situation Research Council (Naigai Seikyoku Kenkyū Kai) was set up by a group of about thirty politicians drawn mainly from the Matsumura, Miki, Nakasone and Fujiyama factions.[59] Thus, by the summer of 1968, positive support for Satō and his policies centred around his own faction and the Fukuda and Ishii groups. The centre of active opposition had shifted from the smaller Fujiyama, Matsumura and Akagi-Ishida factions to the large factions led by Maeo, Miki and Nakasone.[60]

These changes in the Liberal Democratic Party factional balance coincided with the mounting public interest in neutrality discussed in previous chapters. They also occurred at a time marked by growing Japanese-American conflict over economic issues, and signs that two key United States allies, Italy and Canada, were preparing to recognize the People's Republic of China. What the new factional balance implied for Japan's orientation within the security treaty system and, in particular, for the future of the Okinawa question, gradually became apparent in the succeeding months. The development of the government's attitudes to the base problem provided the most reliable barometer of the new climate of opinion.

In May 1968 abnormal levels of radioactivity were detected in Sasebo harbour during the visit of the American nuclear submarine *Swordfish*. This touched off a national outcry on the familiar pattern. What was different this time, however, was the quick response of the government to public sensitivity. The Prime Minister hastened to assure local authorities that port calls by nuclear submarines would be suspended until the cause of contamination became clear.[61] Within the government there was little opposition to the Prime Minister's *démarche*.[62] An expert committee from the Science and Technology Agency reported that contamination had been caused by the *Swordfish* discharging primary coolant water in the port.[63] The United

States, while acceding to the Japanese request temporarily to suspend nuclear sub-marine visits,[64] denied this.[65] The twenty weeks of tortuous Japanese-American negotiations that followed were marked by considerable friction and ill-feeling on both sides.[66] By the end of October, however, the Japanese had received a promise that nuclear submarines would not, in future, discharge primary coolant in port, except in cases of emergency.[67]

At the height of the *Swordfish* controversy an American F-4 Phantom interceptor based at Itazuke crashed into the campus of Kyūshū University, a few yards from the university's nuclear research institute. There were no injuries, although considera-ble damage was caused to university buildings. Yet in the emotionally electric atmos-phere generated by the events of the preceding months, the incident touched off a reaction out of all proportion to its real significance. Even the most 'pro-American' groups in the Liberal Democratic Party began to question the wisdom of locating United States bases near heavily populated areas.[68] The Prime Minister did nothing to prevent public expression of even more radical positions. On 5 June 1968 his loyal Chief Cabinet Secretary Kimura announced that he did not think the presence of American bases was 'an absolute condition' for Japanese security.[69]

Kimura was rebuffed by the Foreign Ministry[70] and the government hastened to assure the United States that it had no intention of requesting retrenchment or with-drawal of bases.[71] Yet there can be no doubt that a major shift in opinion had taken place. In the aftermath of the *Swordfish* and the Phantom affairs, Maeo and Nakasone moved from generalized criticism of Satō's diplomacy to explicit opposi-tion to nuclear-attached reversion of Okinawa.[72] More significantly, perhaps, the party secretary-general, Fukuda Takeo, who had been one of the first to attack the 'nuclear allergy', now announced his conviction that nuclear-attached reversion was 'not very desirable'.[73] There was also evidence that another pillar of the 'pro-Ameri-can' right wing, Funada Naka, chairman of the Security Problems Research Com-mittee, was beginning to waver.[74] The Prime Minister still officially maintained that reversion without nuclear weapons would be 'difficult'.[75] Yet support for nuclear-attached reversion was clearly fading, even among those sections of the party most sympathetic to United States policies in Asia.

This trend was accelerated by the growth of a view that American reliance on Polaris submarines and new developments in air transport were reducing Okinawa's importance, both as a nuclear and as a strategic base. During a visit to the United States in May 1968, Ōhama Shinsen became totally convinced that the United States would, if pressed, consider removal of nuclear weapons from the island.[76]

Opinion within the Foreign Ministry also began to shift, albeit with glacial imper-ceptibility, during the course of 1968. Sometime during the first part of the year, despite the continued intransigence of Ambassador Shimoda in Washington, Mr Chiba, the new director of the First North American Division, and his second-in-command, Satō Yukio, began discussing the possibility of a reversion agreement based on the concept of a non-nuclear Okinawa and full application of the 1960 sec-urity treaty to all facilities remaining on the island. By the end of the year the Foreign Ministry, in a paper presented to the Japanese-American policy planning conference in December, was arguing that imprudent handling of the Okinawan question could muddy the waters of relations between the two countries in the coming decades. It was at this conference, too, that United States officials broadly sympathetic to the concept of 'non-nuclear homeland level' reversion, such as Morton H. Halperin, informally encouraged their Japanese colleagues to press for return of the islands on this basis, suggesting that their position might have more credibility in Washington if it were presented not in terms of strategic considerations but of political pressures in Japan.[77]

The results of three critical elections held in November 1968 demonstrated the compelling nature of these pressures, further restricting the Prime Minister's freedom of manoeuvre *vis-à-vis* the United States. In the Liberal Democratic Party presidential election Satō was elected for a new term with 249 votes. Miki and Maeo, who stood against him, received a total of 203 votes. This represented an increase of 38 per cent in the anti-Satō vote since the 1966 election.[78] The Prime Minister could hardly regard this result as an endorsement of his policies, especially in light of the changes taking place in the outlook of his own supporters. The Cabinet organized after the election represented, to some extent, a return to the 'all-faction' governments of the early Ikeda years. Miki, Maeo and Nakasone refused to participate directly, but two members of the Miki faction, two of Maeo's followers and one member of the Nakasone faction received Cabinet posts. Satō reduced the number of posts given to his own followers from four to three. The Fukuda faction received two posts, other offices went to members of the Ishii and Kawashima factions.[79] The dominant factions could ill afford to antagonize the now powerful dissident groups. Least of all could they confront them on Okinawan policy. Just before the Liberal Democratic Party presidential election, Yara Chōbyō, a candidate supported by the Opposition parties, was returned as Okinawan Chief Executive.[80] His minimum demand was non-nuclear reversion with homeland level bases. Three weeks later another Opposition candidate, Taira Ryōshō, emerged victorious in the Naha mayoral elections.[81] This seemed a clear indication that Okinawans endorsed the Opposition platform of non-nuclear reversion, full application of the security treaty and eventual removal of all bases. The swing to the left in Okinawa was also, perhaps, a sign that the political situation there could become uncontrollable if these expectations were not satisfied.

(v) *The trend of opinion among middle-ranking American bureaucrats, January–December 1968*

The upheavals of 1968 convinced most informed American State and Defence Department officials that it was essential to negotiate return of Okinawa on terms broadly acceptable to the Japanese public. The United States ambassador to Tōkyō, U. Alexis Johnson, had come to believe that while American influence in the Far East was destined to decline, the relationship with Japan would remain of vital importance. The security treaty would not survive, however, unless the

Okinawa problem was settled amicably. Throughout 1968 Johnson made strenuous efforts to persuade United States military officials of the seriousness and urgency of the issue.[82] His views, which were broadly similar to those of Richard Sneider, Morton Halperin and former ambassador Edwin Reischauer, were shared by the newly appointed High Commissioner to the Ryūkyūs, Ferdinand Unger, and his successor, General Lampert. As the political situation in Okinawa became more volatile, Unger, determined to avoid clashes with the civilian population, found himself involved in ceaseless conflict with the United States military bureaucracy. He attempted (unsuccessfully) to prevent port calls by nuclear submarines at Okinawa and to discourage the air force from using the island as a base for B-52 raids on Vietnam.[83]

Those United States officials who were aware of the extraordinary deference of many Japanese Conservative leaders to orthodox American opinion also became concerned that the Satō Cabinet might negotiate a politically unacceptable and potentially destabilizing reversion agreement. Within the limits of the possible, these officials attempted to convince their nervous Japanese counterparts that the American negotiating position might be more flexible than it appeared to be on the surface.[84]

(vi)　Prime Minister Satō decides to aim for nuclear-free reversion with full application of the security treaty, March 1969

On 10 March 1969 Satō announced his intention of negotiating with the United States on the basis of non-nuclear reversion of Okinawa with full application of the security treaty to the bases remaining on the island.[85] This momentous decision was the logical outcome of the events described above. It was also influenced by three new factors.

First, on 5 March, the Prime Minister had received a lengthy report prepared by the Okinawa Base Problems Research Council (Okinawa Kichi Mondai Kenkyū Kai), a working group of Ōhama Shinsen's Okinawan Problems Study Council, chaired by Satō's strategic adviser, the former naval officer and military critic, Kusumi Tadao.*[86] Ōhama, Kusumi and other members of the council had taken advantage of the Japan-United States Kyōto Conference in January 1969 to discuss Okinawa with General Maxwell Taylor, Admiral Arleigh Burke, former ambassador Edwin Reischauer and several other prominent Americans.[88] The council's report made a strong case for non-nuclear return of Okinawa, although it recommended flexibility in applying the prior consultation clauses of the security treaty. Nuclear war in the Far East, the council argued, was highly improbable, conventional war, even in Korea, unlikely. Okinawan nuclear bases, whatever their importance in the past, were now of little significance in the overall regional power balance. Their role had been usurped by Polaris submarines and nuclear bases in the United States itself. Conventional bases in Okinawa had considerable, but declining, importance.

---

* 　Kusumi, a graduate of the Imperial Naval Academy, had served on the Naval Chiefs of Staff, with the Fifth Fleet and the South-Western Regional Force in World War II.[87]

The Okinawan problem was therefore not, in essence, a strategic problem but a problem of political relations between Japan and the United States. An amicable settlement could help consolidate the basis for continued and co-operative relations between the two countries. An unsatisfactory settlement could exacerbate Japanese-American tensions, creating, ultimately, a highly unstable situation throughout Asia and the Pacific.[89]

Second, the Prime Minister's close associate, Tanaka Kakuei, appointed secretary general of the Liberal Democratic Party in November 1968, had decided, on the basis of his talks with Kaihara Osamu, the secretary of the National Defence Council, to support 'immediate and unconditional' return of Okinawa with application of the three non-nuclear principles to American bases remaining on the island. Kaihara had apparently convinced Tanaka that whatever Washington might claim for negotiating purposes, there were no strategic or technical reasons for the United States to continue maintaining nuclear bases on Okinawa.[90]

Third, government-sponsored opinion polls had apparently confirmed the impression, gained from the events of the previous year, that the Japanese public would be very much opposed to the return of Okinawa if the island's nuclear bases remained intact. Towards the end of February, the Prime Minister received the results of a survey conducted by the Cabinet Research Office. This poll showed that 45 per cent of respondents were opposed to immediate reversion of Okinawa if nuclear weapons could not be removed or if Washington insisted on free use of bases; 25 per cent favoured immediate reversion even if the bases remained in their existing state; the other 30 per cent were uncertain.[91] This poll confirmed the results of earlier newspaper surveys. A *Mainichi Shimbun* poll of 3 October 1967 had shown only 1.6 per cent in favour of 'nuclear-attached' reversion, while 32.8 per cent of respondents demanded 'homeland level' bases. Another 14.6 per cent had advocated complete removal of all bases.[92] Another *Mainichi Shimbun* poll taken in May 1969 showed 3.0 per cent in favour of 'nuclear-attached' reversion and free use of bases, 9.0 per cent advocating removal of nuclear weapons and free use of bases, 52.0 per cent supporting 'non-nuclear, homeland level' bases and another 25 per cent demanding complete removal of all American installations on the island.[93] Polls taken later in the year showed basically similar results.

(vii)   The implications of Richard Nixon's victory in the United States presidential elections, November 1968

Richard Nixon's victory in the November 1968 presidential elections set the stage for the most sweeping changes in United States foreign policy since the death of Roosevelt in April 1945. Nixon was, in terms of conventional thinking, a realist, more aware than any President since Eisenhower both of the possibilities and the limitations of American power. At the time of his accession, however, he was regarded, in both the United States and Japan, as an inflexible and uncompromising anti-Communist ideologue, whose Cold War fundamentalism, a product of the early 1950s, showed little promise of further evolution. His attitude towards China was thought to be particularly rigid. This made it seem inevitable not only that Washington would give renewed emphasis to Okinawa's military role, but that pressure for large-scale Japanese rearmament and Japanese participation in regional security organizations would once again mount. Nixon's article in the October 1967 issue of *Foreign Affairs*, advocating a military role for ASPAC, had already caused considerable alarm in Japan.[94] Towards the end of October 1968 Nixon outlined his views on the Okinawan negotiations to a reporter from the *Asahi Shimbun*. The then presidential candidate made two points. First, without referring specifically to the question of Okinawa's nuclear bases, Nixon stressed that

> it must be recognized that the United States facilities on these islands are fulfilling an important role in guaranteeing the security of Japan and the other Free Nations in Asia. My Administration will pay attention to ensuring that no agreement [on the future of Okinawa] undermines in any way the position or the security of Free Asia.

Nixon's second point was that Okinawa would be returned ('eventually', not necessarily 'immediately') 'in correspondence with Japan's continuing leadership in Asia, in the direction of mutual dependence and regional co-operation'. What this meant in concrete terms was spelt out clearly.

> The question of the return of Okinawa is not unrelated to the question of Japan's role in the collective security of Asia... I think it certain that as Japan becomes a leading economic power, she will come to play still greater roles, diplomatically, economically, politically and also militarily, for the maintenance of a sound balance in Asia.[95]

Nixon's electoral victory was thus the cause of much apprehension in Japan. There were gloomy predictions, even in the most pro-American circles, that the new President's schemes, if carried to fulfilment, would be detrimental to the peace of Asia.[96] As in 1958–60, virtually all sections of the Liberal Democratic Party were united in their opposition to direct involvement in regional security organizations. Former Foreign Minister Ōhira, speaking for the dissident factions, remarked that

> Nixon is well aware of Japan's situation and is supposed to know that to raise questions embarrassing to the Japanese government will not be in the interests of the United States ... What the United States has learned in Asia, at dear cost, is that Asian problems cannot be settled militarily. There is no choice but to settle them politically.

A regional military role for Japan, Ōhira declared, was 'impossible'.[97]

In the weeks that followed Nixon's election, these views were reiterated by a distinguished collection of Conservative politicians and former diplomats.[98] Prime Minister Satō, speaking for the dominant factions, observed merely that 'there are things which Japan cannot do'.[99] The new Foreign Minister, Aichi Kiichi, elaborated on this theme in an interview with the *Nihon Keizai Shimbun*. Japan would firmly maintain the three non-nuclear principles, there would be no conscription, no dispatch of troops overseas. ASPAC would not become a military alliance. Aichi emphasized this point strongly, a number of times.[100] Finally, in mid-March 1969, the director of the Legislative Bureau told the House of Councillors Budget Committee that participation in any form of collective defence organization would be, for Japan, unconstitutional.[101]

Immediately after his election, Nixon ordered the establishment of a new, centrally controlled foreign policy decision-making apparatus, centring on the National Security Council. His objective was to concentrate power in the White House, reducing the influence of the Department of State, the Defence Department, the Joint Chiefs of Staff and the Central Intelligence Agency. The council, chaired by the President himself and directed by his National Security Adviser Henry Kissinger, consisted of nine top officials assisted by a specialized staff recruited from the public service, the business world and the universities.

The Okinawan issue was one of the first to be considered by the National Security Council early in 1969. Both Nixon and Kissinger might have treated the matter differently had not Richard Sneider and Morton Halperin joined the National Security Council staff in the last weeks of 1968. On 21 January 1969, Sneider and Halperin, after consultations with the State Department, the Treasury, the Joint Chiefs of Staff and the Department of International Security Affairs in the Office of the Secretary of Defence, submitted a long memorandum (NSSM-J) on American-Japanese relations to the National Security Council Review Group.[102] This memorandum stressed the increasing fragility of the Japanese-American relationship, concluding that early reversion of Okinawa was essential if the 'pro-American' groups in the Liberal Democratic Party, centring around Prime Minister Satō, were to remain in power. The impact of a possible withdrawal of nuclear weapons from Okinawa, it was argued, could be offset by a more 'positive' Japanese attitude to prior consultations under the 1960 arrangements and some clear-cut, public recognition of the importance of South Korea, Taiwan and South Vietnam to Japan's own security. Such a compromise, it was felt, might actually improve the United States strategic position in North-East Asia. The Japanese-American security treaty would be given a new lease of life. An explicit Japanese acknowledgement of the strategic importance of South Korea, Taiwan and South Vietnam, together with a relaxation of the prior consultations clauses, would lock Japan more securely into the United States East Asian alliance system and provide increased freedom of action from bases on the Japanese mainland. United States losses would be minimal, even the Joint Chiefs of Staff having by now concluded that the development of a home-based strategic deterrent had made permanent stationing of nuclear weapons on Okinawa unnecessary. Nevertheless, the Joint Chiefs remained interested in retaining nuclear storage rights on Okinawa. It was perhaps felt that if emergency storage rights could be negotiated as part of a package for 'non-nuclear homeland level' reversion, a precedent would have been established for officially sanctioned emergency introduction of nuclear weapons to other parts of the archipelago.[103]

The Sneider-Halperin memorandum, considered by the National Security Council itself in April 1969, provided the basic frame of reference for United States officials during the subsequent negotiations with Japan. A National Security Council Decision Memorandum authorizing the State Department to begin talks with the

Japanese government on the return of Okinawa was issued on 2 May 1969. While it was agreed that the nuclear question could only be settled at the American-Japanese summit in November, there was, on the United States side, a general consensus that the island's nuclear bases could be scrapped without jeopardizing the strategic equilibrium in the Far East. Since the Japanese government did not know this, it was clearly in Washington's interest to exploit the uncertainty surrounding the nuclear issue to extract maximum concessions from Japan in other areas. This negotiating tactic necessitated the launching of an intensive campaign to convince Japanese policy-makers that the United States continued to attach great importance to Okinawa's nuclear facilities.

III   The negotiations and the final settlement

(i)   The development of American and Japanese positions on the nuclear question and prior consultations, April–November, 1969

Washington's campaign to improve its negotiating position by emphasizing the importance of Okinawa's nuclear bases began immediately after the April 1969 National Security Council meeting. Towards the end of the month Sneider and Halperin told Tōgo Fumihiko, director of the Foreign Ministry's American Affairs Bureau, that while no decision had yet been made, 'nuclear-free, homeland level' reversion of Okinawa would be 'difficult'.[104] American comment on the Kusumi report, circulated privately among State and Defence Department officials in April, was positively discouraging. The former director of the State Department's East Asian Bureau, Mr Yager, reportedly asserted that 'nuclear devices were necessary'. This view was also propogated by the former Deputy Assistant Secretary for Defence, Mr Rowen.[105]

Early in May the Democratic Socialist Party leader Aso Yoshikata had talks in Washington with Sneider, the Senate Minority Whip Mr Scott (Republican) and the then director of the State Department's Japan Desk, Mr Finn. He received the impression that while the Americans were now resigned to the fact that no direct military help could be expected from Japan in the Far East, Washington would insist that nuclear weapons remain on Okinawa. They would also demand that American use of bases be untrammelled by prior consultations.[106] This view was seen to be general among Congressmen, and particularly strong in the House and Senate Armed Services Committees. Two weeks later a special envoy was sent to the United States to explain Japan's position to individual members of Congress. The envoy was given instructions to concentrate his efforts on the chairmen of the two armed services committees and on Senator Scott.[107] His exertions had little apparent effect. About this time the Washington Bureau of the *Sankei Shimbun* circulated questionnaires on the Okinawa problem to 100 Senators. Only ten replies were received. Of these ten only one (unsigned) supported the Japanese position of nuclear-free, homeland level bases. There were four opinions in favour of removal of nuclear weapons and free use of bases. The remaining five were in support of the status quo.[108] Sone Eki (Democratic Socialist Party) could thus receive little comfort when Kissinger told him, enigmatically, towards the end of May, that 'there is nothing which is absolutely necessary'.[109] The presidential adviser could, after all, have been referring to the Japanese Constitution.

As far as can be judged, the Japanese government paid no attention to a report in *The New York Times* on 3 June 1969 that 'President Nixon has decided to remove American nuclear weapons from Okinawa once an overall plan for turning the island back to Japanese rule has been agreed upon'. Nixon and Kissinger's subsequent claim that this revelation seriously undermined the American negotiating position is without foundation.[110]

Talks between Foreign Minister Aichi and President Nixon in June, and the subsequent Aichi-Rogers discussions, produced no clarification of the United States attitude to the nuclear weapons issue. The Americans adopted a hard line on the Chinese nuclear threat, rejecting Japan's indulgent view of Peking's capabilities and intentions. They also refused to accept Japan's optimistic view of the Korean situation. All this suggested a strong interest in preserving the Okinawan status quo.[111]

Japanese efforts to persuade the United States at the Aichi-Meyer talks in mid-July,[112] at the meeting of the United States-Japan Joint Committee on Trade and Economic Affairs towards the end of that month,[113] then at the Aichi-Rogers talks in mid-September met with no apparent success.[114] The Prime Minister, confronted with an intractable situation at home and a barrage of conflicting advice from various quarters, became increasingly uncomfortable. He had staked his political future on the non-nuclear return of Okinawa and was well aware that an unsatisfactory settlement could have disastrous consequences for himself personally, for his own faction and for the future of Conservative rule in Japan. In August, therefore, unknown either to Aichi or the Foreign Ministry, Satō sent a private emissary to Washington to sound out Nixon's attitude. In a series of secret meetings with Kissinger, over an unknown time period, a broad understanding on the outlines of the final agreement was reached.[115]

Yet this cannot have been an easy matter, nor can it have been achieved rapidly. Aichi, unaware of the Prime Minister's secret diplomacy, was so disturbed by the inflexible attitude shown by the Americans in September that, just before his departure for Japan, he telephoned Rogers to make a last-minute appeal on the nuclear question.[116] Despite this he was obliged to report to the party Foreign Affairs Research Council on his return that he had failed to reach agreement with the Americans.[117] The talks between Aichi and the new American ambassador Armin Meyer before Satō's departure for Washington in November also remained deadlocked on the nuclear weapons issue although it seems possible that Satō's emissary and Kissinger had reached agreement on the matter by this time.[118]

As the negotiations developed, the Japanese were also subjected to constant pressure from America's other East Asian allies. On 4 March 1969 South Korean President Pak Chung Hi warned a group of visiting American Congressmen that return of Okinawa to Japan would cause a serious flaw in North-East Asian defence.[119] The same day he suggested to a group of American journalists and businessmen that pressure be put on Japan to rearm and join an Asian collective defence organization.[120] Shortly afterwards an editorial in the semi-official Taipei 'Central Daily News' expressed similar sentiments.[121] Satō also revealed to the Diet that he had been approached by the Nationalist Chinese ambassador, Chen Chi-mai.[122] It was not long before the South Vietnamese became engaged in similar manoeuvres.[123]

Had the Japanese held their ground, they might have been able both to secure non-nuclear, homeland level reversion of Okinawa and avoid unnecessary, dangerous and easily misinterpreted references to the security of third countries in the final agreement, statements which made it extremely difficult for Satō to respond flexibly to the new international situation created by Nixon's overtures to Peking two years later. The United States, after all, was seriously concerned about the state of relations with Japan. There was an almost universal agreement that return of Okinawa, in a manner acceptable to both the Japanese political elite and to public opinion, was necessary to prevent the alliance from foundering. Prime Minister Satō, however, bewildered by the contradictory advice of the Foreign Ministry and his own private counsellors, lacked Yoshida's cunning and talent for tactical procrastination. Kissinger, who was deficient in neither of these qualities, and who was well aware of Satō's domestic difficulties, undoubtedly used his skills to good effect in the secret talks with the Japanese Prime Minister's mysterious envoy. The Japanese government thus gradually moved towards partial acceptance of Washington's demands on prior consultations, despite the continued anxiety caused by America's over-reaction at the time of the *Pueblo* incident. Yet the road to the final compromise was not an easy one.

As early as March 1969 the government began studying a plan whereby American forces could be deployed from Okinawa without consultations in cases of large-scale conflict in areas around Japan. Korea and Taiwan were specifically mentioned as examples of 'areas around Japan'.[124] The Kusumi report also recommended a 'flexible' attitude to prior consultations.[125] The weakness and ambiguity of the prior consultations provisions of the 1960 treaty have already been examined. In some sections of the Liberal Democratic Party, there was an increasingly strong desire to see Japan exert a measure of real control over American actions.[126] Satō himself, disturbed by the implications of the *Pueblo* affair, possibly shared these sentiments. After the presentation of the Kusumi report the Chief Cabinet Secretary told the press that 'the principle of prior consultations is to put on a brake. The policy hitherto taken towards prior consultations will not change at all with the reversion of Okinawa.'[127] In an interview with the *Tōkyō Shimbun* in March 1969 the Chief Cabinet Secretary announced that Japan would decide its attitude at prior consultations 'autonomously' and on the basis of 'national interest'. Japan would probably exercise its power of veto in the case of American action 'in faraway places', for example, 'outside the scope of the Far East'.[128] This suggested an indulgent view towards American deployment to South Korea and the Taiwan area, but not necessarily towards American actions in Vietnam, which fell outside the scope of the Far East as defined in 1960.

On 15 April 1969, five weeks after these indications of the shape of the eventual compromise, an American EC-121 intelligence aircraft based at Atsugi was shot down over North Korea and a situation similar to the *Pueblo* incident threatened to develop. While the approach of the final Okinawa negotiations demanded greater public support for American actions than previously, this incident revived old fears.[129] The positions of the two allies moved further apart. The Americans, urged on by the South Koreans and the Kuomintang, insisted on preserving the right of free take-off. The Japanese worked hard to assert the right to examine American actions on a case-by-case basis.

Immediately after the EC−121 incident the South Korean Deputy Prime Minister Pak Chung Hun conferred with President Nixon and Secretary of State Rogers. He subsequently announced that while Okinawa was a question to be settled between Japan and the United States, South Korea 'could not but be concerned'.[130] The same day (1 May 1969) the Democratic Socialist Party Member of Parliament Aso Yoshikata announced, after talks with 'high-ranking American officials', that the United States attached 'great importance' to the EC-121 incident. Washington intended to make Japanese co-operation in the defence of South Korea a condition for the return of Okinawa, although a direct Japanese military contribution to the security of the area was regarded as impossible.[131] Sone Eki received the same impression from his talks with American officials towards the end of May.[132] After his discussions with President Nixon and Rogers in June, Aichi confessed to reporters that 'the United States seems insistent on free use of bases'.[133]

For a time, the Japanese held their ground. On his return from Washington, Aichi told the Diet that the American bases on Okinawa would, after reversion, be considered on exactly the same level as bases in the homeland. They would cease to have any connection with agreements between the United States and its other Asian allies, such as South Korea and the Philippines.[134] Satō assured the House of Representatives Cabinet Committee that advance agreements on Japan's attitude at prior consultations were impossible.[135] This was repeated by Aichi at a press conference on 20 June 1969. On this occasion the Foreign Minister implicitly warned Washington about its future use of Japanese bases. It was desirable, he said, to create a situation where neither party had to resort to prior consultations. The United States knew that Japan was making an issue of this question and would therefore be careful about using Japanese bases 'for matters which do not concern Japan overmuch'.[136]

Talks on the problem continued, apparently without agreement, throughout the summer and autumn of 1969. By November, however, the Japanese government had decided that while it could not give in advance any unconditional guarantee that it would endorse *all* actions theoretically subject to prior consultations under the 1960 security treaty, it could give the United States an assurance that it would not use the system to apply an automatic veto on American operations. Since Japan's strict legal rights under the 1960 consultations system were minimal, this concession may well have meant very little. At the same time, Satō decided that nothing would be lost by

making an explicit statement of concern for the security of South Korea. It was apparently argued that Japan's commitment to support the American position in Korea
had been made clear in the 1951 Yoshida-Acheson Exchange of Notes and reaffirmed in the Kishi-Herter Exchange of Notes in 1960. A further endorsement of
American policy would thus involve no new departure.[137] Yet had the Japanese been
aware of the real strength of their bargaining position they could also have argued
that a further reaffirmation of these earlier commitments was unnecessary. As it was,
the form of the final statement (see below), devoid of references to the United
Nations action in the peninsula, but uncannily reminiscent of the expression
employed in the 1902 Anglo-Japanese alliance, on the eve of Japan's political and
military advance into the peninsula, caused widespread misunderstanding at home
and abroad. Taiwan and South Vietnam presented even more difficult problems.
The Prime Minister himself, not wishing further to complicate relations with China,
aware of the strength of the 'pro-Peking' groups within the Conservative Party and
mindful of Japanese public opinion, would personally have preferred to avoid any
reference to Taiwan in the agreement. Once again, his failure to recognize the
strength of his position led him to believe this was impossible. On Vietnam, however,
Satō, conscious of the intensity of popular feeling against the war, refused to compromise. In the end, he responded to American pressure only to the extent of agreeing to shelve the question until the actual time of reversion.[138]

(ii)   *The November 1969 Satō-Nixon Joint Communiqué and the terms of the June 1971 agreement*

The Satō-Nixon Joint Communiqué, which laid the basis for the final agreement on
the return of Okinawa, was an extraordinarily ambiguous document, subject to
widely differing interpretations both at home and abroad. The only clearly enunciated agreement was that Okinawa would be returned in 1972, 'subject to the conclusion of ... specific arrangements with the necessary legislative support'.[139]
However, viewed in the context of the Japanese-American negotiations prior to
November 1969, and in the light of subsequent government explanations, the communiqué seemed to mean that nuclear weapons were to be removed from Okinawa
before reversion. Japan, in return, agreed to facilitate implementation of American
policies in South Korea, Taiwan and other areas in the Far East. However, there was
no unequivocal guarantee of prior approval for all American actions in these areas.
More importantly, there was no indication that Japan itself intended to assume wider
military responsibilities within the American alliance system. Its only new commitments were to the defence of Okinawa. This was also made clear in the Arrangement
Concerning Assumption by Japan of the Responsibility for the Immediate Defence
of Okinawa, concluded on the basis of negotiations between the Japanese Defence
Agency and the United States Department of Defence, and approved by the Japan-
United States Security Consultative Committee on 29 June 1971.[140]

(a)   Nuclear weapons

The final reversion agreement, signed by Foreign Minister Aichi Kiichi and Secretary of State Rogers on 17 June 1971, in accordance with established American policy on such matters, made no reference to the question of nuclear weapons. It simply stipulated that 'the reversion of these islands to Japan [should] be carried out on the basis of the [1969] Joint Communiqué.[141]

According to the communiqué:

> The Prime Minister described in detail the particular sentiment of the Japanese people against nuclear weapons and the policy of the Japanese government reflecting such sentiment. The President expressed his deep understanding and assured the Prime Minister that, without prejudice to the position of the United States government with respect to the prior consultations system under the Treaty of Mutual Co-operation and Security, the reversion of Okinawa would be carried out in a manner consistent with the policy of the Japanese government, as described by the Prime Minister.[142]

Both the Prime Minister and Foreign Minister Aichi publicly interpreted this as a pledge on the part of the United States to remove all nuclear weapons from Okinawa by the time of reversion.[143] Subsequent explanations by Aichi and Chief Cabinet Secretary Kimura clarified that while the phrase 'without prejudice to the position of the United States government with respect to the prior consultations system', permitted the United States to raise the subject of re-entry of nuclear weapons, Japan would not permit such weapons to be brought back in unless its own existence were in jeopardy. At all other times, American requests to bring in nuclear weapons would be refused.[144] The subsequent revelations of Admiral Laroque, Professor Reischauer and Daniel Ellsberg (see Chapter VI) raised serious questions concerning American nuclear weapons policy throughout the Japanese archipelago. Despite the consensus reached in State and Defence Department circles in the late 1960s regarding the limited value of Okinawan bases it is by no means clear that Washington fully honoured the commitment to remove all nuclear weapons from the island. On the basis of evidence currently available, it seems likely that Okinawa's role as an active United States strategic nuclear base *did* fall into eclipse after 1972. Nevertheless, in response to pressure from the Joint Chiefs of Staff and, perhaps, other agencies which have left no public record of their activities, storage and transit facilities for nuclear weapons may well have been retained. It is not altogether certain whether Prime Minister Satō, Foreign Minister Aichi and their successors were aware of this.

(b)   South Korea, Taiwan and prior consultations

In Article 4 of the communiqué the Prime Minister 'stated that the security of the Republic of Korea was essential to Japan's own security'.

After President Nixon reaffirmed America's intention to honour its treaty obligations to Taiwan, Satō 'said that the maintenance of peace and security in the Taiwan area was also a most important factor for the security of Japan'.

Article 7 stated that the provisions of the 1960 security treaty and related arrangements would be applied 'without modification' to Okinawa after reversion. This was reaffirmed in Article II of the 1971 reversion agreement. However, according to the joint communiqué,

> the Prime Minister affirmed the recognition of his government that the security of Japan could not be adequately maintained without international peace and security in the Far East ... The Prime Minister was of the view that, in the light of such recognition on the part of the Japanese government, the return of the administrative rights over Okinawa in the manner agreed above [i.e. with full application of the prior consultations and other provisions of the 1960 treaty] should not hinder the effective discharge of the international obligations assumed by the United States for the defence of countries in the Far East, including Japan.

The references to South Korea and Taiwan in Article 4 of the joint communiqué caused much confusion. It was widely assumed that the United States had at last persuaded Japan to assume responsibility for preservation of the political and military status quo in the Korean peninsula and the Taiwan Straits. The Japanese government subsequently stressed that Japan had not agreed to participate actively in any regional military arrangements, that it was undertaking no additional commitments in these two areas and that the constitutional ban on overseas service for the Self Defence Forces still remained. On 17 February 1970 the Prime Minister, after explaining the importance of South Korea and Taiwan to Japanese security, assured the House of Representatives that

> the duty of the Self Defence Forces is to protect Japan from aggression. The provisions of the Constitution make overseas service impossible (*kaigai ni shutsudō suru koto wa kenpō no tatemae jō kara mo ariemasen*).[145]

Thus, as far as can be judged from material publicly available, the joint communiqué was speaking of the Japanese attitude, at prior consultations, to American requests to use Okinawa-based forces for military actions in South Korea and Taiwan.

After his talks with Nixon, Satō told the press that he would handle such situations 'in a forward looking manner' (*maemuki no taido o motte jitai ni taisho suru*).[146] This suggested virtual advance approval of American actions in these areas. However, later explanations indicated the government believed it still retained a right of veto. After his return to Tōkyō, Satō told the press that despite the phrase 'forward-looking', Japan would not necessarily 'co-operate at all times'.[147] Foreign Minister Aichi later elaborated that while it was 'important for the security of the Far East' that the United States fulfill its obligations to Seoul and Taipei, Japan reserved the right to approve or reject American action at prior consultations on a case-by-case basis. Japan's attitude would be decided 'in accordance with its national interests'.[148] The important differences in nuance between these statements and the joint communiqué suggest that Satō and Nixon may have failed to reach complete agreement on the consultations problem.

The Japanese might well have been able to negotiate return of Okinawa on more favourable terms had they called Washington's bluff on the nuclear question, and perhaps been prepared to wait another two years. Nevertheless, it would be difficult to maintain that the 1971 reversion agreement was entirely without redeeming features. Japan's concessions had certainly been considerable. Some of them had undoubtedly been unwise. Yet its gains had also been remarkable. It had reasserted its sovereignty over a strategically important piece of real estate inhabited by nearly a million former Japanese subjects. It had secured a formal American commitment to remove all nuclear weapons from the territory before reversion, thus paving the way for public acceptance of the agreement. While the Americans may have viewed things differently, the Japanese government felt able to claim some degree of control over United States action from Okinawan bases. More importantly, despite the references to South Korea and Taiwan, the agreement did not appear to require direct Japanese participation in any regional security arrangement. On this impor-tant matter of principle, Japan appeared to stand exactly where it had stood in 1951 – allied to the United States, but with no military commitments beyond its own shores. While the Socialist and Communist parties remained understandably scep-tical of the government's explanations of this point, Satō's efforts to negotiate a reversion agreement that did not enmesh Japan even more tightly into the United States global strategic system won high praise from even his bitterest antagonists in the Conservative camp. Former Foreign Minister Sonoda Sunao, for example, once confided to the present writer that

> The Americans were always asking us to do this and to do that, to take over part of the burden of their Far Eastern policies. But all their efforts were sabotaged by one Japanese Cabinet after another. That's why Satō Eisaku got the Nobel Peace Prize. He got it for his accumulated achievements in the field of sabotage. I suppose he is the only Prime Minister ever to have got the Nobel Peace Prize for sabotage.[149]

While the United States was successfully able to turn the political unacceptability of nuclear-attached reversion to its own advantage, without, perhaps, entirely aban-doning Okinawa's strategic nuclear role, it is possible that the relatively favourable outcome of the negotiations from Satō's point of view was not unrelated to Japan's having postponed signing the nuclear non-proliferation treaty until after the 1969 summit. Creating uncertainty was a game the Japanese could play as effectively as their American allies.

CHAPTER X

Japan's nuclear policies and the non-proliferation treaty, 1955–1970

Who among us can dwell with the devouring fire?
Who among us can dwell with everlasting burnings?

Isaiah 33:14

On 3 February 1970, after a long period of hesitation, Japan signed the nuclear non-proliferation treaty sponsored by the United States, the Soviet Union and Great Britain. The Japanese government did not ratify the agreement until 8 June 1976, over six years later, fuelling doubts about the sincerity of its professed intentions to confine its nuclear development programme to peaceful purposes.

In Europe and North America it had been widely believed, for some time, that Japan's re-emergence as a major regional power, its differences with the United States over strategic, political and economic issues, together with a growing sense of insecurity *vis-à-vis* the Communist nations on the continent, would almost inevitably lead to the development of an independent nuclear strike force. As early as January 1964 Brigadier-General Pierre Gallois, one of the architects of the French military nuclear programme, predicted that China's emergence as a nuclear power would render the Japanese-American security treaty ineffective, forcing Japan to rely on its own resources.[1] In August 1969, the American magazine *Newsweek* reported that the Japanese government was undertaking a secret study of whether production of nuclear weapons would be in the national interest.*[2] In the months that followed, speculation about Japan's intentions grew. By July 1971 Senator Hubert Humphrey was writing to the then United States Secretary of Defence Melvin Laird to express his concern.[3] On the eve of the 1972 Satō-Nixon talks at San Clemente the United States Embassy in Tōkyō sent a confidential memorandum to the President suggesting that the Japanese government might soon decide to exercise the nuclear option.[4] It was not long before high-ranking United States officials were voicing their anxieties to third parties, attempting to persuade the Chinese, among others, that the security treaty was worth preserving as a check

---

* The present writer has been assured by a former member of the Japanese Atomic Energy Commission that no such study was ever undertaken.

against Tōkyō's nuclear ambitions.[5]

Japan's ambivalence towards the non-proliferation treaty cannot be understood solely in the context of the Okinawan negotiations. For Japan, as for most other countries, the issue was important in itself. Technically, Japan had been in a position to begin development of a small, independent nuclear strike force since the late 1960s. While the military nuclear option had only limited popular appeal, the attitude of the political establishment to the question was more complex than it seemed on the surface. For twenty years, in all official statements, the government and the Liberal Democratic Party had consistently rejected the concept of an independent military nuclear programme. Japan had opposed nuclear weapons testing by other nations and adopted a strong stand in favour of nuclear disarmament. Nevertheless, successive Cabinets had been anxious to establish the principle that Japan had the constitutional right to exercise a military nuclear option if it chose to do so. While the dominant elements in the Conservative Party remained convinced that subtle diplomacy, a solidly based economy and a high degree of energy security were more effective guarantees of great power status than nuclear weapons, some groups displayed a lively interest in eventual development of an independent *force de frappe*. So, too, did particular individuals in the Foreign Ministry, the Defence Agency and the armed forces. There was also a small academic nuclear weapons lobby.

The Japanese government's cautious approach to the non-proliferation treaty was undoubtedly influenced by the hawkish stand taken by these groups. To a much greater extent, however, it was the outcome of apprehensions about the impact of a non-proliferation agreement on the country's civilian nuclear development programme. These fears were shared by most comparable non-nuclear nations.

I   The Japanese civilian nuclear programme and its military implications

The experience of Hiroshima and Nagasaki, together with the country's delicate international position, combined to ensure that Japan's postwar nuclear industry would be slow to begin operations and subject to unusually strong restraints. It was not until 1955, at the time of the Hatoyama Cabinet, that an Atomic Energy Basic Law, stipulating that the development and application of nuclear power 'be limited to peaceful purposes and performed independently under democratic management', was passed by the Diet. This law also required that the results of all nuclear research 'be made public to contribute to international co-operation'.[6] In 1956, in accordance with the provisions of the new legislation, the Japan Atomic Energy Commission was set up as an organ of the Prime Minister's Office and charged with overall planning and supervision of what was then a rather modest civilian nuclear programme. A complex structure of interlocking governmental, bureaucratic, business and academic organizations was subsequently established. The Japan Atomic Energy Research Institute (1956) (a joint government-business body), the Japan

Atomic Industrial Forum (1956), and the Power Reactor and Nuclear Fuel Development Corporation (1957) (both purely business ventures), were all given responsibility for research into the industrial and commercial applications of nuclear energy. The Radiation Council (1956) and the National Institute for Radiological Sciences of the Science and Technology Agency (1957) were set up to study the possible dangers of radiation and examine appropriate standards and procedures for minimizing exposure. The work of all these bodies was supplemented by broadly based research in the universities and private institutions. In subsequent years, five large nuclear power consortia were established – the First Atomic Power Industry Group, Mitsubishi Atomic Power Industries, the Nippon Atomic Industry Group, Sumitomo Atomic Energy Industries and the Tōkyō Atomic Industrial Consortium.[7]

Two years after the establishment of the Atomic Energy Commission Japan's first nuclear reactor, a small research model obtained from the United States, went into operation. Yet it was only in 1961, with the implementation of the Ikeda Cabinet's high economic growth strategies, that the Atomic Energy Commission completed a concrete, long-term plan for the development and use of nuclear energy. In the early 1960s, on the basis of this plan, important advances were made. The first Japanese-made nuclear reactor went into operation in 1962. The following year an experimental electric power reactor obtained from the United States, then a full-scale commercial nuclear power station of the Calder Hall variety, imported from the United Kingdom, went into operation at Tōkaimura. Shortly afterwards, construction of another nuclear power station was begun at Tsuruga. July 1963 saw the completion of plans for the construction of a nuclear-powered merchant vessel, under the supervision of the Japan Nuclear Ship Development Agency. By 1967 some 10,000 Japanese scientists and technical experts were involved in research and development of nuclear energy. By the middle of the next decade this number had almost doubled.[8]

In 1967, against the background of the emergence of American-Soviet strategic parity, the United States impasse in Indochina, rising tensions in the Middle East and a growing demand for electric power in Japan, the Atomic Energy Commission's 1961 plan for the development and utilization of nuclear energy was substantially revised. Extraordinarily ambitious plans for nuclear development were drawn up. Despite the fact that in 1967 Japan had only a single 160-megawatt commercial nuclear plant in operation and another nearing completion, the new plan provided for a total capacity of 6,000 megawatts by 1975, 15–20,000 megawatts by 1980, 30–40,000 megawatts by 1985. Two new nuclear power stations were to be in operation by 1970, another seven by 1975, a score or so by 1980. Five years later, on the eve of the first oil crisis, another revised plan was announced. The new plan envisaged completion of thirty-eight nuclear power plants between 1971 and 1980, providing some 32,000 megawatts of electricity, and starts on the construction of twenty-eight additional facilities during the same decade.

Whatever foreign observers may have believed, there can be no doubt that Japanese interest in nuclear power was, at this stage, predominantly politico-economic, not military, in character. The government, the Opposition parties, business interests, the academic community and the broad masses of the Japanese people were fully conscious of the implications of the country's increasing dependence on outside sources of oil supply, controlled by Anglo-American multinational corporations, drilled and refined in politically volatile regions, then transported to Japan across vast oceans and through narrow, potentially vulnerable straits. Nuclear power, especially revolutionary developments such as fast breeder reactors (which recreate their own plutonium core every decade), held out the tantalizing prospect of eliminating dependence on the great multinational oil companies, insulating Japan from the vagaries of Middle Eastern politics, reducing concern about the security of the sea-lanes and making possible the realization of energy self-sufficiency by the beginning of the 21st century. The achievement of energy self-sufficiency, by circumventing one of the most effective of George Kennan's 'indirect controls', would have transformed Japan's strategic environment, introducing radically new elements into its relations with the United States, the Soviet Union, China and the countries of the Western Pacific. The Atomic Energy White Paper issued in 1968 was, significantly, subtitled 'the road to autonomous development'. 'Autonomous development' had been a constantly recurring theme in official publications since 1961. The desirability, first, of moving into the field of uranium mining abroad, then of developing an independent domestic capacity to perform all the steps associated with the nuclear fuel cycle, had been much discussed. Since the mid-1960s several concrete steps had been taken to realize these objectives.

It was not clear, however, whether Japan would be in a position to develop rapidly the kind of nuclear autonomy achieved by such established nuclear powers as the United States, the Soviet Union, Great Britain, France and China. From the beginning, the United States had acted as Japan's sole supplier of enriched uranium. Its principal suppliers of uranium ore, too, were the United States itself, Great Britain, South Africa and France. By the beginning of the 1970s two other close American allies, Australia and Canada, were also emerging as significant potential exporters of uranium ore to Japan. Japan's own confirmed natural uranium deposits (estimated at 8,000 metric tons, chiefly in the Ningyō Tōge and Tōno areas of Honshū) fell short of the volume required to fulfil the 1971 nuclear power generation plan (estimated at 7,000 metric tons per annum by 1980, 13,000 metric tons per annum by 1985 and 21,000 metric tons per annum by 1990).[9] This made continued reliance on external sources inevitable, at least until such time as sizeable new reserves were discovered, techniques for extracting uranium from sea water were perfected or the Japanese nuclear power industry was in a position to rely on the output of self-reproducing fast breeder reactors.

By the beginning of the 1970s it was becoming increasingly apparent that the United States would not be in a position to meet its own enriched uranium requirements and those of its allies indefinitely. This realization gave weight to all the arguments traditionally advanced by independently minded nationalists about the dangers of excessive reliance on North America. The Japanese government, therefore, redoubled its efforts to develop an independent enrichment technology, concentrating, in particular, on the centrifugal separation method, which was judged most suitable for Japan's special requirements.[10] Research on the gaseous diffusion method was also continued. At the same time much research was conducted on nuclear fusion, which seemed to offer unusually attractive possibilities for the production of limitless energy from a wide variety of fuels.[11] Much attention, too, was devoted to independent exploration and development of natural uranium deposits in the United States, Canada, Latin America, various parts of Africa, Australia and South-East Asia.[12]

Nuclear explosive devices can be based either on highly enriched uranium or on plutonium. If a Japanese government, in the late 1960s, had decided to construct a uranium-based nuclear weapons stockpile (this assumed perfection of the centrifugal separation method), confirmed domestic uranium reserves would theoretically have permitted the manufacture of 1,200–2,000 usable warheads.[13] Plutonium is produced as a by-product in the normal course of operations in uranium-fuelled power reactors. Admittedly, weapons grade plutonium 239, uncontaminated with plutonium 240 or 242, can only be obtained by burning uranium 235 in particular conditions for a specific period of time, or by reprocessing the spent reactor fuel. The former procedure is an uneconomical one from the viewpoint of the nuclear power industry. In the 1960s Japan's projected nuclear fuel reprocessing facilities, scheduled to begin operations in the middle of the next decade, were relatively small in scale and, like the rest of its nuclear programme, subject to scrutiny by the International Atomic Energy Agency. Nevertheless, as the director of the Atomic Energy Research Institute announced on 16 May 1968, after the Tōkaimura Research Plant had successfully extracted 18 grammes of high-quality plutonium 239, Japan was, theoretically speaking, in a position to begin development of its own plutonium-based nuclear strike force.[14] A month later, the annual report of the Security Research Council (Anzen Hoshō Chōsa Kai) referred, for the first time, to Japan's latent capacity to produce nuclear weapons. It was observed that while production of hydrogen bombs would be difficult, Japan's technological level and existing nuclear facilities would be sufficient to produce both uranium and plutonium bombs. It was estimated that the Tōkaimura facilities could, if converted to military use, manufacture about twenty plutonium-type atomic bombs each year.[15]

Weapons systems already in Japanese possession, or under development in the late 1960s, would theoretically have given Japan the ability to deliver a nuclear payload anywhere in the Kuriles, southern Sakhalin, the Maritime Province of Siberia, the Korean peninsula, north-east and south central China, Taiwan and the Philippines. The Air Self Defence Force F104-J and long-range commercial aircraft operated by Japan Air Lines, such as the Boeing 747 and Douglas DC8, could all have been speedily remodelled to carry nuclear weapons. The F4-Js, which became the mainstay interceptor during the fourth and fifth defence plans (1972–85), were even more admirably suited for this purpose.[16]

The Japanese space research and rocket development programme, begun during the Hatoyama Cabinet in 1955, had reached such a stage of sophistication that Japan was able to launch its first earth satellite in February 1970. Japanese missile technology was, in most respects, comparable to that of France. Despite the country's location in a zone of extreme earthquake activity, and problems with guidance systems and re-entry, Japan's Mu and N rockets could have formed the basis for a land-based, hardened MR/IRBM force.* Japan did not have access to the technology necessary to build a submarine-launched nuclear strike force. It seemed probable, however, that an appropriate technological base could be developed within a decade or so.[17]

Whether this would have provided Japan with a genuinely credible nuclear *force de frappe* able to influence the behaviour of the Soviet Union, the United States, the People's Republic of China and the smaller, non-nuclear nations of South-East Asia and the Pacific was open to question. Yet by the beginning of the 1970s Japan certainly did have the technical capacity to develop an autonomous nuclear force.

II   Japanese attitudes to nuclear weapons development

(i)   *The government and the Liberal Democratic Party*

Discussion of Japanese interest in an independent nuclear *force de frappe* runs the risk of giving the matter more prominence than it deserves. For several years after the occupation the Japanese government, strongly supported by public opinion, had been eager to establish its credentials as a consistent and energetic advocate of nuclear disarmament. At the United Nations and other international forums, Japanese representatives repeatedly criticized nuclear testing by all the great powers, despite the fact that Japan's self-proclaimed reliance on the American nuclear deterrent raised doubts about the severity of its attitude to the United States. Japan's own nuclear research and development, while not without its military implications, was directed almost exclusively towards power generation. Its acceptability to the Opposition parties, the bulk of the scientific community and the general public was based largely on the understanding that its objectives were pacific.

Nevertheless, from the mid-1950s onwards, Japanese Cabinets were anxious to establish the principle that the manufacture, possession and use of nuclear weapons would not contravene Article 9 of the Constitution. Small but significant groups in the Conservative political establishment displayed more than a passing interest in the possibilities of an autonomous *force de frappe*.

Prime Minister Yoshida Shigeru's early support for the concept of an independent nuclear strike force has already been noted. Yoshida doubtless considered a credible Japanese nuclear deterrent an indispensable precondition for disengagement from the American alliance and *rapprochement* with China. Hatoyama's views on nuclear weapons are unknown. It was, however, during the Hatoyama period that the Japanese nuclear and space development programmes were launched.

In May 1957 (almost seven years before the first Chinese nuclear test) Prime Minister Kishi Nobusuke told the House of Councillors Cabinet Committee that

* By July 1983 the Nakasone Cabinet was studying an ambitious plan to construct, independently of United States technology, a large liquid-fuelled rocket able to place a two-ton manmade satellite in orbit by the year 2000. The strategic implications of this project were clearly considerable.

'there would be nothing against using nuclear weapons if they were within the limits of self-defence'. His view, as later elaborated in the House of Councillors Budget Committee, appeared to be that since the right of self-defence was guaranteed by the Constitution, it should be permissible to employ all the discoveries of modern science for this purpose. Most existing nuclear weapons, he conceded, were 'offensive' in character and were thus incompatible with the Constitution. Yet in March 1959 Kishi told the Diet that possession of certain types of weapons (nuclear-tipped Honest John missiles were cited as an example) could be reconciled with Article 9. He stressed that as a matter of policy his government would not attempt to transform Japan into a military nuclear power.[18]

Prime Minister Ikeda Hayato made no public statements on the question of a nuclear strike force. His successor, Satō Eisaku, seems to have at first considered, then rejected the idea of developing an independent deterrent.[19] It was during Satō's period in office that the Japanese position on nuclear weapons was finally – albeit ambiguously – formalized. In December 1967 the Prime Minister enunciated 'the three non-nuclear principles' (*hikaku san gensoku*) and the 'four nuclear policies' (*kaku yon seisaku*). Taken by themselves, the three non-nuclear principles – that Japan would not manufacture, possess or permit the entry of nuclear weapons – represented a significant retreat from the Kishi position. The corollary of the three non-nuclear principles, however, were the four nuclear policies. These were that Japan would adhere to the three non-nuclear principles, make efforts to promote nuclear disarmament, give high priority to its civilian nuclear programme and depend on the American nuclear deterrent for protection against 'international nuclear threats'. This seemed to imply that Japan would adhere to the three non-nuclear principles and remain a non-nuclear power so long as the American deterrent continued to function effectively. This position was reiterated in the 1970 Defence White Paper.[20]

Within the Liberal Democratic Party, none of the bodies responsible for defining foreign and defence policy – the Foreign Affairs Research Council, the Security Problems Research Council and the National Defence Division – had ever called for the development of a nuclear strike force.* On the contrary, the Liberal Democratic Party and its constituent organizations had consistently and publicly opposed the exercise of a nuclear option, although the Security Problems Research Council had argued in its May 1965 report that any decision to disengage from the American alliance would necessitate development of a nuclear *force de frappe*.[21] The council, in this and all subsequent reports, recommended continued adherence to the Japan-United States security treaty system. The 1966 report, compiled after intense struggles between various groups within the party, reiterated this basic position, although an earlier draft, apparently compiled by more tough-minded nationalist and anti-Communist groups, had suggested that nuclear weapons could be 'introduced' into Japan within the framework of the American alliance.[22] The same year, however, the council published a collection of articles on defence and foreign policy for the edifi-

---

*   This remained unchanged at the time of publication in 1988.

cation of the general public. Included among these were two unsigned pieces strongly recommending the nuclear armament of Japan, apparently from a 'pro-American', anti-Communist conservative nationalist standpoint.[23]

At the time of the non-proliferation treaty negotiations there were, within this general framework, various shades of opinion in the government and the Liberal Democratic Party on the question of an independent deterrent. On this, as on most other issues, different views tended to be associated with different faction leaders and supra-factional organizations. Yet discussion of the non-proliferation treaty touched off none of those intense factional struggles so characteristic of the postwar Japanese political process. This was partly because China policy, Korea, Vietnam and Okinawa provided ample opportunity for internecine warfare, partly because the principal difficulty with the non-proliferation treaty was not thought to be Japan's right to preserve a nuclear weapons option (a genuinely controversial issue) but whether the inspection clauses would hinder the country's civil nuclear development programme.

The increasing opposition, both in the nation at large and within the Liberal Democratic Party, to the presence of American nuclear bases on Okinawa has already been discussed. In general, faction leaders opposed to American nuclear bases on Okinawa also appeared uneasy about the concept of an independent deterrent. Fujiyama, Maeo, Matsumura and Miki were opposed on principle to the military application of atomic energy and did not consider that an autonomous *force de frappe* would contribute to Japan's security.[24] Nakasone Yasuhiro, like his mentor Kōno Ichirō, was convinced of the necessity of developing powerful and autonomous military forces. In the late 1960s he did not believe Japan's future lay in exclusive association with the United States. While he had long encouraged efforts to improve relations with Peking he also considered that a future conflict of interests between Japan and China was by no means unthinkable. By the end of the decade he had come to fear the possible implications of a Sino-American *rapprochement* negotiated without regard to Japan's national interests. In order to deal effectively with this contigency, Nakasone proposed, not immediate development of an autonomous deterrent, but heavy investment in civilian nuclear technology and space research to ensure that Japan could not be ignored. He did not publicly explain what steps should be taken if this course of action failed to preserve Japanese interests.[25]

Kishi Nobusuke, Fukuda Takeo, former Vice-Admiral Hoshina Zenshirō, former Air Marshal Genda Minoru and other representatives of the older generation of conservative, militantly anti-Communist nationalists in the Liberal Democratic Party combined an apparently unshakable confidence in the efficacy of the American nuclear umbrella with a view that Japan's own nuclear weapons option should not be surrendered lightly.[26] This position was a natural corollary of the evolutionary view of the Japanese-American relationship held by the leading figures in this group. Only Kaya Okinori seemed strongly opposed to the development of an independent strike force.[27] Among the younger generation of conservative nationalists, Kuraishi Tadao, sometime Minister for Agriculture and Forests, and Nakasone's friend, the patriotic novelist Ishihara Shintarō, emerged as forceful exponents of a nuclear weapons programme. Their position was essentially an emotional one, not an expression of a carefully considered, logical and coherent national defence strategy.

At the time of the *Pueblo* incident in January 1968 Kuraishi, irritated by the fact that American and Soviet naval vessels were repeatedly fouling Japanese fishing nets, told the press that Japan would not be treated so lightly if it had nuclear weapons and a 300,000-man army. His remarks threw the Diet into uproar. After three weeks of governmental chaos he was forced to resign his portfolio. The Prime Minister assured the House of Representatives Budget Committee that 'there is no change in the Cabinet's policy of upholding peace and maintaining the present Constitution'. Kuraishi, unrepentant, declared that since Japan was now 'a first-rate power', there were many things to be reconsidered.[28] His explanation of the circumstances surrounding his outburst reveals the character of his approach to foreign policy and defence issues.

> After the Cabinet meeting the other day I had to go and face this press conference in the cafeteria for Members of the House of Representatives. Well, as far as my own province of agriculture was concerned there was nothing to say. There was nothing at all to say. However, at the press conferences held in the cafeteria they always bring out oranges and coffee and so on. Well, I looked at my watch and found there was still some time before the Budget Committee meeting, so I chatted on about general matters. Just then the director-general of the Fisheries Agency popped in with something about a report and one of the journalists asked what was happening in the Japan Sea. So I told him that Japan was making representations to Russia, America and South Korea. Then I came out with these other statements.[29]

In March 1969 Ishihara Shintarō clarified his position on nuclear weapons in the House of Councillors Budget Committee. The three non-nuclear principles, he declared, were 'products of ignorance'. Japan was destined to become a great power. Great power status was impossible without nuclear weapons, etc. The latter part of Ishihara's discourse was drowned by heckling from the Opposition and gasps of astonishment from female admirers in the gallery. After the former novelist had resumed his seat, Foreign Minister Aichi replied:

> I am old and thinking is somewhat old-fashioned, but there exists a nuclear allergy in the good sense of the term. It is the belief of a majority of the Japanese people that we should persuade ourselves never to be armed with nuclear weapons and I myself share these sentiments.[30]

Aichi later decried the 'dangerous arguments' of 'people on the extreme right' about nuclear weapons.[31] Undeterred, the flamboyant Ishihara (whose election campaign strategies included endorsement by heavy-weight Sumo champions such as Takanohana) elaborated his views in an article in the magazine *Shokun*, where he adopted a decidedly Gaullist posture.[32] National defence could not be based on the shifting sands of feeble and uncertain alliances. The United States nuclear deterrent protected the North American continent alone. Japan's security could only be guaranteed by the construction of an independent *force de frappe* on the French model, based on submarine-launched ballistic missiles. Such views subsequently gained widespread currency in informal Conservative Party organizations such as the Soshinkai (Simple Hearts Society) and the Seirankai (Young Storm Association).

(ii) The bureaucracy

Within the Foreign Ministry and the Defence Agency, too, some groups felt uneasy about the long-term implications of abandoning the nuclear weapons option.[33] Professor Momoi Makoto, of the National Defence College, noting the decline of American influence in East Asia, the strains in the Japanese-American security treaty system, the close economic interdependence between Tōkyō and Canberra and the remarkable stability of Australian society, went so far as to suggest that Japan and Australia might co-operate to develop a joint *force de frappe* should the American deterrent entirely lose its credibility.[34] A joint Australian-Japanese nuclear strike force, he believed, 'might be less provocative to others than a nuclear Japan which has a past record of militarism'. The extent to which Momoi's ideas were shared by others in Defence Agency circles was not clear.

The actual administration of Japan's civil nuclear energy programme was vested in the Science and Technology Agency. The 1955 Atomic Energy Basic Law also gave the Atomic Energy Commission a powerful voice in all decisions on nuclear policy. This commission, whose six members were all appointed by the Prime Minister, included representatives of the scientific community, a few former bureaucrats and professional administrators.[35] As far as the present writer is aware, no member of the commission has ever publicly advocated a Japanese nuclear weapons programme.

(iii) The scientific community

The Japan Science Council (Nihon Gakujutsu Kaigi) also occupied an important, though less formal, position in the nuclear policy decision-making machinery. This body, composed of eminent scientists and other scholars, elected independently by the academic community, had originally been established as a governmental advisory organ on science and education. While it had no legal authority to participate in decisions, its views could not be ignored. In a very real sense, it was the representative of Japan's scientific establishment. No major project in any field requiring the services of advanced technology could be undertaken without its co-operation. Under the leadership of Japan's most eminent nuclear scientists, the Japan Science Council adopted, throughout the period under consideration, a position extremely hostile to the use of atomic energy for military purposes. Especially notable were the declaration against nuclear weapons issued by the council in April 1962 and the resolutions of the second and third congresses of Japanese scientists at Kyōtō in May 1963 and February 1966.[36] One of the principal sources of the 'nuclear allergy' so bitterly criticized in hawkish political circles was, in fact, the Japanese scientific community. Conservative military critics occasionally lamented the fact that even if a governmental decision to develop nuclear weapons were made, it would be virtually impossible to find the four or five hundred scientists necessary to implement the project.[37] The views of the younger generation of Japanese scientists did not seem to diverge markedly from those of their more senior colleagues.

(iv)   *Strategic studies experts, military critics and influential journalists*

In January 1968 the *Yomiuri Shimbun* sought the views of 100 leading intellectuals and military critics on nuclear weapons. Only four were in favour of an autonomous deterrent.[38] Among the handful of individuals advocating a nuclear weapons programme were former Lieutenant-General Doi Akio,[39] Kamigawa Hikomatsu (honorary lecturer at the University of Tōkyō),[40] Kuramae Yoshio (lecturer at Asia University),[41] Maeda Hisashi (writer for the *Asahi Shimbun*),[42] Sekino Hideo (former naval officer and military critic)[43] and Tamura Kosaku (lecturer at Kokushikan University).[44] Other exponents of a Japanese *force de frappe* included former Rear-Admiral Fukutome Shigeru,[45] General Sugita Ichiji (Ground Self Defence Force, retired)[46] and Muramatsu Takeshi.[47] This small group, although composed of men of undoubted experience and integrity, paled into insignificance before the serried ranks of the anti-nuclear weapons activists, among whose number were to be found some of the finest intellects in the country.

The arguments of the nuclear lobby have been examined elsewhere by the present writer and by others.[48] Lieutenant-General Doi Akio contended that nuclear weapons were essentially defensive in nature. Japan should endeavour to build up an independent deterrent in co-operation with the United States. Should Washington refuse to offer assistance a nuclear strike force could be developed independently or in co-operation with nations such as Australia or the Philippines. Doi, like Momoi, was especially interested in the prospects for co-operation with Australia. Commander Sekino Hideo, advancing the traditional Gaullist argument that the United States would be unlikely to unleash its strategic nuclear forces against the Soviet Union or China in the event of an attack on an ally such as Japan, recommended the development of a British- or French-style deterrent by the mid-1970s, preferably with Washington's support. This position was also advocated by Rear-Admiral Fukutome Shigeru in a series of articles published in 1966. Muramatsu Takeshi contended that nuclear weapons were not simply 'military tools'. Rather, they had 'a symbolic importance in international politics'. Possession of an independent *force de frappe*, a symbol of 'racial independence', would liberate Japan from its stifling psychological dependence on the United States.

The most influential elements in the anti-nuclear camp did not (as their opponents frequently contended) base their arguments simply on humanistic opposition to war. Kishida Junnosuke, of the *Asahi Shimbun*, for example, developed the rather sophisticated concept of an 'international nuclear umbrella', based on the American, Soviet, British, French and Chinese forces, locked in a complex relationship of mutual deterrence, guaranteeing the security of most major nations, including non-aligned powers such as Sweden. This mechanism made Japanese nuclear armament – wasteful, socially divisive and potentially destabilizing – totally unnecessary.[49] Kōsaka Masataka, Professor of International Relations at Kyōtō University, while not necessarily rejecting the view that a nuclear deterrent could contribute to Japan's security, argued that the basis of national power was gradually shifting from military force to economic strength and its associated intellectual, scientific and technological skills. Japan's long-term future could best be secured by investing heavily in the latter area rather than in an increasingly irrelevant military nuclear technology.[50] Rōyama Michio, Professor of International Relations at Jōchi (Sophia) University, maintained that it was simply too late in the day for Japan to begin thinking about an independent nuclear strike force. A small Japanese *force de frappe* would have no credibility in Moscow or Washington. It would not intimidate China, whose immense size perhaps gave it some capacity to absorb a nuclear attack. The Japanese archipelago, in contrast, was extremely vulnerable. Japan's acquisition of a nuclear strike force, moreover, would accelerate the tendencies towards proliferation. This would decrease the general level of global security and thus jeopardize Japan's long-term interests. Japan's emergence as an independent nuclear power would also complicate relations not only with Moscow and Peking but also with Washington.[51] Saeki Kiichi, of the Nomura Research Institute, argued that small nuclear forces, such as those of Great Britain and France, had limited credibility. Japan's security could best be preserved by maintaining its alliance with the United States, ideologically the most compatible superpower.[52] Sakamoto Yoshikazu, Professor of International Politics at Tōkyō University, was persuaded that the Japanese archipelago was basically indefensible. Japan's survival could best be guaranteed neither by the American alliance nor by an independent deterrent but by policies based on disarmament and neutrality, and by efforts to strengthen the United Nations.[53]

(v)   Public opinion

Throughout the 1960s and the 1970s, the Japanese public remained overwhelmingly opposed to the development of an independent nuclear deterrent. There were few signs that members of the younger generation were likely to react more favourably to the idea than their parents and grandparents. The political environment in which the Japanese government had to operate was thus very different to that of the United States, Great Britain, France, the Soviet Union, China and non-nuclear countries such as Australia, South Africa, Israel or Argentina.

Since the early 1950s polls conducted by the Prime Minister's Office had attempted to clarify public attitudes to development of an autonomous *force de frappe*. Almost invariably, some 60 per cent of respondents had opposed the idea, 20 per cent had supported it.[54] The major newspapers had begun to examine public attitudes towards a possible Japanese nuclear programme in 1966. The results of various polls have been collated by Professors Shōno Naomi, Nagai Hideaki and Ueno Hirohisa in their excellent study of public opinion on nuclear questions.[55]

Table X.1
Popular attitudes to an independent Japanese nuclear deterrent, 1966–1973.

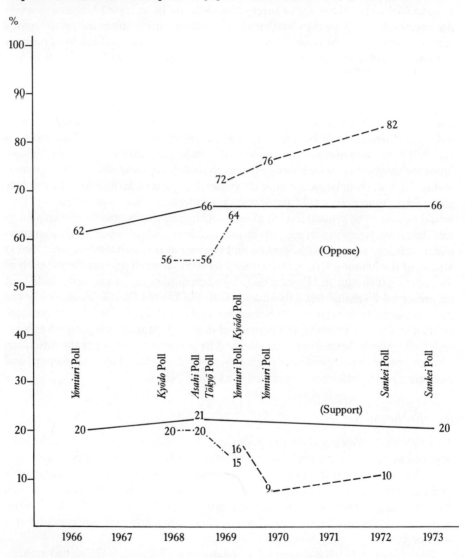

Key:
————————	Is it necessary to manufacture nuclear weapons?
–·—·—·—·–	Would it be safe for Japan to manufacture nuclear weapons?
– – – – –	Is it desirable for Japan to manufacture nuclear weapons?

Source: Shōno Naomi, Nagai Hideaki and Ueno Hirohisa, *Kaku To Heiwa*, Hōritsu Bunka Sha, 1978, p.17.

Table X.2
Political orientation and attitudes to an independent nuclear deterrent, 1972.

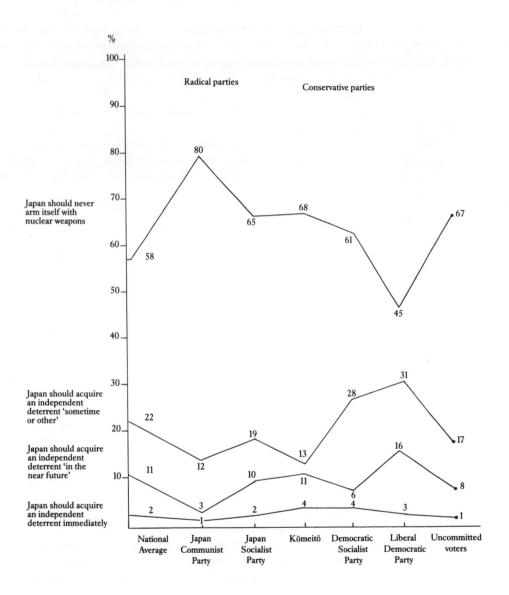

Source: Mainichi Shimbun, 3 May 1972.

Opinion polls also revealed widespread rejection of the official view that the United States nuclear arsenal protected Japan from Soviet or Chinese attack. Rather, all nuclear weapons were seen as threats to regional and world peace.[56] The Japanese public simply did not accept the theory of mutual deterrence. There was very strong support for the 'three non-nuclear principles' (72 per cent in the 1968 *Yomiuri Shimbun* poll, 77 per cent in the 1975 *Asahi Shimbun* poll, with a national average of about 10 per cent opposed*).[57] There was also consistent and generally increasing popular opposition to nuclear testing by the United States, the Soviet Union, Great Britain, France and China (79 per cent in the 1954 *Yomiuri Shimbun* poll, 87 per cent in the 1957 *Asahi Shimbun* poll, 81 per cent in the 1961 *Yomiuri Shimbun* study and 87 per cent in the 1973 *Sankei Shimbun* survey, with an average of around 5 per cent supporting tests).[58]

Opposition to an autonomous nuclear strike force extended right across the political spectrum, although Conservative, Democratic Socialist Party and Kōmeitō voters appeared somewhat more receptive to the idea than supporters of the Socialist Party and the Communist Party.

More recent studies undertaken by Professors Shōno Naomi, Nagai Hideaki and Ueno Hirohisa in Hiroshima and Okayama prefectures have yielded broadly comparable results.[59]

A *Yomiuri Shimbun* survey of Tōkyō University students participating in an anti-security treaty demonstration in 1970 found 4.1 per cent declaring an independent nuclear strike force to be 'highly desirable' for Japan, 2.7 per cent regarding such a force as 'rather desirable', 5.3 per cent expressing indifference, 9.8 per cent considering it 'rather undesirable' and 76.3 per cent resolutely opposed to an autonomous *force de frappe*.[60] Opinion polls of young people conducted throughout the 1970s and the 1980s showed no significant departure from this pattern.[61] Quite clearly, the nuclear issue was one on which a virtually indestructible national consensus had been established.

III   Japan and the international negotiations on nuclear non-proliferation, 1966–70

Talks on non-proliferation had been in progress for some years before any reaction was evident in Japan. This was perhaps understandable. The focus of negotiations up to 1966 had been whether West German 'access' to nuclear weapons under American 'control' (as part of a NATO nuclear-sharing arrangement) would constitute proliferation.[62] Japan was not interested in multilateral security arrangements. There was little possibility of Japanese participation in any North-East Asian multilateral nuclear force sponsored by the United States. Thus the Japanese, while endorsing the general principle of non-proliferation, remained for a time aloof from the negotiations.

---

*   Except in Nagasaki, where some 21.5 per cent did not accept the non-nuclear principles.

During the latter part of 1966, the focus of the non-proliferation debate in the Eighteen Nation Disarmament Committee (of which Japan was not a member) and the United Nations General Assembly moved away from the question of West German access to nuclear weapons. There were also clear indications that some measure of United States-Soviet agreement on non-proliferation was imminent.[63]

Since the submission of the separate American and Soviet draft treaties to the disarmament committee in the autumn of 1965,[64] it had been evident that the nuclear superpowers had little interest in linking non-proliferation to a nuclear test ban or measures for overall disarmament. Moreover, it soon became clear that the United States and the Soviet Union were anxious to bring 'peaceful nuclear explosions' within the scope of the proposed treaty.[65] From the summer of 1967 it also became apparent that while the United States and the Soviet Union hoped to see all the nuclear facilities of non-nuclear weapons states open to inspection by the International Atomic Energy Commission, the Soviet Union would oppose similar scrutiny of its own installations, both civilian and military.[66]

Thus the interest of non-nuclear weapons states, both neutral and aligned, increasingly centred on three questions. First, was participation in a treaty that restricted their own activities but placed no limits on military nuclear weapons powers, either in their own national interests or a genuine contribution to world peace? Second, what effects would the proposed ban on 'peaceful nuclear explosions' have on civil nuclear development? Third, was it reasonable that non-nuclear weapons states be subjected to intensive supervision, while the facilities of established nuclear powers remained immune from scrutiny?

From the beginning, the non-aligned members of the disarmament committee, in particular India, Sweden and the United Arab Republic, had been criticial of the allegedly

> unrealistic and irrational propostion that a non-proliferation treaty should impose obligations only on non-nuclear countries, while the nuclear powers continue to hold on to their privileged status or club membership by retaining and even increasing their deadly stockpiles.[67]

Throughout 1966–7, despite British and Canadian support for the United States-Soviet stand that it would be 'unnecessary as well as imprudent' to insist on commitments to nuclear disarmament prior to the treaty, there was a strong tendency among non-nuclear nations to argue that a treaty with no provisions for nuclear arms control would be meaningless. On 19 August 1966 the eight non-aligned nations on the disarmament committee submitted a memorandum urging that a non-proliferation treaty be 'coupled with or followed by' concrete disarmament measures.[68] More significant, from the Japanese point of view, was the West German memorandum of 7 April 1967 recommending 'more comprehensive solutions' than a 'limited non-proliferation treaty'. (The Germans suggested, specifically, a halt in production of fissionable material for military purposes, a ban on production of delivery vehicles and a comprehensive test ban treaty.)[69] Eventually the British and Canadians, while not going so far as to link the treaty with disarmament measures, came to the conclusion that some commitment to disarmament was important for the long-term stability of the arrangements.[70]

The question of 'peaceful nuclear explosions' was first raised by the United States at the Eighteen Nation Disarmament Committee on 9 August 1966.[71] The United States maintained that since there was little distinction between peaceful and military nuclear explosions, both should come under the provisions of the treaty. Once the agreement was concluded, however, the established nuclear powers would offer their services to all signatory states, conducting nuclear explosions for engineering and other purposes. The American proposal was strongly attacked by the Indians, who understandably saw it as an attempt to enforce 'non-proliferation of science and technology'.[72] This position was also adopted by other countries. The Latin American Nuclear Free Zone Treaty concluded on 14 February 1967 specifically permitted nuclear explosions for peaceful purposes.[73] Brazil and Mexico adopted a particularly strong stand on this issue. In March 1967 the Brazilian Deputy Foreign Minister announced that while Brazil was committed to the principles of non-proliferation,

> we shall not waive the right to conduct research without limitation and eventually to manufacture or receive nuclear explosives that will enable us to perform great engineering works ... to ensure the economic development and the welfare of the Brazilian people.[74]

This was also the West German position. On 1 February Foreign Minister Brandt told the Bundestag that prohibition of peaceful nuclear explosions would affect the civil nuclear programmes of all non-nuclear weapons states.[75] On 27 April, after receiving assurances from Rusk, Brandt announced that while West Germany was 'ready to support everything' to prevent military misuse of nuclear energy, it could not accept restrictions on 'peaceful utilization'.[76]

The non-nuclear weapons states also objected to the proposed inspection arrangements, which appeared to give established nuclear powers free and unilateral access to the fruits of research and development throughout the world. Great Britain and the United States eventually professed a willingness to place their non-military nuclear installations under an inspection system. The Soviet Union, in contrast, refused to permit inspection on its territory. In addition, some nations, while willing to accept inspection, were anxious to be inspected only by friendly powers. This was apparently the position of West Germany and several European nations. Thus the question of whether Euratom safeguards could be regarded as equivalent to the safeguards of the International Atomic Energy Agency arose.[77]

Several nations, moreover, were gravely concerned about the possible effects of the treaty on their security or anxious, for other reasons, to preserve a nuclear weapons option.

It is against the background of these international developments, and in the context of the domestic situation outlined earlier in this chapter, that the evolution of Japanese policy must be understood.

On 9 February 1967, one week after Foreign Minister Brandt revealed West Germany's position to the Bundestag, the Japanese Vice Foreign Minister Shimoda

Takezō (formerly ambassador to Washington) announced that Japan, too, was anxious to preserve a right to conduct 'peaceful' nuclear tests. If guarantees on peaceful nuclear development were not included in the final treaty Japan, despite its commitment to non-proliferation, would be obliged to take 'grave decisions'.[78] The Shimoda statement caused surprise both at home and abroad. There was widespread speculation that Japan's traditional attitude to nuclear weapons had undergone a fundamental change. In order to dispel these suspicions, 'a high government source' hastened to assure the press that Shimoda had merely expressed 'a personal opinion'.[79] This was probably correct. Shimoda was a hawkish personality, whose views on most matters tended to reflect those of the most belligerent conservative nationalists in the Liberal Democratic Party or the most intransigent right-wing opinion in Washington. The director of the Atomic Energy Bureau of the Science and Technology Agency announced that the long-term plans of the Atomic Energy Commission made no provisions for research into 'peaceful nuclear explosions'.[80] On 18 February 1967 Prime Minister Satō told the press that while Japan generally supported non-proliferation, there were undoubtedly possibilities for employing nuclear explosions in large-scale engineering projects, for example, 'in the case of constructing a second Panama Canal'. Satō added, however, that since it was difficult to distinguish between peaceful and military nuclear explosions, 'there is absolutely no possibility of our bringing in or developing nuclear weapons, bound by the Shimoda Statement'.[81] On 9 March the Atomic Energy Commission announced that under present conditions it was 'not desirable for Japan to study or develop nuclear explosions for peaceful purposes'.[82] A fortnight later Foreign Minister Miki (at loggerheads with Satō over several other issues) repeated this statement in the House of Representatives Budget Committee, adding that the view that Japan should develop 'peaceful' nuclear explosions was 'dangerous'.[83] Miki thereafter went to some trouble to distinguish Japan's position from that of nations such as West Germany and Brazil. Thus on 13 April the Foreign Minister told an audience in the Imperial Hotel that Japan's attitude was 'different to that of West Germany'. Japan's overriding interest was in nuclear disarmament. West Germany, according to Miki, had been seeking access to nuclear weapons.[84] Japan had not. Japan's interest subsequently shifted from the concrete issue of peaceful nuclear explosions to more general questions related to civilian nuclear development, in particular to the inspection clauses.

During the first part of 1967, as the shape of the eventual United States-Soviet agreement began to emerge, Japan, like other interested parties, made considerable efforts to influence the specific details of the treaty. In April, former Vice-Foreign Minister Ōno Katsumi was sent to Washington with instructions to urge the Americans to include reference to concrete disarmament measures in the final draft. He was also to press for a special clause eliminating discrimination between nuclear and non-nuclear nations in the peaceful development of atomic energy. He was to explain Japan's hope for some special arrangement whereby established nuclear powers would furnish services and information to non-nuclear weapons states. He was to stress that there should be no difference in the inspection arrangements for nuclear and non-nuclear powers. In addition, a clause permitting reappraisal of the treaty at five-yearly intervals should be included. When the treaty came up for reappraisal under this arrangement, non-nuclear powers would attach importance to the disarmament efforts of the nuclear weapons states during the five-year period. Finally, the United States, Britain and the Soviet Union should do something to ensure the security of the non-nuclear states. Japan's chief concern, however, appeared to be the question of 'peaceful' nuclear development.[85]

What impact Ōno's visit had in Washington remains at present unknown. On 20 April he returned to Tōkyō with the news that the United States would 'bear [Japan's contentions] in mind' when negotiating with the Soviet Union on the treaty draft. The United States, Ōno explained, had not expressed its views on the individual Japanese contentions but he felt confident that Japan's position on 'peaceful' nuclear development would be 'fully adopted'. The Americans, he confessed, had avoided discussion of disarmament. Even so, the treaty was bound to take up this issue 'in one form or another'.[86] Miki's talks with the director of the United States Arms Control and Disarmament Agency in May 1967 also seemed encouraging. The Foreign Minister was given to understand that clauses guaranteeing 'complete equality' in peaceful nuclear development would be incorporated into the final treaty. At the same time, the United States appeared willing to accept some measure of inspection, although the Soviet Union still refused to have any of its own installations opened for examination.[87]

Nevertheless, the joint United States-Soviet draft treaty presented to the Eighteen Nation Disarmament Committee on 24 August 1967 fell short of satisfying the demands of many non-nuclear powers. The draft required signatory nuclear weapons nations

> not to transfer to any recipient whatsoever nuclear weapons or other nuclear explosive devices or control over such weapons or explosive devices directly or indirectly.

Non-nuclear weapons nations were not to

> manufacture or otherwise acquire nuclear weapons or other nuclear explosive devices.

A separate article (Article IV) referred to the 'inalienable right' of all parties to 'develop research, production and use of nuclear energy for peaceful purposes'. The two superpowers had been unable to agree on inspection procedures and the relevant article (Article III) was thus left blank. The treaty preamble referred to the interest of the contracting parties in nuclear disarmament as a step to 'general and complete disarmament' under 'strict and effective international control'. There were no special provisions guaranteeing the security of non-nuclear states. The treaty was to be of unlimited duration, although a review conference was to be held after five years. Provisions could only be amended with the approval of a majority of participatory states, including all the nuclear weapons nations and all members of the board of governors of the International Atomic Energy Agency.[88]

While there was general satisfaction with the reference to the 'inalienable right' to peaceful nuclear development, Mexico, Egypt and Sweden urged that nuclear weapons states recognize a 'duty' to aid non-nuclear nations in this regard. Brazil and India continued to insist on the right to develop and utilize peaceful nuclear explosions. Nigeria not only hoped that non-nuclear states would have access to 'peaceful explosions' through an international agency, but that scientists from such states, by co-operating with scientists from established nuclear powers, could obtain a thorough knowledge of explosion technology. Such was the character of the amendments proposed by Nigeria that the Canadian representative on the Eighteen Nation Disarmament Committee felt compelled to observe that the Nigerians seemed to be asking for 'information on how to make a nuclear explosive device'.[89] As far as inspection was concerned, nations such as Sweden, Brazil, Italy, India, Burma and Nigeria continued to press strongly for the application of uniform inspection procedures to all signatory nations.[90] There was also criticism of the absence of a time limit and of acceptable procedures for reassessment and revision.[91] Moreover, the references to disarmament in the preamble were widely regarded as perfunctory. There were strong demands for some commitment to concrete disarmament measures, and a view that the efforts of the superpowers in this direction should be linked directly to the question of treaty revision.[92] Finally there was, in some quarters, anxiety about the absence of guarantees for the security of non-nuclear nations.[93]

After consideration of these criticisms, the United States and the Soviet Union submitted a joint revised draft to the disarmament committee on 18 January.[94] The articles concerning non-proliferation remained basically unaltered. No exceptions were made for peaceful nuclear explosions. However, Article IV was expanded to suggest that established nuclear powers would co-operate in the peaceful programmes of non-nuclear nations. Another article (Article V) stipulated that the benefits of peaceful nuclear explosions would be extended to non-nuclear nations on a 'non-discriminatory basis'. The interest of signatories in disarmament was expressed in a separate article (Article VI). Still, no concrete disarmament proposals were announced. The previously unlimited duration of the treaty was changed to twenty-five years. Amendment and review procedures remained the same as before.

Article III of the new draft stipulated safeguards and inspection procedures. Only the facilities of the non-nuclear signatories were to be subject to inspection. However, the wording appeared to permit Euratom nations to arrange self-inspection, provided they came to an agreement acceptable to the International Atomic Energy Agency.

The new joint draft referred only generally to the security of non-nuclear powers. However, on 7 March 1968, the United States, Great Britain and the Soviet Union proposed to the disarmament committee to offer the protection of their 'nuclear umbrellas' jointly, through the United Nations Security Council, to non-nuclear signatories of the treaty. This proposal was subsequently accepted by the security council.[95]

These amendments satisfied some of the demands of the non-nuclear powers. Yet much uneasiness remained. Anxiety centred, as before, on the unequal inspection clauses, the provisions for review and the failure to link non-proliferation with concrete disarmament measures. The United States and the Soviet Union eventually accepted a Swedish amendment permitting a majority of signatories to call a review conference every five years. This provision was included in the final draft, but the general dissatisfaction of the non-nuclear powers was not dispelled.[96]

While Japan, unlike Brazil and India, no longer professed any special interest in the right to conduct 'peaceful' nuclear explosions, Japanese reaction to the successive treaty drafts paralleled that of other non-nuclear weapons powers with important civil nuclear programmes. The initial absence of guarantees for the security of non-nuclear nations was noted with regret, but only on the grounds that it was desirable to obtain as wide a participation as possible, particularly from the non-aligned nations. There was no particular expression of concern at the treaty's implications for Japan's own defence.[97] The tripartite proposal on security assurances of 7 March 1968 was naturally welcomed. Yet it was stressed that this was 'of no particular advantage to Japan, since her security has already been assured'.[98]

The main thrust of Japanese criticism was directed at the inspection clauses. Japan's stand was very similar to that of West Germany, Italy and Sweden. Prime Minister Satō and Foreign Minister Miki repeatedly stressed that both nuclear and non-nuclear powers should be subject to inspection.[99] Indications that Britain and the United States would permit inspection of their peaceful nuclear facilities were welcomed. Soviet disinclination to follow their example led to an unofficial decision in April 1968 to bar Soviet inspectors on the International Atomic Energy Agency from Japan.[100] Moreover, while the inclusion of provisions guaranteeing equality in peaceful nuclear development created a favourable impression in Tōkyō, there was considerable uneasiness about how these provisions might be applied. Finally, although there was little objection to the 25-year time limit, there was much interest in arranging reappraisal of the treaty at five-yearly intervals.[101]

Towards the middle of 1968 the Japanese government formally decided to co-ordinate its policies with those of West Germany. Japan, like West Germany, voted in favour of the 12 June 1968 United Nations resolution recommending the treaty,[102] yet declined to participate in the signing ceremony on 1 July.[103] At a press conference shortly afterwards the Chief Cabinet Secretary announced that Japanese signature of the treaty would be considered 'after consultations with West Germany'.[104]

This stand had important consequences. After the Soviet intervention in Czechoslovakia in August 1968, West Germany, Italy and several other European nations adopted an increasingly cautious attitude towards the non-proliferation treaty.[105] Japan followed their example. 'Reserve' towards the treaty was the dominant theme at the meeting of Japanese ambassadors in Europe held in Stockholm in September 1968.[106] This meeting was attended by Miki, who afterwards discussed the treaty with West German Foreign Minister Brandt. Brandt held forth at some length on the unpredictability of Soviet behaviour.[107] On his return from Europe, Miki addressed the Liberal Democratic Party Foreign Affairs Research Council, the Security Research Committee and other interested bodies. His report on the talks with Brandt and the conference of ambassadors persuaded these organizations to adopt formally, for the first time, a 'cautious' position on the treaty.[108] On 16 September 1968 the Chief Cabinet Secretary told the press that the government had originally intended to obtain approval to sign the treaty at the next Diet session. However, 'international developments', in particular the Czechoslovakian question, had impelled a restudy of earlier policies. The Chief Cabinet Secretary specifically mentioned the changing attitudes of West Germany and Italy.[109] Thus when, in mid-October 1968, the United States Senate temporarily shelved ratification of the treaty, advocates of 'caution' in Japan strengthened their position. The final decision was postponed until 1969.[110]

By the time the United States Senate approved ratification of the treaty in March 1969, three new factors had emerged to complicate the situation. First, domestic pressures had forced the Japanese government to demand the return of Okinawa, without nuclear bases, from a new American administration that was believed to attach great importance to those facilities. (see Chapter IX.) As early as May 1969 an unidentified 'government source' suggested to the *Nihon Keizai Shimbun* that signing of the non-proliferation treaty might be used as a lever to ensure a favourable outcome in the Okinawan negotiations.[111] Second, the campaign against the nuclear non-proliferation treaty conducted by the Opposition parties since mid-1967 began to reach a climax. Third, within the Liberal Democratic Party, where interest in the treaty had hitherto been minimal, a powerful movement against unconditional participation began to develop.

Detailed discussion of Opposition attitudes lies beyond the scope of this work. Suffice it to remark that the Socialist Party, the Democratic Socialist Party, the Kōmeitō and the Communists, while rejecting the concept of an autonomous nuclear strike force, considered that the non-proliferation treaty would be as beneficial to the international community as a blood bank administered by a committee of vampires. The Socialists and, to some extent, the Communists and the Kōmeitō, believed the treaty to be, in essence, part of an American-Soviet attempt to dominate and divide the world, consolidate their grip on their own exclusive spheres of influence, and isolate and encircle China. It was thus in no way conducive to the relaxation of tensions.[112]

Sentiments of this kind perhaps motivated some of the 'Asianist' groups in the Liberal Democratic Party. Yet as far as the government itself was concerned, the principal reasons for hesitancy on the treaty were concern over the inspection clauses, interest in the attitude of West Germany, pressure from the nuclear lobby and, perhaps, the desire to preserve a trump card for the final stages of the Okinawan negotiations.

One other important factor must not be overlooked. In 1967–8 the Liberal Democratic Party had shown remarkably little interest in the non-proliferation question. Indeed, in April 1967 it was observed that when a certain Liberal Democratic Party Member of Parliament heard the words '*kakusan jōyaku*' (proliferation treaty), he believed they referred to an agreement sponsored by the then secretary-general of the party, Tanaka Kakuei (affectionately known to his colleagues as 'Kakusan').[113] The party Foreign Affairs Research Council studied the issue for the first time in November 1968, after negotiations had been completed and the treaty was open for signing. Full-scale discussions only began in June 1969.[114] It was probably only then that the faction leaders and the party rank and file realized the true character of the agreement. There was thus an element of delayed reaction in their attitudes, coupled with a pained realization that party organizations had been bypassed in the negotiations, that the government and the Foreign Ministry were about to present the nation with a *fait accompli*.

The strength of Conservative Party anti-treaty sentiment became apparent early in November 1969. On the eve of Satō's departure for Washington the party Executive Council resolved that Japanese participation in the treaty should be decided only after 'careful study'. The Prime Minister did not, therefore, officially clarify his government's stand during the Washington talks, although the matter was on the agenda.[115]

Satō was probably not displeased to be confronted with such a revolt on the eve of the Okinawa negotiations. Rather as one might have expected, the Prime Minister's success in securing the 'nuclear-free' return of Okinawa, then the Conservative victory in the November 1969 general elections, were followed by a drive to win over opponents of the treaty within the Liberal Democratic Party.[116] The formation of a Social Democrat-Free Democrat coalition in West Germany, committed to the cause of non-proliferation, also exerted an important influence on Japanese attitudes. On 26 January 1970 a joint meeting of the Foreign Affairs Research Council, the Security Research Committee and the Special Committee on Science and Technology recommended that although the treaty still contained a number of 'doubtful points', it would be preferable to work for their rectification after the agreement had been signed. The question of signing would be left to the discretion of the government.[117] On 3 February 1970 Cabinet formally decided to sign the treaty.[118] The Japanese ambassadors to the United States, the Soviet Union and Great Britain appended their signatures to the document the same day. Japan's signature, like that of West Germany, Australia and some other nations, was not unconditional. At the time of signing the government issued a long and somewhat obscure statement emphasizing its 'deep interest' in steps towards general disarmament, in the renunciation of force or the threat of force in international disputes and in security guarantees for non-nuclear nations. The statement also expressed the hope that France and China would become parties to the treaty. Yet it would seem that the only actual precondition for Japan's ratification was the arrangement of acceptable inspection procedures. 'The government of Japan intends to give full consideration to this matter before taking steps to ratify the treaty', the statement declared.[119] However this may be, there is little evidence to suggest that the Japanese attitude to the treaty was determined primarily by a desire to retain a nuclear weapons option. In 1970 the 'nuclear allergy' remained one of the most salient features of Japanese society, at all levels.

CHAPTER XI

Japan, the United States and China, 1970–1972

The Four Seas are rising, clouds and waters raging,
The Five Continents are rocking, wind and thunder roaring.
Mao Tse-tung, Reply to Comrade Kuo Mo-jo

I   Super power strategic parity, détente and the emergence of a new world order

By 1970 the changes in the global balance of power had become so marked that none of the great powers, and few of their allies, could afford to ignore them. President Nixon's enunciation of the Guam Doctrine in 1969, the far-reaching accords with the Soviet Union on spheres of influence, arms control and bilateral trade concluded during the first half of the 1970s, the Sino-American *détente* of 1971, the collapse of the Bretton Woods system, the devaluation of the dollar and Washington's retreat from unconditional acceptance of the principles of free trade proceeded from a recognition that the age of American pre-eminence had come to an end, that the Cold War assumptions of the 1950s no longer corresponded to political, strategic and economic realities, that the United States, like its opponents and its allies, had to redefine its role in an increasingly complex and fluid world, where neither Soviet nor Chinese interests were necessarily always antagonistic to its own, nor those of Western Europe, Japan and its other associates always compatible, where the number of international actors – traditional nation states, producer and consumer cartels, great corporations, political parties, special interest groups – had grown significantly, where coalitions cut across national and ideological borders, where spheres of influence were blurred, where the nature of state power had become more and more difficult to anlayse and the efficacy of its conventional instruments difficult to assess.

Nixon and Kissinger, however they may be judged by future historians, were strategic realists. To a far greater extent than any of their successors, they were prepared to recognize the fact that the United States and the Soviet Union had, within the context of their differing geopolitical imperatives, diplomatic traditions, force structures and military doctrines, established a relationship of approximate strategic parity, that this relationship had developed through a process of events largely beyond Washington's control and that it could not be reversed. 'We are coming into a new period', Kissinger declared in the northern summer of 1970. 'No words can explain away the fact that when NATO was created we had an atomic monopoly, and today the Soviets have over a thousand land-based missiles. No presidential decision can take away that change.'[1]

By 1970 the Soviet Union had ceased to be, in military terms, simply a great continental power, with a capacity to deliver nuclear missiles to the strategic heartlands of its major adversaries, a substantial sphere of influence along its East European borders and small naval forces to protect its interests in the Baltic, the Black Sea, the White Sea, the Sea of Japan and the Sea of Okhotsk. An accelerated programme of nuclear weapons development, air force modernization and naval construction implemented in the wake of the 1962 Cuban missile crisis had transformed it into a global superstate, with perceived interests on every continent and in every ocean. Like the United States, the Soviet Union was painfully aware that the relationship between military power and political influence had become more and more tenuous. The great socialist commonwealth, extending across the Eurasian continent from the Elbe to the Pacific, had been shattered beyond repair. Even so, despite China's continued hostility, Soviet diplomacy in the non-European world had made significant advances. By 1971 New Delhi's relationship with Moscow, carefully nurtured throughout the 1960s against the background of the Sino-Soviet dispute, the Sino-Indian border conflict and Washington's antagonism towards the Non-Aligned Movement, had blossomed into a full-scale alliance, less binding than NATO, the Warsaw Pact or the Japanese-American security treaty, but an alliance none the less. The Soviet Union had established itself as India's principal arms supplier. It had gained access to naval facilities at Vishakhapatnam. It was also emerging as an important supplier of arms to Pakistan. Soviet influence in the Middle East, too, had grown. Moscow's decision to station military personnel in Egypt (taken in late 1969) represented a fundamental departure from its traditional policy of avoiding a direct military presence in areas beyond the vital *cordon sanitaire* in Eastern Europe. Within a year of this historic decision the Soviet Union had established itself as the dominant external power in the Red Sea and the Suez Canal. Israeli bombing raids deep inside Egyptian territory in the summer of 1970 further consolidated the Soviet-Egyptian alliance. Soviet military equipment poured into Egypt. Soviet advisers began to play a key role in the Egyptian armed forces at all levels. The Soviet navy gained access to facilities at Alexandria, Port Said, Suez and on the Gulf of Aqaba. Soviet vessels appeared frequently at the ports of Hodeida in Yemen and Berbera in Somalia. The USSR also emerged as the principal supplier of arms to Iraq and the Sudan.[2] Until the collapse of the Soviet-Egyptian alliance in 1975 and the destruction of the Sudanese Communist Party (1975–6) the Russians thus enjoyed an influence in the Islamic world almost comparable to that of their superpower rival.

In South-East Asia, the erratic policies of the Chinese leadership during the Cultural Revolution, China's insensitivity to Vietnamese nationalism, together with the necessity of obtaining an assured supply of sophisticated military equipment compelled Hanoi to attach increasing importance to its ties with the Soviet Union. In the non-Communist countries of the region, too, deep-seated fears of Chinese expansionism, disenchantment with the United States and concern about Japan's future policies created an atmosphere which was by no means inimical to Soviet objectives. The Soviet position in Indonesia, it is true, never recovered from the events of 1965. Even so, the decision of the five members of the Association of South East Asian Nations (ASEAN) in 1971 to work towards the creation of a zone of peace, freedom and neutrality in South-East Asia, while in no sense a victory for Moscow, was at least an indication that the area would remain largely outside the American strategic orbit.

The realization of full Soviet-American strategic parity in no way undermined the structure of mutual deterrence established in the mid-1950s.[3] Nor did Soviet advances in South Asia, the Middle East and Indochina imply that Moscow was about to achieve the near-hegemonic position enjoyed by the United States in the immediate postwar period. The Soviet Union, it was generally recognized by dispassionate observers in the heyday of *détente*, had become the strategic equal of the United States of the 1970s, in the world of the 1970s. Many of the factors that had contributed to America's relative decline as a great power also acted to limit the growth of Soviet influence. Both superpowers operated in a world transformed by the paralysing contradictions of mutual nuclear deterrence, by the economic recovery of Western Europe and Japan, the re-emergence of China as a major force in world politics, the growth of autonomous national capitalism in the Middle East, the Indian subcontinent, South-East Asia and Latin America, the formation of producer cartels such as the Organization of Petroleum Exporting Countries (OPEC), the impact of various forms of highly independent national communism, the revival of Islam, the decline in the efficacy of naval power as an instrument of diplomacy, the demonstrated success of guerilla warfare as a means of overthrowing unpopular governments and frustrating great power aggression, and by the manifold social, political and economic problems that had begun to plague most complex, multi-racial industrial societies. Even so, the final emergence of the Soviet Union as a power equal in almost every respect to the United States represented the end of one era and the beginning of another. President Nixon, in one of his first public speeches after the 1968 elections, made it clear that the United States had at last decided to abandon the chimerical goal of maintaining 'superiority' over the Soviet Union. 'Sufficiency' would be enough. 'When we talk about superiority', Nixon explained, 'that may have a detrimental effect on the other side ... giving great impetus to its own arms race'.[4] Little more was heard about the necessity for the United States to maintain 'superiority' over the Soviet Union until the emergence of the Reagan administration in 1980.

By the time President Nixon visited the Soviet Union in May 1972 the two superpowers had negotiated a Statement of Basic Principles of Relations between the United States of America and the Union of Soviet Socialist Republics, a Treaty on the Limitation of Anti-Ballistic Missile Systems, an Interim Agreement on Certain Measures with Respect to the Limitation of Strategic Offensive Arms, a Protocol on Limitation of Submarine-Launched Ballistic Missiles and Modern Ballistic Missile Submarines, a commercial agreement envisaging a threefold expansion of bilateral

trade by the end of 1975, important accords on scientific and technological co-operation, space exploration, medical research, public health, environmental protection
and the prevention of incidents at sea. At the same time, United States encouragement of the relaxation of tensions between West and East Germany, new agreements
on Berlin and the treaties between Moscow, Warsaw and Bonn, recognizing Soviet
and Polish territorial gains in World War II, were interpreted, correctly as setting
Washington's seal of approval on the postwar settlement in Europe. The issue was
not raised again until President Reagan challenged the validity of the Yalta agreements in the summer of 1984.[5]

   If Nixon was willing to accept the inevitability of American-Soviet strategic parity
and partially restructure United States foreign policy in accordance with the limitations it imposed, he was also prepared to recognize the irreversibility of the Chinese
Revolution of 1949, the legitimacy of the People's Republic and the indivisibility of
China's historic territory, including Taiwan. Nixon's decision to begin a dialogue
with Peking, made, in the most extreme secrecy, on 1 February 1969, twelve days
after his accession to office, represented a complete reversal of all previous American policy towards the Chinese Communists. 'We have to live with Communist
powers and we have no illusions about Communism but we must accept the
realities',[6] he later told the American people. China had clearly re-established its
position as a major power, with a global influence, despite its failure to develop a
credible second-strike capacity, the inability of its armed forces to operate far beyond
its frontiers and the utter disarray into which its policies had fallen during the Cultural Revolution. Its co-operation was thought to be essential if the United States
were to negotiate an end to the Vietnam War and arrange for an orderly withdrawal
of forces from continental South-East Asia. At the same time, Nixon's rejection of
ideology in favour of traditional *realpolitik* led him to believe that a sound relationship
with the People's Republic was essential in the context of America's diplomacy
towards the Soviet Union, Japan and the states of the Indian subcontinent.*

   In February 1969 Nixon requested de Gaulle to inform Peking that he intended
to end the Vietnam War and wished to normalize relations. In August the United
States National Security Council, at an historic meeting, decided that China was not
an expansionist power and posed no threat to American interests. It ought to be possible, the council believed, to develop relations with Peking without jeopardizing
either *détente* with the Soviet Union or United States commitments to Taipei. In
January 1970 the United States discontinued its regular naval patrols in the Taiwan
Straits. At the same time, Sino-American talks were reopened in Warsaw. Other
messages were relayed to Peking through Norway, Pakistan and Romania.

   Nixon's overtures came at a time when the Chinese leadership, still reeling under
the impact of the Cultural Revolution, was entering yet another period of intense
factional-policy conflict. The dominant groups in the Communist Party, the armed

---

*   United States motives in seeking a *rapprochement* with the Chinese Communists closely
paralleled, in many respects, those of the British Empire in negotiating a special relationship
with Japan at the turn of the century.

forces and the bureaucracy continued to regard the machinations of both superpowers with the most profound suspicion. The Czechoslovakian intervention, the proclamation of the Brezhnev Doctrine and the clashes with Soviet forces in the Amur-Ussuri region early in 1969, however, had aggravated China's hostility towards Moscow. It was also clear that United States defeat in Vietnam was inevitable. This suggested that American influence in Asia would further decline. At the same time, Japan's re-emergence as a major regional power was beginning to cause considerable concern.

As far as can be judged from the material available, Mao Tse-tung and Chou En-lai favoured offsetting the potential danger from the Soviet Union, neutralizing the threat of a resurgent Japan, settling the Taiwan question and establishing a framework for withdrawal of American forces from those areas of East and South-East Asia regarded as falling within China's historic sphere of influence through a limited strategic accommodation with the United States. The Minister for Defence, Lin Piao, backed by powerful factions in the army, appears to have opposed the idea of *rapprochement* with the United States, advocating, instead, continued self-reliance, a high level of military spending and careful avoidance of conflict on the Sino-Soviet border.[7] The struggle between the two conflicting tendencies came to a head in September 1971, several weeks after Kissinger's first secret visit to Peking, with the mysterious death of Lin Piao and the eclipse of groups opposed to a unilateral Sino-American *détente*. By the beginning of 1972 Nixon himself was in Peking and the groundwork was being laid not merely for a new American relationship with the People's Republic but for a significantly different international configuration of power.

Washington's interest in promoting *détente* with the Soviet Union and China must to some extent be viewed in the context of its increasingly ambiguous position as leader of the Western alliance system. By the beginning of the 1970s, dissension within NATO, Japanese reluctance to assume greater regional military responsibilities, intensified economic competition from Western Europe and Japan, the continued retreat of United States influence in Asia, Africa and Latin America, coupled with the suspicion that the world was inexorably fragmenting into immense trading blocs, had generated acute public awareness of the contradictions between America's ideological preoccupations and the demands of its economic self-interest. A truce in the Cold War, a halt to the ruinous expenditure of the arms race, were essential if the United States was to preserve the economic foundations of its political pre-eminence in the non-Communist world. There was also a view that the United States might eventually have no alternative but to defend its interests against the EEC, Comecon and other groupings through the creation of its own dollar bloc.

Thus it was that in August 1971, immediately after the Kissinger mission to Peking, the Nixon administration, alarmed by the growing United States balance of payments deficit, the vast and potentially destabilizing accumulation of foreign dollar holdings, the declining international competitiveness of American manufacturers, the inability of major American industries (notably steel and automobiles) to hold their own even in the domestic market, mounting unemployment and social

and convinced that Japanese and European economic nationalism made significant revaluation of foreign currencies improbable, embarked on a series of initiatives designed to strengthen the United States economic position against it allies. These measures, centring around the *de jure* inconvertibility of the dollar, a 10 per cent import surcharge and a wages and price freeze, effectively destroyed the Bretton Woods system, threw the international financial world and trading order into chaos and shook the Western alliance to its foundations. They also failed to achieve the desired results. The United States economic position, relative to its allies, did not improve, despite the substantial devaluation of the dollar and upward revaluation of the mark and the yen negotiated in December 1971. After a further 10 per cent devaluation of the dollar in the spring of 1973, carried out in the midst of turmoil in the world's money markets, a highly unstable system of floating currency blocs came into being. The American alliance system, unlike its Soviet counterpart in the 1960s, emerged from its ordeal intact. Relations among the major non-Communist powers, however, had clearly entered a new era.

II   Japanese domestic politics and foreign policy on the eve of détente

(i)   The 1970 security treaty crisis, Conservative decline and the Liberal Democratic Party succession struggle, June 1970–July 1971

In Japan, the first years of the new decade, like the last years of the old, were characterized by a deepening sense of national crisis. Economic growth continued at a rapid pace. The dense pall of industrial smog extending, almost unbroken, along the New Tōkaidō Line, from the Kantō plains to Hakata, the spread of pollution-related diseases, the launching of the first Japanese earth satellite in February 1970, the opening of the International Exhibition at Ōsaka in March, increasingly serious trade friction with North America and Europe, all symbolized the nation's final re-emergence as a great industrial power. Yoshida Shigeru's boast that a defeated Japan would eventually surpass its conqueror seemed closer to realization than ever before. Nevertheless, the old Conservative establishment, its domestic and foreign policies under constant attack, its electoral fortunes declining, felt itself to be in a state of seige. The Socialist Party, paralysed by endless factional-policy conflict, was in no position to take over the reins of government. Yet by the late 1960s the manifold problems generated by high economic growth, the presence of American military bases and the growing strength of the anti-Vietnam War movement had stimulated renewed interest in a broad alliance of Opposition parties. By 1970 the prospects for some kind of united front seemed brighter than at any time since the end of the occupation.

Prime Minister Kishi's Treaty of Mutual Co-operation and Security between Japan and the United States expired on 22 June 1970. It was automatically extended the following day. This course of action, which enabled either signatory to annul the agreement on one year's advance notice, had been regarded as preferable to renegotiation. Both governments were anxious to avoid any repetition of the 1960 upheaval. Even so, as in the period 1958–60, the Japanese Conservatives prepared for a major confrontation with the anti-treaty forces. Plans to mobilize the Self Defence Forces were again drawn up. The army and the Special Mechanized Police carried out intensive anti-riot training. At the same time the government conducted a large-scale public relations campaign designed to persuade the people of the wid-som of continued association with the United States.

Despite these precautions, the anti-treaty demonstrations organized in the summer of 1970, in the wake of the United States invasion of neutral Cambodia and Japan's participation in the American-sponsored Djakarta Conference, were on a noticeably larger scale than the 1960 movement. According to the Police Agency some 774,000 men and women took part in protests in 416 cities and towns across Japan on 23 June 1970. The organizers of the demonstrations themselves put the figure at more than 2 million. In Tōkyō, 220,000 citizens mobilized by the Socialist Party, the Communist Party and the trade union movement, drawn from some 300 organizations, assembled at Yoyogi Park early in the morning and slowly made their way along Aoyama-dōri, past the Diet and the American Embassy, then on to Shim-bashi, shouting their opposition to Washington's East Asian policies, the security treaty and Japanese rearmament. The immense human tide was still flowing past the United States Embassy late that night, long after the National Railways and the Tōkyō Underground had closed. Throughout the day, while helicopters chattered overhead, thousands of Special Mechanized Police, in their grey uniforms, carrying shields and riot control batons, lined the avenues along the route of the march or waited in quiet streets nearby. Yet there was little violence. As in 1960, Socialist, Communist and trade union leaders insisted that all protest be peaceful. Towards the middle of the afternoon radical anti-Japan Communist Party students marching on the Diet became involved in fierce clashes with police at Kita Aoyama 3-chome crossing. Molotov cocktails and stones were thrown. Clouds of tear gas drifted among the apartment buildings and boutiques of this fashionable quarter. At Hibiya Park the barricades went up and students battled with police until late at night. At Shimizudani Park the Alliance for Peace in Vietnam (Beiheiren) organized a separate demonstration, which attracted some 20,000 participants. Mass meetings, protests and marches also took place in Shinjuku, Nakameguro and Ebisu.[8]

The unrest continued for the greater part of the year, growing in scale and complexity. Calls by Socialist, Communist and trade union leaders for discipline and moderation were increasingly ignored. The autumn saw an intensification of the anti-base struggle, constant clashes between police and ultra-leftist students, savage fratricidal confrontations between rival revolutionary groups. The frenetic activity of the far left was paralleled by a further resurgence of the ultra-nationalist right. On 25 November 1970 the flamboyant novelist Mishima Yukio, leading a group of volunteers from his neo-fascist Society of the Shield, forcibly took over Eastern Army Headquarters at Ichigaya and attempted to incite the Self Defence Forces to stage a *coup d'état*. The assembled officers and men, unmoved by Mishima's oratory, refused to participate, forcing the humiliated patriot to commit ritual suicide.

Despite Mishima's failure to achieve his objectives, his abortive *coup d'état*, by exposing the connections between several Conservative Party politicians, sections of the Self Defence Force officer corps and ultra-nationalist secret societies, sent shock waves throughout the nation. Quite clearly, Mishima was not the Japanese Hitler. Yet it was difficult for many to suppress the uneasy suspicion that his attempted coup, like the Kapp Putsch of 1920, might be a harbinger of things to come.

Once the security treaty crisis had passed, the Conservative Party turned in upon itself. On 29 October 1970 Prime Minister Satō Eisaku won a convincing victory over Miki Takeo in the Liberal Democratic Party presidential elections (353 votes to 111). Satō thus became the longest-serving Prime Minister in Japanese history, surpassing even Itō Hirobumi's record term. His re-election had been made possible by the continuing support of the Fukuda, Maeo, Kawashima, Ishii, Funada, Murakami, Nakasone and Sonoda factions, as well as by the efforts of Fukuda's colleague Shigemune Yūzō, the elderly Yamaguchi oligarch, who had for some years exerted a dominant influence in the House of Councillors. No major redistribution of Cabinet and party posts took place after the election. Fukuda remained as Finance Minister. Aichi Kiichi stayed on as Foreign Minister, Nakasone Yasuhiro as director-general of the Defence Agency, Miyazawa Kiichi as Minister for International Trade and Industry. Satō's associate Hori Shigeru kept his position as Chief Cabinet Secretary. Tanaka Kakuei retained the secretary-generalship of the party. The Prime Minister had made it clear that he would not seek re-election for a fifth term. Thus, almost immediately, party leaders began preparations for the succession struggle. Old, established factions that had preserved their unity through the upheavals of the 1960s made frantic efforts to galvanize their leadership, elevate the morale of their rank and file, consolidate their finances and rethink their strategies. Fragments of once-powerful factions shattered by the convulsions of the previous decade attempted to reconstitute themselves and revive their political fortunes. The smaller factions, subjected to the relentless gravitational pull of the great, manoeuvred either to align themselves with the probable victors, or to forge new coalitions, or to unite with groups having broadly compatible interests and views. Amoeba-like, new factions began to emerge from the bodies of the old. Long-standing alliances were broken down, new constellations of power appeared.

By the winter of 1970–1 the battle lines had been drawn. It was clear that the Prime Minister's chief lieutenant, Tanaka Kakuei, who now commanded the personal allegiance of a substantial grouping within the Satō faction, intended to make a bid for party leadership as soon as his mentor retired. It also seemed clear that Tanaka's ambitions would be strenuously opposed by Fukuda Takeo, Satō's principal factional ally, by Miki Takeo, his chief Conservative critic, and perhaps also by Nakasone Yasuhiro. The Maeo faction, which had been thrown into a crisis over the question of whether to support Satō's re-election for a fourth term, was still paralysed by internal divisions and uncertain of its future course. This situation continued until Ōhira Masayoshi, responding to the dissatisfaction felt by younger members towards Maeo's apparent docility and lack of ambition, took over the reins of leadership in mid-April 1971. It then began to seem possible that Ōhira, too, might announce his candidacy for the next party presidential elections.

The smaller factions, commanded respectively by Shiina Etsusaburō,* Ishii Mitsujirō, Funada Naka, Murakami Isamu and Kōno Ichirō's old disciple Sonoda Sunao, who had thrown their combined weight behind Satō in October, were engaged in complicated manoeuvres to ensure that they retained an important influence on the party and its policies. By the middle of February 1971 the chairman of the Party Policy Board, Mizuta Mikio, together with Nakagawa Ichirō, Watanabe Eiichi, Aoki Masahisa and one or two other members of the Funada faction, had begun secret negotiations with Murakami in the hope of resurrecting the former Ōno faction, from which both groups had originally descended. When Funada voiced his disapproval his faction split. Funada himself, whose followers in the old Ōno faction had decided, unlike Murakami's, to oppose Satō in 1964, now gravitated towards support for Fukuda in the coming contest. Mizuta, while continuing to make cautious overtures to Murakami and other leaders such as Ishida Hirohide, inclined towards support for Tanaka Kakuei. On 14 July 1971, after a convivial meeting at the Tōkyō Hilton, Mizuta succeeded in establishing his own faction of twenty members, the Shinsei Club, made up of Murakami's group, a few of Fujiyama Aiichirō's supporters and his own following from the Funada faction.[9] Towards the end of the year elements within the Nakasone and Sonoda factions became involved in delicate and, eventually, unsuccessful negotiations to reconstitute the former Kōno faction, which had once been such a mighty force within the party. Funada, Ishii and Shiina, too, went into conclave to work out a common strategy for the impending struggle.[10] These moves, while having, ultimately, important policy implications, had no immediate purpose other than to advance the factional interests of the leaders involved.

It was during the last months of the Satō Cabinet, too, that supra-factional, right-wing nationalist groups such as the Lion's Association (Shishikai), organized by relatively young men such as Hamada Kōichi and Hayashi Yoshirō, began to establish a presence in the bewildering galaxy of intra-party organizations, resolutely pressuring the leadership to revise the Constitution, implement tough anti-Communist policies, increase military spending, eradicate 'leftist influence' in schools and universities and reinstitute state support for the Yasukuni Shrine, whatever the attitude of the Socialists, the Communists and the Kōmeitō.[11] The more elderly members of the Conservative Party, worried by the polarization of national opinion, were not necessarily enthusiastic about pursuing these issues. Nor was the party's left. Within a few months, radical liberal members of the Afro-Asian Problems Study Association had set up a rival True Comrades Society (Seishikai) to counteract the burgeoning influence of the New Right.[12]

The right had some cause to worry. The unified local elections held in April 1971 had resulted in overwhelming victories for Socialist-Communist backed candidates in Tōkyō, Kyōto, Ōsaka, and many smaller urban centres across the nation. The fall

---

* Shiina had assumed control of the Kawashima faction after its leader's death in the autumn of 1970.

of Ōsaka, for many years a stronghold of the Liberal Democratic Party, had been a particularly savage blow. At the same time, the Conservatives barely managed to retain their hold on Fukuoka, Kanagawa and Hokkaidō. In the wake of these disasters, the outcome of the June 1971 House of Councillors election, while far from calamitous, was profoundly disappointing. The Liberal Democrats had hoped to increase their representation in the Upper House by 10–15 per cent to a total of about 150 seats. Instead, despite an energetic and expensive campaign, their numbers dropped from 136 seats to 135. The Kōmeitō, too, lost 1 seat, decreasing its representation from 24 to 23. In contrast the Japan Socialist Party increased its strength in the Upper House from 61 to 66, the Democratic Socialist Party from 7 to 13 and the Communist Party from 7 to 10. Especially disturbing was the fact that the Communist Party received almost 12 per cent of the total vote, a figure considerably in excess of the 9.7 per cent obtained in 1949, when its popular support had reached a previous high-water mark.[13]

The Opposition parties, despite their significant advances, fell short of gaining a majority in the House of Councillors. Nevertheless, the Liberal Democratic Party's poor showing proved to be a case of *ari no ana kara tsutsumi no kuzure*, 'the burrowing of an ant destroys the retaining walls'. Within the party, old wounds were reopened, dormant, but never forgotten, quarrels were reactivated. Almost immediately after the election (and the day after the announcement of Nixon's visit to China), Kōno Kenzō, the brother of Satō's late arch-rival Kōno Ichirō, at the head of a coalition comprising his own followers in the Cherry Blossom Association (Sakura Kai) and a majority of the Opposition parties, launched a campaign to prevent the Prime Minister's ally Shigemune Yūzō from securing election as President of the House of Councillors for a fourth term. The success of this campaign and the subsequent disintegration of the 'Shigemune Kingdom' seriously complicated Satō's management of the Diet. It was now by no means inevitable that all bills passed by the House of Representatives, where the Liberal Democratic Party enjoyed an absolute majority, and where the Prime Minister's factional coalition was still intact, would also be accepted by the Upper House. The collapse of Shigemune's influence also jeopardized Fukuda Takeo's future prospects for election as party president. As Shigemune's star waned, Tanaka, Miki and Ōhira began a major drive to increase their own support in the House.[14]

In his reallocation of Cabinet and party posts the Prime Minister, aware of the dangers inherent in this situation, endeavoured to preserve, as far as possible, the existing factional equilibrium. He was also determined to avoid tacitly endorsing any particular candidate for the party leadership. Thus Fukuda Takeo was transferred from the Ministry of Finance to the Foreign Ministry. Hori Shigeru was appointed party secretary-general. Tanaka Kakuei became Minister for International Trade and Industry, Maeo Shigesaburō Minister for Justice, Mizuta Mikio Finance Minister, Akagi Munenori Minister for Agriculture and Forests, Masuhara Keikichi director-general of the Defence Agency. Miki Takeo, while not given any post himself, was at least consulted in the process of Cabinet reorganization. So, too, were the leaders of several smaller factions.[15] In the months that followed, the Opposition parties, heartened by their electoral advances, and the dissident groups in the Conservative camp, encouraged by the erosion of Satō's hegemony, pursued the government mercilessly on foreign and domestic issues, focusing their attention, in particular, on the Prime Minister's support for American East Asian policies, the China question, Japan's relationship with South Korea, the military base problem, the character of the Okinawan Agreement and the Fourth Defence Plan.

(ii) American-Japanese economic friction

George Kennan, John Foster Dulles and Harry Kern had foreseen neither the extent of the postwar Japanese economic recovery nor the possibility of American decline. By the beginning of the 1970s serious fractures had appeared in the structure of economic relationships built up at San Francisco. No doubt the American and Japanese economies had come to enjoy a high degree of mutual interdependence. In many respects, the degree of interdependence had increased remarkably since the early postwar years. Nevertheless, with Japan's emergence as the second-largest industrial power in the non-Communist world, the highly competitive character of the two economies once again became apparent. Japan and the United States, as the *Asahi Shimbun* noted, had been, historically, Pacific rivals, not Pacific allies. The trade disputes that began in the late 1960s continued throughout the 1970s into the 1980s, leaving a legacy of anxiety, frustration and mistrust on both sides of the Pacific. American public criticism of Japan centred around the imbalance in bilateral trade, which had grown steadily since 1965. The changing balance of trade was the inevitable outcome of America's declining economic performance and the operation of the market mechanism. During the late 1960s Japanese exports of iron, steel, automobiles, motor cycles, electrical equipment, household goods and textiles had increased dramatically. Their high quality and competitive prices had made them attractive to American consumers. At the same time, the United States position as the major supplier of raw materials, foodstuffs, capital equipment and manufactured goods to Japan had been challenged by more cost-efficient producers such as Australia, Canada and the developing countries of non-Communist Asia. By 1970, Japan's domestic markets, except in the agricultural sector, were as open to American exports as any markets in Europe. United States businessmen, however, discouraged by linguistic and cultural obstacles, had made little effort to penetrate them. The heavy reliance of the Liberal Democratic Party on rural electorates, especially in the context of Socialist and Communist advances in urban Japan, made liberalization of the agricultural commodities market difficult to realize.[16] Japanese culinary traditions, moreover, made the impact of any such liberalization on bilateral trade difficult to calculate. So, too, did the existence of highly competitive agricultural producers in Australia, Canada, South-East Asia and Latin America, all of whom were eager to negotiate greater access to the Japanese market.

Washington was understandably reluctant to accept the view that the performance of the American economy itself was largely responsible for the trade imbalance. The close links between the Japanese government, the bureaucracy and the business community, it was argued, had for too long given Japan 'unfair' advantages in international trade. The Japanese Ministry of International Trade and Industry rapidly took its place beside the KGB as one of the principal lucifers in the American pantheon of demons. American opinion leaders increasingly saw the solution to the problems posed by 'Japan Incorporated' in terms of *de facto* restrictions on Japanese imports, further liberalization of Japan's domestic markets and a substantial revaluation of the yen. While Japan made it clear that it would under no circumstances voluntarily revalue the yen, that renunciation of agricultural protectionism was politically impossible and that further liberalization of other sectors would probably have only a marginal impact on the bilateral trade imbalance, the business community, in the face of intense American pressure, gradually found itself obliged to implement a series of 'voluntary' restrictions on exports to the United States. These resulted in substantial reductions in Japan's share of the American market for several important commodities.

Between 1969 and 1972, for example, the Japanese steel industry, in order to prevent passage of the protectionist legislation demanded by its American competitors, drastically reduced its reliance on the United States market. The American share of Japan's total steel exports declined from 53 per cent in the mid-1960s to 28 per cent in 1971. Japanese-American friction over steel continued throughout the 1970s. By the end of the decade the United States was buying no more than 20 per cent of Japan's total steel exports.[17]

Serious discord also developed over the question of textiles. In 1969 the Nixon administration had requested Japan to impose temporary limitations on exports of synthetic fibre and woollen goods to the United States. It was widely believed that Nixon wished to strengthen Republican prospects in the next presidential elections by propping up the decaying textile towns of the South. Satō, exploiting the inherent ambiguity of the Japanese language to the fullest extent, had conveyed the impression that he would consider imposing voluntary restrictions. His subsequent dilatoriness and equivocation caused tempers in Washington to flare. The issue dragged on until the conclusion of a government-to-government agreement in the summer of 1971. The combined impact of United States protective measures, 'voluntary restrictions' and the 1971 agreement produced a sharp decline in Japan's share of the American imported textiles market. Between 1966 and 1970 Japan's share of the United States market for chemical and synthetic fibre goods (excluding yarns) decreased from 66.8 per cent to 34.9 per cent, for cotton goods from 22.6 per cent to 21.6 per cent and for woollens from 34.4 per cent to 28.1 per cent.[18] By the middle of the decade the Japanese textile industry had gone into decline and the United States had become a relatively minor market for its products. Even before the textile dispute had come to an end serious problems had arisen over Japanese colour television and automobile exports.

Against the background of Japan's re-emergence as a major world power these bilateral trade disputes, still in their early stages at the beginning of the 1970s, generated a new and far less indulgent American attitude towards Tōkyō. It was not long before influential Americans, in the State Department, the Pentagon and the intelli gence community, began to fear that the economic friction would ultimately develop political and strategic dimensions.[19] Perceptions of Japan as a dangerous competitor spread rapidly not only within the political elite and the business community but also among the general public. An opinion poll on the subject of Japanese-American relations conducted in the United States by the *Asahi Shimbun* and the Harris Corporation in March 1971[20], for example, found that 90 per cent of respondents were aware of Japan's technological progress and that 58 per cent had purchased and highly evaluated Japanese products. Nevertheless, 66 per cent favoured various restrictions on bilateral trade. At the same time, while 85 per cent of respondents agreed that friendship with Japan as essential, there was no enthusiasm to see a wider regional role for the Self Defence Forces. This suggested a certain underlying mistrust of Japan's long-term intentions. In this context, while 64 per cent of respondents maintained that the American decision to use atomic weapons on Japan had been 'unavoidable', 72 per cent were opposed to Japan's own acquisition of an independent nuclear force. Similar trends were evident in many polls conducted during the next ten years.

By the northern summer of 1971, American criticism of Japan's economic policies, while relatively mild compared to the 'Japan bashing' of the 1980s, had reached levels unprecedented in the postwar era. The United States was engaged in a trade war and was on the brink of defeat, Elly R. Carraway Jr, president of Burlington Industries, America's largest textile producer, told the Senate Finance Committee's International Trade Sub-Committee in May 1971.[21] By September he was charging that Japan was pursuing 'a brilliant plan' to become the world's leading power.[22] His sentiments were echoed by many other businessmen. Edsel B. Ford II warned his shareholders that Japanese competition would soon transform the United States into a service economy.[23] Leading executives of the First National Bank of Chicago contended that 'half the responsibility' for the rising protectionist sentiment in the United States lay with Japan.[24] The publication of David Bergamini's *Japan's Imperial Conspiracy* in the spring of 1971, a study of Hirohito's role in World War II, resurrected memories of prewar American–Japanese rivalry in the Pacific. *The New York Times* and the *Wall Street Journal* maintained a relatively sanguine attitude towards the Japanese challenge. Other newspapers were less restrained. *Time*, *Newsweek* and *Forbes Magazine* all ran special issues on the Japanese economy, focusing on the links between government, bureaucracy and business and their impact on bilateral trade problems. *Newsweek* alleged that Japan had launched 'a massive invasion of the world automobile market'.[25] *Time* saw the United States locked in struggle with 'a mighty industrial economy that has been shaped by Oriental history and psychology'.[26]

The Liberal Democratic Party, preoccupied with the impending leadership struggle, and the Foreign Ministry, convinced that Washington's policies would continue to be determined within a Cold War framework, seemed hardly aware of the changes taking place in American perceptions of Japan. The business community had at least observed the storm clouds on the horizon. Any remaining complacency in these quarters was effectively destroyed at the eighth meeting of the United States-

Japan Businessmen's Conference in June 1971. Iwasa Yoshizane, chairman of the board of directors of the Fuji Bank, Uemura Kōgorō, chairman of Keidanren, Kōsaka Tokusaburō, president of Shinetsu Chemicals, Nagano Shigeo, chairman of the board of directors of New Japan Steel, Morita Akio, president of Sony and other members of the Japanese delegation, returned shaken by the aggressive and sustained criticism from their American counterparts. Throughout the discussions, the Americans had relentlessly hammered the trade imbalance, Japanese export strategies, liberalization of the Japanese domestic market and revaluation of the yen, linking these issues to the growing political, economic and social problems in the United States.[27] The American offensive continued at the next meeting of the Businessmen's Conference in September, when the astonished Japanese delegates were treated to a rendition of the popular song 'Import Blues'.

> I got the import blues ... and I got 'em bad.
> I'm a cotton mill man ... and my heart is sad.
> I used to work six days a week, sometimes more ...
> Now it's three days a week ... and I sure am sore.
>
> I'm good at my business, a weaving hot shot
> And still I ain't got ... a heckuva lot.
> I've made big money at the weaving trade
> But now, the people of Jay-Pan have it made.
>
> They make cheap-john goods in a sleazy style
> And ship these goods to the whole world wide.
> And my little wife ... well ... she runs to the store,
> Gobbles 'em up, and says when you gonna get more?
>
> She bought me a shirt that was import made
> And I got mad ... because it hurt my trade.
> She bought a Jap-made mini, way 'bove the knee ...
> You should have seen it after it was washed.[28]

The Japanese, impressed by the depth of the United States political and social crisis, exacerbated by the Vietnam War, yet convinced that Japan could not be blamed for America's domestic problems, began to sense that the time for a far-reaching reassessment of foreign economic policy was fast approaching. Relations with Western Europe, too, were becoming difficult. Uemura thought that a well-planned public relations campaign might help to change Japan's image in the West. Yet it was by no means clear that such an exercise would succeed. The world itself was changing. While there was a general consensus that the United States would remain a crucial market for some time it was also evident that greater efforts would be needed to improve trading links with other powers. The Soviet Union, non-Communist Asia and Oceania clearly offered considerable opportunities. Nevertheless, for historical and cultural reasons, Japanese interest tended to focus on the People's Republic of China.

(iii) China's fears of Japanese militarism and its terms for the normalization of diplomatic ties

A new relationship with China could only be secured at the price of considerable political and strategic accommodation. While the Chinese leadership remained preoccupied with the threat to national security posed by the United States and the Soviet Union, the changing character of the American-Japanese alliance, Japan's re-emergence as a great economic power, its escalating military budget, its ambiguous attitude towards the nuclear non-proliferation treaty, its enunciation of a special interest in Taiwan and the Korean peninsula in the November 1969 Satō-Nixon Joint Communiqué, had all caused much anxiety in Peking. Chinese suspicions of Japan ran deep. The Taiwan clause in the 1969 joint communiqué was inevitably seen as heralding renewed Japanese intervention in the Chinese Civil War. The reference to Korea seemed uncannily reminiscent of the Anglo-Japanese alliance of January 1902, whereby a declining Britain, in order to secure Japanese support against Russia, had given tacit endorsement to Tōkyō's colonial ambitions on the peninsula. In the winter of 1969–70 the Chinese official media launched a massive campaign against the new 'criminal plots of American and Japanese counter-revolutionary circles', 'the reactionary policies of the Satō Cabinet' and the 'revival of Japanese militarism'.[29] At the same time the Chinese government began to lay the groundwork for an anti-Japanese regional coalition. In April 1970 China and the Democratic People's Republic of Korea issued a statement jointly condemning what was seen as the new, more militant character of the American-Japanese alliance, castigating the 'revival of Japanese militarism' and denouncing Japan's 'imperialist designs' both on the peninsula and in the Taiwan Straits.[30] These issues were subsequently raised during the course of discussions with other allies. The prospects for the success of the Chinese campaign seemed bright. The Guam Doctrine, the Satō-Nixon Joint Communiqué and the scale of the Japanese rearmament programme had revived fears of Japanese expansionism throughout Asia and the Pacific, in Communist and non-Communist countries alike. Indonesia, Malaysia, the Philippines and Thailand were increasingly uneasy. Important groups in South Korea, too, had become thoroughly alarmed at the prospect of renewed Japanese domination. The Australian Liberal Party Prime Minister William McMahon, a long-time exponent of containment, was more than a little disturbed by the implications of Japan's Fourth Defence Plan.[31] Gough Whitlam, leader of the Australian Labour Party, soon to succeed McMahon as Prime Minister, confided to Chou En-lai in July 1971 that Australians 'have the same fear of the Japanese as I believe your people have now'. Australia's defence treaty with the United States, Whitlam asserted, had been chiefly intended to protect his country against a possible 'revival of Japanese militarism'.[32]

For some time, the Chinese leadership remained convinced that the national interest would best be served by the traditional policy of encouraging sympathetic Japanese, of all political colourings, to break with Washington and adopt a more independent position in international affairs. It was in this context that Chou En-lai, at the opening of the 1970 Canton Trade Fair, announced a series of new and stringent conditions for Japanese firms wishing to do business with China. Chou's 'Four Conditions', subsequently elaborated in an interview with Matsumura Kenzō, Furui Yoshimi, Fujiyama Aiichirō and other members of the Japanese Memorandum Trade delegation on 19 April 1970, stipulated that

1)   China would not trade with companies assisting Taiwan and South Korea;

2)   China would not trade with companies having investments in Taiwan and South Korea;

3)   China would not trade with companies manufacturing arms for the American war of aggression in Vietnam, Laos and Cambodia;

4)   China would not trade with Japanese companies engaged in joint ventures with American concerns.

The People's Republic, Chou En-lai explained, while recognizing Japan's legitimate right of self-defence, was convinced that the Satō Cabinet was intent on reviving the Greater East Asia Co-prosperity Sphere. China had no intention of assisting 'the Japanese militarists' in any way. It therefore intended to apply the four principles rigorously and would not hesitate to break contracts with firms found to be violating them.

As far as the restoration of Sino-Japanese diplomatic relations was concerned, the Chinese Premier reiterated, with considerable force, Peking's traditional position. Japan should

1)   recognize the government of the People's Republic as the government of all China;

2)   break with the Kuomintang in Taiwan;

3)   abandon its subservience to American imperialism.

The position enunciated by Chou En-lai during this long interview with Matsumura Kenzō's delegation represented the consensus of the inner circles of the Chinese leadership. At one point in the discussions, however, Chou suggested that he himself was not fully convinced that an independent Japan under a Conservative government would always act in ways compatible with China's interests. If this were so, he hinted, the Japanese-American security treaty might have to be viewed in an entirely different light.*[33]

---

*   Chou's remarks, addressed as much to himself as to his Japanese friends, were so subtle that their significance was not fully understood. Observing that the United States, in fact, controlled Japan through its military bases and other facilities on the archipelago, Chou recalled that Fujiyama had fixed a ten-year time limit to the 1960 arrangements. The Satō Cabinet, he said, had apparently extended the treaty indefinitely. When Fujiyama explained that this was not so and that the treaty could now be terminated by either side on one year's notice, the Chinese Premier reflected, enigmatically, 'Then, Mr Fujiyama, your achievement was very great!'

In the months that followed, China's campaign intensified. Japanese delegations visiting Peking were encouraged to issue statements vilifying the Taiwan and Korean clauses in the 1969 Satō-Nixon Joint Communiqué, castigating the revival of Japanese militarism and criticizing America's continued intervention in Indochina. Matsumura Kenzō's Memorandum Trade delegation set the pace with a communiqué proclaiming that the 'revival of Japanese militarism poses a serious threat to the peoples of China, Korea and Indochina, as well as to Asia as a whole'. Matsumura, Furui, Fujiyama and the others promised to redouble their efforts to oppose revanchism and prevent Japan being drawn into aggressive wars in Asia.[34] Peking's criticism of Japan's role in the Djakarta Conference on Cambodia was especially bitter.[35] So, too, was its campaign against the establishment of a joint Japanese-South Korean- Taiwanese commission to exploit the resources of the East China Sea.[36] At the same time Japanese films such as *Yamamoto Isoroku* and *Nihon Kai Dai Kaisen* (The Great Battle in the Japan Sea'), both of which displayed a marked nostalgia for the vanished glories of the Japanese empire, were severely censured by the Chinese media.[37] Mishima Yukio's attempted *coup d'état*, not unexpectedly, also attracted much attention in the Chinese capital. The Mishima incident, *Hsinhua* reported, was 'iron proof' that the revival of Japanese militarism had become a reality.[38]

(iv) Japanese reactions to the Chinese campaign

The Satō Cabinet, rejecting China's assertions that Japan was embarked on a 'militarist' course, advised business firms not to comply with Chou En-lai's 'Four Conditions'. The Prime Minister and his advisers remained convinced that there was no need to depart from established policies in dealings with Peking. United States officials repeatedly assured Japan that no change in China policy was contemplated in Washington.[39] Sino-American hostility seemed likely to continue indefinitely. Despite President Nixon's talk of withdrawing from Vietnam, the constant expansion of the war, first into Cambodia, then into southern Laos, made it seem that the Americans intended to remain in South-East Asia. An intensive American public relations campaign, moreover, had at last managed to persuade the governments of several Asian-Pacific allies that the Indo-China war had entered a new stage and that Washington's efforts would soon be crowned with success. Satō himself, now recovered from the shock of the Tet offensive, was half inclined to believe these claims. If victory was imminent, it would be particularly unwise for Japan to dissociate itself from any aspect of American East Asian policy. Rather, it should endeavour to consolidate its position as America's principal East Asian ally, the representative of 'Western' interests in the non-European world. As former Vice-Foreign Minister Yamada Hisanari, speaking in support of continued Japanese co-sponsorship of the American 'important question formula', designed to keep China out of the United Nations, told the House of Representatives in September 1970:

> If Japan gives up as a co-sponsor [of the American resolution], it will cause a disturbance among the African and Asian Nations. The United States does not want this. Close rela-

tions between Japan and the United States are essential in Japan's own interests. Japan cannot relinquish its co-sponsorship of the American resolution.[40]

On 27 August 1970 Foreign Minister Aichi informed the Liberal Democratic Party Foreign Affairs Research Council that Japan would continue to support the 'important question' formula.[41] The council officially endorsed this policy on 21 September. Thus, when the issue came before the United Nations General Assembly on 18 November 1970 the Japanese ambassador, Tsuruoka Seijin, speaking in favour of the American motion, explained as usual that Japan was 'strongly opposed' to any moves to expel the Republic of China and hand over its seat to the People's Republic.[42] A week later Satō told the Diet that there would be 'no change' in Japan's China policy.[43]

The rigidity of the government's position infuriated both its Conservative critics and the Opposition, many of whom were far from convinced that China's fears of Japanese militarism were groundless. By the autumn of 1970, a few months before the first signs of the Sino-American *détente*, independently minded Conservative nationalists had decided that extraordinary action would be necessary to change the Prime Minister's attitude. On 12 October 1970 the 'pro-Chinese' groups in the Liberal Democratic Party joined with the Socialists, the Kōmeitō, the Democratic Socialists and the Communists to form a non-partisan Parliamentarians' League for the Restoration of Ties with China (Nitchū Kokkō Kaifuku Sokushin Giin Renmei), dedicated to securing China's entry into the United Nations and restoring diplomatic ties on the basis that Peking was the only legal government of China and Taiwan was an integral part of its territory. By mid-December 1970 more than half the membership of the House of Representatives and many members of the House of Councillors, 154 Socialists, 95 Liberal Democrats, 71 members of the Kōmeitō, 36 Democratic Socialists, 21 Communists and 2 Independents, a total of 379 out of 738 parliamentarians, had joined the league, the first organization of its type in postwar Japan.[44]

The scramble of Conservative politicians to join the league was not unrelated to the movement of opinion in the business community. Against the background of rising protectionism in the United States, the enunciation of Chou En-lai's 'Four Conditions' had precipitated a dramatic change in the attitude of Japan's leading financial, industrial and trading houses. Certainly, the Mitsubishi group, Mitsui, Itō-chū, Marubeni-Iida and other firms deeply involved in trade with the United States, Taiwan and South Korea refused to comply with China's demands. Their leading executives remained convinced that Washington's global policies would continue to be determined by the demands of containment. They were also confident that they could ride out the oncoming protectionist storms in North America.[45] Firms already active in the China trade, in contrast, moved rapidly to adjust to the new situation, withdrawing their representatives from the Japan-Republic of China Cooperation Committee, closing down their operations in Taiwan and South Korea, denouncing Japanese militarism and the policies of the Satō Cabinet where appropriate. With the exception of New Japan Steel, moreover, all of the nation's great steel manufacturers, Kawasaki Seitetsu, Kōbe Seikō, Nihon Kōkan and Sumitomo Kinzoku, for many years among the strongest supporters of the Conservative Party's 'pro-American' right wing, accepted Chou's 'Four Conditions' without demur.[46] The fate of New Japan Steel, whose chairman, Nagano Shigeo, enjoyed close personal relations with Prime Minister Satō, served as a salutary example to its competitors. When Nagano, who played a central role in the Japan-Republic of China Co-operation Committee, refused to sever his links with Taiwan, he found his company totally excluded from trade with the continent. Peking's attitude towards this giant corporation further hardened after Nagano attended the fifteenth meeting of the Japan-Republic of China Co-operation Committee on 6–8 July 1971, a gathering that became a battleground between the 'pro-Peking' and 'pro-Taipei' factions in the business community.[47] Sumitomo Kagaku, the big chemical fertilizer company, Komatsu Seisakujo, Kubota Tekkōsho, Hitachi Seiki and Toshiba Kikai, the machinery manufacturers, along with such major textile producers as Tōyō Rayon, Kurashiki Rayon, Yūnichika and Asahi Kasei also quickly accepted the 'Four Conditions'. Kansai-based trading firms such as Ataka Sangyō, Kanematsu Gōshō, Nisshō Iwai and Sumitomo Shōji followed suit. By the spring of 1971 Toyota Motors, which had for some time been exploring the possibility of automobile exports to China, announced that it would refrain from direct investment in Taiwan and South Korea, although established technical services would continue. Following Toyota's lead, Nissan and Honda also accepted Chou En-lai's 'Four Conditions' and thus prepared the way for an advance into the China market.[48]

Peking's exercise in 'ping pong' diplomacy tilted the balance further. In April 1971 Wang Hsiao-yun, managing director of the Chinese People's External Friendship Association, who had accompanied the Chinese table tennis team to the world championships at Nagoya, met with a number of Japanese businessmen eager to explore the possibilities of the China trade. The days when interest in China was confined to relatively peripheral groups in the Japanese business community were clearly over. Among Wang Hsiao-yun's visitors were such influential figures as Imasato Hiroki, president of Nihon Seikō; Iwasa Yoshizane, chairman of the board of directors of the Fuji Bank; Kawai Ryōichi, president of Komatsu Seisakujo; Kikawada Kazutaka, president of Tōkyō Denryoku; Kimura Ichizō, managing director of the Kansai Japan International Trade Promotion Association; Nakayama Sōhei, former president of the Industrial Bank of Japan; Suzuki Haruo, president of Shōwa Denkō and Yamashita Aiichi, managing director of Keizai Dōyūkai.[49]

(v) Straws in the wind

Despite the formation of the Parliamentarians League and the restlessness of the business community Satō continued to hold his ground. In the inner circles of the Liberal Democratic Party preoccupation with the succession struggle hampered serious analysis of international events. Yet the Foreign Ministry, too, remained convinced that the East Asian Cold War would continue indefinitely, that the 1970s would be, in most respects, much the same as the 1960s. The 1971 edition of the Foreign Ministry's Blue Book, *Waga Gaikō No Kinkyō*, for example, noted that while the People's Republic, in the aftermath of the Cultural Revolution, had consolidated its international position, and while the United States had demonstrated 'some flexibility' towards Peking, a marked improvement in bilateral relations would be 'difficult to anticipate', although the future moves of both powers would be 'worthy of note'. Even so, Sino-American differences over Taiwan and Indo-China seemed insurmountable.[50] On the other hand, the Foreign Ministry saw some prospects for improvement in Sino-Soviet relations. The international economic system was regarded as essentially 'calm'. There was no serious discussion of economic friction among the major non-Communist powers, although it was noted that American moves to enforce the Anti-Dumping Act and the emergence of a protectionist EEC closely linked to the Arab world and Black Africa had begun to cast 'a shadow' over the liberal, open structure of world trade set up after 1945. American-Japanese trade friction and the rise of anti-Japanese sentiments in the United States were not examined in any detail.

Japanese complacency regarding the stability of the international economic system was understandable. After all, the Nixon administration itself did not decide on the wages and prices freeze until 2 August 1971. It was only on 13 August that the President decided to impose the 10 per cent import surcharge, suspend the convertibility of dollars into gold and force foreign governments to revalue their currencies.[51]

The Satō Cabinet's thinking on the China question, however, had become so rigid that several signs of a possible shift in both United States and Chinese policies were ignored. On 28 March 1971, Ralf N. Kluff, a member of the State Department Policy Planning Council and chief research officer at the Brookings Institute, told Kamiya Fujii, Professor of International Relations at Keiō University and a close adviser of several Japanese Conservative leaders, that the Nixon administration was 'very interested' in China and that there was 'considerable room for flexibility in the question of policy towards Peking'. 'Both Japan and the United States would probably have to make their decisions on the China question during the course of 1971', Kluff remarked.[52] When Furui Yoshimi visited Peking for the Memorandum Trade talks around the same time, Chou En-lai warned him that China and the United States might soon begin serious negotiations, independently of Japan.[53] This important statement was promptly forgotten, although Nakasone Yasuhiro, at least, remembered it after the event. Finally, the visit of United States Secretary of Defence Melvin Laird to Japan and South Korea in mid-July 1971, on the eve of Nixon's China speech, might have altered sensitive observers to impending changes in Washington's Far Eastern policies. The traditional references to Free World solidarity against a nuclear-armed, expansionist China were notably absent from Laird's public statements, although there was some discussion of a Japanese anti-ballistic missile system to counter a hypothetical Chinese nuclear threat in the 1980s. Nor did Laird specifically describe the Japanese-American relationship as the keystone of United States East Asian strategy. Reference to Japan's maritime forces taking over some of the functions of the American Seventh Fleet was made in the context of remarks about the expansion of Soviet naval power, not containment of China. Laird's delegation, moreover, displayed an unusually ambivalent attitude towards the question of further increases in Japanese military strength. The Secretary of Defence declared himself eminently satisfied with the status quo. Japan's existing military power, he suggested, would be sufficient to fulfil its tasks under the Nixon Doctrine. Deputy Assistant Secretary of Defence Friedheim, on the other hand, gave the impression that the United States might have no objections if Japan wished to acquire an independent nuclear deterrent.[54] These discrepancies perhaps reflected policy debates deep inside the Pentagon. Yet it is difficult to know, in retrospect, whether Friedheim intended to encourage Japan to violate the nuclear non-proliferation treaty or merely to discover, by observing the reaction to his statements, whether the Japanese were in fact really committed to the agreement.

III   The 'Nixon Shocks' and their impact, August 1971

Whatever Chou En-lai and Kluff may have meant to convey, whatever may have been gleaned from Laird's attitude, the sudden shift in United States global strategy in the summer of 1971 caught the Japanese government completely off guard. Prime Minister Satō was given three minutes' advance notice of Nixon's speech on Sino-American relations. He received ten minutes' advance warning of the New Economic Policy. The 'Nixon Shocks' precipitated a major political crisis in Japan, calling into question the very basis of the Satō Cabinet's foreign policy, causing a radical, albeit erratic and spasmodic shift in Conservative thinking about the American alliance, aggravating the already intense factional struggles within the party, paralysing the Foreign Ministry, plunging the business community into confusion and setting in motion a chain of events which, while not of sufficient force to destroy the San Francisco system, further accelerated its prolonged decay, bringing into power a Prime Minister determined to take up once again the cautious Gaullist experiment abandoned by Ikeda in the winter of 1964–5.

Satō himself, in a magnificent display of self-control, publicly welcomed the Nixon speech as a new step towards peace in Asia. Japan, too, he proclaimed, had long hoped for a better climate of Sino-American relations. He himself had always wanted to visit China. The United States certainly had no intention of abandoning Taiwan. Washington's new economic policies were undoubtedly regrettable. Nevertheless, Japan's future could only be secured through a continued close relationship with the United States. The problems caused by America's relative decline could only be overcome by promoting a greater degree of co-operation among the advanced industrial nations of the West. The West, in fact, was entering an era of collective leadership in which Japan would have a vital role to play.[55] In reality, the Prime Minister's faith in the United States had been shattered. 'I have done everything they [the American administration] have asked', he told the Australian Labour leader Gough Whitlam, tears visibly welling in his eyes. 'They let me down.'[56]

Kishi, too, was shocked almost beyond belief. Foreign Minister Fukuda, recuperating in hospital from a gall-bladder operation, made no immediate comment. In subsequent weeks it became clear that Nixon's overtures to Peking had in no way altered his belief that Japan's future lay not with the Chinese mainland but with South Korea, Taiwan and the non-Communist nations of South-East Asia. The Americans might well be about to abandon Kennan's reinterpretation of the Greater East Asia Co-prosperity Sphere. Japan could not afford to do so. While Fukuda eventually edged, slowly and cautiously, towards acceptance of a limited Sino-Japanese *rapprochement*, he seemed under no circumstances prepared to abandon Taiwan. The continued existence of an 'independent' government on that large island was, he believed, a fundamental Japanese national interest.[57] Nevertheless, the mounting evidence that the *Pax Americana* had entered its last decades was not without its impact on Fukuda's world view. In the wake of the 'Nixon Shocks' this tough old hawk, for two decades a pillar of the Conservative Party's 'pro-American' right wing, began a process of spasmodic metamorphosis that led, in time, to his transformation into a reasonably plausible dove, hostile to Communism, no doubt, yet committed to *détente*, minimal defence spending, a non-provocative strategic posture and an Asian-Pacific orientated foreign policy.

Tanaka Kakuei, like Satō, was at first inclined to believe that Japan had no alternative but to follow the direction of American policy, wherever it might lead. In the wake of the 'Nixon Shocks' his public enthusiasm for the American alliance began to display a veritable religious fervour (a phenomenon not unrelated, it may be assumed, to his prime ministerial aspirations). The interests of Japan and the United States were identical, he assured the *Nihon Keizai Shimbun* on 18 August 1971. It was Japan's duty to cooperate wholeheartedly with President Nixon's policies. The Japanese economy was sufficiently dynamic to overcome the problems caused by the 10 per cent import surcharge. The United States and the nations of Western Europe might eventually go their separate ways. Japan and the United States, in contrast, were like 'a couple who cannot get divorced'.[58] As pressure on the yen mounted, Tanaka's position shifted. Even if the American alliance were to remain the corner-stone of Japanese policy, the facts of international life made it necessary to seek out new associations, open up new markets and diversify raw material supplies.[59] This required a far-reaching reassessment of Japan's relations with China, the Soviet Union, South-East Asia, the Middle East and Oceania. Tanaka's closest party colleague, Acting Foreign Minister Kimura Toshio, was more outspoken. The Sino-American *rapprochement*, no doubt, had contributed greatly to the easing of regional tensions.[60] Yet the world was an increasingly complex one. Nixon's New Economic Policy made it clear that the American alliance could no longer provide the only framework for Japanese diplomacy. The United States, while still immensely powerful, had entered an era of decline. The Soviet Union, the People's Republic of China and the nations of Western Europe were of growing importance. So, too, was the Third World. It was no longer prudent to adhere to the political and economic concepts of the past and act by force of habit. The time had come for Japan to move 'positively'.[61]

Hori Shigeru, secretary-general of the party, also saw the writing on the wall. The *Pax Americana* had run its course. The world had entered a critical transition period. While Japanese-American amity would remain important, other possibilities needed to be explored more fully:

> The pre-war world revolved around the central axis of the British Empire, whose naval power dominated the oceans. Towards the end of World War II the United States took over Great Britain's role. For almost a quarter of a century the world has revolved around an American axis. Japan was able to re-emerge from the depths of misery brought on by the defeat and achieve her present position by striving earnestly to adjust her policies to those of the American-dominated world order. However, the world has ceased to revolve around an American axis. The Americans themselves recognize this fact. The world, it is said, has entered a tri-polar era, or a five-polar era ... For Japan, friendship with the United States remains vital. It will be necessary to consolidate this friendship even further to promote our development and prosperity ... At the same time, I believe that it will be necessary for us to recognize, once again, that Japan is an Asian nation.[62]

The restoration of Sino-Japanese relations, Hori considered, should constitute the first step in the process of Japan's reintegration with Asia. At the same time, in order to allay the suspicions of its Asian neighbours, it would be essential for Japan to maintain the pacifist Constitution and keep military expenditure within reasonable limits.

Former Foreign Minister Ōhira Masayoshi shared these views. Japan, he lamented, had been totally outmanoeuvred by its mighty ally.[63] Nevertheless, the government should respond to the situation created by the Sino-American *rapprochement* and Nixon's New Economic Policy by

1) recognizing that relations with Washington had entered an era of 'competitive coexistence' and making conscious efforts to escape from the habit of dependence on the United States, in security as well as in other fields;[64]

2) reducing dependence on foreign trade and attaching more importance to the domestic market;[65]

3) moving as rapidly as possible to normalize relations with China.[66]

By the autumn of 1971 Ōhira had publicly announced his view that relations with the People's Republic could only be restored if Peking were recognized as the sole legal government of all Chinese territory, including Taiwan.[67]

Nakasone Yasuhiro, who had for some years feared that Washington might make approaches to Peking, without much regard for Japan's interests, avoided public comment on the new trends in American policy. Nakasone, at heart, was neither a great admirer of the West nor an Asianist, but a Japan-centred nationalist, profoundly racist in his outlook. Even so, his long-standing friendship with Matsumura Kenzō, together with the fact that Tagawa Seiichi, Matsumura's former private secretary, and Noda Takeo, chairman of the Foreign Affairs Research Council's China Committee, were both members of his faction, made it seem possible that he would at least attempt to persuade the Prime Minister to adopt a more positive stance towards the People's Republic. The wily Nakasone, however, did not show his hand for some time. The China problem was discussed for several hours over bottles of whisky at the faction's annual study camp at Nasu towards the end of July.

Nakasone's own uncertainties and divisions among his followers made consensus difficult to achieve. In the end, the participants went away from this delightful mountain resort with nothing more to show for their efforts than headaches, dry tongues and stiff shoulders.[68] It was not until late September 1971, a month before the United Nations voting on the China issue, that Nakasone finally declared that in his view Sino-Japanese relations could only be established on the premiss that Peking was the sole legal government of China and Taiwan an inalienable part of its territory.[69]

Sonoda Sunao, the leader of the other, smaller offshoot of the old Kōno faction, argued the case for an independent, omnidirectional diplomacy at a study meeting of his faction held on 5 August. The 'Nixon Shocks', he told his followers, made it more necessary than ever before to alter Japan's China policies, launch a major diplomatic offensive towards the Soviet Union and Eastern Europe and re-examine the Fourth Defence Plan.[70]

Former Foreign Minister Kōsaka Zentarō saw the world dividing into gigantic trans-national politico-economic blocs, with the United States dominating all North, Central and South America, the Soviet Union retaining its hegemony of Eastern Europe and the EEC linking up with Africa. China, despite its present weakness, would eventually emerge as the leader of an Asian bloc. Japan, he felt, was in no position to establish its own rival community. Kōsaka was uncertain whether it would be in Japan's best interests to remain within the American sphere of influence, to join hands with China, or to think in terms of a wider organization embracing East Asia, the United States, Australia and New Zealand. For the time being, the most prudent course was a diplomacy *à tous azimuts*.[71]

Miki Takeo, not unexpectedly, rejoiced at the news of the Sino-American *détente*. Nixon's New Economic Policy merely reinforced his long-held conviction that Japan needed to escape from its dependent relationship with the United States and establish its identity as an Asian-Pacific power, enjoying close and mutually beneficial ties with the Americas, the Socialist nations of the continent, non-Communist South-East Asia and Oceania. Japan, he declared, should not simply follow Washington's new policies, but respond creatively to the situation, making its own decisions on the basis of its own judgement. Japan's interests in Asia differed from those of the United States. Nor were they necessarily the same as those of China. Even so, there could be no possibility of developing a healthy relationship with the People's Republic, a matter of fundamental importance, unless Peking was recognized as the legitimate government of all Chinese territory, including Taiwan. It would also be unwise for Japan to think of exploiting Sino-Soviet rivalry in order to contain Russian influence in Asia. Good relations between Moscow and Peking were as essential as the Sino-American *détente* to peace in the Pacific. Any American or Japanese attempt to fish in these troubled waters could only lead to catastrophe.[72] These sentiments were shared by Fujiyama Aiichirō, Furui Yoshimi, Utsunomiya Tokuma and other members of the Conservative Party's 'pro-China' group. Fujiyama, perhaps, manifested somewhat less reluctance to consider alignment with the People's Republic against the Soviet Union. Utsunomiya, the pacific son of the famous pan-Asianist general, while strenuously denying any interest in opposing either Washington or

Moscow, maintained that the decline of America's military and economic hegemony made it essential to re-establish Japan's position as a fully independent Asian power, enjoying close links with the Chinese continent, the Korean peninsula and the lands of South-East Asia. China's conditions for normalization of relations were only reasonable. Taiwan was undoubtedly Chinese territory. Japan had no permanent interests in the island.[73]

Thus, one after another, the elder statesmen, faction leaders and intellectual luminaries of the Liberal Democratic Party revealed their thinking about the shape of the new world and Japan's place in it. In striking contrast to the situation at the time of French recognition of the People's Republic in 1964 there were, even at the highest levels, genuine changes of heart. In the months that followed the 'Nixon Shocks', as the international situation continued to develop, the new winds blew from once section of the party to another, through the factional headquarters, the clubs, the committee rooms and study centres, the expensive hotels, geisha houses, restaurants, bars and coffee shops frequented by Diet members and their staffs, eventually wafting out to trouble the peace of the faithful in the big cities, provincial towns and farming communities across the nation. Within twelve months Conservative Party thinking had undergone a transformation almost as complete as that which had taken place in the period 1945–52. Just prior to the 1969 general election a *Yomiuri Shimbun* survey had found 99 per cent of Liberal Democratic Party candidates in favour of maintaining the Japanese-American alliance. By December 1972, on the eve of the next general election, another *Yomiuri Shimbun* survey found 44.5 per cent of Conservative Party candidates supporting continuation of the security treaty and 47.8 per cent advocating abrogation or revision.[74]

The Foreign Ministry leadership, uncompromisingly 'Westernist' and anti-Communist in outlook, did its best to hold the line. In the business community, too, Mitsubishi, Mitsui and other corporations closely linked both with the dominant factional coalition and its policies, spoke disdainfully of the rush to catch the 'China bus'. Yet, to most businessmen, the 'Nixon Shocks' demonstrated the degree to which the Satō Cabinet had lost touch with global realities. It seemed clear that the American market would continue to contract. It also seemed clear that those same giant American corporations which regarded Japan with such hostility were now poised to enter the China market. 'The game is almost up', Nagano Shigeo commented ruefully after hearing Nixon's speech on China policy.[75] In the wake of the 'Nixon Shocks' the Japanese economy plunged into the worst recession since 1964–5. The iron and steel industry, chemicals and paper announced large-scale production cut-backs. New Japan Steel postponed the opening of its second Ōita furnace. Kawasaki Steel began re-exporting imported scrap iron to overseas producers. By September 1971 Japan's electric power consumption had dropped to a record low level. New export contracts simply ceased to be concluded. Investment in plant and equipment ground to a halt. By the end of August 1971 a *Nihon Keizai Shimbun* survey revealed that forty-eight major companies listed on the Tōkyō Stock Exchange, including such large concerns as New Japan Steel, Sumitomo Kinzoku, Tōray, Unitica and Mitsui Tōatsu, expected either to reduce their annual dividends or to pay no dividends at all. By the end of September over a hundred companies found themselves in this embarrassing situation. Government countermeasures, centring around a supplementary budget appropriating vast sums for public works, tax reductions and additional flotation of government bonds, did little to dispel the gloom.[76]

Quite clearly, this situation could not be permitted to go on forever. From the viewpoint of an increasing number of leading businessmen, the only solution was for Japan to make a complete break with the past and begin negotiating a sound trading relationship with the People's Republic before Washington had fully freed itself from the shackles of the Cold War. It can be assumed that these views were transmitted forcefully to the Liberal Democratic Party and other political organizations dependent on business support. The day after Nixon's China speech, New Japan Steel announced its withdrawal from the Japan-Republic of China and Japan-Republic of Korea co-operation committees. Within less than two months it had accepted Chou En-lai's 'Four Conditions'.[77] The next meeting of the Japan-Republic of China Co-operation Committee virtually collapsed through lack of attendance. In August, much to the irritation of Prime Minister Satō, Nagano Shigeo, together with Iwasa Yoshizane, Imasatō Hiroki, Kikawada Kazutaka and Nakayama Sōhei met with Wang Kuo-chuan, vice-president of the China-Japan Friendship Association.[78] By mid-September a delegation of influential Kansai businessmen, led by the presidents of Nisshō, the Kansai Keieisha Kyōkai, Kansai Keizai Dōyūkai and the Ōsaka Kōgyōkai had left for the People's Republic. A little over a month later a delegation of Tōkyō businessmen, led by Shoji Takeo, former president of Dōyūkai, and including Nagano Shigeo, was touring China. Both delegations issued statements accepting China's position on a wide variety of issues and stressing the need to restore bilateral relations promptly.[79]

The Japanese Opposition parties, for twenty years the most persistent advocates of *rapprochement* with China, found themselves jostled aside in the Conservative stampede. As their rivals thundered past in frantic efforts to outpace the Americans in the race for Peking, the Socialists and the Communists could at least comfort themselves with the thought that their theoretical analysis of the contradictions inherent in the San Francisco system had been vindicated by events. The Japan Socialist Party, the Democratic Socialists and the Kōmeitō were confident that Nixon's overtures to the People's Republic, Sino-Japanese reconciliation and the impending end of the Vietnam War would lay the foundations for a lasting peace in Asia. The Communists, sobered by the experience of their own bitter disputes with Peking, were unaffected by the general euphoria. The Sino-American *détente*, Fuwa Tetsuzō, chairman of the Japan Communist Party Secretariat, declared, was the inevitable outcome of the long-standing crisis of United States imperialism, exacerbated by the strains of the Vietnam War. While the decline of United States imperialism was a welcome development, it was by no means clear that the Sino-American *rapprochement* would lead to peace in Asia. Washington was merely reconstructing its global anti-Communist strategy. China, too, was a great power, with an erratic leadership, ambiguous policies and hegemonistic ambitions.[80]

IV The road to restoration of Sino-Japanese diplomatic ties, August 1971–December 1972

(i) The death of Matsumura Kenzō: funeral diplomacy and factional conflict

On 21 August 1971, a week after the announcement of Nixon's visit to China, Matsumura Kenzō passed away at the Kokuritsu Tokyo Dai-ichi Hospital after a lifetime devoted to the cause of Asian solidarity based on a Sino-Japanese *entente cordiale*. The death of so historic a figure, at so critical a moment, provided the Japanese government with a valuable opportunity to begin discussions with Peking. The Chinese, at this stage, were still prepared to negotiate with the Satō Cabinet. A Sino-Japanese *rapprochement* concluded in the autumn of 1971, before the Nixon visit to the People's Republic, might conceivably have given Japan greater freedom of manoeuvre in its subsequent relations with both Washington and Peking. As it was, Satō's vacillation and the frenzied efforts of almost all factions to exploit Matsumura's death to their own advantage revealed, in a most striking fashion, the depth of the schisms within the Conservative Party, the inability of the contending groups to trust each other fully, let alone co-operate to map out sensible policies in response to the rapidly evolving world situation.

On hearing the news of Matsumura's death, Chou En-lai at once decided to send Wang Kuo-chuan to Tōkyō for the funeral. As vice-president of the China-Japan Friendship Association, Wang was perhaps the highest-ranking official responsible for formulation of policy towards Japan. Chou's decision to dispatch him to Tōkyō was an indication of the Chinese Premier's personal respect for Matsumura. It was also a demonstration of his interest in establishing contact with a wider range of Japanese political leaders, exploring possibilities for the normalization of diplomatic ties, assessing the mood in Tōkyō in the wake of the 'Nixon Shocks' and gathering intelligence on the likely outcome of the Conservative Party succession struggle.

Chou's objectives were fully understood by Prime Minister Satō and his colleagues. On 24 August 1971 Nakasone met Satō and urged him to arrange a meeting with Wang. The Prime Minister, still dazed by the 'Nixon Shocks' and subjected to many different pressures, agreed to do so. Nakasone then visited Tagawa Seiichi, who was in charge of arrangements for the funeral, and tried to persuade him to introduce Wang to Satō. Tagawa hesitated. On 19 August he had been unexpectedly approached by Hori Shigeru. Hori, explaining that the sudden change in American policy had thrown the government into confusion, asked for advice. Tagawa had stated that in his view Japan had no alternative but to break decisively with American policy on China, refuse to co-sponsor the 'reverse important question' formula at the forthcoming session of the United Nations General Assembly, recognize the government of the People's Republic as the sole legal government of China and declare an end to the state of war with that country.[81] Hori had listened carefully, explaining that, in his opinion, it ought to be possible to begin talks with China while Satō was still in office. He himself, he said, would work actively on the Prime Minister to achieve this end. Hori also confided to Tagawa that he was personally opposed to the concept of an 'independent' Taiwan. Tagawa, who had never once spoken with Hori in his entire political life, had been uncertain how to interpret these overtures. Hori had a well-earned reputation for cunning. He was intensely loyal to Satō and doubtless wished to ensure that his leader retired from political life in a blaze of glory, arranging the succession according to his own lights. Tagawa had suspected that the secretary-general was merely seeking to prolong the life of the Cabinet by making some hollow gesture towards China to placate public opinion. Yet it was also possible, Tagawa considered, that the Prime Minister *had* undergone a genuine conversion, that he really *was* prepared to break with the United States and begin realistic negotiations with the People's Republic. Obviously, it would be unwise to pass over any opportunity to normalize relations with Peking. At the same time Tagawa realized that the 'China card', if played effectively, could be used to bring down the Satō structure, significantly alter the complexion of the Conservative Party and establish a coalition of forces led by men who shared, to some extent at least, his own view of Japan and its place in the world. This was a chance that might never come again. He therefore told Nakasone that there would be little point in setting up a Satō-Wang meeting unless the Prime Minister was prepared drastically to overhaul Japan's China policy. The Sino-American *rapprochement*, after all, had only been made possible by Nixon's fundamental re-examination of United States East Asian strategy. Tagawa's suspicion that Satō was merely playing to the gallery deepened when he returned from his meeting with Nakasone to discover that Chief Cabinet Secretary Takeshita had already told the press that the Prime Minister wished to meet Wang and that he (Tagawa) had agreed to act as intermediary.[82]

Tagawa's irritation with the attitude of Satō and his henchmen mounted during the funeral watch next evening. Hori Shigeru, after the ritual burning of incense, edged towards Tagawa and presented him with the Prime Minister's visiting card, urging him to pass it on to Wang. Chief Cabinet Secretary Takeshita, too, crept up and whispered that Satō wished to convey his best regards to Wang. As the incense drifted over the altar Tagawa found it difficult to suppress the feeling that these representatives of the dominant 'pro-American' factions in the party, who had so consistently rejected Matsumura during his lifetime, had come scurrying to his corpse simply because of changes in Washington's global strategy, not out of any genuine desire to embrace the independent policies advocated by the old pan-Asianist. The Prime Minister's interest in meeting Wang, the presence of Hori and Takeshita at the vigil, thus symbolized not a new departure but Japan's continued, humiliating servitude to the United States. It was during the course of this long evening, filled with memories of past struggles, that Tagawa finally decided that he *would* play the 'China card', that he would *not* go out of his way to introduce the Prime Minister to Chou En-lai's personal representative. Instead, he would arrange a meeting between Wang and Satō's arch-enemy, Miki Takeo, whose position on China had been clear for many years and who was once again emerging as a serious contender for the party presidency.[83]

The funeral service itself, held at the great Buddhist temple of Tsukiji No Honganji on the afternoon of 26 August, brought into sharp focus the shifting attitudes of the Japanese establishment and the fierce struggles among its constituent groups. Before the altar, decorated with white chrysanthemums, stood two handsome flower arrangements presented by Their Imperial Majesties the Emperor and Empress. On the left was a bouquet presented by Prime Minister Satō, on the right an arrangement dispatched by Chou En-lai. The 6,000 mourners included the leaders of all Japan's major political parties, representatives from the Ministry of International Trade and Industry, the Ministry of Agriculture and Fisheries, the Ministry of Education, prominent members of the business community, academics and personalities from the mass media. Representatives from the Foreign Ministry, whose dominant factions had fought so long and so hard against the views propounded by Matsumura and his circle, were conspicuous by their absence.[84]

Tagawa and Furui had spent much of the morning planning the seating so that the Prime Minister would be presented with as little opportunity of meeting Wang as possible. Satō was placed on the extreme right of the altar, with the Deputy Speaker of the House of Representatives, Arafune Seijirō, on his left. Wang was seated securely between the President of the House of Councillors, Kōno Kenzō and Furui himself. To the left of Furui sat old Okazaki Kaheita, now the most senior surviving Conservative pan-Asianist, and Chao Tsu-jui, from the China Memorandum Trade Office in Ebisu. In the next row, from right to left, sat Miki Takeo, Fujiyama Aiichirō, Wang Hsiao-lan and Chiang P'ei-kuei, also from the China Memorandum Trade Office. Tagawa and Furui had decided that if Wang arrived at the temple before the service began they should have him wait in a side room so that he could avoid meeting the Prime Minister. If Wang's party arrived after Satō was already seated they should endeavour not to pass in front of him. Yet after they had actually arrived at Tsukiji No Honganji, Furui came to the conclusion that the best way to avoid the Prime Minister would be to have Wang go directly to his seat before Satō appeared.

All this scheming came to nought. Wang himself, who had received careful instructions from Chou En-lai, had different plans. The Chinese official had scarcely taken his seat when Satō walked in. Wang, tall and powerfully built, dressed in a dark, high-collared Chinese jacket, immediately rose to his feet and extended his hand. The Japanese Prime Minister walked past Arafune and Kōno, his fleshy face expressionless, his lips barely moving. He took the proffered hand, mumbled some indistinct greeting, then returned to his seat, gazing fixedly at Matsumura's photograph throughout the rest of the service. Furui, Tagawa, Kōno, Okazaki and the other 'pro-Peking' Conservatives, their earlier efforts to prevent a meeting between Wang and Satō forgotten, watched the scene with a certain grim satisfaction. The most 'pro-American', 'anti-Chinese' Prime Minister in Japan's history had at last been forced to demonstrate his enthusiasm for normalizing Sino-Japanese relations. Yet the fact that this change of heart had come, not spontaneously, from within, but as a result of the new winds blowing from Washington, was a bitter pill to swallow.[85]

The service went on. The priests chanted their sutras. Arafune and Kōno delivered the orations, vowing to continue Matsumura's work. A message of condolence from Chou En-lai was read. The representatives of the Matsumura family, followed by Prime Minister Satō, Arafune, Kōno and Wang, one after the other, rose from their places, walked to the altar, burned incense, bowed, then paused for a moment in silent prayer. As the close family friends and the Chinese representatives were preparing to proceed to the 'leave-taking ceremony' (*kokubetsushiki*), Satō again approached Wang, took him by the hand, asked that his regards be conveyed to Chou En-lai, then walked out into the stifling summer heat. Chief Cabinet Secretary Takeshita again urged Tagawa to arrange a meeting between Wang and the Prime Minister. Tagawa, exhausted by the events of the past few days and disgusted by what he saw as an orgy of hypocrisy, attempted to put him off by observing testily that Sato had already met Wang twice. Outside, much to the alarm of the assembled politicians and security police, Akao Bin, leader of the ultra-rightist Great Japan Patriotic Party, the lifelong, implacable enemy of Chinese Communism, advocate of a close alliance between Japan, South Korea and the Kuomintang, came forward surrounded by a group of supporters, bowing low and sobbing uncontrollably. He, too, had decided to swim with the tide.[86]

The dilemmas that had confronted Japanese governments since the Meiji Restoration and the principles that had determined the nation's foreign policy for over a thousand years before the encounter with the Imperial West had been dramatized in the events of a single afternoon.

(ii)   *Japan's co-sponsorship of the United States 'reverse important question formula' at the United Nations General Assembly, 26 October 1971*

In the weeks after Matsumura Kenzō's funeral the question of Japan's stand on China and Taiwan at the forthcoming meeting of the United Nations General Assembly began to tear the Liberal Democratic Party apart.

Some time in January 1971, at a time when Nixon's secret approaches to Peking were already under way, United States officials had suggested to the Japanese Foreign Ministry that if the rising support for Peking's entry into the world body made the 'important question' formula inoperable, the two allies should co-sponsor a new 'reverse important question' resolution designed to preserve a seat for Taiwan. In view of the fact that the People's Republic was uncompromisingly opposed to the concept of 'two Chinas' and would not take its place in the United Nations unless Chiang Kai-shek's representatives were expelled, this strategy was expected to achieve the same result as the 'important question' formula employed by the United States since December 1961.[87] The Japanese government was astonished when, in the wake of the 'Nixon Shocks', Washington again requested that it co-sponsor this resolution. Satō, stung by Nixon's duplicity, was uncertain what course to adopt. In the Satō faction opinion was divided, with Hori Shigeru, Kimura Toshio and Kuno Chūji arguing forcefully against the policy of co-operating with the United States. The hard core of the Liberal Democratic Party's 'old right', centring around Kaya Okinori and Aikawa Shōroku, recommended continued support for Washington's efforts to preserve the international status of Taiwan. Akagi Munenori, Kōsaka Zentarō, Maeo

Shigesaburō and Nakasone Yasuhiro, in contrast, all argued that Japan should adopt an independent stance and decline to co-sponsor the United States resolution.[88] In the Foreign Ministry, the anti-Communist Westernists who dominated the upper echelons of power, led by Hōgen Shinsaku, found themselves opposed by a host of lesser officials, including such rising stars as Hashimoto Hiroshi, director of the China Division.[89]

On 1 September, at Satō's request, Hori Shigeru met Tagawa Seiichi and asked for advice. Tagawa attempted to persuade the secretary-general that it would not be in Japan's best interests to support the United States. Hori, stressing that he spoke with the Prime Minister's 'understanding', reiterated his personal view that the government of the People's Republic was the only legal government of China, that Taiwan was an indivisible part of Chinese territory and that 'independence' for the island would sow the seeds of future tragedy. Japan, he thought, would probably *not* co-sponsor the American resolution at the United Nations General Assembly. He himself would like to go to Peking and discuss these matters freely with the Chinese leadership. The secretary-general then requested Tagawa to explain his position to the Chinese side. Tagawa, however, again decided to make no approaches to Peking until Satō's intentions had become more clear.[90] Tagawa's suspicions were not altogether unreasonable both in view of Satō's past record and Hori's reputation as an unscrupulous manipulator. Yet it seems probable that Hori's representation of Satō's state of mind, on this occasion, was both honest and accurate. The Prime Minister was, in fact, gradually inclining towards the view that it would be unwise to co-sponsor the American resolution. Later in the month, when Foreign Minister Fukuda visited Washington for the annual meeting of the United States-Japan Joint Committee on Trade and Economic Affairs, he was repeatedly telephoned to ensure that he did not commit Japan to support the American position.[91] When Hori heard that United States Secretary of State William Rogers had earnestly requested Fukuda to promise such support, he, too, contacted the Foreign Minister directly, explaining that such a decision could only be made by Satō himself.[92] It seems unlikely that Hori would have intervened in this way without the Prime Minister's 'understanding'.

In the weeks that followed, the United States exerted extreme pressure on the Japanese government. American officials argued that Japan's failure to give full support to the United States would inevitably affect the attitudes of Australia and New Zealand, hastening the decline of the entire anti-Communist alliance system in Asia.[93] It can also be assumed that Washington intimated that any deviation from the traditional Japanese policy of full support for the United States might have further deleterious effects on bilateral trade relations. The return of Okinawa, too, had not yet been finalized.

Thus, on 26 October 1971, contrary to Hori's predictions, Japan joined the United States in co-sponsoring the new 'reverse important question' formula. The defeat of the American resolution and China's subsequent entry into the United Nations now made restoration of Sino-Japanese relations under the Satō Cabinet virtually impossible.

(iii)   Satō's China policy and the international currency realignments

Satō's reluctance to break with the United States on China was probably also linked to Japan's delicate position in the international currency struggles touched off by Nixon's New Economic Policy. The Japanese government was anxious, above all else, to avoid a large-scale upward revaluation of the yen. Japan had at first aligned its policies closely with those of France, which, unlike West Germany, had been reluctant to allow its currency to float against the dollar.[94] On 28 August, with the collapse of the French position, Japan, too, had adopted a floating rate. Opinion in Japanese government and business cirlces had then split. Some argued that co-operation with the United States was necessary in order to prevent the emergence of an anti-Japanese European coalition. Others recommended joint action with the European powers in order to persuade the United States to remove the 10 per cent import surcharge and desist from settling its internal problems at the expense of its allies. While the record is not yet clear, it would seem that a preoccupation with salvaging the North American market, a belief that the prospects for Japanese trade with Europe were limited, tough American bargaining tactics and lack of information about policy debates in Washington gradually persuaded Japan to align its stance on parity adjustment with that of the United States.[95] Even so, the Japanese remained uneasy. At the Japan-United States Businessmen's Conference held in Hawaii in late August the Americans had told their Japanese counterparts that Washington was thinking in terms of a 15–25 per cent upward revaluation of the yen. Tanaka Kakuei had been mortified, declaring that even 10 per cent would be disastrous.[96] Later in the year United States Secretary for the Treasury John Connally had terrorized the Japanese Cabinet with his talk of a 27–28 per cent upward revaluation.[97] In these circumstances, Prime Minister Satō may have felt he could soften the blow at the Group of Ten meeting in Rome in December by co-operating wholeheartedly with Washington at the United Nations in October. If this was his strategy it failed miserably. At the general adjustment of parities at Rome in November-December 1971 the yen was revalued by 17.9 per cent, rather more than most other delegates had expected.[98] If Satō was attempting to link China policy and currency issues he would probably have got a better bargain in both areas had he broken with the United States decisively in New York and aligned Japan more closely with the European powers at Rome. In the autumn of 1971 serious conflicts had developed within the Nixon administration on the wisdom of the New Economic Policy and the indefinite currency float. Connally and his supporters had argued for continuation of a tough economic nationalist line. Kissinger, Burns and others contended that the impact of the import surcharge and the international monetary confusion were jeopardizing vital United States security concerns, accelerating the trend towards Gaullism in Europe and further eroding support for the American alliance in Japan.[99] Had Japan, at this vital juncture, demonstrated more independence from the United States, it might have been able to normalize relations with China on very favourable terms, and substantially improve its bargaining position both on international currency issues and a wide range of trade questions.

(iv)   The 'Hori Letter', October–November 1971

Had Chou En-lai been made aware of the international and domestic pressures on the Satō Cabinet, Peking might, conceivably, have forgiven Japan's continuing support for American policies at the United Nations. It was Satō's unbending attitude on Taiwan, as much as the voting at New York, that finally made Sino-Japanese reconciliation impossible during his tenure in office. Ironically, the last nail in the coffin was driven home by Hori Shigeru. Some time towards the middle of October, Hori, in close consultation with Satō and Fukuda, wrote a secret letter to Chou En-lai setting out Japan's proposals for establishment of diplomatic ties. This letter almost certainly reflected the thinking of the Prime Minister and the Foreign Minister rather than that of Hori himself. Hori, however, was prepared to take responsibility should the initiative collapse and generate unfavourable publicity. In this way neither Satō nor Fukuda would be damaged. Hori's letter fell short of recognizing the People's Republic as the sole legal government of China. It referred to Taiwan merely as a 'territory of the Chinese people', thus leaving the way open for some kind of internationally recognized separate existence for the island. The letter was delivered to Peking by the Governor of Tōkyō, Dr Minobe Ryōkichi, sometime early in November. Chou En-lai rejected the overture out of hand. Sino-Japanese relations, he insisted, could never be restored on these terms.[100]

(v)   The impact of China's entry into the United Nations, October–December 1971

China's entry into the United Nations, together with the approach of the Nixon visit to Peking, exacerbated the conflicts within the Liberal Democratic Party and accelerated the defection of the business community from support for the Cabinet. Shortly before the voting at the United Nations Fujiyama Aiichirō, chairman of the Parliamentarians League for the Restoration of Ties with China, had led a delegation of five Liberal Democrats, six Socialists, three Democratic Socialists and four members of the Kōmeitō to Peking. The joint communiqué issued at the end of their visit had recognized the People's Republic as the only legal government of all China, reaffirmed that Taiwan was an indivisible part of its territory, urged that the Japan-Republic of China Co-operation Committee be disbanded, that Peking represent China at the United Nations and that United States military power be completely withdrawn from the Far East. On his return to Tōkyō the former Foreign Minister, as chairman of the league, issued a statement castigating Japan's support for the American 'reverse important question' resolution as 'going against the current of the age', and 'forming an obstacle to the restoration of Sino-Japanese relations'.[101] On 26 October, when the Opposition parties proposed a motion of no confidence in Foreign Minister Fukuda, Fujiyama and twelve other Conservative supporters absented themselves from the Diet. They repeated this performance on 23 December when the Opposition proposed a motion of no confidence in the Prime Minister. By the end of the year the Party Discipline Committee, an organ dominated by the extreme anti-Communist right wing, had found Fujiyama guilty of a breach of party discipline and stripped him of all offices. This immediately provoked a strong reaction from the Afro-Asian Problems Study Association and other forces sympathetic to China.[102] The struggle raged furiously through the party organs during the first half of 1972 until it was swept aside by other, greater issues.

The 'anti-China' groups within the party faced an increasingly difficult battle. On 16 December 1971 Uemura Kōgorō, who had supported co-sponsorship of the 'reverse important question' proposal, announced that 'once China has been admitted to the United Nations, we must expect an early resumption of normal relations.'[103] Around the same time, two of the four major trading companies, Itō-Chū and Marubeni Iida, accepted Chou En-lai's Four Conditions and withdrew from the Japan-Republic of China Co-operation Committee. Mitsubishi Shōji and Mitsui Bussan, which had closer links with Taipei and Seoul, did not immediately follow suit. Both companies, while welcoming China's entry into the United Nations, kept up their membership of the Japan-Republic of China committee, although both began to send more junior board members and executives to its meetings. Moreover, Mitsubishi, immediately after the voting at the United Nations, began to make secret plans to send a mission to the People's Republic.[104]

(vi)   *The San Clemente talks, January 1972*

Early in January 1972 Prime Minister Satō flew to the United States for talks with President Nixon prior to the American leader's visit to China. The Satō-Nixon talks at San Clemente, focusing on China, Vietnam and the Okinawan issue, were conducted in an atmosphere of mutual mistrust.* The Japanese Prime Minister emerged from his two days of discussions with no clear picture of the direction in which American policy was moving. The place of the Japanese-American relationship in future United States regional strategy seemed obscure. The United States, he was given to understand, intended to develop relations with China but maintain its commitments to Taiwan. At the same time, the Taiwan and Korean clauses of the 1969 Satō-Nixon Joint Communiqué seemed to have lapsed.[106] Satō found it difficult to suppress the suspicion that Nixon's principal objective in holding the talks had been to forestall independent Japanese initiatives on China. He was probably right. Increasingly, the 'pro-American' right wing of the Liberal Democratic Party began to sense that the San Francisco system had entered its last days. Shortly after the Prime Minister's return to Tōkyō, Ushiba Nobuhiko, Japan's ambassador to the

---

*   On the eve of the discussions the American commentator Jack Anderson had published what was claimed to be the text of secret telegrams from Armin Meyer, the United States ambassador in Tōkyō, to the President, noting that Satō's long-standing 'pro-American' attitudes had been shaken by the events of the previous year, that the Prime Minister was considering independent approaches to China, that anti-American sentiment was growing within the Japanese establishment and that the leadership might soon decide to develop an autonomous nuclear *force de frappe*.[105]

United States, warned that Japanese–American differences on China policy might eventually cause the Asian security structure to collapse.[107] Satō, too, began to speak pessimistically of the long-term future of Japanese-American relations.[108]

(vii)   The Nixon visit to Peking, February 1972

President Nixon and his party arrived in Peking on 21 February 1972. The details of his conversations with Mao Tse-tung and Chou En-lai, had they been known at the time, would have confirmed the Japanese Prime Minister's worst fears.

'What brings us together', Nixon told the Chinese leaders at their first meeting, 'is a recognition of a new situation in the world and a recognition on our part that what is important is not a nation's internal political philosophy. What is important is its policy towards the rest of the world and towards us.' The interests of the United States and China, the American President declared, overlapped in two critical areas. Both were concerned about the policies of the Soviet Union. Both were vitally interested in the future of Japan. Compared with these issues, Korea, Taiwan and Indochina were of secondary importance. 'We must ask ourselves – again in the confines of this room – why the Soviets have more forces on the border facing you than they do on the border facing Western Europe? We must ask ourselves, what is the future of Japan? Is it better – and here I know we have disagreements – from China's standpoint for Japan to be neutral and totally defenceless, or is it better for Japan to have some mutual defence relations with the United States?' The Japanese-American security treaty, Nixon suggested obliquely, should not be viewed simply in a Cold War context. 'If we had no defence arrangement with Japan', he pursued, 'we would have no influence where they were concerned ... If the United States is gone from Asia, gone from Japan ... our protests, no matter how loud, would be like firing an empty cannon. We would have no effect, because thousands of miles away is just too far to be heard.'[109] To the Chinese leaders it must have seemed as if the wheel had turned full circle, that the United States, defeated, exhausted and over-extended, had at last returned to Roosevelt's concept of the Far Eastern balance of power, that Nixon and Kissinger had journeyed to Peking to invite the People's Republic to participate, however indirectly, in the containment of both the Soviet Union and Japan.

Although the substance of these talks was unknown in Tōkyō, Nixon's speech at the banquet given in his honour on 27 February and the text of the Shanghai Communiqué aroused the deepest anxieties among the 'pro-American' right wing of the Liberal Democratic Party. At the banquet, both Nixon and Chou painted a glowing picture of the future of the Sino-American relationship. The United States and China agreed that 'neither should seek hegemony in the Asian-Pacific region and each is opposed to the efforts by any other country or group of countries to establish such hegemony'.[110] There was no suggestion that the American-Japanese security treaty constituted the principal axis of Washington's Far Eastern policy. The communiqué merely observed, in one short sentence, that 'the United States places the highest value on its friendly relations with Japan and will continue to develop the existing close bonds'.[111] The American President did not specifically endorse

China's strong denunciation of 'Japanese militarism'. Nor did he specifically refute it. Contrary to all expectations, the United States came close to accepting, in principle, the Chinese position on Taiwan. The United States, Nixon declared, intended eventually to withdraw all its bases and military installations from this island.[112] No mention was made of Washington's defence treaty with the Chinese Nationalists. The Taiwan question, Nixon agreed, was a matter to be settled by the Chinese people themselves. There was also a certain parallelism between the American and Chinese positions on Korea. Both sides stressed their support for their respective allies on the peninsula. Both expressed interest in a relaxation of tensions. Yet neither Nixon nor Chou En-lai, it seemed, felt that the Soviet Union or Japan had any legitimate interest in the future political evolution of the region. Japan's special concerns in the peninsula, enunciated in the 1969 Satō-Nixon Joint Communiqué, were not mentioned. It was also difficult for observers to dismiss the possibility that the United States and China had engaged in wide-ranging, albeit inconclusive, discussions about future spheres of influence in South-East Asia.

Satō was utterly bewildered. The press conference held after release of the Shanghai Communiqué found him angry, disorientated, almost unable to speak. 'He [Nixon] called this a major event of the century', he mumbled incoherently, then walked out of the room.[113] The visit of United States Assistant Secretary of State Marshall Green to Tōkyō towards the end of the month did nothing to assuage the Japanese Prime Minister's growing indignation. Satō listened, stonily, without comment, to Green's assurances that the United States and China had made no secret agreements, that Washington's commitment to Taiwan remained as firm as ever, that further development of relations with the People's Republic would take time, etc.[114] The Foreign Ministry complained that the United States had kept Japan 'uninformed' of the substance of Nixon's talks in Peking. Green had provided no convincing explanation of America's current policies towards the People's Republic, the Soviet Union or Taiwan. Nor had Kissinger been any more forthcoming when contacted by Ambassador Ushiba early in March.[115]

It was abundantly clear, however, that Washington's attitude towards Japan was undergoing further changes. On 23 March 1972 Foreign Minister Fukuda complained that the United States, in yet another astonishing reversal of policy, had begun to take an ambiguous and evasive attitude towards Japan's claim to the Tiaoyu (Senkaku) islands, a small, uninhabited group lying on the continental shelf between the Ryūkyūs and Taiwan.[116] In 1970, after the discovery of oil in the region, the islands had become the objects of a serious dispute between Tōkyō and Taipei. The People's Republic, too, had staked a claim to the group.[117] On 24 March Prime Minister Satō also voiced his concern at the change in American policy.[118] The new American stand, the Japanese government doubtless suspected, gave some indication of the kind of agreements Nixon, Mao and Chou had secretly concluded in Peking.

(viii)   Conservative Party factional-policy conflict and the emergence of the Tanaka Cabinet, February–July 1972

In the wake of the Nixon visit to China the Japanese Conservatives threw themselves with renewed vigour into the party succession struggle. The outcome of this conflict, and the compromises made during its course, were to have an important impact on Japan's international orientation for several years.

In 1971 it had been generally assumed that Satō intended to transfer the reins of power to Fukuda after his retirement. Tanaka Kakuei, no doubt, was a strong candidate for party leadership. Yet the Prime Minister's long association with Fukuda, the Foreign Minister's friendship with his brother Kishi, the similarity of their views on the American alliance, China policy, Korea and South-East Asia, made it seem probable that Satō would, at the appropriate moment, persuade Tanaka to withdraw his candidacy. Tanaka, as a loyal faction member, would have no alternative but to comply with this request, whatever his personal ambitions.

Confident of the Prime Minister's support, Fukuda remained for some months aloof from the unfolding struggle, cultivating an air of dignified, responsible statesmanship. 'Above the faction is the party and beyond the party is the state', he told those of his supporters who were anxious lest his apparent unwillingness to throw down the gauntlet and enter the fray eventually cost him the prime ministership.[119] He would, he said, base his strategy on the concept of *ben sei shuku shuku*, 'the advance of mounted soldiers with a quiet sound of whipping', maintaining his close ties with the Prime Minister, consolidating his large faction and cultivating support in the party organs and committees.[120] Despite the restlessness of his followers, the Foreign Minister did not deviate from this strategy for some time. Shortly after the San Clemente Conference Tanaka launched a major offensive against Fukuda's forces in the House of Councillors, already demoralized by the collapse of the 'Shigemune Kingdom' in the summer of 1971.[121] By the end of February it was rumoured that he had won over at least half the members of the Seifū Club, the principal grouping of the dominant coalition in the Upper House.[122] Fukuda was still reluctant to move when Tanaka began regular meetings with Ōhira, Miki and Nakasone, or when it became increasingly clear that his rivals were making concerted efforts to forge alliances with minor groups. 'Fukuda has entrenched himself in his castle', knowledgeable people remarked. 'Tanaka has raised an army and is trying to entice him into field operations, which are Tanaka's strongest point. Fukuda, therefore, is cautious about taking action.'[123]

There were several precedents for a party leader using his influence at the last moment to determine the succession in accordance with his own wishes. Fukuda's hopes, however, slowly turned to ashes. During the first half of 1972 the Prime Minister's control over the party, and even over his own faction, weakened by the events of the previous year, went into deeper decline. On 22 February 1972, the day after Nixon's arrival in Peking, the four Opposition parties, encouraged by divisions among the Liberal Democrats, forced the government to revise the estimates for the Fourth Defence Plan, after three weeks of heated debate.[124] The shock of this unprecedented defeat had scarcely subsided when the Socialist Party released the text of three secret Foreign Ministry telegrams, revealing that the government had been obliged to pay the United States rather more than the agreed sum for the purchase of assets, removal of nuclear weapons and other expenses connected with the reversion of Okinawa.[125] At the same time the Liberal Democratic Party's electoral fortunes continued to deteriorate. Popular support for the Satō Cabinet, which had slipped steadily during 1971, plummeted to levels comparable to those of the Kishi Cabinet at the height of the 1960 troubles.[126] In the gubernatorial elections for Fukushima prefecture, held in April, the party decided it had no alternative but to withdraw official recognition from its candidate in order to give him a sporting chance.[127]

It was against this background that the Satō faction, for many years the largest, wealthiest and most powerful in the party, began to disintegrate. By the spring of 1972 the tension between Tanaka Kakuei's supporters and the group sympathetic to Fukuda had reached explosive levels. It had by now become clear that Tanaka Kakuei was his own man, with his own ambitions, and would not necessarily bow to the Prime Minister's wishes. On 14 April Kimura Toshio, leader of the pro-Tanaka forces in the Satō camp, hosted a meeting at a Tōkyō restaurant to lay the groundwork for the establishment of a new faction.[128] Three weeks later, at another, larger meeting organized by Kimura, two-thirds of the Satō faction, altogether eighty-one members of both Houses, declared their allegiance to Tanaka.[129]

The emergence of a quasi-independent Tanaka faction* proved to be a watershed in party history. The leaders of the Fukuda faction, thoroughly alarmed, visited the Prime Minister and requested him to declare publicly his support for their candidate. Satō assured them that he would not permit any member of his faction to act contrary to his wishes.[130] Kimura was virtually expelled from the Satō faction and disciplinary action was taken against some other rebellious followers. Yet the horse had already bolted. In retrospect, it is difficult to suppress the suspicion that the Prime Minister's own views on the succession had changed. Despite his close relationship with Yoshida, Satō had never been an enthusiast for the long-term development of Sino-Japanese relations. If Japan had any permanent interests, he felt, they lay in North America, Korea, Taiwan, South-East Asia and Oceania. Yet it now seemed clear that the country could face a new and, possibly, highly dangerous situation unless relations with Peking were established as rapidly as possible. It was also evident that ties with the People's Republic could not be normalized under a Fukuda cabinet. The Prime Minister's recognition of this fact may, perhaps, explain why he appears to have given his former comrade-in-arms little more than formal support in the crucial period before the Liberal Democratic Party presidential elections. During the last months of his political life, as the special relationship with the United States slowly crumbled, Satō's vision of Japan's future seemed to undergo a significant change. He began to act more and more like Yoshida's disciple, less and less like Kishi's brother.

Aware, perhaps, that the Prime Minister's attitude had shifted, Fukuda went over

---

*   The faction was formally established on 12 September 1972, two months after Tanaka's election as Prime Minister.

to the offensive. It was too late. Tanaka Kakuei and his forces had already captured the high ground. In the Fukuda faction there was desultory talk of an alliance with Miki, and some overtures were made, but they came to nothing. Approaches were also made to Nakasone. The smaller, neutral factions were already leaning heavily towards the Tanaka camp. The Shiina (former Kawashima) faction had a long-standing feud with Fukuda. Funada Naka, too, mistrusted the Foreign Minister, despite the similarity of their views on many policy issues. Sonoda was sympathetic but his faction had been infiltrated by Tanaka supporters and he was uncertain of its loyalty. The Ishii and Mizuta factions, too, were split.[131] Throughout the early summer of 1972 the Foreign Minister's support in the House of Councillors continued to evaporate. By the beginning of June the Tanaka, Ōhira and Miki forces in the Upper House appeared to have the advantage. On 20 June Tanaka's position was further strengthened when Nakasone decided to withdraw from the race and support the candidacy of the energetic Minister for International Trade and Industry.

The final blow to Fukuda's hopes was delivered by the secret agreement between Tanaka, Ōhira and Miki to co-ordinate their strategies in the party presidential elections. Liberal Democratic Party regulations required that the successful candidate for party president either win a clear-cut majority in the first ballot, or, if this proved to be impossible, win a majority in the second, having gained first or second place in the initial, indecisive ballot. Tanaka, Ōhira and Miki agreed that if any of them gained first or second place, alongside Fukuda, in a first, indecisive election, the two losers would mobilize their factions to support their more successful colleague at the next ballot. If, on the other hand, two of their number gained first and second place in an initial, indecisive ballot, they would run against each other in the second.

The three anti-Fukuda candidates also agreed to co-operate closely on China policy after the elections, whatever the outcome. 'Recognizing that the government of the People's Republic of China is the sole legitimate government of China', the secret agreement stated in part, 'we will enter into negotiations with this government with a view to concluding a peace treaty.'[132]

On 5 July 1972, at a special Liberal Democratic Party Conference attended by all Conservative members of the House of Representatives and the House of Councillors, and by representatives of the party's prefectural federations, Tanaka Kakuei defeated Fukuda Takeo 156 to 150 on the first ballot. Ōhira received 101 votes, Miki 69. At the second ballot, Tanaka, supported by the Ōhira, Miki and Nakasone factions, and by several smaller groups, received 282 votes, Fukuda 190. It was thus that this rough-hewn son of a Niigata farmer, a self-made construction millionaire who had hacked his way up through the Conservative establishment by virtue of his native cunning, organizing ability and sheer force of personality, became president of the Liberal Democratic Party and Prime Minister of Japan. He at once proceeded to set up a Cabinet dominated almost completely by his own followers and the factions that had supported his election. Miki Takeo was appointed Deputy Prime Minister. Ōhira Masayoshi took over the Foreign Ministry, Nakasone Yasuhiro became Minister for International Trade and Industry. Altogether the Tanaka faction received six Cabinet posts, the Ōhira faction four, Nakasone's supporters two, Miki, Mizuta and Shiina one each. Tagawa Seiichi's hopes had been realized. Leadership of the party had passed from the 'pro-American' Westernists to nationalists sympathetic to the idea of *rapprochement* with Peking.

Despite efforts at mediation by party elders and business leaders Fukuda refused to join the new Cabinet. In the end his long-time associate Masuhara Keikichi, a man of pacific views, was appointed director-general of the Defence Agency. The mighty Fukuda faction, conscious, like de Gaulle after the collapse of France, that it had lost a battle, not a war, retired from the field to consolidate its unity, repair its finances, rethink its policies and wait for a new opportunity to advance. Within a few weeks, its ranks swollen by Hori's followers and Sonoda's group, it had become the largest single faction in the party.[133]

(ix)   *Prime Minister Tanaka prepares to normalize relations with China, July–October 1972*

Immediately after the formation of the Cabinet, Tanaka, strongly supported by his colleagues, began preparations to establish ties with Peking. There can be no doubt that the new Prime Minister, while relatively inexperienced in foreign affairs, and not previously identified with the 'pro-China' lobby, was fully committed to the enterprise. 'As soon as I become Prime Minister I'll go to China', he had told Fujiyama Aiichirō in mid-March, shortly before the former Foreign Minister had left for Peking to brief Chou En-lai on the likely outcome of the succession struggle.[134] 'I don't know anything about diplomacy, Ōhira', he told his Foreign Minister after the elections. 'I'll leave all that to you. But I'll take full responsibility [for whatever you decide to do].'[135]

Tanaka, unlike Satō, was quite prepared to accept the government of the People's Republic as the sole legitimate government of China and recognize Taiwan as part of its territory. His eagerness to settle the China problem quickly was probably not unrelated to the continued rapid growth of protectionist sentiment in the United States. By the summer of 1972 it had become evident that Nixon's New Economic Policy and the currency adjustments of the previous year would neither restore the health of the American economy nor redress the imbalance in bilateral trade. At the Shimoda Conference (8–11 June), during Kissinger's visit (9–12 June) and at the Japan-United States Businessmen's Conference (15–17 June) Japan was repeatedly warned that Washington expected the trade imbalance to be rectified within two years.[136] In the months that followed, United States pressure for another revaluation of yen mounted.[137] If the trade imbalance were not rectified, Nixon's Special Representative for Trade Negotiations Eberle told Tanaka at the Hakone Conference early in August, Japan would become isolated and pressure for a further upward revaluation of the yen would increase.[138] The remaining 'anti-Chinese' groups in the business community, panic-stricken, ran up the white flag. On 14 August 1972 Tajitsu Wataru, chairman of the Mitsubishi Bank, Fujinō Chūjirō, president of Mitsubishi Shōji and Kōga Shigeichi, the new president of Mitsubishi Heavy Industries, left for Peking, carrying outlines of ambitious projects for the economic reconstruction of the People's Republic and statements of their holdings in Taiwan and South Korea. The Mitsubishi mission was followed by a delegation led by Inayama Yoshihirō, president of New Japan Steel, then by groups from Furukawa,

Fūyō, Mitsui and Sanwa. Virtually the entire Japanese business community had now voted with its feet.[139]

Even so, the Japanese Foreign Ministry remained profoundly hostile to the Chinese Communists. Tanaka, therefore, decided to relegate the ministry to a subordinate, technical role in the forthcoming negotiations. The initial, sensitive contacts with Peking, he resolved, could be carried out by private intermediaries drawn from the Conservative Party's 'pro-China' wing and the Opposition. The new Prime Minister, firm in his own convictions, realized that a broad national consensus on the China question was rapidly being established. He was determined to exploit it to the full.

Unofficial diplomacy, in fact, had already prepared the groundwork for normalization of ties. Fujiyama, Miki and Furui had all visited Peking in the last months of the Satō Cabinet, talked with Chou En-lai and returned fully cognizant of the Chinese position on most major issues. Ninomiya Bunzō, from the Kōmeitō, a party with which Tanaka seemed interested in forming a discreet relationship, had also travelled to China. By the time of the Liberal Democratic Party presidential elections it had become clear, through these channels, that the Chinese attitude to Japan had changed considerably since the time of the Memorandum Trade negotiations two years earlier. While compromise on the issue of Chinese sovereignty over Taiwan was obviously impossible, Chou En-lai's re-evaluation of the security treaty had made Tanaka's task infinitely easier. Early in July the Prime Minister privately informed Sasaki Kōzō, former chairman of the Japan Socialist Party, who was about to leave for China, that he sincerely wished to normalize relations and would accept an invitation to visit Peking.[140] On his return to Tōkyō, Sasaki was able to assure the Prime Minister that China's attitude to most problems was 'flexible'. He urged him to visit the Chinese capital as quickly as possible, preferably before 1 October. Shortly after Sasaki's return, the Tanaka Cabinet, as a gesture of goodwill, approved the use of Export-Import Bank funds to finance industrial plant exports to China, requested the Bank of Japan to reach agreement with its Chinese counterpart on the settlement of accounts in the currencies of both countries, and removed restrictions on Chinese residents visiting the mainland. Tanaka himself also called on Hsiao Hsiang-ch'ien and Sun P'ing-hua at the Tōkyō Imperial Hotel.

The Chinese negotiating positon was further elaborated in some nine hours of talks between Chou En-lai and Takeiri Yoshikatsu, chairman of the Kōmeitō, on 27, 28 and 29 August 1972. China, Chou reiterated, was not insisting on abrogation of the security treaty. It also intended to abandon all claims for war reparations. Restoration of diplomatic relations and the conclusion of a treaty of peace and friendship, moreover, could be considered as separate matters.[141]

Now that he had a clear picture of the Chinese attitude, the Prime Minister felt it would be safe to involve the Foreign Ministry. On Tanaka's instructions a small, closely knit 'China Policy Council', made up of Takashima Masuo, director of the Treaties Bureau, Kuriyama Sōichi, head of the Treaties Division, Yoshida Kenzō, director of the Asian Affairs Bureau and Hashimoto Hiroshi, head of the China Division, was established. Even so, Tanaka remained profoundly mistrustful of the Foreign Ministry bureaucracy. The new Prime Minister made it absolutely clear that the deliberations of the council were to be conducted in the most extreme secrecy and that he would tolerate no mistakes.[142] For this reason, the evolution of China policy at this critical moment was known only in general terms to senior ministry officials. Even within the select group of four, most of the work was done by Hashimoto and Kuriyama. Their two more senior colleagues were often left out of the sensitive discussions with the Cabinet and the Chinese government.[143]

Once it became known, through Takeiri, that the Chinese were not insisting on immediate conclusion of a full peace treaty, the Foreign Ministry team, working closely with Tanaka and Ōhira, set about drafting a joint communiqué acceptable to both countries. During this period, Ōhira consulted carefully with Furui Yoshimi and other members of the Liberal Democratic Party 'China Lobby'. By early September a provisional document, recognizing the government of the People's Republic as the only legally constituted government of China, declaring Japan's 'understanding' and 'respect' for Peking's view that Taiwan was an integral part of its territory and renouncing the earlier peace treaty with Taipei, had been drawn up as a basis for further discussions with the Chinese side. The draft communiqué envisaged a complete break in diplomatic ties with Taiwan, although Japan was to enjoy normal economic and cultural relations with the island.[144] This document was taken to Peking on 9 September by Furui Yoshimi, who had gone to China with Matsumoto Shunichi and Tagawa Seiichi, ostensibly for negotiations on trade. It was shown to Liao Ch'eng-chi the following day. Chou En-lai gave Furui his own comments on the draft two days later and made further suggestions at a meeting held in the small hours of the morning on 20 September, after Furui's return from a tour of Manchuria. The Chinese Premier, thinking of China's future ties with the Soviet Union, the United States and the countries of South-East Asia, was especially anxious to insert in the communiqué a clause explaining that the new Sino-Japanese relationship was not directed against third parties.* He also wanted a general statement indicating Tanaka's acceptance of China's 'Three Principles', a declaration terminating the state of war between the two countries and a clear indication of how and when Japan's ties with the Nationalist regime would lapse. Chou appeared to have no objections to continued economic links between Japan and Taiwan once relations with Peking had been normalized. His attitude suggested that the Four Conditions for Sino-Japanese trade would, at the appropriate moment, be quietly forgotten. On the basis of his conversations with Chou, Furui wrote a detailed report to Ōhira. This was taken back to Tōkyō by Hashimoto, who happened to be in Peking with a delegation of Conservative politicians led by Kōsaka Zentarō. On 24 September, immediately after his return to Tōkyō, Furui met with the Foreign Minister and discussed the Chinese position at length.[145]

Negotiations with Chou En-lai and supervision of the Foreign Ministry proved rather easier than management of the Liberal Democratic Party. No doubt, by the summer of 1971, the majority of Conservatives had come to realize the necessity of

---

*   Chou's intentions, however, should perhaps be interpreted in the context of his remarks to Okazaki Kaheita in the autumn of 1962. See Chapter VII.

normalizing ties with the People's Republic. There was a widespread acceptance of the view that Taiwan was a province of China, not the seat of an independent government. Even so, despite the shift in American attitudes, groups committed to the idea of a militantly anti-Communist foreign policy based on close ties with the Kuomintang, South Korea and other conservative Asian regimes maintained strong positions in the party. Shortly after the formation of the Tanaka Cabinet the hard core of the Taiwan-South Korea Lobby organized a new Foreign Policy Discussion Council (Gaikō Mondai Kondankai). This body, like other organizations dominated by the party's extreme anti-Communist right wing, at once declared its opposition to Japan's acceptance of Chou En-lai's 'Three Principles'. It appeared especially hostile to any apology for prewar Japanese military actions in China.[146]

Tanaka, Miki and Ōhira had no intention of compromising with these elements on issues of substance. The party leadership at first attempted to absorb the right-wing dissidents into the newly formed Council for the Normalization of Japan-China Relations, chaired by that persuasive and easy-going liberal Kōsaka Zentarō and dominated by groups sympathetic to the idea of *rapprochement* with Peking. While this strategy was successful in securing formal party endorsement for Tanaka's visit to Peking it did little to appease the 'pro-Taiwan' elements. Deliberations of the council degenerated into ugly shouting matches as the two sides hurled their irreconcilable principles across the tables. At the same time, Tanaka and Ōhira, mustering all their considerable charm, frequently consulted with Fukuda, Funada, Ishii, Kaya, Kishi and other leaders of the 'anti-China' group, requesting their support and understanding for the course they had decided to adopt.[147] The Prime Minister promised he would do his best to ensure that normalization of ties with the People's Republic would not result in the sacrifice of Japan's economic relations with Taiwan. Since Chou En-lai, anxious to establish a durable relationship with Tōkyō and aware of the strength of the Liberal Democratic Party's right wing, had already indicated that he would not object to continued Japanese trade with Taiwan once the island was recognized as part of the People's Republic, this commitment would clearly not be difficult to fulfil. It seems possible that Tanaka also promised to pay more attention to right-wing views on education policy, the media, the Yasukuni Shrine and other issues. Even so, in the end, as the time of the 1951 security treaty, no real consensus was reached. The Japanese ship of state was launched on its new course over the protesting bodies of the anti-Communist, pro-Taiwan extreme right wing. It was a traumatic experience which its members did not forget easily and which was to have far-reaching consequences once the normal process of factional politics had brought them back into the corridors of power. Yet, for the moment, like Fukuda, their leader, they were cast into the wilderness, unable to exert much influence on the course of events.

(x)   The Honolulu summit and the Shiina visit to Taipei, September 1972

Before setting out on his historic mission to Peking, the Japanese Prime Minister made strenuous efforts to explain his China policies to Washington and Taipei.

At the Japanese-American summit held in Hawaii at the beginning of September Tanaka informed Nixon that he intended to enter into full diplomatic relations with the People's Republic, abrogate the 1952 treaty with Taiwan and recognize Peking's claims to the island. The security treaty, he assured the President, would in no way be affected. The Sino-Japanese *rapprochement* would not impair the position of any political entity in the region, apart from Taiwan. The Honolulu talks, Ōhira later recalled, had been 'difficult'.[148] On the eve of the summit Under-Secretary of State U. Alexis Johnson (a former ambassador to Japan) had publicly warned of the dangers of Western allies, engrossed in the pursuit of narrow national self-interest, competing with each other in making overtures to the Communist powers.[149] At Hawaii, the Americans had apparently listened to Tanaka's explanations in complete silence.[150] The United States, Ōhira reluctantly concluded, did not fully understand Japan's position. This was unfortunate, but it could not be helped. Japan's foreign policy was for Japan alone to determine.

Two weeks later, former Foreign Minister Shiina Etsusaburō, a long-time friend of the Kuomintang, arrived in Taipei for talks with Chiang Ching-kuo, Chiang Kai-shek's son and successor. The Nationalist leader urged Japan to reconsider its course of action. Tanaka's overtures to the Chinese Communists, Chiang insisted, were equivalent to 'making yourselves our enemy again'. Already, the Kuomintang, rejecting Tanaka's offers of aid for the construction of a nuclear power plant and a super expressway, had taken steps to downgrade Taiwan's economic relations with Japan, implementing policies of self-reliance in such strategic industries as chemicals, petroleum, steel and heavy machinery and shifting trade to Europe and North America. Early in September high-ranking officers of the Kuomintang armed forces had held a three-day meeting to 'actively strengthen war preparations'.[151] These events, while causing much excitement in the Liberal Democratic Party right wing, failed to shake Tanaka's resolve. The Prime Minister was well aware that Chiang Ching-kuo was fighting a losing battle. He also knew that the Chinese Nationalists could not apply military pressure against Japan without United States encouragement. This, he felt confident, was unlikely to be forthcoming.

(xi)   *The Tanaka mission to Peking, September 1972*

On 25 September 1972 Tanaka and Ōhira, accompanied by a large party of officials and journalists, left Haneda airport in Tōkyō on a direct flight to Peking, after a rousing farewell by representatives of the Liberal Democratic Party, the Socialist Party, the Democratic Socialists, the Kōmeitō and the Communists. The contrast with Yoshida's visit to San Francisco in August 1951, Kishi's departure for Washington in January 1960 or even Tanaka's own recent visit to Honolulu had been striking.*

---

*   In September 1972 the present writer, walking in western Honshū, discussed Tanaka's diplomacy with the abbot of a large Buddhist temple. It was neither necessary nor seemly, the abbot declared, for the Japanese Prime Minister to have gone all the way to Hawaii to discuss

Never, in the entire history of the postwar period, had there been such a display of unity on a foreign policy issue. The Japanese aircraft touched down in Peking shortly before noon. At the bottom of the ramp Tanaka, who had last set foot on Chinese soil in 1940, as a young recruit in the Imperial Japanese Army, was greeted by Yen Chien-ying, vice-chairman of the Council for National Defence, Foreign Minister Chi Peng-fei, Kuo Mo-jo, vice-chairman of the Standing Committee of the National People's Congress, Liao Cheng-chih, president of the China-Japan Friendship Association, and other dignitaries. As the Prime Minister's party walked across the tarmac, accompanied by their Chinese hosts, a 360-man chorus from the People's Liberation Army burst into a triumphant rendition of the 'Three Main Rules of Discipline, Eight Points of Attention', the battle hymn of the Communists in the pitiless struggles against the invading Japanese forces and the Kuomintang in the 1930s. It was both a reminder of the past and a warning for the future.

Five days later, after intensive discussions among Tanaka, Ōhira, Mao Tse-tung and Chou En-lai, the two parties signed a joint communiqué, terminating the state of war that had existed between them and establishing full diplomatic relations. The Japanese side expressed its regrets 'for causing enormous damages in the past to the Chinese people through war and deeply reproaches itself'. China, 'in the interest of the friendship' between the two peoples, renounced all demands for war indemnities. Japan confirmed its full 'understanding' for China's Three Principles on the normalization of relations, unequivocally recognizing the People's Republic as the 'sole legal government of China' and declaring its 'respect' for Peking's view that Taiwan was an inalienable part of its territory. The two countries, after agreeing to establish 'durable relations of peace and friendship' on the basis of 'mutual respect for sovereignty and territorial integrity, mutual non-aggression, non-interference in each other's internal affairs, equality, mutual benefit and peaceful coexistence', stated that 'neither ... should seek hegemony in the Asian-Pacific region and each ... is opposed to efforts by any other country or group of countries to establish such hegemony'.

The Sino-Japanese relationship, it was stressed, was not directed against other states. The two governments then announced their intention to hold talks on trade, aviation, navigation and fisheries and to begin negotiations with a view to concluding a full-scale treaty of peace and friendship.[152] Tanaka hopefully raised the issue of the Tiaoyu (Senkaku) Islands. Chou En-lai declined to discuss the matter. 'The islands are, after all, tiny specks you can hardly spot on maps and they have become a problem just because oil reserves were found around them', the Chinese Premier remarked.[153] A potentially explosive issue was thus left, unresolved, at the centre of the new relationship from the very beginning.

China with 'that scoundrel Nixon'. If the American President had wanted to talk with Tanaka he could have come to Japan. In contrast, the abbot viewed the Japanese Prime Minister's visit to Peking as 'a great contribution to the peace, stability and prosperity of Asia'. 'Perhaps you think there is a contradiction in my attitude', he said, eyeing me over his cup of tea. 'The fact of the matter is, however, that Japan and China are brother nations, with a common history, a common culture and immense responsibility for the future of Asia. Relations between Japan and the United States are totally different in character.'

Nevertheless, despite the fact that Chou En-lai declined to toast the Japanese Emperor at the welcoming banquet on 25 September,[154] sound personal relations with the Chinese leadership seemed to have been established. During their long meeting at Mao Tse-tung's private residence near Tien An Men on 27 September Tanaka and the Chinese leader discussed East Asian history, Buddhism, cooking and cures for rheumatism, a complaint which apparently plagued them both. Tanaka expressed amazement at Mao's collection of manuscripts. Mao cautioned him against adhering too closely to the classical teachings of Confucianism. Tanaka advised Chou En-lai not to attempt to export revolution. 'I don't like Communism', he told the Chinese Premier. Chou remarked that revolution was 'not something to be exported'. In response to Tanaka's request not to co-operate with the Japanese Communist Party, the Chinese Premier observed that the Japanese Communists were 'no good'.[155] Tanaka presented Mao with a classical Chinese poem, on the subject of Sino-Japanese relations, penned by his own hand. The two countries exchanged gifts of important flora, fauna and cultural artefacts. The atmosphere at Ōhira's final press conference was positively jubilant, with both sides leaving their seats to join in repeated toasts and to exchange expressions of mutual congratulation. By the time he returned to Tōkyō, Tanaka doubtless felt confident not only that he had outflanked the United States in the race to open the world's last remaining unexploited market but also that he had laid the foundations for an enduring peace with the People's Republic, a relationship that might, with the passage of time, develop into the fully fledged political and economic alliance Yoshida had envisaged twenty years before, uniting Asia from Hokkaidō to the Tien Shan.

(xii)　Public opinion

Tanaka's opponents on the anti-Communist right wing of the Liberal Democratic Party could derive little comfort from the Japanese people's reaction to the events of 1971–2. In the wake of the 'Nixon Shocks', the international currency adjustments, China's admission to the United Nations and the American President's visit to Peking, public support for improved relations with China, always strong, had become almost unanimous. There was little concern about the fate of the Kuomintang on Taiwan. Opinion polls taken after the Prime Minister's return from the Chinese capital showed overwhelming approval for the terms on which the settlement was finally reached. A *Tōkyō Shimbun* survey published on 24 November 1972, for example, found 84.9 per cent of respondents welcoming the restoration of Sino-Japanese ties as carried out by the Prime Minister. Only 2.2 per cent declared themselves totally opposed to the settlement.[156]

The global power realignments of 1971–2, the consolidation of the American-Soviet *détente*, the Sino-American *rapprochement*, the restoration of Sino-Japanese ties and the continuing impact of the Vietnam War also coincided with an important shift in Japanese thinking about the relative positions of the United States and China in the international hierarchy. These changes were perhaps influenced by the vigorous debates about the historical origins of the Japanese people, the nature of their links with East Asia, the significance of the Meiji Restoration, modernization, imperialism, domestic political arrangements and foreign policy, all of which reached a peak in the first part of the new decade. While the Japanese people remained, at one level, 'Westernist' in outlook, their assessment of the various Western powers altered significantly during these years. Switzerland, the symbol of modern, capitalist neutralism, remained the most attractive country for Japanese of most age groups and political loyalties. Interest in France also grew. The decline in America's popularity, evident since the mid-1960s, continued unabated. Belief that Japan's future lay in close association with the United States also waned. Paradoxically, popular attitudes to the security treaty did not change. A large minority continued to support some kind of military association with the United States. Another large minority continued to oppose military ties with Washington. At the same time, China's popularity, the appeal of its civilization, its perceived importance as a future political and economic partner, increased dramatically.

Table XI.1
Foreign countries most admired by Japanese, August 1970–April 1973

'List the three countries that you like on the following card.'

	Aug 1970	Aug 1971	Sep 1971	Oct 1971	Jan 1972	9–12 Apr 1973 (like)	(dislike)
America	31.2	29.8	27.8	24.3	24.4	17.9	13.3
Soviet Union	3.0	4.6	4.5	3.0	3.3	2.8	23.8
Great Britain	21.7	25.9	25.0	27.5	23.2	15.5	1.4
France	23.2	29.6	28.5	25.2	25.0	20.8	1.2
West Germany	15.1	15.2	18.2	14.4	14.3	11.3	2.3
Switzerland	35.1	37.5	35.9	34.2	33.5	32.4	0.2
India	3.2	4.6	5.0	3.2	3.9	3.1	4.0
China	3.1	5.5	7.9	4.1	9.1	16.4	4.4
South Korea	1.6	1.6	1.6	1.7	1.6	1.6	10.2
North Korea	0.5	1.4	1.1	0.4	1.0	1.1	15.7

Source: Jiji Press, Monthly Popularity Polls.

Table XI.2a
Tōkyō Shimbun Poll, released 10 September 1972

(i.e. before the Tanaka visit to China)

'On which diplomatic questions should the Government lay greatest emphasis?'

Japanese-American relations	13.0 per cent
Sino-Japanese relations	41.0 per cent
Japanese-Soviet relations	3.0 per cent
The Vietnam question	10.0 per cent
The Korean problem	1.0 per cent
United Nations diplomacy	1.0 per cent
Others	1.0 per cent
Do not know	30.0 per cent

Table XI.2b
Asahi Shimbun Poll, 18 September 1972

(on the eve of the Tanaka visit to China)

'Which country do you think Japan must maintain the most friendly relations with from now on?'

China	38.0 per cent
United States	29.0 per cent
Soviet Union	2.0 per cent
North Korea	0.0 per cent
South Korea	0.0 per cent
Other Asian countries	3.0 per cent
Other countries	1.0 per cent
All countries	7.0 per cent
Other replies	3.0 per cent
No replies	17.0 per cent

Until the United Nations decision on China in 1971, similar polls had traditionally shown the United States at the top of the list of desirable associates, with almost 40 per cent support. China's entry into the United Nations marked, for the Japanese people as a whole, a major watershed. An *Asahi Shimbun* survey taken in December 1971, just after the United Nations decision, showed 33 per cent recommending that priority be given to relations with China, 28 per cent hoping for continued emphasis on ties with the United States. The 18 September 1972 poll showed 40 per cent of supporters of the Tanaka Cabinet attaching the greatest importance to Japan's relations with China, 33 per cent giving priority to ties with America. Among opponents of the Tanaka Cabinet, 50 per cent were for China, 19 per cent for America.

Table XI.3
Tōkyō Shimbun survey, 24 November 1972

(i.e. after the normalization of ties with China)

'What should be done about the security treaty with the United States?'

It should be firmly maintained.	12.1 per cent
It should be continued, with efforts being made to eliminate sources of friction.	25.3 per cent
It should be re-examined, as tension in Asia eases.	23.5 per cent
It should be abolished.	16.5 per cent
Don't know	22.7 per cent

(xiii)   *The December 1972 general election and its impact*

The restoration of diplomatic relations with China, popular as it was, did little to arrest the slow decline of the Liberal Democratic Party. The general elections held on 11 December 1972, just two months after Tanaka's return from Peking, gave the Conservatives a comfortable working majority in the Diet. Liberal Democratic Party representation, however, again dropped significantly, from 297 to 282 seats. Within the party, the Tanaka, Ōhira, Nakasone and Shiina factions marginally improved their positions. The Fukuda faction, still the largest in the Conservative camp, lost many supporters. The Miki, Mizuta and Ishii factions suffered small decreases in representation. Among the Opposition parties, Kōmeitō representation declined from 47 to 29, that of the Democratic Socialist Party from 29 to 19. The Japan Socialist Party, in contrast, increased its strength by some 36 per cent, from 87 to 118 seats.[157] The Communist position improved even more dramatically, from 14 to 38 seats. Conservative Party leaders and their supporters in the business community, frustrated by their inability to appeal to the new generation of well-educated, politically conscious, urban Japanese, and alarmed by the sudden surge of the Socialist and Communist parties, sought to tide over the immediate crisis by the well-tried expedient of an 'all-faction Cabinet'. This necessitated Fukuda's re-entry into the government, a development which made it inevitable that Tanaka's domestic and foreign policies would be, for some time, subjected to greater restraints than he had at first anticipated.

At a deeper level, the 1972 general election marked the beginning of another slow, erratic swing in the pendulum of Liberal Democratic Party attitudes. The dominant factions, a majority of the party perhaps, remained committed to the search for a more autonomous role in world affairs. The lessons of the 'Nixon Shocks' were plain for all to see. Yet for many Conservatives, the growing power of the left suddenly made pursuit of an independent foreign policy seem less desirable. Like Prince Konoye in April 1945, they began to fear, in the marrow of their bones, that a genuinely independent Japan, able to treat with the United States on equal terms, might also be a socialist Japan, that Tanaka Kakuei might unwittingly play John the Baptist to Miyamoto Kenji. Further erosion of the political, economic and social status quo had to be prevented at all costs. Viewed in this light, continued dependent association with an American-centred world order, philosophical acceptance of the arbitrary behaviour of United States presidents and the vagaries of Washington's political life, the comforting presence of the Stars and Stripes fluttering over military bases from Wakkanai to Naha, all seemed infinitely preferable to a Socialist-Communist majority in the Diet, the Red Flag over the Imperial Palace and the transformation of the Self Defence Forces into a People's Army.

CHAPTER XII

Japanese foreign policy in the age of détente, 1972–1978

All things under heaven are predestined to disintegrate. With the passage of time they are inexorably drawn together again. Yet having reconstituted themselves they will inevitably tend to break apart.

Ssu-ma Ch'ien, *Shih-chi*

I Détente and the consolidation of multipolarity

The great power *détente* negotiated in 1971–2, ambiguous as it was, survived for nearly six years, despite continued tensions in the Middle East, the collapse of the Portuguese Empire, upheavals in the Horn of Africa, troubles in Latin America, new waves of unrest in Eastern Europe and the resurgence of American messianic anti-Communism triggered by the fall of Saigon, a deep-seated, grass-roots movement that posed increasingly serious challenges to the *realpolitik* promoted by Nixon, Kissinger and Ford, paving the way for a return to ideology under the Reagan administration.

Until President Carter's tilt to China in the northern spring of 1978, the United States attempted to maintain a certain even-handedness in its dealings with Moscow and Peking. Relations with the People's Republic steadily improved. Efforts were made to broaden the dialogue with the Soviet Union. By the time of First Secretary Brezhnev's visit to Washington in June 1973 the United States and Soviet Union were engaged in far-reaching discussions on further development of the strategic arms limitation agreements, mutual reduction of armed forces in Central Europe, the future of Eastern Europe, the Middle East and Indochina as well as on increased economic exchange. Already, in April 1973, despite the disapproval of anti-Soviet groups in the United States Congress, Occidental Petroleum and several other companies had concluded agreements with the Soviet Union to import $US10 billion worth of Yakut natural gas over a period of twenty-five years. By the end of the Ford administration the future of *détente* seemed reasonably secure, despite Moscow's uneasiness about Washington's China policies, the right-wing military *coup d'état* in Chile and congressional insistence that expansion of trade with Russia be specifically linked to the question of Jewish emigration, a stand that precipitated Soviet abrogation of the 1972 trade agreement before it had run its full course. Nevertheless, the Vladivostok summit of November 1974 and the United States-Soviet Foreign Minister's talks held at Geneva in February 1975 demonstrated, in a dramatic fashion, the continuing interest of both superpowers in efforts to negotiate arms control and at least a partial relaxation of tensions. The Carter administration, too, despite the increasingly anti-Soviet interpretation given to its 'human rights' diplomacy, seemed initially committed to *détente*.

Détente accelerated the erosion of the Cold War alliance systems and the proliferation of new centres of political, military and economic power. In the North Atlantic, conflict between the United States and Western Europe over trade, agricultural policy and investment grew. The cleavages within the American camp were exacerbated by the Arab oil embargo against the states supporting Israel during the Yom Kippur War of 1973. Since the late 1960s, several West European nations, in response to the growth of Arab nationalism, the emergence of the Organisation of Arab Petroleum Exporting Countries (OAPEC) and the declining position of the Anglo-American oil companies, had begun to dissociate their Middle Eastern policies from those of the United States. Immediately after the outbreak of war in October, all European members of NATO, with the single exception of Portugal, denied landing rights to United States aircraft transporting military supplies to Israel. France reiterated its long-standing pro-Arab policies. West Germany banned the transfer to Israel of American arms from bases on its territory. Great Britain refused to supply arms to all belligerents. West European repudiation of the United States stand on such a fundamental issue precipitated the greatest crisis in NATO since de Gaulle took France out of the organization's military wing in 1966. Kissinger, proclaiming that Washington's Middle Eastern policies were founded on elevated concepts of political morality rather than base self-interest, castigated the European attitude as 'craven', 'contemptible', 'pernicious' and 'jackal-like',[1] hinting that the fate of NATO itself lay in the balance. These expressions of American displeasure proved counterproductive. In France, Gaullist attitudes were strengthened. In West Germany, habitually torn between pro-American Atlanticist and pro-French Europeanist tendencies, support for the concept of a United Europe, independent of both superpowers, struck deeper roots. 'In a world whose destiny cannot and should not be determined by the two superpowers alone', Chancellor Willy Brandt declared, 'the influence of a United Europe has become indispensable.'[2] Even in Great Britain, where Atlanticist traditions were stronger than in any other European state, irritation at United States sanctimoniousness was extreme.

Kissinger's concept of a New Atlantic Charter, designed to lock the United States, Western Europe and Japan into a common political, economic and military framework through interrelated agreements on strategic issues, trade and currency evolved in response to this accelerated fragmentation of the Cold War alliance systems. Its contradictions were apparent from the beginning. The United States saw it as an instrument for reimposing its hegemony on the non-Communist world and forcing its policies onto its allies. In the absence of any clearly defined external threat the allies vacillated between the lingering desire to retain the benefits of American leadership and the determination to carve out a wider measure of freedom to pursue their diverse political and economic interests. In this situation, despite the establishment of the Trilateral Commission and the institution of Western economic summits, the New Atlantic Charter almost immediately ran aground on the problems that had originally generated it.

Throughout the 1970s American influence in the Third World contracted at a somewhat greater rate than that of the Soviet Union, creating an impression, not altogether supported by the facts, that Moscow was unfairly taking advantage of *détente* to outflank its superpower rival in these strategic areas. This occurred at a time when the slowdown in industrial growth, the depletion of America's domestic resources and the increasingly competitive relations among the major non-Communist industrial powers had combined to accentuate the importance of the resource-rich, developing countries of Asia, Africa and Latin America in the global equilibrium.

In Latin America, the United States, its position consolidated by the conservative military *coups d'état* of the mid-1960s, as well as by the development of a close politico-economic partnership with Brazil, retained its position as the dominant external power. The Marxist threat to Washington's regional hegemony was temporarily eliminated when the Chilean government of President Salvador Allende, elected in 1970, was ousted by General Pinochet's bloody *coup d'état* in 1973. Radical leftist challenges to the United States and its local allies did not re-emerge until the overthrow of the Somoza dictatorship in Nicaragua by the Sandinistas in 1978. The rift in the Atlantic Alliance, however, inevitably had its repercussions in Latin America. The early 1970s saw several basically conservative Hispanic states, led by Argentina, Colombia, Mexico, Peru and Venezuela, embark on projects to reduce their dependence on the United States and contain the growing power of Brazil by cultivating relations with Europe. The Andean Group (Bolivia, Chile, Colombia, Ecuador and Peru) attempted to stimulate regional trade, restrict the activities of foreign corporations and create a combined merchant marine. The Argentine military government launched a concerted drive to establish independent defence industries with European assistance. These efforts, intensified after the return of Péron from exile in 1973, continued until the death of the former populist dictator and the overthrow of his wife by a pro-American junta in 1976. Right-wing military coups in Bolivia (1971) and Uruguay (1973), together with the successful application of economic pressure on the reformist junta in Peru, also increased United States-Brazilian influence at the expense of conservative Hispanic nationalists, liberals and radical groups. Nevertheless, despite the reassertion of United States authority that had taken place by the end of the decade, Argentina, Colombia, Peru, Venezuela and several other countries continued to make substantial purchases of French military equipment and encourage European investments. To this extent, at least, traditional spheres of influence in Latin America became somewhat blurred.[3]

In the Middle East, the abrogation of the Soviet-Egyptian military alliance, President Sadat's adoption of a generally pro-American foreign policy, the negotiation of the Camp David accords and the destruction of the Sudanese Communist Party represented spectacular victories for American diplomacy. Once again, however, trans-

Atlantic rivalries introduced a new element into these Cold War struggles. It was, significantly, to Great Britain and France, rather than to the United States, that the new Egypt turned for assistance with the development of an independent arms industry. The reassertion of United States influence in Egypt and the Sudan, moreover, was offset by increasing Saudi disenchantment with Washington's pro-Israeli policies in the wake of the 1973 Yom Kippur War, the Soviet alliance with Colonel Mengistu Haile Marian's revolutionary Marxist government in Ethiopia (1977), then the overthrow of the Iranian monarchy by the bitterly anti-American, anti-Communist theocratic regime of the Ayatollah Khomeni in 1978. Towards the end of the decade Colonel Ghaddafi's Libya, too, tacitly encouraged both by the Soviet Union and by Italy, had begun to pursue policies intensely antagonistic to the United States. In sub-Saharan Africa Washington's influence remained marginal. The receding tide of social and political radicalism in black Africa had redounded to the benefit of London and Paris, not Washington. The collapse of the Portuguese Empire in 1975 provided opportunities for covert American–South African intervention in Angola and other territories, a process which led, in turn, to the emergence of radical nationalist regimes dependent, to some extent, on Eastern bloc support for their survival.

In the Indian subcontinent the continuing impact of the Vietnam War, United States hostility towards the Bangladesh independence struggle, then its support for Islamabad in the 1971 Indo-Pakistini conflict, particularly its ill-conceived attempt at gunboat diplomacy in the Bay of Bengal, effectively destroyed what remaining prestige Washington possessed. By the end of 1973 India had achieved virtual hegemony of the subcontinent. Within a year it had exploded its first nuclear device. Its ally, the Soviet Union, found itself the only European power with any significant influence in the vast area extending from the Himalayas to the Gulf of Mannar and from Nagaland to the Thar. In South-East Asia and the Western Pacific, too, United States policy sustained shattering blows. In Indochina the efforts of the Nixon administration to end the war on favourable terms, either through massive application of air and naval power, or through negotiation, ended in failure. By the northern summer of 1975 the flags of three socialist republics, already engaged in complex struggles over the shape of the postwar order, fluttered over territories that had been regarded, for more than a quarter of a century, as vital strategic assets in the global crusade against Communism, indispensable bases for the management of Japan, essential for the survival of the American Republic itself. Despite Washington's close relationship with the Marcos regime in the Philippines the remaining non-Communist states in the region, Indonesia, Malaysia, Thailand and Singapore, had begun to drift, in varying degrees, away from close identification with the United States towards a more generalizd 'pro-Western' non-alignment. Even in Australia and New Zealand, political leaders of all persuasions had begun to question the traditional policy of unwavering support for the United States, moving, discreetly, towards a more self-reliant international stance. The ANZUS treaty survived, in its original form, for the greater part of the next decade. The SEATO alliance, once the regional pivot of United States Cold War strategy, died a natural, albeit lingering death.

II   Japanese responses to multipolarity

Between 1972 and 1978 Japanese governments, like their counterparts in Western Europe, continued the process of cautious adjustment to the changing realities of world politics. Yet their efforts to assert a more independent role, while not entirely unsuccessful, were hampered by a combination of international and domestic factors.

(i)   The Japanese relationship with the United States

By the middle of the decade the Japanese-American security treaty, as an effective military alliance, appeared to have entered a stage of advanced decay. Superpower conflict, nuclear or conventional, seemed increasingly improbable. It also seemed unlikely that the United States would employ either its nuclear arsenal or its conventional forces in Japan's defence against the Soviet Union, China or other potential antagonists. Before the decade had come to an end Washington's unilateral abrogation of its treaty with the Chinese Nationalists on Taiwan had forced even the residual 'pro-American', anti-Communist right wing of the Liberal Democratic Party, still perplexed by the events of 1971–2, to admit that the United States was at best an unpredictable ally.

Japanese governments, citing the necessity of preserving the global balance of power, continued tension in Korea, domestic instability and the growth of the Soviet navy, consistently argued against any downgrading of the military relationship with Washington. Nevertheless, the view that the security treaty should be abandoned or significantly revised gained ground. The balance of power argument cut little ice with the Conservative Party rank and file. Korea, certainly, gave reasons for hesitation. Japan's internal security, too, remained a perennial concern. Yet with the recognition of China and the end of the Vietnam War leftist agitation in Japan had subsided, despite the continued growth in support for the Opposition parties. At the same time, the old arguments about the necessity for Japan to ally itself with the world's greatest naval power, so compelling in Yoshida's day, had begun to lose much of their force. Despite the growing strength of the Soviet fleet in the Sea of Japan and the Sea of Okhotsk, the United States remained, throughout the 1970s, the world's most formidable naval power. Japan's principal suppliers of raw materials, as well as its most important markets, were still located around oceans where the United States Navy sailed virtually unchallenged. The events of the 1970s, however, made it increasingly clear that the efficacy of naval power, not merely as a means of defence, but, more importantly, as an instrument of diplomacy, had undergone a fundamental change. The United States Navy had played a decisive role in the Pacific War. It had played a decisive role in denying Taiwan to the Chinese Communists. American naval forces had exerted an important, albeit less significant influence on the outcome of the Korean War. Yet overwhelming air and naval supremacy, together with massive ground intervention, had not enabled the United States to impose its will on the revolutionary forces of Indochina. The American naval demonstration in the Bay of Bengal had not helped Pakistan suppress the independence movement in

Bangladesh. Naval supremacy in the Atlantic, together with an ability to exert considerable influence in the Indian Ocean, had not enabled the United States to guide the course of events in the former Portuguese colonies after the fall of Salazar. America's navy could do nothing to keep the Shah on the Peacock Throne or protect the Somoza dynasty in Nicaragua. Even if the Seventh Fleet had been mounted on wheels it could not have prevented Soviet intervention in Afghanistan. Most conspicuously, United States naval power had no impact either on the price of oil or on the willingness of the OAPEC nations to supply it. Although naval power still played a significant role in the superpower military balance, it had become apparent, to thoughtful observers, that the days when the destinies of the world were decided by the masters of the seas had passed. The locus of power was returning to the land and to those who controlled the resources beneath its surface. In some parts of the world, no doubt, the controlling interests were American multinational corporations. Yet across large areas of the globe American influence was in full retreat. The initiative had been seized by militantly nationalist governments, by armed masses inspired by revolutionary doctrines and messianic creeds. Against these forces the United States Navy was no more effective than a fleet of toy battleships. The ignominious failure of President Carter's attempts to rescue the American hostages in Teheran in April 1980 symbolized the end of an era.

The argument that the security treaty helped contain potentially dangerous anti-Japanese sentiment in the United States government and Congress, however, was not one that could be dismissed lightly. While the United States retained its position as Japan's single most important market throughout the 1970s, its economic performance continued to deteriorate, trade friction with its allies intensified, pressure for protectionist legislation mounted. In February 1973 the Smithsonian Agreements collapsed, the dollar was devalued a further 10 per cent, the world's money markets were thrown into chaos and the yen, like the European currencies, was forced into an indefinite float. Efforts on the part of the United States, Western Europe and Japan to reconstruct the IMF-GATT system ended in failure. Tanaka Kakuei's grandiose scheme to ease Japanese-American trade friction by shifting the focus of Japanese economic activity away from export-orientated industries towards reconstruction of the home archipelago had only limited results. The fourfold increase in oil prices at the time of the 1973 Yom Kippur War forced the Japanese government to revert to a policy of promoting exports in order to finance its imports of petroleum. In these circumstances the Japanese-American trade imbalance grew out of all proportions. By the end of 1974, at the time of the collapse of the Tanaka Cabinet, it stood at $US1.69 billion. By 1977 it had reached $US7.99 billion. By the end of the decade it had increased sixfold to $US10.41 billion. Disputes over particular commodites continued to cause much bad blood on both sides of the Pacific. Conflict over Japanese steel exports to the United States dragged on until the adoption of the trigger pricing system in 1978. Disputes over colour television sets, automobiles, computers and high technology also generated much acrimony. In 1975, according to polls conducted by Yankelovich, Skelly and White, 25 per cent of Americans favoured protectionist policies. By 1979 this figure had risen to 31 per cent. By the end of 1980 some 40 per cent of Americans declared themselves in favour of protectionism.[4] These sentiments were being increasingly translated into policy. Under the terms of the Orderly Marketing Agreement negotiated by the Carter administration, Japan was obliged to limit its colour television exports to the United States to 1.75 million units per annum during the period 1977–80. The Carter administration also placed extreme pressure on Japan to adopt 'voluntary restraints' in automobile exports. Eventually, when the Japanese automobile industry refused to comply, the United States increased import duties on Japanese light trucks by 25 per cent, thus effectively pricing them out of the market. At the same time Washington applied relentless pressure on the Japanese to increase imports of American agricultural products, raw materials, enriched uranium and high technology.

By the end of the decade Japanese-American economic conflict had become so severe that many observers were convinced that a re-emergence of political and strategic rivalry was imminent. William E. Colby, former director of the Central Intelligence Agency, for example, came to believe that

> Japan and America might be considered to be on a collision course and their interests bound to clash in the new world of the 1980s and 1990s. Having shown her strength in the automotive, steel and electronic fields, Japan is today focusing on the computer and knowledge intensive fields of the future, planning to leave labour intensive industry to the developing nations of East Asia. If it could outpace America in these advanced technological fields it could draw its agricultural products and raw materials from America and move into the leading economic position in the world.
>
> From America's point of view, Japan could be considered as a dangerous threat to its hopes for development of new information intensive industries. America's past leadership in Free World political and strategic matters could be replaced by a Japan strong in the economic and social issues which will dominate the future. The strength of the Japanese economy could transfer the financial leadership of the world to the yen at the expense of the dollar as the international medium of exchange.

The only way a clash could be avoided, Colby argued, foreshadowing a trend of thought that was to achieve greater prominence in the 1980s, was through the full political and economic integration of the two Pacific ally-rivals:

> Japan and the United States must begin to develop a common political framework to permit full operation of their economies within a common framework instead of within two political frameworks. As long as two separate political frameworks exist, competition in the economic field will be reflected in the political field, and the temptation will arise to use political tools to suppress economic competition.[5]

Such integration would clearly be difficult to achieve unless the United States were able to re-establish its position as the world's foremost military power, reassert its global economic supremacy, reimpose its authority on its allies and refurbish its international image. Renewed American hegemony of the non-Communist world, even if it were feasible at all, could not be established in the absence of a common threat. In this sense, the collapse of *détente* and the revival of the Cold War in 1978, like the outbreak of the Korean War in 1950, was a 'gift of the gods'.

(ii)   Sino-Japanese relations

The relationship with China, fraught as it was with contradictions and uncertainties, was the centrepiece of Tanaka's grand design to free Japanese diplomacy from the restraints of the San Francisco system and reduce the level of economic dependence on the United States. In most respects it had, in the short term at least, only limited success. Had Japan's ties with the People's Republic been normalized in the 1950s, in the early 1960s, or even during the last days of the Satō Cabinet, things might have been different. *Tarde venientibus ossa*, as the Romans used to say. The guest who comes late finds only the bones. By the time Tanaka arrived in Peking the United States and the Chinese leadership had reached a tacit agreement that the new Japan, with its mighty industrial power, significant military potential and growing nationalism would be safer under Washington's continued tutelage. This made it inevitable that the Sino-Japanese relationship would, for some time, develop within the framework of Washington's global strategy and not provide an avenue of escape from the San Francisco system. In later years, Chinese officials, eager to forge a global united front against the Soviet Union, and disturbed by the possible implications of Japanese-American economic friction, went to considerable lengths to persuade Japanese exponents of a Tōkyō-Peking axis that Japan's most important ties were with the United States, not with China.[6] Yoshida's vision of a Sino-Japanese alliance independent of both Western superpowers, the East Asian counterpart of General de Gaulle's United Europe, had thus come no closer to realization by 1978 than it had been in 1952, at the end of the occupation.

The development of both American and Japanese relations with China was impeded by the political turmoil that racked all three societies during the first part of the decade.

In 1973 the Watergate scandal plunged the United States into a major constitutional crisis. The conflict between the White House and Capitol Hill reached historically unprecedented levels of intensity. There were calls to limit the powers of the presidency, to restore the traditional balance between the executive and the legislature, curb the activities of the military and the CIA. Public confidence in the political integrity of the American leadership disintegrated. Nixon's resignation in August 1974 did little to retrieve the situation. The Ford administration found its freedom of action in both domestic and foreign affairs severely limited by the political convulsions which continued to shake the republic.

In China, too, factional-policy struggles intensified, reaching a peak after the deaths of Mao Tse-tung and Chou En-lai in 1976, the purge of the radical leftists and the emergence of a new leadership centring around Hua Kuo-feng, Teng Hsiao-ping, Li Hsien-nien and Yeh Chien-ying. It was not until the convening of the Fifth National People's Congress in February–March 1978 that the dust settled, Teng Hsiao-ping established himself as the pre-eminent figure in the new hierarchy and the policies of the regime became clear.

In Japan, allegations of Prime Minister Tanaka's involvement in the Lockheed scandal further discredited the Conservative Party leadership, touching off a new round of savage internecine warfare and ushering in a long period of weak, unstable and relatively powerless governments held in contempt by the electorate. The July of 1974 House of Councillors election produced a situation of approximate strategic parity in the Upper House. The Liberal Democrats were only able to maintain their position by exploiting divisions among the Opposition parties. In national and local elections, while the Conservatives and Socialists stagnated, the Communists continued to make impressive gains. The Kōmeito, too, recovering from its 1972 setback, advanced rapidly. By the end of 1975 the Japan Communist Party had come to an agreement with Sōka Gakkai, the Nichiren Buddhist lay organization which had given birth to the Kōmeitō, designed to pave the way for a grand coalition of all Opposition parties. The Kōmeitō's immediate repudiation of this agreement was greeted with sighs of relief from the Conservative ranks. Yet long-term dangers remained. The Miki Cabinet, established after Tanaka's resignation in December 1974, and dominated by the mutually antagonistic Fukuda, Ōhira and Nakasone factions, was unable either to provide effective leadership or to restore the fortunes of the Liberal Democratic Party. The cabinet lurched from crisis to crisis. The Prime Minister's attempts to eradicate corruption outraged his Conservative colleagues and encountered stiff resistance within the party. The Diet fell into a perennial state of uproar and confusion. Complete paralysis of the legislature was only avoided by enlisting the co-operation of the Democratic Socialists. Fukuda Takeo's 'all-faction Cabinet', formed after Miki's political demise on 24 December 1976, while winning the support of the establishment through its genial indifference to the Lockheed investigations, proved equally unable to provide effective government or inspire public confidence.

These constant political upheavals help explain the exceptionally slow pace of the Sino-Japanese negotiations on aviation, fisheries, navigation, trade and the conclusion of a treaty of peace and friendship. Yet the changing attitude of the Chinese leadership towards its new relationship with Japan also inspired caution in Tōkyō. The fact that the 'third party' clause in the 1972 joint communiqué had been inserted at Chou En-lai's insistence had suggested to Tanaka that the development of relations with the People's Republic would not involve Japan directly in the Sino-Soviet dispute. Yet in China, no less than Japan, the evolution of policy was heavily influenced by the outcome of factional struggles. Chou En-lai proved unable to hold the line against those who wished to confront the Soviet Union more actively. Once negotiations on the Sino-Japanese treaty of peace and friendship opened, therefore, the Chinese began to insist that any agreement commit the contracting states to co-operate against the efforts of third parties to establish 'hegemony' in the Asian-Pacific region. Such a policy, the Chinese now argued, was consistent both with Sino-American objectives as enunciated in the Shanghai Declaration and also with the spirit of the 1972 Sino-Japanese agreements. This course, which would have made Japan the junior partner in a joint Sino-American strategic alliance against the Soviet Union, was regarded with equanimity by sections of the old 'pro-China' lobby, by some 'pro-American' elements and by the militant anti-Soviet right wing. It was rejected by those Conservatives who viewed the events of 1971–2 as providing Japan with an opportunity to break out of the Cold War alliance systems, broaden the base of its diplomacy and play a more creative role in world affairs. This group probably constituted a majority of the party. In 1975, after months of fruitless negotiations, discussion of the peace and friendship treaty was suspended indefinitely. The talks did not resume until the autumn of 1977, on the eve of Carter's tilt to China, a development that precipitated the greatest shift in the regional configuration of power since the collapse of the Chinese Nationalists in 1949.

The immediate, direct economic benefits of the new Sino-Japanese relationship proved less substantial than many 'pro-China' groups in the political and business establishment had expected. Those who had hoped that the People's Republic would rapidly replace, rather than merely supplement, the North American market were sadly mistaken. Despite all the rhetoric about a special Sino-Japanese relationship, competition from American and West European interests in China intensified after 1972. While Japan retained its position as China's single most important trading partner, the Chinese were clearly anxious to avoid excessive dependence on their powerful neighbour. Nevertheless, by 1975, a year after the fall of the Tanaka Cabinet, the volume of trade between Japan and the People's Republic was four times the 1972 level. By 1978 the value of two-way trade had reached some $5,000 million, almost five times the 1972 figure. By the end of the decade China had become Japan's fifth-largest trading partner, after the United States, Saudi Arabia, Indonesia and Australia. On 16 February 1978 a long-term bilateral trade agreement, integrated with China's economic development programmes, was signed in Peking. This agreement, as revised in September 1978, envisaged a fourfold expansion of bilateral trade over the next twelve years, substantially increased Chinese exports of crude oil to Japan, joint development of undersea oil reserves, Japanese participation in the exploitation of oil fields in Sinkiang, joint development of coal reserves in Shantung, Shansi, Hunan and Hupei, along with Japanese participation in hydroelectric power projects along the Yangtse and Yellow rivers. There were also plans for joint exploitation of aluminium, tungsten, tin, copper and lead reserves. Japan, it was generally expected, would supply some 30 per cent of China's capital equipment purchases and technology needs during the new Chinese leadership's modernization campaign. For the Japanese business community these were exciting prospects. Even so, the continual modification of the Chinese modernization programme, together with the erratic nature of China's economic planning and a rather casual approach to contracts, placed, at times, severe strains on the relationship.

(iii)   *Japan's relations with the Soviet Union*

The Tanaka Cabinet had moved boldly to establish its new relationship with the People's Republic of China. While Japan was anxious to avoid involvement in the Sino-Soviet dispute, its approach to the Soviet Union was infinitely more cautious. In their dealings with Moscow, Tanaka and his successors, to a greater extent than many European Conservative leaders, found it difficult to escape from the perspectives of the Cold War. This was not a result of the northern territories issue. Japan had also had territorial disputes with the United States, China and South Korea. To some extent, Japan's hesitation derived from a desire not to offend Washington or Peking. Yet the roots of the problem lay much deeper. Yoshida Shigeru, it will be recalled, had regarded the Russians, unlike the Chinese, as 'real Communists' and therefore especially dangerous. Since the death of the ebullient Kōno Ichirō in 1965 no powerful Conservative Party faction leader had openly embraced the cause of Soviet-Japanese amity. There was thus no coalition of political leaders, business organizations and other interest groups able to counterbalance the almost hysterical anti-Communism of the Liberal Democratic Party's extreme right wing, now roused to new heights of militancy by the Tanaka visit to Peking. At the same time, for historical and cultural reasons, there was no widespread, persistent popular demand for full normalization of ties with Moscow. In the 1970s, as in the 1950s, the Soviet Union remained, for most Japanese, an unknown country with a dark and sinister image. The extent of its postwar recovery and the significance of its new global role were understood only by a limited circle of political leaders, businessmen and academic specialists. Underlying the stereotypes created by three decades of Cold War propaganda was the notion, formed during the Meiji, Taishō and early Shōwa eras, that the Russians were 'backward Europeans', occupying a generally lowly position in the hierarchy of nations, whatever their pretensions to the contrary.

The dominant groups in the Soviet leadership, for their part, had viewed the Sino-American *détente* and the development of the new relationship between Tōkyō and Peking with considerable misgivings. The expansion of Soviet military forces in the Far East during the 1960s had been a direct response to the emergence of an implacably anti-Soviet leadership in Peking. The new emphasis given to the Far East by Soviet military planners in the 1970s must be viewed in the context of the shift in the strategic balance precipitated by the events of 1971–2. Nixon, Kissinger, and, later, Ford, no doubt, hoped to maintain a certain degree of equidistance in their relations with Moscow and Peking. The Russians, on the other hand, feared the emergence of a Washington-Tōkyō-Seoul-Peking axis along their vulnerable eastern borders. Their apprehensions were not entirely groundless. Nixon's visit to Peking (just after the fall of Lin Piao) had coincided with a massive redeployment of Chinese military strength away from the Taiwan Straits onto the Sino-Soviet border. Between 1969 and 1971 the Chinese People's Liberation army had maintained 56 divisions opposite Taiwan and 32 divisions along the Inner Asian frontiers. By the time Nixon arrived in Peking 40 divisions were stationed opposite Taiwan and 45 along the Sino-Soviet border. By the mid-1970s the ratio had been altered to 45:56. Significant redeployments of air and naval power had also taken place.[7] From July 1973, moreover, the Chinese discontinued their inter-continental ballistic missile programme (directed at the United States) and diverted their resources to the development of nuclear-tipped medium and international range missiles targeted against the Soviet Union.[8]

Japan, at the same time, was emerging as a significant factor in the regional military balance. As far as can be judged from documents currently available, neither Tanaka Kakuei nor his immediate successors, Miki Takeo and Fukuda Takeo, viewed the normalization of Sino-Japanese relations as a step towards the forging of an anti-Soviet grand alliance. Moscow's sensitivities were, however, understandable. Whatever the personal views of Tanaka, Miki and Fukuda, the strength of the anti-Soviet elements in the Japanese Conservative establishment was well understood. It also seemed clear to Moscow that Japan's strategic planning developed in the context of discussions between the Defence Agency and the Pentagon and not necessarily in accordance with decisions taken by the Cabinet. The Carter administration's shift towards Peking in the northern spring of 1978, then the rapid conclusion of a Sino-Japanese treaty of peace and friendship incorporating an 'anti-hegemony' clause, confirmed the Kremlin's worst fears, precipitating a vigorous diplomatic counter-offensive and further accelerating the build-up of Soviet forces in the Far East.

While Moscow thus adopted a policy of *si vis pacem para bellum* it also believed Japan's active participation in the emerging hostile coalition might be averted by offering Tōkyō an important role in the development of Siberia. It was doubtless recognized that no Japanese government would willingly replace an irksome dependence on the United States for a equally disagreeable dependence on its superpower rival. Nevertheless, it was hoped that the emergence of the Soviet Union as an important market, source of raw materials and field for investment might eventually result in the formation of a 'pro-Soviet' lobby, comparable to the American, Chinese and Korean lobbies. This, it was thought, would discourage the Japanese government from pursuing policies inimical to Soviet interests. The Russians also assumed that independently minded Japanese nationalists would welcome access to Soviet markets and resources as a means of securing greater freedom of manoeuvre in world politics.

Moscow's calculations proved to be ill founded. On questions of Soviet policy the Japanese government was not prepared either to act independently of the United States or to confront the extreme right. Although the USSR had raised the question of Japanese participation in Siberian development as early as 1966, Tōkyō did not make any positive response until the Nixon-Brezhnev summit of June 1973, then the conclusion of the United States-Soviet trade agreements, had made it seem clear that Washington was committed to *détente*.[9] Even then, despite the fact that Moscow seemed prepared to give Japan a pre-eminent role in the development of the Tyumen oil fields, the exploitation of coal and natural gas in Yakutsk, the development of oil and gas reserves on the continental shelf off Sakhalin, the utilization of Far Eastern forest resources and construction of the port of Wrangel, the Japanese declined to participate at all unless American enterprises also took part. Japan's attitude contrasted dramatically with those of France, West Germany and Italy, which were also beginning to play a more active role in Soviet economic development. Like the Trojan high priesthood in Homer's Illiad, the Japanese establishment sensed some sinister motive behind the apparent generosity of its old ideological antagonist, and was reluctant to move.

Although the USSR acquiesced to Japan's desire, negotiations proceeded at a glacial pace. Tanaka Kakuei's visit to the Soviet Union in September 1973, the first by a Japanese Prime Minister in seventeen years, did little to break the ice. Neither side was prepared to compromise on the territorial issue. The Japanese declined to consider conclusion of a peace treaty unless the Soviet Union promised to return the four northern islands. This immediately aroused Moscow's suspicions. Japan had never made settlement of territorial disputes a precondition for conclusion of treaties with South Korea, Taiwan or the People's Republic, let alone the United States. The Japanese, for their part, felt somewhat alarmed by the colossal scale of the Soviet development projects, the vast sums of money involved and the long-term nature of Soviet economic planning. The political and strategic implications of participation in such titanic enterprises, far greater than anything contemplated in China, Korea, South-East Asia or the Middle East, would obviously be considerable. As originally conceived, the Tyumen oil project, for example, was to have supplied Japan with 25–40 million tons of oil per annum (some 8–14 per cent of total requirements) through a pipeline extending 7,000 kilometres from the region east of the Urals, through Irkutsk in central Siberia to Nahodka on the Japan Sea coast. From Nahodka the oil was to have been transported to the port of Niigata (conveniently close to Tanaka Kakuei's electorate) on the north-west coast of Honshū. To help finance this undertaking, estimated to cost altogether $US2,500 million, the USSR had requested a Japanese Export-Import Bank loan of $US1,000 million. In the spring of 1974, in the wake of the first oil crisis, Moscow announced that for technical reasons it had been forced to abandon the plan for construction of a pipeline all the way to Nahodka. Oil was now to be transported to Japan from Tyumen to Taishet by pipeline, then from Taishet to the Japan Sea coast by means of a new Trans-Siberian railway.[10] The quantity of oil would be 25 million tons annually, rather less than originally estimated. To finance this revised scheme, the USSR requested an Export-Import Bank loan of $US3,200 million from Japan. The Japanese hesitated. On the one hand, it seemed imperative to diversify the nation's sources of oil supply. Massive dependence on the Middle East was clearly dangerous. Reliance on American multinational oil companies had been distasteful and had restricted Japan's independence. Yet it proved impossible for Japanese leaders to abandon the idea that the sheiks of Arabia and the directors of the Seven Sisters would always be easier to deal with than the Communist Party of the Soviet Union. In the United States, Senator Henry Jackson, the most implacable opponent of Nixon's policy of *détente* with the Soviet Union, had launched his campaign against the Soviet-American treaty and was advocating that Japan's interest be directed towards Alaskan oil resources.[11] There were also projects for oil development in China. At the meeting of the United States-Japan Economic Co-operation Committee held in June 1974 the Japanese were told that, for strategic and economic reasons, Washington was not enthusiastic about the development of Siberian resources.[12] About the same time, Assistant Secretary of State Ingersoll told the Senate Foreign Relations Committee that the United States had made no commitment either to the Soviet Union or to Japan on Siberian development.[13] By the end of the year it was clear that Japan, too, would pull out of the Tyumen project.

Even so, despite the virtual abrogation of the United States-Soviet Trade Agreement in January 1975, Russo-Japanese trade increased steadily throughout the 1970s. Various small-scale resource projects went ahead. The Soviet Union emerged as a Japanese export market approximately comparable in importance to Australia,

Great Britain, Canada, Indonesia, Saudi Arabia, Iran, Taiwan or Singapore. By the middle of the decade Russia had become Japan's fourth largest steel market (after the United States, China and South Korea), its third largest market for plant and machinery (after the United States and South Korea), its fourth largest supplier of forest products (after the United States, Indonesia and Malaysia) and its second most important source of cotton (after the United States).[14] The relationship clearly had some future.

(iv) *Japan's relations with the Korean peninsula*

The great power realignments of 1971–2 had initially improved the prospects for relaxation of tensions in Korea. In both Seoul and Pyongyang, alarm at the unpredictability of allies and concern about the future of Japan stimulated interest in the possibility of national reconciliation. Nevertheless, the 4 July 1972 North-South Joint Communiqué and the formation of a co-ordinating committee to promote political, economic and cultural exchange between the two states, with a view to eventual reunification, failed to achieve significant results. The international and domestic obstacles to settlement of the Korean problem seemed insurmountable. The American-Soviet *détente* and the new climate in relations between the United States and China were not followed by a *rapprochement* between Washington and Pyongyang. China and the Soviet Union did not move to develop relations with Seoul. By the end of 1972 the governments of both Koreas, in expectation of a new era of intensified ideological competition, had begun to consolidate their domestic political structures. In the South, Pak Chung Hi moved to implement constitutional changes designed to establish a near-absolute presidential dictatorship. The South Korean leader, already in an exceptionally strong position as Chief Executive and Supreme Commander of the Armed Forces, assumed additional powers over the legislature and the judiciary, reserving the right to dissolve the National Assembly, disband political parties, appoint all judges, proclaim martial law and take any emergency measures deemed necessary in the areas of defence, diplomacy, administration, justice and national economy. The new constitution also made it possible for the President to remain in office indefinitely.[15] Inauguration of the New Order was followed almost immediately by draconian repression of the nation's residual Opposition parties, trade unions, nonconformist religious groups, dissident academics and student activists. In the North, Kim Il Sung strengthened his hold on the reins of power, launching a renewed drive for self-sufficient economic modernization and endeavouring to persuade the party, the armed forces and the intelligence organizations that a dynastic succession offered the best prospects for long-term stability. By the end of the decade, an unparalleled family personality cult, incorporating elements derived from the ancient kingdom of Koguryŏ, Stalinism and Maoism, had been created to buttress the foundations of the world's first socialist monarchy.

These events disturbed wide sections of public opinion in Japan, on the right and on the left. Nevertheless, important groups in the Liberal Democratic Party, the Foreign Ministry, the Defence Agency, the armed forces and the business community remained convinced that a dependent, anti-Communist regime in Seoul was a vital strategic asset. Tanaka's *rapprochement* with China, indeed, had enhanced the importance of South Korea in the eyes of the Japanese right. Chiang Kai-shek had been ignominiously sacrificed on the altar of political expediency. The right was determined that the same fate would not befall Pak Chung Hi. There remained, however, a general (albeit not universal) consensus that Japan itself could not play a direct military role on the peninsula. In these circumstances there seemed no alternative to continued reliance on the United States. For this reason the Japanese government energetically opposed American plans for a graduated withdrawal of ground forces from South Korea. Pressure from the Fukuda Cabinet undoubtedly influenced President Jimmy Carter's decision to retain a strong military presence in the peninsula, despite his belief that a reduced American profile could contribute to *détente* and regional stability.

Japan's economic position in South Korea was further consolidated during the first half of the decade. United States influence, in contrast, continued to recede. The totalitarian character of the Korean state, the commitment of its leadership to high economic growth within a free market framework, low wage levels and the obstacles confronting trade unions and anti-pollution campaigners encouraged many Japanese corporations, expecially in the fields of aluminium, petro-chemicals, shipbuilding and steel, to transfer all or part of their operations to South Korea. By 1976 Japanese investment accounted for some 64 per cent of all foreign investment in the republic. The United States, the second-largest investor, trailed a long way behind with 17 per cent. The Masan Export Processing Zone, where some 90 per cent of all investment was Japanese, had become, in many respects, a continental extension of the Japanese archipelago. After the United States, Japan was South Korea's largest source of foreign loans and credits. In 1977 the republic absorbed 5.1 per cent of Japan's total exports, making it the country's largest market after the United States and non-Communist South-East Asia. In the same year some 3.0 per cent of Japan's imports originated in South Korea. The balance of trade was so heavily in Tōkyō's favour that in the period 1965–75 the Japanese trade surplus was three times the total value of Japanese aid and investment in the republic. Some 30 per cent of South Korea's trade, moreover, was in the hands of Japanese trading companies.[16]

Since the early 1960s Japanese governments had found themselves under constant pressure from the liberal elements in the Conservative Party, from the Opposition, the press and public opinion, on the moral issues involved in support for the Pak Chung Hi regime. The problems resembled, in many aspects, those posed by British Commonwealth, European and American relations with the Republic of South Africa or the Greek colonels. They became more acute as the Pak Chung Hi dictatorship, undermined by Byzantine palace intrigue and military-bureaucratic factionalism, confronted by mounting popular opposition, and shaken by the world economic crisis of the mid-1970s, slowly lurched towards its inevitable end.* In the

---

* On 26 October 1979 Pak Chung Hi was assassinated at a dinner party by the Director of the Korean Central Intelligence Agency, Kim Jae-kyu.

face of public disenchantment with its Korean policies, the Japanese government, like its Western counterparts, retreated into ambiguity and equivocation, launching, where necessary, elaborate campaigns of deception punctuated by ritual denunciations of the misdemeanours of its protégé. These strategies, while successfully preserving the relationship with Seoul, and the American military guarantees which underpinned it, did not necessarily enhance the image of the South Korean state or inspire public confidence in the integrity of the Japanese government.

It would be tempting to view the political conflicts that racked South Korea in the 1970s partly in terms of Japanese-American rivalry. Nixon, Kissinger, Ford and Carter were anxious to scale down the level of American military involvement in the peninsula. Washington's enthusiasm to have Japan assume the burdens of containment had temporarily faded. So long as *détente* continued, this gave the United States a certain interest in promoting North-South dialogue, a process which might have been facilitated by restoration of democratic government in Seoul. Japan, on the other hand, having replaced the United States as the dominant economic power in South Korea desired the American military presence to continue. This gave Japan a certain interest in maintaining the political status quo in Seoul. Such an interpretation, while not without its merits, would be too simplistic. In reality, it would appear that as the storms unleashed by the events of 1971–2 swept through Seoul, a variety of Japanese and American organizations, official and unofficial, interlocking, overlapping and competing in complex ways, sought to advance their interests by the age old technique of promoting rival Korean factions. This made co-ordination of policy between Tōkyō and Washington, at the highest level, more and more difficult to achieve. It also complicated formulation of Korean policy in both capitals. These tendencies were well illustrated by the Kim Dae Jung affair of 1973.

On 8 August 1973 Kim Dae Jung, the principal luminary in the South Korean liberal democratic opposition, a moderate Catholic of middle class background who had been narrowly defeated by Pak Chung Hi in the 1971 general elections* and had subsequently taken refuge in the United States, was abducted from a Tōkyō hotel by agents of the South Korean Central Intelligence Agency (KCIA), taken to Seoul, temporarily released, then arrested, tried and sentenced to prison on charges of violating presidential decrees. The facts of the case were well known to both the United States and Japanese governments. The United States government, doubtless suspecting that Pak Chung Hi had ordered his rival's abduction, and aware of the serious threat to Kim's life, took a strong line against Seoul. On 21 August 1973 Philip Habib, the United States ambassador to Seoul, wrote to Secretary of State William Rogers informing him that the incident had been masterminded by the KCIA and explaining that he had lost no opportunity to remind South Korean leaders of its gravity. Kissinger, alarmed, gave instructions that the United States government provide protection for Kim should he request it.[17] Powerful elements in the Japanese government, in contrast, seemed not altogether ill disposed towards the KCIA's

---

*   Some observers maintained that Kim had actually won the election, although the official count had found the incumbent President to be victorious.

action. At about the same time that Habib was writing to Rogers, the Japanese Minister for Justice, Tanaka Isaji, told the Diet that he suspected the abduction had been planned and executed by 'the secret police of a foreign government'. Some years later Tanaka confided to the *Mainichi Shimbun* that on the day of Kim's abduction, before the incident was reported in the mass media,

> a high government official came into my office without even going through my secretary He stood erect in front of me and reported that Kim Dae Jung had been kidnapped ... When I asked who the culprits were, the high official moved up to me and whispered into my ear: 'The secret police of the Republic of Korea, the KCIA.'

Tanaka Isaji always refused to identify the name and position of his informant, on the grounds that 'if I talked, it would mean that law enforcement authorities knew about the kidnapping [before it happened]'.

Whatever the involvement of high-ranking Japanese officials like Tanaka's mysterious visitor, the Foreign Ministry and the Police Agency did not take an indulgent view of the abduction. Japanese police investigators announced that fingerprints found at the scene of the crime were those of Kim Dong Un, a First Secretary at the South Korean Embassy in Tōkyō and a suspected KCIA agent. The Foreign Ministry, outraged at this blatant violation of Japanese sovereignty by secret agents of another power, urged that the government act promptly to (1) secure an apology from South Korea, (2) ensure that Seoul punish the persons responsible for the abduction, (3) have Kim Dae Jung returned safely to Tōkyō and, (4) obtain assurances that similar incidents would not occur in the future.[18]

As usual the Foreign Ministry found its views totally ignored. Whatever Washington may have felt, the Tanaka Cabinet had no intention of embarrassing Pak Chung Hi. Prime Minister Tanaka, who himself attached considerable importance to Japan's ties with Seoul, was also acutely conscious of the strength of the Fukuda faction and uneasy about the growing restiveness of the party's extreme right. He was therefore anxious to negotiate a 'political settlement'. The United States, too, eventually came around to this view. Foreign Minister Ōhira, accordingly, announced in the Diet that Japan and South Korea would set up a joint commission to investigate the matter. Japan, he maintained, was in no position to demand that Kim Dae Jung be returned to Tōkyō or that the offenders be punished.* While pandemonium reigned in the Diet and demonstrators gathered in the streets, secret emissaries shuttled back and forth across the Tsushima Straits. Eventually, in the winter of 1973, the South Korean Prime Minister (and former director of the KCIA) Kim Jong Pil called on Tanaka and, explaining that the identity of the abductors remained unknown, apologized, in general terms, for 'the trouble Koreans caused

---

* Japan's attitude contrasted strikingly with that of West Germany. In 1967 the KCIA had kidnapped seventeen Korean scholars and students resident in the Federal Republic and taken them to Seoul, where they were tried for a variety of alleged offences against the state. Bonn strongly denounced Seoul's infringement of its sovereignty, effectively suspended diplomatic relations and cut off all aid to the Pak Chung Hi government.

the government of Japan'. No mention was made of any violation of Japanese sovereignty. Kim Dae Jung remained under detention, despite the South Korean Prime Minister's assurance that he would be free to leave the country if he wished to do so.

Both governments thereafter considered the matter closed. Important groups in the Liberal Democratic Party, however, were far from satisfied. Utsunomiya Tokuma, Fujiyama Aiichirō, Akagi Munenori, Kimura Toshio, Tagawa Seiichi and Kōno Yōhei (the late Kōno Ichirō's son), supported by the entire membership of the Afro-Asian Problems Study Association, in all about a hundred Conservative politicians, insisted that Japan press for Kim Dae Jung's release, postpone the scheduled meeting of the Japan-South Korea Ministerial Talks until Pak Chung Hi freed his former opponent and exercise more discretion in future economic co-operation with Seoul.[19] The Foreign Ministry, the Ministry of Justice, the Police Agency, most of the Opposition parties and a large body of public opinion, too, were scandalized by the government's attitude. The dispute dragged on acrimoniously. Japanese opponents of the Pak Chung Hi regime began to recall the territorial dispute over Takeshima (Dokto) and make embarrassing comparisons between the Cabinet's attitudes to Seoul and Moscow. In June 1974 Professor Edwin O. Reischauer, the former American ambassador to Japan, added fuel to the fire by delivering a stinging attack on the Pak Chung Hi dictatorship in an interview with the *Mainichi Shimbun*. The fate of Kim Dae Jung, Reischauer asserted, was an 'international question'. Unless democracy was restored South Korea would ultimately collapse.[20] By the autumn of 1974, as the South Korean economy reeled under the impact of the first oil crisis, sections of the Japanese business community, which had previously viewed the Kim Dae Jung affair as a minor irritant in an otherwise extremely satisfactory relationship, began to express concern about the future of the Pak Chung Hi regime.[21] Eventually, in July 1975, the South Korean government, in a *note verbale* to Miki Takeo's Foreign Minister, Miyazawa Kiichi, explained that its own investigations had revealed that Kim Dong Un had in no way been involved in the affair (despite his fingerprints having been found at the scene of the crime). Miki, his attention increasingly diverted from foreign policy by the upheavals in his own party, felt nothing could be gained by pursuing the matter further.

Even so, the Kim Dae Jung affair refused to die. In 1977 a new crisis broke when Kim Hyung Wook, a former director of the KCIA, told the United States Congress House of Representatives Committee on International Relations that his own organization had been responsible for the abduction. This testimony was confirmed by the 'accidental' release of secret United States diplomatic documents in 1979.[22] Although these revelations were dismissed by the Fukuda Cabinet as 'mere hearsay', their impact on public perceptions of the relationship with South Korea was considerable. Anxiety about the South Korean connection further intensified after the trial and imprisonment of the dissident poet Kim Chi Ha, the severe punishments meted out to a number of student activists and the arrest of two Japanese citizens on espionage charges.[23] Evidence that the KCIA had penetrated Japanese political parties, sections of the bureaucracy, the mass media and the academic community also caused increasing concern.

While the Tanaka, Miki and Fukuda Cabinets were eager to maintain good relations with Seoul, they were not necessarily opposed to improvement of ties with Pyongyang. If the anti-Communist right wing of the Liberal Democratic Party insisted that preservation of the Pak Chung Hi regime in Seoul was an absolute condition of Japanese security, other Conservatives, like the majority of Socialists and Communists, contended that Japan's true interests would best be served by efforts to promote relaxation of regional tensions and, eventually, peaceful reunification of the peninsula. Japan, it was argued, should gradually move towards a policy of equidistance between Seoul and Pyongyang. Kim Il Sung's Democratic People's Republic was not viewed as a prospective middle-class liberal democracy or as an egalitarian socialist paradise. Nevertheless, it was felt that *détente* provided opportunities for establishing potentially valuable economic, political and cultural contacts. Initially, the outlook seemed promising. The North Koreans, whose economy had made notable advances during the 1960s, were anxious to reduce the level of dependence on the Soviet Union, hitherto their main source of expensive capital equipment. Pyongyang was also determined to acquire the world's most advanced automation, computer and electronic equipment in order to upgrade its industrial base. The prospects for reconciliation with the United States seemed limited. Particular emphasis, therefore, was placed on developing ties with Japan and the countries of Western Europe.

In the autumn of 1972 a North Korean economic delegation led by Kim Syok Jin, a high-ranking official of the International Trade Promotion Committee, arrived in Japan for private talks with business leaders. The Democratic People's Republic, Kim stressed, was committed to a policy of economic self reliance. Still, North Korea was interested in importing chemical plants, high-grade iron and steel, automobiles and other items. It was ready to export non-ferrous metals (gold, silver, lead, zinc, cadmium), magnesium clinker, anthracite, fish products and herbal medicines to Japan. A government-to-government trade agreement could be negotiated if necessary. The Democratic People's Republic was not interested in Japanese loans, Kim said. It was, however, hopeful of negotiating long-term low interest deferred payments.[24] Prime Minister Tanaka, echoing remarks made by Foreign Minister Ōhira, told the Diet that Japan did not adopt a hostile attitude towards Pyongyang. Nevertheless, his government was neither considering recognition of the Democratic People's Republic nor promoting its entry into the United Nations. For various reasons, it would be difficult to adopt a policy of equidistance between the two states on the peninsula.[25]

The slight thaw in relations between Tōkyō and Pyongyang was followed by a marginal increase in bilateral trade. During the early part of the 1970s the Democratic People's Republic invested heavily in the purchase of sophisticated industrial plant and equipment, much of which was obtained from Japan on short-term credit. In the wake of the 1973 oil crisis, however, the North Korean economy, like its southern counterpart, ran into severe difficulties. Energy costs rose, export prices for the country's minerals fell. Increasingly serious domestic political struggles, inefficient economic management, poor planning, inadequate port facilities and unfamiliarity with the conventions of foreign trade also caused problems. Export contracts were unfulfilled, debts were rescheduled.[26] The resultant lack of confidence among the nation's trading partners caused a sharp decline in economic contacts with the outside world. Pyongyang's international reputation also suffered from scandals concerning the conduct of some of its diplomats in Western Europe. Trade with Japan did not fully recover until the end of the decade. Political relations, too, failed to develop. On 9–10 August 1974 Kim Il Sung told Utsunomiya Tokuma that he had no intention of normalizing ties with Japan in such a way as would consolidate the division of the peninsula. 'Cross recognition' was out of the question. Nor could diplomatic ties be established until Article 3 of the 1965 Japan-Republic of Korea Basic Treaty, which implied (to the North Koreans) that Seoul was the only legal government on the peninsula, was declared null and void.[27] In view of the attitudes of the United States and South Korea, and the delicate factional balance in the Liberal Democratic Party, it was clear that efforts to develop the new relationship beyond this point were doomed to failure.

(v)   *Japan's relations with the Middle East, South-East Asia and Oceania*

The Yom Kippur War delivered the first serious blow to George Kennan's strategy of indirectly controlling Japan through oil supply. In November 1973, in the wake of the Arab oil embargo against nations supporting Israel, Japan, like France and most of America's NATO allies, moved to distance itself from Washington's policies in the Middle East. The break was not decisive and Japan continued to encourage American regional initiatives in many ways. Nevertheless, Japanese involvement in the Middle East began to develop in directions totally unforeseen by United States global strategists in the early postwar period.[28]

On 19 October 1973, two days after the OAPEC oil ministers' meeting in Kuwait had decided to reduce oil production 'until such a time as the international community compels Israel to relinquish [the occupied Arab] territories', the Saudi ambassador, accompanied by his colleagues from nine other Arab countries, called on Foreign Minister Ōhira to request his support in the ongoing struggle. Ōhira, having just confronted the United States on China policy, was not anxious to alienate the Americans further. Japan had traditionally adopted a 'pro-Western' but generally even-handed policy towards the Middle East. The region was seen to lie outside any conceivable Japanese sphere of influence. There was a strong desire to avoid involvement in its explosive political conflicts. While Israel was clearly a United States client state, the antagonism between Arabs and Jews did not readily lend itself to analysis in Asianist-Westernist terms. Views in the Liberal Democratic Party were divided. Ōhira, therefore, told the Saudi ambassador that Japan hoped for an early settlement of the conflict and would continue to support the 1967 United Nations resolution calling on Israel to withdraw from occupied Arab territories.

This attitude, formally outlined in 'A Statement of Japan's Position on the Fourth Middle East War', drafted by Vice-Foreign Minister Hōgen Shinsaku, did not satisfy the Saudi ambassador. Japan was therefore not classified as a 'friendly' country eligible for special consideration under the terms of the 17 October OAPEC resolution. The Saudi authorities subsequently ordered Japan's Arabian Oil Company to cut back production. The international oil majors followed suit.

Early in November another Arab oil ministers' meeting in Kuwait decided on even more stringent measures against nations seen to be supporting the American-Israeli axis. Within a few days the major European nations had begun to shift, in varying degrees, towards a more 'pro-Arab' position. Kissinger, profoundly disturbed, flew into Tōkyō, urging Japan to co-operate wholeheartedly with the United States. Concessions to the Arab world at this juncture, he declared, would further stimulate nationalist passions, making a Middle Eastern settlement more difficult to achieve. Kissinger was in no position, however, to guarantee Japan access to oil from either Alaska or the American mainland. In this situation, fierce struggles erupted in the Japanese government. The Foreign Ministry, stressing the overriding importance of relations with the United States, argued against altering the nation's basic policy towards the Middle East. MITI, supported by the dominant groups in the business community, and impressed by the attitude of the European nations, recommended a greater measure of support for the Arab cause. Inside the Liberal Democratic Party, Prime Minister Tanaka, unfamiliar with the Middle Eastern problem, adopted a neutral attitude. Foreign Minister Ōhira, too, vacillated. Nakasone, in contrast, energetically advocated a complete break with United States policies. 'The era of blindly following has come to an end', he declared.

Nakasone and his supporters carried the day. On 22 November 1973 a meeting of Arab oil ministers in Vienna announced the suspension of sanctions against all EEC countries except the Netherlands in response to the revision of their attitudes towards Israel. Three days later the Japanese government, following the example set by America's European allies, declared that any settlement of the Middle Eastern problem should include withdrawal of Israeli forces from territories occupied since 1967 and recognition of 'the legitimate rights of the Palestinian people'. Prime Minister Tanaka announced suspension of jet fuel supplies to United States air force bases in Japan from 1 January 1974. Deputy Prime Minister Miki at once made preparations for an extensive tour of the Middle East. As a goodwill gesture $5 million was immediately earmarked for Palestinian refugees. The result was predictable. On Christmas Day 1973 another Arab oil ministers' meeting in Kuwait, noting the changes in Japanese policy, decided to place Japan on the 'friendly' list. The United States, certainly, found Japan's pro-Arab tilt "regrettable." American Jewish organizations threatened to boycott Japanese products. Yet the efficacy of a diplomacy based on the principle of *nagai mono ni makareyō* had seldom been more dramatically demonstrated. Japan's oil supply shortfall during the crisis was a mere 3 per cent, compared with 11 per cent for the United States and 19 per cent for Western Europe.

In the years that followed, the Japanese ship of state, constantly tacking in accordance with new winds and currents, continued to steer a careful course through the treacherous waters of the Middle East. In the United Nations, the adjustments in Japanese policy remained largely at the rhetorical level. Japan's actual voting behaviour changed little.[29] This doubtless helped to repair relations with the United

States and the American Jewish community. At the same time, Japan's profile in the Islamic world, hitherto obscure and ill-defined, expanded considerably. Deputy Prime Minister Miki's tour of December 1973 encompassed Saudi Arabia, Egypt, Abu Dhabi, Kuwait, Qatar, Syria, Iraq and Iran. Nakasone visited Iraq and Iran. In January 1973 Kōsaka Zentarō embarked on an odyssey that took him from Morocco to Yemen. Wherever they went the Japanese dignitaries uttered sentiments interpreted as sympathetic to the Arab cause. They also promised economic and technical aid on a scale generous even by early postwar American standards. By the end of 1974, moreover, the Palestine Liberation Organization (PLO) had established a liaison office in Tōkyō. Reflecting the new trends, Islamic studies experienced a minor boom in Japanese institutions of higher learning.

It is difficult to argue with success. Once it had taken place, the shift in Japan's Middle Eastern policies won approval from all groups in the Liberal Democratic Party, from the Opposition and from the general public. The entire issue of the Middle East remained closed until the Iranian Revolution of 1978–9.

Détente, then the end of the Indochina War, also brought the complexity of the Japanese-American relationship in South-East Asia into sharper focus. Undoubtedly, Tōkyō and Washington continued to believe they shared important interests in this region. Yet it was very clear, as it had been in the 1950s and the 1960s, that these interests were not necessarily always convergent. The 1970s saw Japan's final emergence as the dominant economic power in non-Communist South-East Asia. This development occurred at a time when American influence in the area was in full retreat. Japanese investment in all ASEAN countries except Thailand had increased rapidly since the late 1960s. American investment, in contrast, had declined in all states except Malaysia. In 1971 Japan's share of total foreign investment in ASEAN countries had been 15.62 per cent. The American share had been 36.40 per cent. By 1976 the Japanese share had increased to 36.44 per cent, while the American share had declined to 26.02 per cent. By the end of the decade some 20.60 per cent of Japan's total direct overseas investment had been channelled into ASEAN countries. Investment in ASEAN represented two-thirds of all Japanese investment in Asia. Between 2,000 and 3,000 Japanese companies operated in the region. Giant corporations like National, Toyota and Matsushita had come to exercise an enormous influence on the local economies. Their political influence, too, was by no means negligible. Medium and small Japanese enterprises were also active. Following the pattern established in the 1960s, Japanese investment was especially heavy in Indonesia (almost 40 per cent of the total share by 1976), where it far exceeded that of any other nation. By the middle of the decade Japan had also become the largest single foreign investor in Malaysia (21.42 per cent of the total share), Singapore (26.57 per cent) and the Philippines (34.93 per cent). Only in Thailand was the overall share of Japanese investment declining. The Japanese aid programme in the five ASEAN countries, too, was very substantial.[30]

During the early 1970s several conservative Japanese strategic thinkers, following the example of their American counterparts in the years before *détente*, began to argue the case for a more active military role in the region.[31] The violent anti-

Japanese demonstrations during Tanaka's visits to Bangkok and Djakarta in January 1974 made even the most hawkish elements in the government and Liberal Democratic Party realize that such notions were, for the time being at least, unrealistic. The persistence of anti-Japanese sentiment throughout South-East Asia thus forced many conservatives to conclude, somewhat reluctantly, perhaps, that they had no alternative but to persuade Washington to continue acting as the military guarantor of the status quo, despite the fact that its efforts had been so far notably unsuccessful.

Even so, the Japanese government, conscious of its powerful economic position, redoubled its efforts to distinguish its policies from those of its North American ally. Many groups in the United States, for example, had initially regarded ASEAN as an emerging economic bloc that might, like the EEC, eventually act in ways contrary to Washington's interests.[32] Japan, in contrast, decided to encourage the organization from the beginning. The Tanaka Cabinet increased economic assistance to the nations of non-Communist South-East Asia, launched a vigorous programme of cultural exchange and made a concerted effort to promote a greater sense of social responsibility among Japanese firms operating in the area. On the eve of the first ASEAN Prime Ministers Conference in Bali (February 1976) Prime Minister Miki Takeo suggested that he would like to arrange a meeting with the five South-East Asian leaders immediately after the summit. At this time, the five Prime Ministers turned down his request as 'premature'. Japan revealed its 'positive' attitude towards the organization at the second ASEAN leaders' meeting, held at Kuala Lumpur, in August 1977, and attended by Prime Ministers Fukuda Takeo, Malcolm Fraser of Australia and Robert Muldoon of New Zealand. At Kuala Lumpur, Fukuda, stressing his country's 'special and extremely close ties with ASEAN', committed Japan to act as 'an equal partner' in the region's development. A 'heart-to-heart dialogue', he maintained, was essential. Specifically, Fukuda held out the prospect of Japanese participation in five major ASEAN projects, doubling Japan's aid to all developing countries over a period of five years and giving ASEAN special priority. Japan would reassess its aid and investment programme, give sympathetic consideration to the ASEAN countries' desire to process at least some raw materials and co-operate to increase access to Japanese markets for the region's exports. Support for increased cultural exchanges, both between Japan and ASEAN, and among the member states themselves, was also promised. Fukuda, like his predecessors, stressed Japan's lack of interest in any regional military role.[33]

At the same time, with the end of the Indochina War, the Japanese government, in striking contrast to the United States, made considerable efforts to place its relations with Vietnam on a sound footing. It also discreetly encouraged dialogues between Hanoi and the capitals of non-Communist South-East Asia. Japan's policies closely paralleled those of France, Sweden and the Australian Labour government. Both the Japanese government and the business community showed a lively appreciation of Vietnam's future potential as a political influence in South-East Asia, as a market for plant and equipment and as a source of raw materials. In the years after the war, Japan-Vietnam trade, although small in volume, expanded steadily. In 1976 the total volume of two-way trade was $US215.5 million. By 1977 it had grown to $US242 million. Japan's trade with the Socialist Republic of Vietnam, while in no way comparable to its trade with any of the ASEAN countries, was approximately the same value as trade with Austria, Finland or North Korea, and rather more significant than trade with Bulgaria, Czechoslovakia, East Germany and Hungary.[34] It clearly had considerable capacity for growth. In 1975–6, Japan also extended some $US25 million in aid to Vietnam. So promising did the future of Japanese relations with Vietnam appear that in 1976 Prime Minister Fukuda was obliged to assure ASEAN leaders that Japan's ties with Hanoi would in no way alter its attitude to ASEAN.[35]

By the end of 1977, the situation in South-East Asia appeared to be developing in a direction generally favourable to Japanese perceptions of their interests in the area. The erosion of United States influence had not encouraged a Soviet advance. The fall of Saigon had not stimulated Communist movements in neighbouring countries. While there were signs of increasing Sino-Vietnamese tension, culminating in China's total suspension of aid to Hanoi and the massive exodus of ethnic Chinese from Vietnam, Vietnam's relations with the ASEAN powers improved steadily. Between 28 December and 12 January 1978 the Vietnamese Deputy Prime Minister and Foreign Minister Nguyen Duy Trinh visited all the ASEAN countries except Singapore to discuss trade and regional security problems. His tour, which was welcomed in Japan, appeared to have met with considerable success. The communiqué issued after his visit to Thailand spoke eloquently of progress towards the development of mutually advantageous relations, of the contribution both countries could make to the cause of peace, independence and neutrality in South-East Asia. During the course of 1978, despite worsening relations between Hanoi and Peking, and clashes on the Vietnamese-Cambodian border, the *rapprochement* between Vietnam and ASEAN continued to develop.

It was during the halcyon days of *détente*, too, that Japanese governments came to attach increasing importance to relations with Australia and New Zealand. The Whitlam government in Australia, during its first few weeks in office, had recognized the People's Republic of China, initiated moves to improve relations with Moscow, established diplomatic relations with Hanoi and announced the withdrawal of Australian forces from Vietnam. Overtures were also made to North Korea. In the years that followed, the Australian Labour government assumed an increasingly independent position within the American alliance system, maintained a policy of equidistance between Moscow and Peking, further consolidated Australia's established ties with non-Communist South-East Asia and the nations of the Indian subcontinent, negotiated political, economic and cultural agreements with the Democratic Republic of Vietnam, and launched a vigorous diplomatic offensive to refurbish Australia's image in Africa and the Middle East. The collapse of the Whitlam government in November 1975 was followed by a breakdown in Australia's relations with the Soviet Union and a strategic tilt to China. In most other respects the conservative Fraser Cabinet continued Whitlam's policies. Economic issues apart, the Australian experiment interested a wide range of Japanese political, business and intellectual leaders. It was during the Whitlam and Fraser years that the Japanese-Australian relationship entered its period of greatest intimacy. Bilateral trade reached record levels. Vast resources projects were planned. Japanese investment in Australia increased. More significantly, perhaps, the two nations became involved in a dialogue on a wide range of regional and global issues. By October 1973 Whitlam and Tanaka had agreed to negotiate a treaty of friendship and co-operation. This was eventually signed by Prime Ministers Malcolm Fraser and Miki Takeo in 1976. Thereafter, while historical, cultural and politico-economic constraints precluded the development of any exclusive special relationship, the policies of the two nations began to be shaped, to some extent at least, by a mutual recognition of their common interests in the Western Pacific area.

(vi) Japanese nuclear policies and ratification of the non-proliferation treaty

The decline in United States global influence, multipolarity, the intensification of economic rivalries in the non-Communist world, anticipated shortages in enriched uranium supply and the 1973 oil crisis all had considerable impact on Japan's nuclear policies. It is in this context that the government's extraordinary delay in ratifying the nuclear non-proliferation treaty must be understood.

In July 1974 the United States informed Japan that it would not be able to conclude new agreements to supply enriched uranium for the period after 1982. The anticipated seriousness of enriched uranium supply problems in the 1980s left Japan with four alternative courses of action. It could endeavour to negotiate access to United States uranium enrichment technology and establish joint ventures with American firms. It could attempt to diversify its sources of supply. It could develop an independent enrichment capacity. Or it could endeavour to work out some appropriate combination of all three strategies. In the end, the Japanese government and the nuclear industry decided on the fourth option. Particular emphasis was placed, however, on the development of an independent enrichment capability.

In July 1971 Washington had indicated its willingness to share enrichment technology with the European Community, Great Britain, Japan, Australia and Canada 'on condition that arrangements are made with the United States on financial plans and the preservation of secrets'. Talks between Japan and the United States on enrichment technology sharing began in November 1972 and continued inconclusively for most of the following decade. The Japanese Uranium Enrichment Project Research Council and the American firms of Betchel, Union Carbide and Westinghouse conducted feasibility studies on the establishment of a joint enrichment plant in the United States. Japanese power interests also examined the possibility of participating in joint ventures with General Electrics and Exxon for setting up a centrifugal separation plant. These schemes eventually came to nothing.

By the mid-1970s Soviet offers to supply enriched uranium to Japan at competitive prices were being studied by the Japanese government. So, too, was Japan's possible participation in a joint British, Dutch and West German project to build a series of centrifugal enrichment plants by 1980, and in an ambitious French scheme to set up a Pacific Basin gaseous diffusion enrichment plant, as regional a counterpart to a similar European scheme involving France, Great Britain, West Germany, Belgium and Italy. The prospects for joint ventures with Australia or Canada also aroused a certain amount of interest. Again, most of these projects were eventually shelved because of political, economic or technological difficulties.[36]

At the same time, Japan intensified its own research efforts, focusing, in particular, on the centrifugal separation method. By 1970 the Japanese nuclear industry had virtually perfected the process of converting enriched uranium hexafluoride into the uranium dioxide pellets employed in the fuel elements of nuclear reactors. In 1972 the major nuclear fuel manufacturers in Japan, the Japan Nuclear Fuel Company (Toshiba, 30 per cent, Hitachi, 30 per cent and General Electrics, 40 per cent), Sumitomo Electric Industries (which had licensing agreements with the American firm of Gulf United Nuclear) and Mitsubishi Atomic Power Industries (Mitsubishi Heavy Industries, 20 per cent, Mitsubishi Metal Mining, 40 per cent, with participation from the American firm of Westinghouse), were joined by a new, wholly Japanese owned concern, the Nuclear Fuel Industry Company, set up jointly by the Furukawa Electric Company and Sumitomo Electric Industries. Japan's first fuel reprocessing plant was scheduled to begin operation in the mid-1970s. Research into nuclear waste disposal was also being carried out.[37]

The Japanese government and the nuclear power industry had also begun to display considerable interest in plutonium-fuelled fast breeder reactors. Two experimental fast breeder reactors, the Joyo and the Monju, became critical in the mid-1970s. By July 1983 Japanese scientists had successfully extracted plutonium oxide from the spent fuel rods of the Joyo reactor and had begun processing it into reusable fuel. The optimists in the nuclear power industry were persuaded that large-scale commercial introduction of fast breeder reactors could begin in the mid-1980s and that by the year 2000 all newly established facilities and all replacements would be fast breeders.[38] There was also much interest in advanced thermal reactors.[39]

Japanese missile technology also made significant advances during the 1970s. These developments inevitably enhanced Japan's capacity to construct an independent nuclear strike force. While public opinion remained strongly opposed to the exercise of this option, the upheavals of the early 1970s hardened the views of the small nuclear weapons lobby in the Liberal Democratic Party. On 13 March 1973 Prime Minister Tanaka Kakuei, a man of generally pacific views, assured the House of Representatives Budget Committee that nuclear weapons were essentially offensive in character and therefore incompatible with the Constitution. This statement provoked such a strong reaction from sections of the Liberal Democratic Party that Tanaka was obliged to retract it. On 14 March, in a surprisingly unambiguous 'Unified View', the Prime Minister's statement was amended to imply that possession of tactical nuclear weapons would not contravene the spirit of Article 9.[40] Then, on 18 March, Tanaka told the House of Councillors Budget Committee that while defensive nuclear weapons would not be unconstitutional, nuclear weapons were generally regarded as being offensive in character. In this sense, they *did* run counter to the provisions of the Japanese Constitution. In any case, the government intended to adhere to the three non-nuclear principles and had no intention of acquiring atomic weapons.[41] Two days later Tanaka told the committee that while Japan could not acquire 'offensive nuclear weapons', some kinds of nuclear weapons might not be incompatible with the Constitution. The director-general of the Cabinet Legislative Bureau reportedly told the committee that it was 'difficult' to know whether nuclear weapons were 'offensive' or 'defensive'.[42]

The continued proliferation of nuclear weapons during the 1970s strengthened the position of the Liberal Democratic Party hardliners and their supporters in the bureaucracy, the business community and the academic world. Nevertheless, the government remained opposed to the concept of an independent *force de frappe*. The Indian nuclear test of 18 May 1974 had little impact on the mainstream of Japanese Conservative opinion. Chief Cabinet Secreatry Nikaidō Susumu criticized the Indian decision to develop a military nuclear capacity on the grounds that it was inimical to the cause of non-proliferation, would undermine the basis for regional *détente* and was incompatible with Japan's opposition to nuclear testing. All the Opposition parties issued statements of protest.[43] On 23 May the House of Representatives passed a unanimous resolution condemning the Indian test.[44] The major Japanese newspapers, too, castigated the Indian decision.[45] Opinion polls showed that these sentiments were shared by the vast majority of the Japanese people – 70 per cent of respondents in the 23 May 1974 *Sankei Shimbun* survey regarded the test as 'impermissible', although only 26 per cent felt concerned about the possible implications for Japan's security.[46] The Japanese government announced that its aid to India through the international consortium would not be increased and that it would not participate in United Nations sponsored efforts to help India overcome the effects of the oil crisis.[47]

Far more disturbing than the Indian nuclear programme was President Nixon's announcement in June 1974 that the United States would provide both Egypt and Israel with nuclear reactors and uranium. Since Israel was not even a signatory to the non-proliferation treaty, and was widely believed to be secretly developing a military nuclear capability, this decision called into question Washington's own commitment to the cause of non-proliferation. Japanese observers may also have felt that if the United States could provide nuclear assistance to Israel, it could provide the same kind of assistance to its South Korean allies, to Taiwan, or even to the People's Republic of China, with unforeseeable consequences for Japan's security.

As in the late 1960s, however, the Japanese government's attitude to the non-proliferation treaty was determined not so much by military-security considerations as by anxiety about the potential impact of the agreement on the country's civil nuclear programme. This clearly had foreign policy implications. In many circles, the non-proliferation treaty had come to be seen as an updated version of George Kennan's strategy to exercise 'veto power' over Japanese diplomacy through control of energy supply. While the nuclear power industry was aware that refusal to ratify the treaty would complicate access to uranium, enrichment services and nuclear technology, and was prepared, as early as 1972, to declare that the safeguards were not entirely unacceptable, it was also persuaded that non-proliferation treaty was basically an 'unequal treaty'.[48] By the beginning of 1973 this view seems to have become firmly rooted in the government and the bureaucracy, especially in the Science and Technology Agency.[49] In January 1973 the government announced that the demands it had made at the time of signing the treaty in 1970 had not been satisfied and that it would therefore postpone ratification at least until 1974. Singled out for special mention was Japan's requirement that International Atomic Energy Agency inspection of its facilities be neither unfavourable nor discriminatory.[50] The conclusion of an agreement between the European Atomic Energy Community and the International Atomic Energy Commission in April 1973, permitting Euratom to carry out virtual autonomous inspection, set a precedent for subsequent Japanese demands.[51] The establishment of a European Association for Centrifuge Enrichment, comprising Great Britain, the Netherlands and West Germany, in June 1973, increased the sense of caution felt in Japanese government circles. Since Great Britain was an established nuclear power, it was argued, the European Association for Centrifuge Enrichment guaranteed West German access to important nuclear technology.[52] Japan, in contrast, was the only advanced industrial power placed 'in an unfavourable position as to inspection'.[53] Japan's decision to ratify the treaty on 8 June 1976 temporarily put an end to the controversy. It did not solve the problem.

CHAPTER XIII

The Self Defence Forces, 1960–1978

The roar of the lion, the voice of the fierce
  lion, the teeth of the young lions, are broken.
The strong lion perishes for lack of prey,
  and the whelps of the lioness are scattered.

Job 4:10–11

I Japanese military power, the American alliance and the strategies of the three services, 1960–78

With the completion of the First Defence Power Consolidation Plan in 1960, the Japanese armed forces developed in accordance with guidelines laid down in the Second (1962–6), Third (1967–71), and Fourth (1972–6) Defence Plans. In 1976, at the height of *détente*, the Miki Cabinet decided that future defence planning would be based on the assumption that there was 'little possibility' of a full-scale super-power conflict, or a major confrontation leading to such a clash, or even of a limited military engagement in Japan's immediate region. Japan, it was announced, would continue to rely on the United States deterrent to counter possible nuclear threats to its security. It would endeavour to repel 'limited', 'small-scale' conventional attacks on its territory 'in principle without external assistance'. It would also attempt to resist large-scale aggression single-handedly until such time as American assistance was forthcoming. Domestic security would remain a Japanese responsibility. After 1976 defence planning continued on an annual basis until the adoption of the Mid-Term Defence Programme Estimate (FY 1983–7) in the very different international environment of the early 1980s.

Dissimilar strategic requirements, divergent traditions of military thought, differing alliance policies, technological levels, leadership, experience and, above all, perhaps, intangible psychological factors make it difficult to compare the military power of one nation with that of another. The historic tendency of Japanese governments to promote their perceived interests through association with the dominant world power, the extreme vulnerability of the archipelago's heavily populated industrial cities to both nuclear and conventional attack, reliance on overseas supplies of raw materials and foreign markets, conflicting traditions of militarism and popular

pacifism, the psychological legacy of defeat in World War II and the highly factionalized nature of the nation's political life make the effectiveness of its armed
forces, whether as a contribution to deterrence, an adjunct to diplomacy or an instrument for war, particularly difficult to estimate.

Certainly, by the middle of the 1970s, Japan's military power, conventionally
calculated in terms of the number of men under arms, weapons systems, operational range and industrial support capability, had re-emerged as an important
factor in Western Pacific politics. It was by no means clear that the lack of an
independent nuclear capability undermined the basis of national defence. Japanese
air and naval forces, it is true, were no match, in quantitative terms, for those
deployed by the two nuclear superpowers in the Western Pacific. Yet the weakness
of the Soviet strategic position in the Far East, the vast distances separating Siberia
from the Russian industrial heartland, the impossibility of reinforcing the Soviet
Pacific Fleet in time of war except across potentially hostile seas far from protective air cover, the low operational rate of Soviet nuclear submarines and
military aircraft, all need to be taken into account when making comparisons
with Japan. The Ground Self Defence Forces were certainly comparable, at least in
terms of numerical strength, with Soviet ground forces stationed in eastern Siberia,
Kamchatka, Sakhalin and the Kuriles. The three Japanese services were nearly
twice as large as American forces stationed in the Far East after the fall of Saigon.
Evidence suggested that the quality of individual Japanese units, in limited exercises,
was very much higher than that of their American counterparts.[1] Comparisons
with China were difficult to make. The Japanese forces were relatively modest
in size compared with those of Taiwan, the two Koreas and Vietnam. Even so,
the military forces maintained by these smaller East Asian states lacked the balance
and potential flexibility of their Japanese counterparts. The disparity between
Japanese military power and that of all non-Communist South-East Asian countries, except Indonesia, was even more striking. By almost every conventional
index of military arithmetic the Self Defence Forces (SDF) completely overshadowed their counterparts in the Philippines, Thailand, Malaysia, Burma, Singapore, Australia, New Zealand and the small societies of the Southwest Pacific. (See
tables XIII.1, XIII.2 and XIII.3)

Japan's early postwar military planners had been determined to lay the foundations for a fully independent national defence system. Complete integration of the
Self Defence Forces into United States Far Eastern strategy, it was argued, was to
be resisted at all costs (see Chapters III and IV). Complex, indecisive struggles between the Pentagon, Japanese nationalists and exponents of a more intimate alliance
with the United States continued throughout the 1960s and 1970s. During this
period, within the framework of the security treaty and the government's policy
against overseas service, Japan's forces continued to develop in close co-operation
with those of the United States, despite the strong dissatisfaction felt by more independently minded officers. The chief function of the Air Self Defence Force, for
example, remained the protection of American offensive power from Soviet attack or
counter-attack.[2] Adoption of the BADGE semi-automatic aerial warning control

system, linked, through American Fifth Air Force Headquarters, with United States installations in Korea and Okinawa, significantly increased the level of bilateral military co-operation.[3] The links between the Maritime Self Defence Force and the Seventh Fleet also deepened.[4] It was generally assumed that in the event of an American–Soviet conflict the Japanese navy would block the straits leading from the Sea of Japan to the Pacific and undertake convoy duties as far south as Guam and the Philippines. As was to be expected, Japanese naval exercises placed heavy emphasis on anti-submarine operations, as well as routine coastal patrols, port defence and minesweeping.

For the Ground Self Defence Forces, too, the main hypothetical external antagonist remained the Soviet Union.[5] Thirty per cent of Japan's ground strength, including its only fully mechanized division and its strongest artillery units, were concentrated in the northernmost island of Hokkaidō. There were no comparable concentrations along the west coast of Honshū, or in Kyūshū, the Japanese island closest to the Asian continent. The forces in Hokkaidō could be regarded either as the frontline for the defence of the home archipelago against Russian attack or as the advance guard for a combined Japanese-American assault on the Soviet Far East.* Acting in conjunction with the United States, the Japanese army also possessed a capacity to conduct offensive operations in the Korean peninsula, China and South-East Asia.

In the wake of the 1960 crisis the Japanese army also paid increasing attention to internal security. The growth of Soviet and Chinese power, continuing tension in Korea, the struggles in South-East Asia, the resurgence of the Japanese Communist Party, together with the presence of a large, urban-based Korean minority, it was argued in some military circles, had further exacerbated the nation's chronic internal instability, creating favourable conditions for a left-wing seizure of power. The Soviet Union or China, it was believed, might attempt to precipitate a Communist revolution in Japan by launching a limited invasion of the home archipelago or through attacks on vital shipping-lanes. The sweeping reorganization of the army in 1960–2, the change-over from an organization based on six large regional forces and four mixed brigades to one based on thirteen smaller, more mobile and more mechanized divisions, was partly designed to counter these perceived threats. So too was the reversion to the Police Reserve Force arrangement of concentrating large forces within easy striking distance of Tōkyō and the industrial cities along the shores of the Inland Sea.[6] The superpower *détente* of the early 1970s, the Sino-American *rapprochement* and the Tanaka visit to Peking do not seem to have influenced thinking about such matters in the higher echelons of the Japanese military leadership.

---

* Offensive military action in the Kuriles and southern Sakhalin, officially regarded in Tōkyō either as Japanese national territory or as being of undetermined international status, could certainly have been presented as being compatible with Article 9 of the Constitution. A legal basis for action in other areas would have been more difficult (albeit not impossible) to establish.

Were the Japanese forces capable of fulfilling their functions? Since the ultimate test of military power remains success in war this question is impossible to answer. The great upheavals of the late twentieth century, the Chinese Revolution, the Korean War, the Algerian War of Independence, the Cuban Revolution, the long struggles in Indochina, successive Arab–Israeli conflicts, the collapse of the Pahlevi Dynasty in Iran, have clearly demonstrated that possession of superior military forces provides no guarantee of victory. Time and chance, as the writer of Ecclesiastes observed, happen to them all.

By the middle of the 1970s the Self Defence Forces were certainly capable of delivering a crushing blow to any domestic revolutionary movement – provided, always, that they could preserve their own ideological unity.

They were probably also capable of mounting a creditable, short-term defence of the home archipelago against foreign invasion. Expert opinion on the length of time resistance could be sustained differed. General Nakamura Ryūhei, Chief of the Ground Self Defence Force Staff (1971–2), hoped that implementation of the Fourth Defence Plan would enable Japan to hold off a large-scale, conventional attack for 'several months'.[7] Kaihara Osamu, who served for many years as Chief of the Secretariat at the National Defence Council, was convinced that the entire Japanese military machine would be destroyed during the first day, perhaps, even, within the first hour of any conflict involving the Soviet Union.[8] Even a major Japanese military expansion programme, Kaihara was inclined to believe, would do little to alter the real power relationship between the two countries. It should be noted, however, that a full-scale Soviet invasion of Japan was (and remains) highly improbable. To be reasonably sure of victory in such operations an attacking side needs at least a three-to-one margin of superiority over the defending side. Soviet forces in the Far East did not have the capacity to transport to Japan even the twelve divisions that would be necessary to take Hokkaidō. The USSR had not developed such a capability even by the mid-1980s, long after the breakdown of *détente* and the emergence of a much closer American-Japanese strategic relationship.

A joint Japanese-American amphibious assault on the Soviet Far East in the context of a superpower conflict would inevitably have provoked a massive Russian counter-offensive from the air and sea, resulting, if Kaihara's assumptions were correct, in the total destruction of the archipelago. Even if it had proved possible to protect the Japanese islands from the anticipated Russian counter-offensive, an attack on the Soviet Far East would probably have been suicidal. The entire Ground Self Defence Force would have had little chance of overcoming Soviet defences in these territories, except, perhaps, in the southern Kuriles and Sakhalin.

The outcome of a hypothetical Sino-Japanese confrontation was more difficult to predict. In the absence of support from a superpower ally neither country possessed the physical means to land large forces on the other's territory. Joint Japanese-American operations against China, even if they had ever been contemplated, would probably have had little prospect of success. The Japanese air force had a theoretical capacity to conduct bombing operations over a wide area of north-east, central and south China. Japan itself, in turn, was vulnerable to Chinese missile and bomber attack. Acting in co-operation with the Seventh Fleet the Maritime Self Defence Force could probably have protected the sea-lanes linking the archipelago with the Middle East, South-East Asia and Australia from Chinese submarine activity. Their ability to perform this task on their own was uncertain. Japan's capacity to project its military power into South-East Asia and the Southwest Pacific remained limited. Neither the Japanese navy nor the air force maintained an independent capability to transport and sustain large expeditionary forces overseas. The lessons of the Sino-Japanese War and the American experience in Vietnam suggested that Japanese intervention in Korea or South-East Asia, either unilaterally or within the framework of the security treaty, would have ended in unmitigated disaster.

Table XIII.1 Japanese and other military forces, 1969–70 and 1977–8

A. 1969–70	Total full-time regular armed forces	Paramilitary forces	Trained reservists	Total men of military age (18–45 years)	Percentage of regular armed forces to men of military age
a. Japan	250,000	–	30,000	25,500,000	1.0
b. Comparable NATO and West European powers					
Britain	405,000	–	268,000	10,700,000	3.8
Canada	98,300	–	26,600	4,060,000	2.4
France	503,000	80,000	390,000	10,600,000	4.7
West Germany	465,000	30,000	750,000	11,760,000	4.0
Italy	420,000	76,000	635,000	11,650,000	3.6
Netherlands	124,000	3,000	220,000	2,650,000	4.7
c. Comparable Warsaw Pact powers					
Czechoslovakia	230,000	35,000	300,000	3,180,000	7.2
East Germany	137,000	77,000	200,000	2,870,000	4.8
Poland	275,000	45,000	440,000	6,800,000	4.0
Rumania	193,000	50,000	250,000	4,450,000	4.3
d. Comparable neutral and non-aligned powers					
India	925,000	100,000	110,000	100,000,000	0.9
Sweden	76,000	–	674,000	1,620,000	4.7

e. Asian and Pacific
   states

Australia	87,150	–	43,350	2,500,000	3.5
Burma	142,500	–	–	–	–
Cambodia	38,500	–	–	–	–
China	2,821,000	300,000	–	150,000,000	1.9
Indonesia	365,000	110,000	100,000	21,000,000	1.7
North Korea	384,000	25,000	110,000	–	–
South Korea	620,000	–	2,000,000	–	–
Malaysia	44,750	–	–	–	–
Philippines	37,500	–	–	–	–
Taiwan	550,000	–	–	–	–
Thailand	126,000	–	–	–	–
North Vietnam	457,000	–	–	–	–
South Vietnam	472,000	573,000	–	–	–

f. Soviet and American
   forces in the Far East

Soviet Union	The Soviet Union was believed to maintain ground forces totalling 240,000 men in the Far East.
United States	Exclusive of forces in Vietnam the United States maintained about 126,000 men in its Far Eastern ground and naval forces. The number of air force personnel was highly variable.

Sources: *The Military Balance, 1969–70*, The Institute for Strategic Studies, 1969.
      Nihon No Bōei, *Bōei Hakusho*, Bōei Cho, 1970.

B. 1977–78	Total full-time regular armed forces	Paramilitary forces	Trained reservists	Total men of military age (18–45 years)	Percentage of regular armed forces to men of military age
a. Japan	238,000	–	39,000	26,400,000	0.9
b. Comparable NATO and West European powers					
Britain	339,150	–	249,000	10,598,000	3.2
Canada	80,000	–	19,100	5,000,000	1.6
France	502,100	76,000	450,000	10,458,000	4.8
West Germany	489,000	20,000	1,179,500	12,868,000	3.8
Italy	330,000	167,000	694,800	11,000,000	3.0
Netherlands	109,700	–	176,500	2,794,000	3.9

c. Comparable Warsaw
    Pact powers

Czechoslovakia	181,000	132,500	350,000	3,016,000	6.0
East Germany	157,000	73,000	255,000	3,340,000	4.7
Poland	307,000	97,000	605,000	7,487,000	4.1
Rumania	180,000	37,000	345,000	4,500,000	4.0

d. Comparable neutral
    and non-aligned powers

India	1,096,000	300,000	200,000	137,000,000	0.8
Sweden	68,550	–	500,000	1,594,000	4.3

e. Asian and Pacific
    States

Australia	69,650	–	33,331	2,786,000	2.5
Burma	169,500	73,000	–	–	–
Cambodia	90,000	–	–	–	–
China	3,950,000	up to 111,000,000	–	179,545,000	2.2
Indonesia	247,000	112,000	–	24,700,000	1.0
North Korea	500,000	between 1–2,000,000	–	–	–
South Korea	635,000	1,000,000	1,215,000	7,383,000	8.6
Malaysia	64,000	213,000	27,000	2,370,000	2.7
Philippines	99,000	65,000	45,000	8,250,000	1.2
Taiwan	460,000	100,000	170,000	–	–
Thailand	211,000	66,000	500,000	7,535,000	2.8
Vietnam, Socialist Republic of	615,000	1,570,000	–	–	–

f. Soviet and American
    forces in the Far East

Soviet Union	The Soviet Union was believed to maintain ground forces totalling 300,000 men in its Far Eastern territories.
United States	Excluding its forces based on the west coast and in Alaska, the United States maintained 48,600 military personnel in Japan, 39,900 in South Korea, 42,700 in Hawaii, 23,900 in other Pacific locations, 25,600 aboard the Seventh Fleet and small forces in Thailand, a total of 180,850 throughout the region.

Sources The Military Balance, the Institute for Strategic Studies (successive issues). Bōei Cho(ed.), *Bōei Hakusho*, successive issues.

Table XIII.2 Japanese and other naval forces, 1970–1 and 1977–8

Type of vessel	Japan	Britain	France	West Germany	Italy	Netherlands	India	Sweden	Australia	Burma	Cambodia	China	Indonesia	North Korea	South Korea	Malaysia	Philippines	Taiwan	Thailand	North Vietnam	South Vietnam
	1970–1	Comparable NATO and West European powers					Comparable neutrals			Asian and Pacific Countries											
Large aircraft carriers	–	2	–	–	–	–	–	–	–	–	–	–	–	–	–	–	–	–	–	–	–
Light aircraft carriers	–	2	2	–	–	–	1	–	1	–	–	–	–	–	–	–	–	–	–	–	–
Escort, helicopter and commando carriers	–	2	2	–	–	–	–	–	–	–	–	–	–	–	–	–	–	–	–	–	–
Command ships, communication amphibious force flag ships	–	–	–	–	–	–	–	–	–	–	–	–	–	–	–	–	–	–	–	–	–
Nuclear-powered submarines	–	8	–	–	–	–	–	–	–	–	–	–	–	–	–	–	–	–	–	–	–
Conventionally powered submarines	10	33	20	12	8	6	4	24	4	–	–	33	12	2	–	–	–	–	–	–	–
Cruisers	–	3	2	–	4	2	2	1	–	–	–	–	1	–	–	–	–	–	–	–	–
Leaders, large destroyers, frigates (DLG)	–	8	2	–	4	–	–	–	3	–	–	–	–	–	–	–	–	–	–	–	–
Destroyers	27	11	17	12	4	12	3	8	5	–	–	4	7	–	3	–	–	10	–	–	–
Destroyers, escorts, frigates, escorts (& APD)	13	68	27	21	13	6	19	7	9	1	–	19	11	–	13	2	1	18	5	–	–
Corvettes (incl. PCE)	–	–	–	6	21	6	–	–	–	3	–	–	13	–	11	–	7	4	–	–	7
Patrol vessels, submarine chasers (PC)	20	–	14	–	7	–	–	–	–	4	–	24	11	18	6	–	7	21	14	–	7
Missile and torpedo boats, fast gunboats, patrol boats	10	4	–	40	15	–	–	42	–	5	–	394	61	42	–	4	–	48	–	–	22
Fleet minelayers, fast minelayers, mine support ships	–	1	–	2	–	3	–	1	–	–	–	–	–	–	–	–	–	–	–	–	–
Coastal minelayers	2	5	–	–	–	–	–	10	–	–	–	–	–	–	–	–	–	1	2	–	–

	Japan	Britain	France	West Germany	Italy	Netherlands	India	Sweden	Australia	Burma	Cambodia	China	Indonesia	North Korea	South Korea	Malaysia	Philippines	Taiwan	Thailand	North Vietnam	South Vietnam
Ocean minesweepers, fleet minesweepers	–	–	15	–	4	3	–	–	–	1	–	21	6	10	–	–	–	2	1	–	–
Coastal minesweepers, minehunters	33	66	64	24	37	36	4	18	6	–	–	6	15	–	11	6	2	15	4	–	3
Inshore minesweepers, minesweeping boats	6	22	15	51	20	16	4	17	3	–	–	–	–	24	1	2	–	2	–	–	–
Motor launches, motor patrol craft, river gunboats	27	4	13	24	–	5	15	31	20	34	–	22	74	15	–	25	28	50	8	–	–
Landing ships	4	2	9	–	3	–	1	–	–	–	–	44	6	–	20	–	6	44	5	–	25
Landing craft	48	26	10	24	23	12	3	23	–	9	–	26	7	–	–	–	–	21	8	19	–
Boom defence vessels, net layers	–	20	12	–	2	–	–	–	–	–	–	6	–	–	–	–	–	–	–	–	–
Survey ships	–	13	9	8	2	3	4	12	5	–	–	2	4	–	–	1	1	2	1	–	–
Depot ships, repair ships, maintenance ships	3	8	10	16	1	1	2	2	1	–	–	1	3	–	1	–	1	2	–	–	–
Transports	–	–	10	–	6	–	–	–	–	1	–	–	2	–	1	–	1	6	1	–	–
Supply ships	–	11	16	6	–	2	–	1	–	–	–	8	–	–	6	–	–	–	–	–	2
Oilers	3	38	10	10	2	1	4	3	1	–	–	5	4	–	4	–	1	4	4	–	3
Training ships	2	4	4	3	4	3	–	2	–	–	–	2	–	–	–	–	–	1	–	–	–
Tugs	3	70	20	18	26	8	1	–	1	–	11	1	–	2	–	4	6	5	16	–	–
Miscellaneous	326	185	50	40	80	10	5	20	10	2	375	2	70	6	2	5	63	3	19	–	–

1977–1978

Note: Vietnam

	Japan	Britain	France	West Germany	Italy	Netherlands	India	Sweden	Australia	Burma	Cambodia	China	Indonesia	North Korea	South Korea	Malaysia	Philippines	Taiwan	Thailand	Vietnam
Large aircraft carriers	–	1	–	–	–	–	–	–	–	–	–	–	–	–	–	–	–	–	–	–
Light aircraft carriers	–	1	2	–	–	–	1	–	1	–	–	–	–	–	–	–	–	–	–	–
Cruisers/light cruisers	–	10	2	–	3	–	2	–	–	–	–	–	–	–	–	–	–	–	–	–
Destroyers	31	3	21	11	8	12	–	6	5	–	–	9	–	–	9	–	–	20	–	–
Frigates	15	56	29	6	11	6	25	4	6	2	–	12	11	2	9	3	10	11	6	–
Corvettes	12	–	–	6	13	6	–	–	–	4	–	40	–	–	10	–	12	3	–	–
Nuclear-powered ballistic missile submarines	–	4	4	–	–	–	–	–	–	–	–	–	–	–	–	–	–	–	–	–

	Japan	Britain	France	West Germany	Italy	Netherlands	India	Sweden	Australia	Burma	Cambodia	China	Indonesia	North Korea	South Korea	Malaysia	Philippines	Taiwan	Thailand	Vietnam
Conventionally powered ballistic missile submarines	–	–	1	–	–	–	–	–	–	–	–	1	–	–	–	–	–	–	–	–
Nuclear or conventionally powered cruise missile submarines	–	–	–	–	–	–	–	–	–	–	–	–	–	–	–	–	–	–	–	–
Fleet submarines	–	9	–	–	–	–	–	–	–	–	–	1	–	–	–	–	–	–	–	–
Patrol submarines	15	18	22	24	10	6	8	18	4	–	–	65	3	13	–	–	–	2	–	–
FAC missile	–	–	5	30	–	–	16	1	–	–	–	140	19	18	8	8	–	1	3	–
FAC torpedo	5	–	–	10	6	–	–	41	–	–	–	240	5	157	–	–	–	8	–	–
FAC gun	–	–	–	–	4	–	–	–	–	–	–	438	–	44	–	6	9	–	–	–
Patrol craft	9	19	34	–	–	5	8	27	12	71	–	40	27	51	38	22	46	14	47	–
Mine layers	1	1	–	–	–	–	–	49	–	–	–	–	–	–	–	–	–	1	6	–
Ocean minesweepers	–	–	8	–	4	–	–	–	–	–	–	18	5	–	–	–	–	2	–	–
Coastal minesweepers, minehunters	29	22	31	40	30	11	4	18	3	–	–	–	2	–	10	6	2	14	4	–
Inshore minesweepers	–	5	–	18	10	16	4	20	–	–	–	–	–	–	–	–	–	–	–	–
Minesweeping boats	6	–	–	–	–	–	–	–	–	–	–	–	–	1	–	–	–	8	10	–
Assault ships	–	2	2	–	–	–	–	–	–	–	–	–	–	–	–	–	–	–	–	–
Landing ships	6	7	5	–	2	–	1	–	–	–	–	36	9	–	21	3	39	29	10	–
Landing craft	–	59	31	41	59	11	6	140	6	–	–	467	2	90	1	–	71	22	39	–
Depot repair maintenance ships	4	3	9	14	8	4	1	5	1	–	–	1	4	–	1	1	1	1	–	–
Survey ships (large and small)	6	4	10	1	4	3	3	1	4	2	–	11	4	–	3	1	–	3	4	–
Supply ships	–	7	6	12	1	2	–	–	–	–	–	14	–	–	6	–	–	–	–	–
Large tankers	–	17	5	–	1	–	21	–	1	–	–	–	1	–	–	–	–	–	–	–
Small tankers	1	6	5	11	–	–	35	1	–	–	–	10	7	–	–	–	7	7	4	–
Hydrofoils and ACUs	–	5	–	–	1	–	–	–	–	–	–	70	–	–	–	–	4	–	–	–
Miscellaneous	62	200	168	504	97	24	86	43	15	10	–	400	5	105	2	28	33	42	12	–

Source: Compiled from *Jane's Fighting Ships*, 1970–71 and 1977–8. Sampson, Lowe, Marston & Company.

Table XIII.3 Japanese and other air forces

	Number of front-line combat aircraft, with no distinction as to type, range, modernity or performance	
	1969–70	1977–8
A. Japan	518	364
B. Comparable NATO and West European powers		
Britain	750	550
Canada	300	210
France	475	557
West Germany	600	509
Italy	450	336
Netherlands	145	162
C. Comparable Warsaw Pact powers		
Czechoslovakia	600	558
East Germany	270	416
Poland	750	745
D. Comparable neutral and non-aligned powers		
India	625	670
Sweden	650	504
E. Asian and Pacific states		
Australia	230	120
China	2,800	5,200
North Korea	590	630
South Korea	215	335
Taiwan	375	296
Vietnam	133 (North) 125 (South)	310 (SRVN)
F. Soviet Far Eastern Air Force	2,000 (estimate only)	2,000 (estimate)
United States Far Eastern Air Force	400 aircraft attached to air force 550 to navy	300 attached to air force 250 to navy.

Source: The Military Balance, The Institute for Strategic Studies (successive issues).

II   Japanese military spending 1960–78

While Japan's annual military spending in the decades after the occupation remained within 1 per cent of GNP (the smallest percentage for any comparable nation) and represented a declining proportion of the national budget (13.5 per cent in 1954, 9 per cent in 1960, 7.7 per cent in 1967, 5.9 per cent in 1977) the annual rate of increase in its actual military expenditure was the highest in the world. In 1955 Japan's total military expenditure (exclusive of MSA aid) was $US368 million. By 1960 this had risen almost 40 per cent to $508 million. Defence spending in 1966 totalled $US958 million, almost double the 1960 figure. By 1969 it had risen to $US1,344 million, three and half times the size of the 1955 military budget. Japanese military expenditure in 1969 almost equalled the combined defence budgets of Burma, Thailand, Malaysia, Indonesia, Laos, Cambodia, South Vietnam, the Philippines, Taiwan and South Korea. Japan's military spending in 1970 was approximately equal to the entire Thai budget and more than twice the size of the Philippines budget.[9] By the mid-1970s these disparities had become even more marked.

The increases in the Japanese military budgets, both in absolute terms and relative to expenditure in South-East Asia, were paralleled by increased military spending in most comparable industrial nations. Nevertheless, the Japanese increases were steeper than most. Japan's relative position in the international hierarchy of military budgets changed significantly during the 1960s and early 1970s.

In 1955 Japanese defence spending, while very substantial compared with that of non-Communist South-East Asia, was only a fraction of that of the major NATO powers – less than 10 per cent of the British military budget, about 15 per cent of the French or West German, a little more than half the size of the Italian. Japanese military spending in the early post-occupation period was approximately comparable with that of Australia, Belgium, Holland, India or Sweden. During the 1960s the gap between Japan and the principal NATO allies narrowed. The level of Japanese military spending, too, gradually began to outpace that of Belgium and the Netherlands, a development not altogether unrelated to the disintegration of these powers' colonial empires in Africa and South-East Asia. Nevertheless, Japanese military budgets remained generally comparable with those of Australia, India or Sweden. By the mid-1970s, while Japanese defence expenditure was still only half that of Great Britain, less than half that of the French Republic and a third of that of West Germany, Japan had decisively overtaken Australia, India and Sweden in the international hierarchy. Japanese outlays were also considerably larger than those of middle-ranking NATO powers such as Italy. Japan itself, however, had been eclipsed by the Shah's Iran and by Saudi Arabia, two American allies then being groomed for important regional roles in Washington's global strategy. (See table XIII.4, XIII.5)

The extraordinary increases in Japanese military spending had undoubtedly strengthened the Self Defence Forces, providing them with greater fire-power, better equipment, improved training facilities and enhanced mobility. By 1978 the Self Defence Forces had become more formidable, in every respect, than they had been two decades earlier. Nevertheless, much of Japan's spiralling military expenditure, like that of other comparable nations, had been caused by rising costs of manpower, equipment and maintenance. The fifth annual report of the United States Arms Control and Disarmament Agency in May 1971 estimated that 60 per cent of the increase in the world's defence spending in 1970 alone had been caused by inflation.[10] In Japan the impact of inflation on military budgets was possibly even greater. Personnel costs, which accounted for almost 44 per cent of Japan's annual military expenditure (as opposed to 33.4 per cent in the case of Great Britain, 30.1 per cent in France, 36.7 per cent in Italy, 21.2 per cent in West Germany and 21.4 per cent in Sweden) increased dramatically in the period 1960–78.[11] Salaries doubled between 1960 and 1967. By the end of the decade it was two and a half times as costly to recruit and equip one infantryman and twice as costly to maintain a sailor or an airman than it had been in 1960. By the end of the 1970s salaries alone had increased a staggering 616 per cent on the 1967 figure.[12]

The percentage of the Japanese defence budget consumed by purchase of weapons and equipment (40.9 per cent), while higher than that of France (31.2 per cent) and Italy (26.9 per cent), was roughly comparable with that of West Germany (37.1 per cent), Sweden (40.2 per cent) and Great Britain (41 per cent). Here, too, costs continuously escalated. In 1953 domestic construction of the 3,400-ton escort vessel *Harukaze* cost Y2,159 million. Annual maintenance costs averaged at that time Y306 million. In contrast, production of the 3,050-ton *Amatsukaze*-type anti-aircraft escort vessel in 1965 cost Y6,696 million, three times the price of the *Harukaze*. Annual maintenance costs had doubled. The absolute cost to Japan of the F86 jet fighter during the first and second defence plans was Y101 million per unit. Average annual maintenance costs were Y35.5 million. On the other hand the F104-J, which constituted Japan's mainstay fighter during the Third Defence Plan, cost Y409 million, with annual maintenance expenses of Y86.73 million. This represented a fourfold increase in the cost of the fighter and a twofold increase in maintenance charges.[13]

The changing ratio of domestic procurement, foreign purchases, reimbursable and non-reimbursable aid had also had a significant impact on the growth of Japan's military expenditure, at least until the end of the Second Defence Plan in 1966. This was largely because the figures for non-reimbursable American aid, which made such an important contribution to the growth of the Self Defence Forces in the late 1950s and early 1960s, were not included in the Japanese government's annual budget statements, giving a somewhat misleading impression of the extent of the country's military build-up. Between 1958 and 1960, for example, the Self Defence Forces had obtained annually arms and equipment valued at Y150,031 million. Of this, 62.6 per cent had been procured at home, 2.4 per cent had been imported and 3.7 per cent received as reimbursable aid. However, additional arms and equipment, valued at Y46,831 million, or 31.2 per cent of the total, had been obtained gratis from the United States. With the curtailment of the American assistance programme in the 1960s Japan was increasingly obliged to rely on domestic procurement and foreign imports, paid for in hard cash. Costs inevitably escalated. The true extent of

Table XIII.4 Japanese and other military expenditure, 1955–78
($ million)

	1954–5	1959–60	1963–4	1965	1966	1967	1968	1969	1970	1971	1972	1973	1974	1975	1976	1977	1978
A. Japan	369	508	669	953	958	1,059	1,172	1,344	1,582	1,864	2,600	3,530	3,835	4,484	5,058	6,090	8,567
B. Comparable NATO and West European powers																	
Belgium	388	364	444	–	520	550	501	519	677	594	724	990	1,079	1,821	2,013	2,476	–
Britain	4,300	4,502	5,140	5,937	6,081	6,200	5,450	5,438	5,712	6,108	6,900	8,673	8,721	10,380	10,734	11,214	13,579
Canada	1,826	1,599	1,480	1,438	1,461	1,569	1,589	1,678	1,741	1,687	1,967	2,141	2,429	2,960	3,231	3,348	3,635
France	2,543	3,378	4,062	4,465	4,465	4,879	6,104	5,586	5,874	5,202	6,241	8,488	7,913	12,250	12,857	13,740	17,518
West Germany	2,202	2,571	4,607	4,850	4,335	4,625	5,108	5,301	6,111	5,961	7,568	11,083	10,764	16,260	15,220	16,602	21,355
Italy	674	1,075	1,510	1,984	1,982	2,075	1,940	1,930	2,416	2,651	3,244	3,964	3,673	4,220	3,821	4,416	5,610
Netherlands	334	428	618	750	750	817	898	940	1,075	1,161	1,562	2,102	2,303	2,936	2,825	3,357	4,208
C. Comparable Warsaw Pact powers																	
Czechoslovakia	–	–	789	715	754	1,452	1,538	1,576	1,635	1,765	1,875	1,336	1,384	1,542	1,805	1,614	1,818
East Germany	–	–	650	665	785	1,063	1,715	1,873	1,990	2,124	–	2,031	2,171	2,333	2,729	2,889	–
Poland	–	–	911	978	1,052	1,662	1,830	2,080	2,220	2,220	2,350	1,799	2,073	2,170	2,252	2,438	2,545
Rumania	–	–	342	–	265	530	551	574	745	798	725	528	572	647	759	824	923
D. Comparable neutral powers																	
India	424	649	1,858	2,100	1,171	1,292	1,452	1,491	1,467	1,656	1,817	2,386	2,443	2,660	2,812	3,445	3,571
Sweden	390	610	787	865	856	–	1,008	1,099	1,129	1,192	1,510	1,883	1,641	2,475	2,418	2,833	2,946
Switzerland	176	222	292	–	387	–	415	412	422	459	561	799	884	1,041	1,221	1,280	1,547

E. Asian and Pacific
States

Australia	442	458	669	864	1,090	1,378	1,375	1,225	1,261	1,149	1,500	1,907	2,661	2,492	2,837	2,678	–
Burma	83	86	–	–	–	–	112	111	104	100	91	101	–	–	113	–	–
Cambodia	–	–	–	–	50	55	63	64	–	335	–	–	98	–	–	–	–
China (estimated)	–	–	–	–	6,000	7,000	7,000	7,250	7,600–8,550	8,000–16,000	8,000–16,000	4,000–12,000	4,000–12,000	5,000–15,000	23,000–28,000	35,000	35,000
Indonesia	253	–	980	–	900	–	113	229	272	287	287	452	601	1,108	1,024	1,349	1,691
North Korea	–	–	–	–	–	–	629	692	746	849	443	620	770	–	–	–	1,030
South Korea	–	229	165	–	146	180	234	290	333	411	427	476	742	943	1,500	1,800	2,600
Malaysia	–	46	–	–	126	128	130	132	183	186	315	311	385	445	353	544	699
Philippines	84	76	79	72	70	104	115	123	110	136	92	136	312	407	410	420	793
Taiwan	–	–	–	147	270	300	300	302	482	601	–	878	1,000	1,007	–	–	–
Thailand	69	68	75	93	104	125	125	154	240	260	250	332	430	542	639	–	–
North Vietnam	–	–	–	–	350	–	500	500	584	–	–	–	–	–	–	–	–
South Vietnam	–	–	–	–	300	193	312	444	1,028	564	436	570	672	–	–	–	–

Sources: The Military Balance, The Institute for Strategic Studies (successive issues).
Nihon No Bōei, Bōei Hakusho, Bōei Cho, 1978. (– indicates figures unavailable or of doubtful reliability).

Table XIII.5 Japanese and other military expenditure as a percentage of Gross National Product, 1965–77

	Defence expenditure as a percentage of Gross National Product												
	1965	1966	1967	1968	1969	1970	1971	1972	1973	1974	1975	1976	1977
Japan	1.3	1.0	0.9	0.8	0.8	0.8	0.8	0.9	0.8	0.9	C.9	0.9	0.9
Comparable NATO and West European powers													
Britain	6.3	6.0	5.7	5.3	5.1	4.8	4.8	4.9	4.9	5.1	4.9	5.2	5.0
Canada	3.2	2.8	2.7	2.5	2.5	2.1	1.9	1.9	1.8	2.1	2.2	1.8	1.8
France	5.6	5.4	5.3	5.3	4.4	3.5	3.5	3.4	3.1	3.6	3.9	3.7	3.6
West Germany	4.4	4.8	4.3	3.9	3.5	2.9	2.9	3.1	2.9	3.6	3.7	3.5	3.4
Italy	2.9	2.9	2.9	2.7	2.9	2.7	3.0	3.0	2.9	2.9	2.6	2.5	2.4
Netherlands	4.3	4.1	4.0	3.9	3.7	3.5	3.4	3.3	3.3	3.4	3.6	3.3	3.6
Comparable Warsaw Pact powers													
Czechoslovakia	5.7	5.7	5.7	5.7	5.6	3.8	3.7	3.8	3.8	3.8	3.8	3.9	3.8
East Germany	3.0	3.3	3.7	5.7	5.9	5.1	5.2	5.2	5.3	5.4	5.5	5.7	5.9
Poland	5.1	5.3	5.4	4.8	5.0	4.1	4.1	3.9	3.7	3.0	3.1	3.0	3.0
Comparable neutral powers													
India	3.8	3.6	3.3	3.6	3.5	3.0	3.4	3.1	3.1	2.7	3.0	3.1	3.1
Sweden	4.4	4.2	3.9	3.8	4.0	3.5	3.3	3.4	3.1	3.4	3.4	3.4	3.4
Switzerland	2.5	2.6	2.4	2.5	2.2	2.1	2.0	1.9	1.7	1.8	1.8	2.0	1.9

Asian and Pacific
States

Australia	3.7	4.7	4.9	4.8	4.0	3.9	3.8	3.6	3.3	3.6	3.2	3.0	2.9
China	8.5	8.9	9.2	9.0	9.0	–	–	–	–	–	–	10.0	8.5
North Korea	–	–	–	–	24.9	–	–	–	–	–	–	11.2	10.5
South Korea	3.8	4.4	3.9	4.5	4.0	3.9	4.1	4.4	3.8	4.3	5.1	6.2	6.5
Taiwan	9.0	8.3	7.9	7.6	9.2	10.2	10.0	9.7	9.4	7.2	–	9.3	8.3

Sources: The Military Balance, The Institute for Strategic Studies (successive issues).
Nihon No Bōei Hakusho, Bōei Chō (successive issues). (– indicates figures unavailable or of doubtful reliability).

the nation's defence expansion programme at last came to be reflected in the budget. During the Second Defence Plan, the Self Defence Forces obtained annually weapons and equipment valued at some Y134,938 million. Eighty per cent of this was domestically produced, 5.5 per cent purchased overseas and 6.1 per cent received in the form of reimbursable aid. Non-reimbursable United States military aid accounted for no more than 7.5 per cent of the total.[14]

The meagre annual allocation of resources to research and development was probably an indication of the extent to which the Japanese defence budget was eroded by administrative costs, personnel expenses, rising prices and the effects of decreasing American assistance. The National Defence Council Secretariat estimated that, during the 1960s, 3.6 per cent of the West German, 4 per cent of the Swedish, 9 per cent of the British and 21.3 per cent of the French military budgets were channelled into research and development. In contrast, only 1 per cent of the Japanese defence budget was spent on research. This was even more significant in view of the great differences in scale between the Japanese and most European military budgets. It meant that in 1964–5, for example, while France spent $US855.8 million on military research (more than the entire Japanese defence budget for that year), Great Britain spent $US563.9 million, West Germany spent $US175 million and Sweden spent $US30.6 million, Japan spent a mere $US7.5 million, 1.3 per cent of Britain's expenditure and 24.5 per cent of Sweden's.[15] These trends continued through the 1970s. In 1976, the last year of the Fourth Defence Plan, Japan was still spending a mere 0.9 per cent of its military budget on research and development.

III   The character of the Self Defence Forces

(i)   Rank, experience and educational background

Like all military organizations, the Self Defence Forces were highly stratified and complex. In all three services, officers and petty officers enjoyed lifetime employment. They constituted, in every sense, a military elite, a class apart. The rank and file, who made up the overwhelming majority of the 240,000 men under arms, entered the forces on renewable two- or three-year contracts. In many cases, their objective was simply to learn a trade, save money and return to the private sector. It was difficult to recruit them. It was also difficult to retain them. Some 20–30,000 men resigned and re-entered civilian life each year. Their attitudes to the Self Defence Forces varied. Some remembered their years of service fondly. Others found the demands of an extremely hierarchical and disciplined military life stifling, to say the least.

The officer corps itself comprised three fairly distinct groups. The Old Guard was made up almost entirely of former members of the Imperial Japanese Army and Navy. The younger officers were generally graduates of the postwar National Defence Academy (Bōei Daigakkō) with no experience of active military service.

Men who entered the forces after graduating from normal state or private universities, or from high schools, constituted another separate group. In 1961 former members of the Imperial Army and Navy occupied most Self Defence Force officer posts above the rank of captain, naval lieutenant and flight lieutenant.[16] By 1968 former Imperial officers occupied no more than about 15 per cent of such posts.[17] By 1982, only 127 former Imperial Army and Naval personnel remained in an officer corps numbering more than 42,000.[18] Nevertheless, the highest positions in all three services remained their exclusive preserve. To this extent, at least, the traditions of the Imperial Japanese Army and Navy lived on in the Self Defence Forces.

(ii)   Regional patterns of recruitment

Regional origin, as well as age, experience and educational background, remained a factor of some importance in the informal structure of the Self Defence Forces. As in the Meiji, Taishō and early Shōwa periods, a disproportionate number of officers and men came from the farming villages and small towns of western and northern Japan, especially from areas where samurai traditions had been strong. These regions, which had given birth both to the great patriotic secret societies and to some of Japan's most determined radical revolutionaries had been characterized, even in the prewar period, by an exceptionally intense conservative nationalism, a deep attachment to the traditional, emphatically masculine values of the warrior class and an unusually high level of socio-political conflict between the dominant right and the dissident left. Their social ethos, history and political culture differed, in several significant respects, from those of the rest of Japan. The extraordinarily high percentage of Corsicans in the French armed forces, the tendency of Americans from the Deep South to embark on military careers or the domination of the prewar German officer corps by Prussian *junkers* provided interesting parallels.

Particularly striking was the strong representation from Kyūshū. By the early 1980s, the seven prefectures of Kyūshū, accounting for only 11.08 per cent of the entire Japanese population, provided 30.73 per cent of senior Self Defence Force officers, 29.74 per cent of petty officers and 28.78 per cent of the rank and file, altogether 29.10 per cent of men under arms. Kagoshima alone, the heartland of the old Satsuma domain, with a mere 1.52 per cent of the Japanese population, was the source of 5.87 per cent of Self Defence Force personnel. Kumamoto, too, the home of many a turbulent Restoration samurai, and one of the major recruiting grounds of prewar Japan, was exceptionally well represented. Also notable was the heavy recruitment from Hokkaidō, the Tōhoku region and Yamaguchi prefecture, the centre of the former Chōshū domain. In contrast, the seven prefectures of the Kantō district, incorporating the immense connurbations of Tōkyō and Yokohama, and containing altogether 29.80 per cent of the Japanese population, supplied only 13.66 per cent of Self Defence Force personnel. The Kinki region, centring around the historic capitals of Nara and Kyōtō, and the industrial cities of Ōsaka and Kōbe, and containing altogether 18.12 per cent of the Japanese population, provided no more than 6.12 per cent of the officers and men in the Self Defence Forces. This was only

Table XIII.6 **Regional origins of Self Defence Force members on the eve of the Mid-Term Defence Programme Estimate.**

Region	Prefecture	Population (% of national total)	Officers %	Petty officers %	Men %	Total SDF
Tōhoku	Aomori	1,524,000	759	127	7,806	8,692
		1.30%	1.99%	3.01%	3.90%	3.59%
	Akita	1,257,000	481	83	3,898	4,462
		1.07%	1.26%	1.97%	1.95%	1.84%
	Iwate	1,422,000	428	70	4,631	5,129
		1.21%	1.12%	1.66%	2.32%	2.12%
	Miyagi	2,082,000	999	191	6,781	7,971
		1.78%	2.62%	4.53%	3.39%	3.29%
	Yamagata	1,252,000	552	69	4,177	4,798
		1.07%	1.45%	1.64%	2.09%	1.98%
	Fukushima	2,035,000	724	128	6,259	7,111
		1.74%	1.90%	3.01%	3.13%	2.93%
	TOTAL	9,572,000	3,943	668	33,552	38,163
		8.18%	10.34%	15.82%	16.78%	15.75%
Kantō	Ibaraki	2,558,000	777	122	4,678	5,577
		2.19%	2.04%	2.90%	2.34%	2.30%
	Tochigi	1,792,000	517	67	2,885	3,469
		1.53%	1.36%	1.59%	1.44%	1.43%
	Gumma	1,849,000	518	90	3,401	4,009
		1.58%	1.58%	2.13%	1.70%	1.65%
	Saitama	5,420,000	599	76	2,808	3,483
		4.63%	1.57%	1.80%	1.40%	1.47%
	Tōkyō-to	11,615,000	2,118	125	5,147	7,390
		9.92%	5.55%	2.97%	2.57%	3.05%
	Kanagawa	6,924,000	1,214	139	3,298	4,651
		5.91%	3.18%	3.30%	1.65%	1.92%
	Chiba	4,735,000	881	87	3,561	4,529
		4.05%	2.31%	2.07%	1.78%	1.87%
	TOTAL	34,893,000	6,624	706	25,778	33,108
		29.80%	17.36%	16.76%	12.89%	13.66%

Region	Prefecture	Population (% of national total)	Officers %	Petty officers %	Men %	Total SDF
Chūbu	Niigata	2,451,000 2.09%	623 1.63%	86 2.04%	4,578 2.29%	5,277 2.18%
	Toyama	1,103,000 0.94%	325 0.85%	26 0.62%	1,319 0.66%	1,670 0.69%
	Ishikawa	1,119,000 0.96%	453 1.19%	28 0.66%	1,733 0.87%	2,214 0.91%
	Fukui	794,000 0.68%	348 0.91%	37 0.88%	1,336 0.67%	1,721 0.71%
	Shizuoka	3,447,000 2.94%	· 677 1.78%	84 1.99%	3,990 1.99%	4,751 1.96%
	Yamanashi	804,000 0.69%	305 0.80%	40 0.95%	1,322 0.66%	1,667 0.69%
	Nagano	2,084,000 1.78%	558 1.46%	87 2.07%	3,103 1.55%	3,748 1.55%
	Aichi	6,222,000 5.32%	676 1.77%	48 1.14%	2,947 1.47%	3,671 1.51%
	Gifu	1,960,000 1.67%	382 1.00%	42 1.10%	2,319 1.16%	2,743 1.13%
	TOTAL	19,984,000 17.07%	4,347 11.39%	478 11.34%	22,647 11.32%	27,472 11.33%
Kinki	Shiga	1,080,000 0.92%	177 0.46%	15 0.36%	909 0.45%	1,101 0.45%
	Kyōtō-fu	2,527,000 2.16%	520 1.36%	64 1.52%	2,060 1.03%	2,644 1.09%
	Ōsaka-fu	8,473,000 7.24%	535 1.40%	9 0.21%	2,493 1.25%	3,037 1.25%
	Nara	1,209,000 1.03%	157 0.41%	6 0.14%	742 0.37%	905 0.37%
	Wakayama	1,088,000 0.93%	187 0.49%	17 0.40%	1,073 0.54%	1,277 0.53%
	Mie	1,687,000 1.44%	365 0.95%	37 0.88%	1,805 0.90%	2,207 0.91%

Region	Prefecture	Population (% of national total)	Officers %	Petty officers %	Men %	Total SDF
	Hyōgō	5,145,000 4.00%	740 1.94%	50 1.18%	2,848 1.42%	3,638 1.50%
	TOTAL	21,209,000 18.12%	2,681 7.03%	198 4.70%	11,930 5.96%	14,809 6.12%
Chūgoku	Okayama	1,871,000 1.60%	727 1.91%	71 1.69%	2,556 1.28%	3,354 1.38%
	Hiroshima	2,739,000 2.34%	1,335 2.34%	158 3.75%	4,522 2.26%	6,015 2.48%
	Yamaguchi	1,587,000 1.36%	1,094 2.87%	88 2.09%	4,260 2.13%	5,442 2.25%
	Tottori	604,000 0.52%	307 0.80%	35 0.83%	1.843 0.96%	2,185 0.90%
	Shimane	785,000 0.67%	435 1.14%	36 0.85%	2,729 1.36%	3,200 1.32%
	TOTAL	7,586,000 6.48%	3,898 10.22%	388 9.21%	15,910 7.99%	20,196 8.33%
Shikoku	Kagawa	1,000,000 0.85%	660 1.73%	60 1.42%	1,997 1.00%	2,717 1.12%
	Ehime	1,507,000 1.29%	805 2.11%	74 1.76%	3,210 1.60%	4,089 1.69%
	Tokushima	825,000 0.70%	473 1.24%	50 1.89%	1,917 0.96%	2,440 1.01%
	Kochi	831,000 0.71%	452 1.19%	35 0.83%	2,220 1.11%	2,707 1.17%
	TOTAL	4,163,000 3.56%	2,390 6.27%	219 5.20%	9,344 4.67%	11,953 4.93%
Kyūshū	Fukuoka	4,554,000 3.89%	2,249 5.90%	203 4.82%	8,827 4.41%	11,279 4.65%
	Ōita	1,229,000 1.05%	1,313 3.44%	112 2.66%	5,890 2.94%	7,315 3.02%

	Miyazaki	1,152,000	1,173	160	7,217	8,550
		0.98%	3.08%	3.80%	3.61%	3.53%
	Saga	866,000	965	99	4,549	5,613
		0.74%	2.53%	2.53%	2.27%	2.32%
	Nagasaki	1,591,000	1,301	141	8,549	9,991
		1.36%	3.41%	3.35%	4.27%	4.12%
	Kumamoto	1,790,000	2,300	249	11,028	13,577
		1.53%	6.03%	5.91%	5.51%	5.60%
	Kagoshima	1,784,000	2,421	289	11,510	14,220
		1.52%	6.34%	6.86%	5.75%	5.87%
	TOTAL	12,966,000	11,722	1,253	57,570	70,545
		11.08%	30.73%	29.74%	28.78%	29.10%
Ryūkyū	Okinawa	1,107,000	27	1	1,355	1,383
		0.95%	0.07%	0.02%	0.68%	0.57%
Hokkaidō	Hokkaidō	5,576,000	2,506	311	21,947	24,764
		4.76%	6.57%	7.38%	10.97%	10.22%

Source: Compiled from *Bōei Handobukku*, Asagumo Shuppan Sha, 1982 and Yano Tsuneta Kinenkai (ed.), *Nihon Kokusei Zue*, Kokusei Sha, 1982.

slightly more than the tiny prefecture of Kagoshima. The commercially minded young men of Ōsaka appeared even more reluctant than their colleagues in Tōkyō to take up a military career. Interesting, too, was the extremely small number of recruits from Okinawa. This, perhaps, reflected the absence of an historical, indigenous military tradition, the intense local pacifism induced by the horrors of World War II and the presence of American military bases, the anxiety of the Defence Agency recruitment organizations about the strength of radical political movements in the prefecture, or simply the traditional prejudices of mainlanders, and particularly of the bureaucratic classes, towards the inhabitants of this outlying archipelago. Whatever the explanation, Okinawa, with 0.94 per cent of the Japanese population, provided only 0.07 per cent of senior Self Defence officers, 0.02 per cent of petty officers and 0.68 per cent of the rank and file, altogether 0.57 per cent of men under arms. (See tables XIII.6, XIII.7)

The pattern of student intake into the Defence Academy made it clear that these trends would continue indefinitely. Indeed, it seemed probable that the passage of time would consolidate the virtual hegemony already enjoyed by officers from Kyūshū in the forces. During the period 1959–78 between 26.9 per cent and 39.6 per cent of Defence Academy students came from this rich, subtropical southern island. Among these, students from Kagoshima were almost always the most numer-

Table XIII.7   Regional origins of Defence Academy students

Year	Hokkaidō	Tōhoku	Kantō	Chūbu	Kinki	Chūgoku	Shikoku	Kyūshū
1959	3.4%	5.7%	16.2%	13.3%	8.8%	11.8%	7.9%	32.9%
1960	3.9%	4.8%	16.2%	13.4%	9.0%	11.9%	6.7%	31.1%
1961	5.7%	5.6%	19.4%	12.0%	8.1%	12.2%	6.6%	27.9%
1962	3.6%	5.4%	20.0%	18.8%	8.8%	10.7%	8.9%	28.8%
1963	4.2%	5.1%	24.1%	9.2%	10.3%	9.7%	7.8%	30.2%
1964	2.8%	5.9%	19.5%	13.4%	10.5%	11.1%	8.6%	28.2%
1965	3.1%	4.1%	15.9%	14.1%	12.3%	11.7%	7.9%	30.9%
1966	2.8%	4.2%	20.9%	13.9%	9.7%	15.9%	5.5%	26.9%
1967	2.3%	4.5%	19.2%	13.9%	13.1%	9.9%	9.8%	27.3%
1968	5.0%	6.3%	18.8%	11.1%	7.3%	12.5%	10.3%	28.7%
1969	3.2%	7.7%	15.4%	13.8%	10.9%	10.6%	9.3%	29.1%
1970	6.1%	7.6%	16.3%	11.4%	10.4%	9.4%	5.7%	31.0%
1971	4.1%	9.0%	16.4%	9.9%	7.7%	9.0%	5.5%	38.4%
1972	2.8%	8.2%	21.8%	10.0%	8.8%	7.5%	7.0%	33.6%
1973	4.6%	9.9%	17.9%	11.0%	11.4%	7.0%	5.1%	33.6%
1974	4.8%	10.2%	14.9%	11.6%	10.1%	7.7%	4.5%	36.2%
1975	7.0%	5.4%	15.8%	11.4%	11.2%	5.2%	4.4%	39.6%
1976	5.7%	7.1%	18.8%	14.0%	12.7%	7.1%	7.1%	27.5%
1977	2.8%	10.9%	14.9%	15.9%	13.8%	5.7%	5.2%	29.3%
1978	4.4%	8.7%	13.1%	16.3%	14.1%	6.3%	5.6%	31.2%

Source: Okuda Toshitsune, *Bōei Daigakkō*, Kyōiku Sha, 1979, p.109.

ous. The old Satsuma oligarchs could thus rest comfortably in their graves.

(iii)   Political and ideological trends in the Self Defence Forces

Even in the most democratic societies the philosophical controversies, policy debates and factional conflicts within the military forces tend to be hidden from outside observers. It is only after successful war or violent revolution have forced the state to reveal its innermost secrets that the complexity of military politics becomes apparent. The military is a glandular thing, a monstrosity, Robert A. Lovett once told John F. Kennedy. In normal times, the interested bystander attempting to evaluate its collective state of mind, and the divisions of opinion within it, faces much the same sort of problems as a tracker endeavouring to determine the emotional condition of an unseen elephant on the basis of occasional footprints and random droppings. The task is not completely impossible. The evidence, when it can be found, is often impressive. Yet conclusions must always be tentative. Much of the most vital information will always be lacking. Elephants, too, are volatile creatures. Their emotions are subject to sudden, if not inexplicable, changes.

In June 1958 the Japanese military critic Yoshiwara Kōichirō* conducted a survey of the socio-political attitudes, international outlook and personal lives of 403 Self Defence Force members at Nerima, Kita Furukawa, Matsudo and Kurihama.[19] In April 1965 he undertook a more wide-ranging study of 77 Self Defence Force personnel, selected from the elite First Airborne Group (Dai-ichi Kūtei Dan), the Eighth Guards Unit (Dai-hachi Gōei Tai), the Defence Agency and students at the National Defence Academy. This second survey examined the views of two major-generals, six colonels, one lieutenant-colonel, three captains, two first lieutenants, twelve second-lieutenants, one sergeant first class, three sergeants second class, six sergeants third class, ten corporals and eight privates first class. Yoshiwara's surveys were some of the few non-official studies of Self Defence Force members ever taken. His findings, while based on numerically limited and possibly somewhat unrepresentative samples, therefore remain of great interest.

Generally speaking, the officers and men who responded to Yoshiwara's questionnaires revealed themselves to be politically conservative, albeit critical of the 'weakness' and 'corruption' of the Japanese government, prepared, with some reservations, to accept the principle of civilian control but confused about the purposes of the SDF. There was strong interest in constitutional revision. While there was a high degree of support for the Japanese-American security treaty there appeared to be a marked disinclination to view world politics in Cold War terms. A large majority of Yoshiwara's respondents opposed development of an independent nuclear *force de frappe*. They were also singularly unenthusiastic about the idea of overseas service.

The overwhelming majority of Self Defence Force personnel surveyed, in all ranks and all units, declared themselves to be supporters of the Liberal Democratic Party. A small minority in the First Airborne Group supported the Democratic

* An opponent of the security treaty.

Table XIII.8 Support for political parties in the Self Defence Forces, April 1965

Political Party	First Airborne Group		Eighth Guards Unit		Defence Academy	Defence Agency		Total
	Captains 1st Lieuts 2nd Lieuts	Sergeants Corporals Privates	Captains 1st Lieuts 2nd Lieuts	Sergeants Corporals Privates		Major-Generals	Colonels Lt-Colonels Majors	
Liberal Democratic Party	7	11	3	4	13	–	4	42
Democratic Socialists	2	–	–	–	–	–	–	2
Kōmeitō	–	2	–	–	–	–	–	2
Socialists	–	–	–	–	–	–	–	–
Communists	–	–	–	–	–	–	–	–
None	1	1	1	1	8	1	1	14
No answer	2	9	1	–	2	1	2	17
TOTALS	12	23	5	5	23	2	7	77

Source: Yoshiwara Kōichirō, *Nanajūnen Ampo To Nihon No Gunjiryoku*, Nihon Hyōron Sha, 1969, p.261.

Table XIII.9   Support for political parties among officer graduates of the Defence Academy, April 1965

Political Party	Captains	First Lieuts	Second Lieuts	Total
Liberal Democratic Party	1	1	5	7
Democratic Socialists	–	–	2	2
Kōmeitō	–	–	–	–
Socialists	–	–	–	–
Communists	–	–	–	–
None	1	–	1	2
No answer	–	–	4	4
TOTALS	2	1	12	15

Source: Yoshiwara, op. cit., p.261

Socialist Party or the Kōmeitō. A large minority of Defence Academy students declared themselves to be essentially apolitical. There was no evidence of support for the Japan Socialist Party or the Communist Party. Yoshiwara's informants, in fact, were vituperative in their comments about the Communist Party ('Not an independent Japanese party', 'An advance guard for the Soviet Union and China', 'Not real Communism', 'I bear an unspeakable hatred towards it').[20] (See tables XIII.8, XIII.9)

Despite their loyalty to the Liberal Democratic Party, only a minority of Self Defence Force members were satisfied with the performance of the Japanese government, regarding it as 'corrupt' or 'too weak'. Clearly, however, few felt that the Opposition parties offered any acceptable alternatives. Their criticism of the government and its policies was from the right, not the left. (See table XIII.10)

While they appeared to have clear-cut domestic political allegiances, albeit little confidence in their favourite party, the majority of the Self Defence Force personnel surveyed, including the two major-generals and seven senior officers in the Defence Agency, found themselves unable, or unwilling, clearly to explain the purposes of the organization to which they belonged. The Defence Academy students were no more forthcoming on this rather fundamental matter than their more senior colleagues. (See table XIII.11)

It is possible that the philosophical confusion of Yoshiwara's respondents had its origins in the traditional manly inarticulateness of the samurai class. Patriotic emotions are, at the best of times, difficult to explain. Yet it is also possible that all

Table XIII.10 Attitudes of Self Defence Forces members towards the Japanese government, April 1965

Opinion	First Airborne Group		Eighth Guards Unit		Defence Academy	Defence Agency		Total
	Captains 1st Lieuts 2nd Lieuts	Sergeants Corporals Privates	Captains 1st Lieuts 2nd Lieuts	Sergeants Corporals Privates		Major-Generals	Colonels Lt-Colonels Majors	
Too weak	5	2	5	–	7	–	4	23
Corrupt	2	5	–	–	5	–	–	12
Should be changed	–	–	–	–	–	–	–	–
Best as is	4	3	–	3	10	1	3	24
Don't know	1	5	–	1	1	–	–	8
No answer	–	8	–	1	–	1	–	10
TOTALS	12	23	5	5	23	2	7	77

Source: Yoshiwara op. cit., p.262.

Table XIII.11 **What are you defending? April 1965**

Opinion	First Airborne Group		Eighth Guards Unit		Defence Academy	Defence Agency		Total
	Captains 1st Lieuts 2nd Lieuts	Sergeants Corporals Privates	Captains 1st Lieuts 2nd Lieuts	Sergeants Corporals Privates		Major-Generals	Colonels Lt-Colonels Majors	
The peace and independence of Japan as a nation based on democracy	–	–	–	–	1	–	–	1
Japan	1	–	–	–	–	–	–	1
The Japanese race	1	–	–	–	1	–	–	2
The State	–	–	–	–	1	–	–	1
The land and people	–	–	–	–	1	–	–	1
Land, people, peace	1	–	–	–	–	–	–	1
Our own way of life	–	–	1	–	–	–	–	1
Don't know	–	–	–	–	2	–	–	2
No answer	9	23	4	5	17	2	7	67
TOTALS	12	23	5	5	23	2	7	77

Source: Yoshiwara, op. cit., p.273

but eight of the seventy-seven officers and men surveyed by Yoshiwara could not define the objectives of the Self Defence Forces because they had never thought much about the matter. The limited reading diet of many Self Defence Force members certainly suggested a lack of intellectual curiosity. Almost half of Yoshiwara's sample, including, again, the two major-generals and seven senior officers in the Defence Agency, could not recall what magazines and books they had read in the weeks prior to the survey. The minority who did read, however, inclined towards fairly serious weekly and monthly magazines, biographies, classics and popular novels. The officers and men of the First Airborne Group and students at the Defence Academy had noticeably more catholic tastes than their colleagues in the Eighth Guards Unit and the Defence Agency bureaucracy. Intellectual interests appeared to follow no particular ideological line. While John Stuart Mill, Jefferson, Marx, Lenin, Mao Tse-tung, Che Guevara, Fukuzawa Yukichi and Kita Ikki were notably absent, Russian literature, pre-revolutionary and post-revolutionary, was just as popular (or unpopular) as English, French or German.[21]

Civilian control of the armed forces seemed to be widely understood and accepted. Yet it should be noted that some 40 per cent of Yoshiwara's respondents ventured no opinion on the question of whether the right of command should be held by the emperor (as in the prewar period) or the Prime Minister (in accordance with the provisions of the 1954–6 defence laws). A not entirely insignificant minority, moreover, asserted that it would *not* be prepared to abide by the principle of civilian control if any of the Opposition parties came to power. Another substantial minority was unable to answer whether it would *always* obey the orders of a legally constituted civilian government. In principle, mobilization of the Self Defence Forces to suppress domestic revolutionary movements did not appear to be strongly opposed. The 'Three Arrows' exercise, in contrast, which seemed to assume a future overseas role for the forces, generated widespread uneasiness. Those who supported the Defence Agency's right to conduct such paper exercises, in fact, were outnumbered by those who were opposed, did not know or could not answer. (See tables XIII.12, XIII.13, XIII.14, XIII.15)

The majority of Self Defence Force personnel surveyed favoured constitutional revision, establishment of a full Ministry of Defence and formal recognition of the SDF as an army, navy and air force. A not inconsiderable minority favoured continuation of the status quo. Only a tiny minority advocated a return to the arrangements that had prevailed at the time of the Imperial Army and Navy. Support for overseas service was minimal. The percentage of Self Defence Force personnel interested in an independent nuclear deterrent appeared to be somewhat smaller than it was among the general population. (See tables XIII.16, XIII.17.)

Attitudes to the Japanese-American alliance were complex. The vast majority of respondents (71.43 per cent), including the two major-generals and all the senior officers in the Defence Agency, accepted the government's view that the security treaty was 'necessary'. A minority (7.79 per cent) felt that the alliance should be strengthened. Only one interviewee (a member of the First Airborne group) declared that the security treaty ought to be discarded. It should be noted, however, that almost 20 per cent of respondents did not venture any opinion on this issue. (See table XIII.18)

Table XIII.12 Right of command, April 1965

Opinion	First Airborne Group		Eighth Guards Unit		Defence Academy	Defence Agency		Total
	Captains 1st Lieuts 2nd Lieuts	Sergeants Corporals Privates	Captains 1st Lieuts 2nd Lieuts	Sergeants Corporals Privates		Major-Generals	Colonels Lt-Colonels Majors	
Should be held by the emperor	–	2	–	–	–	–	–	2
Should be held by the Prime Minister	7	9	4	4	19	1	–	44
Don't know	–	–	–	–	1	–	–	1
No answer	5	12	1	1	3	1	7	30
TOTALS	12	23	5	5	23	2	7	77

Source: Yoshiwara op. cit., p.267.

Table XIII.13 Attitude to civilian control in the case of Opposition parties forming a government, April 1965

Opinion	First Airborne Group		Eighth Guards Unit		Defence Academy	Defence Agency		Total
	Captains 1st Lieuts 2nd Lieuts	Sergeants Corporals Privates	Captains 1st Lieuts 2nd Lieuts	Sergeants Corporals Privates		Major-Generals	Colonels Lt-Colonels Majors	
Would obey if the government were legally constituted	8	7	4	4	18	2	5	48
Would not obey	2	3	–	–	1	–	1	7
Would obey even if it were a revolutionary government	–	–	–	–	1	–	–	1
Don't know	–	–	–	–	1	–	–	1
No answer	2	13	1	1	2	–	1	20
TOTALS	12	23	5	5	23	2	7	77

Source: Yoshiwara, op. cit., p.267.

Table XIII.14 Attitude to mobilization for domestic law and order enforcement.

Opinion	First Airborne Group		Eighth Guards Unit		Defence Academy	Defence Agency		Total
	Captains 1st Lieuts 2nd Lieuts	Sergeants Corporals Privates	Captains 1st Lieuts 2nd Lieuts	Sergeants Corporals Privates		Major-Generals	Colonels Lt-Colonels Majors	
Obey orders	12	18	5	5	18	2	6	66
Not obey orders (but depends on the situation)	–	–	–	–	3	–	–	3
Don't know	–	4	–	–	2	–	1	7
Resign at once	–	1	–	–	–	–	–	1
No answer	–	–	–	–	–	–	–	–
TOTALS	12	23	5	5	23	2	7	77

Source: Yoshiwara, op. cit., p.267.

Table XIII.15 Attitude to 'Three Arrows' exercise (Mitsuya Kenkyū), April 1965

Opinion	First Airborne Group		Eighth Guards Unit		Defence Academy	Defence Agency		Total
	Captains 1st Lieuts 2nd Lieuts	Sergeants Corporals Privates	Captains 1st Lieuts 2nd Lieuts	Sergeants Corporals Privates		Major-Generals	Colonels Lt-Colonels Majors	
Natural to conduct such research	9	6	4	2	20	1	5	47
Should not be undertaken	–	1	–	–	1	1	2	5
Don't know	1	13	1	3	1	–	–	19
No answer	2	3	–	–	1	–	–	6
TOTALS	12	23	5	5	23	2	7	77

Source: Yoshiwara, op. cit., p.268.

Table XIII.16   Attitude to the Constitution, April 1965

Opinion	First Airborne Group		Eighth Guards Unit		Defence Academy	Defence Agency		Total
	Captains 1st Lieuts 2nd Lieuts	Sergeants Corporals Privates	Captains 1st Lieuts 2nd Lieuts	Sergeants Corporals Privates		Major-Generals	Colonels Lt-Colonels Majors	
Should be revised	10	8	5	–	21	1	4	49
The present constitution should be defended	–	6	–	–	2	–	3	11
Don't know	–	9	–	–	–	–	–	9
No answer	2	–	–	5	–	1	–	8
TOTALS	12	23	5	5	23	2	7	77

Source: Yoshiwara, op. cit., p.262.

Table XIII.17 Hopes for the future of the Self Defence Forces, April 1965

Opinion	First Airborne Group		Eighth Guards Unit		Defence Academy	Defence Agency		Total
	Captains 1st Lieuts 2nd Lieuts	Sergeants Corporals Privates	Captains 1st Lieuts 2nd Lieuts	Sergeants Corporals Privates		Major-Generals	Colonels Lt-Colonels Majors	
Hope for establishment of a full Defence Ministry	8	15	5	4	21	5	5	63
Status quo all right	1	2	–	1	2	–	2	8
Hope for restoration of Imperial armed forces	–	3	–	–	–	–	–	3
Should arm with nuclear weapons	3	1	–	–	8	–	–	12
Hope for overseas service as part of the Free World	–	2	–	–	–	–	–	2
TOTALS	12	23	5	5	31	5	7	88

Source: Yoshiwara, op. cit., p.265.

Table XIII.18 Attitudes to the Japanese–American alliance, April 1965

Opinion	First Airborne Group		Eighth Guards Unit		Defence Academy	Defence Agency		Total
	Captains 1st Lieuts 2nd Lieuts	Sergeants Corporals Privates	Captains 1st Lieuts 2nd Lieuts	Sergeants Corporals Privates		Major-Generals	Colonels Lt-Colonels Majors	
Necessary	10	9	4	3	20	2	7	55
Should be strengthened	2	1	1	–	2	–	–	6
Should be abolished	–	1	–	–	–	–	–	1
No answer	–	12	–	2	1	–	–	15
TOTALS	12	23	5	5	23	2	7	77

Source: Yoshiwara, op. cit., p.262.

Despite their support for the alliance, only a minority of the officers and men surveyed declared themselves willing to act under American command in time of war. This minority included one of the major-generals and three of the seven senior officers in the Defence Agency. A much smaller minority categorically asserted it would refuse to serve under American command. A somewhat larger group declared that it would be prepared to act according to the requirements of the security treaty, but not under American command. Most of Yoshiwara's respondents, however, either gave no answer to this question or confessed that they did not know what they would do in time of crisis. (See table XIII.19)

Self Defence Force support for the security treaty was probably a function of loyalty to the government and the Liberal Democratic Party rather than an expression of inherently 'pro-American' sentiment. Whatever their domestic political positions, the Self Defence Force officers and men surveyed by Yoshiwara did not view the world in terms of the Truman Doctrine. There was no strong tendency to see Japan standing shoulder to shoulder with the United States and its Free World allies in the apocalyptic struggle against Communist tyranny. The majority of respondents (93.5 per cent) did not venture any opinion about Japan's hypothetical enemies. Only a tiny minority (5.19 per cent) regarded the Soviet Union, the People's Republic of China and the Democratic People's Republic of Korea as potential antagonists. (See table XIII.20)

Memoirs, books and articles written by Self Defence Force members provided additional information about the outlook of the postwar military establishment. To some extent, the literary evidence tended to confirm Yoshiwara's findings. It also brought to light aspects of the forces not readily discernable from public opinion polls. Those senior military officers who wrote extensively on international affairs, defence policy and domestic politics, or whose activities attracted public attention in other ways, were generally conservative in outlook, ranging from unreconstructed right-wing militarists at one end of the spectrum, through an assortment of relatively apolitical technocrats, to reasonably liberal conservative nationalists at the other end. The precise location of the ideological centre of gravity of the higher officer corps was impossible to judge. So, too, was its movement over time. Yet it ought to be noted that extremely conservative, bellicose nationalists, of a type apparently uncharacteristic of the forces as a whole, men who remained highly dissatisfied with the postwar order, were not infrequently able to rise to powerful positions.

Consider, for example, the case of General Sugita Ichiji, Chief of the Ground Staff from 1960 to 1962 and subsequently president of the Japan Veterans Association (Nihon Goyū Renmei), an organization with a national membership of some 446,000 dedicated to 'the propagation of defence consciousness, the development of a civil defence system and the honour of fallen heroes'.[22] During the Greater East Asia War Sugita had served as a staff officer with the Imperial Japanese Army in Malaya, Sumatra, the Solomons, at Guadalcanal and in New Guinea.[23] On entering the National Security Force, after his release from the purge in 1952, he had attended a one month's reorientation course designed to acquaint him with the working of Japan's new democratic system.[24] This course had apparently failed to alter his most cherished political beliefs. General Sugita's unabashed nostalgia for

Table XIII.19   Attitudes to the Self Defence Forces acting under United States command within the framework of the security treaty, April 1965

Opinion	First Airborne Group		Eighth Guards Unit		Defence Academy	Defence Agency		Total
	Captains 1st Lieuts 2nd Lieuts	Sergeants Corporals Privates	Captains 1st Lieuts 2nd Lieuts	Sergeants Corporals Privates		Major-Generals	Colonels Lt-Colonels Majors	
Willing to act under American command	5	1	1	2	4	1	3	17
Not willing	–	3	–	–	–	–	–	3
Willing to act according to security treaty but not under US command	1	2	–	–	5	–	2	10
Don't know	1	3	–	–	2	–	–	6
No answer	5	14	4	3	12	1	2	41
TOTALS	12	23	5	5	23	2	7	77

Source: Yoshiwara, op. cit., p.271.

Table XIII.20 Japan's hypothetical enemies

Opinion	First Airborne Group		Eighth Guards Unit		Defence Academy	Defence Agency		Total
	Captains 1st Lieuts 2nd Lieuts	Sergeants Corporals Privates	Captains 1st Lieuts 2nd Lieuts	Sergeants Corporals Privates		Major-Generals	Colonels Lt-Colonels Majors	
Not told about any in particular	3	5	2	1	12	–	1	24
Said to be the USSR, Communist China, North Korea	1	–	–	–	–	1	–	2
Cannot write	2	3	–	–	–	–	–	5
Natural to have hypothetical enemies	–	–	–	–	1	–	–	1
Generally Communist countries	–	–	–	–	1	–	–	1
Countries not in the same camp	–	–	–	–	1	–	–	1
Judge according to common sense	–	–	–	–	–	–	1	1
The hypothetical enemies in the Three Arrows exercise	–	–	–	–	–	1	–	1
No answer	6	15	3	4	8	–	5	41
TOTALS	12	23	5	5	23	2	7	77

Source: Yoshiwara, op. cit., p.269.

the Restoration Order and Japan's imperial past was evident throughout his writings and speeches. According to the former Chief of Staff, the greatness of prewar Japan had been founded on its imperial institutions, patriotic education system and powerful military forces. The dismantling of the Imperial system during the occupation, the trials of 'war criminals', the dissolution of the military forces, the fostering of popular pacifism, the reorganization of educational institutions, imposition of an 'ethical charter' on the Japan Teachers' Federation, constitutional revision, recognition of the Communist Party, revision of the police system and attempts to alter the structure of the family had all been intended to emasculate Japan, to prevent its revival as an independent great power. The scale and character of the damage inflicted on Japan by the Allies during the occupation, he argued, particularly the attempt to limit the political influence of the armed forces, was comparable to Stalin's 1940 Katyn Forest massacre of 20,000 loyal and brave Polish officers because of fear of a Polish revival. Sugita conceded that the onset of the Cold War had obliged the Americans to realize the error of their ways and promote Japan's economic reconstruction and rearmament. Nevertheless, he lamented, no efforts had been made to correct the damage done to the nation's political, social and spiritual order. The result had been a society lacking in firm and inspired leadership, served by colourless and venal politicians, rent by internal political disorders, sapped of its vitality by intellectual egoism and 'confusion of thought', despising time-honoured military values, ignorant of its glorious past and unmindful of its current global responsibilities.[25]

Anglo-American liberal institutions, General Sugita suggested, were not altogether appropriate for Japan's particular culturo-historical traditions. Sugita's view of Japanese history centred around the Imperial institution, the armed forces, the development of a powerful, authoritarian, modern state after the Meiji Restoration and the nation's subsequent rise to great power status. The Pacific War, he believed, had been a glorious failure, defeat an inevitable consequence of inexperienced leadership.[26] His ideal remained a strong, hierarchical national state, essentially Confucian in its values, united around the Imperial house. Only if Japan were true to itself, he asserted, could it re-emerge as a genuinely independent power and assume its natural role in the world.

> The way to peace lies first in correction of our own posture. Japan must reveal its true self before Asia and before the world, its politicians acting [correctly] as politicians, its industrialists [correctly] as industrialists, its scholars [correctly] as scholars, the members of the Self Defence Forces [correctly] as soldiers, its teachers as teachers, its workers as workers, its students as students.[27]

Like all Japanese conservatives, Sugita regarded Western liberalism as posing a rather less serious threat than Marxism to traditional institutions and values. The former Chief of Staff exhibited extreme hostility towards the Socialist and Communist parties. The Japan Teachers' Federation, the academic establishment, trade unions, Japan's Korean residents, students and the peace movement were also the objects of scathing comment.[28] Quite clearly, in Sugita's view, the major Opposition parties and their supporters had no real legitimacy. Regarding the assassination of the Socialist Party leader Asanuma Inejirō in 1960 by the ultranationalist son of one of his own officers, Sugita made the following remarks:

> The security treaty crisis created an atmosphere in which laws and regulations were successively trampled underfoot. The responsibility for this lay largely with the Communist and Socialist parties ... Not only that, but Asanuma had gone to Communist China and grandly announced in a joint communiqué with the Chinese that 'American imperialism is the common enemy of the Chinese and Japanese peoples'. This announcement subservient to Communist China provoked great and numerous repercussions. History frequently shows that in this sort of situation, young people burning with a sense of righteousness and justice are unable to stand things any longer and resort to violent action. Postwar Japanese society has even gone so far as to create a general impression that justice and righteousness are no longer recognized as justice and righteousness, that injustice has become justice, vice has become virtue ... In any case, the Asanuma assassination was an unfortunate event invited by Japanese society itself.[29]

It is interesting to compare Sugita's attitude with that of long-time ultranationalist activists such as Kageyama Masuharu, organizer of the abortive 1933 'Heaven-Sent Soldiers' Plot' (*Shinpei Tai Jihen*) to assassinate the Cabinet and inaugurate the Shōwa Restoration. Kageyama, who, after his release from the purge re-emerged as a prominent figure on the extreme right, expressed his views on Asanuma's assassination in the following terms:

> Yamaguchi [Asanuma's youthful assassin] fought the pro-Communist and un-Japanese [*hanminzokuteki*] character of the Socialist Party with the sacrifice of his life. The assassination was a national tragedy, both from the point of view of the assassin and the assassinated. However, the growing national consciousness among the younger generation is an encouraging tendency. Still, we have not yet reached the stage where terror should be practised.[30]

The former Chief of Staff was unhappy with the civilian control system embodied in the 1954–6 defence laws. Certainly, he protested, he had 'no objection' to the *actual principle* of civilian control and acknowledged that in any modern democratic state 'military affairs must be absolutely dependent on politics'. The military leaders of the Taishō and early Shōwa periods, he declared, had 'misused' their power.[31] Nevertheless, he asserted, the postwar civilian control system had been 'misinterpreted' to mean that the views of 'civilian bureaucrats' should take precedence over those of military men.[32] His remarks, in a letter to Prime Minister Ikeda, that 'the balance between the civil and the military has not been found', revealed something of his true state of mind.[33] In Sugita's opinion, many of the Defence Agency's civilian bureaucrats were time-serving, uninspired, ignorant, not interested in defence, unsympathetic towards the military and prejudiced against former Imperial officers.[34] The administrative changes he advocated to overcome these problems would, in fact, have drastically altered the civilian control system as it had operated since 1954. He proposed, for example, that the Crown Prince, as future head of state, be given proper instruction in military affairs; that a system enabling political and military leaders to determine national policies 'in the closest co-operation' be established;[35] and that responsibility for the national budget be taken out of the hands of the Finance Ministry and entrusted instead to an independent National Budget Compilation Agency (Kokka Yōsan Henseikyoku). Such an arrangement would overcome the problems caused by the Finance Ministry's 'way of thinking about defence' and enable the Prime Minister (working in close collaboration with high-ranking officers) to determine the size of defence and other appropriations 'from a broad national standpoint'.[36] He also recommended that short-sighted and obstructionist personnel in the Defence Agency's internal bureaux should be replaced by men with greater defence consciousness and a more suitable general attitude. At the same time, former Imperial officers and serving defence force members should not be prevented from working in those sections of the Defence Agency traditionally reserved for civilians.[37]

General Sugita also had strong views on several diplomatic issues. In particular, he believed that the preservation of the status quo on the Korean peninsula and in Taiwan were essential Japanese security interests. Failing success by other means, he seemed prepared to recommend Japanese military intervention, in Korea at least, to protect the national interest as he saw it. As far as can be judged from the public record this has not been the policy of any Japanese government since the Pacific War. Despite this, during his years as Chief of Staff, Sugita apparently not only strove to promote acceptance of his views through normal channels but also attempted, albeit on a small scale and without success, to conduct his own private diplomacy, somewhat independently of the government (see Chapter VIII).

Sugita's philosophical outlook, powerful personality and tendency to interpret government policy in an unusually flexible manner perhaps help explain Akagi Munenori's refusal, as director-general of the Defence Agency, to order mobilization of the forces against student demonstrators on 19 June 1960 (see Chapter VI). Quite apart from the fact that this action, requested by Prime Minister Kishi and several other Conservative Party leaders, would have unleashed *de facto* civil war, liberal 'small Japanists' like Akagi doubtless shrank before the prospect of again conferring such awesome power on the representatives of the old Imperial armed forces officer corps. Even a limited mobilization of the forces, Akagi perhaps reasoned, might have precipitated consequences out of all proportion to its causes.

Sugita's views were by no means exceptional in the higher echelons of the Self Defence Force officer corps. Air Marshal Genda Minoru, too, one of the principal planners of the Pearl Harbor operation, Chief of the Air Self Defence Force Staff 1958–62 and subsequently a prominent Conservative Party spokesman on strategic affairs, remained steadfastly loyal to the institutions, values and policies of an earlier era. 'I have no regrets about Pearl Harbor', he declared on more than one occasion. 'If I have any regrets it is only that we did not go back and bomb it two or three times again.'[38]

Like Sugita, Genda had strong views about domestic politics. He also advocated a highly activist foreign policy. The outcome of World War II and the dangers posed by Bolshevism to all conservative governments made the American alliance acceptable, at least as an interim measure. Nevertheless, in Genda's opinion, responsibility for preserving the status quo in the ring on non-Communist countries extending from Korea to Burma should be borne by Japan. The American intervention in Indochina, he felt, had been 'unnatural'.

First let Japan perform the task and where we cannot do it all, the Americans should help us. As a matter of principle, the freedom of Asia should be defended by the hands of Asians and Japan should act as the leader.[39]

This position was consistent, in every way, with the mainstream of conservative American thinking about Japan's place in the Western alliance system, at least until the reconstruction of United States global strategy under Nixon and Kissinger. It came into prominence again during the Carter and Reagan administrations. Yet American advocates of a more active Japanese regional role always assumed Japan would remain, indefinitely, an American satellite. Genda's conviction that Japan would re-emerge as a fully independent great power, together with his interest in an autonomous nuclear strike force, suggested that he saw non-Communist Asia eventually constituting a more or less exclusive Japanese sphere of influence. His enthusiasm for a more assertive military role, albeit within the context of the American alliance, could therefore be interpreted as a strategy to reimpose Japanese regional hegemony, in much the same way as the Marquis de Chauvelin, Louis XV's far-sighted Foreign Minister, sought, successfully, to bring Corsica under French control through a policy of careful co-operation with its decaying suzerain power, Genoa.

General Mitsuoka Kenjirō, a graduate of the Imperial Military Academy, Staff Officer at Imperial General Headquarters during the Greater East Asia War and subsequently Chief of Staff of the Ground Self Defence Force Third Division, Chief of Staff of the Central Regional Force, Chief of Staff of the Ninth Division and director of the Education Section at the Officers Staff College, also drew his philosophical inspiration from the Meiji ideal of a unified and hierarchical Confucian state. For Mitsuoka, as for Sugita and Genda, power remained the paramount factor in international politics. A civilization not founded on power was a civilization doomed to extinction.[40] While Mitsuoka certainly did not regard Communism in a favourable light, his thinking about contemporary international politics was only marginally influenced by the Cold War. His world was composed of competing national states, not conflicting ideologies. He was therefore not prone to wax lyrical about such topics as the preservation of freedom and the defence of the West.

> We must judge which countries might pose a threat to Japan, and thus become the object of our defence policies, on the basis of their offensive capacities and intentions, in the context of the international situation. However, since intentions are often very unclear until just before an attack, we must base our judgements largely on offensive capacity. If we take various factors into consideration [it will be apparent] that the countries in the region whose military power we should take into consideration are, provisionally, the Soviet Union, China and North Korea. Among these, China possesses nuclear weapons and a vast army, but an attack on Japan would be unthinkable in the near future because of her [limited] maritime and air transport capacities.
>
> The same could be said of North Korea. Moreover, South Korea lies between us and the North. For this reason we must assume that the Soviet Union poses the principal threat ... To posit a country as a hypothetical enemy certainly does not mean that friendly relations with it should be jeopardized in times of peace. The judgement is one about a country's ability, not about its intentions. We are doing no more than establishing hypotheses about

things that might happen. In the future, if China modernizes and strengthens her armed-forces, we will naturally be obliged to consider her as a potential antagonist.[41]

Mitsuoka's support for the Japanese-American alliance was a highly qualified one. The United States, he believed, also posed a threat to Japan, even within the context of the security treaty system.

> The United States would not go to war for Japan's interests, but for its own interests. If the United States judges that co-operation in the defence of Japan is against its own interests there is no doubt that it would abandon Japan. If it abandons Japan it is unlikely to hand the country over for the use of the Soviet Union. When it withdraws, it will naturally destroy the country completely, so that it will not fall into enemy's hands, just as it did after the retreat from Hungnam during the Korean War. From the American point of view, it would be very much simpler to destroy Japan and abandon it in the case of a serious Soviet attack, rather than dispatch its own armed forces and defend the country with the blood of American youths.[42]

Like Sugita, Mitsuoka was unhappy with many aspects of the postwar civilian control system. The Defence Agency was dominated by civilians without military knowledge who devoted themselves solely to 'supervising, fettering and interfering with the work of uniformed officers'. The United States, he maintained, lost the war in Vietnam largely because it adhered too rigidly to a 'theoretical system of military control'. Japan had adopted the same system and was trudging dutifully in America's footsteps towards its own ruin.[43]

Many other senior officers, in contrast, appeared satisfied with the postwar constitutional order, accepted the civilian control system and avoided provocative comment on either domestic political issues or international affairs. Like General Mitsuoka, most of these men appeared to be exponents of foreign policies based on traditional, state-centred realism rather than ideological anti-Communism. Admiral Nakayama Sadayoshi, for example, a graduate of the Imperial Naval Academy, staff officer at Imperial General Headquarters during World War II and Chief of the Maritime Self Defence Force Staff 1961–3, rarely publicized his views on internal social and political matters. He did, however, make it clear that he understood and fully supported the civilian control system embodied in the 1954–6 defence laws. American-Soviet rivalry, he argued, was simply a fact of international life. In this context, the security treaty would be necessary 'so long as Japan maintains the policy of acting in concert with the Free World', despite the general trend towards greater autonomy within the Cold War alliance systems.[44]

General Nakamura Ryūhei, too, Chief of the Ground Self Defence Force Staff, 1971–2, was reluctant to discuss domestic politics. His public comments suggested a strong interest in creating a national consensus on defence, persuading all Japanese, including Socialists and Communist supporters, to recognize the necessity of the forces. Nakamura had a clear understanding of the postwar democratic order and unequivocally endorsed the principle of civilian control.[45] His experience in the Imperial Japanese Army, while not as extensive as that of Sugita or Genda, had given him considerable insight into the complexities of international politics. As a young officer he had been instructed by the legendary pan-Asianist Ishiwara Kanji. The end of the war had found him at General Headquarters planning the defence of the home islands against the anticipated American onslaught. Within a few years, like many of his colleagues, he was serving in an American-dominated gendarmerie held in contempt by large sections of the general public. Nakamura, to a far greater extent than anti-Communist officers such as Sugita, seemed anxious to re-establish a Japanese national identity outside the framework of the Cold War. In his discussions of international politics he therefore carefully eschewed one-sided moral judgements and ideological posturings. His view of international society was pragmatic, evolutionary and essentially pacific. In 1972 he told the strategic studies specialist Kotani Hidejirō that

> Japan does not consider any particular country as a hypothetical enemy. Japan's national policies are based on peace. We live in an age which stresses peaceful coexistence. Japan exists as part of an international community and [is eager] to promote international co-operation. Since Japan's [prosperity] depends on trade, this political posture is [an eminently reasonable one]. Politically, I believe it is natural for us to promote friendly relations with all countries, whether they be Socialist or whatever ... However, there are various countries in Japan's region. The military power currently maintained by these countries is a matter of military interest. Naturally, we do not know how these countries might intend to use their military power. I consider that the amount, the quality of the military power currently maintained by these countries, their possible intentions, their strategic thinking and their [military] tactics are natural objects for consideration by [those responsible] for the defence of Japan.[46]

General Nakamura did not consider that the Self Defence forces, whatever their origins might have been, existed in order to further the global interests of one particular superpower. On the contrary,

> the task of the Ground Self Defence Force is to defend the peace and security of Japan. To elaborate further, this means that their task is to protect the national territory and the people, to protect the property of the people, to protect their traditions and to protect their culture ... I believe we must pay particular attention to the lives of the people.[47]

Effective fulfilment in this task required larger defence expenditure, a powerful intelligence organization[48] and greater public awareness of international strategic issues. It did not require military commitments outside Japan. Nor, ideally, should it require alliance with a foreign power.

> I want Japanese soil to be defended by the hands of the Japanese people, without the assistance of the American army.[49]

Not surprisingly, General Nakamura displayed particular interest in the defence policies of countries such as France and Switzerland.[50]

Senior officers such as Air Marshal Ishikawa Tsurayuki, Chief of the Air Self Defence Force Staff 1971–2,[51] or Admiral Ishida Suteo, Chief of the Maritime Self Defence Force Staff 1972–3,[52] as well as relatively younger men such as Captain Karube Tsutomu, Associate Professor at the National Defence Academy and member of the Defence Research Institute, while supporting the Japanese-American security treaty on the basis of balance of power and deterrence theories, also displayed little evidence of strong ideological preferences in either domestic or global politics. Like Admiral Nakayama and General Nakamura, they avoided public comment on the policies of any political party. At the same time they tended to view the United States and the Soviet Union simply as rival global superpowers, each with its own strengths and weaknesses, its own peculiar interests and sensibilities, essentially amoral in their behaviour. Japan's current alignments were not so much a matter of choice as of historical necessity, the outcome of its failure to wrest Pacific hegemony from the United States in the Greater East Asia War. Generally speaking, these apolitical military technocrats, conscious of the fluidity of international society and the manifold potentialities latent in any evolving situation, did not seem convinced that United States claims to moral superiority over its superpower rival should decisively influence Japanese policies. Captain Karube's analysis of the capabilities, objectives and methods of the two superpowers, for example, was remarkable for its dispassionate strategic objectivity.

> At sea, the two superpowers employ their competing naval presences as the principal vehicle of their diplomacy. Whether we like it or not, Japan, as a West Pacific country, cannot escape being drawn into the vortex of their struggles. The Chief of United States Naval Operations, lamenting the situation in the Japan Sea [the growing strength of the Soviet navy] has appealed for expansion of the Maritime Self Defence Forces ... Even if the Soviet Union enjoys naval supremacy in the Japan Sea, it would be possible to adopt a policy of blockading the straits and containing this power in the Japan Sea area ... Naval supremacy in vast oceans is an extremely fluid thing. To seize it and maintain it is the accumulated result of will-power and of decisions taken in time of peace. Japan, which depends upon the seas for its survival, must, in peacetime, in a situation confused by the presence of both the United States and Soviet navies, before any emergency requiring direct defence of the national territory actually arises, demonstrate a readiness to preserve its political freedom of choice, respond to the demands of the national interest and be prepared to exercise a policy of give and take in its relations with other countries.[53]

The higher officer corps was not, of course, without its committed enthusiasts for Japan's membership of the Western Community, men who accepted the philosophical assumptions of the Cold War, seemed thoroughly at home working in the context of a transnational, global alliance system and did not necessarily view the security treaty simply as a means to realize traditional Japanese objectives. Air Vice-Marshal Suzuki Ryūgorō, for example, commander of the Fiftieth Naval Attack Squadron in the Pacific War and subsequently Chief of Staff of the Northern Regional Air Force a.d Deputy Chief of the Air Staff, while lamenting the failure of Japan's prewar drive for Asian-Pacific hegemony, was convinced that the United States 'was not an opponent that we could have taken on with any hope of victory in the first place'. Postwar Japan, he believed, owed its thirty years of peace and prosperity to the 'help and protection of the United States military occupation' and the subsequent development of an 'intimate bilateral economic co-operation and common defence system'. Japan's defence was based on the security treaty and on virtual alliances with South Korea, Taiwan, the Philippines and America's other Pacific partners. The Soviet Union, powerful, expansionist, intent on world revolution and actually occupying Japanese territory in the north, was 'the single greatest threat' to the Japanese state. This situation could be expected to continue indefinitely.[54]

There were also high-ranking officers who believed, like General Umezu Yoshij-irō in the last months of the Pacific War, that the national interest demanded close ties with America's superpower rival. On 18 January 1980 Major-General Miyanaga Yukishisa, the scion of an old military family, a graduate of the Imperial Officers Staff College (1940–54th class) with a record of distinguished service in World War II, who had entered the Police Reserve Force in 1951, eventually serving as Chief of Intelligence in the Self Defence Force Northern Army Command and deputy director of the Intelligence School, was arrested on charges of spying for the Soviet Union. Two accomplices, Lieutenant Kashi Eiichi and Lieutenant Ōshima Suketoshi, were taken into custody at the same time. While the evidence is as yet far from clear it seems that Major-General Miyanaga and his group, who had worked undetected for the Soviet Union since the mid-1960s, had decided to betray their government for philosophical reasons. During the preliminary police investigations, Miyanaga, described by his astonished colleagues as 'an intellectual', 'serious-minded', 'quiet', 'diligent' and 'meticulous', insisted that he had gone over to the Soviet interest because of his ideological belief in Communism, 'not for the sake of money or women'.[55]

Historical assessment of General Miyanaga must be suspended until further material becomes available. Nevertheless, the persistence of a deep-rooted tradition of dissidence in the Japanese armed forces cannot be overlooked. Prince Konoye's adviser Ozaki Hotsumi, the central Japanese figure in Richard Sorge's Tōkyō spy ring, had been convinced that a Greater East Asia Co-prosperity Sphere could only be founded on the basis of an alliance among the Soviet Union, a Communist China and a revolutionary Japan. While Ozaki had worked in isolation the Imperial Japanese Army and Navy, too, had contained a powerful radical wing, dedicated to domestic reconstruction along socialist lines and a foreign policy based on pan-Asianist principles. In 1945, it will be recalled, Prince Konoye and his circle had advised the emperor to surrender to the United States in order to forestall a seizure of power by this group. Prime Minister Yoshida Shigeru's opposition to rearmament had been, in part, motivated by fears that radical nationalist 'left wing' elements would inevitably infiltrate any new military organization. In view of the extraordinary vigilance subsequently exercised by all Japanese governments in the selection of both officers and enlisted men, it might be thought that it would have been as easy for a camel to pass through the eye of a needle as for a radical 'Marxist' revolutionary to enter the Self Defence Forces. Yet apparently this was not the case. As the old proverb goes, *Kōbō mo fude no ayamari*, 'Even the Great Monk Kōbō sometimes makes a mistake with the brush'. On 5 October 1969 Pilot Officer Konishi Makoto, of the Forty-Sixth Electronic Communications Group, Air Self Defence Force, based on the island of Sado, off Niigata, in the Japan Sea, began openly conducting a campaign against the domestic 'peace-keeping' role of the SDF. On 18 October he refused to participate in 'special duties exercises' (*tokubetsu keibi kunren*) and 'peace-keeping exercises' (*chian shutsudō kunren*). Shortly afterwards he was arrested and charged with 'instigation to sabotage', 'conduct of a kind likely to undermine the effectiveness of government action' and sundry violations of the Self Defence Forces Law.

Konishi was not a conscientious objector. Appalled by what he saw as postwar Japan's subservience to the United States and the corruption of the Liberal Democratic Party government, he had gradually abandoned the conservatism of his early youth in favour of a revolutionary Marxism with strong nationalist overtones.

> Although I was living on an isolated island far out in the Japan Sea, I heard the voice of the people, of real human beings, swelling up from among their ranks. Those voices sank deep into my mind and forced me to make a decision. I resolved to live as a true soldier who had sworn his allegiance to the workers and peasants. I wrote that on my last anti-war poster, 'Against the Security Treaty'. I appealled for the setting-up of a Red Army, an alliance of all the revolutionary Communists in the Self Defence Forces.[56]

Konishi, widely regarded in the West as representing Japan's 'new left', had no connection with any established political party. He was highly critical of the nation's major Opposition groupings, believing they had little appreciation of the role of military power either in international society or domestic politics.[57]

> Modern warfare is a struggle involving the entire people. This proposition is demonstrated by the local conflicts in Indochina and the Middle East. For this reason, the armed forces, the principal vehicles of war, cannot exist without the overwhelming support and admiration of the people.[58]

The Konishi affair brought to light the existence of a group of revolutionary Marxist junior officers and enlisted men, opposed to the Japanese-American alliance, alienated from the domestic status quo, no more attached to the concept of civilian control than their colleagues on the extreme right, committed to radical transformation of the Self Defence Forces and the total reconstruction of Japanese society. Corporal Ōshiro Seigo, one of the few officers of Okinawan origin, who had attended his first demonstration against the security treaty as a third-year high school student and later participated in the prolonged struggle against the expropriation of farmland at Sanrizuka for the construction of Narita International Airport, explained his decision to embark on a military career in the following manner:

> I would like to make it clear why I entered the Self Defence Forces. I entered because I wanted to become a solider in a Red Army. That's why I went in. That's why I threw myself into the drills. That's why I built up my knowledge.[59]

Private Kawai Masaji, of the Ground Self Defence Force, had begun to reassess his philosophical position after he became sceptical about the official pantheon of hypothetical enemies and the real purposes of his training:

> What exactly is the purpose of the things that we do every day? We are taught that we are defending our country from Chinese and Soviet aggression ... but have the Soviet Union

and China ever once attacked Japan? If it is impossible to believe Soviet and Chinese protestations that they will not attack unless they themselves are attacked first, it is also impossible to believe that the Self Defence Forces exist solely for the purposes of self defence.
Any country intending to invade Japan would need an enormous number of transport
vessels to ship a vast army (to our shores). The Chinese navy hardly deserves the name. It
consists of nothing but obsolete small coastal vessels. The Soviet Union's capacity to transport forces overseas is also small – nothing compared to that of the United States – and it
would be impossible to employ it solely against Japan.

What kind of exercises do we ourselves do? Naturally, if we were to be fighting only in
self defence, the Self Defence Forces would not be dispatched overseas. We would fight
inside Japan when some other army had landed on our shores. Japan's geography being
what it is, this would naturally mean that most of the fighting would be done in cities. But
in that case, why is it we do the kind of exercises we are doing now, travelling tens of
kilometres in large formations of mechanized divisions, pouring out of tanks, armoured
cars and helicopters in wide open spaces, then engaging in hand-to-hand combat. You'll
see what I mean if you spread out a map of Japan and try to find a place (apart from the
exercise grounds) where you can do that sort of thing. Of course, matters would be different if the enemy decided not to seize Tōkyō or Ōsaka, but to occupy the exercise grounds.
But actually the continent, the Asian continent, is the only place you can fight that kind of
war.[60]

For Private Kawai, only one course of action seemed acceptable:

What should the members of the Self Defence Forces be defending? In order to protect
the interests of the capitalists, should we act as the capitalists' mercenaries, invade Asia
and turn our weapons against our parents, our brothers and our friends? Or, in order to
protect the people's interests, should we turn our weapons against the capitalists and fight
as the soldiers of the workers and peasants? We must choose one or the other alternative.
We must understand that we are not mercenaries of the capitalists, but soldiers of the workers and peasants. We must make it clear that our weapons are directed towards the
capitalists.[61]

In all probability, Konishi, Ōshiro, Kawai and their colleagues constituted a tiny,
isolated minority in the Self Defence Forces. The Mishima affair suggested that the
extreme right, encouraged by prominent Conservative politicians and high-ranking
officers, enjoyed greater opportunities to extend its organizations and promote its
views. Yet it is also possible to underestimate the strength of leftist sentiment. The
most intelligent radical officers were unlikely to draw public attention to their
activities or reveal their true sentiments to scholars conducting opinion surveys. The
Japanese are extremely adept at forming and maintaining secret societies. Pilot
Officer Konishi, while admitting that he himself had been something of an isolated
figure in his unit, asserted that 'radical views' were to be found 'rather frequently'
among graduates of the Defence Academy, officers who had entered the forces from
state and private universities, and among the large body of technical experts working
within the military establishment.[62] In this connection, Private Asaoka Tetsu's
experience was of considerable interest:

One day I happened to turn on the television and saw the farmers at Sanrizuka battling with the Special Mechanized Police (Kidōtai). The spectacle of the police, snarling like enraged animals, dragging off farmers who had chained themselves to trees and refused to move, utterly sickened me. The Self Defence Forces, after all, also do 'law and order' training.... At first I didn't notice it, but a few of the other blokes had also come in to watch the television. Most of them cursed the farmers. But there were a few who thought about them. I don't know whether they had the same ideas as me, but it was a relief to know that some of them thought about the farmers.... One night I opened up and discussed the Vietnam war, 'law and order' training and a lot of other things with one of the other fellows. I was astonished to find out how left-wing his views were and was greatly encouraged to find out that there were such men in the forces. Two or three days after that we had 'law and order' training. I had decided to refuse to do it but then thought it would be better to wait for some future time. The squad leader instructed us enthusiastically but the men appeared to have mixed feelings. At the present time I am working hard to become a conscientious member of the Self Defence Forces and hope to become an officer. I would like, however, to make one point clear. Together with the [Japanese] people, the students, the workers and [my comrades] in one section of the Self Defence Forces, I intend to resolutely oppose the dispatch of the SDF to Okinawa, refuse to co-operate in 'law and order' training, strive to crush militarism and oppose war. We will work towards dissolution of the Self Defence Forces ... with the ultimate objective of rebuilding them into a Red Army which will overthrow the state.[63]

Regardless of its size and influence, the fact that this group existed at all was in itself of considerable significance. It is frequently forgotten how rapidly situations can change. In 1914 the Imperial Russian Army and Navy, along with the Holy Orthodox Church, were rightly regarded as impregnable bastions of the Tsarist state. The Bolsheviks who had infiltrated the ranks of the armed forces were a tiny, apparently insignificant minority. Within three years the old regime had fallen, the Communist Party had assumed supreme political power and the Bolshevik officers, enthusiastically supported by tens of thousands of former Imperial soldiers, were leading the Red Army to victory in the Civil War. In the Imperial Japanese Army and Navy, too, the ideological equilibrium changed rapidly between 1920 and 1930 and again between 1930 and 1941. There was no reason to assume that the order established in 1950–6 would endure forever. Moreover, while the conservative, nationalist right clearly occupied the strategic heights of power in all three services, it was by no means inevitable that change would necessarily work in its interests. A serious domestic crisis, involving full mobilization of the police and army against demonstrators (a situation only narrowly avoided in 1960), or participation in a protracted and unpopular war in Korea, South-East Asia or the Northern Territories, could, given the existence of powerful Socialist and Communist parties in Japan itself, have promoted conditions favourable to the growth of radical left-wing influence in the Self Defence Forces. Much to the relief of established political leaders of all persuasions, *détente*, the great peace which settled over much of East Asia after the end of the Vietnam War, the corresponding subsidence of domestic unrest and the relaxation of American pressure on the rearmament issue, reduced the possibility of Japan's involvement in any such conflict. The Pandora's box of the Japanese armed forces was not again taken down from the shelf until the early 1980s.

CHAPTER XIV

Defence policy decision-making, 1960–1978

So, naturalists observe, a flea
Hath smaller fleas that on him prey;
And these have smaller fleas to bite 'em,
And so proceed ad infinitum.

Jonathan Swift

I Defence Planning and civilian control: the operation of the 1954–6 defence laws

On 19 July 1978, General Kurisu Hiroomi, chairman of the Joint Staff Council, announced that 'since there are many inadequacies in the present Self Defence Forces Law, it is possible that the forces might be obliged to take extra-legal action [*chōhōkiteki kōdō*] in time of emergency'.[1]

Kurisu, who later emerged as a prominent advocate of an independent nuclear strike force, also suggested that the chairman of the Joint Staff Council should be made an 'attested official' (Ninshokan), directly responsible to the emperor, in the same manner as Cabinet ministers, judges of the Supreme Court, the Attorney General, the director-general of the Imperial Household Agency and the Imperial Grand Chamberlain.[2] His proposals represented a direct challenge, of the most fundamental kind, to the entire postwar order. The changes he advocated would have gone a long way towards restoring the powerful domestic position occupied by the armed forces under the Meiji Constitution. As such, they were unacceptable both to the Japanese government and to the public at large. Within two weeks Kurisu had been dismissed from office. Totally unrepentant, the former chairman of the Joint Staff Council launched an energetic campaign against the postwar civilian control system. 'If I am to speak frankly', he told the magazine *Shūkan Bunshun*, 'the [Defence Agency's] internal bureaux are, at the present time, excessively powerful. They have everything in their hands. The uniformed officers are little more than their assistants'.[3] This situation, he claimed, caused serious problems in relations with the United States.

The Kurisu affair resulted in a decisive victory for those in favour of upholding the status quo. Yet the episode inevitably focused public attention, once again, on to the

question of defence policy decision-making and the wider issue of civil-military relations. Understandably, interest centred not merely on how the institutions established under the 1954–6 laws operated but on whether the principle of civilian control enshrined in these laws had actually been applied in practice.

Two general points should be made before we proceed to examine the inner workings of the Defence Agency and its related institutions.

First, while the distinction between civilian and military made in the 1954–6 laws
generally conforms to the usage of the Anglo-American world, the popular belief
that the domination of one by the other will automatically produce certain predictable effects is questionable. Effective operation of civilian control in a democratic society will perhaps ensure that defence policy is formulated by legally constituted civilian authorities ultimately answerable to the electorate. It does not guarantee that the
government's military posture will be rational and non-provocative, that the media
will adopt balanced and responsible attitudes in its reporting of foreign affairs, that
public opinion will not succumb to bouts of aggressive jingoism. Militarism has
never been the exclusive property of the professional officer class. In its most viru-
lent form it is a condition affecting entire societies. It has, as often as not, found its
most energetic champions among civilians. Many eminent professional soldiers, in
contrast, have been exponents of moderate and pacific policies. Disraeli and Salis-
bury, Joseph Chamberlain, Winston Churchill, Jules Ferry, President McKinley and
Theodore Roosevelt probably contributed more to the growth of belligerent, expansionist nationalism in their respective countries than any of the generals and
admirals who served their governments. In both world wars, the General Staffs of all
the major powers dutifully followed the dictates of their political masters. Truman,
no doubt, was wise in rejecting advice from the Chiefs of Staff to attack the USSR.
He was prudent in opposing MacArthur's desire to expand the Korean War. Yet this
merely shows that Truman was more far-sighted than his Chiefs of Staff and more
sensible than MacArthur, not that civilians are generally less belligerent than military officers. It was, after all, General Charles de Gaulle who extracted France from
the disastrous and costly wars initiated by the Fourth Republic; Dwight D.
Eisenhower, the four-star general, who negotiated the Korean armistice, decided
against intervention in Indochina, promoted a limited United States-Soviet *détente*
and warned the American people of the dangers posed by the military-industrial
complex. The most calamitous war in American history was launched by an
administration notably lacking in men with real military experience, on the basis of
doctrines formulated largely by desk generals, armchair strategists and civilian
academic advisers.

Second, as far as Japan is concerned, the historical record simply will not sustain
the view that a handful of ultra-nationalist military officers drove the entire Japanese
nation unwillingly along the road to empire. Japan's expansion in Asia and the
Pacific, in the decades before World War II, did not occur because the Chiefs of Staff
enjoyed a constitutional position equal to that of the Prime Minister. Since the Meiji
Restoration, the dominant groups in the Japanese government, civilian and military,
the political parties, the bureaucracy, the business community and the mass media

had all favoured expansionist policies. It had been well understood that the pursuit of these policies could involve Japan in a clash with the Anglo-American powers, the Soviet Union and the forces of Chinese nationalism. After 1945, the democratic mythology of the American Republic combined with the self-interest of the old Japanese court oligarchy, the new Conservative political establishment, the bureaucracy and the great corporations to make the Imperial Armed Forces the scapegoats for everything disagreeable that had occurred since the Meiji Restoration. As the demands of the Cold War drew the United States leadership and the old Japanese political elite closer together, this fiction became increasingly satisfactory for both parties. Yet it was in no way consistent with the facts.

(i)   The Cabinet and the National Defence Council

Under the 1954–6 defence laws, the ultimate power of decision on all matters relating to defence and foreign policy was vested in the Cabinet. By the beginning of the 1960s, however, the National Defence Council, originally established as a consultative body, had effectively replaced the Cabinet as the ultimate decison-making organ, at least to the extent that its recommendations tended automatically to become Cabinet decisions.[4] Meetings of the National Defence Council, it will be recalled, were to be attended by the Prime Minister, the Minister of Finance, the director-general of the Defence Agency, the Foreign Minister and the director-general of the Economic Planning Agency, all of whom enjoyed the right to participate in the decisions. By the middle of the 1960s it had also become customary for meetings to be attended by the Chief Cabinet Secretary, the director of the Science and Technology Agency and the Minister for International Trade and Industry. The chairman of the Joint Staff Council, the chief of the National Defence Council Secretariat and various high-ranking civil servants were also usually present in an advisory capacity. Given the political climate of postwar Japan it would be rash to assume that the chairman of the Joint Staff Council did anything more than offer advice. At the same time, in a situation where few members of the Liberal Democratic Party and fewer Cabinet ministers have been noted for their knowledge of military affairs, it would be wrong to imagine that the recommendations of Japan's highest-ranking professional soldier on technical and, perhaps, at times, wider strategic questions, could have habitually gone unheeded.

From the inception of the Joint Staff Council in July 1954 until the autumn of 1964, the chairmanship was occupied continuously by General Hayashi Keizō, whose relative innocence in the military field has already been noted. Hayashi's successors, Admiral Sugie Ichizō, General Amano Yoshihide, Air Marshal Muta Hirokuni, Admiral Itaya Ryūichi, General Kinugasa Hayao, General Nakamura Ryūhei, Air Marshal Shirakawa Motoharu, Admiral Samejima Hirokazu and General Kurisu Hiroomi were all former Imperial officers with distinguished records and strong personalities. The civilian members of the National Defence Council probably experienced more difficulty arguing with these men than with Hayashi. Hayashi had been a bureaucrat dressed up as a general. After his retirement the National Defence Council had to deal with real generals.

At meetings of the National Defence Council, the Prime Minister's dependence on the chairman of the Joint Staff Council for technical and strategic advice was reduced by the presence of the chief of the National Defence Council's own secretariat. This secretariat had been set up under the 1956 law in order to collect intelligence and conduct research. It consisted of twenty permanent civilian officials responsible to a civilian chief secretary appointed by the Prime Minister, ten part-time secretaries appointed from the public service, three full-time and six part-time councillors appointed from other administrative organizations.[5] Although its true purpose had not been explicitly spelled out in the original legislation, the secretariat had, in fact, been designed to act as an informed counterweight to the views of the Joint Staff Council and the uniformed officers in the Defence Agency. While it would be incorrect to assume that the civilian bureaucrats invariably espoused the cause of pacific external policies and minimal defence spending, while the Self Defence Force officer corps favoured an assertive foreign policy and more substantial military budgets, the National Defence Council secretariat and the Joint Staff Council clashed frequently.[6]

Although the National Defence Council had effectively taken over functions originally vested in the Cabinet, the infrequency of its meetings suggested that the more important concrete decisions on defence planning and policy were made elsewhere. The National Defence Council met only fifteen times during the eleven years between its inception in 1956 and the final decision on the Third Defence Plan in 1967, that is, an average of 1.4 times each year. Even if the council's forty-three informal discussion meetings held during this period are included, the average comes to no more than 5.13 meetings per year, less than one meeting every two months.[7] Between 1967 and 1977 it held only eighteen major meetings.[8] Many of the council's decisions were of a relatively trivial nature. One of its first acts, for example, was to 'decide' the so-called Basic Policy of National Defence (*Kokubō No Kihon Hōshin*), which is

> To prevent direct and indirect aggression, to resist aggression in the improbable event of its occurrence and to defend the peace and independence of our country, which stands on the basis of democracy.[9]

As specific measures to achieve these goals, the Basic Policy recommended support for the United Nations, reliance on the security treaty, stabilization of the people's livelihood and gradual strengthening of the Self Defence Forces. Quite a number of the council's meetings between 1956 and 1977 resulted in 'decisions' of this type. The Second, Third and Fourth Defence Plans were all officially 'decided' by the council after a single meeting, or at the most two or three meetings, most of which lasted for no more than an hour. The same could be said of the council's decisions on the successive mainstay fighters for the air force.[10]

No less remarkable was the fact that the council apparently never discussed many issues directly affecting Japanese security. It has already been seen how the initial decision to renegotiate the 1951 security treaty was made by Prime Minister Kishi alone. The National Defence Council was not consulted during the entire course of the negotiations or at any time during the crisis that ensued. Kishi's initial project was frustrated because of opposition from the Liberal Democratic Party, at least some of which was of a personal and factional character, totally unconnected with the issues ostensibly at stake. The problem of whether to mobilize the Self Defence Forces against the anti-treaty demonstrators was debated, not by the National Defence Council, but in a highly informal fashion by the Prime Minister, the director-general of the Defence Agency, assorted Cabinet ministers and members of the Liberal Democratic Party. The complex issues involved in policy towards China, Korea, South-East Asia and the Middle East were thrashed out in the Cabinet, in the Liberal Democratic Party and in the various ministries and agencies concerned. So too was the Okinawan question. The National Defence Council was never once consulted. Nor was it consulted on the issue of the nuclear non-proliferation treaty. The decision to extend the security treaty automatically after 1970, too, was the product of a gradual unification of opinion within the Liberal Democratic Party and of prolonged consultations with Washington. The National Defence Council played no role.

(ii)   Decision-making and civilian control within the Defence Agency

The general direction of Japan's foreign policy and its overall strategic posture were thus determined not by the National Defence Council but by the state of the Liberal Democratic Party factional balance. Within this framework, the Defence Agency was responsible largely for the technical details of defence planning. Inside the Defence Agency, power of decision on all matters ranging from the agency's draft budget to details of operational plans and the promotion of high-ranking officers was, under the director-general, vested in seven internal bureaux (the Secretariat, the Defence Bureau, the Educational Bureau, the Personnel Bureau, the Medical Bureau, the Paymaster's Bureau and the Weapons Bureau) employing a total of about two hundred civilian officials, and in the councillors meeting, attended by the director-general, the two vice-ministers and the seven bureau chiefs.[11] At the time of the National Security Agency uniformed officers were completely excluded from the internal bureaux. This regulation was subsequently waived. Nevertheless, it became customary not to permit uniformed men to occupy posts above the rank of section chief in these bureaux.[12] The two vice-ministers and the seven bureau chiefs remained, of course, civilians. During the mid-1960s strenuous efforts were made to ensure that civilian dominance of the internal bureaux was not further eroded. Newly recruited civilian officials, for example, had at one time been temporarily assigned to sections staffed largely by uniformed men. After a period of apprenticeship in military affairs they had then been placed in one of the internal bureaux. This practice was subsequently abandoned because it was felt that excessive exposure to military officers was having an undesirable influence on the views of the new civilian appointees.[13]

From what, exactly, were these civilian officials being protected? It is difficult for an outsider to judge such matters accurately. The strategic perceptions of the civilian bureaucrats did not seem to differ radically from those of their uniformed colleagues. The former Home Ministry officials who dominated the civilian bureaucracy perhaps remained, to a somewhat greater extent than the military leadership, preoccupied with domestic threats to Japan's security.* Yet high-ranking officers like General Sugita Ichiji, too, spent many sleepless nights worrying about the machinations of the Communist Party, the Socialist Party, the trade union leadership, the peace movement, student organizations and Japan's Korean residents. Occasionally, prominent representatives of the two camps clashed over the interpretation of international strategic developments, domestic political, economic and social trends and the policy options open to Japan. In 1978, for example, the Defence Agency bureaucracy clashed with General Kurisu about the significance of Soviet manoeuvres in the disputed northern islands. The civilian analysts asserted that the Russians were 'constructing a base'. Kurisu maintained they were carrying out 'landing exercises',[14] the implication presumably being that the Soviet Union was preparing for a possible future invasion of Japan. These two conflicting interpretations of Soviet activity required two significantly different Japanese responses. Yet the frequency and extent of such conflicts should not be exaggerated. Hawks and doves were to be found in both the civilian bureaucracy and the officer corps. Tough-minded conservative nationalist officers like General Sugita and Air Marshal Genda certainly had their counterparts among the Defence Agency's civilian officials. The policies advocated by high-ranking civilian functionaries such as Kaihara Osamu and Toga Hiroshi, whose writings stressed the stability and relative security of Japan's strategic environment, opposing heavy rearmament and wider commitments overseas, did not seem, in essence, to be very different from those espoused by moderate officers such as Admiral Nakayama or General Nakamura.

The available evidence suggests that civilian-military conflict in the Defence Agency during this period centred less around policy issues than questions of status and power. High-ranking military officers, particularly those brought up in the pre-war system, resented their subordination to men whom they regarded as bumbling amateurs. Civilian bureaucrats understandably viewed the uniformed officers, frequently men with charismatic personalities, extensive military experience and considerable capacity for intrigue, as threats to their newly acquired supremacy.

These conflicts were perhaps more significant than they appeared on the surface. Civil-military rivalry, not directly related to questions of external policy, has a long history in Japan. The Defence Agency civilian officials, while owing their postwar supremacy to the occupation settlement, were the heirs to a hoary bureaucratic tradition. The attitudes of the most senior uniformed officers had been moulded by the Imperial Japanese Army and Navy, whose Chiefs of Staff had stood, under the emperor, on equal terms with the Prime Minister. Behind the Imperial Army and Navy hovered the shades of a long line of military oligarchs and their mighty war hosts, extending back, like the endless rows of granite statues in Buddhist grave-

---

* Until the end of the Pacific War the Home Ministry, through the agency of the regular and secret police, had been responsible for suppressing political and religious dissent throughout the Japanese Empire. Much of the postwar leadership of the Opposition parties, in particular the Communist Party, had experienced considerable discomfort as a result of its activities.

yards, to the very origins of the Japanese state. Japan's civil and military traditions, overlapping, interpenetrating and interacting in complicated, constantly changing, unpredictable patterns, derived, to a far greater extent than those of other, comparable modern societies, from fundamentally divergent philosophical assumptions, premisses which had given birth, during the course of the nation's turbulent history, to very different views about the nature of civilization, the institutional arrangements necessary to ensure its continuity, the relationship between the emperor and the state, the state and the people, the community and the individual, the meaning of human life itself. Both traditions were intensely culturo-centric, elitist, hierarchical, mistrustful of popular democracy. One tended towards materialistic rationalism, the other towards an almost mystical belief in the national destiny. One was preoccupied with the pursuit of stability, status and power, the other with masculinity, honour and death. Too close an association with men whose lives embodied these ancient military values, the agency's civilian leadership perhaps felt, posed great dangers, especially to young and impressionable personnel. However this may be, the stern measures taken to reinforce the civilian control system after the 1961 Sammu incident (when a group of former Imperial officers was arrested while planning a *coup d'état*) and the Kurisu affair made it clear that the divisions within the Defence Agency, whatever their origins, were extremely deep.[15]

It has been claimed that the desire to protect the Defence Agency from 'contamination by the military mind' resulted in policies deliberately designed to encourage a rapid turnover of the civilian staff in the internal bureaux.[16] This was believed to result in either effective domination of the Defence Agency by military men or in a complete paralysis of its activities.

Until the late 1960s the director-general of the Defence Agency usually held his post for six to eight months. This was a much shorter term than a politician could expect to serve in any other ministry.[17] The Defence Agency was not a prestige appointment. It was not a particularly useful stepping-stone on the road to the prime ministership. Many incumbents did not bother to do their homework. Several directors-general displayed appalling ignorance of military matters. In October 1961 Esaki Masumi, a man of commendably broad vision on larger, more general issues, was asked, in his capacity as a former director-general of the Defence Agency, to comment on the Soviet Union's explosion of a 50-megaton bomb. 'Fifty megatons is fifty million tons and fifty million tons is 13,350 *kan**', he gravely told the reporters. 'The thing is *very* heavy.'[18] It seems highly probable that such birds of passage, their gaze fixed upon more distant and glorious fields, paid little attention to the internal workings of the agency they nominally headed.

The staff of the seven internal bureaux was drawn largely from former Home Ministry officials, from the Ministry of Finance, the Police Agency, the Foreign Ministry and the Ministry of International Trade and Industry. The realities of civilian control ought to have been apparent at this level. Naturally enough, little data on the quotidian operations of the bureaux was available to the public. Nor was it poss-

---

* An old Japanese measure of weight.

ible to obtain a wide range of detailed statistics on personnel movements. Neverthe-less, the following few examples of key changes over a limited period suggest that the turnover of high-ranking civilian officials was not as rapid as opponents of the sys-tem claimed. At least some of the Defence Agency's civilian employees lacked neither the knowledge nor the experience necessary to assert their legal supremacy, should they have wished to do so.

In the autumn of 1963, with the retirement of the then Administrative Vice-Minis-ter, Toga Muneo, the Defence Agency's internal bureaux and related institutions were subjected to a major personnel reshuffle. Toga's successor was Katō Yōzō, the then chief of the Secretariat. Katō, a former Home Ministry official, had entered the Defence Agency about 1960 after continuous postwar service with the Police Agency. Katō's successor in the vital post of chief of the Secretariat was Miwa Yoshio, also brought in directly from the Police Agency. Before the war Miwa had been a Home Ministry official, specializing in agricultural problems. To an outsider unacquainted with his personality and qualifications, Miwa's wartime experience as a conscript army paymaster in Mongolia, his reputed taste for military songs and the pleasures of the cup, then his service in the police force, would hardly seem to have provided the experience necessary to counter pressure from the uniformed men in the Defence Agency and on the National Defence Council. In contrast, the new director of the Education Bureau, Hotta Masataka, had seven years' continuous experience in the Defence Agency. Like Katō and Miwa, Hotta was a former Home Ministry official who had entered the Police Agency after the war. In the Defence Agency he had already served as public information section chief and counsellor to the Secretariat. The new Personnel Bureau director, Obata Hisao, whose influence on promotions of high-ranking officers gave him particular importance, had served ten years in the Defence Agency, to which he had come in 1954 after a closely related career in the Maritime Safety Agency. Finally, Yamagami Nobushige, the new chief of the Procurement Office, who, along with the chiefs of the Defence Agency's Defence Bureau and Weapons Bureau, could have been expected to influence the selection of weapons systems and equipment, had spent thirteen years with the Defence Agency. By the time he became Procurement Office chief Yamagami had had a year's experience as chief of the Control and Supply Staff of the Police Reserve Force, two years as chief of the General Affairs section of the National Security Agency, three years as deputy director of the Defence Agency Construction Office, three years as deputy director of the Procurement Office, two years as deputy direc-tor of the Technical Research Institute and another two years as deputy director of the Defence Facilities Agency. All other things being equal, the most determined military officer would have found Yamagami a formidable opponent in the case of a conflict between the uniformed and civilian components of the Defence Agency. That is to say, of five key appointments made to the agency at this time, four were of men with considerable experience in the Defence Agency. The other was a relative newcomer.[19]

(iii)   The Finance Ministry and defence planning

Throughout the 1960s and the 1970s, as in the 1950s, the Ministry of Finance, not the Defence Agency, exercised the ultimate power of decision on the level of military spending. The ministry's approach to the military aspect of national security was a parsimonious and conservative one, a fact which explains why hawkish officers such as General Sugita were anxious to see its influence circumscribed.

The Defence Agency's initial draft for the Second Defence Plan (released as the 'Akagi Proposal' in October 1959) requested a total defence expenditure of Y1.3 billion over the five-year period 1961–5. This was calculated on the expectation of Y150 thousand million in free United States military aid over the same period. Although it soon became clear that American aid would amount only to Y90 thousand million (60 per cent of the original estimate) the plan that was eventually approved by the National Defence Council (on 18 July 1961), after tortuous negotiations between the Defence Agency and the Finance Ministry, envisaged only Y1.15 billion in defence spending over the five-year period, a reduction of about 12 per cent.[20]

Similarly, the Defence Agency's original estimate of the total expenditure for the Third Defence Plan was Y3.1 billion.[21] By the time the agency's first drafts were published in April 1966 estimated expenditure for the five-year period (1966–71) had been reduced to Y2.7 billion.[22] Even this substantial reduction was not enough for the Finance Ministry, which argued that the projected expansion rate was too fast and would exert unacceptable pressure on expenditure in other areas.[23] From early June 1966, the chief of the National Defence Council Secretariat and officials from the Finance Ministry, Defence Agency, Economic Planning Agency, Ministry of International Trade and Industry and Foreign Ministry met to discuss the problem. The Finance Ministry adamantly refused to compromise. Moreover, the Economic Planning Agency was still in the process of compiling a long-term economic plan and resistance to the Defence Agency's demands was also felt in these quarters. Prime Minister Satō's statement to the House of Representatives Budget Committee on 19 July 1966 that defence expenditure must be related to the expansion of the economy as a whole, to social security, housing and so on, represented an endorsement of the views of these two powerful ministries.[24] In response to these pressures the director-general of the Defence Agency proposed that the original five-year plan be converted into a six-year plan divided into two three-year periods. During the first three-year period, it was suggested, great efforts should be made to realize the objectives for expenditure on equipment. While the objectives for the second period could be published, operation of the plan thereafter should be 'flexible'.[25] Debate on this and other proposals continued throughout the autumn of 1966. No decision had been reached by the time the generalized outline of the Third Defence Plan was released by the Defence Agency in November.[26] Early in the new year the Prime Minister announced enigmatically that the scale of spending under the Third Plan should be 'not less than our defence efforts in the past'.[27] This suggested a stand in favour of the Ministry of Finance. It was thus not long before the Defence Agency abandoned its target of Y2.7 billion spent over five years and announced it was willing to compromise at Y2.4 billion.[28] Encouraged by the Prime Minister's attitude the Finance Ministry proceeded to demand a further reduction to Y2.2 billion.[29] The dispute dragged on until March when the Prime Minister decided that expenditure should Y2.34 billion ± Y25 thousand million,[30] approximately midway between the positions of the two ministries, but only 75 per cent of the Defence Agency's original demands.

The attitude of the Japanese Ministry of Finance, no doubt, reflected the innate tight-fistedness of all treasuries. Yet its treatment of the Self Defence Forces was especially severe. In 1961 the ministry obliged all military officers to carry home-packed lunches to field exercises, abandoning the earlier practice of permitting them to dine more expansively at local restaurants.[31] This caused not inconsiderable outrage. The ministry's dominant factions, brought up under the influence of such pacific Conservatives as Ikeda Hayato and Miyazawa Kiichi, were apparently convinced that sound diplomacy, not military force, was the surest guarantee of national security and that the danger of domestic revolution could be removed by raising popular living standards. This partly explains why the ministry did not offer comparable resistance to expenditure on social security, education, science and public works. It also partly explains why expenditure on these items in the decades after the occupation increased much more rapidly than the military budget. In 1950 expenditure on social security was about one-sixth of expenditure on defence. In 1959 expenditure on these two items was approximately equal. By 1970 twice as much was being spent on social security as on defence. By 1978 the social security budget was over three and a half times the size of the defence budget. The breakdown of *détente*, the Japanese-American strategic *rapprochement* that took place during the first part of the 1980s and the subsequent expansion of Japanese military expenditure did not dramatically affect this basic trend. (See table XIV.1)

II Public opinion

Public opinion continued to act as one of the most important constraints on government policy. Between 1960 and 1978 there was no overwhelming popular support for further consolidation of the American alliance, increased military spending, expansion of the Self Defence Forces or constitutional revision. Despite their growing self-confidence, the Japanese people were not eager to see their country play a more assertive role in international affairs. Until the collapse of the American-Soviet *détente* in 1978 there was no widespread anxiety about possible threats to Japan's security. Even then, there seemed no strong belief that these threats could or should be countered by military means.

(i) The American alliance

Throughout the 1970s a large number of Japanese believed that the relationship with the United States remained of paramount importance to their country. In an *Asahi Shimbun* survey published on 1 January 1978, for example, 37 per cent of respondents declared that Japan should devote its greatest efforts to cultivation of close ties with Washington. The next largest group (20 per cent) thought that the relationship with Peking should take priority.[32] A national consensus on the question

Table XIVl Japanese defence and other expenditure, 1966–77
(Y100 million)

Item	1966 Amount	Increase %	Total %	1967 Amount	Increase %	Total %	1968 Amount	Increase %	Total %	1969 Amount	Increase %	Total %	1970 Amount	Increase %	Total %	1971 Amount	Increase %	Total %
General Expenditure	43,143	17.9	100.0	49,509	14.8	100.0	58,186	17.5	100.0	67,396	13.8	100.0	79,498	17.9	100.0	94,143	18.4	100.0
Social Security, etc.	6,236	20.3	14.5	7,215	15.7	14.6	8,157	13.1	14.0	9,470	16.1	14.0	11,408	20.5	14.3	13,441	17.8	14.3
Education, Culture, Science	5,433	14.3	12.6	6,245	15.0	12.6	7,024	12.5	12.1	8,057	14.7	12.0	9,258	14.9	11.7	10,790	16.6	11.5
Public Works	8,762	18.8	20.3	10,005	14.2	20.1	10,701	7.0	18.4	12,064	12.7	17.9	14,099	16.9	16.7	16,656	18.1	17.7
	(7,809)	(17.2)	(18.1)	(9,142)	(17.1)	(18.4)	(9,736)	(6.5)	(16.7)	(11,235)	(15.4)	(16.6)	(13,300)	(18.4)	(17.7)	(15,927)	(19.7)	(16.9)
Defence	3,407	13.0	7.9	3,809	11.8	7.7	4,221	10.8	7.3	4,838	14.6	7.2	5,695	17.7	7.2	6,709	17.8	7.1

Item	1972 Amount	Increase %	Total %	1973 Amount	Increase %	Total %	1974 Amount	Increase %	Total %	1975 Amount	Increase %	Total %	1976 Amount	Increase %	Total %	1977 Amount	Increase %	Total %
General Expenditure	114,677	21.8	100.0	142,841	24.6	100.0	170,994	19.7	100.0	212,888	24.5	100.0	242,960	14.1	100.0	285,143	17.4	100.0
Social Security, etc.	16,414	22.1	14.3	21,145	28.8	14.8	29,908	36.7	16.9	39,269	35.8	18.4	48,076	22.4	19.8	56,920	18.4	20.0
Education, Culture, Science	13,047	20.9	11.4	15,703	20.4	11.0	19,633	25.0	11.5	26,401	34.5	12.4	29,689	14.5	12.2	33,578	13.8	11.8
Public Works	21,485	29.0	18.7	28,408	32.2	19.9	28,407	0.0	16.6	29,095	2.4	13.7	35,272	21.2	14.5	42,810	21.4	15.0
	(20,130)	(26.4)	(17.5)	(25,757)	(28.0)	(18.0)	(26,688)	(3.6)	(15.6)	(26,688)	(0.0)	(12.5)	(31,946)	(19.7)	(13.1)	(38,553)	(20.7)	(13.5)
Defence	8,002	19.3	7.0	9,355	16.9	6.5	10,930	16.8	6.4	13,273	21.4	6.2	15,124	13.9	6.2	16,906	11.8	5.9

The figures given in parentheses under public works do not include special unemployment countermeasures appropriations, expenditure for restoration after natural disasters, etc.

Source: Bōei Handobuktu, Asagumo Shimbun Sha (successive issues).

of whether the American alliance contributed to Japan's security or posed a serious danger to the peace of the Far East remained difficult to achieve. An *Asahi Shimbun* survey of 27 September 1971 found 30 per cent of respondents declaring that the alliance made a positive contribution to the security of Japan and the peace of Asia, 33 per cent asserting that it was a dangerous arrangement, increasing international tensions and the risk of involvement in war.[33] Towards the middle of the decade, with the apparent consolidation of superpower *détente* and the end of the Indochina conflict, popular concern about the security treaty subsided, despite the fact that the lines of cleavage evident in 1950–2 remained essentially unaltered. By the beginning of the 1980s, with the collapse of *détente* and the emergence of the Reagan administration, Japanese uneasiness about the military relationship with the United States again mounted. A *Newsweek* survey published on 11 July 1983 found 52 per cent of Japanese respondents declaring that a strong American military presence around the world increased the chances of war. Only 27 per cent thought that the stationing of United States forces abroad enhanced the prospects for peace. Popular Japanese suspicions of the United States, while less marked than those of the Mexicans or Brazilians polled by *Newsweek*, were considerably deeper than those to be found in Washington's major European allies.[34]

There was no great confidence in the treaty's efficacy, even among its most committed supporters. Only 21.2 per cent of Japanese questioned by the *Yomiuri Shimbun* in April 1978 thought that the United States would really come to Japan's assistance in time of crisis. Some 38 per cent, including 34 per cent of Conservative voters, declared that the United States could not be relied upon.[35] (See tables XIV.2, XIV.3 and XIV.4)

TABLE XIV. 2 Popular Japanese perceptions of United States military power
(in global perspective)

Newsweek 11 July 1983	Overall, do you think a strong American military presence around the world tends to increase the chance of peace or tends to increase the chance of war?					
	Japan	France	West Germany	Great Britain	Brazil	Mexico
	%	%	%	%	%	%
Increase the chance of peace	27.0	32.0	39.0	39.0	19.0	18.0
Increase the chance of war	52.0	46.0	25.0	43.0	62.0	74.0
Neither (volunteered)	17.0	7.0	13.0	7.0	6.0	3.0

(ii)   The Self Defence Forces

Following the pattern established in the 1950s, a majority of Japanese con-

TABLE XIV. 3 Popular Japanese perceptions of the reliability of the American alliance

Yomiuri Shimbun 17 Apr 78

Do you think the United States would really defend Japan under the security treaty in an emergency? Or do you think it would not defend Japan?

	Total	Males	Females	Liberal Democratic Party voters	Socialist Party voters	Kōmeitō voters	Democratic Socialist Party voters	Communist Party voters	New Liberal Club voters	Social Alliance (Shaminren) voters	Other	Non-partisan
The US would defend Japan.	21.2	27.8	15.1	26.4	18.9	18.8	28.6	10.3	37.9	23.8	–	17.2
The US would not defend Japan.	38.0	39.5	36.6	34.0	45.6	47.5	39.0	67.2	39.7	47.6	33.3	38.1
Don't know, no answer	40.9	32.6	48.4	39.6	35.5	33.8	32.5	22.4	22.4	28.6	66.7	44.8

TABLE XIV. 4 Popular Japanese threat perceptions

Newspaper or Organ	Date	Feel no anxiety %	Uncertain	Feel anxiety %	Source of anxiety				
					USSR %	USA %	China %	Communist countries %	North Korea %
Shūkan Asahi	5 Apr 68	66.8	Question not asked	18.8	Question not asked				
Mainichi Shimbun	1 Jul 68	45.0	43.0	3.0	Question not asked				
Asahi Shimbun	5 Jan 69	52.0	Question not asked	32.0	15.0	6.0	5.0	2.0	Not asked
Sankei Shimbun	18 May 69	42.0	Question not asked	19.0	6.0	1.0	3.0	3.0	2.0
Mainichi Shimbun	3 May 72		External attack totally impossible	External attack unlikely			External attack possible		External attack likely
			8	39			43		4
			Internal uprising supported financially and ideologically by foreign power totally impossible	Internal uprising supported financially and ideologically by foreign power unlikely			Internal uprising supported financially and ideologically by foreign power possible		Internal uprising supported financially and ideologically by foreign power likely
			12	46			31		3

	Feel no anxiety	Other, no answer	Feel anxiety	USSR	USA	China	South Korea	North Korea	Other
Asahi Shimbun 1 Jan 78	54.0	13.0	33.0	–	–	–	–	–	–
	No countries threaten Japan	Don't Know	Certain countries do pose a threat to Japan						
Yomiuri Shimbun 17 Apr 78	10.4	25.0	64.6	52.7	10.8	10.5	4.8	8.6	0.7

tinued to accept the Self Defence Forces but remained uneasy about their expansion beyond a certain point. An *Asahi Shimbun* poll taken in January 1971 showed 64 per cent of respondents agreeing with the proposition that military forces were necessary, 26 per cent in favour of complete disarmament.[36] Urban and rural Japanese held basically similar views on this issue. In the 1968 *Shūkan Asahi* poll 51 per cent of those interviewed in Tōkyō maintained that some forces were necessary. A further 32.4 per cent agreed that military forces were conditionally necessary (i.e. depending on size and character). Only 13.8 per cent asserted that Japan did not need military forces to protect its security. The figures for rural Kagawa prefecture were 56.1 per cent, 28.9 per cent and 7.8 per cent respectively.[37]

Later polls showed broadly similar results. Generally speaking, support for the maintenance of military forces appeared strongest among males in the 50–59 age group. Men aged 20–29 were almost equally divided in their opinions, as were women of any age.[38] Not surprisingly, Conservatives felt the need for military forces more acutely than supporters of the Socialist and Communist parties. A *Mainichi Shimbun* survey of 14 June 1971, for example, revealed that whereas 88 per cent of Liberal Democratic Party supporters, 79 per cent of Democratic Socialist Party voters, 58 per cent of Kōmeitō supporters and 64 per cent of uncommitted voters considered the Self Defence Forces necessary, only 55 per cent of Socialists and 47 per cent of Communists were of this opinion. Japanese of all political persuasions, significantly, viewed the Self Defence Forces essentially as vehicles for the maintenance of domestic order or for disaster relief work. Even among Liberal Democratic Party supporters, only a minority regarded the Self Defence Force as an army.[39] The *Yomiuri Shimbun* survey of Japanese academics, critics, journalists, businessmen, trade union officials, bureaucrats, military officers and students published in June 1973 also revealed that support for the Self Defence Forces, while generally high in the upper echelons of Japanese society, was strongest among government officials and businessmen, weakest in trade union circles and among students.[40] (See tables XIV.5, XIV.6)

For the greater part of the period under consideration, a clear majority of the public remained opposed to constitutional revision, increases in the level of military spending, large-scale expansion of the Self Defence Forces or drastic changes in their strategic role. (See tables XIV.7, XIV.8, XIV.9, XIV.10) Within this general framework, popular attitudes were significantly influenced by the impact of global political trends. During the early years of *détente*, in the wake of China's campaign against 'Japanese militarism', while support for the Self Defence Forces remained high, a substantial minority of Japanese (including, significantly, up to one third of Conservative voters) came to believe that Japan's rearmament was beginning to pose a threat to neighbouring countries. There was widespread anxiety about a possible revival of Japanese militarism, especially in the context of American pressure for an accelerated arms build-up. Many appeared uneasy about the adequacy of the civilian control system. There was little confidence that Japan's re-emergence as a great military power would be advantageous either to the nation or its people. (See tables XIV.11, XIV.12, XIV.13, XIV.14, XIV.15)

Table XIV.5 Necessity of military forces

Newspaper or Organ	Date	Military forces are necessary	Military forces are conditionally necessary	Military forces are unnecessary
Prime Minister's Office	March 1966	82.0	Question not asked	5.0
Prime Minister's Office	February 1968	49.0	Question not asked	35.8
Shūkan Asahi	5 April 1968	51.3 (56.1)	32.4 (28.9)	13.8 (7.8)
Asahi Shimbun	5 January 1969	64.0	Question not asked	26.0
Yomiuri Shimbun	1 June 1969	60.0	Question not asked	16.0
Mainichi Shimbun	14 June 1971	71.0	Question not asked	24.0
Sankei Shimbun	17 September 1973	58.0	Question not asked	18.0
Defence Agency Survey	September 1977	83.0	–	–

(Figures in parentheses are for Kagawa prefecture)

Table XIV. 6   Necessity of Military forces as seen by supporters of various political parties

Mainichi Shimbun 14 January 1971	All Voters	Liberal Democratic Party voters	Socialist Party voters	Kōmeitō voters	Democratic Socialist Party voters	Japan Communist Party voters	Uncommitted voters
The Self Defence Forces are necessary:	71	88	55	58	79	47	64
(i) for defence against external aggression	14	22	9	4	15	5	10
(ii) for preservation of public order	24	32	21	21	28	13	17
(iii) for disaster relief work	22	20	21	23	22	23	27
(iv) Because all nations have armed forces	6	8	3	6	8	5	7
(v) Other, no answer	5	6	1	4	6	1	3

Table XIV.7 Constitutional revision

Newspaper or organ	Date	Article 9 should be revised so Japan can possess an army	Oppose revision of Article 9
		%	%
Asahi Shimbun	17 August 1962	26.0	61.0
Shūkan Asahi	5 April 1968	21.6	72.1
		(22.6)	(60.6)
Asahi Shimbun	5 January 1969	19.0	64.0
	(Figures in parentheses are for Kagawa prefecture)		

Yomiuri Shimbun Survey 27 June 1973	The Constitution should be revised and made to conform with reality
Academic circles	5 (8.1%)
Critics	2 (7.7%)
Press	2 (15.4%)
Business community	1 (8.3%)
Labour circles	0 (0.0%)
Government Circles	2 (12.5%)
Self Defence Forces	5 (25.0%)
Total	17 (10.1%)
Students	20 (5.5%)

(Figures in parentheses refer to the percentage of the sample adhering to this particular view)

Polls conducted in the northern spring of 1978, against the background of mounting American-Soviet tension, continued American withdrawal from continental Asia, the Carter administration's strategic tilt towards Peking, growing trade problems with the United States and increasingly severe congressional criticism of Japan's military contribution to the Western alliance revealed a substantial (albeit temporary) erosion of these traditional attitudes. Threat perceptions remained essentially unchanged. Nevertheless, 31.1 per cent of respondents questioned by the *Yomiuri Shimbun* in April 1978 agreed that Japan should strengthen its *autonomous* defence system in the context of the United States withdrawal from Asia, in particular the projected pull-out of ground forces from South Korea; 22.3 per cent remained opposed to strengthening the nation's military power, 46.6 per cent expressed no opinion. A majority of Conservative voters (42.5 per cent) favoured consolidation of Japan's autonomous defence system. Only 14 per cent of Liberal Democratic Party supporters opposed this course of action. Socialist and Communist voters remained hostile to any expansion of the Self Defence Forces. Overall, some 28.2 per cent of respondents thought that the Self Defence Forces should be strengthened in the interests of better relations with the United States; 35.2 per cent

Table XIV. 8   Attitude to military spending and support for political parties

Mainichi Shimbun
14 Jun 71

	Defence spending should be increased/decreased						
	All voters	Liberal Democratic Party voters	Socialist Party voters	Kōmeitō voters	Democratic Socialist Party voters	Japan Communist Party voters	Uncommitted voters
Should be increased	8	14	4	6	7	2	3
Should remain at current levels	38	49	32	20	43	24	30
Should be decreased	28	19	37	41	37	27	34
Should be abolished	11	3	16	21	6	38	14
Other, no answer	15	15	11	12	7	9	19

Yomiuri Shimbun
17 Apr 78

There is no need to be particular in observing the 1% GNP ceiling on defence spending in the future

	All voters	Males	Females	Liberal Democratic Party voters	Socialist Party voters	Kōmeitō voters	Democratic Socialist Party voters	Communist Party voters	New Liberal Club voters	Social Alliance voters	Other	Non-partisan voters
Agree	25.2	35.7	15.6	34.7	18.6	23.8	42.9	12.1	32.8	38.1	–	18.0
Do not agree	27.0	32.3	22.1	19.6	45.9	33.8	23.4	51.7	25.9	42.9	33.3	27.2
Don't know, no answer	47.9	32.1	62.3	45.6	35.5	42.5	33.8	36.2	41.4	19.0	66.7	54.8

Table XIV. 9 Strengthening the Self Defence Forces

Newspaper or organ	Date	Self Defence Forces should be strengthened	Self Defence Forces should be left at present level	Self Defence Forces should be reduced or abolished
		%	%	%
Prime Minister's Office	November 1965	19.0	50.0	3.0
Shūkan Asahi	5 April 1968	25.4 (28.7)*	50.1 were opposed (40.2)* the forces	to strengthening
Mainichi Shimbun	1 July 1968	18.0	58.0	17.0
Asahi Shimbun	5 January 1969	19.0	55.0	13.0
Sankei Shimbun	18 May 1969	23.0	53.0	13.0
Tōkyō Shimbun	10 December 1969	17.9	40.5	25.7
Yomiuri Shimbun	19 October 1971	10.3 (34.3 felt that the SDF would inevitably be strengthened)	40.4 regarded strengthening SDF as 'undesirable'.	
Sankei Shimbun	October 1972	19.0	45.0	32.0 (8.0 for total abolition)
Sankei Shimbun	17 September 1973	12.0	50.0	33.0 (9.0 for total abolition)
Asahi Shimbun	1 January 1978	23.0	54.0	15.0 (5.0 for total abolition)

* Figures for Kagawa prefecture.

did not believe Washington's criticisms of Japan's 'free ride' should influence decisions on defence policy. Conservative voters seemed especially sensitive to United States attitudes. A majority of Liberal Democratic Party supporters (41.1 per cent) felt that Japan should respond positively to American criticisms of its efforts in the defence field. Only 25.5 per cent of Conservatives believed Japan should continue to resist American demands. Socialist and Communist voters, not unexpectedly, were overwhelmingly opposed to suggestions that the Self Defence Forces should be strengthened to please the United States.[41] (See tables XIV.16, XIV.17)

III Pressure groups

Despite the generally pacific character of Japanese public opinion, there existed a variety of organizations and individuals advocating higher levels of defence spend-

Table XIV. 10 The purpose and range of Self Defence Force activities

Newspaper or Organ	Date	The SDF should devote their attention to national defence	The SDF should devote their attention to preservation of public order	The SDF should devote their attention to disaster relief work	The SDF should devote their attention to public welfare work
		%	%	%	%
Prime Minister's Office Poll	November 1965	15.0	16.0	40.0	12.0
Yomiuri Shimbun	22 Apr 68	24.0	19.0	37.0	10.0

Yomiuri Shimbun survey 27 Jun 73	It is not possible to establish limits to defence power	Japan's defence power should be established at minimum peace-time level	Since military power is unconstitutional it is meaningless to discuss limits
	%	%	%
Academic circles	21 (33.9)	24 (38.7)	14 (22.6)
Critics	10 (38.5)	8 (30.8)	4 (15.4)
Press	5 (38.5)	7 (53.8)	1 (7.7)
Business community	5 (41.7)	7 (58.3)	0 (0.0)
Labour circles	3 (15.8)	9 (47.4)	7 (36.8)
Government circles	10 (62.5)	6 (37.5)	0 (0.0)
Self Defence Forces	16 (80.0)	3 (15.0)	0 (0.0)
Total	70 (41.7)	64 (38.1)	26 (15.5)
Students	77 (21.0)	166 (45.4)	117 (32.0)

Yomiuri Shimbun survey 27 Jun 73	SDF operations should be strictly limited to defence of territorial waters and air space	SDF should maintain command of sea and air space around Japanese archipelago	SDF should not set limits to maritime escort operation	Not necessary to set limits SDF activities
	%	%	%	%
Academic circles	31 (50.0)	8 (12.9)	0 (0.0)	3 (4.8)
Critics	8 (30.8)	5 (19.2)	1 (3.8)	3 (11.5)
Press	9 (69.2)	2 (15.4)	0 (0.0)	0 (0.0)
Business Community	6 (50.0)	4 (33.3)	1 (8.3)	1 (8.3)
Labour circles	7 (36.8)	2 (10.5)	0 (0.0)	0 (0.0)
Government circles	7 (43.8)	6 (37.5)	0 (0.0)	1 (6.3)
Self Defence Forces	4 (20.0)	11 (55.0)	1 (5.0)	3 (15.0)
Total	72 (42.9)	38 (22.6)	3 (1.8)	11 (6.5)
Students	142 (38.8)	52 (14.2)	3 (0.8)	9 (2.5)

(Figures in parentheses represent the percentage of each subgroup adhering to a particular view.)

Table XIV. 11   The Self Defence Forces: a threat to Japan's neighbours?

Mainichi Shimbun 14 June 1971	Is Japan's Fourth Defence Plan a threat to other countries?					
	All voters	Liberal Democratic Party voters	Socialist Party voters	Kōmeitō voters	Democratic Socialist Party voters	Communist voters	Uncommitted voters
	%	%	%	%	%	%	%
Does pose a threat	41	33	53	50	42	67	41
Does not pose a threat	37	46	30	34	44	24	33
Others, no answer	22	21	17	16	14	9	26
Mainichi Shimbun 14 June 1971	Do the Japanese Self Defence Forces pose a threat to other countries?					
	%	%	%	%	%	%	%
Do pose a threat	27	21	37	40	30	41	27
Do not pose a threat	54	63	48	42	61	49	50
Others, no answer	19	16	15	18	9	10	23

Table XIV. 12   Revival of Japanese militarism

Newspaper or organ	Japanese militarism has revived	Japanese militarism is reviving	Revival of Japanese militarism is possible	Japanese militarism is not reviving	Other, no answer
	%	%	%	%	%
Mainichi Shimbun 18 October 1971	3.0	21.0	39.0	28.0	9.0
Yomiuri Shimbun 19 October 1971	7.3	42.5	not asked	31.4	18.8
Asahi Shimbun 3 January 1972	not asked	24.0	17.0 (of the 53% declaring militarism not revived)	53.0	23.0

ing, larger military forces and a more assertive foreign policy. The concrete objectives of such organizations differed considerably. So too did the kind of pressure they could exert on the government and the bureaucracy.

Table XIV. 13 American pressure and wider role for the Self Defence Forces in Asia

Newspaper or organ	Think that the SDF will take over the US role in Asia	Do not think the SDF will take over the US role in Asia	Others, don't know, no answer
	%	%	%
Yomiuri Shimbun 19 October 1971	33.6	35.6	30.7
Asahi Shimbun 3 January 1972	27.0	42.0	31.0

Table XIV.14 Public perceptions of civilian control

Yomiuri Shimbun survey 27 June 1973	The present level of civilian control of the SDF is adequate	The present level of civilian control of the SDF is inadequate	Since the SDF is unconstitutional it is meaningless to discuss civilian control
	%	%	%
Academic circles	14 (22.6)	36 (58.1)	11 (17.7)
Critics	4 (15.4)	17 (65.4)	2 (7.7)
Press	2 (15.4)	11 (84.6)	0 (0.0)
Business Community	6 (50.0)	6 (50.0)	0 (0.0)
Labour Circles	3 (15.8)	10 (52.6)	6 (31.6)
Government Circles	8 (50.0)	7 (43.8)	0 (0.0)
Self Defence Forces	15 (75.0)	4 (20.0)	0 (0.0)
Total	52 (31.0)	91 (54.2)	19 (11.3)
Students	56 (15.3)	199 (54.4)	97 (26.5)
(Figures in parentheses represent the percentage of each subgroup adhering to a particular view.)			

(i) *Rightist and ultranationalist organizations*

Throughout the postwar period, the most persistent and effective pressure for large-scale Japanese rearmament undoubtedly came from the United States. Within the Liberal Democratic Party, the Security Problems Research Council, the National Defence Division and the Domestic Weapons Production Committee, all dominated by the hawkish 'pro-American' right, also relentlessly advocated constitutional revision, rearmament and more forceful external policies. Nevertheless, the pressure groups that excited most attention overseas, especially in the wake of the novelist Mishima Yukio's abortive attempt to stage a *coup d'état* in 1970, were undoubtedly those tough-minded ultra-nationalist organizations, akin to the neo-

Table XIV. 15   **What would be the impact of a revival of militarism on your life?**

Asahi Shimbun 3 January 1972	What would be the impact of a revival of militarism on your life?
Austerity	16
Loss of liberty	38
Peaceful coexistence impossible	15
Inflation	7
Conscription	32
Danger of war	31
Good for business	3
Other answers	1
No effects	3
No answers	7

fascist groupings in West Germany and Italy, which, in society at large, in the business community and the universities, competed with the left for influence on the uncommitted.

During the latter part of the 1960s these organizations, many of which were direct descendants of the Genyōsha, the Kokuryūkai and other prewar ultra-nationalist groups, rapidly expanded their membership and activities. In 1966 the Police Agency estimated the total membership of all right-wing organizations at about 60,000. By mid-1967 it was estimated that there were some 400 right-wing organizations with a total membership of about 110,000.[42] By mid-1973 the Police Agency put the total number of ultra-nationalist groupings at 500, with an estimated membership of 120,000.[43] Steady growth continued throughout the decade, stimulated by increasing disenchantment with the United States and the waves of anti-Soviet sentiment which swept the nation after the collapse of *détente*.

All ultra-nationalist organizations advocated a 'Shōwa Restoration' to consolidate the Imperial system and purge Japanese society of undesirable foreign influences. They also urged revision of the 1946 Constitution, establishment of fully independent military forces, radical changes in education policy to emphasize nationalist values, domestic and foreign policies based on hardline anti-Communism, recovery of the Kuriles and other former Japanese possessions in the northern seas, close relations with South Korea and Taiwan and opposition to the People's Republic of China.

Despite the overall unity of views on domestic reconstruction and external policies, the ultra-nationalist camp, like the extreme left, was fragmented along regional and factional lines. In the Tōkyō area, right-wing organizations were clustered around seven major councils. Some eighty-eight groups were affiliated with the National Council of Patriotic Organizations (Zenkoku Aikokusha Dantai Kaigi or Zenai Kaigi), chaired, until his death on 14 April 1972, by Sagoya Yoshiaki, who had

Table XIV. 16

Yomiuri Shimbun 17 Apr 78   There is a view that Japan should strengthen its autonomous defence system as a response to the American withdrawal from Asia, the pull-out of US ground forces from South Korea, etc. Do you agree or disagree?

	All voters	Males	Females	Liberal Democratic Party voters	Socialist Party voters	Kōmeitō voters	Democratic Socialist Party voters	Communist Party voters	New Liberal Club voters	Social Alliance voters	Other	Non-partisan voters
%	%	%	%	%	%	%	%	%	%	%	%	%
Agree	31.1	42.5	20.7	42.5	22.6	38.8	41.6	12.1	55.2	28.6	33.3	22.7
Disagree	22.3	28.4	16.7	14.0	40.2	13.8	15.6	51.7	10.3	38.1	–	26.0
No answer, don't know	46.6	29.1	62.7	43.6	37.2	47.5	42.9	36.2	34.5	33.3	66.7	51.2

Table XIV. 17

Yomiuri Shimbun 17 Apr 78

Japan has been criticized in the United States for receiving a 'free ride' in defence. Do you think Japan's defence strength should be increased in order to preserve a good climate of relations with the United States?

	All voters	Males	Females	Liberal Democratic Party voters	Socialist Party voters	Kōmeitō voters	Democratic Socialist Party voters	Communist Party voters	New Liberal Club voters	Social Alliance voters	Other	Non-partisan voters
	%	%	%	%	%	%	%	%	%	%	%	%
Yes	28.2	36.2	20.9	41.1	15.9	32.5	42.9	10.3	37.9	23.8	–	20.2
No	35.2	41.3	29.7	25.5	57.1	35.0	29.9	67.2	39.7	52.4	–	38.1
No answer, don't know	36.5	22.5	49.4	33.4	27.0	32.5	27.3	22.4	22.4	23.8	100.0	41.8

achieved fame in the prewar period as the assassin of Prime Minister Hamaguchi. The National Council was subsequently led by a coalition drawn from the Greater Japan People's Party (Dai Nippon Kokumintō), the Imperial Way Comrades' Association (Kōdō Dōshikai), the Japan League (Nippon Renmei) and the Patriotic Youth League (Aikoku Seinen Renmei). Another twenty groups were connected with the All Japan Federation of Patriotic Organizations Situation Countermeasures Co-operation Committee (Zen-Nippon Aikoku Dantai Rengō Jikyoku Taisaku Kyōgikai), led by Fukuda Motoaki, sometime editor-in-chief of the prewar Kōdō (Imperial Way) News Agency. A further forty-four groups had links with Kodama Yoshio's Youth Thought Research Association (Seinen Shisō Kenkyū Kai or Seishikai), the principal vehicle of which was the Rising Sun Youth Corps (Hinomaru Seinen Tai). Several organizations were connected with the Japan Renovation Council (Nippon Kakushin Kaigi), centring around the Right-Wing Activist Anti-Communism Volunteer Corps (Kōdō Uyoku Bōkyō Teishin Tai). Prominent also were the All Japanese Patriots' Consultative Council (Zen-Nippon Aikokusha Kondan Kai), the Amur River Club (Kokuryū Kurabu), the Kōfu Club (Kōfu Kurabu) and the Japanese Race Association (Nippon Minzoku Kurabu). In the Kansai area the ultra-nationalist landscape was dominated by the Sanyōkai (a regional offshoot of Zenai Kaigi, chaired by Sagoya's old associate Adachi Satoru), the Kansai Patriotic Volunteers Club (Kansai Aikoku Yūshi Kurabu) and the All-Kyōtō Council of Patriotic Movements (Zen-Kyōtō Aikoku Undō Kyōgikai). In Kyūshū, the birthplace of the Genyōsha, the All-Kyūshū Nationalist Council (Zen-Kyūshū Minzoku Kyōgi Kai) had imposed a certain degree of unity among the traditionally turbulent and combative right-wing groups on that island.

In the northern summer of 1973, an extreme right-wing organization, the Young Storm Association (Seiran Kai), centring around such figures as Watanabe Michio, Nakagawa Ichirō, Nakao Eiichi and Ishihara Shintarō, and drawing its membership largely from the Fukuda and Nakasone factions, was established within the Liberal Democratic Party itself. Its links, both ideological and personal, with ultra-nationalist bodies outside the party, were close and extensive.[44]

The folly of exaggerating the importance of these organizations need hardly be stressed. They did not exert a dominant influence on the Japanese government. They did not determine the country's foreign policy. They did not shape its defence policy. They represented only one small constellation of power in the immense firmament of postwar Japanese politics.

This said, a number of important qualifications should be made. At their lowest level, right-wing organizations of the type described above merged into the shadowy empire of the Japanese underworld. At the highest level, however, some right-wing organizations had direct and continuous access to the corridors of power. A single organization could act simultaneously on both levels, maintaining a wide range of contacts in the political, business, military, academic, student and gangster worlds. Yotsumoto Yoshitaka, a key member of the Blood Brotherhood League (Ketsumeidan), sentenced to fifteen years' hard labour in 1932 for an attempt on the life of Count Makino Nobuaki, Lord Keeper of the Privy Seal, emerged, in the postwar period, as a confidant of Prime Ministers Yoshida Shigeru (Makino's son-in-law),

Ikeda Hayato, Satō Eisaku and Nakasone Yasuhiro.[45] Kodama Yoshio, whose pre-war activities ranged from involvement in ultra-nationalist terrorist organizations to advising the government of Prince Higashikuni, cultivated close personal relations with such postwar political leaders as Hatoyama Ichirō, Kishi Nobusuke, Kōno Ichirō, Miki Bukichi and Ogata Taketora.[46] In their student days both Kishi and Kodama had been connected with the ultra-nationalist academic Uesugi Shinkichi, first president of the National Founding Association (Kenkoku Kai). In 1945 Kodama had supplied Hatoyama's fledgeling Liberal Party with vast quantities of much-needed funds.[47] His Youth Thought Research Association and its offshoot the Japan Youth Seminar (Nihon Seinen Kōza) maintained links not only with certain Liberal Democratic Party Diet members, prominent personalities from several universities and colleges, various conservative clubs and veterans' groups, but also with at least two gangster-type organizations, the Gijin Tō (Martyr's Party) and the Tōseikai Society. Hamaguchi's assassin Sagoya Yoshiaki (see above) and Shirai Tameo, who had been involved in the 1933 'Heaven Sent Soldiers' Plot', the *Shinpei Tai Jihen*, were also on the board of directors of the Japan Youth Seminar.[48] Moreover, Kodama's private army, like the late Mishima Yukio's Society of the Shield (Tate No Kai), was permitted to make full use of Self Defence Force facilities for training and, presumably, for the propagation of its views.[49] The unsympathetic reaction of the assembled officers and men on the occasion of Mishima's dramatic suicide suggests organizations of this kind were not regarded favourably by the rank and file of the forces.[50] However, high-level sympathy and protection obviously existed and were strong enough to enable these neo-fascist groupings to obtain officially endorsed training facilities, at least until Mishima's attempted *coup d'état* apparently put an end to the practice.

Kodama's network of conservative political connections was highly evaluated by foreign aircraft manufacturers and armaments industries. In the late 1960s, for example, he acted as a secret consultant for the Lockheed Corporation in Japan, using his influence with former Prime Minister Kishi and his brother Satō Eisaku in an attempt to promote sales of his client's civilian and military aircraft.[51] It is not clear whether he was able to exert influence on wider policy matters as well.

The extraordinary proliferation of films, popular novels and comic books depicting the glories of Imperial Japan, the incremental erosion of historical objectivity in school social science textbooks, the formal admission of the spirits of General Tōjō Hideki and other wartime leaders executed by the Allies into the Yasukuni Shrine, together with the *de facto* re-emergence of Shintō as a state-supported religion may, perhaps, to some extent at least, be attributed to the activities of the extreme right. These developments, especially in the area of education policy, had far-reaching, long-term implications. In general, however, the principal roles of Japan's extreme right-wing organizations, during the period under consideration, would appear to have been propagandist and persuasive. Certainly, these groupings had objectives and programmes of their own. At the same time, they provided militarily-minded businessmen, politicians and public servants with one convenient vehicle to promote the revival of strong-armed nationalism. Any romantic aura they managed to generate through association with noted literary eccentrics such as Mishima Yukio might hopefully attract wider public support. Moreover, the splendid muscles cultivated by so many of their members often proved useful to the ultra-nationalist cause, on the campus, in the streets or even in the Diet, when all other means of persuasion had failed. Bitter clashes between right-wing and radical leftist students raged on most Japanese campuses until the mid-1970s. Japanese academics critical of the Emperor system, prewar expansionist policies in Asia and other causes espoused by the extreme right not infrequently received anonymous letters urging them to 'reflect' upon their mistaken views or face serious albeit unspecified consequences. The annual conferences of the Japan Teachers' Federation (Nikkyōsō) were habitually disrupted by gangs of physically robust right-wing demonstrators. It will also be recalled that many of the 'private secretaries' brought into the Diet by Prime Kishi during the 1960 crisis displayed cuts, bruises and dark glasses that betrayed their origins.[52] In short, the capacity of the extreme right to apply strong, albeit not necessarily decisive, pressure, at all levels of the Japanese political hierarchy, was not to be dismissed lightly.

(ii)   Ex-servicemen's groups

Japan's major veterans' associations, along with substantial numbers of former Imperial field marshals, generals and admirals who had remained aloof from the Self Defence Forces, also took an active interest in military affairs. During the Yoshida era they were given little opportunity to promote their views. After Hatoyama's accession to office in 1954 it was observed that such former officers began to gain easy access to Prime Minister's Residence and the Defence Agency, where they became, in effect, unofficial advisers.[53] What advice they gave and how seriously it was taken remain unknown. At times, the subjects discussed at these advisory meetings appeared somewhat peripheral to the major issues of national security. In April 1962, for example, Field Marshal Hata, General Imamura and other distinguished Imperial officers called on Prime Minister Ikeda to request that the statue of the Russo-Japanese War hero General Ōyama, then abandoned in the backyard of the Ueno Art Museum, remain in Tōkyō instead of being sent back to the hero's birthplace in Kagoshima.[54] Nevertheless, a month later, three of these inveterate old warriors (General Imamura, General Okamura and Admiral Sawamura) were being welcomed at the Defence Agency for a formal conference on national security policy with the Chiefs of Staff.[55] Such formal meetings were, in fact, rather frequent. Informal meetings were even more regular. Readers of Sugita's memoirs will recall that the Chief of Staff was attending an old soldiers' reunion the afternoon he heard of his appointment. One gathers it was a fairly convivial affair, as many of these meetings probably were.[56] Whatever the influence of these former Imperial Army and Navy officers on their colleagues and erstwhile subordinates in the Self Defence Forces, the fact that serving Chiefs of Staff spent time hobnobbing with such doughty old warriors was not without its significance. Group loyalty based on shared experience and common aspirations is a powerful emotion.

The former Imperial officers involved in the 1961 Sammu plot were apparently known to some Self Defence Force members, whose co-operation they had attempted to secure.[57] The serving officers approached sensibly refused to participate in the attempted coup. Yet they compromised themselves and the forces by apparently failing to report the approaches immediately and by their subsequent efforts to cover up their contacts.[58] Incidents of this kind reinforced the popular impression that the former Imperial officers' group, both within and outside the Self Defence Force, constituted a closely knit, alienated and potentially explosive subculture.

(iii)   Private advisers

It has been seen that in 1953–4 Yoshida's Liberals opposed the Democratic (Progressive) Party scheme for seating private citizens of 'learning and experience' in the National Defence Council, on the grounds that this arrangement would undermine the principles of civilian control and Cabinet responsibility, facilitating infiltration of the defence policy decision-making machinery by ultra-nationalist groups. When Ikeda first appointed nineteen private citizens as 'advisers' to the Defence Agency in June 1962 similar apprehensions were expressed. A cursory glance at the list of nineteen citizens appointed by Ikeda, however, would suggest that these fears were groundless. The group had no particular association with the extreme right, the prewar officers' clique or defence industry circles. Nor were most of its members known for their knowledge of or interest in defence matters. It included the historian and literary critic Ikeshima Shimpei (associated with Keio University and the magazine *Bungei Shunjū*), the former Imperial cook and television personality Egami Tomi, novelists Shibata Renzaburō, Ōzaki Shirō and Sono Ayako, dramatist Hōjō Makoto, poets Fujiura Ko and Nakamura Teijo, critics Sakanishi Shihō, Shibusawa Hideo and Fukuda Tsuneari (a noted translator of Shakespeare) and the patriotic entertainers Tokugawa Musei, Fujiyama Ichirō and Raymond Hattori. It also included Okuno Shintarō, a Keio University specialist on Chinese literature, a Rikkyō University social studies lecturer, Koyama Eizō, and Sugawara Tsūsai, the Kamakura art collector, social reformer and noted man of independent means. Sugawara was concurrently vice-president of the Society for Social Purification (Shakai Junketsuka Kyōkai) and president of the Society for Banishment of the Three Evils (San Aku Tsuihō Kyōkai).[59] It is difficult to imagine that these figures became the vehicles through which sinister outside influences penetrated the Defence Agency. The institution of the advisers system was obviously no more than a public relations exercise. Nevertheless, it can be assumed that the Defence Agency was also advised by a variety of scholars and other specialists whose services were not widely advertised.

(iv)   Military industries

Japan's military industries were in a position to influence the technical details of defence planning, if not the overall direction of national security policy. So, too, were foreign suppliers of military equipment to the Japanese government.[60]

The basis of Japan's present defence industry was laid during the last years of occupation, after the United States abandoned its attempt to destroy the prewar military-industrial complex. Although the industry had been greatly stimulated by

Table XIV.18   Defence Agency procurement as a percentage of total sales of
particular Japanese companies
(Units: Y100 million)

Rank	Company	1975			1976		
		Total Sales	Defence Contracts	Ratio %	Total Sales	Defence Contracts	Ratio %
1.	Mitsubishi Heavy Industries	10,729.0	911.8	8.5	12,179.0	981.5	8.1
2.	Ishikawajima-Harima Heavy Industries	6,249.5	564.5	9.0	6,961.7	579.6	8.3
3.	Kawasaki Heavy Industries	4,901.0	218.6	4.5	5,399.1	252.7	4.7
4.	Mitsubishi Electrics	5,917.0	207.7	3.5	6,962.8	200.4	2.9
5.	Hitachi Shipbuilding	3,292.7	41.3	1.2	3,324.2	103.3	3.1
6.	Nippon Electrics	4,274.0	91.3	2.1	4,859.2	101.4	2.1
7.	Shinmeiwa Industries	478.0	64.3	13.5	449.4	78.7	17.5
8.	Fuji Heavy Industries	2,003.7	52.3	2.6	2,540.1	65.6	2.6
9.	Tōkyō Shibaura Electrics	8,939.0	82.4	0.9	9,642.8	62.8	0.7
10.	Nihon Seikōjo	1,124.0	61.2	5.4	1,217.6	61.4	5.0
11.	Komatsu Seisakujo	3,608.0	54.7	1.5	3,153.7	59.9	1.9
12.	Hitachi Seisakujo	10,895.0	30.8	0.3	12,948.7	58.3	0.5
13.	Nippon Kōki	48.0	38.3	79.8	48.2	50.5	104.8
14.	Nihon Sekiyū	15,436.0	40.8	0.3	17,638.1	49.5	0.3
15.	Daikin Kōgyō	796.0	29.4	3.7	886.3	48.2	5.4
16.	Shimazu Seisakujo	576.1	45.6	7.9	614.8	36.5	5.9
17.	Nissan Motor Company	17,701.0	26.6	0.2	20,246.2	36.3	0.2
18.	Mitsubishi Precision	60.8	20.9	34.4	63.8	34.5	54.1
19.	Maruzen Sekiyū	8,608.0	27.1	0.3	9,904.9	31.4	0.3
20.	Idemitsu Kōsan	13,673.3	20.3	0.1	15,325.2	30.6	0.2

Source: Nagamatsu Keiichi, *Nihon No Bōei Sangyō* Kyōiku Sha, 1979, pp. 16–17

the Korean War it only became significant after the phasing out of American MSA aid in the mid-1960s. By 1965 it was estimated that 87.2 per cent of the Self Defence Forces' weapons, equipment and other needs were being manufactured in Japan.[61] Domestic production of armaments more than doubled in the first two decades after the end of the occupation.[62] The importance of military industries in the Japanese economy as a whole, however, was not to be exaggerated. With the exception of the munitions and aircraft industries, both of which were heavily dependent on Defence Agency orders, military production accounted for only a small percentage of the output of individual industries. In 1966, for example, the Defence Agency purchased some 65 per cent of production in the aircraft industry and 50–70 per cent of the output of most munitions manufacturers. Yet it was claimed that no more than 4 per cent of Mitsubishi Heavy Industry's sales in 1966–7 had been to the Defence Agency. Even such munitions firms as Hōwa Industries were allegedly selling only 10 per cent of their wares to the agency.[63] By the mid-1970s, however, with the continued trend towards domestic production, the reliance of particular firms on Defence Agency orders had increased substantially. Nevertheless, few Japanese firms were as heavily dependent on Defence Agency orders as the giant corporations at the centre of the United States military-industrial complex. (See tables XIV.18, XIV.19)

Except in the case of the aircraft and munitions industries, Defence Agency requirements continued to absorb only a tiny fraction of Japan's total industrial production. Between 1954 and 1975, in fact, the ratio of military production to total industrial output decreased significantly.[64] (See table XIV.20)

A significant feature of Japan's postwar military industry was the fact that ten or a dozen companies monopolized more than 65 per cent of production. Among these companies a mere four, Mitsubishi Heavy Industries, Ishikawajima-Harima Heavy Industries, Kawasaki Heavy Industries and Mitsubishi Electrics occupied the dominant position. Moreover, within this exclusive group of four companies, all of which were concerned with production of aircraft, aircraft engines, naval vessels and communications equipment, Mitsubishi Heavy Industries clearly led the field. In 1965 Mitsubishi Heavy Industries manufactured 38.7 per cent of military equipment produced by the ten leading companies. Ishikawajima-Harima manufactured 17.5 per cent, Kawasaki 8.3 per cent, Mitsubishi Electrics 6.9 per cent. By 1969 Mitsubishi Heavy Industry's share had risen to 47.9 per cent, Kawasaki's to 14.6 per cent, Mitsubishi Electrics' to 7.8 per cent. In contrast, Ishikawajima-Harima's share had dropped to 13 per cent.[65] In 1975, Mitsubishi Heavy Industries produced 39.7 per cent of all domestically manufactured military equipment. Ishikawajima-Harima produced 24.6 per cent, Kawasaki Heavy Industries 9.2 per cent and Mitsubishi Electrics 9.1 per cent.[66]

Throughout the 1960s and the 1970s, despite the relative unimportance of military production in the Japanese economy as a whole, the four principal employers organizations, Keidanren, Nikkeiren, Nisshō and Keizai Dōyūkai, were all enthusiastic exponents of a stronger defence posture, greater military spending and a higher level of domestic procurement.[67] The actual degree of influence enjoyed by these four organizations was not always easy to ascertain. Certainly, Keidanren, Nikkeiren, Nisshō and Keizai Dōyūkai, with their extensive connections in the bureau-

Table XIV.19 Military procurement as a percentage of total sales of particular
American companies (1976)
(Units:)

Rank	Company	Defence Contracts	Total Sales	Ratio %
1.	McDonnell Douglas Corp.	2,464,563	3,583,775	68.8
2.	Lockheed Aircraft Corp.	1,509,845	3,397,600	44.4
3.	Northrop Corp.	1,480,182	–	–
4.	General Electric Corp.	1,346,925	15,971,600	8.4
5.	United Technologies Corp.	1,233,115	5,192,945	23.7
6.	Boeing Corp.	1,176,346	3,989,916	29.5
7.	General Dynamics Corp.	1,072,978	2,562,394	41.9
8.	Grumman Corp.	982,026	1,523,122	64.5
9.	Litton Industries, Inc.	978,225	3,354,552	29.2
10.	Rockwell International Corp.	965,954	5,232,300	18.5

Source: Nagamatsu Keiichi, op-cit., p. 19. Compiled from *Moody's Industrial Manual* and *Aviation Week and Space Technology*, 10 October 1977.

cracy, the defence forces and the academic world, their control of strategic sections of the mass media and their network of official and private ties overseas, appeared in a unique position to place pressure on the government. United action by the four organizations played an important, indeed, a decisive role during several crises in Japan's postwar political history. The four organizations had diverted funds from Yoshida to Hatoyama in 1954 and from Kishi to Ikeda in 1960. After Ikeda's retirement, they had supported Satō against Kōno and Fujiyama.[68] Nevertheless, these were efforts to preserve stable Conservative government, not to change established policies. It has yet to be convincingly demonstrated that the organized business community has been able to force a well-entrenched government to change its policies against the inclinations of the dominant factional coalition and the advice of the bureaucracy. Certainly, in the area of defence policy, business has not always had its way, as Yoshida's rejection of Keidanren's ambitious rearmament projects in the mid-1950s demonstrates.

The strongest business pressure for large-scale rearmament came not from Keidanren, Nikkeiren, Nisshō and Keizai Dōyūkai but from a number of groups connected exclusively with military production, in particular from Keidanren's Defence Production Committee, the Japan Aviation Industry Association, the Japan Weapons Industry Association and the Japan Rocket Development Council. The extreme statements emanating from some of these organizations stood in marked contrast to the publicly enunciated views of the rest of the industrial world.[69]

On the surface these organizations represented a wide range of defence-based industries. There were some eighty-eight companies affiliated with the Japan Weapons Industry Association[70] and over a hundred connected with Keidanren's Defence Production Committee.[71] In reality, the organizations were dominated by

Table XIV.20   The place of military production in Japanese industry
(Units: Y100 million)

Sector	Defence Agency procurement in Japan (A)	Special procurement (B)	Total defence production (C)=(A)+(B)	Total industrial production (D)	Ratio (C)/(D)(%)
Shipbuilding	58,726		58,726	3,178,264	1.85
	50,075		50,075	3,008,508	1.66
Aircraft	197,979	1,348	199,327	229,396	86.89
	214,220	1,222	215,442	243,077	88.63
Motor vehicles	9,481		9,401	10,890,525	0.09
	10,302		10,302	12,741,992	0.08
Arms and	62,228		62,228	62,674	99.29
ammunition	71,229		71,229	71,333	99.85
Electric com-					
munications	75,346		75,346	9,978,934	0.76
equipment	80,041		80,041	13,006,323	0.62
Oil products	27,038		27,038	6,531,645	0.41
	31,714		31,714	7,675,384	0.41
Coal	1,153		1,153	167,255	0.69
	1,715		1,715	204,997	0.84
Textiles	6,237		6,237	6,159,605	0.10
	6,459		6,459	7,071,712	0.09
Medical	2,090		2,090	1,626,812	0.13
supplies	2,224		2,224	1,809,491	0.12
Foodstuffs	31,261		31,261	12,545,810	0.25
	28,843		28,843	14,438,256	0.20
Other	29,054		29,054	59,168,153	0.05
	30,615		30,615	66,292,785	0.05
Total	500,593	1,348	501,941	110,539,093	0.45
	527,437	1,222	528,659	126,563,858	0.42

Note: Upper figures are for 1975, lower figures are for 1976.
Source: Nagamatsu Keiichi, op. cit., pp. 24–5.

the four leading defence-based companies. Mitsubishi's influence was preponderant. It would be no exaggeration to claim that the two most important of the four organizations, the Japan Weapons Industry Association and the Keidanren Committee, were no more than Mitsubishi pressure groups and that the remaining two were strongly under Mitsubishi's influence.[72]

Fulfilment of production targets associated with successive defence plans required close and continuous government liaison with these organizations. They thus had well-trodden paths into the Liberal Democratic Party, the Defence Agency and the Self Defence Forces. On the political level they maintained ties with the

Liberal Democratic Party's Security Problems Research Committee and Domestic Weapons Production Committee.[73] Both committees, it will be recalled, were dominated by the party's 'pro-American' conservative nationalists, centring around the 'old soldiers' group'. They were thus somewhat isolated from the mainstream of party opinion and their extremely hawkish recommendations apparently had little impact on government policy during these years. The fact that the weapons industry represented such an insignificant sector of the Japanese economy as a whole probably strengthened the hand of the less bellicose elements in the Liberal Democratic Party and government.

The weapons industry groups and associated companies also maintained close ties with the Defence Agency. Obviously, the agency found it convenient to know what equipment could be domestically produced, in what time and at what cost before decisions could be taken on long-term defence plans. Industry representatives and the top civilian leadership of the Defence Agency thus held frequent round-table conferences.[74] During the course of these discussions defence industry leaders were presumably given opportunities to influence the technical details of the agency's plans. It would also have been surprising if they did not explain their views on the overall direction of Japan's defence policy. Yet since the rate of Japan's military expansion programme during the period under consideration consistently fell far short of the industry's hopes, these explanations presumably had little effect.

From the latter part of the 1960s attention was drawn to the increasingly intimate connections between defence-based industries and the Self Defence Force officer corps. In March 1968 it was revealed that almost three hundred former high-ranking officers had, after retirement from the forces, found employment in private firms.[75] Most of the firms involved were associated with military production. Moreover, it was disclosed that the thirty leading defence-based firms were at that time employing a total of sixty-eight retired high-ranking officers. Significantly, Mitsubishi Heavy Industries topped the list with two vice-admirals, one rear-admiral, one lieutenant-general, two air vice-marshals and one air marshal employed as advisers. Ishikawajima-Harima Heavy Industries employed one vice-admiral, one rear-admiral, two major-generals and an air marshal. Kawasaki had managed to obtain the services of a former vice-admiral and a rear-admiral. Mitsubishi Electrics was employing a vice-admiral, a rear-admiral, two major-generals and one air marshal. Even relatively small firms like Japan Electronics, Kyōdō Oil or Japan Radio had managed to enlist the services of the odd rear-admiral or major-general. All the appointments had been made since 1962 and the majority since 1965.[76] Evidence of links between serving officers and former Imperial officers employed in defence-based firms also came to light.[77]

There were, of course, rather compelling economic reasons for Self Defence Force officers to seek employment after retirement. Retiring ages were low (fifty-eight for lieutenant-generals, fifty-six for major-generals, fifty-three for colonels, fifty for lieutenant-colonels, majors, captains, first and second lieutenants), wages were not high by private industry standards, pensions were small.[78] Air Vice-Marshal Yamaguchi, whose suicide in suspicious circumstances first brought to light the connections between the defence forces and private firms, was to have received a mere Y2 million in retirement allowances after thirteen years of service. His family was to have received an annual pension of Y300,000,[79] a paltry sum by any standards. Pay scales improved dramatically in the 1970s but were still not comparable to those in the private sector. It was thus natural that, as retirement approached, high-ranking officers made frenzied efforts to find other employment. For obvious reasons they were drawn to defence-based industries. In a technocratic and rather anti-military society the prospects for an unemployed officer could be forlorn. In 1963 Major-General Sano Tsunemitsu, commandant of the Self Defence Force Physical Training School, committed suicide after a futile search for post-retirement employment.[80]

It would be difficult to show that these connections had much influence on defence policy and planning. Yet the government, prompted by the Opposition, occasionally felt it necessary to blow the whistle. In 1967, when it was revealed that four high-ranking Ground Self Defence Force Staff Officers had made an overnight trip to Sengokubara (Hakone) for a game of golf with two former lieutenant-generals employed by Itō-Chū and Japan Aviotronics, the Defence Agency director-general warned the officers concerned and prohibited future contacts.[81] Yet such warnings appear to have been relatively ineffective. Throughout the 1960s and the 1970s, ties of mutual obligation, common interests and parallel philosophical positions continued to draw Japan's small defence-based industries and its new military forces closer together.

In the late 1970s it began to seem as if United States aerospace companies had also, through a variety of highly questionable practices, exerted an extraordinary influence, for at least a decade, not only on the technical details of Japanese military procurement, but also on personnel movements in the Defence Agency. As early as 1974, Arimori Kunio, former acting head of Nisshō-Iwai's Aircraft Department, which in the late 1960s had been involved in a campaign to sell the McDonnell Douglas F-4E Phantom to the Defence Agency, revealed that in order to undermine the efforts of Itō-chū to promote the cause of Northrop's F-5 fighters, his company had enlisted the support of former Prime Minister Kishi, Tanaka Ryōsuke (sometime Prime Minister Ikeda Hayato's private secretary and subsequently an influential Conservative member of the House of Representatives) and Matsuno Raizō, director-general of the Defence Agency, to have Kaihara Osamu removed as Chief of the National Defence Council Secretariat.[82] Kaihara (known for his relatively sanguine assessment of Japan's strategic environment) had favoured purchase of the F-5. In February 1979 evidence was tendered to the Diet suggesting that Nisshō-Iwai had also attempted to persuade Kishi and Matsuno to influence the careers of particular uniformed officers with a view to promoting sales of the F-4E Phantom.[83] Kishi was presumably to have used his influence with his younger brother, Prime Minister Satō Eisaku, to effect these changes. Notes allegedly written by Kaifu Hachirō, then primarily responsible for Nisshō-Iwai's aircraft sales drive, suggested that large sums of money had changed hands during the course of these operations.[84] Matsuno subsequently admitted to the Diet that he had received Y400–500 million in political donations from Nisshō-Iwai in the late 1960s and early 1970s, although he denied that any corrupt practices had been involved.[85] He had apparently forgotten to include this windfall in his taxation returns. During the course of investigations it was also noted that a florist's shop in a condominium built by Nisshō-Iwai was registered under the name of Matsuno's wife.[86] On 25 January 1979, Shimada Mitsuhiro, former executive director of Nisshō-Iwai, told police prosecutors of the existence of a secret agreement between his company and Kishi's close American friend, Harry Kern, founder of the Japan Lobby and sometime consultant to Grumman International. On 1 February 1979, before further details could be elicited, Shimada leapt to his death from his Tōkyō office.[87]

Diet investigations into the affair, unlike those into the Lockheed scandal, proved somewhat inconclusive. The leading figures involved seemed far less vulnerable than former Prime Minister Tanaka Kakuei. Some important witnesses, such as Arimori, who had agreed to testify only after receiving a guarantee of his personal safety, and who was accorded police protection because of threats against his life, refused to answer crucial questions on the grounds that they might thereby incriminate themselves.[88] Others, such as the unfortunate Kaifu, trembling violently when shown copies of a memorandum, allegedly in his handwriting, ordering substantial payments to 'Mr Matsuno and Mr Fukuda, under instructions from Mr Kishi' pleaded ignorance or deficiency of memory.[89]

Whatever the truth of the matter, the ability of foreign companies, assisted by malleable elements in the Japanese political world, to influence equipment purchases and Defence Agency personnel movements, and, therefore, the strategic judgements, threat perceptions and contingency plans on which Japan's policies were ultimately based, posed at least as great a threat to the evolution of a rational, balanced national security policy as did the activities of agents of hostile powers.

Japan, the United States and East Asia after the collapse of détente, 1978–1987

> Whatever stars may glow or burn
> O'er lands of East and West,
> The wandering heart of man will turn
> To one it loves the best.
>
> Henry Lawson, *The Never-Never Land*

The special relationship with the United States, as Prince Konoye and Yoshida Shigeru had hoped, enabled Japan to preserve at least the elements of the Imperial system, hold off the challenges posed by the Communist Party and radical elements in the armed forces and re-establish its position as a major world power. China's ambivalence towards Japan had, for the time being, made negotiation of an exclusive partnership with Peking impossible. Nevertheless, superpower strategic parity, *détente* and the erosion of the Cold War alliance systems provided an international environment conducive to Japan's adoption of an Asian-orientated omnidirectional diplomacy. Domestic political trends, too, provided a solid foundation for more independent policies. Had *détente* continued and had the Conservative establishment been able to overcome its suspicions of the Soviet Union, Japan might gradually have disentangled itself from the San Francisco system, carefully balancing its relationships with Washington, Moscow and Peking, avoiding strategic commitments in Korea, consolidating its very powerful positions in South-East Asia, strengthening ties with Australia and continuing to pursue an autonomous course in the Middle East. The Self Defence Forces, supported by a strong, indigenous military industry might have emerged as a genuine national army, navy and air force, committed, exclusively, to the defence of Japanese territory. In this way they might have contributed significantly to a reduction of superpower tension in North-East Asia. An independent nuclear capability would not have been necessary for the Japanese forces to perform this task. Swedish-style neutrality would have been welcomed by a large body of public opinion. A certain aloofness from international affairs was, in every way, as consistent with the Japanese historic tradition as alignment with the hegemonic power.

The collapse of *détente* in 1978–9, against the background of the Polish crisis, heightened instability in Central America, the upheavals in Iran, unrest in Saudi Arabia and Soviet intervention in Afghanistan, brought Japan's incremental disengagement from the San Francisco system to an abrupt end. The United States, rebounding from the trauma of Vietnam and Watergate, embarked on a concerted drive to re-establish its military superiority over the Soviet Union, reassert its pre-eminence in the Western alliance, reimpose its authority in the Middle East and consolidate its position in the Western Pacific through negotiation of a strategic *entente* with the Chinese Communists. The resurgence of American self-confidence, the revival of conservative values and the rout of the liberal left made a profound impression on Japanese leaders. Conservative westernisers hailed the dawning of "a new American century". Nevertheless, many observers doubted whether the massive American arms build-up that began during the latter part of the Carter administration and continued, at an accelerated pace, throughout the Reagan era, would undermine the superpower strategic parity established during the 1960s. President Reagan's Strategic Defence Iniative (SDI) programme, even if it were to achieve its objectives, seemed likely to give the United States no more than a temporary advantage over its rival. The strengthening of United States naval forces in the Pacific and Indian Ocean areas, the adoption of the Lehman 'forward offensive strategy' in North-East Asia, the creation of a special deployment force for service in the Middle East, all seemed of doubtful utility in a world where sea-power was clearly losing its effectiveness. The sceptics were right. At the end of the Reagan era superpower strategic parity remained as much a fact of international life as it had been twenty years before. In the Middle East the United States, still reeling under the impact of the Iranian Revolution, remained on the defensive. American naval and air power had been unable either to influence the outcome of the Lebanese Civil War or to topple Colonel Ghaddafi's government in Libya. By the summer of 1987 the proud United States Navy, expanded and refurbished by the Reagan administration at a cost of billions of dollars, was being constantly humiliated in the Persian Gulf by two regional powers equipped with relatively antiquated technology.

Throughout the 1980s, United States economic decline continued unabated, conflict with its major trading partners intensified. By the middle of the decade the United States had become the world's largest debtor. Nevertheless, the emergence of pro-American governments in Great Britain, France and West Germany facilitated, for a time, Washington's efforts to promote Western unity. Attempts to coordinate Western approaches to global strategic, political and economic issues gathered momentum. While the success of these moves was, in most cases, more apparent than real, it became increasingly difficult for Japan to appear the odd man out. Far more significant, from Japan's point of view, was the *de facto* Sino-American alliance that developed in the wake of the Carter administration's tilt to China in the spring of 1978. The Sino-American strategic *rapprochement* drastically altered the regional balance of power. At one stroke the United States recovered all the ground lost during the Vietnam War and placed itself in an extremely favourable position *vis-à-vis* its rivals in the Far East. The new coalition appeared far more formidable, in every respect, than the Sino-Soviet alliance of 1950. Washington was determined to exploit it to the full. 'The American-Chinese relationship is a central element in our global policy', Carter's national security adviser Zbigniew Brzezinsky told the Japan Society in New York on the eve of Prime Minister Fukuda's visit to the United States in April 1978.[1] By the middle of the year Richard Holbrooke, Under-Secretary of State for Far Eastern Affairs, was recommending that the United States, Japan and China co-ordinate their strategies against the Soviet Union.[2] The possibility of forging a grand Pacific anti-Soviet alliance, centring on the United States and incorporating Japan, China, South Korea, the ASEAN nations, Australia and New Zealand was widely discussed at the time of Vice-President Walter Mondale's tour of South-East Asia and Oceania in the summer of 1978. Brzezinsky also raised the issue during his visit to China, Japan and South Korea.[3] The idea appealed strongly to the new leadership in Peking. It was highly appreciated in Seoul. Canberra, too, expressed interest. The ASEAN countries were divided. Singapore and Thailand seemed receptive. Indonesia and Malaysia, mistrustful of Washington, antagonistic towards China and suspicious of Japan, were less enthusiastic. The Indian government was profoundly alarmed.

Once the decision to play the 'China card' had been taken, America's ties with the People's Republic expanded rapidly, despite fears of possible Soviet counteraction. Scores of bilateral economic, scientific, technological and cultural agreements were signed in the first month after the final normalization of diplomatic relations in January 1979. These included an extremely significant accord on nuclear co-operation. By the end of 1979 over sixty major American firms had established offices in China. Bilateral trade doubled in the course of a single year. It grew steadily throughout the following decade. Sino-American strategic co-operation also developed at a brisk pace, stimulated by the build-up of Soviet naval and air power in the Far East, the emergence of a close Soviet-Vietnamese alliance and Soviet intervention in Afghanistan. Exchanges of intelligence were expanded.[4] Teng Hsiao-ping discussed China's plans to 'punish' Vietnam during his visit to Washington in February 1979 in the wake of the Kampuchean crisis.[5] The Carter administration leaned heavily towards the Chinese side during the conflict. In subsequent years, China and the United States, co-operating closely with the Thai military regime, worked energetically to weaken and isolate the government in Hanoi. In the West, China moved to consolidate its long-standing relationship with Pakistan. The United States, too, began to repair ties with Islamabad. In the north the Chinese, while maintaining their alliance with Pyongyang, effected a limited *rapprochement* with Seoul and made it clear they did not wish to see an American withdrawal from South Korea. During his visit to Peking in January 1980 United States Defence Secretary Harold Brown stressed the convergence of Sino-American interests in the strongest terms.[6] The visit of the Chinese Defence Minister Geng Biao to Washington in the summer of 1980 resulted in an American decision to sell military support equipment to the People's Republic.[7] Despite President Ronald Reagan's personal ambivalence towards the Chinese Communists, the close Sino-American strategic relationship negotiated during the Carter era survived until the mid-1980s, when Peking began to repair its ties with the Soviet Union and shift to a policy of equidistance between the two superpowers. This development, in turn, stimulated Washington's interest in a closer strategic relationship with Japan and South Korea.

So long as it endured, the Sino-American strategic partnership exerted a powerful impact on Japanese policies. From the spring of 1978 Japanese governments found themselves under increasing pressure from both Washington and Peking to adopt a positive attitude towards the new coalition and play a more active role in containment of the Soviet Union. These pressures were a logical outcome of the informal Sino-American understandings on Japan negotiated earlier in the decade. At the Carter-Fukuda talks in May 1978, the American President encouraged Japan to press ahead with the difficult negotiations on the Sino-Japanese Treaty of Peace, Friendship and Mutual Co-operation, held up chiefly by disagreements on the inclusion of an 'anti-hegemony clause'. The Chinese leadership, in turn, urged Japan to give the highest priority to preserving a harmonious relationship with the United States. In Washington, Japan's potential role in the modernization of China's armed forces and strategic industries caused much excitement. Brzezinsky and other Carter administration officials expressed the hope that Japan would eventually emerge as one of China's principal suppliers of sophisticated military equipment.[8] While the Japanese government made it clear that it would continue to uphold its traditional policies towards arms exports, the strong position of 'pro-American' Westernizers and 'pro-Chinese' Asianists in the Liberal Democratic Party, together with the absence of a substantial 'pro-Soviet' lobby, made these pressures difficult to resist.

The intensification of Japanese-American trade friction and Washington's growing tendency to link strategic and economic issues made Japan's position even more difficult. By 1987 America's trade deficit with Japan stood at $80 billion. Criticism of Japan's trade practices became more acute. So, too, did attacks on Japan's alleged 'free ride' in the Western alliance. In 1978 Congress adopted the first of a number of resolutions demanding big increases in Japanese defence spending. On 14 December 1982 the Senate Foreign Relations Committee called on Japan to expand its military budget and acquire what the United States judged to be sufficient defence capability by 1990. The defence appropriations bill approved by Congress in September 1983 specifically noted Japan's commitment to defend its sea-lanes out to 1,000 miles from the home islands. In July 1985 Congress passed a resolution calling on Japan to strengthen its military forces and extend its defence perimeters or face the possibility of retaliation in the field of trade.[9] In June 1987, shortly after the United States had imposed wide-ranging sanctions on imports of Japanese electronic goods, the House of Representatives approved a resolution requiring the Secretary of State to initiate talks with Japan on increasing its military spending to at least 3 per cent of GNP or providing Washington with an equivalent amount of cash as a security fee.[10] There was a growing interest in encouraging Japan to play a more active role in the Persian Gulf as well as in the Western Pacific. Two weeks after the passage of this resolution the Senate voted overwhelmingly to ban imports of Toshiba products into the United States for two to five years in retaliation for the Japanese corporation's sale of computer software and machine tool manufacturing equipment to the Soviet Union in violation of COCOM rules. In scenes reminiscent of the anti-German hysteria that swept the Anglo-American powers during World War I, enraged Congressmen, holding aloft a hangman's noose, publicly demolished a $30 Toshiba radio with sledgehammers, reducing the offending item to a tangled heap of plastic and metal.[11]

American and Chinese pressure, in the context of the rapidly changing global balance of power, touched off factional upheavals in Japan on the familiar pattern. By the beginning of the 1980s the Japanese government had formally abandoned the concept of 'omnidirectional diplomacy'. Instead, Japan closely aligned its policies with those of the United States and China, giving the two powers full and unequivocal support over Afghanistan, the Kampuchean question, the Korean peninsula, the Philippines and the South-West Pacific. The Japanese government responded positively to United States requests to increase economic assistance to distant, unstable and highly vulnerable American allies such as Egypt, Pakistan, Thailand and Turkey. As trade problems exacerbated anti-Japanese feeling in the United States, official pronouncements about Japan's place in the world focused more and more on its membership of the Western alliance system. The Japanese conservative revival that began to gather strength in the late 1970s, forcing the Socialist and Communist parties on to the defensive, persuaded the government that this rhetorical shift would cause minimal difficulties with the electorate. 'Japan is a member of the Western camp', Prime Minister Ōhira Masayoshi assured President Jimmy Carter in 1980. By 1983 Prime Minister Nakasone Yasuhiro was portraying the Japanese archipelago as a virtual eastern extension of NATO, 'an unsinkable aircraft carrier putting up a tremendous bulwark of defence against infiltration of the [Soviet] backfire bomber'.[12]

During the Reagan-Nakasone years, Japanese-American co-operation in the field of joint defence planning, military manoeuvres, manpower training, logistics, communications and intelligence deepened. Wide ranging agreements on military technology exchange were concluded, although the details surrounding their actual implementation remain obscure. After a long internal debate Japan eventually decided to participate in President Ronald Reagan's Strategic Defence Initiative programme. There was much talk of promoting interoperability of Japanese and American forces at all levels. At the same time, to facilitate United States operations in South-East Asia, the Indian Ocean and the Middle East in time of war, the Japanese government publicly agreed, for the first time, both to assume responsibility for the defence of the sea-lanes up to 1,000 nautical miles from the home archipelago and to participate in joint efforts to prohibit 'access by Soviet naval vessels from bases in eastern Siberia into the Pacific'.[13] The range and strike power of the Japanese air force was to be extended. Naval and ground forces were to be further strengthened through updating of equipment. Japanese military spending rose steadily. In 1986, the Nakasone Cabinet abandoned the 1 per cent GNP ceiling for military expenditure set by Prime Minister Miki ten years before. The 1986–90 Mid-Term Defence Programme Estimate laid the groundwork for increases in military power of a kind that could eventually project Japanese influence far beyond the shores of the home archipelago.[14] By 1987 officials travelling with Foreign Minister Kuranari on his tour of Australia, New Zealand and the South-West Pacific were speaking of a Japanese 'Monroe Doctrine' to counter perceived

Soviet influence in Oceania.[15]

At the same time, in order to offset the problems caused by the rise of protectionism in North America, Japanese capital poured into the United States. Japan began to finance an increasingly large proportion of the Federal deficit. By 1986 Japanese investors were purchasing an estimated 35–40 per cent of United States government bonds. The Japanese government, retreating from its traditional support for market principles, sought to alleviate the bilateral trade imbalance by encouraging industry to purchase raw materials, foodstuffs and other commodities from United States producers, regardless of cost. Japanese reliance on the United States market, which had been steadily declining for many years, reached unprecedented levels.

By the end of the decade William E. Colby's recommendation that the United States and Japan should work to overcome their differences through development of a 'common political framework' seemed close to realization. Some Americans, admittedly, remained sceptical of the wisdom of encouraging Japan to adopt too assertive a regional role. In January 1987 Henry Kissinger, for example, warned that 'major [Japanese] rearmament would set in motion developments and tendencies not deducible from contemporary pronouncements ... Japan's increased military contribution', he argued, 'is largely unnecessary to maintaining global equilibrium'.[16] Zbigniew Brzezinsky, in contrast, his enthusiasm for a special relationship with China dampened by the realities of the mid-1980s, had begun to wax lyrical about the imminent formation of 'Amerippon', a gigantic North Pacific superstate characterized by 'overlapping elites, corporate structures, and increasingly, joint political planning'.[17] Even Mike Mansfield, United States ambassador to Japan, a man rather less given to hyperbole, was convinced that the two nations were rapidly approaching full strategic, political and economic integration. The next logical step in this historic process, he argued, was a bilateral free trade agreement, 'the prelude to a vast free trade arrangement embracing much of the Pacific Rim'.[18]

Brzezinsky, Mansfield and other exponents of a close and exclusive American-Japanese partnership doubtless felt they had grounds for optimism. Yet it was not altogether clear that their hopes were any more realistic than those of Harry Kern, George Kennan and John Foster Dulles thirty years before. Chuang-tzu's observation that governments pontificate most earnestly about virtue in times of social collapse can equally be applied to the field of international relations. The increasingly intimate strategic co-operation of the 1980s did not necessarily demonstrate the 'inevitable harmony' of Japanese and American interests. It simply represented the Japanese government's adjustment, on the basis of the age-old principle of *nagai mono ni makareyō*, to a particular set of international circumstances. The return to bilateralism was resisted strongly by many elements in the Japanese political and business establishment. It was not welcomed by Japanese popular opinion, despite a sustained public relations campaign. By the end of the decade, the dawning of a new era of superpower *détente*, the failure of Ronald Reagan's efforts to reimpose the *Pax Americana*, the emergence of a reformist regime in the Soviet Union, China's return to policies of equidistance and continuing Japanese-American economic fric tion had set the stage for further changes in Japan's international orientation. During the summer of 1987 Cabinet criticism of United States policies mounted. The humiliating apology extracted from the Toshiba Corporation for its violation of COCOM agreements, United States insistence that Japan abandon plans for domestic manufacture of the next generation of Self Defence Force ground support fighters and constant pressure from the American agricultural lobby increased the deep-seated frustrations with the Japanese-American relationship felt by large sections of the business community. On 31 July 1987 the Tōkai Bank recommended that Japan should seek to reduce its excessive dependence on the United States through the formation of an Asian Common Market organized along the lines of the European Community.[19] Inoki Masamichi, former commandant of the National Defence Academy, saw Japanese-American relations reaching 'a critical stage' and drew parallels with the situation in 1940–1.[20] Public opinion polls, too, revealed a persistent, widespread and growing belief, among Japanese of all age-groups, that the nation's most significant long-term interests lay not with North America but with China, South-East Asia and the societies of the Western Pacific. Scepticism about the value of the United States connection seemed strongest among high school and university students, superficially, at least, the most Americanized element in Japanese society. The majority of Japanese teenagers surveyed by Dr Benjamin C. Duke in 1985 expressed only 'a little respect' for American civilization, were convinced that the United States was an unreliable ally and argued that American bases in their country served purely American purposes. They appeared strongly opposed to the development of closer bilateral ties.[21] By August 1987, forty-two years after the nuclear bombings of Hiroshima and Nagasaki, 49 per cent of Japanese junior high school students surveyed by the *Asahi Shimbun* were declaring that if their country were to go to war again the enemy would be the United States. Only 41 per cent saw the Soviet Union as the chief hypothetical antagonist. A mere 3 per cent envisaged a future conflict with China.[22]

Japan's greatly enhanced international status, above all, the immense strength of the Japanese economy and the nation's emergence as the world's principal creditor, made it inevitable that the next swing of the pendulum would have more far-reaching consequences than those produced by the 'Nixon Shocks' of 1971. Even if the security treaty survived the anticipated upheaval, it seemed distinctly possible that the United States Pacific alliance system, like the Roman Empire after the death of Theodosius, would gradually divide into Eastern and Western segments, politically autonomous, economically self-sustaining and culturally distinct, evolving in accordance with their own traditions and requirements.

NOTES

Chapter I

1. For an excellent discussion of Japan's relations with East and South-East Asia in ancient and medieval times, see Tōma Seita, *Higashi Ajia Sekai No Keisei*, Shunjū Sha, 1977.
2. See Inoue Mitsusada, *Nihon Kokka No Kigen*, Iwanami Shoten, 1968 and Saeki Arimasa, *Kodai No Higashi Ajia To Nihon*, Kyōiku Sha, 1977.
3. Mori Katsumi, *Nissō Bōeki No Kenkyū*, Kokusho Kankōkai, 1975; Tōma, op. cit., pp. 183–204 and Rekishigaku Kenkyū Kai-Nihon Shi Kenkyū Kai (eds), *Kōza Nihon Shi*, Volume 2, Tōkyō Daigaku Shuppan Kai, 1970.
4. Sasaki Ginya, 'Kaigai Bōeki To Kokunai Keizai', in Rekishigaku Kenkyū Kai-Nihon Shi Kenkyū Kai (eds), op. cit., Volume 3, pp. 161–87.
5. Tōma, op. cit., p. 74. It is not clear whether these useful items ever reached the Chinese continent.
6. Sasayama Haruo, *Kodai Kokka No Guntai*, Chūō Kōron Sha, 1975, pp. 17–19.
7. Fukuzawa Yukichi, 'Datsu-A Ron', *Jiyū Shimpō*, 16 March 1885. Keiō Gijuku (ed.), *Fukuzawa Yukichi Zenshū*, Volume 10, Iwanami Shoten, 1960, pp. 238–40.
8. Donald Keene, *The Japanese Discovery of Europe, 1720–1830*, Stanford University Press, Stanford, Calif., 1969, Chapters 4, 5 and Appendix.
9. *Dai Hon'ei Rikugun Bu, Dai Tōa Sensō Kaisen Ni Kansuru Kosatsu*, Senshi Kenkyū Shiryō, HRO–5, Bōei Kenshūjo Senshi Shitsu, 1976, p.3. See also Naratomo Tatsuya, *Yoshida Shōin*, Iwanami Shoten, 1951.
10. Keiō Gijuku (ed.), *Fukuzawa Yukichi Zenshū*, Volume IV, 1959, p.16. Quoted in Bannō Junji, 'Japan's foreign policy and attitudes to the outside world, 1868–1945', in Peter Drysdale and Hironobu Kitaōji (eds), *Japan and Australia*, Australian National University Press, Canberra, 1981, p.30.
11. Kaneko Kentarō (ed.), *Itō Hirobumi Den*, Tōkyō, 1940, Volume 11, pp. 337–8. Quoted in Bannō, op. cit., p.30.
12. Tamamuro Taijō, *Saigō Takamori*, Iwanami Shoten, 1960.
13. Hasegawa Yoshiki, *Tōyama Mitsuru Hyōden*, Hara Shobō, 1974. E. H. Norman, 'The Genyōsha: a study in the origins of Japanese imperialism', *Pacific Affairs*, XVII, September 1944, pp. 261–84.
14. *Kita Ikki Sho Sakushū* (2 volumes), Misuzu Shobō, 1971, passim.
15. Katō Bunzō *et al.*, *Nihon Shi*, Volume 2, Shin Nihon Shuppan Kaisha, 1967, pp. 121–2.
16. Ibid., p.122.

17. Ibid.
18. Ibid.
19. Ibid., p.156.
20. Miyazaki Tōten, *Sanjū San Nen No Yume*, Tōyō Bunkō, Heibon Sha, 1967, p. 22.
21. Kawakami Tetsutarō (ed.), *Uchimura Kanzō Shū*, Chikuma Shobō, Tōkyō, 1967, p. 131. Quoted in Bannō, op. cit., p. 11.
22. Tsunoda Jun (ed.), *Ishiwara Kanji Shiryō*, Hara Shobō, 1973, pp. 422–32.
23. Professor Ian Nish does not view the impact of British policy in this light. Great Britain, he suggests, cannot be held responsible for the Sino-Japanese war or its consequences. See Ian H. Nish, *The Anglo-Japanese Alliance, The Diplomacy of Two Island Empires, 1894–1907*, Athlone Press, London, 1966. For a counter-argument see John Welfield, 'The Anglo-Japanese alliance and Japan's imperial expansion', *Bulletin of the Graduate School of International Relations*, IUJ, no. 3, July 1985, pp. 55–83.
24. Komura Gaikōshi, I, pp. 277–80. Quoted in Nish, op. cit., pp. 383–5 (Nish's translation).
25. Ibid.
26. Itō Hirobumi Hiroku, no. 48, Itō To Katsura, 13 December 1901. Quoted in Nish, op. cit., p. 387.
27. R. A. Esthus, 'The Taft-Katsura Agreement – reality or myth?' *Journal of Modern History*, XXX, 1959, p. 50ff.
28. James Crowley, *Japan's Quest for Autonomy*, Princeton University Press, Princeton, NJ, 1966, pp. 10–11.
29. R. M. Dawson (ed.), *William Lyon Mackenzie King*, Volume I, Methuen, London, 1958, pp. 150–66; D. C. Gordon, 'Roosevelt's smart Yankee trick', *Pacific Historical Review*, 30, 1961, pp. 351–8.
30. Luella J. Hall, 'The abortive German-American entente of 1907–8', *Journal of Modern History*, I, 1929, pp. 219–35.
31. Burton F. Beers, *Vain Endeavour: Robert Lansing's Attempts to End the American-Japanese Rivalry*, Duke University Press, Durham, NC, 1962. See also Ian H. Nish, *Alliance in Decline: A Study in Anglo-Japanese Relations*, 1908–23, Athlone Press, London, 1972, pp. 221–5 and Shinobu Seisaburō, *Nihon Gaikō Shi*, Volume I, Mainichi Shimbun Sha, 1974, pp. 281–2.
32. *Teikoku Kokubō Hōshin*, 28 February 1923. The writer is deeply indebted to General Kinugasa Hayao, former chairman of the Japanese Joint Staff Council, for providing the Japanese text of this document.
33. Nish, *Alliance in Decline*, pp. 158, 180, 219–221.
34. Shinobu, op. cit., pp. 247–8.
35. Kitamura Keichoku (ed.), *Yume No Nanajūyonen Nishihara Kamezō Jiden*, Tōyō Bunkō, Heibon Sha, 1965, pp. 82–6. Shinobu, op. cit., pp. 277–9.
36. Viscount Kikujiro Ishii, *Diplomatic Commentaries* (translated and edited by William R. Langdon), Johns Hopkins University Press, Baltimore, MD, 1936, p. 129.
37. *Teikoku Kokubō Hōshin*, 28 February 1923.
38. Dai Hoh'ei Rikugun Bu, *Dai Tōa Sensō Kaisen Ni Kansuru Shisatsu*, Senshi Kenkyū Shiryō, HRO–5, Bōei Kenshūjo Senshi Shitsu, 1976, p. 81.
39. Ibid.
40. Ibid., pp. 83–4.
41. Ibid., pp. 84–5.
42. Ibid., pp. 83–4.

43. Ibid., pp. 112–13.

Chapter II

1. Walter Lafeber, *America, Russia and the Cold War, 1945–1967*, John Wiley & Sons, New York, 1968, p.9.
2. Lafeber, op. cit., p. 14, and Daniel Yergin, *Shattered Peace*, Penguin, Harmondsworth, 1977, p.64.
3. Nikita S. Khruschev, *Khruschev Remembers*, Penguin, Harmondsworth, 1977, Volume I, 1973, p.502ff.
4. Ernest R. May, *'Lessons' of the Past: The Use and Misuse of History in American Foreign Policy*, Oxford University Press, New York, 1973, p.30.
5. For the evolution of American policy see Stephen Ambrose, *Rise to Globalism; American Foreign Policy, 1938–1970*, Penguin, Harmondsworth, 1973; Lafeber, op. cit.; May, op. cit.; Michael Schaller, *The American Occupation of Japan: The Origins of the Cold War in Asia*, Oxford University Press, New York, 1985 and Yergin, op. cit.
6. For the views of Truman's Under-Secretary of State Joseph C. Grew, Assistant Secretary of State for European, Asian, Near Eastern and African Affairs, James Clement Dunn, H. Freeman Matthews, director of the State Department's European Office and Loy Henderson, director of the Office of Near Eastern and African Affairs, see May, op. cit., pp.24–5. For George Kennan, see Yergin, op. cit., p.40. John Foster Dulles' prewar atittudes to Nazi Germany are discussed in Townsend Hoopes, *The Devil and John Foster Dulles*, André Deutsch, London, 1974, p.47.
7. *Treaty of Peace Between the Allied Powers and Japan*, Chapter 2, Article II.
8. Ibid., Chapter 2, Article III.
9. *Security Treaty between the United States of America and Japan* (signed at San Francisco, 8 September 1951; entered into force 28 April 1952).
10. *Exchange of Notes*, 8 September 1951.
11. James E. Auer, *The Postwar Rearmament of Japanese Maritime Forces, 1945–1971*, Praeger, New York, 1973, p.63ff.
12. Akira Iriye, 'Japan and the Cold War', a paper prepared for the International Symposium on the International Environment in Postwar Asia, Kyōtō, November 1975, sponsored by the Japanese Ministry of Education and the Japan Foundation.
13. Schaller, op. cit., pp.12–13, 93.
14. Ibid., pp. 9–13, 17, 93–4. See also Howard Schonberger, 'The Japan Lobby in American diplomacy', *Pacific Historical Review*, Volume XLVI, no. 3, August 1977.
15. Schaller, op. cit., pp.17–18.
16. United States Department of State, *Foreign Relations of the United States*, Volume VII, pp.842, 845.
17. *The China White Paper*, Wedemeyer Report, p.811.
18. Quoted in Schaller, op. cit., p.90.
19. George F. Kennan, *Memoirs, 1925–1950*, Atlantic, Little, Brown, Boston, Mass., 1961, pp.359, 374–5, 381.
20. Schaller, op. cit., p.104.
21. Ibid., p.179.
22. Ibid., p.182.
23. Ibid., p.104.

24. Ibid., p.141ff.
25. Ibid., p.179.
26. Ibid., pp.103–4.
27. United States Department of Defence, *United States–Vietnam Relations, 1945–1967*, Washington DC, 1971, pp.239–42.
28. *The New York Times*, 30 May 1950.
29. The writer is indebted to Nishimura Kumao, former head of the Japanese Foreign Ministry Treaties Bureau, for this perspective on MacArthur's thinking. (Talk with Nishimura Kumao, 17 January 1977.) See also Schaller, op. cit., p.124.
30. David Alan Rosenberg, 'The origins of overkill', *International Security*, Spring 1983.
31. Schaller, op. cit., pp.55–6.
32. Ibid., p.90.
33. Ibid., p.110.
34. Cited in Schonberger, op. cit.
35. Schaller, op. cit., pp.167–8.
36. Schonberger, op. cit.
37. For details of this group and its activities see J. W. Dower, *Empire and Aftermath: Yoshida Shigeru and the Japanese Experience, 1878–1954*, Harvard University Press, Cambridge, Mass., 1979, p.231ff.
38. Ibid., p.230.
39. Yabe Teiji, *Konoye Fumimaro*, Yomiuri Shimbun Sha, 1975, p.671.
40. Ibid., p.673.
41. Iriye, op. cit., p.63.
42. Hayashi Fusao, *Yoshida Shigeru To Senryō Kenpō*, Rōman, 1974, pp.32–3.
43. Yabe, op. cit., p.698.
44. See Stalin's comments to Byrnes at the Moscow Conference of Foreign Ministers in December 1945. 'The Soviet Government would have no objection if the United States wishes to leave its troops [in China] but they would merely like to be told about it'. Stalin also complained to Bevin that 'the United Kingdom had India and her possessions in the Indian Ocean in her sphere of influence; the United States had China and Japan, but the Soviets had nothing'. (Yergin, op. cit., p.150.)
45. Yabe, op. cit., pp.702–4. The writer is grateful to Prince Konoye's former private secretary, Ushiba Tomohiko, for verifying the text of this document. (Discussion with Ushiba Tomohiko, 15 February 1977.)
46. Yabe, op. cit., p.704.
47. Schaller, op. cit., p.10.
48. *The Japan Times*, 16 April 1986.
49. Discussion with Ushiba Tomohiko, 15 February 1977.
50. Yabe, op. cit., p.681.
51. George McTurnan Kahin, *Nationalism and Revolution in Indonesia*, Cornell University Press, Ithaca, NY, 1952, pp.114–25.
52. Tanabe Toshihiro's *Kike Wa Datsumi No Koe*, Tōkyō Daigaku Shuppan Kai, 1949, a collection of letters and poems from students at the front, provides a rare glimpse into the attitudes of young educated Japanese to the war. Iwate-ken Nōson Bunka Kondan Kai (ed.), *Senbotsu Nōmin Heishi No Tegami*, Iwanami, 1969, a collection of the letters of peasant soldiers killed in action, is a profoundly moving chronicle of the impact of war on the lives of ordinary men and women. So too is the 56-volume study compiled by the Sōka Gakkai

Youth Division, an abridged version of which has been published in English under the title of *Cries For Peace* (2 volumes), by *The Japan Times*, 1978.

53. Dower's *Empire and Aftermath*, already cited, is probably the most incisive biography of Yoshida in any language. See also Yoshida Shigeru, *The Yoshida Memoirs*, Heinemann, London, 1961; Kōsaka Masataka, *Saisho Yoshida Shigeru Ron*, Chūō Kōron Sha, 1968; Tadamiya Eitarō, *Yoshida-Hatoyama Jidai*, Tosho Shuppan Sha, 1976; Miyazawa Kiichi, 'Ampō Jōyaku Teiketsu No Ikisatsu', *Chūō Kōron*, May 1957; Hayashi Fusao, *Yoshida Shigeru Tō Senryō Kenpō*, Rōman, 1974; etc. The picture of Yoshida painted by the present writer has been compiled not only on the basis of a study of his writings, speeches and political actions, but in the light of extensive discussions with his daughter, Mrs Asō Kazuko; his private secretary (for forty years), Kitazawa Naokichi; his military adviser, Lieutenant-General Tatsumi Eiichi; one of his most illustrious disciples, former Prime Minister Satō Eisaku, and several of his political opponents, including former Prime Minister Katayama Tetsu, Tagawa Seiichi (of the New Liberal Club) and former Foreign Ministers Fujiyama Aiichirō and Sonoda Sunao.

54. Dower, op. cit., p.271.

55. This interpretation of Yoshida's prewar attitudes is based largely on information provided by Kitazawa Naokichi (2 April 1975) and Lieutenant-General Tatsumi Eiichi (8 February 1977).

56. Yoshida, op. cit., p.8.

57. Discussions with Mrs Asō Kazuko (28 April 1975), Lieutenant-General Tatsumi Eiichi (8 February 1977) and Kitazawa Naokichi (2 April 1975).

58. Schaller, op. cit., p.298.

59. Hayashi, op. cit., p.115.

60. Schaller, op. cit., pp.188–9.

61. Discussions with Mrs Asō Kazuko, Lieutenant-General Tatsumi Eiichi and Kitazawa Naokichi. Mrs Asō insisted that her father's aspirations went far beyond the mere *normalization* of ties with Peking. His ultimate goal, she maintained, was a Sino-Japanese *alliance*.

62. *Ugaki Kazunari Nikki*, Misuzu Shobō, 1971, Volume III, p.1729.

63. Ashida Hitoshi, 'Jiyū To Heiwa No Tame No Tatakai', *Bungei Shunjū*, March 1951; 'Eisei Chūritsu Fukanō Ron', *Bungei Shunjū* (Kinkyū Zōkan), 1950; 'Jiei Busō Ron', *Daiamondo*, 1 February 1951.

64. Katayama Tetsu, *Kaigan Tō Tenbō*, Fukumura Shuppan Kan, 1967, p.195ff.

65. Discussions with Katayama Tetsu, 20 February 1977.

66. Talk with Nishimura Kumao, 17 January 1977.

67. Yoshida, op. cit., p.263. This is corroborated by the testimony of Okazaki Katsuo, Permanent Secretary of the Foreign Ministry during the Katayama Cabinet and later Foreign Minister under Yoshida, before the Commission on the Constitution, 6 May 1959. (*Kenpō Chōsa Kai*, Dai San Iinkai, Dai Sanjukkai Gijiroku, pp.2–3.)

68. Ibid., p.3.

69. Ibid.

70. The Socialist component of the coalition was in a weak position from the beginning. As the price for a coalition, Ashida insisted on exclusion of left-wing Socialists from the Cabinet and six posts for his own Democrats (compared with the Socialists' seven). See Koyama Kōken and Shimizu Shinzō, *Nihon Shakaitō Shi*, Hoga Shoten, 1965, p.50ff.

71. When interviewed by the present writer in February 1977, Katayama's memory of these events appeared hazy. Former Foreign Minister Okazaki, when questioned on this point

by Nakasone Yasuhiro at the Commission on the Constitution hearings, could only reply that he 'did not know whether the Prime Minister's co-operation or approval had been obtained'. He thought that Chief Cabinet Secretary Nishio, who knew of Ashida's plans, might have spoken to Katayama, but stressed that this was pure speculation. (*Kenpō Chōsa Kai*, op. cit., p.24.) Okazaki himself was certainly consulted.

72. The writer is indebted to Nishimura Kumao for the text of this document.
73. Discussion with Nishimura Kumao, 17 January 1977.
74. One copy of the memorandum was given to the Australian Minister for External Affairs, Dr Evatt, when he visited Japan later in the year. (*Kenpō Chōsa Kai*, op. cit., p.3.)
75. Discussions with Nishimura Kumao, 17 January 1977.
76. Nishimura Kumao was quite adamant on this point in his discussions with the present writer. 'I am sure that only [Chief Cabinet Secretary] Nishio, *not* Prime Minister Katayama, was consulted.'
77. For extracts from some stirring prewar speeches by Nishio, see Katayama, op. cit., p.188ff.
78. The writer is indebted to Nishimura Kumao for providing access to this document. See also *Kenpō Chōsa Kai*, op. cit., p.4 (Okazaki's testimony).
79. Discussion with Nishimura Kumao, 17 January 1977.
80. Yoshida, op. cit., p.265.
81. Schaller, op. cit., p.164ff.
82. Discussion with Nishimura Kumao, 17 January 1977.
83. Miyazawa, op. cit., pp.68–70.
84. Dower, op. cit., p.389ff.
85. Ibid., p.316.
86. Kōsaka, op. cit., p.106.
87. *Kenpō Chōsa Kai*, op. cit., p.12 (Nishimura Kumao's testimony).
88. Ibid., pp.13–14. (Nishimura Kumao's testimony). See also Nishimura Kumao, 'San Furanshisuko No Omoide', *Chūō Kōron*, May 1957.
89. Townsend Hoopes, op. cit., pp.104–7.
90. Ibid., p.107.
91. Ibid., pp.107–8.
92. Martin E. Weinstein, *Japan's Postwar Defence Policy, 1947–1968*, Columbia University Press, New York, 1971, p.62. See also *Kenpō Chōsa Kai*, p.13.
93. *Kenpō Chōsa Kai*, op. cit., p.15 and Nishimura, op. cit., p.76.
94. Weinstein, op. cit., p.59.
95. Nishimura, op. cit., p.76 and Kōsaka, op. cit., p.107.
96. This was revealed by Yoshida in an NHK television interview on 29 August 1965. See Weinstein, op. cit., p.61.
97. Kōsaka, op. cit., p.107.
98. Nishimura, op. cit., p.76.
99. Ibid., p.76.
100. *Bōei Nenkan*, Boei Nenkan Kankō Kai, 1955, p.20.
101. Nishimura, op. cit., p.76.
102. Yoshida, op. cit., p.267.
103. Nishimura, op. cit., p.76. See also Nishimura's testimony before the Committee on the Constitution in *Kenpō Chōsa Kai*, op. cit., p.15.
104. The Vandenberg Resolution had been adopted as the basis for American participation

in NATO.
105. Kōsaka, op. cit., p.107.
106. Yoshida, op. cit., p.267.
107. Discussion with Mrs Asō Kazuko, 28 April 1975.
108. Yoshida, op. cit., p.263.
109. Townsend Hoopes, op. cit., p.111.
110. Discussion with Mrs Asō Kazuko, 28 April 1975
111. Townsend Hoopes, op. cit., p.112.
112. Ibid.
113. Ibid.
114. Tagawa Seiichi, *Matsumura Kenzō To Chūgoku*, Yomiuri Shimbun Sha, 1972, passim. Tagawa Seiichi was, for many years, Matsumara's private secretary. For Kitamura's position see Kitamura Tokutarō, 'Tankoku Kōwa To Yatō No Shuchō', *Sekai*, October 1950, p.140ff; 'Atarshii Jitai Ni Taisho Shite', *Sekai*, April 1952, p.196ff; 'Bimbō Kara No Kaihō', *Sekai*, October 1952, p.116ff; 'Seiji No Yoru', *Chūō Kōron*, July 1952.
115. Schaller, op. cit., p.179.
116. Yanaga Chitoshi, *Big Business in Japanese Politics*, Yale University Press, New Haven, Conn., 1968, Chapter 9.
117. 'Sensō To Heiwa Ni Kansuru Nihon No Kagakusha No Seimei', *Sekai*, March, 1949.
118. 'Kōwa Mondai Ni Tsuite No Seimei', *Sekai*, March 1950.
119. 'Mitabi Heiwa Ni Tsuite', *Sekai*, December 1950.
120 For a comprehensive discussion see Terasawa Hajime, 'Anzen Hoshō Ni Kansuru Zasshi Ronchō', *Kokusai Hō Gaikō Zasshi*, January 1951.
121. Unpublished poll, courtesy of the *Yomiuru Shimbun*.
122. Courtesy of the *Yomiuru Shimbun*.
123. *Mainichi Shimbun*, 21 November 1949.
124. *Mainichi Shimbun*, 3 September 1950.

Chapter III

1. Lewe Van Aduard, *Japan from Surrender to Peace*, Martinus Nijhoff, 1953, Appendix i.
2. Roger Buckley, 'Defeat, occupation and reconciliation: Anglo-Japanese relations, 1945–52', in Chihiro Hosoya (ed.), *Japan and Postwar Diplomacy in the Asian Pacific Region*, International University of Japan, 1984, p. 145.
3. James E. Auer, *The Postwar Rearmament of Japanese Maritime Forces, 1945–71*, Praeger, New York, 1973, p. 40.
4. Hata Ikuhiko, *Shi Roku: Nihon Saigunbi*, Bungei Shunjū, 1976, p. 174.
5. Auer, op. cit., p. 40.
6. Self Defence Forces Law, Article 76; Defence Agency Establishment Law, Article 25.
7. *Kampō* (Dai Jūkyū Kai Kokkai, Sangiin Kaigiroku, Dai Gojūshichi Go, 2 June 1954), p. 35ff.
8. This section closely follows the account given in D.C.S. Sissons, 'The pacifist clause in the Japanese Constitution', *International Affairs*, Volume 37, no. 1, January 1961.
9. See Theodore McNelly, 'The Japanese Constitution, Child of the Cold War', *Political Science Quarterly*, no. 2, June 1959, p. 179ff.
10. *Military Situation in the Far East: Hearings Before the Committee on Armed Services and the Committee on Foreign Relations*, United States Senate, 82nd Congress, 1st Session; Part I,

p.223. See Sissons, op. cit., p.46.

11. Supreme Commander for the Allied Powers, *Political Reorientation of Japan*, Government Section (Washington, US Government Printing Office), pp.98–102. See Sissons, op. cit., p.45.

12. Douglas MacArthur, *Reminiscences*, McGraw-Hill, New York, 1964, p.304.

13. See T. Miyazawa, *Nihon Kokukenpō Kommentaru*, Tōkyō, 1955, Volume 2, p.60ff, as quoted in Sissons, op. cit., p.46.

14. Auer, op. cit., p.47.

15. Sissons, op. cit., p.47.

16. Ibid., p.48.

17. Arisue Seizō, *Arisue Kikan Cho No Shuki*, Fūyō Shobō, 1976, Volume II, p.140ff.

18. Ibid., p.257ff.

19. John Powell, 'Japanese germ war tests: US cover-up', *The National Times*, 1–7 November, 1981.

20. Arisue, op. cit., Volume II, pp.205–7.

21. Ibid.

22. Hironaka Toshio, *Sengo Nihon No Keisatsu*, Iwanami Shoten, 1970, passim; Ōno Tatsuzō, *Nihon No Seiji Keisatsu*, Shin Nihon Shuppan Sha, 1974, chapters IV and V.

23. Hata, op. cit., p.156.

24. Ibid., p. 157.

25. Tsuji Masanobu, *Senkō Sanzen Ri*, Kokusha Kankō Kai, 1958.

26. Auer, op. cit., p.70. Hata, op. cit., p.175.

27. Auer, op. cit., pp.49–52.

28. Ibid., p.53ff.

29. Supreme Commander for the Allied Powers, op. cit., p.305.

30. Auer, op. cit., pp.51, 55.

31. Supreme Commander for the Allied Powers, op. cit., p.305–6, 1090–4.

32. Ibid., p.1092.

33. Talk with Mrs Asō Kazuko, 28 April 1975.

34. Arisue, op. cit., p.258.

35. United States Department of State, *Foreign Relations of the United States*, 1948, pp.857–62.

36. Howard Schonberger, 'The Japan Lobby in American diplomacy, 1947–1952', *Pacific Historical Review*, Volume XLVI, no. 3, August 1977.

37. Michael Schaller, *The American Occupation of Japan: The Origins of the Cold War in Asia*, Oxford University Press, New York, 1985, p.170.

38. Masuhara Keikichi, 'Jieitai No Enkaku To Nihon No Anzen', in Nihon Kokusai Mondai Kenkyūjo, Kajima Kenkyūjo (Ed.), *Nihon No Anzen Hoshō*, Kajima Kenkyūjo Shuppan Kai, 1964, p.405.

39. For the same reason MacArthur discounted the possibility of Soviet or Chinese intervention in Korea. See his interview with Bob Considine in *The New York Times*, 9 April 1964. See also William Manchester, *American Caesar*, Dell Books, New York, 1979, pp. 693–702.

40. For the phantom Sakhalin prisoner armies, see Hata, op. cit., p.170.

41. W. Douglas Reeve, *The Republic of Korea*, Oxford University Press, 1963, p.32, and D.F. Flemming, *The Cold War and its Origins, 1917–1960*, Allen & Unwin, London, 1961, p.592.

42. Yoshida Shigeru, *The Yoshida Memoirs*, Heinemann, London, 1961, p.180.

43. Hata, op. cit., p.142.

44. Ibid., p.142–3.
45. Ibid., p.152.
46. Ibid., p.140.
47. Masuhara, op. cit., p.408.
48. Ibid. p.407.
49. Ibid., pp.408–9. See also *Asahi Shimbun*, 19 October 1951.
50. *Bōei Nenkan*, Bōei Nenkan Kankō Kai, 1955, p.11.
51. Hata, op. cit., pp.165–6.
52. Masuhara, op. cit., pp.409–10.
53. Hata, op. cit., p.173.
54. Ibid., pp.165–9.
55. Masuhara, op.cit., pp.410–11.
56. Hata, op. cit., pp.170–1. See also *Asahi Shimbun*, 21 March 1951 and *Bōei Nenkan*, 1955, p.35.
57. Hata, op. cit., p.171–3.
58. *Asahi Shimbun*, 9 August 1951.
59. Auer, op. cit., pp.73–6.
60. Ridgeway began requesting Yoshida to strengthen the Police Reserve as early as June 1951. See *Asahi Shimbun*, 4 July 1951.
61. For details, see Auer, op. cit., pp.77–89.
62. *Bōei Nenkan*, 1955, p.54. *Asahi Shimbun*, 1 February 1952.
63. *Bōei Nenkan*, 1955, pp.50–4.
64. Ibid., p.56.
65. Ibid., pp.54–6.
66. Ibid., pp.57–9.
67. Ibid., p.57.
68. *Yomiuri Shimbun*, 15 August 1950.
69. See *Bōei Nenkan*, 1955, p.45. *Asahi Shimbun*, 2 October 1952.
70. *Asahi Shimbun*, 3 October 1952. The right-wing Socialists increased their representation from thirty to sixty-seven seats, the left-wing Socialists from sixteen to fifty-four seats. Communist representation dropped from twenty-two to zero seats.
71. *Asahi Shimbun*, 14 November 1952.
72. *Asahi Shimbun*, 20 November 1952.
73. *Asahi Shimbun*, 23 November 1952.
74. Yoshida, op. cit., p. 188.
75. *Asahi Shimbun*, 24 April 1953.
76. *Asahi Shimbun*, 28 May 1953.
77. *Asahi Shimbun*, 26 June 1953. *Bōei Nenkan*, 1955, pp.63–4.
78. Ibid., p.65.
79. *Asahi Shimbun*, 14 July 1953.
80. *Asahi Shimbun*, 17 July 1953.
81. *Asahi Shimbun*, 18 July 1953.
82. *Asahi Shimbun*, 20 April 1953.
83. *Asahi Shimbun*, 27 and 28 September 1953.
84. *Asahi Shimbun*, 27 September 1953.
85. *Bōei Nenkan*, 1955, p.89. *Asahi Shimbun*, 11 and 14 November 1953.
86. For Matsumura Kenzō's views, see *Mainichi Shimbun*, 3 December 1964.
87. *Asahi Shimbun*, 8 February, 21 March, 1 April, 5–6 June 1952, 16 September 1953.

88. This discussion is based on analysis of the successive texts of draft laws and accompanying commentaries, as reported in the *Asahi Shimbun*, 23 November, 14, 15, 16, 26, 31 December 1953 and 14, 20, 28 January, 2 February, 6, 7, 9 March 1954.

Chapter IV

1. United States Department of Defense, *United States' Vietnam Relations, 1945–67*, US Government Printing Office, Washington, DC, V.B. 2, The Truman Administration, 1945–52, Book 2 (1950–52), pp. 434–5.
2. A State Department memorandum of May 1949 described Indonesia as the 'southern anchor' of United States' regional policies, the 'base from which a beginning could be made in rolling back the communist tide in Asia'. Michael Schaller, *The American Occupation of Japan*, Oxford University Press, New York, 1985, p. 156.
3. 'United States objectives and courses of action with respect to Southeast Asia', The New York Times, *The Pentagon Papers*, Bantam Books, 1971, pp.27–32.
4. Carl Oglesby and Richard Shaull, *Containment and Change*, Macmillan, New York, 1967, p.128.
5. *The New York Times*, 14 April 1956.
6. Arisawa Hiromi, *Shōwa Keizai Shi*, Nihon Keizai Shimbun Sha, 1977, pp.326–9. Keizai Kikaku Chō (ed.), *Shiryō: Keizai Hakusho Nijūgonen*, Nihon Keizai Shimbun, 1974, pp.53–8.
7. Cited in Schaller, op. cit., p.182.
8. Terao Gorō *et al.*, 'Nikkan Kaidan', in Ajia-Afurika Kōza, *Nihon To Chōsen*, Keiso Shobō, 1970, pp.61–2.
9. *The New York Times*, 5 September 1951.
10. J.W. Dower, *Empire and Aftermath: Yoshida Shigeru and the Japanese Experience, 1878–1954*, Harvard University Press, Cambridge, Mass., 1979, pp.388–9.
11. Discussion with Kitazawa Naokichi (Prime Minister Yoshida's former private secretary), 2 April 1975.
12. *Asahi Shimbun*, 15, 21 October 1953.
13. Arisawa, op. cit., pp.356–60.
14. Yūichirō Hama, 'Japan's iron-steel industry and Australian iron ore', in Kiyoshi Kojima (ed.), *Australia, Japan and the Resource Goods Trade*, Japanese-Australian Project Reports no. 2, Tōkyō, June 1974, p.83.
15. Arisawa, op. cit., p.359.
16. Peter R. Odell, *Oil and World Power*, Pelican, Harmondsworth, 1975, p.123ff. Miyajima Nobuo, *Sekiyū Sensō To Nihon Keizai*, Sanichi Shobō, 1974, p.69ff.
17. Odell, op. cit., p.127.
18. Miyajima, op. cit., p.77.
19. Ibid., p.78.
20. Hata Ikuhiko, *Shi Roku: Nihon Saigunbi*, Bungei Shunjū, 1976, p.197.
21. Miyazawa Kiichi, 'Amerika No Tai-Nichi Bōei Yōsei', *Sekai*, July 1957, p.49.
22. *Asahi Shimbun*, 23 November 1952.
23. *Asahi Shimbun*, 24 November 1952.
24. *Asahi Shimbun*, 7 September 1953.
25. *Bōei Nenkan*, 1955, p.61. *Asahi Shimbun*, 6 April 1953.
26. *Asahi Shimbun*, 4 May 1953.

27. *The New York Times*, 16 May 1953.
28. Miyazawa, op. cit., p.49.
29. *Asahi Shimbun*, 9 May 1953.
30. Uemura Kōgorō, 'MSA Kyohi Wa Keizai No Hametsu', *Ekonomisuto*, 11 July 1953. Yanaga Chitoshi, *Big Business in Japanese Politics*, Yale University Press, New Haven, Conn., 1968, p.254ff.
31. *Bōei Nenkan*, 1955, p.62.
32. *Asahi Shimbun*, 26 May 1953.
33. *Asahi Shimbun*, 29 May 1953.
34. *Asahi Shimbun*, 30–1 May 1953.
35. *Bōei Nenkan*, 1955, p.63.
36. *Asahi Shimbun*, 26 June 1953. *Bōei Nenkan*, 1955, p.64.
37. *Asahi Shimbun*, 12 June 1953.
38. *Asahi Shimbun*, 17 June 1953.
39. *Bōei Nenkan*, 1955, p.65.
40. *Bōei Nenkan*, 1955, p.65ff. Miyazawa op. cit., p.49.
41. Public Law 165, Chapter 47a, *United States Statutes at Large*, 1951, Volume 65, p.373ff.
42. *Asahi Shimbun*, 11 August 1953.
43. Ibid. *The New York Times*, 11 August 1953.
44. *Bōei Nenkan*, 1955, p.67ff.
45. *The New York Times*, 4 and 5 September 1953. *Bōei Nenkan*, 1955, pp.72–3 and *Asahi Shimbun*, 4 September 1953.
46. Matsumoto Saburō, 'Hoshu Renkei To MSA', *Chūō Kōron*, November 1953. *Asahi Shimbun*, 25 September 1953.
47. Miyazawa Kiichi, 'Ampō Jōyaku Teiketsu No Ikisatsu', *Chūō Kōron*, May 1957, p.72.
48. *Asahi Shimbun*, 6 October 1953.
49. *Asahi Shimbun*, 10 October 1953.
50. *Asahi Shimbun*, 13, 16, 19, 23, 30 October 1953.
51. *Asahi Shimbun*, 16 October 1953.
52. *Asahi Shimbun*, 17 October 1953.
53. *Asahi Shimbun*, 20 October 1953.
54. *Asahi Shimbun*, 22 October 1953.
55. *Asahi Shimbun*, 1 November 1953.
56. *Asahi Shimbun*, 23 October 1953.
57. Dwight D. Eisenhower, *Mandate for Change, 1953–6*, Heinemann, London, 1963, p.126ff. See also P. M. S. Blackett, *Studies of War, Nuclear and Conventional*, Oliver & Boyd, 1962, pp.25–6.
58. The shortcomings of air power became particularly evident after entry of Chinese troops into the war in the winter of 1950, and later, after the Communists developed the technique of tunnelling artillery positions and defensive works deep under hillsides.
59. *Asahi Shimbun*, 23 October 1953.
60. For details see Terasawa Hajime, 'Saigunbi Sansei Ron, Hantai Ron No Tenbō', *Chūō Kōron*, November 1952.
61. Ōno Shinzō, as quoted by Terasawa, op. cit., p.24.
62. Nakada Minoru *et al.*, *Nihon No Bōei To Keizai*, Asahi Shimbun Anzen Hoshō Mondai Chōsa Kai, Asahi Shimbun Sha, 1969, p.172ff.
63. Dōba Hajime, *Nihon No Jieiryoku, Jieitai No Uchimaku*, Yomiuri Shimbun Sha, 1963,

pp.96–7.

64. I.I. Morris, *Nationalism and the Right Wing in Japan: A Study of Postwar Trends*, Oxford University Press, London, 1960, p.445.

65. Nabeyama Sadachika, 'Buryokuteki Jiei No Soshiki O', *Sekai Shūhō*, no. 154, 1950, p.28ff. Dōba, op. cit., pp.96–7.

66. Watanabe Tetsuzō, *Ware-ware Saigunbi O Shuchōsu*, Watanabe Keizai Kenkyūjo, February 1951.

67. Nomura Kichisaburō, 'Kokudo Hozen No Tame', *Keizai Ōrai*, 2 September 1950, and Dōba, op. cit., pp.96–7.

68. Dōba, op. cit., pp.97–8.

69. Tsuji Masanobu, *Jiei Chūritsu*, Tōa Shobō, 1952, p.202ff.

70. For other examples see Lieutenant-General Andō Kisaburō (former Minister of Home Affairs in the Tōjō Cabinet), 'Nihon Saigunbi O Kentō Suru', *Jitsugyō Tenbō*, February 1951; Itō Masanobu, 'Nihon Kokubō No Saizen Hōshiki', *Bungei Shunjū*, October 1950; 'Aete Saigunbi O Teian Suru', *Bungei Shunjū*, October 1951; Ōno Shinzō, 'Nihon No Saibusō Ron, *Nihon Shūhō*, 1 January 1951; 'Yobitai De Wa Bōei Dekinai – Jiei Soshiki Ron', *Nihon Shūhō*, 22 January 1951; 'Saigunbi O Dō Suru Ka', *Gekkan Yomiuru* (Kiki No Nihon), February 1951; Rear Admiral Takagai Sōkichi (sometime head of the Research Section, Imperial Japanese Naval Ministry), 'Nihon Jiei No Gunbi To Senryaku', *Nihon Hyōron*, February 1951; 'Nihon Wa Dō Gunbi Sareru Ka', *Jitsugyō No Nihon*, 1 March 1951; 'Nihon Ga Kokubōgun O Motsu To Shitara', *Mainichi Jōhō*, April 1951.

71. See Masuhara Keikichi, 'Jieitai No Enkaku To Nihon No Anzen', *Nihon No Anzen Hoshō*, Nihon Kokusai Mondai Kenkyūjo, Kajima Kenkyūjo Shuppan Kai, 1964, pp.416–17.

72. Masuhara, op. cit., p.419; *Asahi Shimbun*, 19 October 1950.

73. Sakanaka Tomohisa *et al.*, *Nihon No Jiei Ryoku*, Asahi Shimbun Sha, 1967, p.88, and Dōba, op. cit., p.91.

74. Sakanaka *et al.*, op. cit., p.88. Dōba, op. cit., pp.92–3.For Yoshida's attitude to the scale of planning, see Masuhara, op. cit., p.420. For the Finance Ministry's views, see *Asahi Shimbun*, 22 September and 11 November 1953.

75. *Asahi Shimbun*, 2, 7 September, 7 October, 11, 24, 27 November, 29 December 1953.

76. *Asahi Shimbun*, 22 and 29 December 1953.

77. *Asahi Shimbun*, 1 February, 3 March 1954. *Bōei Nenkan*, 1955, p.85.

78. Eisenhower, op. cit., p.346.

79. Ibid., p.347.

80. Mutual Defence Assistance Agreement between the United States of America and Japan, *Department of State Bulletin*, Vol. XXX, no. 771, 5 April 1954, p.520ff.

81. *Asahi Shimbun*, 9 March 1954.

82. Statement by Ambassador Allison, Press Release 119, 8 March, *Department of State Bulletin*, Vol. XXX no. 771, 5 April 1954, p.519.

83. Ibid., p.521.

84. Ibid., p.523.

85. Agreement between Japan and the United States of America Regarding the Guarantee of Investments, ibid., p.524.

86. Yanaga, op. cit., p.262.

87. Discussion with Kaihara Osamu, former Secretary-General of the National Defence Council, 24 March 1975.

88. US Department of State, 'Joint Statement of August 31, 1955', *Department of State Bulletin*, Vol. XXXIII, no. 846, 12 September 1955, pp.419–20. *Asahi Shimbun*, 3 September 1955.
89. *Asahi Shimbun*, 1 September 1955 (evening edition).
90. *The New York Times*, 1 September 1955.
91. *Asahi Shimbun*, 14, 15 September 1955.
92. *Asahi Shimbun*, 2, 3 September 1955; *Mainichi Shimbun*, 3 September 1955; *Yomiuri Shimbun*, 9 September 1955.
93. *Asahi Shimbun*, 15 September 1955; *Bōei Nenkan*, 1956, p.146.
94. For of the Radford 'strategy', see Townsend Hoopes, *The Devil and John Foster Dulles*, André Deutsch, London, 1974, pp.191–201; Eisenhower, op. cit., p.451ff. Kishida Junnosuke, *Amerika No Kyokutō Senryaku*, Asahi Shimbun Sha, 1967, p.36ff.
95. Eisenhower, op. cit., p.454; Hoopes, op. cit., p.194.
96. Eisenhower, op. cit., p.454.
97. *Bōei Nenkan*, 1957, p.192ff; 1958, p.168ff; 1959, p.177ff. *Jieitai*, Asahi Shimbun Sha, 1968, p.266.
98. On 27 June 1955 Foreign Minister Shigemitsu Mamoru told the House of Representatives Cabinet Committee that he had been assured by the American Ambassador first, that United States forces in Japan were not armed with nuclear weapons, second, that such weapons would not be brought in without Japan's consent. *Bōei Nenkan*, 1956, p.163. For subsequent developments, see *Bōei Nenkan*, 1958, p.173 and *Bōei Nenkan*, 1960, p.132.
99. *Mainichi Shimbun*, 17 May 1981.
100. *Bōei Nenkan*, 1957, p.193.
101. See Sakanaka Tomohisa, *Amerika Senryakuka No Okinawa*, Asahi Shimbun Sha, 1967, p.38ff.
102. Dōba, op. cit., p.122ff.
103. Ibid., p.103ff.
104. James E. Auer, *The Postwar Rearmament of the Japanese Maritime Forces, 1945–71*, Praeger, New York, 1973, pp.95–6.
105. Genda Minoru, 'Kokubō-Kyokuchi Sen, Zenmen Sen To Nihon No Tachiba', in *Nihon No Anzen Hoshō*, Nihon Kokusai Mondai Kenkyūjo, Kajima Kenkyūjo Shuppan Kai, 1964, p.506.
106. See Sakanaka, op. cit., p.61ff and *Jieitai*, op. cit., p.40ff.
107. *Yomiuru Shimbun*, 22 March 1968.
108. *Bōei Nenkan*, 1956, p.155ff; 1957, p.187ff; 1959, p.164ff.

Chapter V

1. For Conservative Party factionalism see Shinobu Seisaburō, *Ampo Tōsō Shi*, Sekai Shoin, 1968; Haruhiro Fukui, *Party in Power: The Japanese Liberal-Democrats and Policy-Making*, Australian National University Press, Canberra, 1970; J.A.A. Stockwin, *Japan: Divided Politics in a Growth Economy* (second edition), Weidenfeld & Nicolson, London, 1982 and Nathaniel B. Thayer, *How the Conservatives Rule Japan*, Princeton University Press, Princeton, NJ, 1969.
2. *Ekonomisuto*, 7 July 1959. See also Fujiyama Aiichirō, *Seiji Waga Michi*, Asahi Shimbun Sha, 1976, p.11. and Alec Dubro & David E. Kaplan, *Yakuza*, Futura Books, London, 1987, passim.

3. For Kishi's background, see Kishi Nobusuke, Yatsugi Kazuo and Itō Takashi, *Kishi Nobusuke No Kaisō*, Bungei Shunjū, 1981; Hayashi Fusao, *Yoshida Shigeru To Senryō Kenpō*, Rōman, 1974, pp.265–301; Iwakawa Takashi, *Kyōkai: Kishi Nobusuke Kenkyū*, Daiyamondo Sha, 1978; Shinobu, op. cit., pp.16–18, p.29ff; Tajiri Ikuzō, *Kishi Nobusuke*, Gakuyō Shobō, 1979; Yoshimoto Shigeyoshi, *Kishi Nobusuke Den*, Tōyō Shokan, 1957 and Dan Kurzman, *Kishi and Japan: The Search for the Sun*, Ivan Obolensky, New York, 1960.

4. Yoshimoto, op. cit., pp.31–2.

5. Ibid., p.53.

6. Ibid., p.66.

7. Ibid., p.67.

8. Discussion with Kishi Nobusuke, 8 April 1975.

9. Yoshimoto, op. cit., pp.117–18.

10. Discussion with Kishi Nobusuke, 8 April 1975.

11. The importance of the North American market to the Japanese steel industry had grown rapidly during the 1950s. See Kawasaki Tsutomu, *Nihon Tekkōgyō*, Tekkō Shimbun Sha, 1982, p.413.

12. Even so, speaking to the *Tōkyō Shimbun* about his fear of the Soviet Union on 19 May 1968, Kishi declared: 'If Communist China were to change in the future, I would personally feel much closer to her than to the Soviet Union.'

13. Yoshimito, op. cit., pp.158–60.

14. Discussion with Kishi Nobusuke, 8 April 1975.

15. Chung Kyungmo, 'Aru Minzokushugisha No Shōgai', *Sekai*, December 1975.

16. John Roberts, 'The Rebirth of Japan's Zaibatsu', *Insight*, July 1978, passim.

17. In an interview with the present writer on 8 April 1975 Kishi remarked that while the security of the Western Pacific was currently guaranteed by the United States, it was not permissible to imagine that this system would continue forever. Formation of an independent military bloc in the Western Pacific would not be possible in the 'near future'. Kishi therefore recommended that the non-Communist nations of the region encourage the United States to remain in Asia, strengthen their economic ties and develop a regional security policy based on the UN.

18. Talk with Kishi Nobusuke, 8 April 1975.

19. *Nihon Keizai Shimbun*, 30 September 1973.

20. Satō Yūichi, *Fukuda Takeo, Seiji Rosen To Sono Jinmyaku*, Jūtaku Shinpōsha, 1974, pp.84–8.

21. Discussion with Fujiyama, 4 February 1977.

22. Fujiyama, op. cit., p.166.

23. Ibid., p.167.

24. Ibid., p.169.

25. Ibid., p.36.

26. Ibid., p.37.

27. Ibid., pp.2–12.

28. Ibid., pp.44–6.

29. Ibid., p.34.

30. Ibid., pp.64–8.

31. Ibid., p.170.

32. Ibid.

33. Ibid., pp.14–15.

34. Ibid., p.13.
35. Ibid., pp.64–8.
36. For Ishii's recollections, see Ishii Mitsujirō, *Kaisō Hachijū Hachi Nen*, Karuchā Shuppan Sha, 1975.
37. Ishii, op. cit., pp.334–5.
38. Ibid., pp.384–5; Fujiyama, op. cit., pp.44–6.
39. Ishii, op. cit., p.403.
40. Ibid., p.423.
41. For Ikeda see Haji Fumio, *Ningen Ikeda Hayato*, Kodan Sha, 1967 and Hayashi Fusao, *Ikeda Hayato*, Sankei Shimbun Sha, 1968.
42. *Ekonomisuto*, 10 January 1959, 26 May 1959 and *Nihon Keizai Shimbun*, 30 July 1960.
43. Hayashi, op. cit., p.71.
44. *Asahi Shimbun*, 22 April 1971.
45. Discussion with former Prime Minister Satō Eisaku, 16 May 1975.
46. Hayashi, op. cit., p.329.
47. Kaburagi Seiichi, *Nihon No Seijika Hyaku Sen*, Akita Shoten, 1972.See also Dubro & Kaplan, op. cit., passim.
48. Kōno Ichirō, *Kōno Ichirō Jiden*, Tokuma Shoten, 1965.
49. Nakasone was a much more orthodox Conservative than his leader. He had been a member of the National Territory Defence Research Association (Kokudo Bōei Kenkyū Kai), established in 1950 by the former Communist Ōyama Iwao to promote rearmament and popular defence consciousness and to defeat left-wing strategy in Japan. This organization had connections with ultra-nationalist groups such as the Japan Sound Youth Association (Nihon Kensei Kai). See I.I. Morris, *Nationalism and the Right Wing in Japan: A Study of Postwar Trends*, Oxford University Press, London, 1960 p.198, note 3. Nakasone, like Kishi and Ishii, was also a member of the Asian Peoples' Anti-Communist League. (*Tōkyō Shimbun*, 24 September 1962, evening edition.)
50. *Ekonomisuto*, 10 January 1959. See also Dubrow & Kaplan, op. cit., passim.
51. Kōno Ichirō, *Nihon No Shōrai*, Kobun Sha, 1965, p.26ff.
52. *Ekonomisuto*, 10 January 1959.
53. For Miki's background, see Miki Yōnosuke, *Miki Takeo*, Sankei Drama Books, 1975.
54. Tagawa Seiichi, *Matsumura Kenzō To Chūgoku*, Yomiuri Shimbun Sha, 1972.
55. Ibid., pp.89–90.
56. Ibid., p.134.
57. Ibid., pp.76–7, 82–3.
58. *Ekonomisuto*, 10 January 1959.
59. For Ishibashi, see Chō Yukio (ed.), *Ishibashi Tanzan, Hito To Shisō*, Tōyō Keizai Shinpō Sha, 1974. See also Ishibashi Tanzan Zenshū Hensō Iinkai (Ed.), *Ishibashi Tanzan Zenshū*, Tōyō Keizai Shinpō Sha, 15 volumes, 1970–2.
60 Ishikawa Tadao, Nakajima Mineo and Ikei Yū (eds), *Sengō Shiryō: Nitchū Kankei*, Nihon Hyōron Sha, 1970, p.130.

Chapter VI

1. For the 1960 crisis see Fujii Shōichi and Ōe Shinobu, *Sengō Nihon No Rekishi*, Aoki Shoten, 1974, Volume II, v; Rekishigaku Kenkyū Kai (ed.), *Sengō Nihon Shi*, Volume IV, Aoki Shoten, 1975; Shinobu Seisaburō, *Ampo Tōsō Shi*, Sekai Shōin, 1968, and, in English,

George R. Packard, *Protest in Tokyo: The Security Treaty Crisis of 1960*, Princeton University Press, Princeton, NJ, 1966.

2. These included Miki, Matsumura and eleven members of their faction; Ishibashi Tanzan and five followers; Kōno Ichirō and four supporters; one member of the Ishii faction and a single member of the Ōno faction. Eleven other members, including former Prime Minister Yoshida, alleged 'sickness' or 'travel commitments' as their reason for not putting in an appearance.

3. Fujiyama Aiichirō, *Seiji Waga Michi*, Asahi Shimbun Sha, 1976, pp.106–10.

4. See Itō Masami, 'Gikaishugi No Hametsu O Fusegu Tame Ni', *Jiyū*, July 1960; Shinohara Hajime, 'Gikaishugi No Kokufuku', *Jiyū*, July 1960; Yanaihara Tadao, 'Minshūshugi O Mamoru Yūki O', *Shūkan Asahi*, 3 July 1960 and 'Minshūshugi No Genri Wa Kō Shite Yaburareta', *Gekkan Shakai Tō*, July 1960.

5. See Sugita Ichiji (then Chief of the Ground Staff), *Wasurerarete Iru Anzen Hoshō*, Jiji Tsūshin Sha, 1967, p.90ff.

6. Akagi Munenori, *Ima Dakara Iu*, Bunka Sōgō Shuppan, quoted in Kishi Nobusuke, Yatsugi Kazuo, Itō Takashi, 'Ampo Jōyaku Kaitei To Hantai Undō', *Chūō Kōron*, May 1980, p.233.

7. Fujiyama, op. cit., p.106.

8. Miyamoto's achievement is recognized even by his political opponents. See Kishi, Yatsugi, Itō, op. cit., p.240.

9. Ibid., p.240.

10. Packard, op. cit., p.319ff. See also Kinoshita Hanji, *Nihon Uyoku No Kenkyū*, Gendai Hyōron Sha, 1977, pp.225–341.

11. The most authoritative works on the legal aspects of the 1960 treaty remain Kamimura Shinichi, *Sōgo Kyōryoku Anzen Hoshō Jōyaku No Kaisetsu*, Jiji Tsūshin Sha, 1965, and Kurahara Koreaki, *Nichi-Bei Ampo Jōyaku No Shoten*, Asahi Shimbun Sha, 1967.

12. Treaty of Mutual Co-operation and Security between the United States of America and Japan (signed at Washington, 19 January 1960; entered into force, 23 June 1960), Article VI.

13. Ibid., Article X.

14. *Agreed Minute to the Treaty of Mutual Co-operation and Security* (dated at Washington, 19 January 1960).

15. *Exchange of Notes* (dated at Washington, 19 January 1960).

16. For a detailed discussion, see Kamimura, op. cit., p.75ff.

17. *Asahi Shimbun*, 8 May 1960. See also *Bōei Nenkan*, 1961, p.127.

18. See the record of an interview with former Prime Minister Kishi in the *Tōkyō Shimbun*, 19 May 1968. As far as the present writer is aware no such consultations have been held between this date and the time of publication of the present work.

19. *Mainichi Shimbun*, 17 May 1981.

20. Fujiyama, op. cit., p.85.

21. On 19 April 1960 the Defence Agency director-general Akagi Munenori made it clear to the House of Representatives Security Treaty Special Committee that military activity by the United States Fifth Air Force stationed in Okinawa or South Korea, even if undertaken on the orders of Fifth Air Force Headquarters in Tōkyō, could not be a subject for prior consultations (*Asahi Shimbun*, 20 April 1960). It was thus possible to imagine a situation where units of the Fifth Air Force stationed, say, in Korea, became involved in a local conflict which rapidly escalated, automatically drawing in the Fifth Air Force in Japan and,

inevitably, the Japanese Air Self Defence Forces as well.

22. Nishi Haruhiko, 'Nihon Gaikō O Ureru', *Chūō Kōron*, February 1960, p.99. Nishi added: 'Over the past year I have listened to people in various fields, including the Defence [Agency] authorities, and no one has denied this.' See also his remarks in 'Nihon Gaikō O Urete Futatabi', *Chūō Kōron*, April 1960, pp.39–40.

23. *Asahi Shimbun*, 15 April 1960 (evening edition). See also Watanabe Yōzō and Okakura Kōshirō (eds), *Nichi-Bei Ampo Jōyaku, Sono Kaisetsu To Shiryō*, Rōdō Junpō Sha, 1968, p.457. This is also the interpretation advanced by Kamimura Shinichi. (Kamimura, op. cit., p.78.)

24. *Asahi Shimbun*, 5 May 1960. See also Watanabe and Okakura, op. cit., p.464.

25. *Nihon Keizai Shimbun*, 17 March 1969 (evening edition).

26. Discussion with Kishi Nobusuke, 8 April 1975.

27. Discussion with Kishi Nobusuke, 8 April 1975. See also Fujiyama, op. cit., p.60.

28. Fujiyama, op. cit., p.59.

29. Discussion with Fujiyama Aiichirō, 4 February 1977.

30. Fujiyama, op. cit., pp.59–60.

31. Ibid., p.61.

32. Ibid., pp.61–2.

33. Ibid., p.68.

34. Nishimura Kumao, *Anzen Hoshō Jōyaku Ron*, Jiji Tsūshin Sha, 1960, p.123.

35. US Department of State, 'Joint Statement of 11 September 1958, issued to the Press after meeting of 11 September 1958, between Secretary of State Dulles and Foreign Minister Fujiyama', *Department of State Bulletin*, Volume XXXIX, 6 October 1958, pp.532–3.

36. Discussions with Kishi Nobusuke, 8 April 1975.

37. Fujiyama, op. cit., pp.81–2.

38. Discussion with Asaki Kōichirō, February 1977.

39. Fujiyama, op. cit., p.72.

40. Ibid., pp.82–3.

41. *Asahi Nenkan*, 1959, p.188ff.

42. *The Times*, 22 May and 31 May 1958.

43. *Asahi Shimbun*, 24 May 1958.

44. Kishi Nobusuke, Yatsugi Kazuo and Itō Takashi, 'Nichi-Bei Shin Jidai To Keishoku Hō Sawagi', *Chūō Kōron*, March 1980.

45. *Asahi Shimbun*, 24 June 1958. See also *Asahi Nenkan*, 1959, p.173ff.

46. *Asahi Shimbun*, 24 June 1958. See also *Asahi Nenkan*, 1959, p.201ff.

47. *Asahi Shimbun*, 5 September 1958.

48. *Asahi Shimbun*, 19 September 1958.

49. The chairman of the council at the time was the militantly anti-Communist Funada Naka, of the Ōno faction.

50. *Asahi Shimbun*, 2 September 1958.

51. *Asahi Shimbun*, 19 September 1958.

52. *Asahi Shimbun*, 25 September 1958.

53. Fujiyama, op. cit., pp.94–5. Discussion with Fujiyama, 4 February 1977.

54. *Tōkyō Shimbun*, 21 September 1958 (an account of an interview with Yoshida two days after his eightieth birthday).

55. Packard, op. cit., p.61.

56. For details of these Sino-Soviet talks and their outcome, see Nikita S. Khruschev, *Khruschev Remembers*, Penguin, Harmondsworth, 1977, Volume 1, pp.502–3.

57. Fujiyama, op. cit., p.94.

58. *Asahi Shimbun*, 3 October 1958.

59. *Asahi Shimbun*, 7 October 1958.

60. 'The introduction of the Police Law was such a sudden thing', Fujiyama recalls. 'I was not consulted about it in any way beforehand. There were quite a few other Cabinet Ministers who, like me, could claim to have known absolutely nothing about it.' Fujiyama, op. cit., pp.78–9.

61. Fujii and Oe, op. cit., pp.37–55; Rekishi Gaku Kenkyū Kai (ed.), *Sengō Nihon Shi*, Volume III, p.177ff; and Packard, op. cit., pp.52, 90, 101, 103, 126.

62 Fujiyama, op. cit., p.86.

63. Ibid., p.76.

64. See, for example, Nishimura, op. cit., p.122ff. While Nishimura was no longer head of the Foreign Ministry Treaties Bureau at the time of the negotiations he had access to official material in the preparation of his book.

65. Ibid., p.123 and *Yomiuri Shimbun*, 20 January 1959. The American request for a treaty covering the Western Pacific is also mentioned in *Asahi Shimbun*, 29 October 1958 and in the official *Bōei Nenkan*, 1961, p.161.

66. Fujiyama, op. cit., pp.82–3.

67. *Asahi Shimbun*, 23 October 1958.

68. Fujiyama, op. cit., pp.81–2.

69. See *Bōei Nenkan*, 1960, p.120; *Asahi Shimbun*, 25 November 1958.

70. *Asahi Shimbun*, 1 November 1958.

71. *Asahi Shimbun*, 3 December 1958.

72. *Asahi Shimbun*, 4 December 1958. Kōno clarified his views on 29 January 1959, during the course of a visit to the United States Embassy to discuss treaty revision with Ambassador MacArthur. See *Asahi Shimbun*, 29 January 1959.

73. *Asahi Shimbun*, 1 February 1959.

74. *Bōei Nenkan*, 1960, pp.132–5.

75. Fujiyama's first draft treaty, presented to Kishi, Akagi and Fukuda on 18 February, had definitely excluded Okinawa and the Bonins (*Asahi Shimbun*, 18 February 1959). For the text of the second, amended draft, see *Asahi Shimbun*, 7 April 1959.

76. *Asahi Shimbun*, 29 May 1959.

77. Dai Sanjūyon-Kai Kokkai, Shūgiin, Yōsan Iinkai, Giroku, Dai-Yongo, 8 February 1960, pp.10–13.

78. Dai Sanjūyon-Kai Kokkai, Shūgiin, Yōsan Iinkai, Giroku, Dai-Rokugo, 10 February 1960.

79. Dai Sanjūyon-Kai Kokkai, Shūgiin, Yōsan Iinkai, Giroku, Dai-Jūgo, 25 March 1960.

80. Fujiyama, op. cit., pp.84–5.

81. *Asahi Shimbun*, 28 July, 3, 13, 25 August, 6, 15 September 1959.

82. Fujiyama, op. cit., pp.82–3.

83. Ibid., pp.81–2. *Asahi Shimbun*, 13 February 1959.

84. *Asahi Shimbun*, 18 February 1959.

85. *Asahi Shimbun*, 20 February 1959.

86. *Asahi Shimbun*, 21 February 1959.

87. *Asahi Shimbun*, 4 April 1959.

88. *Asahi Shimbun*, 3 April 1959.
89. *Asahi Shimbun*, 4 April 1959.
90. *Asahi Shimbun*, 8 April 1959.
91. *Bōei Nenkan*, 1960, pp.121–2.
92. *Asahi Shimbun*, 8 September 1959.
93. *Asahi Shimbun*, 9 September 1959.
94. Fujiyama, op. cit., pp.95–6.
95. *Asahi Shimbun*, 8 September 1959.
96. *Asahi Shimbun*, 26 September 1959.
97. *Asahi Shimbun*, 8 October 1959.
98. *Asahi Shimbun*, 14 October 1959.
99. *Asahi Shimbun*, 22 October 1959.
100. *Asahi Shimbun*, 27 October 1959.
101. Shinobu, op. cit., p.495ff. See also Yanaga Chitoshi, *Big Business in Japanese Politics*, Yale University Press, New Haven, Conn., 1968, p.273ff, and Haruhiro Fukui, *Party in Power: The Japanese Liberal-Democrats and Policy-Making*, Australian National University Press, Canberra, 1970, p.163.
102. For the line taken by the anti-treaty camp, see Heiwa Mondai Danwa Kai, 'Ampo Kaitei Mondai Ni Tsuite No Seimei', *Sekai*, February 1960. Arguments by the pro-treaty forces can be found in *Anzen Hoshō Taisei No Kenkyū* (2 volumes), Jiji Tsūshin Sha, 1960 and in Tanaka Naokichi, *Shin Nichi-Bei Ampo Jōyaku No Kenkyū*, Yūshindo, 1969.
103. Hatada Shigeo, *Shin Ampo Taisei Ron*, Aoki Shoten, 1969, pp.49–54.
104. Ōhira Zengo, *Nihon No Anzen Hoshō To Kokusai Hō*, Yūshindo, 1960, p.156. Quoted in Packard, op. cit., p.341 (Packard's translation).
105. 'Yoshida Shigeru Ga Kataru Gaikō Hiwa', NHK Television interview, 29 August 1965.

Chapter VII

1. Charles de Gaulle, 'Conférence de presse tenue au Palais de l'Elysée', *Discours et Messages*, Plon, 1970, p.355.
2. For French foreign policy during this period see Charles de Gaulle, *Mémoires d'Espoir, Le Renouveau, 1958–62*, Plon, 1970; Charles Ailleret, *L'Aventure Atomique Française*, Paris, 1968; Guy de Carmoy, *Les Politiques Etrangères de la France, 1944–1966*, Paris, 1967; R. Massip, *De Gaulle et l'Europe, 1958–1969*, Paris, 1971 and Alexander Werth, *de Gaulle*, Penguin, Harmondsworth, 1969.
3. Yano Tsuneta Kinenkai (ed.), *Nihon Kokusei Zue, 1978*, Kokusei Sha, 1978, p.170.
4. 'Mission to South-East Asia, India and Pakistan', memorandum from Vice-President Lyndon B. Johnson to President Kennedy, 23 May 1961, *The Pentagon Papers* (*The New York Times* edition), Bantam Books, 1971, pp.127–30.
5. De Gaulle, *Mémoires d'Espoir, Le Renouveau*, pp.268–9.
6. *The Pentagon Papers*, op. cit., pp.150–3.
7. Roger Hilsman, *To Move a Nation*, Delta Books, 1967, pp.310–15.
8. 'Vietnam and South-East Asia', memorandum from General Maxwell D. Taylor, chairman of the Joint Chiefs of Staff, to Secretary of Defence McNamara, 22 January 1964. The Pentagon Papers, op. cit., pp.274–7.
9. Sakanaka Tomohisa, *Amerika Senryakuka No Okinawa*, Asahi Shimbun Sha, 1967, p.42.
10. For details see Kishida Junnosuke, *Amerika No Kyokutō Senryaku*, Asahi Shimbun Sha,

1967, especially parts V and VI.

11. For the Sino-Soviet conflict see Jean Baby, *La Grande Controverse Sino-Soviétique, 1956–66*, Editions Bernard Grasset, 1966; O.E. Clubb, *China and Russia: The 'Great Game'*, Columbia University Press, NY, 1971; Edward Crankshaw, *The New Cold War: Moscow vs Peking*, Freeport, New York, 1970; and John Gittings, *Survey of the Sino-Soviet Dispute*, Oxford University Press, 1968.

12. *Asahi Shimbun*, 19 July 1960. In later years Stanislav Levchenko, a KGB official who defected to the United States, was to identify Ishida Hirohide as a Soviet agent. The present writer, taking into consideration the international and domestic context of Levchenko's revelations, is inclined to discount these claims. For Levchenko's account, see Stanislav Levchenko, *KGB Today: the Hidden Hand*, Readers Digest, May 1983.

13. Fujii Shōichi and Ōe Shinobu, *Sengō Nihon No Rekishi*, Aoki Shoten, 1974, Volume 2, pp.184–8.

14. Fujiyama Aiichirō, *Seiji Waga Michi*, Asahi Shimbun Sha, 1976, p.130.

15. Fujii and Ōe, op. cit., pp.130–45; Isiah Frank and Ryōkichi Hironō (eds), *How the United States and Japan See Each Other's Economy*, Committee for Economic Development, New York, 1974, pp.2–94.

16. OECD, *National Accounts of OECD Countries, 1960–1970*, cited in Isiah and Hirono, op. cit., p.11.

17. Ibid., p.35.

18. Ibid., pp.52–7.

19. *Asahi Shimbun*, 8 December 1960.

20. *Asahi Shimbun*, 18 July 1961 (evening edition).

21. *Asahi Shimbun*, 13 December 1961; *Asahi Shimbun*, 25 February 1962 (evening edition).

22. *Asahi Shimbun*, 13 December 1961; *Yomiuri Shimbun*, 29, 30 April 1963.

23. Haruhiro Fukui, *Party in Power: The Japanese Liberal Democrats and Policy Making*, Australian National University Press, Canberra, 1970, p.111.

24. *Asahi Shimbun*, 3 January 1963. See also Kōno Ichirō, 'Nihon No Iiwake, Soren No Iiwake', *Bungei Shungū*, July 1962.

25. Kōno Ichirō, 'Nisso Kōryū Ni Tsuite Kokumin Ni Uttaeru', *Chūō Kōron*, July 1962, p.197.

26. The *Sankei Shimbun*, while condemning this act as 'foolish', recommended that the gangsters concerned be handled 'lightly'. *Sankei Shimbun*, 16 July 1963.

27. In February 1962, Satō's close associate Tanaka Kakuei, then chairman of the Party Policy Affairs Research Council, suggested to Robert Kennedy that the United States encourage constitutional revision and rearmament in Japan. The Minister for Justice, Yamanaka Sadanori (Kōno faction), was also present at the talks with Kennedy and hastened to assure the President's brother that 'Tanaka has only expressed a personal view, and it is not shared by us.' In the uproar that followed, Satō strongly defended Tanaka and made no attempt to dissociate himself from these views. See *Asahi Shimbun*, 7 February 1962 (evening addition); *Mainichi Shimbun*, 8 February 1962.

28. *Asahi Shimbun*, 11 November 1961 (evening edition).

29. *Asahi Shimbun*, 14 November 1962 (evening edition).

30. *Nihon Keizai Shimbun*, 11 February 1962 (evening edition). *Mainichi Shimbun*, 1 and 4 November 1962.

31. *Mainichi Shimbun*, 7 July 1962.

32. *Asahi Shimbun*, 14 July 1962 (evening edition).

33. Fujiyama, op. cit., p.132.
34. *Asahi Shimbun*, 12, 15, 18 July 1962; 15, 16 July 1962 (evening editions).
35. *Asahi Shimbun*, 20 July 1960.
36. Gene T. Hsiao, 'Communist China's trade treaties and agreements (1949–64)', *Vanderbilt Law Review*, Volume XXI, no. 5, October 1968, p. 640; Tagawa Seiichi, *Nitchū Kōshō Hiroku*, Mainichi Shimbun Sha, 1973, pp.32–3.
37. Takasaki Tatsunosuke, 'Shu On-rai To Kaidan Shite', *Chūō Kōron*, February 1961
38. Hilsman, op. cit., pp.307–8.
39. *Nihon Keizai Shimbun*, 16 November 1962.
40. *Yomiuri Shimbun*, 19 May 1962.
41. *Nihon Keizai Shimbun*, 8 July 1962 (evening edition).
42. Dōba Hajime, *Nihon No Gunji Ryoku*, Yomiuri Shimbun Sha, 1963, p.66ff.
43. *Asahi Shimbun*, 1 August 1962, *Tōkyō Shimbun*, 1 August 1962 (evening edition).
44. *Nihon Keizai Shimbun*, 29 January 1963.
45. *Jimintō Gaikō Chōsa Kai Chūgoku Shoiinkai Kaiinchō Matsumoto Shun'ichi No 'Chūkyō Mondai Ni Kansuru Chūkan Hokoku'* 15 May 1961, from the text in Ishikawa Tadao *et al.* (eds), *Sengō Shiryō: Nitchū Kankei*, Nihon Hyōron Sha, 1970, pp.199–201.
46. Even in these circles, however, attitudes to China were extremely complicated. Some sections of the ultra-conservative Soshinkai had apparently not given up hope of Chiang Kai-shek's reconquest of the mainland (*Asahi Shimbun*, 2 June 1962). Yet in June 1961 Utsunomiya Tokuma had taken Hasegawa Takeshi, an active member of the Soshinkai, together with two other Conservative Members of Parliament, on a visit to Peking. The four had chatted for three hours with Chou En-lai. Hasegawa had been much impressed, announcing on his return to Japan that the Liberal Democrats should take the lead in promoting 'a mood of friendship with China' (*Mainichi Shimbun*, 5 July 1961).
47. Tagawa, op. cit., pp.31–51. Tagawa accompanied the mission as Matsumura's private secretary.
48. Ibid., pp.45–7.
49. Ibid., p.37–8.
50. Okazaki Kaheita, *Watakushi No Kiroku*, Tōhō Sensho, 1979, p.141.
51. *Mainichi Shimbun*, 24 November 1962 (evening edition).
52. *Yomiuri Shimbun*, 13 December 1962 (evening edition).
53. *Tōkyō Shimbun*, 7 December 1962.
54. *Asahi Shimbun*, 5 and 7 December 1962; *Mainichi Shimbun*, 6 and 9 December; *Yomiuri Shimbun*, 7 December 1962; *Sankei Shimbun*, 7 December 1962.
55. *Mainichi Shimbun*, 20 December 1962 (evening edition).
56. See *Bōei Nenkan*, 1964, p.107. *Asahi Shimbun*, 25 January 1963.
57. See *Bōei Nenkan*, 1964, p.110. The Japanese delegates to the committee replied that these questions were not pressing, since the Chinese were engaged in internal construction.
58. *Asahi Shimbun*, 9 December 1962.
59. *Yomiuri Shimbun*, 7 December 1962.
60. *Asahi Shimbun*, 9 December 1962.
61. *Nihon Keizai Shimbun*, 2 November 1962.
62. *Sankei Shimbun*, 19 January 1963 (evening edition).
63. *Nihon Kōgyō Shimbun*, 18 April 1963.
64. *Nihon Kōgyō Shimbun*, 18 April 1963.

65. *Yomiuri Shimbun*, 14 August 1963. *Asahi Shimbun*, 15 August 1963.

66. See *Yomiuri Shimbun*, 27 June 1963; *Nihon Kōgyō Shimbun*, 29 June 1963; *Sankei Shimbun*, 11 July 1963.

67. *Mainichi Shimbun*, 10 September 1963.

68. *Nihon Keizai Shimbun*, 18 September 1963.

69. *Mainichi Shimbun*, 9 October 1963.

70. Fujii and Ōe, op. cit., p.172.

71. *Mainichi Shimbun*, 25 January 1963.

72. *Mainichi Shimbun*, 3 September 1963.

73. Concrete plans for the construction of this vessel had actually been drawn up by July 1963, although work did not begin until 1967. See Genshi Ryoku Iinkai (ed.), *Genshi Ryoku Hakusho*, Okura Sho Insatsu Kyoku, 1968, p.11ff.

74. These views were particularly strong in the Foreign Ministry. See *Tōkyō Shimbun*, 3 June 1962 (evening edition).

75. *Tōkyō Shimbun*, 25 January 1963.

76. *Tōkyō Shimbun*, 24 January 1963. See also *Bōei Nenkan* 1964, p.110.

77. The *Yomiuri Shimbun* (9 February 1963) reported that the Defence Agency and Foreign Ministry saw the Gilpatric visit as an American attempt to stem the tide in favour of peaceful coexistence in the Ikeda Cabinet.

78. *Asahi Shimbun*, 30, 31 January, 1 February 1963. See also *Bōei Nenkan*, 1964, p.107.

79. *Asahi Shimbun*, 2, 15, 17 February 1963.

80. *Asahi Shimbun*, 18 March 1963 (evening edition).

81. *Asahi Shimbun*, 12 April 1963.

82. *Asahi Shimbun*, 26 March 1963.

83. *Asahi Shimbun*, 28 March 1963.

84. *Yomiuri Shimbun*, 23 April 1963.

85. *Asahi Shimbun*, 27 April 1963.

86. *Yomiuri Shimbun*, 23 April 1963 (evening edition).

87. *Asahi Shimbun*, 2 May 1963 (evening edition).

88. *Mainichi Shimbun*, 30 December 1963.

89. The Liberal Democrats won a total of 283 seats, compared with 296 in the 1960 general election and 286 seats actually held at the time of dissolution. *Asahi Shimbun*, 22 November 1963.

90. *Nihon Keizai Shimbun*, 1 December 1963.

91. *Asahi Shimbun*, 12 December 1963.

92. *Asahi Shimbun*, 31 May 1964 (evening edition).

93. *Asahi Shimbun*, 10 July 1964 (evening edition).

94. *Asahi Shimbun*, 18 July 1964.

95. *Asahi Shimbun*, 10 November 1964; *Mainichi Shimbun*, 10 November 1964.

96. *Asahi Shimbun*, 12 January 1964. *Nihon Keizai Shimbun*, 12 January 1964.

97. *Sankei Shimbun*, 21 January 1964.

98. *Asahi Shimbun*, 21 January 1964.

99. *Nihon Keizai Shimbun*, 23 January 1964.

100. *Asahi Shimbun*, 28 January 1964.

101. *Asahi Shimbun*, 21 January 1964 (evening edition).

102. *Sankei Shimbun*, 22 January 1964.

103. *Asahi Shimbun*, 31 January 1964 (evening edition).

104. *Asahi Shimbun*, 6 February 1964 (evening edition).
105. *Asahi Shimbun*, 13 February 1964.
106. *Asahi Shimbun*, 18 February 1964.
107. *Asahi Shimbun*, 1 March 1964 (evening edition).
108. *Tōkyō Shimbun*, 8 March 1964 (evening edition).
109. Discussion with Asakai Kōichirō, February 1977.
110. This is the present writer's personal interpretation of Yoshida's strategy.
111. See his remarks as reported in the *Asahi Shimbun*, 20 February 1964 (evening edition).
112. *Mainichi Shimbun*, 20 February 1964.
113. *Asahi Shimbun*, 4 March 1964 (evening edition).
114. *Sankei Shimbun*, 3 March 1964. *Asahi Shimbun*, 5 March 1964 (evening edition).
115. *Yomiuri Shimbun*, 18 March 1964.
116. *Tōkyō Shimbun*, 15 March 1964 (evening edition).
117. *Mainichi Shimbun*, 3 April 1964.
118. Tagawa, op. cit. pp.52–60.
119. Asahi Shimbun Shimin Kyōshitsu (eds), *Shiryō: Nihon To Chūgoku, '45–'71*, Asahi Shimbun Sha, 1972, p.194.
120. *Asahi Shimbun*, 5 July 1964.
121. *The Pentagon Papers*, op. cit., p.265.
122. *Asahi Shimbun*, 10 August 1964 (evening edition).
123. *Yomiuri Shimbun*, 9 September 1964; *Nihon Keizai Shimbun*, 9 September 1964.
124. *Asahi Shimbun*, 11 July 1964.
125. *Asahi Shimbun*, 18 August 1964.
126. *Asahi Shimbun*, 28 August 1964.
127. *Asahi Shimbun*, 10 July 1964.
128. *Asahi Shimbun*, 17 October 1964.
129. *Yomiuri Shimbun*, 18 October 1964.
130. *Sankei Shimbun*, 4 November 1964.
131. 'Soren No Seisaku Oyobi Chūkyō No Kaku Jikken Ga Waga Kuni No Anzen Hoshō Ni Oyobosu Eikyō, Narabi Ni Kore Ni Taisuru Waga Kuni No Toru Beki Hōsaku' (adopted by the Committee on 28 November 1964). Watanabe Yōzō and Okakura Koshirō (eds), *Nichi-Bei Ampo Jōyaku, Sono Kaisetsu To Shiryō*, Rōdō Junpō Sha, 1968, p.119ff.
132. 'Waga Kuni No Anzen Hoshō Ni Kansuru Chūkan Hōkoku', in Watanabe and Okakura, op. cit., p.148ff, and 'Kyokutō Jōsei To Waga Kuni No Anzen Hoshō', ibid., p.126ff.
133. *Mainichi Shimbun*, 10 November 1964. Matsumura Kenzō, Kawasaki Hideji, Furui Yoshimi and others interested in Sino-Japanese reconciliation broke with Miki in November 1964 over the issue of co-operation with Satō. See *Asahi Shimbun*, 22 November 1964 (evening edition).
134. This, at least, was Satō's own belief. (Discussions with former Prime Minister Satō, 16 May 1975.)
135. Cited in Ishikawa *et al.*, op. cit., p.330.
136. *Tōkyō Shimbun*, 27 November 1964.
137. *People's Daily*, 24 and 25 November 1964.
138. *Sankei Shimbun*, 2 December 1964.
139. *Nihon Keizai Shimbun*, 1 December 1964.
140. *Nihon Keizai Shimbun*, 3 December 1964 (evening edition).
141. *Nihon Keizai Shimbun*, 3 December 1964 (evening edition). *Asahi Shimbun*, 4 December

1964.

142. *Asahi Shimbun*, 24 January 1965.

143. *Tōkyō Shimbun*, 25 December 1965. *Yomiuri Shimbun*, 31 March 1965 (evening edition).

144. *Asahi Shimbun*, 4 June 1965; *Tōkyō Shimbun*, 4 June 1965.

145. *Yomiuri Shimbun*, 13 August 1965 (evening edition). See also *Yomiuri Shimbun*, 22 August 1966; *Mainichi Shimbun*, 29 June 1966 (evening edition); *Mainichi Shimbun*, 20 July 1966 and *Sankei Shimbun*, 13 December 1966 (evening edition).

146. *Yomiuri Shimbun*, 22 March 1966.

147. *Yomiuri Shimbun*, 22 March 1966.

148. The American ambassador singled out two reporters, Ōmori of the *Mainichi Shimbun* and Hata of the *Asahi Shimbun*, for particular criticism. *Asahi Shimbun*, 9 October 1965. Ōmori subsequently replied at length to these criticisms. See Ōmori Minoru, *Ishi Ni Kaku, Raishyawa Jiken No Shinsō*, Ushio Shuppan Sha, 1971.

149. *The New York Times*, 31 October 1965.

150. *Mainichi Shimbun*, 25 December 1965 (evening edition).

151. *The New York Times*, 22 December 1965.

152. Philip W. Quigg, 'Japan in neutral', *Foreign Affairs*, Volume 44, no. 2, January 1966.

153. *Nihon Keizai Shimbun*, 4 January 1966.

154. *Yomiuri Shimbun*, 4 March 1966.

155. *Asahi Shimbun*, 25 November 1965.

156. *Asahi Shimbun*, 27 November 1965.

157. *Nihon Keizai Shimbun*, 11 December 1965 (evening edition).

158. *Yomiuri Shimbun*, 30 March 1966.

159. *Asahi Shimbun*, 10 May 1966 (evening edition).

160. *Asahi Shimbun*, 10 May 1966 (evening edition).

161. *Asahi Shimbun*, 27 November 1965.

162. Wakaizumi Kei, 'Makunamara Bei Kokubō Chōkan Tandoku Kaiken Ki', *Chūō Kōron*, September 1966.

163. For typical examples of 'neo-idealist' writing see Sakamoto Yoshikazu, *Kaku Jidai No Kokusai Seiji*, Iwanami Shoten, 1968; Seki Hiroharu, *Kiki No Ninshiki*, Fukumura Shuppan, 1969; and Ishida Takeshi, *Heiwa No Seijigaku*, Iwanami Shinsho, 1968.

164. 'Neo-realist' writing on defence and diplomacy was exemplified by Kōsaka Masataka, *Kaiyō Kokka Nihon No Kōsō*, Chūō Kōron Sha, 1965; Etō Shinkichi, 'Nihon No Anzen Hoshō Ryoku O Dō Takameru Ka', *Chūō Kōron*, May 1965; Etō Shinkichi and Okabe Tatsumi, 'Chūkyō Taigai Seisaku No Kōdō Gensoku', *Jiyū*, March 1965; Nagai Yōnosuke, *Heiwa No Daishō*, Chūō Kōron Sha, 1967; Wakaizumi Kei, 'Chūgoku No Kaku Busō To Nihon No Anzen Hoshō', *Chūō Kōron*, February 1966.

165. See Wakaizumi's contributions to the *Mainichi Shimbun*, 15 and 17 May 1967 (evening editions).

166. See Kōsaka's article in the *Yomiuri Shimbun*, 30 May 1966 (evening edition); Nagai's articles in the *Mainichi Shimbun*, 18 April 1966, and in the *Yomiuri Shimbun*, 13 May 1966, and the same author's 'Beikoku No Sensōkan To Mō Taku-tō No Chosen' in *Heiwa No Daishō*, op. cit., pp.64–6. For Etō's views on this aspect of the subject, see his 'Nihon No Anzen Hoshō Ryoku O Dō Takameru Ka', op. cit.

167. Nagai Yōnosuke, 'Nihon Gaikō Ni Okeru Kōsoku To Sentaku' in *Heiwa No Daishō*, op. cit., pp.119–20.

168. *Yomiuri Shimbun*, 22 April 1968.

169. *Asahi Shimbun*, 5 January 1969.
170. *Yomiuri Shimbun*, 14 April 1968.
171. For a detailed analysis of this subject see Hayashi Chikio, 'Chōsa: Betonamu O Dō Miru Ka', *Jiyū*, October 1965.

Chapter VIII

1. *Sekai Shūhō*, 7 March 1963.
2. *Chosun Ilbo* (Seoul), 4 October 1964.
3. Terao Gorō *et al.*, 'Nikkan Kaidan', in Ajia-Afurika Kōza (ed.), *Nihon To Chōsen*, Keiso Shobō, 1965, pp.76–7.
4. For a perceptive analysis of the character of the Pak Chung Hi regime see Mura Tsuneo, *Kankoku Gunsei No Keifu: Ri Sho-ban Kara Boku Sei-ki E*, Miraisha, 1966.
5. *Nihon Keizai Shimbun*, 14 October 1969 (evening edition).
6. Fukuda Takeo, 'Kenpō Kaisei No Hata Wa Takaku', *Jiyū*, August 1964, p.56.
7. From Ōno's address at Pak Chung Hi's inauguration ceremony. *Asahi Shimbun*, 20 December 1963.
8. Quoted in Nikkan Kankei O Kenkyū Suru Kai, *Shiryō: Nikkan Kankei, I*, Gendai Shi Shuppan Kai, 1976, p.36.
9. Funada Naka, 'Anzen Hosho To Sho Shisaku No Saikento', in *Nihon No Anzen Hoshō*, 18 October 1962.
10. Quoted in Nikkan Kankei O Kenkyū Suru Kai, op. cit., p.39.
11. *Tōkyō Shimbun*, 11 January 1963.
12. *Asahi Shimbun*, 23 September 1962.
13. *The Japan Times*, 28 June 1958. In subsequent questioning by the House of Representatives Foreign Affairs Committee, Sawada explained that he had really meant that Japan's interests required the formation of a united Korea. Unity was to be achieved through democratic elections in both parts of the divided peninsula.
14. Discussions with Morita Yoshio, formerly counsellor at the Japanese Embassy in Seoul, April 1973.
15. Sugita Ichiji, *Wasurerarete Iru Anzen Hoshō*, Jiji Tsūshin Sha, 1967, p.271.
16. Ibid., pp. 270–2.
17. Ibid., p. 275.
18. Ibid.
19. Ibid.
20. Ibid. p. 276–9.
21. Ibid., p. 280.
22. For good discussions of the Mitsuya Kenkyū ('Three Arrows Research') and its implications, see Sakanaka Tomohisa *et al.*, *Nihon No Jiei Ryoku*, Asahi Shimbun Sha, 1967, p.72ff and Fujii Shōichi and Ōe Shinobu, *Sengō Nihon No Rekishi*, Aoki Shoten, 1974, pp.179–81. A document purporting to be the full text of the research project has been published by Hayashi Shigeo, *Zenbun: Mitsuya Sakusen Kenkyū*, Bansei Sha, 1979.
23. *Asahi Shimbun* (evening edition), 10 February 1965.
24. *Asahi Shimbun*, 20, 21, 22 July 1961.
25. *Ekonomisuto*, 21 November 1961.
26. Hatada Shigeo, 'Nikkan Kaidan To Bei Kyokutō Senryaku', in Ajia-Afurika Kōza (ed.),

Nihon To Chōsen, Keiso Shobō, 1965 p.123, and *Asahi Shimbun*, 12 May 1962.

27. For a full report see *Newsweek*, 23 July 1962, p.29.
28. *Asahi Shimbun*, 1 August 1962.
29. *Asahi Shimbun*, 20 January 1962.
30. *Asahi Shimbun*, 8 February 1963.
31. Terao, op. cit., p.82.
32. Ibid.
33. *Asahi Shimbun*, 10 October 1963.
34. For the text of the treaty and related agreements, see *Hōritsu Jihō*, May 1969, p.414ff.
35. Soon Sung-Cho, 'Japan's two Koreas and the problems of Korean unification', *Asian Survey*, Volume VII, no. 10, October 1967, p.707.
36. Ibid., p.709.
37. *Tōkyō Shimbun*, 13 October 1965.
38. *Nihon Keizai Shimbun*, 24 June 1965.
39. *Asahi Shimbun*, 15 October 1965.
40. *Asahi Shimbun*, 6 November 1965.
41. See Foreign Minister Shiina's statement as reported in the *Asahi Shimbun*, 27 November 1965 (evening edition).
42. See the remarks by the Defence Agency director-general, Matsuno Raizō, as reported in the *Asahi Shimbun*, 4 December 1965.
43. *Sankei Shimbun*, 14 May 1966.
44. *Tōkyō Shimbun*, 23 June 1965.
45. *Tōkyō Shimbun*, 23 June 1965.
46. *Survey of Current Business*, Volume 49, no. 12, December 1969.
47. *Christian Science Monitor* (Western edition), 7 August 1965.
48. Okazaki Kaheita, *Watakushi No Kiroku*, Tōhō Sensho, 1979, pp.119–22.
49. *Mainichi Shimbun*, 10 June, 1 September 1965.
50. *Asahi Shimbun*, 1 July 1966.
51. *Mainichi Shimbun*, 29 October 1966.
52. *Asahi Shimbun*, 18 January 1965.
53. *Asahi Shimbun*, 1 April 1965.
54. *Yomiuri Shimbun*, 8 June 1965; *Asahi Shimbun*, 7 July 1966 and *Nihon Keizai Shimbun*, 13 February 1968.
55. Haruhiro Fukui, *Party in Power: The Japanese Liberal-Democrats and Policy-Making*, Australian National University Press, Canberra, 1970, p.251ff and Uchida Kenzō, 'Jimintō Daigishi No Chūgokukan', *Chūō Kōron*, July 1965.
56. *Yomiuru Shimbun*, 24 December 1964 (evening edition).
57. See Uchida, op. cit., and Fukui, op. cit., p.251ff.
58. *Mainichi Shimbun*, 29 November 1966.
59. *Mainichi Shimbun*, 13 September 1966 (evening edition).
60. *Tōkyō Shimbun*, 27 September 1966.
61. *Nihon Keizai Shimbun*, 6 October 1966.
62. *Mainichi Shimbun*, 29 November 1966.
63. Fukui, op. cit., p.253.
64. *Asahi Shimbun*, 20 May 1966.
65. *Yomiuri Shimbun*, 15 June 1966.
66. *Tōkyō Shimbun*, 7 June 1966.

67. *Mainichi Shimbun*, 2 November 1966; *Yomiuri Shimbun*, 1 December 1966.
68. *Mainichi Shimbun*, 1 December 1966 (evening edition); *Tōkyō Shimbun*, 4 December 1966.
69. Tsūsho Sangyō Sho, *Tsūsho Hakusho*, Kakuron, 1972 and Tsūsho Sangyō Sho Kōzan Sekitan Kyoku, *Shigen Mondai No Tenbō*, 1971, passim.
70. Masashi Nishihara, *The Japanese and Sukarno's Indonesia, Tokyo-Jakarta Relations, 1951–1966*, University Press of Hawaii, Honolulu, 1975, is by far the best study of this question in any language. The present writer has drawn heavily on it in preparing this section.
71. Ibid., p.108.
72. Ibid., p.112.
73. Ibid., pp.136–7.
74. Ibid., pp.47, 52, 69, 72, 74, 81, 109–11, 112, 129, 163.
75. Ibid., pp.137–9.
76. Kajima Morinosuke, 'The Road to Pan-Asia', *The Japan Times*, 1975.
77. Nishihara, op. cit., pp.106, 115.
78. Ibid., pp.113–17 and *passim*.
79. Ibid., p.162.
80. Ibid., pp.158–61.
81. Ibid., p.130.
82. Ibid., pp.131–3.
83. Ibid., p.133.
84. Ibid., p.133.
85. Ibid., pp.133–4.
86. Ibid., p.134.
87. Ibid., p.136.
88. Ibid., pp.138–40.
89. Ibid., p.197.
90. Ibid., p.198.
91. Ibid., p.201.
92. Ibid., p.202.
93. Ibid., p.203.
94. Ibid.
95. Ibid., p.206.
96. Ibid., pp.142–3.
97. Ibid., pp.191–2.
98. Ibid., p.191.
99. Ibid., pp.195–7.
100. See Sir John Crawford and Dr Saburo Ōkita (eds), *Australia, Japan and Western Pacific Economic Relations*, Australian Government Publishing Service, Canberra, 1976 and Peter Drysdale and Hironbu Kitaōji (eds), *Japan and Australia: Two Societies and their Interaction*, Australian National University Press, Canberra, 1981.

Chapter IX

1. Priscilla Clapp, 'Okinawa reversion: bureaucratic interaction in Washington, 1966–1969', a paper presented at the Conference on Okinawa Reversion, Hakone, Japan, 10–13 January 1975, pp. 7–12.

2. US Department of State, 'Joint Communiqué', *Department of State Bulletin*, Volume XLV, no. 1150, 10 July 1961, pp. 57–8.
3. 'United States-Japanese Political Relations', Centre for Strategic Studies, Georgetown University, Washington DC, Special Report Series, no. 7, 1968, p.35. Cited in Clapp, op. cit., pp.14–15.
4. Edwin O. Reischauer, *Trans-Pacific Relations*, Charles E. Tuttle Co., Tōkyō, 1969, pp. 79–80.
5. For details see Kawamura Hiroo *et al.*, *Okinawa Henkan, Tsuki: Asahi Shimbun Yoron Chōsa*, Asahi Shimbun Sha, 1968; Nakano Yoshio (ed.), *Okinawa*, Nihon Hyōron Sha, 1969; and Watanabe Akio, *The Okinawa Problem: A Chapter in Japan-US Relations*, Melbourne University Press, Melbourne, 1970.
6. Kusuda Minoru, 'Tokumei E No Jōnetsu', *Bungei Shunjū*, September 1974, pp. 96–8.
7. Fukui Haruhiro, 'Okinawa reversion: decision-making in the Japanese government', a paper presented at the Conference on Okinawa Reversion, Hakone, Japan, 10–13 January 1975, pp.15–16.
8. Clapp, op. cit., pp.18–36.
9. *Yomiuri Shimbun*, 31 January 1967.
10. *Asahi Shimbun*, 30 January 1967 (evening edition) and 31 January 1967.
11. *Sankei Shimbun*, 18 April 1967.
12. *Sankei Shimbun*, 18 April 1967; Fukuda lamented that the Liberal Democrats 'could not even put up an election poster' without having to hire assistance, while the Communist Party had 'hundreds of young men' willing to devote their time and energy to advancing its cause.
13. *Tōkyō Shimbun*, 20 April 1967.
14. *Nihon Keizai Shimbun*, 20 April 1967 (evening edition).
15. The Prime Minister assured reporters that the four-nation conference had been no more than 'a morning tea party, a social get-together' (*Mainichi Shimbun*, 3 July 1967).
16. *Asahi Shimbun*, 13 October 1967.
17. For accounts of Chiang Cheng-kuo's activities during his visit to Japan, see *Sankei Shimbun*, 28 November 1967 and *Nihon Keizai Shimbun*, 29 November 1967.
18. *Tōkyō Shimbun*, 7 July 1967 and *Nihon Keizai Shimbun*, 8 July 1967 (evening edition). While Satō was in Seoul and Miki in Bangkok, representatives of the party's 'Asianist' groups were in China. In July Utsunomiya Tokuma returned from a visit to the People's Republic full of praise for the discipline, vigour and humanity of the Chinese army. In these qualities, Utsunomiya declared, the People's Liberation Army was far superior to the Imperial Japanese Army at the height of its power. (*Mainichi Shimbun*, 10 July 1967.)
19. *Mainichi Shimbun*, 25 July 1967.
20. *Tōkyō Shimbun*, 11 October 1967.
21. Fukui, op. cit., pp.10, 17, 19–20. *Mainichi Shimbun*, 4 October 1967; *Yomiuri Shimbun*, 4 October 1967.
22. Fukui, op. cit., pp.19–20.
23. Ibid., p.21.
24. Ibid., p.20.
25. *Asahi Shimbun*, 3 October 1967 (evening edition).
26. Fukui, op. cit., pp.21–2.
27. Clapp, op. cit., p.38. Fukui, op. cit., p.22.
28. Satō-Johnson Communiqué, Article VII, US Department of State, *Department of State*

Bulletin, Volume XLVII, no, 1484, 4 December 1967, pp.744–7.

29. Ibid.
30. *Sankei Shimbun*, 15 November 1967.
31. *Nihon Keizai Shimbun*, 21 November 1967 (evening edition).
32. *Sankei Shimbun*, 14 December 1967 (evening edition)) *Asahi Shimbun*, 18 December 1967.
33. *Mainichi Shimbun*, 31 December 1967.
34. *Tōkyō Shimbun*, 31 December 1967; 17 January 1968.
35. *Asahi Shimbun*, 17 January 1968.
36. *Mainichi Shimbun*, 16 January 1968.
37. *Asahi Shimbun*, 25 November 1967.
38. *Asahi Shimbun*, 7 December 1967 (evening edition).
39. *Asahi Shimbun*, *Yomiuri Shimbun*, 19 December 1967.
40. *Kokkai Ampo Ronsō, Sokkiroku Tō Yōten Kaisetsu*, Yomiuri Shimbun Sha, 1968, Volume 1, p.206.
41. Ibid., Volume II, pp.121–2.
42. *Mainichi Shimbun*, 26 November 1967; *Nihon Keizai Shimbun*, 30 November 1967 (evening edition).
43. *Asahi Shimbun*, 2 November 1967 (evening edition).
44. *The Times on Sunday*, 4 January 1987.
45. *Yomiuri Shimbun*, 23 January 1968 (evening edition).
46. The government had, in fact, distributed some 60,000 pamphlets in support of the visit within the city of Sasebo. For details see *Yomiuri Shimbun*, 18 January 1968.
47. *Asahi Shimbun*, 22 January 1968 (evening edition).
48. *Asahi Shimbun*, 23 January 1968.
49. *Mainichi Shimbun*, 25 January 1968.
50. *Asahi Shimbun*, 30 January 1968 (evening edition).
51. *Nihon Keizai Shimbun*, 8 February 1968.
52. *Asahi Shimbun*, 9 February 1968.
53. *Tōkyō Shimbun*, 3 April 1968 (evening edition).
54. *Yomiuri Shimbun*, 2 April 1968.
55. *Tōkyō Shimbun*, 2, 10 April 1968 (evening edition).
56. *Mainichi Shimbun*, 20 April 1968; *Yomiuri Shimbun*, 21 April 1968.
57. *Mainichi Shimbun*, 9 February, 11 March 1968.
58. *Sankei Shimbun*, 26 March, 11 April 1968.
59. *Yomiuri Shimbun*, 6 April 1968.
60. *Asahi Shimbun*, 25 April 1968 (evening edition).
61. *Asahi Shimbun*, 14 May 1968.
62. The Foreign Ministry, however, took a strong line against the view that the *Swordfish* had been responsible for the radioactivity. This attitude was publicly rebuked by Chief Cabinet Secretary Kimura. See *Nihon Keizai Shimbun*, 14 May 1968.
63. *Asahi Shimbun*, 14 May 1968.
64. *Yomiuri Shimbun*, 21 May 1968.
65. *Asahi Shimbun*, 30 May 1968.
66. For details see *Asahi Shimbun*, 24, 30, 31 May 1968; *Asahi Shimbun* and *Yomiuri Shimbun*, 19 June 1968.
67. *Sankei Shimbun*, 4 September 1968.

68. *Asahi Shimbun*, 4 June 1968 (evening edition); *Yomiuri Shimbun*, 4 June 1968 (evening edition); *Yomiuri Shimbun*, 5 June 1968; *Nihon Keizai Shimbun*, 4 June 1968 (evening edition) and *Sankei Shimbun*, 4 June 1968 (evening edition).
69. *Mainichi Shimbun*, 6 June 1968.
70. *Tōkyō Shimbun*, 16 June 1968.
71. *Sankei Shimbun*, 19 June 1968.
72. *Tōkyō Shimbun,* 19 June 1968; *Nihon Keizai Shimbun*, 9 August 1968.
73. *Nihon Keizai Shimbun*, 10 July 1968.
74. *Asahi Shimbun*, 12 June 1968.
75. *Yomiuri Shimbun*, 5 July 1968 (evening edition).
76. *Sankei Shimbun*, 14 May 1968.
77. Fukui, op. cit., pp.24–5.
78. *Asahi Shimbun*, 27 November 1968 (evening edition).
79. *Nihon Keizai Shimbun*, 31 November 1968 (evening edition).
80. *Asahi Shimbun*, 11 November 1968 (evening edition).
81. *Asahi Shimbun*, 1 December 1968 (evening edition).
82. Clapp, op. cit., pp.41–3.
83. Ibid., pp.43–6.
84. Ibid., pp.46–8.
85. *Yomiuri Shimbun*, 11 March 1969.
86. *Nihon Keizai Shimbun*, 18 February 1968.
87. For Kusumi's strategic thought, see Kusumi Tadao, *Sensō, Senryaku, Nihon*, Hayashi Shoten, Tōkyō (no publication date).
88. Fukui, op. cit., p.28.
89. *Asahi Shimbun* and *Sankei Shimbun*, 9 March 1969.
90. Fukui, op. cit., pp.29–30.
91. *Mainichi Shimbun*, 26 February 1969.
92. *Mainichi Shimbun*, 3 October 1967.
93. *Mainichi Shimbun*, 12 May 1969.
94. Richard M. Nixon, 'Asia after Vietnam', *Foreign Affairs*, Volume 46, no. 1, October 1967.
95. *Asahi Shimbun*, 22 October 1968.
96. See, for example, the editorials in *Mainichi Shimbun*, 7 November 1968, *Yomiuri Shimbun*, 9 November 1968 and *Tōkyō Shimbun*, 8 November 1968.
97. *Tōkyō Shimbun*, 7 November 1968.
98. *Mainichi Shimbun*, 7 November 1968; *Asahi Shimbun*, 8 November 1968; *Nikkan Kōgyō Shimbun*, 8 November 1968.
99. *Nihon Keizai Shimbun*, 15 November 1968 (evening edition).
100. *Nihon Keizai Shimbun*, 1 December 1968.
101. *Yomiuri Shimbun*, 11 March 1969.
102. Clapp, op. cit., pp.51–5.
103. This is the view of the present writer, not of Ms Clapp.
104. *Asahi Shimbun*, 29 April 1969 (evening edition), 30 April 1969; *Mainichi Shimbun*, 30 April 1969 (evening edition); *Sankei Shimbun*, 29 April 1969 (evening edition), 30 April 1969 (evening edition).
105. *Tōkyō Shimbun*, 30 April 1969.
106. *Yomiuri Shimbun*, 3 May 1969 (evening edition).
107. *Tōkyō Shimbun*, 15 May 1969 (evening edition).

108. *Sankei Shimbun*, 20 May 1969.
109. *Mainichi Shimbun*, 29 May 1969 (evening edition).
110. For Nixon's allegations, see Richard M. Nixon, *The Memoirs of Richard Nixon*, Arrow Books, London, 1978, p.389. For Kissinger's claims, see Statement of Information Submitted on Behalf of President Nixon, Hearings before Committee on the Judiciary, House of Representatives, 93rd Congress, 2nd Session, pursuant to H.R. 803, Book IV, White House Surveillance Activities, p.148. Cited in Clapp, op. cit., p.55.
111. For the Aichi-Nixon talks (at which the Japanese Foreign Minister received a golf ball personally signed by the President, and an assurance that 'no President has been better informed on Japan and Asia than I'), see *Asahi Shimbun*, 3 and 8 June 1969, *Tōkyō Shimbun*, 4 June 1969. For the Aichi-Rogers talks, see *Asahi Shimbun*, 5 June 1969 (evening edition), *Yomiuri Shimbun*, 5 June 1969 (evening edition) and *Tōkyō Shimbun*, 6 June 1969 (evening edition).
112. *Asahi Shimbun*, 18 July 1969.
113. *Mainichi Shimbun*, 30 July 1969.
114. *Asahi Shimbun*, *Nihon Keizai Shimbun* and *Yomiuri Shimbun*, 16 September 1969.
115. Fukui, op. cit., pp.37–8.
116. *Mainichi Shimbun*, 25 September 1969 (evening edition).
117. *Nihon Keizai Shimbun*, 3 October 1969.
118. *Tōkyō Shimbun*, 2 November 1969.
119. *Tōkyō Shimbun*, 5 March 1969.
120. *Asahi Shimbun*, 5 March 1969.
121. *Asahi Shimbun*, 10 March 1969.
122. *Asahi Shimbun*, 8 March 1969 (evening edition).
123. *Yomiuri Shimbun*, 2 June 1969.
124. *Yomiuri Shimbun*, 1 March 1969.
125. *Asahi Shimbun* and *Sankei Shimbun*, 9 March 1969.
126. *Tōkyō Shimbun*, 19 June 1968; *Nihon Keizai Shimbun*, 10 July 1968, 31 March 1969 (evening edition).
127. *Asahi Shimbun* and *Tōkyō Shimbun*, 12 March 1969.
128. *Tōkyō Shimbun*, 15 March 1969.
129. According to the *Sankei Shimbun* (28 April 1969), the Prime Minister was only told of the incident three hours after it occurred, and some time after both the American forces based in Japan and the Japanese Air Self Defence Force had gone on the alert. The Prime Minister had, according to this report, been informed not by the United States, but by the Defence Agency.
130. *Sankei Shimbun*, 30 April 1969; *Mainichi Shimbun*, 2 May 1969 (evening edition); *Asahi Shimbun*, 6 May 1969 (evening edition).
131. *Yomiuri Shimbun*, 3 May 1969 (evening edition).
132. *Mainichi Shimbun* and *Yomiuri Shimbun*, 2 June 1969 (evening edition).
133. *Asahi Shimbun*, 4 June 1969 (evening edition).
134. *Asahi Shimbun*, 18 June 1969.
135. *Asahi Shimbun*, 20 June 1969.
136. *Sankei Shimbun*, 20 June 1969 (evening edition).
137. Fukui, op. cit., p.35.
138. Ibid., pp.35–6.
139. The Satō-Nixon Joint Communiqué, Article 6, *The New York Times*, 22 November 1969.

140. *Arrangement Concerning Assumption by Japan of the Responsibility for the Immediate Defence of Okinawa*, from the text in *Hōritsu Jihō*, October 1971, pp.322–4.
141. *Agreement between Japan and the United States of America Concerning the Ryūkyū and Daitō Islands*, from the text in *Hōritsu Jihō*, October 1971, pp.306–13.
142. The Satō-Nixon Joint Communiqué, Article 8.
143. *Asahi Shimbun*, 27 November 1969; *Yomiuri Shimbun*, 4 December 1969.
144. *Nihon Keizai Shimbun*, 23 November 1969; *Yomiuri Shimbun*, 5 December 1969.
145. "Dai 63 Kokkai Ni Okeru Satō Sōri No Hatsugen Roku", *Toki No Ugoki*, 15 May 1970, p.24.
146. *Asahi Shimbun*, 23 November 1969 (evening edition).
147. *Asahi Shimbun*, 27 November 1969.
148. See Aichi's explanations in the round table discussion reported in *Yomiuri Shimbun*, 5 December 1969.
149. Discussion with Sonoda Sunao, 14 March 1975.

Chapter X

1. *Mainichi Shimbun*, 30 January 1964.
2. *Newsweek*, 11 August 1969.
3. *Yomiuri Shimbun*, 10 July 1971.
4. *Mainichi Shimbun*, 16 January 1972.
5. Ibid.
6. The Atomic Energy Basic Law, Law Number 186, 19 December 1955, partially revised by Law Number 72, 20 July 1967.
7. John E. Endicott, *Japan's Nuclear Option: Political, Technical and Strategic Factors*, Praeger, New York, 1975, p.113 ff. Endicott's discussion is the best on the subject.
8. For detailed discussions see, in English, Victor Gilinsky and Paul Langer, *The Japanese Civilian Nuclear Program*, Rand Corporation, Memorandum RM-5366-PR, August 1967; Endicott, op. cit.; and, in Japanese, Genshi Ryokū Iinkai (ed.), *Genshi Ryoku Hakusho, 1968*, Ōkura Sho Insatsu Kyoku, 1968.
9. US Atomic Energy Commission, 'Remarks by Clarence E. Larson, Commissioner, US AEC, at the Symposium on Energy, Resources and the Environment, Kyōtō, Japan', USAEC News Release, 9 August 1972, p.4. *Atoms in Japan*, May 1971, Supplement I, p.12. Cited in Endicott, op. cit., p.116.
10. *Yomiuri Shimbun*, 16 March 1968; *Atoms in Japan*, August 1972, p.10.
11. *Atoms in Japan*, July 1972, pp.31–2.
12. *Atoms in Japan*, June 1971, p.34; April 1972, p.46; May 1972, p.37.
13. Anzen Hoshō Chōsa Kai, *Nihon No Anzen Hoshō, 1970 Nen E No Tenbō*, Asagumo Shuppan Sha, 1968, p.314 ff. Endicott, op. cit., p. 134.
14. *Asahi Shimbun*, 16 May 1968.
15. Anzen Hoshō Chōsa Kai, op. cit.
16. Endicott, op. cit., p.150ff.
17. Ibid., Appendix D, pp.245–8.
18. *Bōei Nenkan*, 1958, p.174 and *Bōei Nenkan*, 1960, p.132.
19. Discussion with anonymous but well-placed informant, July 1972. Satō's Nobel Peace Prize in 1974 was specifically awarded for his contributions to nuclear non-proliferation.
20. Defence Agency of Japan, *The Defence of Japan*, Tōkyō, 1979, p.40.

21. Jiyūminshūtō Anzen Hoshō Chōsa Kai, 'Kyokutō Jōsei To Waga Kuni No Anzen Hoshō,' May 1965, and 'Kyokutō Jōsei To Waga Kuni No Azen Hoshō Taisaku', June 1965. From the text in Watanabe Yōzō and Okakura Kōshirō (eds.), *Nichi-Bei Ampo Jōyaku, Sono Kaisetsu To Shiryō*, Rōdō Junpō Sha, 1968, pp.126–147.

22. Jiyūminshūtō Anzen Hoshō Ni Kansuru Chōsa Kai, 'Waga Kuni No Anzen Hoshō Ni Kansuru Chūkan Hōkoku', June 1966. From the text in Watanabe and Okakura, op. cit., pp.148–67.

23. 'Nihon No Kaku Hibusōron O Hihansu' and ' "Hikaku Busō Sengen" No Inbō', in Jimintō Anzen Hoshō Chōsa Kai (ed.), *Nihon No Anzen To Bōei*, Hara Shobō, 1966, pp.863–924.

24. *Sankei Shimbun*, 14 December 1967 (evening edition). See also *Yomiuri Shimbun*, 2 March 1968.

25. *Mainichi Shimbun*, 26 October 1967 (evening edition).

26. *Yomiuri Shimbun*, 2 March 1968; *Nihon Keizai Shimbun*, 15 March 1969.

27. *Yomiuri Shimbun*, 2 March 1968.

28. *Mainichi Shimbun*, 24 February 1968; *Yomiuri Shimbun*, 24 February 1968.

29. Yomiuri Shimbun Sha Seiji Bu (ed.), *Kokkai Ampo Ronsō*, op. cit., Volume 1, p.52ff.

30. For details of this interesting episode, see the *Nihon Keizai Shimbun*, 16 March 1969.

31. *Mainichi Shimbun*, 15 November 1969.

32. *Shokun*, October 1970.

33. *Nihon Keizai Shimbun*, 22 April 1966.

34. Momoi Makoto, 'Japan and Australia', undated paper (circa 1970) in possession of present writer.

35. *Genshi Ryoku Hakusho*, op. cit., pp.137–41.

36. *Nihon Gakujutsu Kaigi Dai-36-Kai Sōkai Seimei*, 25 April 1962; *Dai-2-Kai Kagakusha Kyōtō Kaigi Seimei*, 9 May 1963; *Dai-3-Kai Kagakusha Kyōtō Kaigi Seimei*, 2 July 1966. From the text in the appendix of Yūkawa Hideki, Tomonaga Shinichirō and Sakata Shōichi, *Heiwa Jidai O Sōzō Suru Tame Ni*, Iwanami Shoten, 1967. For the views of various scientists see, in addition to this work, Yūkawa Hideki *et al.*, *Kaku Jidai O Koeru*, Iwanami Shoten, 1968, and Toyoda Toshiyuki, *Kaku Senryaku Hihan*, Iwanami Shoten, 1966.

37. Makoto Kazumaro, 'Hikaku Chūkyū Kokka No Bōei Seisaku', *Ushiō*, Spring 1966, p.121.

38. *Yomiuri Shimbun*, 1 January 1968.

39. *Yomiuri Shimbun*, 29 February 1968; Kaihara Osamu, *Nihon Rettō Shubitai Ron*, Asagumo Shuppan Sha, 1972, pp.325–7.

40. Kamigawa Hikomatsu, 'Kaku Kakusan Bōshi Jōyaku No Shōrai To Waga Shin Kaku Koku Seisaku No Jūritsu', *Minzoku To Seiji*, July 1968.

41. Kuramae Yoshio, 'Nihon No Unmei O Kessuru Kakubō Jōyaku No Mondaiten', *Ronsō Jānaru*, September 1968.

42. Maeda Hisashi, 'Kaku Kakubō Jōyaku To Nihon No Kaku Seisaku', *Kokubō*, August 1968.

43. Sekino Hideo, 'Kaku Heiki Kaihatsu No Jōkyō To Sono Eikyō', *Kōmei*, August 1968. Kaihara Osamu, *Nihon Rettō Shubitai Ron*, Asagumo Shuppan Sha, pp.326–7.

44. Tamura Kosaku, 'Kakubō Jōyaku O Ikani Atsukau Ka', *Gaikō Jihō*, 11 December 1968.

45. Kaihara, op. cit., pp.322–4.,

46. Sugita Ichiji, *Wasurerarete Iru Anzen Hoshō*, Jiji Tsūshin Sha, 1967, p.173.

47. Jiji Mondai Kenkyū Kai (ed.), *Kaku Naki Nihon No Anzen Hoshō*, Jiji Tsūshin Sha, 1967,

pp.178–81.
48. See Endicott, op. cit., pp.62–4 and John Welfield, *Japan and Nuclear China*, Canberra Papers on Strategy and Defence, no. 9, Australian National University Press, Canberra, 1970.
49. Kishida Junnosuke, 'Nihon No Kaku Seisaku To Hikaku Sengen No Imi', *Ushiō*, Spring 1968.
50. Kōsaka Masataka, 'Kaiyō Kokka Nihon No Kōsō, *Chūō Kōron*, September 1964; 'Kokusai Seiji No Tagenka', *Chūō Kōron*, December 1964, p.103ff.
51. Rōyama Michio, 'Nihon No Anzen Hoshō To Chūgoku No Imi', *Ushiō*, Spring 1966.
52. Saeki Kiichi, *Nihon No Anzen Hoshō*, Nihon Kokusai Mondai Kenkyūjo, 1966, pp 44–64.
53. Sakamoto Yoshikazu, *Kaku Jidai No Kokusai Seiji*, Iwanami Shoten, 1968.
54. For details see Shōno Naomi, Nagai Hideaki and Ueno Hirohisa, *Kaku To Heiwa*, Hōritsu Bunka Sha, 1978, pp.16–17.
55. Ibid., p.17.
56. See Welfield, op. cit., p.35ff.
57. Shōno, Nagai and Ueno, op. cit., p.16.
58. Ibid., p.15.
59. Ibid., pp.139–70.
60. *Yomiuri Shimbun*, 19 June 1970.
61. See, for example, *Soka Gakkai News*, Volume 7, no. 162, September 1982, pp.2–3.
62. *International Negotiations on the Treaty on the Nonproliferation of Nuclear Weapons*, United States Arms Control and Disarmament Agency, Publication 48, released January 1969, p.9ff.
63. Ibid., p.32ff.
64. Ibid., p.17ff.
65. Ibid., p.52.
66. Ibid., p.81.
67. Ibid., pp.19–20.
68. Ibid., p.53.
69. Ibid., p.75.
70. Ibid., p.76.
71. Ibid., p.52.
72. Ibid., p.68.
73. Ibid., p.65.
74. Ibid., p.67.
75. Ibid., p.63.
76. Ibid., p.64.
77. Ibid., p.70.
78. *Sankei Shimbun*, 10 February 1967.
79. *Sankei Shimbun*, 10 February 1967.
80. *Sankei Shimbun*, 10 February 1967.
81. *Nihon Keizai Shimbun*, 19 February 1967.
82. *Mainichi Shimbun*, 10 March 1967 (evening edition). *Sankei Shimbun*, 10 March 1967 (evening edition).
83. *Asahi Shimbun*, 22 March 1967 (evening edition).
84. *Asahi Shimbun*, 20 April 1967.

85. *Yomiuri Shimbun*, 12 April 1967.

86. *Tōkyō Shimbun*, 22 April 1967.

87. *Sankei Shimbun*, 9 May 1967 (evening edition).

88. *International Negotiations on the Treaty on the Nonproliferation of Nuclear Weapons*, op. cit., pp.146–9.

89. Ibid., pp.83–6.

90. Ibid., pp.81–2.

91. Ibid., p.90.

92. Ibid., p.86ff.

93. Ibid., pp.89–90.

94. Ibid., pp.150–5.

95. Ibid., p.155.

96. Ibid., pp.101–13.

97. *Asahi Shimbun*, 25 August 1967. *Tōkyō Shimbun*, 29 August 1967.

98. *Mainichi Shimbun*, 9 March 1968.

99. *Asahi Shimbun*, 2 February 1968; *Mainichi Shimbun*, 11 February 1968; *Sankei Shimbun*, 30 April 1968 and *Asahi Shimbun*, 1 June 1968 (evening edition).

100. *Sankei Shimbun*, 30 April 1968.

101. *Mainichi Shimbun*, 11 February 1968.

102. *Sankei Shimbun*, 12 June 1968.

103. *Mainichi Shimbun*, 3 July 1968.

104. *Mainichi Shimbun*, 3 July 1968.

105. *Yomiuri Shimbun*, 4 September 1968.

106. *Asahi Shimbun*, 18 September 1968.

107. *Nihon Keizai Shimbun*, 17 September 1968 (evening edition).

108. *Nihon Keizai Shimbun*, 27 September 1968 (evening edition).

109. *Tōkyō Shimbun*, 16 September 1968.

110. *Asahi Shimbun*, 13 October 1968.

111. *Nihon Keizai Shimbun*, 21 May 1969 (evening edition); *Sankei Shimbun*, 20 June 1969.

112. For Opposition views see *Mainichi Shimbun*, 6 November 1969 and *Akahata*, 8 November 1969.

113. *Asahi Shimbun*, 20 April 1967.

114. *Asahi Shimbun*, 28 April 1969.

115. For details of the complicated manoeuvres in the Liberal Democratic Party prior to Satō's departure for Washington, see *Sankei Shimbun*, 8 November 1969 and *Tōkyō Shimbun*, 15 November 1969.

116. *Asahi Shimbun*, 9 January 1970.

117. *Tōkyō Shimbun*, 26 January 1970.

118. *Asahi Shimbun*, 4 February 1970.

119. *Kaku Heiki Fukakusan Jōyaku Shōmei No Sai No Nihon Seifu Seimei*.

Chapter XI

1. Cited in Henry Brandon, *The Retreat of American Power*, The Bodley Head, London, 1972, p.82.

2. T.B. Millar, *Soviet Policies in the Indian Ocean Area*, Canberra Papers on Strategy and Defence, no. 7, Australian National University Press, Canberra, 1970.

3. Walter Slocombe, *The Political Implications of Strategic Parity*, Adelphi Papers, no. 77, International Institute for Strategic Studies, London, 1971.
4. Brandon, op. cit., p.71.
5. *The New York Times*, 18 August 1984.
6. Quoted in Brandon, op. cit., p.184.
7. C.P. Fitzgerald, 'The emergence of China: internal dynamics', in *East Asia and the World System, Part II, The Regional Powers*, Adelphi Papers, no. 92, International Institute for Strategic Studies, London, 1972, pp.3–5.
8. *Asahi Shimbun*, 24 June 1970.
9. *Mainichi Shimbun*, 15 July 1971; *Yomiuri Shimbun*, 15 July 1971.
10. *Mainichi Shimbun*, 10 May 1971.
11. *Mainichi Shimbun*, 12 May 1971.
12. *Asahi Shimbun*, 20 November 1971.
13. *Asahi Shimbun*, 28 June 1971 (evening edition).
14. *Asahi Shimbun*, 16 July 1971.
15. *Asahi Shimbun*, 16 July 1971.
16. James C. Abegglen and Thomas M. Hout, 'Facing up to the trade gap with Japan', *Foreign Affairs*, Volume 57, no. 1, Fall 1978.
17. *Nihon Kokusei Zue* (successive issues).
18. *Nikkan Kōgyō*, 4 March 1971.
19. William E. Colby, 'Japan and the U.S.: an intelligence projection', *The Japan Times*, 13 February 1979.
20. *Asahi Shimbun*, 15 and 16 March 1971.
21. *Nihon Keizai Shimbun*, 23 May 1971.
22. *The New York Times*, 23 September 1971.
23. *Nihon Keizai Shimbun*, 23 May 1971.
24. Ibid.
25. *Newsweek*, 3 May 1971.
26. *Time*, 10 May 1971.
27. *Nikkan Kōgyō*, 25 June 1971.
28. *Tōkyō Shimbun*, 2 September 1971.
29. *Radio Peking*, 24 November 1969; *Renmin Ribao* (editorial), 28 November 1969; *Radio Peking*, 26 December 1969; *Radio Peking*, 22 January 1970.
30. *Rodong Sinmun* (Pyongyang), 9 April 1970. For the English text see *Korea Today*, no. 165, 1970.
31. *Current Notes on International Affairs*, Department of Foreign Affairs, Canberra, June 1971, pp.42–6.
32. *Sydney Morning Herald*, 7 July 1971.
33. Tagawa Seiichi, *Nitchū Kōshō Hiroku*, Mainichi Shimbun Sha, 1973, pp.257–63.
34. Asahi Shimin Kyōshitsu (eds), *Shiryō: Nihon To Chūgoku, '45–71*, Asahi Shimbun Sha, 1972, p.216.
35. See, for example, *Rodong Sinmun*, 9 April 1970; the official statements issued after the Indochinese Leaders' Conference held at an unknown location near the Chinese border on 24–5 April 1970; the Sino-Khymer Joint Communiqué of 27 April 1970 and the lengthy statements published by the government of the People's Republic on 4–5 May 1970.
36. *Renmin Ribao*, 29 December 1970.
37. *Kuang Ming Ribao*, 4 November 1970; *Kuang Ming Ribao*, 13 December 1970.

38. *Hsinhua*, 28 November 1970.
39. For Ambassador Armin Meyer's assurances to Foreign Minister Aichi, see *The Japan Times*, 17 November 1970.
40. *The Japan Times*, 3 September 1970.
41. *The Japan Times*, 28 August 1970.
42. *The Japan Times*, 19 November 1970.
43. *The Japan Times*, 26 November 1970.
44. *The Japan Times*, 10 December 1970.
45. Ogata Sadako, 'The business community and foreign policy: a process leading to Japan's recognition of the People's Republic of China' (undated paper in possession of the present writer), pp.19–20.
46. Ibid., p.17.
47. Ibid., pp.20–1.
48. Ibid., p.28.
49. Ibid., p.29.
50. Asahi Shimbun, 7 January 1971.
51. Brandon, op. cit., pp.221–4.
52. *Mainichi Shimbun*, 28 March 1971.
53. *Asahi Shimbun*, 16 July 1971 (evening edition).
54. *Mainichi Shimbun*, 11 July 1971.
55. *Nihon Keizai Shimbun*, 6 October 1971 (evening edition).
56. Graham Freudenberg, *A Certain Grandeur: Gough Whitlam in Politics*, Sun Books, 1977, p.211.
57. *Mainichi Shimbun*, 26 September 1971.
58. *Nihon Keizai Shimbun*, 11 September 1971 (evening edition).
59. *Nihon Keizai Shimbun*, 20 December 1971.
60. *Tōkyō Shimbun*, 17 July 1971.
61. *Nihon Keizai Shimbun*, 19 August 1971.
62. *Jiyū Shimpō*, 7 December 1971.
63. *Jiyū Shimpō*, 2 November 1971.
64. *Asahi Shimbun*, 9 January 1972.
65. *Tōkyō Shimbun*, 10 August 1971.
66. *Tōkyō Shimbun*, 10 August 1971.
67. *Nihon Keizai Shimbun*, 9 September 1971 (evening edition).
68. *Nihon Keizai Shimbun*, 29 July 1971 (evening edition).
69. *The Japan Times*, 3 and 13 September 1971.
70. *Tōkyō Shimbun*, 10 August 1971.
71. *Mainichi Shimbun*, 13 September 1971.
72. *Tōkyō Shimbun*, 10 August 1971; *Jiyū Shinpō*, 26 October 1971.
73. Utsunomiya Tokuma, *Tenkan Suru Bei-Ajia Seisaku To Nihon*, Hayashi Shobō, 1972, passim.
74. *Yomiuri Shimbun*, 5 December 1972.
75. Ogata, op. cit., p.30.
76. *Nihon Keizai Shimbun*, 1 October 1971.
77. Ogata, op. cit., p.30.
78. Ibid., p.31.
79. Ibid., pp.33–4.

80. *Yomiuri Shimbun*, 17 July 1971; *Mainichi Shimbun*, 15 August 1971.
81. Tagawa Seiichi, *Matsumura Kenzō To Chūgoku*, Yomiuri Shimbun Sha, 1972, pp.179–82.
82. Ibid., p.157.
83. Ibid., p.158.
84. Ibid., p.136.
85. Ibid., p.164ff; *Asahi Shimbun*, 26 August 1971 (evening edition).
86. *Asahi Shimbun*, 26 August 1971 (evening edition).
87. Haruhiro Fukui, 'Tanaka goes to Peking: a case study of foreign policy making', in T.J. Pempel (ed.), *Policy Making in Contemporary Japan*, Cornell University Press, Ithaca, NY, 1977, pp.60–102.
88. Tagawa, *Matsumura Kenzō To Chūgoku*, p.191.
89. Fukui, op. cit., p.69.
90. Tagawa, *Matsumura Kenzō To Chūgoku*, p.186ff.
91. Ibid., p.192; Fukui, op. cit., p.69.
92. Fukui, op. cit., p.69.
93. Tagawa, *Matsumura Kenzō To Chūgoku*, p.192.
94. *Mainichi Shimbun*, 29 August 1971; interview with Finance Minister Mizuta.
95. *Mainichi Shimbun*, 29 August 1971; *Mainichi Shimbun*, 28 October 1971; *Nihon Keizai Shimbun*, 18 August 1971; *Nihon Keizai Shimbun*, 19 August 1971; *Yomiuri Shimbun*, 25 August 1971; *Mainichi Shimbun*, 29 August 1971; *Tōkyō Shimbun*, 11 September 1971 (evening edition); *Nihon Keizai Shimbun*, 11 September 1971 (evening edition).
96. *Nikkan Kōgyō*, 26 August 1971.
97. *Asahi Shimbun*, 12 November 1971.
98. Brandon, op. cit., p.242.
99. Ibid., pp.230–6.
100. Jiji Tsūshin Sha Seiji Bu (ed.), *Nitchū Fukkō*, Jiji Tsūshin Sha, 1972, pp.81–95.
101. Fujiyama Aiichirō, *Seiji Waga Michi*, Asahi Shimbun Sha, 1976, p.203.
102. Ibid., p.210.
103. Ogata, op. cit., p.37.
104. Ibid., pp.37–8.
105. *Yomiuri Shimbun*, 6 January 1972 (evening edition).
106. *Asahi Shimbun*, 8 January 1972 (evening edition).
107. *Sankei Shimbun*, 13 January 1972.
108. *Sankei Shimbun*, 19 January 1972.
109. Richard M. Nixon, *The Memoirs of Richard Nixon*, Arrow Books, London, 1978, pp.562–7.
110. *The New York Times*, 28 February 1972.
111. Ibid.
112. Ibid.
113. Ibid., 24 February 1972.
114. *Nihon Keizai Shimbun*, 29 February 1972; *Mainichi Shimbun*, 29 February 1972.
115. *Nihon Keizai Shimbun*, 14 March 1972.
116. *Nihon Keizai Shimbun*, 23 March 1972.
117. *Sekai*, September 1971, pp.133–6.
118. *Tōkyō Shimbun*, 24 March 1972.
119. *Asahi Shimbun*, 11 May 1972.
120. *Yomiuri Shimbun*, 21 May 1972.
121. *Mainichi Shimbun*, 23 February 1972; *Nihon Keizai Shimbun*, 13 March 1972.

122. *Nihon Keizai Shimbun*, 13 March 1972.
123. *Asahi Shimbun*, 11 May 1972.
124. *Asahi Shimbun*, 23 February 1972.
125. *Yomiuri Shimbun*, 28 March 1972.
126. *Asahi Shimbun*, 3 January 1972.
127. *Mainichi Shimbun*, 19 April 1972; *Asahi Shimbun*, 26 April 1972.
128. *Mainichi Shimbun*, 19 April 1972.
129. *Asahi Shimbun*, 16 May 1972.
130. *Yomiuri Shimbun*, 21 May 1972.
131. *Mainichi Shimbun*, 24 May 1972.
132. *Asahi Shimbun*, 3 July 1972.
133. *Asahi Shimbun*, 7 July 1972.
134. Fujiyama, op. cit., p.212.
135. Furui Yoshimi, 'Nitchū Kokkō Seijōka No Hiwa', *Chūō Kōron*, December 1972, p.147.
136. *Nihon Keizai Shimbun*, 24 June 1972 (day and evening editions).
137. *Mainichi Shimbun*, 19, 20, 21 October 1972.
138. *Yomiuri Shimbun*, 5 August 1972.
139. Ogata, op. cit., pp.38–40.
140. Fukui, op. cit., p.82.
141. Ibid., pp.80–1.
142. Ibid., p.87.
143. Ibid., pp.80–90.
144. Furui, op. cit., p.146.
145. Ibid., pp.138–9.
146. *Mainichi Shimbun*, 15 July 1972.
147. Fukui, op. cit., p.76.
148. *Yomiuri Shimbun*, 2 September 1972.
149. *Tōkyō Shimbun*, 28 August 1972 (evening edition).
150. *Yomiuri Shimbun*, 2 September 1972 (interview with Ōhira).
151. Gene T. Hsiao, 'The Sino-Japanese rapprochement: a relationship of ambivalence', in Gene T. Hsiao (ed.), *Sino-American Détente and its Implications*, Praeger, New York, 1974.
152. *The New York Times*, 30 September 1972.
153. *The Japan Times*, 2 October 1972.
154. *The Japan Times*, 26 September 1972.
155. *The Japan Times*, 2 October 1972.
156. *Tōkyō Shimbun*, 24 November 1972.
157. *Asahi Shimbun*, 11, 12, 13 December 1972.

Chapter XII

1. Theodore Draper, 'Detente', *Commentary*, June 1974, cited in Mary Kaldor, *The Disintegrating West*, Penguin, Harmondsworth, 1978, p.151.
2. James R. Goldsborough, 'France, the European crisis and the alliance', cited in Kaldor, op. cit., p.151.
3. Kaldor, op. cit., pp.161–8.
4. *The Financial Australian*, 9 December 1980.
5. *The Japan Times*, 13 February 1979.

6. Discussions with Tagawa Seiichi, 12 March 1975.
7. Michael Yahuda, 'China's new role in world affairs', a paper presented at the Asian Studies Association of Australia Conference, May 1976, p.7.
8. Ibid., p.8.
9. *Nihon Keizai Shimbun*, 2 July 1973 (evening edition).
10. *Mainichi Shimbun*, 3 and 4 April 1974 (evening edition).
11. *Sankei Shimbun*, 5 April 1974.
12. *Nihon Keizai Shimbun*, 5 September 1974.
13. Ibid.
14. Ogawa Kazuo, *Nisso Bōeki No Jitsujō To Kadai*, Kyōiku Sha, 1979, pp.126–34.
15. *Asahi Shimbun*, 2 November 1972 (evening edition).
16. Gavan McCormack and Mark Seldon (eds), *Korea North and South: The Deepening Crisis*, Monthly Review Press, New York, 1979, p.177ff. For detailed statistics see Nikkan Kankei Kenkyū Kai (ed.), *Nikkan Kankei No Kisō Chishiki*, Tabata Shoten, 1975.
17. Confidential documents obtained from the US State Department by Kyōdō News Service in May 1979 under the Freedom of Information Act. For the English text, see *The Japan Times*, 13 May 1979. The authenticity of the documents was implicitly confirmed by the State Department when it subsequently announced that they had been released 'by mistake'. See *The Japan Times*, 17 May 1979.
18. *Mainichi Shimbun*, 19 May 1979; *The Japan Times*, 25 May 1979.
19. *Mainichi Shimbun*, 14 December 1973.
20. *Mainichi Shimbun*, 12 June 1974.
21. *Mainichi Shimbun*, 8 August 1974.
22. *The Japan Times*, 13, 17, 25 May 1979.
23. *Asahi Shimbun*, 12 July 1974.
24. *Mainichi Shimbun*, 24 October 1972.
25. *Asahi Shimbun*, 1 November 1972 (evening edition).
26. McCormack and Seldon, op. cit., pp.143–4.
27. *Mainichi Shimbun*, 21 August 1974.
28. For Japan's involvement in the Middle East see Kenneth I. Juster, 'Foreign policy making during the oil crisis', *The Japan Interpreter*, Volume XI, no. 3, 1977; Manohar Prasad Bhattarai, 'Japan's resource dependency: oil diplomacy in the Middle East', Master's Degree thesis, International University of Japan, 1987, and Kweku Ampiah, 'Japan's oil diplomacy, relations with the Middle East, 1968–1982', Master's Degree thesis, International University of Japan, 1987.
29. For details, see Ampiah, op. cit., Chapter IV.
30. Mari Pangestu, *Japanese and Other Foreign Investment in the ASEAN Countries*, Australia-Japan Research Centre, Australian National University, (no date), Canberra, passim.
31. For details, see Kaihara Osamu, *Nihon Rētto Shubitai Ron*; Asagumo Shuppan Sha, 1972, p.43ff.
32. Alejandro Melchor, Jr, 'United States interests in Southeast Asia: friends and former enemies', Australian Institute of International Affairs, Seventh National Conference, 14–16 April 1977.
33. *Asahi Shimbun*, 5, 18 August 1977, *Nihon Keizai Shimbun*, 8 August 1977, *Mainichi Shimbun*, 17 August 1977. See also Ogiso Isao, *ASEAN*, Kyōiku Sha, 1978, p.60ff, p.124ff.
34. *Nihon Kokusei Zue* (successive issues).
35. The Parliament of the Commonwealth of Australia, *Australia-Japan Relations*, Parliamen-

tary Paper, no. 197, 1978, Commonwealth Government Printer, 1978, pp.141–2.
36. For a detailed analysis of Japan's nuclear policies during this period see John E. Endicott, *Japan's Nuclear Option: Political, Technical and Strategic Factors*, Praeger, New York, 1975. The present writer had drawn heavily on Endicott's work in preparation of this section.
37. Ibid., pp.126–7.
38. *The Japan Times*, 1 July 1983.
39. Endicott, op. cit., p.131.
40. *Asahi Shimbun*, 15 March 1973.
41. *Asahi Shimbun*, 18 March 1973.
42. *Asahi Shimbun*, 21 March 1973.
43. *Asahi Shimbun*, 19 May 1974.
44. *Asahi Shimbun*, 23 May 1974.
45. For commentaries see *Asahi Shimbun, Mainichi Shimbun, Yomiuri Shimbun*, 19 May 1974.
46. *Sankei Shimbun*, 23 May 1974.
47. Endicott, op. cit., p.75.
48. Ibid., p.69.
49. Ibid., p.70ff.
50. Ibid., p.71
51. *Mainichi Shimbun*, 4 June 1974.
52. Endicott, op. cit., p.72.
53. Ibid.

Chapter XIII

1. Iwashima Hisao, 'Problems in Japan's Defence', Orientation Seminars on Japan, no.9, The Japan Foundation, Tōkyō, 1982, pp.5–6.
2. Sakanaka Tomohisa *et al.*, *Nihon No Jiei Ryoku*, Asahi Shimbun Sha, 1967, p.61ff; Genda Minoru, 'Kokubō-Kyokuchi Sen, Zenmen Sen To Nihon No Tachiba', in *Nihon No Anzen Hoshō*, Nihon Kokusai Mondai Kenkyūjo, Kajima Kenkyūjo Shuppan Kai, 1964, p.506; *Jieitai*, Asahi Shimbun Sha Hen, 1968, pp.20–47; and Suzuki Ryōgoro, *Nihon No Bōku Taisei*, Kyōiku Sha, 1979.
3. Sakanaka *et al.*, op. cit., p.66ff.
4. Ibid., p.52ff. See also Nakayama Sadayoshi, 'Kaijō Jieitai To Nihon No Anzen', in *Nihon No Anzen Hoshō*, Nihon Kokusai Mondai Kenkyūjo, Kajima Kenkyūjo Shuppan Kai, 1964, p.529ff and Karube Tsutomu, *Bei-So Kaijō Senryaku To Nihon No Kaijō Bōei*, Kyōiku Sha, 1979.
5. See Sakanaka *et al.*, op. cit., p.42ff; Mitsuoka Kenjirō, *Nihon No Rikujō Bōei Senryaku To Sono Tokusei*, Kyōiku Sha, 1979; Hokkaidō Heiwa Iinkai, *Hokkaidō Kokusho, Ampo Taisei Ka No Jieitai*, Rōdō Junpō Sha, 1969.
6. Some analysts believe that the 1960–2 reorganization was a prelude to equipping the Self Defence Forces with tactical nuclear weapons. See Yoshiwara Kōichirō, *Nanajū-Nen Ampo To Nihon No Gunji Ryoku*, Nihon Hyōron Sha, 1969, p.30ff.
7. Nakamura Ryūhei, 'Rikujō Jieitai Wa Donna Sentō Yōsō O Kangaete Iru Ka?', in Kotani Hidejirō (ed.), *Bōei No Jittai*, Nihon Kyōbun Sha, 1972, p.117.
8. Kaihara Osamu, *Nihon Rettō Shubitai Ron*, Asagumo Shuppan Sha, 1972, p.69.
9. Hayashi Naomichi, 'Nihon Gunkokushugi Fukkatsu No Keizaiteki Kiso', *Gendai To Shisō*, October 1970, p.234.

10. *The Australian*, 8 May 1971.
11. Nakada Minoru *et al.*, *Nihon No Bōei To Keizai*, Asahi Shimbun Sha, 1967, p.107ff.
12. In December 1961 the monthly salary of a private, second class (Nito Shi), the rank comprising the greatest number of personnel in all three services, was Y8,000. By January 1967 this had risen to Y15,000. By the end of the 1970s, privates, second class were receiving Y96,200 per month. (Bōei Cho (ed.), *Bōei Handobukku*, Asagumo Shuppan Sha, 1982, p.138.)
13. Nakada *et al.*, op. cit., pp.107–11. The picture was complicated by the fact that the fighters for the Japanese air force had either been imported directly from the United States or constructed in Japan under licence from American firms. For a comprehensive discussion of this subject see Takase Shōji, 'Gunji Gijutsu To Bōei Seisan', in Nakada et al., op. cit., p.184ff. The situation in the 1970s is examined in Nagamatsu Keiichi, *Nihon No Bōei Sangyō*, Kyōiku Sha, 1979.
14. Nakada op. cit., pp.109–10.
15. Ibid., p.107.
16. *Yomiuri Shimbun*, 17 December 1961.
17. *Jieitai*, Asahi Shimbun Sha, 1968, p.200ff.
18. *Bōei Handobukku*, 1982, p.127.
19. Yoshiwara Kōichirō, op. cit., pp 239–76. Yoshiwara Kōichirō, *Sengo Nihongun No Ronri*, Gendai Shi Shuppan Kai, 1973, pp.71–104.
20. Ibid., p.90.
21. Ibid., pp.74–7.
22. *Bōei Handobukku*, 1982, p.442.
23. Sugita Ichiji, *Wasurerarete Iru Anzen Hoshō*, Jiji Tsūshin Sha, 1967, p.27ff.
24. Ibid., p.23.
25. Ibid., pp.127, 160–6, 188–9 and generally throughout his memoirs.
26. Ibid., pp.126–7.
27. Ibid., p.459.
28. Ibid., pp.90ff, 110ff, 186ff.
29. Ibid., pp.190–1.
30 *Asahi Shimbun*, 16 October 1960.
31. Sugita, op. cit., p.157.
32. Ibid., p.125.
33. Ibid., pp.278–9.
34. Ibid., pp.118–35 and generally throughout the work.
35. Ibid., pp.184–5.
36. Ibid., p.457.
37. Ibid., pp.116–18, 124–5.
38. Hoshino Yasusaburō and Hayashi Shigeo, *Jieitai, Sono Futatsu No Kao*, Sanichi Shobō, 1973, p.127. For Genda's views see also his articles, 'Sonae Areba Urei Nashi – Nihon Bōei Sai-Kentō No Toki', *Sekai Shūhō*, 22 August 1967, 'Kokubo O Kataru (Mishima Yukio To No Taiwa)', *Kokubō*, April 1968 and 'Nihon No Bōei Ni Tsuite', *Yoron*, June 1969.
39. Genda Minoru, 'Tōkai No Rakuen, Anitsu Wa Bōkoku No In', *Sekai Shūhō*, 30 July 1968.
40. Mitsuoka, op. cit., pp.157–9.
41. Ibid., pp.81–2.
42. Ibid., pp.124–5.
43. Ibid., p.146.

44. Nakayama, op. cit., pp.542–3.
45. Nakamura, op. cit., pp.137–41.
46. Ibid., p.103.
47. Ibid., p.111.
48. Ibid., pp.112–13.
49. Ibid., p.126.
50. Ibid., pp.120–1, 129.
51. Ishikawa Tsurayuki, 'Semete Aite No Katte Demo Kiriotoseba', in Kotani Hidejirō (ed.), *Bōei No Jittai*, Nihon Kyōbun Sha, 1972, p.151ff.
52. Ishida Suteo, 'Kaijō Kōeisen Wa Doko Made Nobaseba Yoi Ka', in Kotani Hidejirō (ed.), *Bōei No Jittai*, Nihon Kyōbun Sha, 1972, p.185ff.
53. Karube, op. cit., pp.102–5.
54. Suzuki, op. cit., pp.7–9.
55. *Mainichi Shimbun*, 19 January 1980, *Asahi Shimbun*, 21 January 1980, *Yomiuri Shimbun*, 22 January 1980.
56. Konishi Makoto, 'Hangun Tōsō No Ronri To Sono Tenkai', in Konishi Hangun Saiban Shien Iinkai (ed.), *Jieitai*, Gendai Hyōron Sha, 1972, p.259.
57. Ibid., p.265.
58. Ibid., p.259.
59. Ōshiro Seigo, 'Okinawa Shusshin Taiin To Shite', in Konishi Hangun Saiban Shien Iinkai (ed.), *Jieitai*, Gendai Hyōron Sha, 1972, p.249–50.
60. Kawai Masaji, 'Shihonka No Yōhei O Kyohi Suru', in Konishi Hangun Saiban Shien Iinkai (ed.), *Jieitai*, Gendai Hyōron Sha, 1972, p.230ff.
61. Ibid., pp.232–3.
62. Konishi, op. cit., p.270.
63. Asaoka Tetsu, 'Sanritsuka Tōsō Ni Shokuhatsu', in Konishi Hangun Saiban Shien Iinkai (ed.), *Jieitai*, Gendai. Hyōron Sha, 1972, pp.245–6.

Chapter XIV

1. *Asahi Shimbun*, 20 July 1978; *Yomiuri Shimbun*, 25 and 26 July 1978; *Mainichi Shimbun*, 27 July 1978.
2. Hirose Kiyoshi, *Tōbaku Gichō No Chii To Kengen*, Kyōiku Sha, 1979, pp.8–10.
3. Ibid., pp.12–17.
4. See Maeda Kotobuki, *Nihon No Bōei Seisaku*, in Sakanaka Tomohisa *et al.*, *Nihon No Jiei Ryoku*, Asahi Shimbun Sha, 1967, p.234ff.
5. *Kokubō Kaigi No Kōsei Nado Ni Kansuru Hōritsu*, Article 8.
6. See, for example, Kaihara Osamu's criticisms of the initial draft of the Fourth Defence Plan, *Sankei Shimbun*, 27 October 1969 (evening edition).
7. Maeda, op. cit., p.240ff.
8. *Bōei Handobukku*, 1982, pp.81–3.
9. Watanabe Yōzō and Okakura Kōshirō (eds), *Nichi-Bei Ampo Jōyaku, Sono Kaisetsu To Shiryō*, Rōdō Junpō Sha, 1968, p.431.
10. For observations on the operation of the National Defence Council, see Sugita Ichiji, *Wasurerarete Iru Anzen Hoshō*, Jiji Tsūshin Sha, 1967, p.116.
11. See Katō Shunsaku, *Jieiai To Shibirian Kontrōru, Seidoteki Sokumen O Chūshin Ni Shite*, Kantō Gakuin Daigaku Keizai Gakkai Kenkyū Ronshū, Keizai Kei, Dai-70 Shū,

November 1966; Sakanaka Tomohisa, 'Jieitai No Jittai', in Sakanaka Tomohisa *et al.*, *Nihon No Jiei Ryoku*, Asahi Shimbun Sha, 1967, p.38ff; Sugita, op. cit., p.118ff.

12. Sugita, op. cit., p.53. *Asahi Shimbun*, 5 December 1967.
13. *Asahi Shimbun*, 5 December 1967.
14. Hirose, op. cit., p.10.
15. For details see *Tōkyō Shimbun*, 13 December 1961, 4 September 1962. In view of rumours that the civilians in the Defence Agency had deliberately not been informed of contacts between the plotters and uniformed men, director-general Shiga ordered the Ground Staff Office to prepare a full report. Shiga was said to believe that the attitude of the Imperial officers' clique was a 'cancer' in the new forces, and major personnel changes were subsequently effected.
16. Sugita, op. cit., p.118. *Asahi Shimbun*, 5 December 1967.
17. Sugita, op. cit., p.122.
18. *Tōkyō Shimbun*, 25 October 1961.
19. *Yomiuri Shimbun*, 2 August 1963, *Sankei Shimbun*, 18 November 1964.
20. Sakanaka Tomohisa, 'Bōei Ryoku Seibi Keikaku No Suii', in Sakanaka Tomohisa *et al.*, *Nihon No Jiei Ryoku*, Asahi Shimbun Sha, 1967, p.95.
21. Ibid., p.94ff. *Nihon Keizai Shimbun*, 26 March 1963.
22. Sakanaka, 'Bōei Ryoku Seibi Keikaku No Suii', p.96.
23. *Nihon Keizai Shimbun*, 18 June 1966.
24. Sakanaka, 'Bōei Ryoku Seibi Keikaku No Suii', p.96.
25. *Mainichi Shimbun*, 14 August 1966; *Nihon Keizai Shimbun*, 22 September 1966; *Tōkyō Shimbun*, 23 September 1966.
26. *Sankei Shimbun*, 29 November 1966 (evening edition).
27. Sakanaka, 'Bōei Ryoku Seibi Keikaku No Suii', p.99.
28. *Asahi Shimbun*, 7 February 1967.
29. *Tōkyō Shimbun*, 17 February 1967.
30. *Tōkyō Shimbun*, 14 March 1967 (evening edition).
31. Sugita, op. cit., p.234.
32. *Asahi Shimbun*, 1 January 1978.
33. *Asahi Shimbun*, 27 September 1971.
34. *Newsweek*, 11 July 1983.
35. *Yomiuri Shimbun*, 17 April 1978.
36. *Asahi Shimbun*, 5 January 1971.
37. *Shūkan Asahi*, 5 April 1967.
38. Prime Minister's Office poll, February 1968; *Shūkan Asahi* survey, 5 April 1968.
39. *Mainichi Shimbun*, 14 June 1971.
40. *Yomiuri Shimbun*, 27 June 1973.
41. *Yomiuri Shimbun*, 17 April 1978.
42. *Yomiuri Shimbun*, 29 June 1967.
43. *Asahi Shimbun*, 13 May 1974 (evening edition), 15 July 1975.
44. *Asahi Shimbun*, 14 July 1973; *Mainichi Shimbun*, 26 July 1973; *Yamato Shimbun*, 16 January 1974; *Sankei Shimbun*, 6 February 1974; 9, 10, 12 March 1974.
45. *The Japan Times*, 12 April 1983.
46. I.I. Morris, *Nationalism and the Right Wing in Japan: A Study of Postwar Trends*, Oxford University Press, London, 1960, pp.443–4. See also Alec Dubro and David E. Kaplan, *Yakuza*, Futura, London, 1987, passim. Kishi and Kodama frequently appeared together on public

platforms to promote extreme nationalist causes. See, for example, *The Australian*, 24 July 1970.

47. Haruhiro Fukui, *Party in Power: The Japanese Liberal Democrats and Policy-Making*, Australian National University Press, Canberra, 1970, p.43.

48. *Yomiuri Shimbun*, 29 June 1967.

49. *The Australian*, 24 July 1970. *Nihon Keizai Shimbun*, 27 November 1970 (evening edition).

50. For a full account of the Mishima affair, see *Asahi Shimbun*, 26 November 1970. For a study of Mishima's political thought see Scott Johnson, 'Japanese culture and ultra-nationalism: the case of Mishima Yukio', Master's Degree thesis, International University of Japan, 1987.

51. Kiyoaki Murata, 'The Kaifu memos', *The Japan Times*, 23 February 1979.

52. *Mainichi Shimbun*, 20 May 1960.

53. *Bōei Nenkan*, 1956, p.167.

54. *Yomiuri Shimbun*, 12 April 1962.

55. *Tōkyō Shimbun*, 17 May 1962.

56. Sugita, op. cit., p.45.

57. *Tōkyō Shimbun*, 13 December 1961.

58. *Tōkyō Shimbun*, 4 September 1962.

59. *Nihon Keizai Shimbun*, 20 June 1962 (evening edition).

60. For comprehensive accounts of the Japanese weapons industry see Akagi Shōichi, *Nihon No Bōei Sangyō*, Sanichi Shobō, 1969 and Nagamatsu Keiichi, *Nihon No Bōei Sangyō*, Kyōiku Sha, 1979.

61. Takase Shōji, 'Bōei Sangyō No Saiken', in Nakada Minoru *et al.*, *Nihon No Bōei To Keizai*, Asahi Shimbun Sha, 1969, p.178 (Table 8).

62. Ibid., p.179 (Table 9).

63. Takase Shōji, 'Shōhin To Shite No Heiki', in Nakada, op. cit., pp.220–1.

64. Ibid., p.179.

65. Calculations based on the data given in *Jieitai*, Asahi Shimbun Sha, 1968, p.278ff and Hayashi Naomichi, 'Nihon Gunkokushugi Fukkatsu No Keizaiteki Kiso', *Gendai To Shisō*, October 1970.

66. Calculations based on data in Nagamatsu, op. cit., pp.16–17.

67. See, for example, *Keidanren Geppō*, June 1969; *Mainichi Shimbun*, 21 May 1969, 27 October 1969; *Nikkeiren Taimuzu*, 30 October 1969; *Nihon Keizai Shimbun*, 25 December 1969.

68. Shinobu Seisaburō, 'Dokusen Shihon To Seiji', in Oka Yoshitake (ed.), *Gendai Nihon No Seiji Katei*, Iwanami Shoten, 1958, pp.224–36. Fukui, op. cit., p.163.

69. In the early 1970s, the president of the Japan Weapons Industry Association (Nihon Heiki Kōgyō Kai), Ōkubo Ken, for example, urged spending 4 per cent of GNP (over four times the level of the 1960s) on defence and promoting Japanese weapons exports to South-East Asia. He also made ambiguous remarks about the desirability of a nuclear weapons programme. See Hayashi, op. cit., p.243.

70. *Mainichi Shimbun*, 29 May 1969.

71. *Mainichi Shimbun*, 10 June 1969.

72. Hayashi, op. cit., p.251.

73. *Mainichi Shimbun*, 10 June 1969.

74. *Nihon Keizai Shimbun*, 21 February 1967.

75. The revelations were made after the questioning of an ex-Major Aoki, the arrest of a Col-

onel Kawasaki and the sudden suicide of a Air Vice Marshal Yamaguchi in connection with alleged leakage of defence secrets to private firms.
76. *Tōkyō Shimbun*, 6 March 1968.
77. For example Sejima Ryūzō, a relative of the former War Minister Hayashi Senjirō, an honours graduate of the Imperial Military Academy and Staff Officer at Imperial Headquarters, had been barred from the Self Defence Forces because of his war record and close association with Hattori Takushirō. He subsequently became managing director of Itō-chū, a firm with considerable interest in defence procurement. Sejima's former classmate at the Imperial Military Academy, Hara Shirō, had managed to enter the Self Defence Forces, where he eventually rose to be Chief of Intelligence in the air force. On his retirement he took, at Sejima's invitation, a post at Itō-chū. (*Mainichi Shimbun*, 12 March 1968).
78. *Mainichi Shimbun*, 6 March 1968.
79. *Mainichi Shimbun*, 6 March 1968.
80. *Mainichi Shimbun*, 6 March 1968.
81. *Mainichi Shimbun*, 6 March 1968.
82. *The Japan Times*, 13 February 1979.
83. *Mainichi Daily News*, 19 February 1979.
84. *The Japan Times*, 23 and 26 February 1979.
85. *The Japan Times*, 25 May 1979.
86. *The Japan Times*, 13 February 1979.
87. *The Japan Times*, 18 February 1979.
88. *The Japan Times*, 16 and 17 February 1979.
89. *The Japan Times*, 17 February 1979.

Epilogue

1. *The Japan Times*, 29 April 1978.
2. *Mainichi Shimbun*, 17 June 1978.
3. *The New York Times*, 9, 11, 19, 21, 22, 23, 24, 26, 28, 29 May 1978.
4. *The National Times*, 24 February 1979.
5. *Mainichi Shimbun*, 4 May 1979.
6. *Time*, 21 January 1980.
7. *Newsweek*, 7 July 1980.
8. *Mainichi Shimbun*, 11 July 1979.
9. Aurelia George, *The Nakasone Challenge*, Legislative Branch, Parliament of the Commonwealth of Australia, Discussion Paper no. 2, 1986–7, pp.8, 22. Yoshikazu Sakamoto, 'Major power relations in East Asia', *Bulletin of Atomic Scientists*, February 1984, p.19ff.
10. *The Japan Times*, 20 June 1987.
11. *The Japan Times*, 3 July 1987.
12. *Washington Post*, 19 January 1983.
13. Larry A. Niksh, 'Japanese defence policy: Suzuki's shrinking options', *Journal of Northeast Asian Studies*, Volume 1, no. 2, June 1982, p.84.
14. George, op. cit., p.31ff.
15. *The Australian*, 15 January 1987.
16. Henry Kissinger, 'The rearming of Japan and the rest of Asia', *Washington Post*, 29 January 1987.

17. *The Japan Times*, 20 May 1987.
18. Ibid.
19. *The Japan Times*, 4 August 1987.
20. *The Sydney Morning Herald*, 13 August 1987.
21. Benjamin C. Duke, 'A difference of opinion', *The Japan Times*, 2 April 1986.
22. *Asahi Shimbun*, 7 August 1987.

Select Bibliography

Readers are advised to consult the footnotes for a more complete list of books, articles, documents and other materials used in preparing the present work.

Books in English

Ambrose, Stephen, *Rise to Globalism: American Foreign Policy, 1938–1970*, Penguin, Harmondsworth, 1973.

Auer, James E., *The Postwar Rearmament of Japanese Maritime Forces, 1945–1971*, Praeger, New York, 1973.

Brandon, Henry, *The Retreat of American Power*, The Bodley Head, London, 1972.

Crawford, Sir John and Ōkita, Dr Saburo (eds), *Australia, Japan and Western Pacific Economic Relations*, Australian Government Publishing Service, Canberra, 1976.

Crowley, James B., *Japan's Quest for Autonomy: National Security and Foreign Policy, 1930–1938*, Princeton University Press, Princeton, NJ, 1966.

Dower, J.W., *Empire and Aftermath: Yoshida Shigeru and the Japanese Experience, 1878–1954*, Harvard University Press, Cambridge, Mass., 1979.

Dunn, Frederick, S., *Peace-Making and the Settlement with Japan*, Princeton University Press, Princeton, NJ, 1963.

Endicott, John E., *Japan's Nuclear Option: Political, Technical and Strategic Factors*, Praeger, New York, 1975.

Flemming, Denna F., *The Cold War and its Origins, 1917–1960*, Allen & Unwin, London, 1961.

Frank, Isiah and Hironō, Ryōkichi (eds), *How the United States and Japan See Each Other's Economy*, Committee for Economic Development, New York, 1974.

Fukui, Haruhiro, *Party in Power: The Japanese Liberal Democrats and Policy-Making*, Australian National University Press, Canberra, 1970.

Hoopes, Townsend, *The Devil and John Foster Dulles*, André Deutsch, London, 1974.

Horowitz, David, *From Yalta to Vietnam: American Foreign Policy in the Cold War* (rev. edn), Penguin, Harmondsworth, 1967.

Kaldor, Mary, *The Disintegrating West*, Penguin, Harmondsworth, 1978.

Kennan, George F., *Memoirs, 1925–1950*, Atlantic, Little, Brown, Boston, Mass., 1961.

——, *Memoirs: 1950–1963*, Little Brown & Company, Boston, Mass., 1972.

Kurzman, Dan, *Kishi and Japan: the Search for the Sun*, Ivan Obolensky, New York, 1960.

Lafeber, Walter, *America, Russia and the Cold War, 1945–1966*, John Wiley & Sons, New York, 1968.

MacArthur, Douglas, *Reminiscences*, McGraw-Hill Book Co., New York, 1964.

Manchester, William, *American Caesar: Douglas MacArthur, 1880–1964*, Dell Books, New York, 1979.

May, Ernest R., *'Lessons' of the Past: The Use and Misuse of History in American Foreign Policy*,

Oxford University Press, New York, 1973.

Morris, I.I., *Nationalism and the Right Wing in Japan: A Study of Postwar Trends*, Oxford University Press, London, 1960.

Nish, Ian H., *The Anglo-Japanese Alliance: The Diplomacy of Two Island Empires, 1894–1907*, Athlone Press, London, 1966.

——, *Alliance in Decline: A Study in Anglo-Japanese Relations, 1908–23*, Athlone Press, London, 1972.

Nishihara Masashi, *The Japanese and Sukarno's Indonesia, Tokyo-Jakarta Relations, 1951–1966*, University Press of Hawaii, Honolulu, 1975.

Nixon, Richard M., *The Memoirs of Richard Nixon*, Arrow Books, London, 1978.

Odell, Peter R., *Oil and World Power*, Pelican, Harmondsworth, 1975.

Packard, George R., *Protest in Tokyo: The Security Treaty Crisis of 1960*, Princeton University Press, Princeton NJ, 1966.

Pempel, T.J. (ed.), *Policy Making in Contemporary Japan*, Cornell University Press, Ithaca NY, 1977.

Reischauer, Edwin O., *Trans-Pacific Relations*, Charles E. Tuttle Co., Tōkyō, 1969.

Schaller, Michael, *The American Occupation of Japan: The Origins of the Cold War in Asia*, Oxford University Press, New York, 1985.

Stockwin, J.A.A., *Japan: Divided Politics in a Growth Economy* (2nd edn), Weidenfeld & Nicolson, London, 1982.

Thayer, Nathaniel B., *How the Conservatives Rule Japan*, Princeton University Press, Princeton, NJ, 1969.

Watanabe, Akio, *The Okinawa Problem: A Chapter in Japan-US Relations*, Melbourne University Press, Melbourne, 1970.

Weinstein, Martin E., *Japan's Postwar Defence Policy, 1947–1968*, Columbia University Press, New York, 1971.

Yanaga, Chitoshi, *Big Business in Japanese Politics*, Yale University Press, New Haven, Conn., 1968.

Yergin, Daniel, *Shattered Peace: The Origins of the Cold War and the National Security State*, Penguin, Harmondsworth, 1977.

Yoshida, Shigeru, *The Yoshida Memoirs*, Heinemann, London, 1961.

Books in Japanese

Arisawa, Hiromi, *Shōwa Keizai Shi*, Nihon Keizai Shimbun Sha, 1977.

Arisue, Seizō, *Arisue Kikan Cho No Shuki*, 2 volumes, Fūyō Shobō, 1976.

Asahi Shimin Kyōshitsu (eds), *Shiryō: Nihon To Chūgoku, '45–71*, Asahi Shimbun Sha, 1972.

Dōba, Hajime, *Nihon No Gunji Ryoku, Jietai No Uchimaku*, Yomiuri Shimbun Sha, 1963.

Fujii, Shōichi and Ōe, Shinobu, *Sengo Nihon No Rekishi*, 2 volumes, Aoki Shoten, 1974.

Fujiyama, Aiichirō, *Seiji Waga Michi*, Asahi Shimbun Sha, 1976.

Hasegawa, Yoshiki, *Tōyama Mitsuru Hyōden*, Hara Shobō, 1974.

Hata, Ikuhiko, *Shi Roku: Nihon Saigunbi*, Bungei Shunjū, 1976.

Hatada, Shigeo, *Shin Ampo Taisei Ron*, Aoki Shoten, 1969.

Hayashi, Fusao, *Yoshida Shigeru To Senryō Kenpō*, Rōman, 1974.

Hironaka, Toshio, *Sengo Nihon No Keisatsu*, Iwanami Shoten, 1970.

Hirose, Kiyoshi, *Tōbaku Gichō No Chii To Kengen*, Kyōiku Sha, 1979.

Hoshino, Yasusaburō and Hayashi, Shigeo, *Jieitai, Sono Futatsu No Kao*, Sanichi Shobō, 1973.

Hosoya, Chihiro; Saitō, Makoto; Imai, Seiichi; Rōyama, Michio, *Nichi-Bei Kankei Shi*, 4 volumes, Tōkyō Daigaku Shuppan Kai, 1971.

Inoue, Mitsusada, *Nihon Kokka No Kigen*, Iwanami Shoten, 1968.

Ishii, Mitsujirō, *Kaisō Hachijū Hachi Nen*, Karuchā Shuppan Sha, 1975.

Ishikawa, Tadao; Nakajima, Mineo and Ikei, Yu, (eds), *Sengō Shiryō: Nitchū Kankei*, Nihon Hyōron Sha, 1970.

Jiji Tsūshin Sha Seiji Bu (ed.), *Nitchū Fukkō*, Jiji Tsūshin Sha, 1972.

Kaihara, Osamu, *Nihon Rettō Shubitai Ron*, Asagumo Shuppan Sha, 1972.

Kamimura, Shinichi, *Sōgo Kyōryoku Anzen Hoshō Jōyaku No Kaisetsu*, Jiji Tsūshin Sha, 1965.

Karube, Tsutomu, *Bei-So Kaijō Senryaku To Nihon No Kaijo Boei*, Kyōiku Sha, 1979.

Katayama, Tetsu, *Kaigan To Tenbō*, Fukumura Shuppan Kan, 1967.

Kawakami, Tetsutarō (ed.), *Uchimura Kanzō Shū*, Chikuma Shobō, Tōkyō, 1967.

Kawamura, Hiroo *et al.*, *Okinawa Henkan, Tsuki: Asahi Shimbun Yoron Chōsa*, Asahi Shimbun Sha, 1968.

Kinoshita, Hanji, *Nihon Uyoku No Kenkyū*, Gendai Hyōron Sha, 1977.

Kishida, Junnosuke, *Amerika No Kyokutō Senryaku*, Asahi Shimbun Sha, 1967.

Kōno, Ichirō, *Kōno Ichirō Jiden*, Tokuma Shoten, 1965.

——, *Nihon No Shōrai*, Kobun Sha, 1965.

Kurahara, Koreaki, *Nichi-Bei Ampo Jōyaku No Shoten*, Asahi Shimbun Sha, 1967.

Kusumi, Tadao, *Sensō, Senryaku, Nihon*, Hayashi Shoten, Tōkyō (no date).

Miki, Yōnosuke, *Miki Takeo*, Sankei Drama Books, 1975.

Mitsuoka, Kenjirō, *Nihon No Rikujō Bōei Senryaku To Sono Tokusei*, Kyōiku Sha, 1979.

Miyajima, Nobuo, *Sekiyū Sensō To Nihon Keizai*, Sanichi Shobō, 1974.

Miyazaki, Tōten, *Sanjū San Nen No Yume*, Tōyō Bunkō, Heibonsha, 1967.

Mura, Tsuneo, *Kankoku Gunsei No Keifu: Ri Sho-ban Kara Boku Sei-ki E*, Miraisha, 1966.

Nakada, Minoru *et al.*, *Nihon No Bōei To Keizai*, Asahi Shimbun Anzen Hoshō Mondai Chōsa Kai, Asahi Shimbun Sha, 1969.

——, *Nanajū Nen Ampo No Shintenkai*, Asahi Shimbun Sha, 1969.

Nakano, Yoshio (ed.), *Sengo Shiryō: Okinawa*, Nihon Hyōron Sha, 1969.

—— and Arasaki, Moriteru, *Okinawa Mondai Nijū Nen*, Iwanami Shoten, 1968.

Nikkan Kankei Kenkyū Kai (ed.), *Nikkan Kankei No Kisō Chishiki*, Tabata Shoten, 1975.

Nishimura, Kumao, *Anzen Hosho Jōyaku Ron*, Jiji Tsūshin Sha, 1960.

Ogawa, Kazuo, *Nisso Bōeki No Jitsujō To Kadai*, Kyōiku Sha, 1979.

Ōhira, Zengo, *Nihon No Anzen Hoshō To Kokusai Hō*, Yūshindo, 1960.

Okazaki, Kaheita, *Watakushi No Kiroku*, Tōhō Sensho, 1979.

Ōmori, Minoru, *Ishi Ni Kaku, Raishyawa Jiken No Shinsō*, Ushio Shuppan Sha, 1971.

Ōtake, Hideo, *Nihon No Bōei To Kokunai Seiji*, Sanichi Shobō, 1983.

Rekishigaku Kenkyū Kai (ed.), *Sengo Nihon Shi*, 5 volumes, Aoki Shoten, 1962.

Rekishigaku Kenkyū Kai-Nihon Shi Kenkyū Kai (eds), *Kōza Nihon Shi*, 10 volumes, Tōkyō Daigaku Shuppan Kai, 1970.

Saeki, Arimasa, *Kodai No Higashi Ajia To Nihon*, Kyōiku Sha, 1977.

Saeki, Kiichi, *Nihon No Anzen Hoshō*, Nihon Kokusai Mondai Kenkyūjo, 1966.

Saitō, Makoto; Nagai, Yōnosuke; Yamamoto, Mitsuru, *Shiryō: Nichi-Bei Kankei*, Nihon Hyōron Sha, 1970.

Sakamato, Yoshikazu, *Kaku Jidai No Kokusai Seiji*, Iwanami Shoten, 1968.

Sakanaka, Tomohisa, *Amerika Senryakuka No Okinawa*, Asahi Shimbun Sha, 1967.

—— *et al.*, *Nihon No Jiei Ryoku*, Asahi Shimbun Sha, 1967.

Sasayama, Haruo, *Kodai Kokka No Guntai*, Chūō Kōron Sha, 1975.

Satō, Yūichi, *Fukuda Takeo, Seiji Rosen To Sono Jinmyaku*, Jūtaku Shinpōsha, 1974.

Sengo Kaikaku Kenkyū Kai (ed.), *Sengo Kaikaku*, 7 volumes, Tōkyō Daigaku Shuppan Kai, 1974.

Shinobu, Seisaburō, *Sengo Nihon Seiji Shi, 4 volumes, Keisō Shobō, 1967.*

———, *Ampo Tōsō Shi*, Sekai Shōin, 1968.

———, *Nihon Gaikō Shi*, 2 volumes, Mainichi Shimbun Sha, 1974.

Shōno, Naomi; Nagai, Hideaki and Ueno, Hirohisa, *Kaku To Heiwa*, Hōritsu Bunka Sha, 1978.

Sugita, Ichiji, *Wasurerarete Iru Anzen Hoshō*, Jiji Tsūshin Sha, 1967.

Suzuki, Ryōgoro, *Nihon No Bokū Taisei*, Kyōiku Sha, 1979.

Tagawa, Seiichi, *Matsumura Kenzō To Chūgoku*, Yomiuri Shimbun Sha, 1972.

———, *Nitchū Kōshō Hiroku* , Mainichi Shimbun Sha, 1973.

Tanabe, Toshihiro, *Kike Wa Datsumi No Koe*, Tōkyō Daigaku Shuppan Kai, 1949.

Tōma, Seita, *Higashi Ajia Sekai No Keisei*, Shunjū Sha, 1977.

Toyoda, Toshiyuki, *Kaku Senryaku Hihan*, Iwanami Shoten, 1966.

Tsuji, Masanobu, *Senkō Sanzen Ri*, Kokusha Kankō Kai, 1958.

———, *Jiei Chūritsu*, Tōa Shobō, 1952.

Tsunoda, Jun (ed.), *Ishiwara Kanji Shiryō*, Hara Shobō, 1973.

Utsunomiya, Tokuma, *Tenkan Suru Bei-Ajia Seisaku To Nihon*, Hayashi Shobō, 1972.

Watanabe, Tetsuzō, *Ware-ware Saigunbi O Shuchōsu*, Watanabe Keizai Kenkyūjo, 1951.

Watanabe, Yōzō and Okakura, Kōshirō (eds), *Nichi-Bei Ampo Jōyaku, Sono Kaisetsu To Shiryō*, Rōdō Junpō Sha, 1968.

Yabe, Teiji, *Konoye Fumimaro*, Yomiuri Shimbun Sha, 1975.

Yoshimoto, Shigeyoshi, *Kishi Nobusuke Den*, Tōyō Shokan, 1957.

Yoshiwara, Kōichirō, *Nanajū Nen Ampo To Nihon No Gunji Ryoku*, Nihon Hyōron Sha, 1969.

———, *Sengo Nihongun No Ronri*, Gendai Shi Shuppan Kai, 1973.

Yukawa, Hideki *et al.*, *Kaku Jidai O Koeru*, Iwanami Shoten, 1968.

Articles in English

Abegglen, James C. and Hout, Thomas M., 'Facing up to the trade gap with Japan', *Foreign Affairs*, Volume 57, no. 1, Fall 1978.

Bannō, Junji, 'Japan's foreign policy and attitudes to the outside world, 1868–1945', in Peter Drysdale and Hironobu Kitaōji (eds), *Japan and Australia: Two Societies and their Interaction*, Australian National University Press, Canberra, 1981.

Esthus, R.A., 'The Taft-Katsura Agreement – reality or myth?', *Journal of Modern History*, Volume XXX, 1959.

Gordon, D.C., 'Roosevelt's smart Yankee trick', *Pacific Historical Review*, Volume 30, no. 4, November 1961.

Hall, Luella J., 'The abortive German-American entente of 1907–8', *Journal of Modern History*, Volume I, 1929.

Hama, Yuichiro, 'Japan's iron-steel industry and Australian iron ore', in Kojima Kiyoshi (ed.), *Australia, Japan and the Resource Goods Trade*, Japanese-Australian Project, Report no. 2, Tokyo, 1974.

Hsiao, Gene T., 'The Sino-Japanese rapprochement: a relationship of ambivalence', in Gene T. Hsiao (ed.), *Sino-American Detente and its Implications*, Praeger, New York, 1974.

McNelly, Theodore, 'The Japanese Constitution, child of the Cold War', *Political Science Quarterly*, Volume LXXIV, no. 2, June 1959.

Quigg, Philip W., 'Japan in neutral', *Foreign Affairs*, Volume 44, no. 2, January 1966.

Roberts, John, 'The rebirth of Japan's Zaibatsu', *Insight*, July 1978.

Rosenberg, David Alan, 'The origins of overkill: nuclear weapons and American strategy, 1945–1960', *International Security*, Volume 7, no. 4, Spring 1983.

Schonberger, Howard, 'The Japan Lobby in American diplomacy, 1947–1952', *Pacific Historical Review*, Volume XLVI, no. 3, August 1977.

Sissons, D.C.S., 'The pacifist clause in the Japanese Constitution', *International Affairs*, Volume 37, no. 1, January 1961.

Slocombe, Walter, 'The political implications of strategic parity', *Adelphi Papers*, no. 77, International Institute for Strategic Studies, London, 1971.

Soon Chung-Cho, 'Japan's two Koreas and the problems of Korean unification', *Asian Survey*, Volume VII, no. 10, October 1967.

Welfield, John, 'The Anglo-Japanese alliance and Japan's imperial expansion', *Bulletin of the Graduate School of International Relations*, International University of Japan, no. 3, July 1985.

Yung-Hwan Jo, 'Japanese-Korean relations and Asian diplomacy', *Orbis*, Volume XI, no. 2, Summer 1967.

Articles in Japanese

Ashida, Hitoshi, 'Jiyū To Heiwa No Tame No Tatakai', *Bungei Shunjū*, March 1951.

Fukuda, Takeo, 'Kenpō Kaisei No Hata Wa Takaku', *Jiyū*, August 1964.

Fukuzawa, Yukichi, 'Datsu-A Ron', *Jiyū Shimpō*, 16 March 1885.

Furui, Yoshimi, 'Nitchū Kokkō Seijōka No Hiwa', *Chūō Kōron*, December 1972.

Genda, Minoru, 'Kokubō – Kyokuchi Sen, Zenmen Sen To Nihon No Tachiba', *Nihon No Anzen Hoshō* Nihon Kokusai Mondai Kenkyūjo, Kajima Kenkyūjo Shuppan Kai, 1964.

——, 'Tōkai No Rakuen, Anitsu Wa Bōkoku No In', *Sekai Shūho*, July 1968.

Hayashi, Naomichi, 'Nihon Gunkokushugi Fukkatsu No Keizaiteki Kiso', *Gendai To Shisō*, 1970.

Itō, Masami, 'Gikaishugi No Hametsu O Fusegu Tame Ni', *Jiyū*, July 1960.

Kamigawa Hikomatsu, 'Kaku Kakusan Bōshi Jōyaku No Shōrai To Waga Shin Kaku Koku Seisaku No Jūritsu', *Minzoku to Seiji*, July 1968.

Kishi, Nobusuke, et. al., 'Ampo Jōyaku Kaitei To Hantai Undō', *Chūō Kōron*, May 1980.

Kishida Junnosuke, 'Nihon No Kaku Seisaku To Hikaku Sengen No Imi', *Ushio*, Spring 1968.

Kitamura Tokutarō, 'Tandoku Kōwa To Yatō No Shuchō', *Sekai*, October 1950.

Konishi, Makoto, 'Hangun Tōsō No Ronri To Sono Tenkai' Konishi Hangun Saiban Shien Iinkai (ed.), *Jietai*, Gendai Hyōron Sha, 1972.

Kōno, Ichirō, 'Nissō Kōryū Ni Tsuite Kokumin Ni Uttaeru', *Chūō Kōron*, July 1962.

Kosaka, Masataka, 'Kaiyō Kokka Nihon No Kōsō', *Chūō Kōron*, September 1964.

Kuramae, Yoshio, 'Nihon No Unmei O Kessuru Kakubō Jōyaku No Mondaiten', *Ronsō Janaru*, September 1968.

Maeda, Hisashi, 'Kaku Kakubō Jōyaku To Nihon No Kaku Seisaku', *Kokubō*, August 1968.

Makoto, Kazumaro, 'Hikaku Chūkyū Kokka No Bōei Seisaku', *Ushio*, Spring 1966.

Masuhara, Keikichi, 'Jieitai No Enkaku To Nihon No Anzen', *Nihon No Anzen Hoshō*, Nihon Kokusai Mondai Kenkyūjo, Kajima Kenkyūjo, Kajima Kenkyūjo Shuppan Kai, 1964.

Matsumoto, Saburō, 'Hoshu Renkei To MSA', *Chūō Kōron*, November 1953.

Miyazawa, Kiichi, 'Amerika No Tai-Nichi Bōei Yōsei', *Sekai*, July 1957.

——, 'Ampō Jōyaku Teiketsu No Ikisatsu', *Chūō Kōron*, May 1957.

Nabeyama, Sadachika, 'Buryokuteki Jiei No Soshiki O', *Sekai Shūhō*, No.154, 1950.

Nakamura, Ryūhei, 'Rikujō Jieitai Wa Donna Sentō Yosō O Kangaete Iru ka', Kotani Hidejirō, *Bōei No Jittai*, Nihon Kyōbun Sha, 1972.

Nakayama, Sadayoshi, 'Kaigō Jieitai To Nihon No Anzen', *Nihon No Anzen Hoshō*, Nihon Kokusai Mondai Kenkyūjo, Kajima Kenkyūjo Shuppan Kai, 1964.

Nishi, Haruhiko, 'Nihon Gaikō O Ureru', *Chūō Kōron*, February 1960.

Nomura, Kichisaburō, 'Kokudo Hozen No Tame', *Keizai Ōrai*, 1950.

Ōshiro, Seigo, 'Okinawa Shusshin Taiin To Shite', Konishi Hangun Saiban Shien Iinkai (ed.), *Jieitai*, Gendai Hyōron Sha, 1972.

Rōyama, Michio, 'Nihon No Anzen Hoshō To Chūgoku No Imi', *Ushio*, Spring 1966.

Shinobu, Seisaburō, 'Dokusen Shihon To Seiji', Oka Yoshitake (ed.), *Gendai Nihon No Seiji Katei*, Iwanami Shoten, 1958.

Takasaki, Tatsunosuke, 'Shu On-rai To Kaidan Shite', *Chūō Kōron*, February 1961.

Tamura Kosaku, 'Kakubō Jōyaku O Ikani Atsukau Ka', *Gaikō Jihō*, 11 December 1968.

Terao, Goro, et.al., 'Nikkan Kaidan', Ajia-Afurika Kōza, *Nihon To Chōsen*, Keiso Shobō, 1965.

Terasawa, Hajime, 'Anzen Hoshō Ni Kansuru Zasshi Ronchō', *Kokusai Hō Gaikō Zasshi*, January 1951.

——, 'Saigunbi Sansei Ron, Hantai Ron No Tenbō, *Chūō Kōron*, November 1952.

Wakaizumi Kei, 'Makunamara Bei Kokubō Chōkan Tandoku Kaiken Ki', *Chūō Kōron*, September 1966.

——, 'Chūgoku No Kaku Busō To Nihon No Anzen Hoshō', *Chūō Kōron*, February 1966.

Uemura Kōgorō, 'MSA Kyohi Wa Keizai No Hametsu', *Ekonomisuto*, 11 July 1953.

INDEX